# The Wiley Handbook on the Cognitive Neuroscience of Memory

# The Wiley Handbook on the Cognitive Neuroscience of Memory

Edited by

**Donna Rose Addis, Morgan Barense, and Audrey Duarte**

**WILEY** Blackwell

This edition first published 2015
© 2015 John Wiley & Sons, Ltd.

*Registered Office*
John Wiley & Sons, Ltd., The Atrium, Southern Gate, Chichester, West Sussex, PO19 8SQ, UK

*Editorial Offices*
350 Main Street, Malden, MA 02148-5020, USA
9600 Garsington Road, Oxford, OX4 2DQ, UK
The Atrium, Southern Gate, Chichester, West Sussex, PO19 8SQ, UK

For details of our global editorial offices, for customer services, and for information about how to apply for permission to reuse the copyright material in this book please see our website at www.wiley.com/wiley-blackwell.

The right of Donna Rose Addis, Morgan Barense, and Audrey Duarte to be identified as the authors of the editorial material in this work has been asserted in accordance with the UK Copyright, Designs and Patents Act 1988.

*Library of Congress Cataloging-in-Publication Data*
The Wiley handbook on the cognitive neuroscience of memory / edited by Donna Rose Addis, Morgan Barense, Audrey Duarte.
     pages   cm
  Includes index.
  ISBN 978-1-118-33259-7 (hardback)
1. Memory.   2. Cognitive neuroscience.   3. Brain–Imaging.   I. Addis, Donna Rose, 1977–
II. Barense, Morgan, 1980–   III. Duarte, Audrey, 1976–
  QP406.W55 2015
  612.8′23312–dc23
                                        2015000669
A catalogue record for this book is available from the British Library.

Cover image: Background © happyperson / Shutterstock; profile head © amasterphotographer / Shutterstock

Set in 10/12pt Galliard by SPi Publisher Services, Pondicherry, India
Printed and bound in Malaysia by Vivar Printing Sdn Bhd

1   2015

# Contents

# About the Editors

**Donna Rose Addis** is an Associate Professor and Rutherford Discovery Fellow in the School of Psychology at The University of Auckland. She received her PhD from the University of Toronto in 2005 and completed a postdoctoral fellowship at Harvard University. She has published 60 articles and chapters on autobiographical memory, future thinking, and identity. Dr. Addis has received a number of honors for her work in this area, including the prestigious New Zealand Prime Minister's MacDiarmid Emerging Scientist Prize and the Cognitive Neuroscience Society Young Investigator Award.

**Morgan Barense** is an Associate Professor in the Department of Psychology at the University of Toronto. She received her PhD from the University of Cambridge in 2006. Dr. Barense has published extensively on how memory functions are organized within the human brain and how memory relates to other cognitive processes, such as perception. She has received many accolades for this work, including a Canada Research Chair in Cognitive Neuroscience, the Early Investigator Award from the Society of Experimental Psychologists, and a Scholar Award from the James S. McDonnell Foundation.

**Audrey Duarte** is an Associate Professor in the School of Psychology at the Georgia Institute of Technology. She received her PhD from the University of California, at Berkeley in 2004. She has published numerous EEG, fMRI, and neuropsychological studies on age-related changes in episodic memory functioning, and held the Early Career Goizueta Professor Chair at the Georgia Institute of Technology.

# About the Contributors

**David Badre** is an Associate Professor of Cognitive, Linguistic, and Psychological Sciences at Brown University and an affiliate of the Brown Institute for Brain Science. His lab at Brown studies cognitive control of memory and action, with a focus on frontal lobe function and organization. He was named an Alfred P. Sloan Fellow in 2011 and a James S. McDonnell Scholar in 2012, and currently serves on the editorial boards of *Cognitive Neuroscience* and *Psychological Science*.

**Caitlin R. Bowman** is a PhD student in cognitive psychology at the Pennsylvania State University studying with Dr. Nancy A. Dennis. Her work focuses on the neural basis of age differences in memory processing, particularly false memories. Her recent focus has been investigating the neural resources older adults utilize to avoid false memories. Her long-term goal is to identify causes of age-related memory decline and ways to enhance memory in older adults.

**Alexis M. Chambers** is a graduate student in the Cognition, Brain, and Behavior program at the University of Notre Dame. Her research spans a variety of domains, including sleep, memory, and emotion. Specifically, she is interested in exploring how sleep promotes selective emotional memory processing.

**Christopher R. Cox** is a graduate student in the Department of Psychology at the University of Wisconsin–Madison. His research focuses on the application of state-of-the-art methods for fMRI pattern analysis to questions about the neural bases of semantic memory.

**Felipe De Brigard** is an Assistant Professor of Philosophy at Duke University, and core faculty at the Center for Cognitive Neuroscience and the Duke Institute for Brain Sciences. He did his PhD at the University of North Carolina, Chapel Hill, and then spent two years as postdoctoral fellow in the Department of Psychology at Harvard University. His research centers on the interaction between memory and imagination, as well as the relationship between attention, consciousness, and recollection.

**Nancy A. Dennis** is an Assistant Professor at Pennsylvania State University, where she directs the Cognitive Aging and Neuroimaging Lab. Dr. Dennis is affiliated with the Center for Healthy Aging, the Social, Life, & Engineering Sciences Imaging Center, the Center for Brain, Behavior and Cognition, and the Huck Institute of Life Sciences.

Her research addresses the cognitive and neural mechanisms underlying age-related differences in memory. Her current work focuses on cognitive control, false memories, and association memories across the lifespan.

**Ilana T. Z. Dew** is a postdoctoral scholar at the Center for Cognitive Neuroscience at Duke University, where she uses behavioral and functional neuroimaging techniques to study human memory and emotion in young and older adults. She received her PhD in psychology from the University of North Carolina at Chapel Hill.

**Danielle Douglas** is a PhD student in psychology at the University of Toronto, studying cognitive neuroscience under the joint supervision of Andy Lee and Morgan Barense. Their research focuses on understanding memory processing in the human brain, particularly how memory interacts with perception.

**Yana Fandakova** is a postdoctoral research fellow at the University of California, at Berkeley. She studied psychology in Berlin and received her doctorate in psychology from the Humboldt Universität zu Berlin in 2012. Her primary research interests are the cognitive and neural mechanisms of developmental change across the lifespan, with a focus on episodic memory and cognitive control development in childhood and aging.

**Chris M. Fiacconi** is a Post-Doctoral Fellow in the Brain and Mind Institute at the University of Western Ontario. His research interests center broadly on human memory, with a focus on the relation between memory and affect, and the influence of prior experience on current perception and action. His research involves the use of cognitive experiments, psychophysiology, and the assessment of cognitive impairment in patients with various neurological conditions, including dementia and disorders of consciousness.

**Kelly S. Giovanello** is an Associate Professor of Psychology at the University of North Carolina at Chapel Hill, with appointments in the Biomedical Research Imaging Center and the Institute on Aging. She received her PhD in neuroscience from Boston University. Her research combines behavioral, patient-based, and functional neuroimaging approaches to investigate the cognitive neuroscience of human learning and memory.

**Rebecca Gomez** is an Associate Professor in the Psychology Department at the University of Arizona in Tucson. She completed a PhD at New Mexico State University before conducting postdoctoral research at the University of Arizona. Her research spans such topics as implicit learning, language acquisition, sleep-dependent memory consolidation, memory reconsolidation, and early learning systems, all with the aim of better understanding learning and memory mechanisms.

**Cheryl L. Grady** is a Senior Scientist at the Rotman Research Institute at Baycrest Centre in Toronto, Ontario. She is a Professor in the Departments of Psychiatry and Psychology at the University of Toronto, and holds a Tier I Canada Research Chair in Neurocognitive Aging. Her research focuses on age differences in large-scale functional connectivity of brain networks, the influence of lifelong experience (such as bilingualism) on brain structure/function, and variability of brain activity.

**Andrea Greve** is a Research Scientist at the MRC Cognition and Brain Sciences Unit in Cambridge, UK. Her primary research concerns the cognitive and neural basis of human memory. One central question guiding her work focuses on how previously acquired knowledge influences the ways in which novel information is learned and retrieved. Her work aims to elucidate the interplay between episodic and semantic memories by combining different methods including behavioral, computational, and neuroimaging techniques.

**Angela Gutchess** is an Associate Professor of Psychology at Brandeis University, with appointments in Neuroscience and the Volen Center for Complex Systems. She received her PhD in Psychology from the University of Michigan. Her research investigates the influence of age and culture on memory and social cognition, using both behavioral and neuroimaging (fMRI) methods. She is particularly interested in how aging affects memory for self-relevant information and impressions of others.

**Richard Henson** is an MRC Programme Leader and Director for Neuroimaging at the MRC Cognition and Brain Sciences Unit in Cambridge, UK. His research focuses on the neural bases of memory, including the relationship between recollection, familiarity, and priming. He uses fMRI and EEG/MEG to examine brain activity as healthy volunteers attempt to remember information, and relates these findings, via computational modeling, to the memory problems in aging, amnesia, and dementia.

**Michael Hornberger** is a Senior Research Associate at the Department of Clinical Neurosciences, University of Cambridge, UK. His research focuses on memory processes in neurodegenerative patients to delineate underlying mechanisms of memory. At the same time, he develops novel memory and neuroimaging biomarkers to improve diagnostics and disease tracking in neurodegenerative disorders.

**Almut Hupbach** is an Assistant Professor of Psychology at Lehigh University. She received her PhD from the University of Trier, Germany. Her research focuses on the circumstances permitting induction of plasticity in human long-term memory. In particular, she studies the conditions that allow episodic memories to be modified and updated with new information. She is interested in unintentional and intentional processes of memory change, and studies these processes in children and adults.

**Muireann Irish** is a Research Fellow in the School of Psychology at the University of New South Wales, in Sydney, Australia. She conducts her research at Neuroscience Research Australia, Sydney, and is an Associate Investigator in the Australian Research Council Centre of Excellence in Cognition and its Disorders. Her research focuses on the disruption of episodic memory processes, such as autobiographical memory and future thinking, in neurodegenerative disorders, including Alzheimer's disease and frontotemporal dementia.

**Jeffrey D. Johnson** is an Assistant Professor in the Department of Psychological Sciences at the University of Missouri. His research focuses on understanding the cognitive and neural processes that contribute to episodic memory encoding and retrieval, through the use of electrophysiology (EEG and ERP), functional neuroimaging (fMRI), and pattern classification techniques.

**Elizabeth A. Kensinger** received her PhD from the Massachusetts Institute of Technology (MIT) and is Professor of Psychology at Boston College, where she directs the Cognitive and Affective Neuroscience laboratory. Her laboratory researches the intersection between emotion and memory across the adult lifespan. She has co-authored numerous scientific publications on this topic and is the author of the book *Emotional Memory Across the Adult Lifespan* (Psychology Press, 2009).

**Kerstin H. Kipp** is a Senior Research Scientist at the Transfer Center for Neurosciences and Learning (ZNL) at Ulm University, Germany. After obtaining a dual degree in psychology and in communication and speech she defended her doctoral degree in cognitive psychology in 2003 at Saarland University in Saarbrücken. In 2011 she habilitated in the field of cognitive neuropsychology about episodic memory, its development and pathologies.

**Stefan Köhler** is a faculty member in the Department of Psychology and the Brain and Mind Institute at the University of Western Ontario, and is affiliated with the Rotman Research Institute, Toronto, Canada. His research addresses the neural and cognitive mechanisms of human memory, and the interface between memory and perception. His approach focuses on functional neuroimaging, cognitive experiments, and the study of memory impairments associated with various neurological conditions, including epilepsy and Alzheimer's disease.

**Andy Lee** is an Assistant Professor of Psychology at the University of Toronto and Adjunct Scientist at the Rotman Research Institute at the Baycrest Centre for Geriatric Care, Toronto. His research focuses on the contributions of the medial temporal lobe structures to mnemonic and perceptual processes.

**Jackson C. Liang** is a PhD candidate in the Institute for Neuroscience at the University of Texas at Austin under the mentorship of Dr. Alison Preston. His research focuses on the unique contributions of medial temporal lobe subregions to remembering category-level perceptual details and understanding how category representations are used to support memory-guided decisions.

**Ulman Lindenberger** directs the Center for Lifespan Psychology at the Max Planck Institute for Human Development, Berlin, Germany. He is an honorary professor at Freie Universität Berlin, Humboldt Universität zu Berlin, and Saarland University, Saarbrücken, Germany. His research interests are behavioral and neural plasticity across the lifespan, brain–behavior relations across the lifespan, multivariate developmental methodology, and formal models of behavioral change. He received the Gottfried Wilhelm Leibniz Prize from the Deutsche Forschungsgemeinschaft in 2010.

**David Maillet** is a Postdoctoral fellow at Harvard University. He has received postgraduate scholarships from the Natural Science and Engineering Research Council of Canada throughout his graduate training and is recipient of the FRQ-S Étudiants-chercheurs étoiles Award. He is interested in understanding how aging impacts the neural networks involved in episodic memory.

**Chris B. Martin** is a doctoral candidate in the Department of Psychology and the Brain and Mind Institute at the University of Western Ontario. His research is generally focused on human memory, with a specific interest in the cognitive and neural mechanisms that support familiarity-based recognition. His recent work has used functional neuroimaging to examine whether the neural correlates of familiarity assessment are organized in a category-specific manner in the medial temporal lobes.

**Victoria C. McLelland** is a postdoctoral fellow in the Department of Psychology at the University of Toronto, and her research is focused on the neural correlates of episodic memory. She received her PhD from the University of Auckland, where she investigated the role of the hippocampus in imagining and encoding future episodic events.

**Axel Mecklinger** is Full Professor for Neuropsychology at Saarland University in Saarbrücken and Speaker of the International Research Training Group "Adaptive Minds". Prior to this he worked as a Senior Research Scientist at the Max Planck Institute for Human Cognitive and Brain Sciences in Leipzig. In 1999 he received the Distinguished Scientific Award for Early Career Contributions to Psychophysiology from the Society for Psychophysiological Research. His research interests lie in the cognitive neuroscience of learning, memory, and cognitive control.

**Laurie A. Miller** is a Clinical Neuropsychologist at Royal Prince Alfred Hospital, Chief Investigator in the Australian Research Council Centre of Excellence in Cognition and Its Disorders as well as Senior Clinical Lecturer at the University of Sydney, Australia. She obtained a BSc degree from Westminster College in Pennsylvania and then Master's and PhD degrees in psychology from McGill University under the supervision of Professor Brenda Milner at the Montreal Neurological Institute. She pursued a two-year postdoctoral position at the University of Auckland and previously worked as a clinician and researcher at University Hospital in London, Ontario. Her interests include the study of memory disorders and their remediation.

**Lynn Nadel** is Regents' Professor of Psychology and Cognitive Science at the University of Arizona in Tucson. He proposed, with John O'Keefe, the "cognitive map" theory of hippocampal function and, with Morris Moscovitch, the "multiple trace" theory of memory and memory consolidation. He has worked on the role of the hippocampus in human memory, context, stress and anxiety disorders, and Down syndrome, bringing ideas in cognitive map theory to a wide range of research domains.

**Erika Nyhus** is a postdoctoral Research Associate in Cognitive, Linguistic, and Psychological Sciences at Brown University. She studies the neural processes involved in higher-level cognition, including executive functioning and episodic memory. Her research has addressed these topics through behavioral and neuroimaging (EEG, ERP, and fMRI) methods. This research has shown how frontal cortex, parietal cortex, and hippocampus transiently interact in support of controlled retrieval of episodic memories.

**Jessica D. Payne** is an Assistant Professor and Nancy O'Neill Collegiate Chair in Psychology at the University of Notre Dame. She is the Director of the Sleep Stress and Memory (SAM) Lab. Her research focuses on how sleep and stress independently and interactively influence human memory, emotion, performance, and creativity.

**Bradley R. Postle** is a Professor of Psychology and Psychiatry at the University of Wisconsin–Madison. He has over 60 peer-reviewed publications in scientific journals, many of these on the neural bases of human working memory and attention, and is associate editor at the *Journal of Cognitive Neuroscience* and *Cortex*.

**Alison R. Preston** received her PhD from Stanford University and is an Associate Professor of Psychology and Neuroscience at the University of Texas at Austin and a Fellow in the Center for Learning and Memory and the Institute for Neuroscience. Her research combines behavioral and brain imaging techniques to study how we form new memories, how we remember past experiences, and how memory for the past influences what we learn and do in the present.

**Kylie A. Radford** is a postdoctoral researcher at Neuroscience Research Australia, Clinical Neuropsychologist at Prince of Wales Hospital, and Conjoint Lecturer at the University of New South Wales, Sydney. She completed Doctorate of Clinical Neuropsychology/PhD degrees at the University of Sydney under the supervision of Dr. Laurie A. Miller and Dr. Suncica Lah. Her doctoral project focused on the impact of group-based rehabilitation of memory for patients with neurological disorders at Royal Prince Alfred Hospital.

**M. Natasha Rajah** is an Associate Professor in the Department of Psychiatry at McGill University, and Director of the Douglas Mental Health University Institute's Brain Imaging Centre. Her research focuses on using neuroimaging methods to understand how healthy and pathological forms of aging impact the neural structures, functions, and network interactions important for successful episodic memory encoding and retrieval.

**Timothy T. Rogers** is an Associate Professor in the Department of Psychology at the University of Wisconsin–Madison. His research focuses on the cognitive, neural, and computational bases of semantic memory. He is the author, with Jay McClelland, of *Semantic Cognition: A Parallel Distributed Processing Approach* (MIT Press, 2004).

**Michael D. Rugg** is Distinguished Professor in Behavioral and Brain Sciences and co-director of the Center for Vital Longevity at the University of Texas at Dallas. His research interests are in the cognitive and neural bases of human memory and the effects of aging and neurodegenerative disease on memory function.

**Anthony J. Ryals** is a postdoctoral fellow in the Department of Medical Social Sciences and the Interdepartmental Neuroscience Program, Northwestern University Feinberg School of Medicine, Chicago. Dr. Ryals studies how explicit and implicit processes operate in episodic memory by using behavioral experimentation as well as electrophysiology and functional neuroimaging. He also studies how subjective meta-cognitive awareness (or lack of awareness) relates to performance, brain function, and life quality in healthy and memory-impaired populations.

**Daniel L. Schacter** is William R. Kenan, Jr. Professor of Psychology at Harvard University. He received his PhD from the University of Toronto in 1981, and has since published over 350 research articles and chapters on various aspects of memory and the brain. He is the author of *The Seven Sins of Memory* (Houghton Mifflin, 2002) and several other books, and has received a number of awards for his research, including election to the National Academy of Sciences.

**Yee Lee Shing** is a research scientist at the Center for Lifespan Psychology at the Max Planck Institute for Human Development in Berlin, Germany. She received her doctorate in psychology from the Humboldt University Berlin in 2008. She is primarily interested in the development and plasticity of cognitive mechanics across the lifespan, with a focus on brain–behavior relations of episodic memory components. She received the Heinz Maier-Leibnitz Prize from the Deutsche Forschungsgemeinschaft in 2012.

**Volker Sprondel** is currently a postdoctoral researcher at Saarland University in Saarbrücken. After graduating in psychology from the University of Konstanz, he started working as a doctoral researcher at Saarland University, from which he received his PhD in 2011. His research focuses on human memory and its development during childhood and adolescence from a cognitive neuroscience perspective.

**Peggy L. St. Jacques** is a Lecturer in the School of Psychology at the University of Sussex, Brighton, UK. She received her PhD from Duke University and completed a postdoctoral fellowship at Harvard University where she was the recipient of the L'Oréal USA for Women in Science Fellowship. Her research investigates autobiographical memory retrieval, aging, and emotion, and how reconstruction processes during retrieval can alter memory.

**Indira C. Turney** is a PhD student in cognitive psychology at the Pennsylvania State University, studying cognitive neuroscience under the supervision of Dr. Nancy Dennis. Her research examines the influence of age on a variety of memory processes. Her recent work focuses on the age-related neural markers underlying cognitive decline using functional and structural neuroimaging methods. Specifically, she is interested in understanding the cognitive and neural mechanisms mediating both true and false memories.

**Melina R. Uncapher** is a research scientist in the Stanford Memory Laboratory at Stanford University. Her research program focuses on the cognitive and neurobiological mechanisms that support learning and remembering, with an emphasis on understanding interactions between memory and attention. A prominent focus of her research involves the use of advanced neuroimaging techniques to investigate the functional heterogeneity of parietal cortex, and the role of this region in learning and remembering.

**Joel L. Voss** is an Assistant Professor based in the Department of Medical Social Sciences and the Interdepartmental Neuroscience Program, Northwestern University Feinberg School of Medicine, Chicago. Dr. Voss directs the Laboratory for Human Neuroscience, which studies brain mechanisms for memory and their disruptions due to neurological injury.

# Preface

Experimental psychologists have been working to understand the cognitive processes that contribute to human memory for more than 100 years. Their research has yielded many important models and hypotheses regarding the cognitive and neural mechanisms that underlie short- and long-term memory. Neuroscience methods have advanced our understanding of human memory considerably, but many of these methods, including functional magnetic resonance imaging (fMRI), are relatively new and have been somewhat limited in their ability to resolve many of the controversies and mysteries of human memory functioning. Over the last several years, however, tremendous advances have been made in both the methods themselves and the analysis techniques used to examine the data. For example, due to the increased prevalence of higher field scanners and robust imaging sequences, the spatial resolution of neuroimaging methods has improved dramatically. This advancement has been instrumental in allowing cognitive neuroscientists, including contributors to this handbook, to distinguish the roles of human hippocampal subfields in episodic memory encoding and retrieval. Furthermore, highly sensitive multivariate statistical methods are being applied with increasing frequency, such that it is now possible to determine the extent to which a retrieved memory representation recapitulates that associated with initial encoding. Contributors to this volume use these and other cutting-edge approaches to address a wide variety of topics in the field of human memory, including the effects of healthy aging and dementia on episodic and semantic memory and their underlying neural substrates, the nature of the visual representations maintained in working memory and perception, the potential of therapeutic interventions for memory disorders, among many others.

Given the recent technological developments in neuroscience methods and the number of publications applying these methods, we felt that the timing was apt for this handbook. Although other excellent books on the topic of memory have been published over the last few years, this volume is unique in that it is focused on the recent neuroscience studies that have advanced our understanding of human memory. This book both summarizes this literature and makes predictions about the future studies that will advance our understanding further.

The contributors to this handbook represent many of the best cognitive neuroscientists working in the domain of human memory. We have endeavored to include a wide range of research areas and approaches in this volume. Each author has provided an excellent review of the work being done in his or her own research area. The chapters are comprehensive enough that graduate students with some experience with the relevant literature can understand them; but also thought-provoking enough that experienced human memory researchers will find them interesting. We imagine that this book might also be useful for professors planning graduate seminars on topics of human memory.

We would like to extend our thanks to the authors who graciously accepted our invitation to contribute to this volume, and to the expert reviewers who provided invaluable feedback that helped perfect it. Needless to say, this handbook would not have been possible without their collective efforts.

Donna Rose Addis, Morgan Barense, and Audrey Duarte

# 1

# What We Have Learned about Memory from Neuroimaging

## Andrea Greve and Richard Henson

## Introduction

Functional neuroimaging techniques, such as functional magnetic resonance imaging (fMRI) and electro/magnetoencephalography (EEG/MEG), have had a major impact on the study of human memory over the last two decades. This impact includes not only new evidence about the parts of the brain that are important for memory ("functional localization" or "brain mapping"), which extends what was previously known from patients with brain damage, but also arguably informs our theoretical understanding of how memory works (e.g., Henson, 2005; Poldrack, 2006; though such claims have been questioned, e.g., Coltheart, 2006; Uttal, 2001). In this chapter, we illustrate ways in which functional neuroimaging has influenced our understanding of memory, going beyond research that was previously based primarily on behavioral techniques. We focus in particular on how memory processes might be implemented in the brain in terms of average levels of activity in certain brain areas, patterns of activity within areas, and connectivity between brain areas.

## Theoretical Concepts That are Difficult to Measure Behaviorally, e.g., Retrieval States

Tulving (1983) theorized that we adopt a particular mind-set during episodic memory retrieval, a so-called "retrieval mode," which optimizes recovery of information from memory, and allows us to interpret that information as having come from the past (rather than from sensations in the present). Until recently, however, it has been difficult to evaluate theories like this owing to the difficulty of measuring such states behaviorally. Neuroimaging, on the other hand, is able to measure sustained brain activity directly associated with a state. This ability has reinvigorated such theories, leading to new hypothetical states that are assumed to be important for the encoding and retrieval of information, and even prompting new behavioral measures to investigate such theories further (see Chapter 5).

*The Wiley Handbook on the Cognitive Neuroscience of Memory*, First Edition.
Edited by Donna Rose Addis, Morgan Barense, and Audrey Duarte.
© 2015 John Wiley & Sons, Ltd. Published 2015 by John Wiley & Sons, Ltd.

An early example of this use of neuroimaging is the study of Düzel and colleagues (1999), who recorded EEG during sequences of four words. Prior to each sequence, a cue instructed participants to decide whether or not each word was seen in a previous study phase ("episodic task"), or whether each word denoted a living or nonliving entity ("semantic task"). Düzel *et al.* found a sustained positive shift over right frontal electrodes for the episodic task relative to the semantic task. This positive shift emerged shortly after the instruction onset, but prior to the presentation of the first word (i.e., before any retrieval had taken place), and so was interpreted as evidence of a preparatory state for episodic retrieval, i.e., a retrieval mode.

This neuroimaging finding in turn prompted new theoretical proposals. Rugg and Wilding (2000) proposed that there may be different states even within a retrieval mode, in which people are oriented towards retrieving different types of episodic information. They called these "retrieval orientations." For example, Herron and Wilding (2004) reported a more positive-going left frontocentral EEG shift when participants prepared to retrieve the type of encoding task under which an item was studied, compared to when they prepared to retrieve the location in which an item was studied. Another example is the study of Ranganath and Paller (1999), which examined event-related potentials (ERPs) locked to the onset of correctly rejected, new (unstudied) items in a recognition memory test. Because such correct rejections are unlikely to elicit any episodic retrieval, any difference in their associated ERPs as a function of retrieval instructions is likely to be a consequence of a different retrieval orientation. In this case, Ranganath and Paller compared a retrieval task in which participants had to endorse objects that had appeared at study, regardless of their size on the screen ("general task"), with another task in which participants were only to endorse items as studied if they appeared in the same size as at study ("specific task"). A more positive-going ERP waveform to correct rejections was found post-stimulus onset over left frontal electrodes for the specific than for the general task.

It is also possible to measure such state-related brain activity with fMRI, though given its worse temporal resolution relative to EEG, special designs are needed that allow statistical modeling to separate state-related from item-related blood-oxygen-level-dependent (BOLD) responses. For example, Donaldson and colleagues (2001) showed state-related activity associated with blocks of a recognition memory task (relative to blocks of a fixation task) in bilateral frontal opercular areas. Moreover, the same brain areas also showed greater item-related activity for correct recognition (hits) than correct rejections, suggesting that frontal operculum supports both a sustained retrieval mode and transient processes associated with successful retrieval. A subsequent fMRI study by Otten, Henson, and Rugg (2002) provided analogous evidence for dissociable "encoding orientations". These authors found that the mean level of state-related activity during blocks of words varied as a function of the number of words later remembered within each block, independent of item-related activity associated with whether or not individual words were successfully remembered. Furthermore, this relationship between state-related activity and subsequent memory occurred in different brain areas as a function of the study task: occurring in left prefrontal cortex when participants performed a semantic (deep) task, and superior medial parietal cortex when participants performed a phonemic (shallow) task.

Importantly, the neuroimaging studies described above have not only led to new theoretical development (e.g., the concepts of retrieval and encoding orientations), but also prompted new behavioral experiments to further test these concepts. Building on the ERP studies such as that of Ranganath and Paller (1999) described above, Jacoby *et al.* (2005) conducted behavioral investigations of retrieval orientation. They used a second memory test to probe the fate of correctly rejected new items (foils) in a first recognition test, as a function of the retrieval orientation that was adopted during that first memory test. Participants studied one list of items under a semantic (deep) task, and another list of items under a phonemic (shallow) task. In the first recognition test, participants were expected to be oriented towards semantic information when distinguishing foils from deeply encoded targets, but oriented towards phonemic information when distinguishing foils from shallowly encoded targets. If so, the foils in the semantic condition should be processed more deeply than the foils in the phonemic condition, and hence themselves be remembered better on the final recognition test. This is exactly what the authors found. Thus, this (indirect) behavioral assay supported the theories of retrieval orientations that originated from neuroimaging research. Furthermore, this assay has been used to examine how retrieval orientations become less precise as people get older.

## Supplementing Behavioral Dissociations with Neuroimaging Dissociations, e.g., Dual-Process Theories

Another situation in which neuroimaging data can complement behavioral data arises when seeking functional dissociations between hypothetical memory processes. For example, there has been a long-standing debate about whether behavioral data from recognition memory tasks are best explained by single- versus dual-process models. Single-process models claim that a single memory-strength variable is sufficient to explain recognition performance, normally couched in terms of signal detection theory (Donaldson, 1996; Dunn, 2004, 2008; Wixted, 2007; Wixted and Mickes, 2010). Dual-process models, however, assume that recognition involves at least two different processes, such as recollection, associated with retrieval of contextual information, and familiarity, providing a generic sense of a previous encounter, but without contextual retrieval (Aggleton and Brown, 1999; Diana *et al.*, 2006; Rotello and Macmillan, 2006; Yonelinas, 2002; see also Chapter 9). It is not clear that behavioral data have yet resolved this debate (though the main protagonists may disagree!). One possible solution is to examine neuroimaging data from the same task: if conditions assumed to entail recollection produce qualitatively, rather than just quantitatively, different patterns of activity across the brain compared to conditions assumed to entail familiarity, then this would appear to support dual-process models (see Henson, 2005, 2006, for further elaboration and assumptions of this type of "forward inference").

A methodological question then becomes how to define a "qualitatively" different pattern of brain activity. With classical statistics, it is not sufficient, for example, to find a significant difference in one brain area for a contrast of a recollection-condition against a baseline condition, and in a different brain area for the contrast of a familiarity-condition with that baseline. This is simply because the failure to find significant activation for each condition in the other brain area could be a null result.

However, even finding a significant interaction between two brain areas and two such contrasts is not sufficient, because we do not know the "neurometric" mapping between fMRI/EEG/MEG signal and the hypothetical processes of interest. This mapping may not be linear (i.e., a doubling in memory strength may not necessarily mean a doubling in BOLD signal or ERP amplitude). Moreover, the neurometric mapping may differ across different brain areas. Indeed, there may be a positive relationship between the neuroimaging signal and a memory process in one area (e.g., increasing BOLD signal associated with increasing memory strength in hippocampus), but a negative relationship between the neuroimaging signal and the same memory process in another area (e.g., decreasing BOLD signal associated with increasing memory strength in perirhinal cortex; Henson, 2006; Squire, Wixted, and Clark, 2007). These considerations mean that even a significant crossover interaction between two areas and two conditions does not refute single-process theories.

Fortunately, there is a method to solve this problem of unknown neurometric mappings, which assumes only that these mappings are monotonic (in other words, the neuroimaging signal must always increase, or always decrease, whenever engagement of the hypothetical process increases, even if it does not increase or decrease in equal steps). This method is called "state-trace analysis," and it was developed in the psychological literature by Bamber (1979). The "reversed association" pattern described by Dunn and Kirsner (1988), and by Henson (2005), is a special case of state-trace analysis. This method requires at least two dependent variables, e.g., neuroimaging signal in two brain areas, and at least three levels of the independent variable, e.g., three memory conditions. When plotting the data from each condition in a space whose axes are defined by the two independent variables, if the resulting "state-trace" is neither monotonically increasing nor monotonically decreasing, then one can refute the hypothesis that there is a single underlying process (for further elaboration, see Newell and Dunn 2008).

This analysis has been recently applied to neuroimaging data, for the first time, by Staresina *et al.* (2013b). These authors examined the amplitude of the initial evoked component (peaking around 400 ms) in ERPs recorded directly from human hippocampus and perirhinal cortex during a recognition memory task. The task enabled definition of three trial types: (1) trials in which an unstudied item was correctly rejected, (2) trials in which a studied item was recognized but its study context was not identified, and (3) trials in which a studied item was recognized and its study context was identified. According to single-process models, conditions 1–3 should be ordered along an increasing continuum of memory strength. However, Staresina *et al.* were able to reject this hypothesis by demonstrating a non-monotonic state-trace, concluding that at least two different processes were occurring in these two brain areas.

While this finding overturns previous claims that a single dimension of memory strength can explain neuroimaging data in the medial temporal lobe during recognition memory tasks (Squire, Wixted, and Clark, 2007; Wixted, 2007), it is important to note that it does not necessarily support specific dual-process memory theories. State-trace analysis only imputes the dimensionality of the underlying causes (assuming a monotonic mapping from those causes to each measurement); it does not constrain what those dimensions are. Thus further theorizing, concerning the precise nature of the experimental conditions, is necessary to infer the nature of the two or more processes that differed across the three conditions in the study by Staresina *et al.*

(2013b). For example, one process may have related to memory strength, while the other could have reflected differences in some other non-mnemonic process that happened to also differ across the three conditions. Note also that, even if there are multiple memory signals in the brain, they may still be mapped onto a single dimension of "evidence of oldness" in order to make a typical old/new recognition decision, i.e., conform to single-process theory in terms of behavioral data.

The use of state-trace analysis for "forward inference" of course resembles the classical "dissociation logic" commonly used in cognitive psychology and neuropsychology (Henson, 2005; Shallice, 2003). In the extreme case, such inferences do not care where in the brain (or when in time) qualitative differences in brain activity are found (cf. "reverse inference," considered in the next section). Indeed, even when brain location may be of interest – such as hippocampus versus perirhinal cortex in the above example of Staresina *et al.* (2013b) – there are limitations to the specificity of such localization. As argued by Henson (2011), for example, as soon as one allows for nonlinear and recurrent transformations of a stimulus (experimental input) by other brain areas, the finding of a non-monotonic state-trace across two measured areas does not necessitate that the processes of interest occur in those areas: the dissociable neuroimaging signals in those areas might instead be due to differing inputs from other (non-measured) areas.

## Inferring Memory Processes Directly from Local Brain Activity (Reverse Inference)

In contrast to the dissociation logic above, one of the most common types of psychological inference from neuroimaging data is based on association: namely, that a memory process occured within an experimental condition because a certain brain area was active. The assumptions and limitations of this type of "reverse inference" have been discussed at length (Poldrack, 2006, 2008). In the extreme case, this inference is only valid under a strict form of functional localization: i.e., when there exists a one-to-one mapping between a specific brain area and a specific cognitive process (Henson, 2005). We return to these limitations later, but first give some examples of this type of inference.

One example of a recent MEG study to use reverse inference was reported by Evans and Wilding (2012). This study tested a particular type of the dual-process theories of recognition memory described above: the independent-dual-process model of Yonelinas and colleagues (Diana *et al.*, 2006; Yonelinas, 2002). According to this model, recollection is a probabilistic event whose occurrence is independent of familiarity. This independence assumption has been questioned by others, however (Berry *et al.*, 2012; Pratte and Rouder, 2012; Wixted and Mickes, 2010), and is difficult to test with behavioral data alone, since the independence assumption is normally necessary in order to score the data.

Evans and Wilding (2012) combined MEG with Tulving's (1985) remember/know procedure, which instructs participants to make a *remember* (R) judgment when they can retrieve any contextual information associated with prior study of an item, a *know* (K) judgment if the item seems familiar to them, but they cannot remember any context, or a *new* (N) judgment if the item does not seem familiar. The basis of Evans and Wilding's reverse inference was an extensive EEG literature in which familiarity is believed to occur from 300 to 500 ms post-stimulus, while recollection is believed to occur later, from 500 to 800 ms (Bridson *et al.*, 2009; Donaldson, Wilding, and Allan, 2003; Greve, van Rossum, and Donaldson, 2007; Mecklinger, 2000; Rugg and Curran, 2007; Tendolkar *et al.*, 2000). They therefore measured the amplitude of the event-related fields (ERFs) in these two time-windows for R, K, and N judgments to studied items (i.e., R hits, K hits, and N misses).

According to Yonelinas's model (and in common with signal-detection theories), for a K judgment to be given, the strength of a familiarity signal needs to exceed some criterion (otherwise an N judgment is given instead). This means that, if R judgments are given only when recollection occurs, and the probability of this recollection is independent of the level of familiarity, then the mean level of familiarity for R judgments will be less than that for K judgments (since the occurrence of recollection means that familiarity does not also need to exceed some criterion in order to make an R judgment). Single-process theories, on the other hand, which assume R and K judgments are quantitatively rather than qualitatively different, always predict that memory strength will be highest for R judgments. Thus the rank order of the ERF from 300 to 500 ms should be N–R–K according to the independent dual-process model, but N–K–R according to single-process theories. Evans and Wilding (2012) found support for the first pattern, with ERF amplitude between 300 and 500 ms for R judgments falling in between that for N and K judgments. For the later time-window of 500–800 ms, on the other hand, the order was N = K < R, consistent with a separate, later recollection effect. This finding therefore supports dual-process models in which recollection and familiarity are independent.

Another recent example of a reverse inference in the context of dual-process models of recognition memory comes from the fMRI study of Taylor, Buratto, and Henson (2013). This study combined R/K judgments with brief, masked primes that occurred immediately prior to each item during a recognition memory test. These primes were masked so effectively that participants were rarely able to identify them. Under such conditions, Jacoby and Whitehouse (1989) found that participants are more likely to endorse test items (targets) as previously studied when the preceding prime was the same item (primed condition), relative to when the preceding prime was a different item (unprimed condition). This memory illusion occurs even for new test items that are not in fact studied, and subsequent studies showed that this increased bias to respond "old" is associated with K judgments, not R judgments (Kinoshita, 1997; Rajaram, 1993). This bias is naturally explained within a dual-process framework by assuming that matching primes increase the familiarity of test items, and this increased familiarity is attributed to the study phase (erroneously in the case of new items).

Taylor, Buratto, and Henson (2013) compared the effects of masked "repetition" primes, of the type discussed above, with the effects of masked "conceptual" primes, which were different but semantically related to the target item (though not associatively related; cf. Rajaram and Geraci, 2000). These conceptual primes increased R but not K judgments, thus showing the opposite effect to repetition primes. This finding is difficult to explain along the conventional dual-process lines described above, i.e, in terms of increased fluency being attributed to familiarity (though see Taylor, Buratto, and Henson 2013, for some suggestions). However, one trivial explanation is that the crossover interaction between repetition versus conceptual primes and R versus K judgments was an artefact of the mutually exclusive nature of the R/K procedure. That is, if the repetition and conceptual primes produced different types of fluency (perceptual versus semantic, for example), participants might feel obliged to indicate this by using K judgments for one type of fluency and R judgments for the other. Indeed, this mutually exclusive responding has been claimed to be a weakness of the standard R/K procedure; when participants are asked to give continuous and parallel ratings of both "remembering" and "knowing" for each item, many experimental manipulations are found to affect both R and K ratings (see Brown and Bodner, 2011; Kurilla and Westerman, 2008).

Taylor, Buratto, and Henson (2013) therefore combined their masked priming paradigm with fMRI, and leveraged on previous fMRI studies that have implicated inferior parietal activation in recollection. The authors replicated the increased BOLD signal in these parietal areas for R versus K judgments, but importantly also found that masked conceptual primes, but not masked repetition primes, increased this parietal activation further (relative to the unprimed case). This observation suggests that the conceptual primes were genuinely increasing recollection. This is therefore an example of where a reverse inference from neuroimaging data can be used to rule out an alternative theoretical account: here, that the interaction between R/K judgments and repetition/conceptual primes was a methodological artefact of the mutually exclusive R/K procedure.

Assuming the reverse inferences used by Evans and Wilding (2012) and Taylor, Buratto, and Henson (2013) are valid, both of these neuroimaging studies not only provide additional constraints on theories of recognition memory; they also offer methodological guidance for analysis of behavioral data, such as whether R and K judgments can be assumed to be independent (rather than redundant or exclusive; Knowlton and Squire, 1995; Mayes, Montaldi, and Migo, 2007). However, as mentioned earlier, the assumption of reverse inference, in its most extreme form, requires that the 300–500 ms ERF amplitude (in the Evans and Wilding example) reflects differences in, and only in, familiarity, and that the inferior parietal BOLD amplitude (in the Taylor and colleagues example) reflects differences in, and only in, recollection. If instead the 300–500 ms ERF or parietal BOLD amplitude reflect differences between R, K, and N categories other than their mean familiarity or recollection respectively (e.g., differences in some confounding variable), then the theoretical (reverse) inferences do not follow. For example, electrophysiological signals from 300–500 ms in recognition tasks have been argued not to reflect familiarity per se, but rather forms of implicit conceptual fluency (Paller, Voss, and Boehm, 2007; see also Chapter 3). Likewise, the BOLD signal in parietal cortex might not reflect recollection per se, but rather differences in endogenous or exogenous attention, or perhaps even differences related to motor preparation (given that "old" decisions associated with R judgments tend be made faster on average).

The nature of the mapping between brain measure and cognitive process is of course at the heart of cognitive neuroscience. The extreme form of functional localization assumes that each distinct brain area supports one unique hypothetical function (Figure 1.1a). To avoid making this one-to-one mapping between neuroimaging measure and cognitive process (which may not be provable in the strict sense: Henson, 2005), Poldrack (2006) suggested reverse inferences as probabilistic, according to a Bayesian framework. According to the Bayes' theorem, the probability that a cognitive function F1 was engaged when activity in a certain brain area A1 is observed depends on how likely it is that this brain area is active when function F1 is known to have

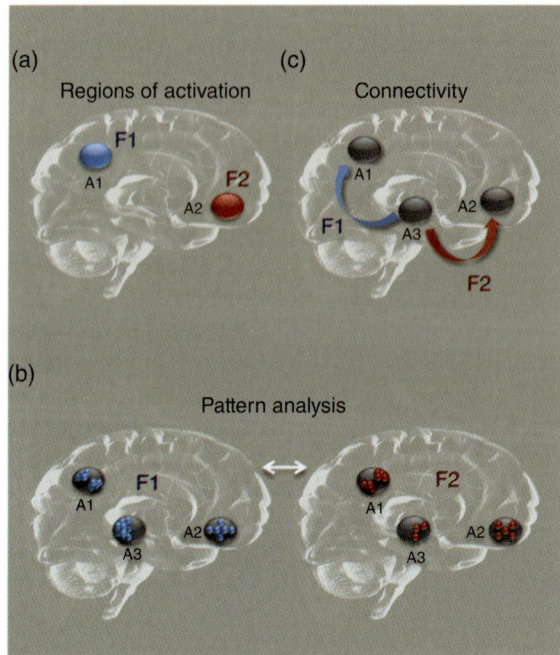

**Figure 1.1** Schematic drawings of the human brain that illustrate different potential mappings of distinct memory functions (F1, F2) onto neural activity within and across distinct brain areas (A1, A2, A3). Changes in cognitive function can give rise to modulations in: (a) average levels of activity in different brain areas, (b) the pattern of activity within and across different regions, and (c) the nature of connectivity between multiple brain areas.

occurred, multiplied by the prior probability that function F1 generally occurs, and divided by the baseline probability that brain area A1 is generally active. While the likelihood of A1 being activated, whether or not F1 is assumed to have occurred, can be estimated from databases or meta-analyses, estimating the prior probability of function F1 occurring is problematic (though see Poldrack, 2006, for a possible solution).

In general terms, the implication of this Bayesian formulation is that, even if activity in a certain brain area is very likely to occur with a specific function – for example, a cognitive process reliably activates that area – this is not particularly informative if the same area is also activated in many other situations where that function is not involved. This has led many to criticize the weakness of reverse inferences. More recently, Hutzler (2014) argued that, if one further conditionalizes the probability of a brain area being activated on a subset of tasks (e.g., just those experiments that examined activity during a recognition memory task), then reverse inferences become stronger. In other words, if a brain area has consistently been activated in association with a specific memory process *in the context of recognition memory tasks* (ignoring how often it is activated in other types of tasks), then its activation in a new recognition memory experiment can provide strong evidence that this process has occurred. Thus, if the 300–500 ms ERF and parietal BOLD effects in the Evans and Wilding (2012) and Taylor, Buratto, and Henson (2013) studies have been consistently associated with familiarity and recollection respectively by prior neuroimaging experiments of recognition memory (regardless of whether they occur in other contexts), then this would bolster the reverse inferences described above.

The problem with Hutzler's (2014) argument is that it requires a definition of the subset of tasks over which to estimate the prior probability of activation (e.g., recognition memory tasks just with visual stimuli, or with any type of stimulus?). This debate then returns to the persistent question of cognitive theory, that is, the ontology of basic cognitive processes and their engagement in specific tasks. If this ontology can be established on purely independent grounds (e.g., from behavioral data alone), then reverse inference might become valid, but ironically neuroimaging is then no longer necessary for informing the ontology. An alternative pragmatic approach, suggested by Henson (2005), is that reverse inferences may start as being weak, but can still be used to inform and/or revise the cognitive ontology, leading to new experiments and iterated inferences until there is (hopefully) a convergence of brain mapping and cognitive ontology, such that a one-to-one mapping between brain area and cognitive process is established; at which point, reverse inference then becomes valid (see also Gonsalves and Cohen, 2010; Poldrack and Wagner, 2004).

## Anatomical and Functional Scale, High-Resolution fMRI, and Contact with Animal Models

The above discussion raises the important issue of granularity (Henson, 2005): that is, at what level of specificity to define a cognitive process and at what spatial scale to define a "brain area." In terms of memory processes, for example, it is possible that recollection is not a unitary construct, in that retrieval of spatial context might be a dissociable function from retrieval of temporal context (e.g., Duarte *et al.*, 2010) and likewise, familiarity might encompass fluency of multiple different types of processing, e.g., orthographic, phonological, semantic, etc. In terms of brain areas, on the other hand, it is possible that trying to ascribe a single function to the hippocampus is inappropriate because it in fact contains several distinct subfields that each serve a different function, e.g., dentate gyrus (DG), CA1, CA3, and subiculum (Deguchi *et al.*, 2011; Lee *et al.*, 2004; Leutgeb *et al.*, 2004; Schmidt, Marrone, and Markus, 2012; Vazdarjanova and Guzowski, 2004; see also Chapter 6). In this case, averaging activity over all voxels within the hippocampus will obscure such functional differences. Analogously, had Evans and Wilding (2012) averaged over all time samples between 300 ms and 800 ms in their MEG study, then no difference between familiarity and recollection might have been observed.

It is possible that the appropriate level of anatomical granularity will only be found when the spatial resolution of neuroimaging techniques such as fMRI is increased. Indeed, in the extreme, we would like to be able to measure activity in individual neurons (or even individual synapses). This is of course possible in animals, but rarely in humans. Nonetheless, there are many computational models of the hippocampus (and other brain areas) that are based on such single-cell data from animals (Hasselmo and Howard, 2005; Lisman and Otmakhova, 2001; Treves and Rolls, 1994), some of which have hypothesized specialized functions for hippocampal subfields. The advent of high-resolution fMRI means that some of these subfields can now be imaged in humans, which in turn allows a bridge between human and animal data and models. For example, two concepts popularized in computational (neural network) models of the hippocampus are *pattern separation* and *pattern completion* (for more discussion, see Chapter 6). Pattern separation refers to the ability to orthogonalize similar input patterns (e.g., to separate two episodes that occurred in similar contexts), whereas pattern completion refers to the ability to group together different input patterns (e.g., to complete the details of an episodic memory given only a partial cue).

Several recent models attribute pattern separation to the DG. Inputs from cortical areas are assumed to reflect distributed patterns of activity, which are transformed into unique hippocampal representations via the DG and its subsequent sparse projections to the CA3 field. The recurrent connectivity within CA3, on the other hand, is thought to support pattern completion, via conjunctive representations of co-occurring elements. When a noisy or partial cue is presented, these conjunctive codes and recurrent connections enable completion of associated information (which is then projected back into the cortex via other subfields such as CA1 and subiculum). Most fMRI studies to date (which typically have a resolution of 3 mm isotropic) have been unable to resolve these hippocampal subfields, and so it has been difficult to test theories about pattern separation and completion, given that these processes co-occur.

Bakker *et al.* (2008), however, used the higher resolution (1.5 mm isotropic) afforded by recent advances in fMRI to separate BOLD signal across hippocampal subfields. They presented participants with a series of images, in which some images were either the same as previous images in the series, or were similar but not identical. If participants noticed this slight change, the DG showed a novelty response that was also observed for new items, but was absent when exact replicas of previously studied images were shown (though it was not possible to distinguish DG and CA3 even at this resolution). Bakker *et al.* interpreted this pattern as supporting a role of human DG in pattern separation. Neural populations in CA1 and subiculum areas, on the other hand, did not show a novelty response for the similar items and did not differentiate between the similar and identical items, and were interpreted as contributing to pattern completion (see also Johnson, Muftuler, and Rugg, 2008).

Clearly today's high-resolution fMRI is unlikely to be sufficient to reveal all functional subdivisions in our brains, and this may remain the case even if we reach theoretical limits on fMRI resolution, for example, in terms of vascular coverage. Nonetheless, the finer level of spatial granularity offered by higher-resolution fMRI is still likely to furnish insights beyond those afforded by our current resolutions, and thereby further reduce the gap between human and animal models. High-resolution fMRI is also likely to increase the amount of information extracted by multivariate pattern analyses, as discussed next.

## Multivariate Pattern Analysis: Processes Versus Representations?

Multivariate pattern analysis (MVPA) is a relatively recent method that uses powerful pattern classification algorithms to determine whether different types of stimuli or cognitive processes can be classified on the basis of patterns of activity over voxels (in fMRI, e.g., Haxby *et al.*, 2001; Norman *et al.*, 2006; Polyn *et al.*, 2005), or over sensors/time-points/frequencies (in MEG/EEG, e.g., Jafarpour *et al.*, 2013). Thus in an fMRI experiment, for example, rather than comparing two conditions in terms of the average BOLD signal across voxels within a region of interest (ROI), the traditional "univariate" approach, MVPA compares them in terms of patterns of signals across voxels within that ROI, which may not necessarily differ in the average signal (Figure 1.1b). These methods have been shown to offer the remarkable ability to "decode" brain activity, for example, to determine what stimulus a person is looking at from the brain activity alone (see Norman *et al.*, 2006, for review; for more discussion of MVPA, see Chapters 2 and 6).

Some caution should be exercised concerning the recent excitement around MVPA, however, which again has to do with the questions of granularity and functional–anatomical mapping. If one were to include all voxels within the brain, then it would not be particularly surprising if MVPA could distinguish two stimuli that were perceivably different. Analyses of this kind are more theoretically interesting when participants have no reportable access to the processes of interest, or when patterns are restricted to various ROIs: for example, to discover that episodic memories can be classified above chance within one ROI, e.g., hippocampus (Chadwick *et al.*, 2010), but not within another, e.g., cerebellum. Yet it should be noted that this latter use of MVPA to "decode" brain activity within ROIs describes another form of functional localization, albeit one that may be more sensitive than traditional analyses that only consider the mean activity within an ROI[1]. Indeed, this use of MVPA is analogous to the issue of spatial resolution discussed in the previous section: a standard-resolution voxel can be viewed as an ROI that averages over what might be quite distinct patterns of activity had a higher resolution been used (i.e., one scanner's voxel is another scanner's ROI!).

Nonetheless, there has been a more important shift in perspective triggered by MVPA, in terms of characterizing the nature of neural representations. One example of this is the development of methods to test whether neural representations are sparse or distributed (e.g., Morcom and Friston, 2012). Another example, which is likely to have a significant effect on the field, is representational similarity analysis (RSA), in which the activity patterns for a large number of different stimuli are compared in terms of their similarity (see Chapter 6). The emergence of structure within the resulting stimulus-by-stimulus "similarity matrix" then gives clues to what an ROI is representing (e.g., animate versus inanimate visual objects; Kriegeskorte *et al.*, 2008). Thus the focus is not so much on whether or not patterns can be classified according to two or more experimentally defined categories, but on letting the data reveal the nature of the categories represented by an ROI (its "representational geometry"). Moreover, the similarity spaces observed in neuroimaging data can then be compared to those predicted by competing computational models (by applying RSA to model outputs, when the models are "presented with" the same stimuli). This approach offers an interesting potential way to test the computational models of the MTL described in the previous section (e.g., in terms of pattern separation and completion).

Moreover, the greater sensitivity of MVPA classification methods over traditional univariate methods should not be dismissed, because it has allowed researchers to track the presence of neural activity patterns (representations) over time in continuous – and hence noisy – brain activity. This has been particularly influential in memory research, where reactivation of memories can be examined by training a classifier on stimuli presented during the study phase, and then testing that classifier's ability to detect the same patterns during retrieval (when the stimuli are no longer present, e.g., cued by a different stimulus). One of the first examples to use this approach was the fMRI study of Polyn *et al.* (2005). These authors wanted to test the contextual reinstatement hypothesis (Bartlett, 1932; Tulving and Thomson, 1973), which states that people retrieve specific episodic details by first activating information about the general properties of such episodes. Polyn *et al.* did this by asking participants to study famous faces, famous locations, and common objects. An MVPA classifier was trained to distinguish these three categories from fMRI data acquired during the study phase. Then, using the fMRI data acquired when participants later freely recalled the names of the studied stimuli, the classifier predicted the category that participants were thinking about, on a moment-by-moment basis. Consistent with the contextual reinstatement hypothesis, high classification about a given category emerged several seconds before specific examples of that category were recalled.

MVPA has also been used in MEG, at least in the context of maintenance in short-term memory. Fuentemilla *et al.* (2010) trained an MVPA classifier to distinguish indoor or outdoor scenes, and then looked for above-chance classification (across sensors) at various times and frequencies during a 5-second retention interval. Interestingly, reactivations of above-chance classification were common in the theta frequency range (around 6 Hz) and correlated with memory performance, although only for blocks in which configural information needed to be retained during that interval. The authors argued that these data support animal models in which theta-coupled replay supports maintenance of information in working memory. Evidence for reactivation during a longer-term retention interval has also recently been found with fMRI. Staresina and colleagues (2013a) tracked the fMRI activity patterns occurring during a retention interval in which participants performed an odd/even distractor task, comparing their similarity to patterns evoked by individual stimuli during the study phase. Greater similarity was found for stimuli that were recalled in the subsequent test phase than for stimuli that were not, which supports the hypothesis that long-term memories are retained and/or consolidated by offline reactivation.

These examples thus illustrate a more subtle effect of the advent of MVPA, namely the theoretical shift in interpreting neuroimaging data in terms of processes versus representations. Results from univariate tests within an ROI are normally interpreted in terms of processes, i.e, the degree to which recollection or familiarity occurred, whereas MVPA results are normally interpreted in terms of representations. In reality, of course, it is impossible to define processes in the absence of representations (and vice versa), and defining both is often only possible in the context of formal models. Greve, Donaldson, and van Rossum (2010), for instance, described a neural network model that simulates two kinds of retrieval processes that operate on the same memory representation. This model simulated both familiarity-based and recollection-based discrimination of old and new items, which paralleled the characteristics reported in the empirical literature. Simulations like this demonstrate how the psychological processes of recollection and familiarity may reflect qualitatively distinct retrieval (read-out) operations that act on the same representations within a single brain area. More generally, explicit neural models like those described by Greve and colleagues, coupled with a subtle shift in perspective between characterizing processes and characterizing representations, may alter the way neuroimaging data are used to inform memory theories.

# Functional and Effective Connectivity in Memory, e.g., within MTL

A further logical possibility is that some memory processes/representations are most visible in changes in the connectivity between brain areas, rather than in average activity or activity patterns within each area (Figure 1.1c). Given that memories are likely to be stored in terms of changes in synaptic strengths, and that those occur between as well as within brain areas, it would seem likely that those synaptic changes would alter the functional connectivity between areas. Recollection, for example, might correspond not simply to high activity levels within hippocampus, but rather to high levels of connectivity between hippocampus and other cortical areas, which represent the content of recollected memories (see also Chapter 13). Indeed, it is also possible that the same set of brain areas could enable different memory functions depending on changes in the effective connectivity between them; that is, the same anatomical network could "re-wire" into different functional networks according to different memory processes.

Some of the first fMRI studies to investigate memory-related changes in functional connectivity were performed by Maguire, Mummery, and Büchel (2000). These authors used structural equation modeling (SEM), a technique that tests competing models against each other, to evaluate explicit network models defined over a small number of ROIs. Assuming a model provides a satisfactory fit to the time-series data in each ROI, SEM coefficients for individual connections can then be interpreted in terms of "effective connectivity" between ROIs. Effective connectivity in this context goes beyond functional connectivity (e.g., in Figure 1.1a, simple pairwise correlation between activity in two areas A1 and A2) in that it allows for indirect connections (e.g., in Figure 1.1c, testing whether the correlation between A1 and A2 is actually due solely to a common input from a third area A3, assuming that all the areas that modulate activity within the network have been included in the model). Maguire *et al.* used SEM to address a theoretical debate about the distinction between semantic and episodic memory. The multiple-memory systems view (Tulving 1987) holds that separate memory systems are specialized for processing episodic and semantic information, supported by functionally independent networks. The alternative unitary system view proposes a single declarative memory system (McIntosh, 1999; Rajah and McIntosh, 2005; Roediger, 1984), in which memories can vary along a contextual continuum. Maguire and colleagues tested these theories by acquiring fMRI data while participants judged the accuracy of sentences about four different types of information: autobiographical events, public events, autobiographical facts, and general knowledge. They then defined a memory retrieval network by comparing activity common to all four of these types of sentence against a scrambled sentence baseline condition. This network included medial frontal cortex, left temporal pole, left hippocampus, left anterolateral middle temporal gyrus, parahippocampal cortex, posterior cingulate, retrosplenial cortex, and temporoparietal junction.

SEM then revealed several differences in effective connectivity between areas within this retrieval network as a function of the type of information retrieved. For example, connectivity from temporal pole to parahippocampal gyrus increased during retrieval of autobiographical relative to public events. Connectivity from temporal pole to lateral temporal cortex, on the other hand, increased during retrieval of public relative to autobiographical events. The authors argued that this pattern of results is more consistent with the view that episodic and semantic memories originate from separate systems that differ in the way information is processed, than with the view that semantic and episodic memories emerge from a continuum of representations that differ in contextual detail. Furthermore, the data suggest that brain areas can have multiple functions during memory retrieval, depending on their connectivity with other brain areas.

Gagnepain *et al.* (2010) provided another example of the different perspectives offered by local activity versus effective connectivity. These authors used dynamic causal modeling (DCM) of fMRI data, which can be thought of as an extension of SEM that includes a more sophisticated model of the dynamics of neural interactions and their expression via the haemodynamic (BOLD) response. DCM was applied to fMRI data from a study phase in which participants performed an incidental task on auditory words, and memory was tested 24 hours later using a remember/know procedure. Of primary interest was how neural activity that predicted subsequent R versus K judgments varied as a function of whether or not words at study had been primed via pre-study exposure. Unprimed words showed the usual pattern of greater hippocampal activity for words later attracting R judgments than for words later receiving K judgments. For primed words, however, this pattern was reversed, with decreased activity for words that attracted R than K judgments. This suggests that local hippocampal activity alone is not sufficient to predict subsequent memory. Instead, DCM analysis showed that subsequent R judgments were associated with increased effective connectivity to the hippocampus from the superior temporal gyrus – an area that showed the usual reduction in activity for primed relative to unprimed words. This was explained in terms of priming improving the transmission of sensory information to hippocampus, resulting in stronger associations between that information and its spatiotemporal context. Regardless of whether this explanation is correct, the more important issue for present purposes is that some causes of successful memory encoding may be found in the functional coupling between areas, rather than in local activity within those areas.

Given that much communication between brain areas during memory encoding and retrieval is likely to occur on the scale of tenths of a second, methods for testing effective connectivity are likely to be more theoretically illuminating when applied to MEG/EEG data than fMRI data, because changes in connectivity over such rapid timescales will be invisible to fMRI. Intracranial EEG data acquired directly from the medial temporal lobes of patients about to undergo surgery, for example, have shown transient increases in coupling between hippocampus and perirhinal cortex in the gamma frequency band (around 40 Hz) associated with successful memory encoding (Fell *et al.*, 2001). Recent methods that use DCM to compare different network models of extracranial MEG and EEG data may also prove a useful approach when intracranial data are not available (Kiebel *et al.*, 2008).

## Closing the Loop: Inferring Causality from Neuroimaging Data

It is often stated that neuroimaging data are only correlational, and therefore brain activity may be incidental to a memory process of interest, rather than causing that process. This is sometimes then taken to mean that neuroimaging data are somehow inferior to behavioral data. The latter claim, however, would be mistaken, since both measures of brain activity and measures of behavior (for example, accuracy or speed) are measurements of the same neural/cognitive system. Indeed, the behavioral responses only reflect the final output, with less information about the intermediate stages between stimulus and response. In most cognitive neuroscientific (hypothetical-deductive) frameworks, neither type of measurement can directly "cause" a cognitive process; this would only make sense if one measurement were used as a surrogate for a process of interest, according to some theory (for further discussion of this issue, see Henson, 2005). Thus, claims that neuroimaging differences are confounded by concurrent behavioral differences are usually invalid: behavioral differences cannot cause activity differences; rather, brain activity and behavioral responses are normally both considered as the consequence of some hypothetical process. In the context of more mechanistic models of information flow, sensory input can be said to cause activity in one brain area, which can then be said to cause activity in another area, ultimately causing motor output (i.e., a behavioral response).

Of course, what is normally meant by the statement that neuroimaging data are only correlational is that they cannot tell us about the causal role of a brain area in a cognitive process in the same way that lesion data do. This issue would appear to be undeniable, and of course raises the question about how to define causality (Henson, 2005; Weber and Thompson-Schill, 2010). Without getting into philosophical debate, one recent step towards inferring causality from neuroimaging data was made by Yoo *et al.* (2012). Normally, a stimulus or task is manipulated experimentally, and brain and behavioral data are measured in response. Yoo *et al.*, on the other hand, used brain data to control when a stimulus was presented, and measured the consequence for subsequent behavior (i.e., the brain data were used to define the independent variable, rather than being the dependent variable). More precisely, they used real-time fMRI to measure online activity in the parahippocampal place area (PPA), and then presented visual scenes when PPA activity corresponded to either a "good" or "bad" state, where those states were defined by a prior experiment in which PPA activity was related to subsequent memory for scenes. Later testing outside the scanner then showed that recognition memory for the scenes presented during the "good" brain state was superior to that for scenes presented during the "bad" state. This finding thus bolsters the claim for a causal role in PPA activity during memory encoding. This approach still does not correspond to experimental manipulations that directly affect neural activity in a brain area (e.g., transcranial magnetic stimulation, TMS) – in that it relies on spontaneous rather than controlled changes in PPA state – but it is another interesting example of how neuroimaging data can be used to inform neuroscientific theories about how our brains enable our memories.

## Conclusion

We have presented a number of examples of neuroimaging studies that we believe have enriched our understanding of human memory. For example, we have illustrated cases where neuroimaging has been informative in investigating memory processes that are difficult to access behaviorally. In other cases, neuroimaging provides additional sources of constraints (e.g., dissociations) that can be used to distinguish competing memory theories. Moreover, neuroimaging has not only offered additional ways to test existing theories, but has also facilitated the development of new experimental paradigms for behavioral studies, and provided the ability to address assumptions underlying some behavioral analysis methods.

We have emphasized that the value of neuroimaging hinges on the types of analysis and inference employed. While most neuroimaging studies have focused on the average activity within brain areas (or within time/frequency windows) and have been portrayed solely in terms of localizing a presumed memory process (in space or time), some neuroimaging studies have tried to reverse this inference, using neuroimaging data to determine whether a memory process occurred in a certain context. Furthermore, recent analysis techniques have started to utilize patterns of activity over voxels or times/frequencies, rather than just averaging that activity, and to consider what these patterns might represent. Other analyses have focused on memory-related changes in the communication between brain regions in terms of effective connectivity. These new analyses in turn force memory researchers to think carefully about how memory processes might be implemented in terms of neural representations and synaptic changes between neural populations. Such thoughts are best formalized in computational models of neuronal networks, which can then be tested in more detail with animal experiments.

Having said this, there are still deep philosophical issues that need to be considered when interpreting neuroimaging data. Issues related to the granularity of cognitive processes and resolvable brain areas, for example, must be considered when interpreting neuroimaging data, for example, for reverse inferences. We also acknowledge that not all neuroimaging studies of memory have made useful contributions to memory theories, and that the neuroimaging field continues to be plagued by tricky statistical issues that may question some published findings. Nonetheless, we do not think these are reasons to "throw the baby out with the bathwater."

## Note

1   This also raises the question of how the ROIs are defined in the first place, which is often based on traditional mass univariate analyses that search through the whole brain, though analogous searchlight methods exist to apply MVPA within a fixed volume, the center of which can be traversed across the entire brain image (Kriegeskorte *et al.* 2008).

## References

Aggleton, J.P., and Brown, M.W. (1999). Episodic memory, amnesia, and the hippocampal–anterior thalamic axis. *Behavioral and Brain Sciences*, 22 (3), 425–444.

Bakker, A., Kirwan, C.B., Miller, M., and Stark, C.E.L. (2008). Pattern separation in the human hippocampal CA3 and dentate gyrus. *Science*, 319, 1640–1642. doi: 10.1126/science.1152882.

Bamber, D. (1979). State-trace analysis: a method of testing simple theories of causation. *Journal of Mathematical Psychology*, 19 (2), 137–181. doi:10.1016/0022-2496(79)90016-6.

Bartlett, F.C. (1932). *Remembering: A Study in Experimental and Social Psychology*. Cambridge: Cambridge University Press.

Berry, C.J., Shanks, D.R., Speekenbrink, M., and Henson, R.N. (2012). Models of recognition, repetition priming, and fluency: exploring a new framework. *Psychological Review*, 119 (1), 40–79. doi: 10.1037/a0025464

Bridson, N.C., Muthukumaraswamy, S.D., Singh, K.D., and Wilding, E.L. (2009). Magnetoencephalographic correlates of processes supporting long-term memory judgments. *Brain Research*, 1283, 73–83. doi: 10.1016/j.brainres.2009.05.093.

Brown, A.A., and Bodner, G.E. (2011). Re-examining dissociations between remembering and knowing: binary judgments vs. independent ratings. *Journal of Memory and Language*, 65, 98–108.

Chadwick, M.J., Hassabis, D., Weiskopf, N., and Maguire, E.A. (2010). Decoding individual episodic memory traces in the human hippocampus. *Current Biology*, 20 (6), 544–547. doi: 10.1016/j.cub.2010.01.053.

Coltheart, M. (2006). What has functional neuroimaging told us about the mind (so far)? (Position paper presented to the European Cognitive Neuropsychology Workshop, Bressanone, 2005). *Cortex*, 42, 323–331

Deguchi, Y., Donato, F., Galimberti, I., *et al.* (2011). Temporally matched subpopulations of selectively interconnected principal neurons in the hippocampus. *Nature Neuroscience*, 14 (4), 495–504.

Diana, R.A., Reder, L.M., Arndt, J., and Park, H. (2006). Models of recognition: a review of arguments in favor of a dual-process account. *Psychonomic Bulletin Review*, 13 (1), 1–21.

Donaldson, D.I., Petersen, S.E., Ollinger, J.M., and Buckner, R.L. (2001). Dissociating state and item components of recognition memory using fMRI. *NeuroImage*, 13 (1), 129–142. doi: 10.1006/nimg.2000.0664.

Donaldson, D.I., Wilding, E.L., and Allan, K. (2003). Fractionating retrieval from episodic memory using event-related potentials. In *The Cognitive Neuroscience of Memory: Episodic Encoding and Retrieval* (ed. E.L. Wilding, A.E. Parker, and T.J. Bussey). Hove, UK: Psychology Press, pp. 39–58.

Donaldson, W. (1996). The role of decision processes in remembering and knowing. *Memory and Cognition*, 24, 523–533.

Duarte, A., Henson, R.N., Knight, R.T., *et al.* (2010). Orbito-frontal cortex is necessary for temporal context memory. *Journal of Cognitive Neuroscience*, 22 (8), 1819–1831. doi: 10.1162/jocn.2009.21316.

Dunn, J.C. (2004). Remember–know: a matter of confidence. *Psychological Review*, 111, 524–542.

Dunn, J.C. (2008). The dimensionality of the remember–know task: a state-trace analysis. *Psychological Review*, 115 (2), 426–446. doi: 10.1037/0033-295x.115.2.426.

Dunn, J.C., and Kirsner, K. (1988). Discovering functionally independent mental processes: the principle of reversed association. *Psychological Review*, 95 (1), 91–101. doi: 10.1037/0033-295x.95.1.91.

Düzel E., Cabeza, R., Picton, T.W., *et al.* (1999). Task-related and item-related brain processes of memory retrieval. *Proceedings of the National Academy of Sciences of the USA*, 96, 1794–1799.

Evans, L.H., and Wilding, E.L. (2012). Recollection and familiarity make independent contributions to memory judgments. *Journal of Neuroscience*, 32 (21), 7253–7257. doi: 10.1523/jneurosci.6396-11.2012.

Fell, J., Klaver, P., Lehnertz, K., *et al.* (2001). Human memory formation is accompanied by rhinal-hippocampal coupling and decoupling. *Nature Neuroscience*, 4 (12), 1259–1264.

Fuentemilla, L., Penny, W.D., Cashdollar, N., *et al.* (2010). Theta-coupled periodic replay in working memory *Current Biology*, 20 (7), 606–612. doi: 10.1016/j.cub.2010.01.057.

Gagnepain, P., Henson, R.N., Chételat, G., *et al.* (2010). Is neocortical–hippocampal connectivity a better predictor of subsequent recollection than local increases in hippocampal activity? New insights on the role of priming. *Journal of Cognitive Neuroscience*, 23 (2), 391–403. doi: 10.1162/jocn.2010.21454.

Gonsalves B.D., and Cohen, N.J. (2010). Brain imaging, cognitive processes, and brain networks. *Perspectives on Psychological Science*, 5, 744–752.

Greve, A., Donaldson, D.I., and van Rossum, M.C.W. (2010). A single-trace dual-process model of episodic memory: a novel computational account of familiarity and recollection. *Hippocampus*, 20 (2), 235–251. doi: 10.1002/hipo.20606.

Greve, A., van Rossum, M.C.W., and Donaldson, D.I. (2007). Investigating the functional interaction between semantic and episodic memory: convergent behavioral and electrophysiological evidence for the role of familiarity. *NeuroImage*, 34 (2), 801–814.

Hasselmo, M.E., and Howard, E. (2005). Hippocampal mechanisms for the context-dependent retrieval of episodes. *Neural Networks*, 18 (9), 1172–1190. doi: 10.1016/j.neunet.2005.08.007.

Haxby, J.V., Gobbini, M.I., Furey, *et al.* (2001). Distributed and overlapping representations of faces and objects in ventral temporal cortex. *Science*, 293 (5539), 2425–2430. doi: 10.1126/science.1063736.

Henson, R.N. (2005). What can functional neuroimaging tell the experimental psychologist? *Quarterly Journal of Experimental Psychology, Section A: Human Experimental Psychology*, 58 (2), 193–233. doi: 10.1080/02724980443000502.

Henson, R.N. (2006). Forward inference using functional neuroimaging: dissociations versus associations. *Trends in Cognitive Sciences*, 10 (2), 64–69. doi: 10.1016/j.tics.2005.12.005.

Henson, R.N. (2011). How to discover modules in mind and brain: the curse of nonlinearity, and blessing of neuroimaging. A comment on Sternberg (2011). *Cognitive Neuropsychology* 28 (3–4), 209–223. doi: 10.1080/02643294.2011.561305.

Herron J.E., and Wilding, E.L. (2004). An electrophysiological dissociation of retrieval mode and retrieval orientation. *NeuroImage*, 22, 1554–1562.

Hutzler, F. (2014). Reverse inference is not a fallacy per se: cognitive processes can be inferred from functional imaging data. *NeuroImage*, 84, 1061–1069. doi: 10.1016/j.neuroimage.2012.12.075.

Jacoby, L.L., Shimizu, Y., Daniels, K.A., and Rhodes, M.G. (2005). Modes of cognitive control in recognition and source memory: depth of retrieval. *Psychonomic Bulletin and Review*, 12 (5), 852–857.

Jacoby, L.L., and Whitehouse, K. (1989). An illusion of memory: false recognition influenced by unconscious perception. *Journal of Experimental Psychology: General* 118 (2), 126–135. doi: 10.1037/0096-3445.118.2.126.

Jafarpour, A., Horner, A.J. Fuentemilla, L., *et al.* (2013). Decoding oscillatory representations and mechanisms in memory. *Neuropsychologia*, 51 (4), 772–780. doi: 10.1016/j.neuropsychologia.2012.04.002.

Johnson, J.D., Muftuler, L.T., and Rugg, M.D. (2008). Multiple repetitions reveal functionally and anatomically distinct patterns of hippocampal activity during continuous recognition memory. *Hippocampus*, 18 (10), 975–980. doi: 10.1002/hipo.20456.

Kiebel, S., Garrido, M., Moran, R., and Friston, K. (2008). Dynamic causal modelling for EEG and MEG. *Cognitive Neurodynamics*, 2 (2), 121–136. doi: 10.1007/s11571-008-9038-0.

Kinoshita, S. (1997). Masked target priming effects on feeling-of-knowing and feeling-of-familiarity judgments. *Acta Psychologica*, 97 (2), 183–199.

Knowlton, B.J., and Squire, L.R. (1995). Remembering and knowing: two different expressions of declarative memory. *Journal of Experimental Psychology: Learning, Memory, and Cognition*, 21 (3), 699–710.

Kriegeskorte, N., Mur, M., Ruff, D.A., *et al.* (2008). Matching categorical object representations in inferior temporal cortex of man and monkey. *Neuron* 60 (6), 1126–1141. doi: 10.1016/j.neuron.2008.10.043.

Kurilla B.P., and Westerman, D.L. (2008). Processing fluency affects subjective claims of recollection. *Memory & Cognition*, 36, 82–92.

Lee, I., Yoganarasimha, D., Rao, G., and Knierim, J.J. (2004). Comparison of population coherence of place cells in hippocampal subfields CA1 and CA3. *Nature*, 430 (6998), 456–459.

Leutgeb, S., Leutgeb, J.K., Treves, A., *et al.* (2004). Distinct ensemble codes in hippocampal areas CA3 and CA1. *Science*, 305 (5688), 1295–1298. doi: 10.1126/science.1100265.

Lisman, J.E., and Otmakhova, N.A. (2001). Storage, recall, and novelty detection of sequences by the hippocampus: elaborating on the SOCRATIC model to account for normal and aberrant effects of dopamine. *Hippocampus*, 11 (5), 551–568. doi: 10.1002/hipo.1071.

Maguire, E.A., Mummery, C.J., and Büchel, C. (2000). Patterns of hippocampal–cortical interaction dissociate temporal lobe memory subsystems. *Hippocampus* 10 (4), 475–482. doi: 10.1002/1098-1063(2000)10:4<475::aid-hipo14>3.0.co;2-x.

Mayes, A., Montaldi, D., and Migo, E. (2007). Associative memory and the medial temporal lobes. *Trends in Cognitive Sciences*, 11 (3), 126–135. doi: 10.1016/j.tics.2006.12.003.

McIntosh, A.R. (1999). Mapping cognition to the brain through neural interactions. *Memory*, 7 (5–6), 523–548. doi: 10.1080/096582199387733.

Mecklinger, A. (2000). Interfacing mind and brain: a neurocognitive model of recognition memory. *Psychophysiology*, 37 (5), 565–582. doi: 10.1111/1469-8986.3750565.

Morcom, A.M., and Friston, K.J. (2012). Decoding episodic memory in ageing: a Bayesian analysis of activity patterns predicting memory. *NeuroImage*, 59 (2), 1772–1782. doi: 10.1016/j.neuroimage.2011.08.071.

Newell, B.R., and Dunn, J.C. (2008). Dimensions in data: testing psychological models using state-trace analysis. *Trends in Cognitive Sciences*, 12 (8), 285–290.

Norman, K.A., Polyn, S.M., Detre, G.J., and Haxby, J.V. (2006). Beyond mind-reading: multi-voxel pattern analysis of fMRI data. *Trends in Cognitive Sciences*, 10 (9), 424–430. doi: 10.1016/j.tics.2006.07.005.

Otten, L.J., Henson, R.N., and Rugg, M.D. (2002). State-related and item-related neural correlates of successful memory encoding. *Nature Neuroscience*, 5 (12), 1339–1344.

Paller, K.A., Voss, J.L., and Boehm, S.G. (2007). Validating neural correlates of familiarity. *Trends in Cognitive Sciences*, 11 (6), 243–250. doi: 10.1016/j.tics.2007.04.002.

Poldrack, R.A. (2006). Can cognitive processes be inferred from neuroimaging data? *Trends in Cognitive Sciences*, 10 (2), 59–63. doi: http://dx.doi.org/10.1016/j.tics.2005.12.004.

Poldrack, R.A. (2008). The role of fMRI in cognitive neuroscience: where do we stand? *Current Opinion in Neurobiology*, 18 (2), 223–227. doi: 10.1016/j.conb.2008.07.006.

Poldrack, R.A., and Wagner, A.D. (2004). What can neuroimaging tell us about the mind? Insights from prefrontal cortex. *Current Directions in Psychological Science*, 13, 177–181.

Polyn, S.M., Natu, V.S., Cohen, J.D., and Norman, K.A. (2005). Category-specific cortical activity precedes retrieval during memory search. *Science*, 310 (5756), 1963–1966.

Pratte, M.S., and Rouder, J.N. (2012). Assessing the dissociability of recollection and familiarity in recognition memory. *Journal of Experimental Psychology: Learning, Memory, and Cognition*, 38 (6), 1591–1607. doi: 10.1037/a0028144.

Rajah, M.N., and McIntosh, A.R. (2005). Overlap in the functional neural systems involved in semantic and episodic memory retrieval. *Journal of Cognitive Neuroscience*, 17 (3), 470–482. doi: 10.1162/0898929053279478.

Rajaram, S. (1993). Remembering and knowing: two means of access to the personal past. *Memory & Cognition*, 21 (1), 89–102. doi: http://dx.doi.org/10.3758/bf03211168.

Rajaram, S., and Geraci, L. (2000). Conceptual fluency selectively influences knowing. *Journal of Experimental Psychology: Learning, Memory, and Cognition*, 26 (4), 1070–1074. doi: 10.1037/02/8-7393.26.4.1070.

Ranganath, C., and Paller, K.A. (1999). Frontal brain potentials during recognition are modulated by requirements to retrieve perceptual detail. *Neuron*, 22 (3), 605–613.

Roediger, H.L. (1984). Does current evidence from dissociation experiments favor the episodic/semantic distinction? *Behavioral and Brain Sciences*, 7, 252–254.

Rotello, C.M., and Macmillan, N.A. (2006). Remember–know models as decision strategies in two experimental paradigms. *Journal of Memory and Language*, 55 (4), 479–494. doi: 10.1016/j.jml.2006.08.002.

Rugg, M.D., and Curran, T. (2007). Event-related potentials and recognition memory. *Trends in Cognitive Sciences*, 11 (6), 251–257. doi: 10.1016/j.tics.2007.04.004.

Rugg M.D., Wilding, E.L. (2000). Retrieval processing and episodic memory. *Trends in Cognitive Sciences*, 4, 108–115.

Schmidt, B., Marrone, D.F., and Markus, E.J. (2012). Disambiguating the similar: the dentate gyrus and pattern separation. *Behavioural Brain Research*, 226 (1), 56–65. doi: 10.1016/j.bbr.2011.08.039.

Shallice, T. (2003). Functional imaging and neuropsychology findings: how can they be linked? *NeuroImage*, 20, Supplement 1, S146–S154. doi: 10.1016/j.neuroimage.2003.09.023.

Squire, L.R., Wixted, J.T., and Clark, R.E. (2007). Recognition memory and the medial temporal lobe: a new perspective. *Nature Reviews Neuroscience* 8 (11), 872–883.

Staresina, B.P., Alink, A., Kriegeskorte, N., and Henson, R.N. (2013a). Awake reactivation predicts memory in humans. *Proceedings of the National Academy of Sciences of the USA*, 110 (52), 21159–21164. doi: 10.1073/pnas.1311989110.

Staresina, B.P., Fell, J., Dunn, J.C., *et al.* (2013b). Using state-trace analysis to dissociate the functions of the human hippocampus and perirhinal cortex in recognition memory. *Proceedings of the National Academy of Sciences of the USA*, 110 (8), 3119–3124. doi: 10.1073/pnas.1215710110.

Taylor, J.R., Buratto, L.G., and Henson, R.N. (2013). Behavioral and neural evidence for masked conceptual priming of recollection. *Cortex*, 49, 1511–1525.

Tendolkar, I., Rugg, M., Fell, J., *et al.* (2000). A magnetoencephalographic study of brain activity related to recognition memory in healthy young human subjects. *Neuroscience Letters*, 280 (1), 69–72. doi, 10.1016/S0304-3940(99)01001-0.

Treves, A., and Rolls, E.T. (1994). Computational analysis of the role of the hippocampus in memory. *Hippocampus*, 4 (3), 374–391. doi, 10.1002/hipo.450040319.

Tulving, E. (1983). *Elements of Episodic Memory*. New York, NY: Oxford University Press.

Tulving, E. (1985). Memory and consciousness. *Canadian Psychology/Psychologie Canadienne*, 26 (1), 1–12. doi: 10.1037/h0080017.

Tulving, E. (1987). Multiple memory systems and consciousness. *Human Neurobiology*, 6 (2), 67–80.

Tulving, E., and Thomson, D.M. (1973). Encoding specificity and retrieval processes in episodic memory. *Psychological Review*, 80 (5), 352.

Uttal, W.R. (2001). *The New Phrenology: The Limits of Localizing Cognitive Processes*. Cambridge, MA: MIT Press.

Vazdarjanova, A., and Guzowski, J.F. (2004). Differences in hippocampal neuronal population responses to modifications of an environmental context: evidence for distinct, yet complementary, functions of CA3 and CA1 ensembles. *Journal of Neuroscience*, 24 (29), 6489–6496. doi: 10.1523/jneurosci.0350-04.2004.

Weber, M.J., and Thompson-Schill, S.L. (2010). Functional neuroimaging can support causal claims about brain function. *Journal of Cognitive Neuroscience*, 22 (11), 2415–2416. doi: 10.1162/jocn.2010.21461.

Wixted, J.T. (2007). Dual-process theory and signal-detection theory of recognition memory. *Psychological Review*, 114 (1), 152–176. doi: 10.1037/0033-295x.114.1.152.

Wixted, J.T., and Mickes, L. (2010). A continuous dual-process model of remember/know judgments. *Psychological Review*, 117 (4), 1025–1054. doi: 10.1037/a0020874.

Yonelinas, A.P. (2002). The nature of recollection and familiarity: a review of 30 years of research. *Journal of Memory and Language*, 46 (3), 441–517. doi: 10.1006/jmla.2002.2864.

Yoo, J.J., Hinds, O., Ofen, N., *et al.* (2012). When the brain is prepared to learn: enhancing human learning using real-time fMRI. *NeuroImage*, 59 (1), 846–852. doi: 10.1016/j.neuroimage.2011.07.063.

# 2

# Activation and Information in Working Memory Research

Bradley R. Postle

## Introduction

In a 2006 review I wrote that "working memory functions arise through the coordinated recruitment, via attention, of brain systems that have evolved to accomplish sensory-, representation-, and action-related functions" (Postle, 2006a). By and large, ensuing developments in cognitive, computational, and systems neuroscience have been consistent with this perspective. One salient example is a 2011 special issue of *Neuropsychologia* that is devoted to the interrelatedness of the constructs of attention and working memory (Nobre and Stokes, 2011). Interestingly, however, the past several years have witnessed developments in the analysis of high-dimensional datasets, including those generated by functional magnetic resonance imaging (fMRI), electroencephalography (EEG), and multi-unit extracellular electrophysiology, that, in some cases, call for a reconsideration of the interpretation of many of the studies that feature in the Postle (2006a) review and, indeed, in some of those in the more recent, above-mentioned special issue of *Neuropsychologia*. This chapter will consider some of the implications of these recent developments for working memory and attentional research. A second theme that has recently been gaining in prominence in working memory research, although by no means a "new development", is the critical role of network-level oscillatory dynamics in supporting working memory and attentional functions. This second theme has been covered extensively elsewhere, including in a recent chapter by this author (Postle, 2011), and so will not be addressed in detail here.

## Activation and Information in the Interpretation of Physiological Signals

### The signal-intensity assumption

The idea of sustained activity as a neural basis of the short-term retention (STR) of information (i.e., the "storage" or "maintenance" functions of short-term memory [STM] and working memory) has been a potent one that can be traced back at least as far as the reverberatory trace in Hebb's dual-trace model of long-term memory

*The Wiley Handbook on the Cognitive Neuroscience of Memory*, First Edition.
Edited by Donna Rose Addis, Morgan Barense, and Audrey Duarte.
© 2015 John Wiley & Sons, Ltd. Published 2015 by John Wiley & Sons, Ltd.

(LTM) formation: the active reverberation within a circuit being the initial trace that served the function of the STR of the memory until synapses making up the circuit could be strengthened to create the (second) long-lasting trace (Hebb, 1949). Since the 1970s, neurons in the monkey (and other species) that demonstrate sustained activity throughout the delay period of delay tasks have been seen as a neural embodiment of this trace. First observed in prefrontal cortex (PFC) and mediodorsal thalamus by Fuster and Alexander (1971), sustained delay-period activity has since been observed in many brain areas, including not only "high level" regions of parietal and temporal cortex (e.g., Gnadt and Andersen, 1988; Nakamura and Kubota, 1995; Suzuki, Miller, and Desimone, 1997), but also, in a modality-dependent manner, in primary sensory cortex (e.g., Super, Spekreijse, and Lamme, 2001; Zhou and Fuster, 1996). In the human, delay-period neuroimaging signal with intensity that is elevated above baseline has long been considered a correlate of the STR of information (e.g., Courtney *et al.*, 1997; Jonides *et al.*, 1993; Zarahn, Aguirre, and D'Esposito, 1997), and the strength of this elevated signal, in comparison with other conditions, used to support models of the neural organization of working memory function. Thus, for example, statistically greater delay-period activity for, say, object information versus spatial information has been taken as evidence for the neural segregation of the STR of these two types of information (e.g., Courtney *et al.*, 1996; Owen *et al.*, 1998). The gold standard of evidence that a signal represents the STR of information has been evidence of monotonic increases in signal intensity with increasing memory load ("load sensitivity"; e.g., Jha and McCarthy, 2000; Leung, Seelig, and Gore, 2004; Postle, Berger, and D'Esposito, 1999; Todd and Marois, 2004; Xu and Chun, 2006).

Last to be reviewed here is the use of functional localizers to identify putatively category-selective regions of the brain. The classic example is that of the "fusiform face area" (FFA), a region in mid-fusiform gyrus that is typically found to respond with stronger signal intensity to the visual presentation of faces than of objects from other categories, such as houses (Kanwisher, McDermott, and Chun, 1997). In working memory and attention research, a commonly used strategy has been to identify "category-specific" regions of cortex with functional localizer scans (e.g., alternating blocks of faces versus houses), then to see how activity in these regions of interest (ROIs) varies during cognitive tasks that feature stimuli from these same categories. Thus, for example, a neural correlate of object-based attention is inferred when signal intensity in the FFA and in an analogous region of "house-selective" cortex is positively correlated with endogenous attentional cues, despite the fact that face and house stimuli are always present in a superimposed, translucent display (O'Craven, Downing, and Kanwisher, 1999). Similarly, neural correlates of the STR of face versus scene information are inferred from the fact that delay-period activity in an FFA ROI is greater for face memory than for house memory, and the converse is true for a "parahippocampal place area" (PPA) ROI (Ranganath, DeGutis, and D'Esposito, 2004).

Each of the types of experimental strategy reviewed in the preceding paragraph draws on a common underlying assumption, which is that one can infer the active representation of a particular kind of information from the signal intensity in a local area of the brain (see also Chapter 1). For expository expediency, I will refer to this as the *signal-intensity assumption*. In recent years, however, it has become increasingly clear that the signal-intensity assumption is subject to important limitations. Empirically, this has been seen in an increasing number of studies in which it fails to account for working memory performance. And, as we shall see, an increasing appreciation for the multivariate nature of neuroimaging datasets (and, indeed, of brain function) provides a perspective from which the limitations of the signal-intensity assumption become clearer.

First, a brief review of empirical demonstrations reveals that the seemingly straight-forward interpretation of elevated delay-period activity as serving a mnemonic function can be problematic. These can be organized into two categories: failures of specificity, and failures of sensitivity. The former refers to instances in which elevated delay-period activity can be shown to serve a function other than the STR of information; the latter, to instances in which behavioral performance makes clear that the subject is successfully remembering information, yet no evidence of elevated delay-period activity can be found.

Examples of failures of specificity include the finding that neurons with elevated delay-period activity in a memory task exhibit similarly sustained activity during the "delay" period of a visually guided saccade task, when no memory is required (Tsujimoto and Sawaguchi, 2004). Moreover, neurons that in a "standard" paradigm seem to encode a sensory representation of the to-be-remembered sample stimulus can be shown in a rotation condition to dynamically change during a single delay period from retrospectively representing the location of the sample to prospectively representing the target of the impending saccade (Takeda and Funahashi, 2002, 2004, 2007). Another example is a study designed to dissociate the focus of spatial attention from the focus of spatial memory that finds the majority of delay-active neurons to track the former (Lebedev *et al.*, 2004). (Limits of the specificity assumption will also factor importantly in the consideration of "reverse inference" in neuroimaging, which appears further along, in the section on *Implications of MVPA for ROI-based analyses.*)

Examples of failures of sensitivity include the finding that, in the monkey, STM for the direction of moving dots in a sample display can be excellent, despite the failure to find directionally tuned neurons, in either area MT or the PFC, that sustain elevated activity across the delay period (Bisley *et al.*, 2004; Zaksas and Pasternak, 2006). In a human fMRI study in which subjects maintained one of two different memory loads across a 24-second delay period, sustained, elevated delay-period activity was observed in several frontal and parietal sites during the delay, but none showed load sensitivity, leaving uncertain whether these regions were actually involved in storage (Jha and McCarthy, 2000).

Against this backdrop, there has been an increased appreciation for limitations of the univariate analytic framework within which hypotheses about differences in signal intensity are most commonly tested (see Chapter 1). With neuroimaging data, the most familiar approach is to solve the general linear model (GLM) in a mass univariate manner (e.g., Friston *et al.*, 1995). That is, the GLM is solved effectively independently at each of the (typically) thousands of data elements in a dataset. Typically, this approach leads to the identification of elevated or decreased signal intensity in voxels occupying a several-cubic-millimeter (or larger) volume of tissue, and the pooling across these voxels to extract a spatially averaged time-course. Using this univariate approach to implement the signal-intensity assumption often engages a second assumption that can also be problematic, that of homogeneity of function. That is, by pooling across "activated" (or "deactivated") voxels, one is assuming that all pooled voxels are "doing the same thing." Finally, the interpretation of the activity from this cluster of voxels often entails a third, often implicit, assumption, which is that this locally homogeneous activity can be construed as supporting a mental function independent of other parts of the brain (i.e., modularity).[1] Each of these assumptions is difficult to reconcile with the increasingly common recognition that neural representations are high-dimensional, and supported by anatomically distributed, dynamic computations (e.g., Bullmore and Sporns, 2009; Buzsaki, 2006; Cohen, 2011; Kriegeskorte, Goebel, and Bandettini, 2006; Norman *et al.*, 2006).

## Information-based analyses

An important conceptual advance in neuroimaging methods occurred with the publication by Haxby and colleagues (2001) of evidence that meaningful information about neural representations can be obtained from the patterns of activity in unthresholded fMRI data. This breakthrough was soon followed by the application of powerful machine-learning algorithms to fMRI datasets in an approach that has come to be known as multivariate pattern analysis (MVPA) (e.g., Haynes and Rees, 2006; Kriegeskorte, Goebel, and Bandettini, 2006; Norman *et al.*, 2006; Pereira, Mitchell, and Botvinick, 2009; see also Chapters 1 and 6). As the name implies, MVPA differs fundamentally from signal-intensity-based approaches in that it treats neural datasets as single high-dimensional images, rather than as a collection of independent low-dimensional elements. Therefore, it affords the detection and characterization of information that is represented in patterns of activity distributed within and across multiple regions of the brain. A detailed explication of the details underlying MVPA and its implementation to neuroimaging datasets is beyond the scope of this chapter, but what bears highlighting here is that MVPA is not subject to many of the problematic assumptions associated with signal-intensity-based analyses. This includes not only the assumptions of homogeneity of function and of modularity, but also, and most importantly for the topic of this chapter, the very assumption that the STR of information is accomplished via sustained, elevated activity. Indeed, tests of this assumption are the first applications of MVPA to working memory research that I will review here.

The possibility that the STR of information may not depend on sustained activity that is elevated above a baseline (typically, the inter-trial interval) was demonstrated by two MVPA studies of visual STM that focused on primary visual cortex (V1). These studies demonstrated that, although V1 did not show elevated activity during the delay period, it nonetheless contained representations of the to-be-remembered stimuli that spanned the delay period (Harrison and Tong, 2009; Serences *et al.*, 2009). In addition to building on what had been reported from V1 in the monkey (Super, Spekreijse, and Lamme, 2001), these studies clearly demonstrated the increased sensitivity of MVPA relative to signal-intensity-based analyses, in that no studies applying the latter to an fMRI dataset had previously implicated V1 in the STR of visual information.

A clear next step would be a direct test of the assumption that elevated delay-period activity carries trial-specific stimulus information. To implement it, Riggall and Postle (2012) acquired fMRI data during delayed recognition of visual motion, and analyzed the data with both GLM and MVPA. The former identified sustained, elevated delay-period activity in superior and lateral frontal cortex and in intraparietal sulcus (IPS), regions that invariably show such activity in studies of STM and working memory.

When we applied MVPA, however, the pattern classifiers implementing the analysis were unable to recover trial-specific stimulus information from these delay-active regions (Figure 2.1). This was not merely a failure of our MVPA methods, because the same classifiers successfully identified trial-specific stimulus information in posterior regions that had not been identified by the GLM: lateral temporo-occipital cortex, including the MT+ complex, and calcarine and pericalcarine cortex. Nor was it the case that the frontal and parietal regions were somehow "unclassifiable," because pattern classifiers were able to extract trial-specific task instruction-related information from these regions. Specifically, MVPA showed the frontal and parietal regions to encode whether the instructions on a particular trial were to remember the speed or the direction of the moving dots that had been presented as the sample stimulus, a finding consistent with previous reports from the monkey (Freedman and Assad, 2006; Swaminathan and Freedman, 2012). Thus, it is unlikely that the failure to recover stimulus-specific information from the frontal and parietal regions (i.e., that the to-be-remembered direction of motion was 42°, 132°, 222°, or 312°) is because they encode information on a finer spatial scale than the posterior regions for which item-level decoding was successful.[2] Rather, our conclusion is that the elevated delay-period activity that is measured with fMRI may reflect processes other than the storage, per se, of trial-specific stimulus information. Further, and consistent with previous studies (Harrison and Tong, 2009; Serences *et al.*, 2009), it may be that the short-term storage of stimulus information is represented in patterns of (statistically) "sub-threshold" activity distributed across regions of low-level sensory cortex that univariate methods cannot detect.

The finding from Riggall and Postle (2012) has potentially profound implications for our understanding of the neural bases of the STR of information, because it calls into question one of the more enduring assumptions of systems and cognitive neuroscience. We have reason to believe that it will hold up, because other groups are reporting

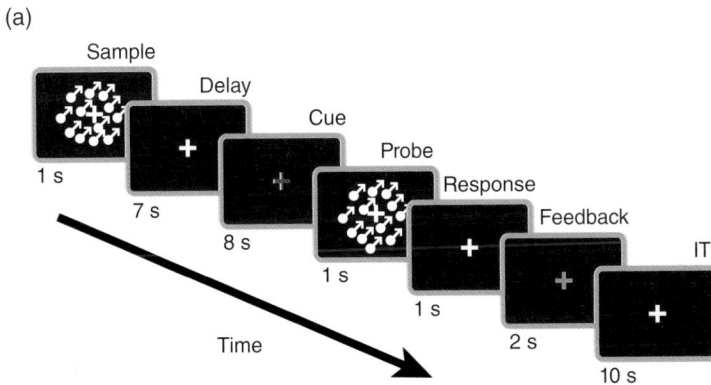

**Figure 2.1** (a) Behavioral task from Riggall and Postle (2012). Subjects maintained the direction and speed of a sample motion stimulus over a 15-second delay period. Midway through the delay period, they were cued as to the dimension on which they would be making an upcoming comparison against the remembered sample, either direction or speed. At the end of the delay period, they were presented with a probe motion stimulus and had to indicate with a button press whether it did or did not match the sample stimulus on the cued dimension.

(b)

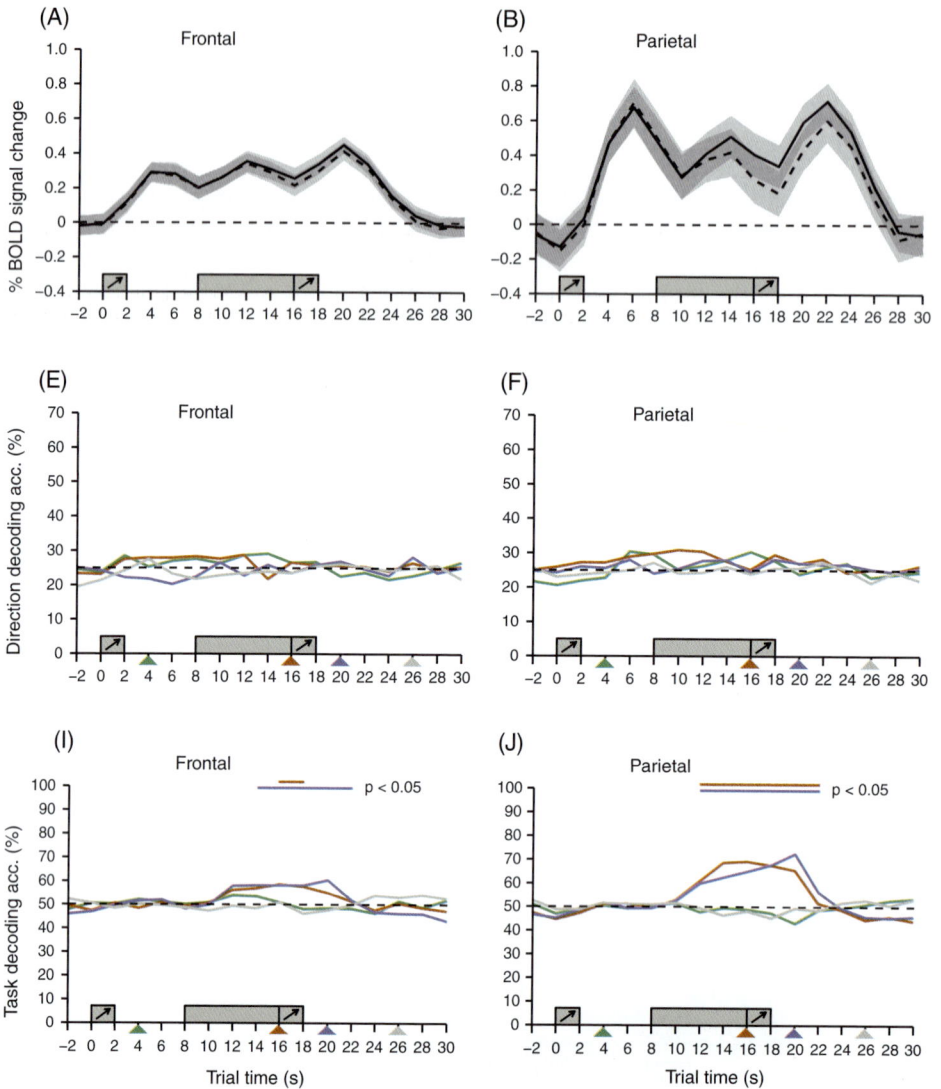

**Figure 2.1** (continued) (b) BOLD and MVPA time-courses from four ROIs. Sample presentation occurred at 0 seconds, and at 8 seconds subjects were cued that either direction or speed of sample motion would be tested on that trial. (A–D) Average ROI BOLD activity. Data from direction-cued trials use solid lines and speed-cued trials use dashed-lines, bands cover average standard error across subjects. (E–H) ROI stimulus-direction decoding results and (I–L) ROI trial-dimension decoding results. Each waveform represents the mean direction-decoding accuracy across subjects ($n=7$) for a classifier trained with data limited to a single time-point in the trial and then tested on all time-points in the hold-out trials (e.g., the green line illustrates the decoding

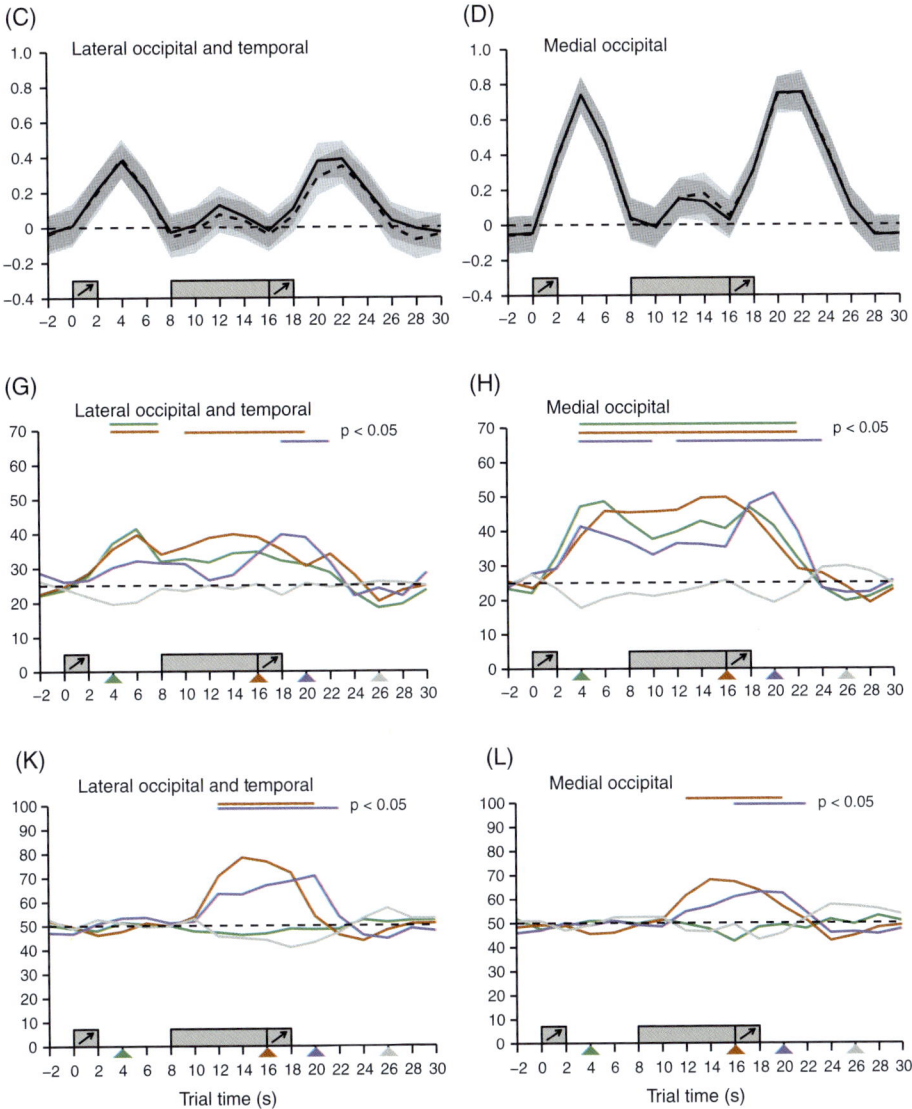

**Figure 2.1** (continued) time-course from a classifier trained on only data from time-point 4, indicated by the small green triangle along the *x*-axis.) Horizontal bars along the top indicate points at which the decoding accuracy for the corresponding classifier was significantly above chance ($p < 0.05$, permutation test). Schematic icons of trial events are shown at the appropriate times along the *x*-axis. Data are unshifted in time. From Riggall, A.C., and Postle, B.R. (2012). The relation between working memory storage and elevated activity, as measured with fMRI. *Journal of Neuroscience*, 32, 12990–12998. © 2012. Reproduced with permission of the Society for Neuroscience.

compatible findings. For example, Linden and colleagues (2012) have reported a failure with MVPA to recover delay-period stimulus category information from frontal and parietal cortex, and Christophel, Hebart, and Haynes (2012) reported a failure to recover delay-period information specific to complex artificial visual stimuli from frontal cortex. The distinction between classifying at the item level (e.g., Christophel, Hebart, and Haynes, 2012; Riggall and Postle, 2012) versus at the category level (as by, e.g., Linden *et al.*, 2012) is an important one, in that the former provides the stronger evidence for memory storage, per se.

At this point it is useful to introduce the idea of an *active neural representation*. To illustrate, although Riggall and Postle (2012) contrasted signal intensity, a traditional index of "activation," versus classifiability, it is important to note that successful classification also depended on evaluation of levels of activity within individual voxels. Thus, there is an important distinction to be made between signal-intensity-based *activation*, which can be construed as a first-order physiological property,[3] and a multivariate-pattern-based *neural representation*, a second-order property (not just activity, but the pattern of activity) that is detectable with MVPA but not with univariate approaches. Nonetheless, a MVPA-detectable neural representation is an active representation, in the sense that neural activity must organize itself to create this pattern, and the neural representation is only present (i.e., only active) for the span of time that we assume it to be psychologically active. For example, Riggall and Postle (2012) found that MVPA of stimulus direction was only successful during a trial, when subjects were presumed to be thinking about a stimulus, and not during the inter-trial interval, when it is assumed that they were not.

Another way to illustrate this idea of an active neural representation is to consider information held in LTM. For example, Polyn *et al.* (2005) and Lewis-Peacock and Postle (2008) assumed that all of the US-citizen participants for their studies were familiar with the American actor John Wayne prior to volunteering for the studies. However, it is also assumed that none of them were *actively* thinking about John Wayne prior to being shown his image during the course of the study. Thus, there existed in the brains of these subjects an *inactive* neural representation of John Wayne that was not detectable by MVPA during portions of the experiment when subjects were not thinking about John Wayne. This neural representation became *active* when subjects were viewing an image of the actor, or retrieving this image from memory, and MVPA was sensitive to this change in the state of the LTM representation. The concept of an active neural representation is of central importance to the next studies to be reviewed here.

One of the questions raised by the Riggall and Postle (2012) findings is: What is the function of the sustained, delay-period activity that has been reported in the hundreds (if not more) of published studies on the neural correlates of STM and working memory since the 1970s? Several possible answers to this question (and it is almost certainly true that there are several answers) have been reviewed in the first section of this chapter. Our group has also begun addressing this question from the theoretical perspective that working memory performance may be achieved, in part, via the temporary activation of LTM representations. First, in a study employing MVPA that will not be reviewed in detail here, we established the neural plausibility of this idea (Lewis-Peacock and Postle 2008). In two more recent studies, we have worked from models that posit multiple states of activation, including, variously, a capacity-limited focus of attention, a region of direct access, and a broader pool of temporarily activated representations, all nested within the immense network of latently stored LTM (Cowan, 1988; McElree, 2001; Oberauer, 2002). Importantly, these models distinguish the STR of information – which can be accomplished in any of the activated states of LTM – from attention to information – which is a capacity-limited resource that can be applied only to a small subset of highly activated representations.

The first of two studies that will be reviewed in this context (Lewis-Peacock *et al.*, 2012) was an fMRI study of a multi-step delayed-recognition task (adopted from Oberauer, 2005) (Figure 2.2). Each trial began with the presentation of two sample stimuli, always selected from two of three categories (lines, words, and pronounceable pseudowords), one in the top half of the screen and one in the bottom half (Figure 2.2b). After offset of the stimulus display and an initial delay period, a retrocue indicated which sample was relevant for the first recognition probe, followed by a second delay, followed by an initial Y/N recognition probe (and response). Critically, during the second delay both items needed to be kept in STM, even though only one was relevant for the first probe. This is because the first probe was followed by a second retrocue that, with equal probability, would indicate that the same item (a "repeat" trial) or the previously uncued item (a "switch" trial) would be tested by the trial-ending second Y/N recognition probe (and response). Thus, the first delay was assumed to require the active retention of two items, whereas the second delay would feature an "attended memory item" (AMI) and an "unattended memory item" (UMI).[4] The third delay would only require the retention of an AMI, because it was certain that memory for the item not cued by the second retrocue would never be tested. This design therefore allowed us to assess the prediction that there are different levels of neural activation corresponding to different hypothesized states of activation of LTM representations (Cowan, 1988; McElree, 2001; Oberauer, 2002).

Prior to performing this task, subjects were first scanned while performing a simple delayed recognition task (Figure 2.2a), and the data from this phase-1 scan were used to train the classifier that was then applied to the data from the multi-step task described in the previous paragraph. For phase 1, subjects were trained to indicate whether the probe stimulus matched the sample according to a category-specific criterion – synonym judgment for words, rhyme judgment for pseudowords, and an orientation judgment for line segments. Our rationale was that by training the classifier (separately for each subject) on data from the delay period of this task, we would be training it on patterns of brain activity related to the STR of just a single representational code: phonological (pseudoword trials), semantic (word trials), or visual (line trials). This, in turn, would provide the most unambiguous decoding of delay periods entailing the STR of two AMIs versus one AMI and one UMI versus one AMI.

In all trials, classifier evidence for both trial-relevant categories rose precipitously at trial onset and remained at the same elevated level until the onset of the first retrocue. This indicated that both items were encoded and sustained in the focus of attention across the initial memory delay, while it was equiprobable that either would be relevant for the first memory response. Following onset of the first retrocue, however, classifier evidence for the two memory items diverged. Post-cue brain activity patterns were classified as highly consistent with the category of the cued item, whereas evidence for the uncued item dropped precipitously, becoming indistinguishable from the classifier's evidence for the stimulus category not presented on that trial (i.e., not different from baseline). If the second cue was a repeat cue, classifier evidence for the already-selected memory item remained elevated and that of the uncued item remained indistinguishable

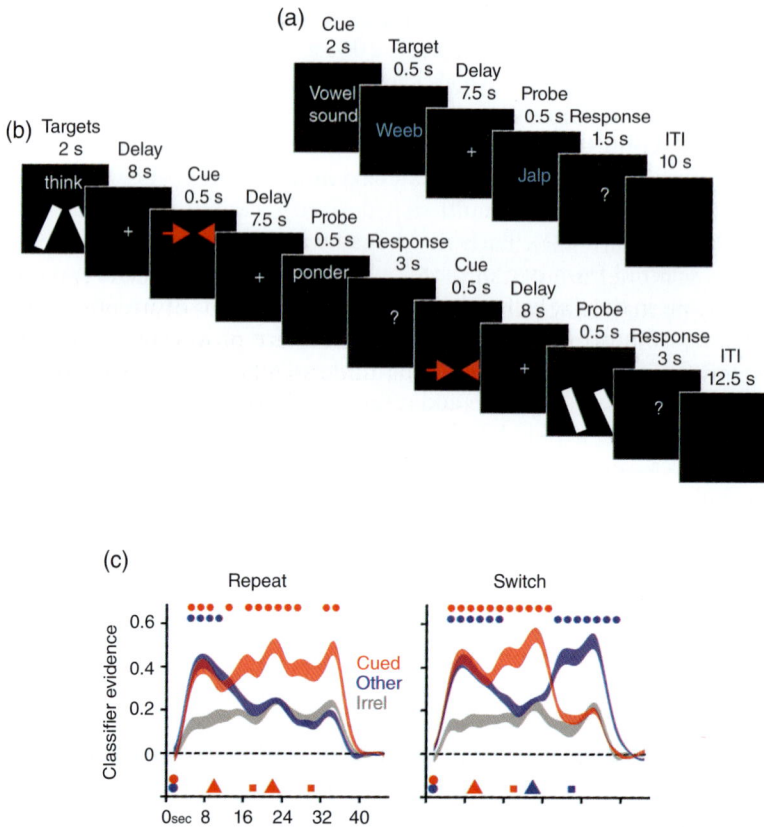

**Figure 2.2** (a,b) Behavioral tasks from Experiment 2 of Lewis-Peacock *et al.* (2012). (a) In the first phase, subjects performed short-term recognition of a pseudoword (phonological STM), a word (semantic STM), or two lines (visual STM). (b) In the second phase, during the same scanning session, subjects performed short-term recognition with two stimuli (between-category combinations of pseudowords, words, and lines). On half of the trials, the same memory item was selected as behaviorally relevant by the first and second cues (repeat trials), and on the other half of trials the second cue selected the previously uncued item (switch trials). (c) Classifier decoding from Experiment 2 of Lewis-Peacock *et al.* (2012). Results are shown separately for repeat (left) and switch (right) trials. Classifier evidence values for phonological, semantic, and visual were relabeled and collapsed across all trials into three new categories: *cued* (red, the category of the memory item selected by the first cue), *other* (blue, the category of the other memory item), and *irrel* (gray, the trial-irrelevant category). The colored shapes along the horizontal axis indicate the onset of the targets (red and blue circles, 0 seconds), the first cue (red triangle, 10 seconds), the first recognition probe (red square, 18 seconds), the second cue (red or blue triangle, 22 seconds), and the final recognition probe (red or blue square, 30 seconds). Data for each category are shown as ribbons whose thickness indicate ±1 SEM across subjects, interpolated across the 23 discrete data points in the trial-averaged data. Statistical comparisons of evidence values focused on within-subject differences. For every 2-second interval throughout the trial, color-coded circles along the top of each graph indicate that the classifier's evidence for the *cued* or *other* categories, respectively, was reliably stronger ($p < 0.002$, based on repeated-measures *t*-tests, corrected for multiple comparisons) than the evidence for the *irrel* category. Reproduced with permission from Lewis-Peacock, J.A., Drysdale, A., Oberauer, K., and Postle, B.R. (2012). Neural evidence for a distinction between short-term memory and the focus of attention. *Journal of Cognitive Neuroscience*, 23, 61–79. © 2012 Massachusetts Institute of Technology.

from baseline (Figure 2.2, Repeat). If, in contrast, the second cue was a switch cue, classifier evidence for the previously uncued item was reinstated, while evidence for the previously cued item dropped to baseline (Figure 2.2, Switch).

These results suggest that only AMIs are held in an active state. Classifier evidence for an active representation of UMIs returned to baseline levels, despite the fact that they could quickly be reactivated if cued during the second half of the trial. This point is important because, despite the apparent loss of sustained activity, UMIs were nonetheless easily remembered after a brief delay. Thus, it may be that STM can be preserved across a brief delay despite the apparent loss of sustained representations. Further, it may be that delay-period activity reflects the focus of attention, rather than the STR per se, of information. These possibilities are provocative, and would have potentially profound implications for our understanding of working memory and attention. There are, however, several concerns and possible alternative explanations that need to be considered before these conclusions can be viewed as definitive. Some of these are taken up in the study of LaRocque *et al.* (2013), to be considered next.

One important caveat about the Lewis-Peacock *et al.* (2012) findings is that they were derived solely from fMRI data. The possibility exists, however, that UMIs may be retained in an active state via a mechanism to which the BOLD signal measured by fMRI is not sensitive. One candidate for such a mechanism is neuronal oscillations. There is considerable evidence that oscillatory dynamics in large populations of neurons are sensitive to, and may underlie, the STR of information (e.g., Fuentemilla *et al.*, 2010; Jensen *et al.*, 2002; Palva and Palva, 2011; Sauseng *et al.*, 2009; Uhlhaas *et al.*, 2009). Because the relationship between the BOLD signal and the broad band of frequencies at which different neural systems can oscillate is poorly understood, and certainly indirect, current fMRI methods are poorly suited to measure neural oscillatory dynamics. Therefore, we (LaRocque *et al.*, 2013) designed this follow-up study to replicate the critical features of Lewis-Peacock *et al.* (2012), with the exception that we concurrently measured neural activity with the electroencephalogram (EEG) rather than with fMRI. In addition to being sensitive to neuronal oscillations across a broad, physiologically relevant range of frequencies, EEG has the additional property of affording greater temporal resolution than fMRI, which could permit more nuanced interpretations of the time-course of the activation and deactivation of neural representations.

In brief, the findings from LaRocque *et al.* (2013) replicate the principal finding from Lewis-Peacock *et al.* (2012): MVPA of the EEG signal failed to find evidence that information that was outside the focus of attention, but nonetheless in STM (i.e., UMIs), was retained in an active state (Figure 2.3). An additional analysis also ruled out the possibility that a neural representation is represented differently when being retained as a UMI versus when being retained as an AMI; if this were the case, MVPA of data trained on AMIs from phase 1 might be expected to fail to detect UMIs during phase 2. This was achieved by implementing MVPA by training and testing on data from delay 2 (i.e., following the first retrocue, when there was one AMI and one UMI) via the leave-one-out cross-validation procedure. These results qualitatively replicated those from the train-on-phase-1-test-on-phase-2 analysis.

In order to characterize the time-course of the removal of memory items from the focus of attention in the EEG classification data, we focused on the first retrocue because this cue initiates the "unloading" of uncued items from the focus of attention (Oberauer, 2005; LaRocque *et al.*, 2013). The estimate was made simply by

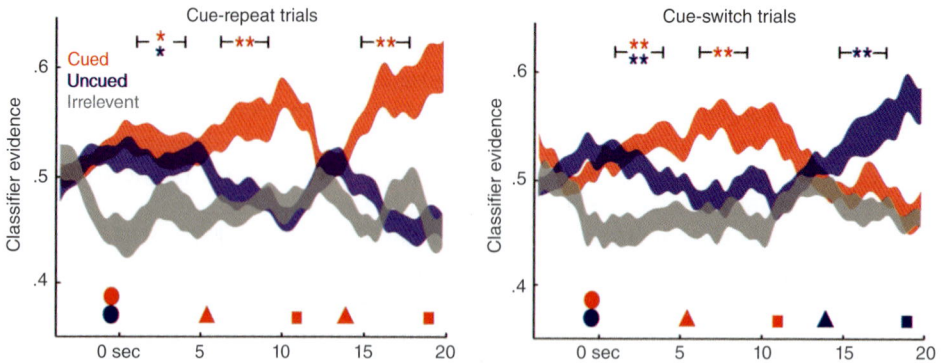

**Figure 2.3** Classifier decoding from EEG study of LaRocque *et al.* (2013). Results are shown separately for cue-repeat (left) and cue-switch trials (right). Graphical conventions are the same as in Figure 2.2, with the exception that the width of the brackets surrounding significance markers denotes the extent of the delay period used for statistical analysis; *p<0.05, **p<0.005. Reproduced with permission from LaRocque, J.J., Lewis-Peacock, J.A. Drysdale, A., *et al.* (2013). Decoding attended information in short-term memory: an EEG study. *Journal of Cognitive Neuroscience*, 25, 127–142. © 2013 Massachusetts Institute of Technology.

determining the time-point following retrocue onset at which evidence for an active neural representation of the UMI was lost (i.e., the time-point at which classifier evidence for the UMI did not differ statistically from classifier evidence for the category that was not presented on that trial, an empirically derived baseline). The estimate derived from the EEG data of the time required for the neural representation of a single UMI to fall to baseline was 1.25 seconds (LaRocque *et al.*, 2013).

The principal finding from the Lewis-Peacock *et al.* (2012) and the LaRocque *et al.* (2013) studies is that UMIs are not maintained in an active state. This observation is at odds with theoretical models positing one or more intermediate levels of activation between the focus of attention and unactivated LTM (Cowan, 1988; McElree, 2001; Oberauer, 2002; Olivers *et al.*, 2011). Additionally, there are empirical studies that, in contrast to the studies reviewed here, have reported data derived from signal-intensity-based analyses that could be interpreted as neural evidence for an intermediate state of activation for UMIs (e.g., Lepsien and Nobre, 2007; Nee and Jonides, 2008; Peters, Roelfsema, and Goebel, 2012). Thus, resolving these empirical inconsistencies will be important for progress to be made on the theoretical front. In the following section it will be argued that these inconsistencies may be attributable to inferential limitations of the signal-intensity assumption.

## Implications of MVPA for ROI-Based Analyses

One corollary of the signal-intensity assumption – the assumption of the category specificity of neuroimaging signal measured from ROIs that have been defined either anatomically or functionally – has underlain many cognitive neuroscience studies of working memory (including many performed by this author). This section will examine this assumption in the context of the AMI/UMI distinction, and will conclude that it can lead to incorrect inference. Note that although the argumentation will be framed in the relatively narrow terms of this question in the working memory literature, its logic may generalize more broadly to many domains of cognitive and systems neuroscience in which signal from "domain-specific ROIs" or "stimulus-selective neurons" is interpreted.

There are compelling intuitive and theoretical (Cowan, 1988; Oberauer 2002; McElree, 2001; Olivers *et al.*, 2011) reasons to posit an intermediate level of activation occupied by UMIs relative to AMIs and inactive LTM representations. This section will draw on two studies whose results can be seen as consistent with these multiple-levels models, and thus at odds with the findings from Lewis-Peacock *et al.* (2012) and LaRocque *et al.* (2013) that were reviewed in the previous section. One of these studies comes from Nobre and colleagues, who have been studying this question from the perspective that attention may modulate internal representations in a manner similar to its influence on perceptual processing (Griffin and Nobre, 2003; Nobre *et al.*, 2004). In particular, Lepsien and Nobre (2007) used a procedure very similar to that described for Lewis-Peacock *et al.* (2012) and LaRocque *et al.* (2013): subjects viewed the serial presentation of two stimulus items, one a face and one a scene, and during the ensuing delay period viewed a retrocue indicating one of the two stimulus categories, and then, roughly 5 seconds later, a second cue that instructed subjects to "switch" their attention to the previously uncued category or to "stay." The combination of cues was 100% informative about which stimulus would be tested with a recognition probe. Of principal relevance for this chapter are the modulations of activity measured from ROIs determined independently to respond more strongly to faces than to scenes (and located in fusiform gyrus), or more strongly to scenes than to faces (and located in parahippocampal gyrus). Signal intensity within these ROIs was seen to increase and decrease in a manner congruent with the category indicated by each cue (Griffin and Nobre, 2003). Although the authors make no explicit claims about multiple levels of activation in working memory, this aspect of their results can be interpreted as evidence for such models.

A second group, Nee and Jonides (2008, 2011), has explicitly tested multiple-levels models. In one study they followed the rapid serial visual presentation of three words with a recognition probe, reasoning that the level of activation to recognition probes matching the most recently presented item (the "*–1 item*"), which was assumed to be held in a 1-item focus of attention, would differ from probes matching the other two serial positions, which, being outside the focus of attention, were presumed to make greater demands on retrieval processes (Nee and Jonides, 2008). Their results showed that probes matching the *–1 item* evoked higher-magnitude responses in inferior temporal cortex relative to probes matching the *–2* and *–3 items*, whereas the latter increased evoked higher-magnitude responses in the medial temporal lobe and left mid-ventrolateral prefrontal cortex (Nee and Jonides, 2008).

What is particularly germane for this chapter is that Lepsien and Nobre (2007), in summarizing their findings, characterize their fusiform and parahippocampal ROIs as "involved in maintaining representations of faces and scenes respectively" (p. 2072), and that Nee and Jonides (2008) characterize the inferior temporal cortex as "inferior temporal representational cortex" (p. 14228).[5] That is, both of these publications articulate the assumption (pervasive within the cognitive neuroimaging literature) that, under certain circumstances, activity in carefully selected regions can be interpreted as being specific to a particular function. These are examples of reasoning based on reverse inference (see Chapter 1), reasoning "backward" from the presence of elevated activity in a certain area of the brain (in this case, e.g., a fusiform gyrus ROI), to the engagement of a particular cognitive function (e.g., the STR of face information).[6]

The practice of reverse inference is widespread in the cognitive neuroimaging literature, despite the fact that one often hears it being disparaged in conversation with cognitive neuroscientists. And it is certainly true that, in some cases, reverse inference can lead to incorrect inferences. For example, it can be incorrect to conclude from an observation of elevated activity in the PFC during a task that working memory was engaged during the task. The reason for this is that "human prefrontal cortex is not specific for working memory" (D'Esposito *et al.*, 1998); it can support many functions other than working memory. An influential paper by Poldrack (2006) has cogently made the point that the validity of reverse inference depends critically on the specificity of the pattern of activity that is being interpreted. To illustrate this point quantitatively, he evaluated the proposition that "activation in Broca's area implies engagement of language function" by computing a Bayes factor (ratio of the posterior odds to the prior odds) with data from the BrainMap database (tabulating, for "language studies" and "not language studies" in the database, the number of contrasts for which Broca's area was "activated" versus "not activated"). The resultant Bayes factor of 2.3 was considered only weak evidence for this inference. In a concluding section of his paper, however, Poldrack (2006) notes that "There are two ways in which to improve confidence in reverse inferences: increase the selectivity of response in the brain … or increase the prior probability of the cognitive process in question" (p. 62). The former factor is critical for this chapter: MVPA can support stronger reverse inferences than can univariate techniques because it measures high-dimensional neural representations that have markedly higher selectivity than do univariate activation peaks. Early evidence for this was demonstrated for face perception and the FFA by Haxby and colleagues (2001), who showed that faces could be discriminated from six other visual categories from the multivariate signal from ventral temporal cortex even when the FFA was excluded from the MVPA. Additionally, they showed a high level of discriminability for all categories (except shoes) when the MVPA was restricted to only the FFA (Haxby *et al.*, 2001). Against this backdrop, we now return to the question of whether UMIs are represented at an intermediate level of activity between that of AMIs and inactive LTM.

In part to explore the contradictory findings regarding the physiological state in which UMIs are maintained, Lewis-Peacock performed a head-to-head comparison of the results of univariate versus multivariate analyses on the data from Lewis-Peacock *et al.* (2012). To do so, he first identified voxels that were selectively sensitive in terms of univariate signal intensity to the STR of just one of the three visual categories used in the experiment (visual, semantic, phonological). These voxels correspond to what we call "exclusive" ROIs in that they showed elevated delay-period signal intensity (versus inter-trial interval baseline) for only *one* of the three categories of stimulus. Second, he observed that the fluctuations of signal intensity levels in these regions followed the pattern that would be predicted by multiple-state models: higher delay-period activity when a region's "specific" category was an AMI; lower, but above-baseline, delay-period activity when a region's "specific" category was a UMI. When the same ROI-specific signal was submitted to MVPA, however, a different pattern emerged: the multivariate patterns of activity in exclusive ROIs reflected which stimulus category was currently in the focus of attention, regardless

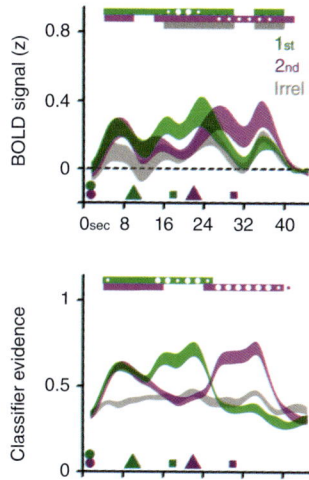

**Figure 2.4** Signal intensity versus MVPA in "category-selective" ROIs. Trial-averaged decoding of phase 2 switch trials from Lewis-Peacock and Postle (2012), using the GLM method (top row) and the MVPA method (bottom row). Data for each category (*1st*, the first cued category; *2nd*, the second cued category; *irrel*, the trial-irrelevant category) are shown as ribbons whose thickness indicate ±1 SEM across subjects. The colored shapes along this horizontal axis indicate the onset of the targets (green and purple circles), the first cue (green triangle), the first probe (green square), the second cue (purple triangle), and the second probe (purple square). Statistical comparisons focused on within-subject differences: for every 2-second interval throughout the trial, color-coded bars along the top of each graph indicate that the signal intensity (GLM) or classifier evidence (MVPA) for each category was above baseline. Activation baseline is mean signal intensity during rest, whereas information baseline is mean classifier evidence for *irrel* at each time-point. Circles inside and outside these bars indicate that the value for one trial-relevant category was stronger than the value for the other trial-relevant category (small circles: $p < 0.05$; big circles: $p < 0.002$, Bonferroni corrected). Reproduced with permission of Elsevier Science Ltd, Lewis-Peacock, J.A., and Postle, B.R. (2012). Decoding the internal focus of attention. *Neuropsychologia* 50, 470–478.

of whether or not that category was the one for which the ROI might be assumed to be "selective" (Figure 2.4). For example, multivariate patterns of activity in the voxels whose GLM-defined activity was specific to STM for phonological stimuli reliably conveyed, on trials featuring a semantic and a visual stimulus, which was the current AMI (Lewis-Peacock and Postle, 2012).

This finding has two implications that will be emphasized here. First, with regard to the narrower question of the neural representation of items in STM, it demonstrates empirically that a univariate "read out" of signal intensity from an ROI, despite its univariate specificity, cannot be used as a reliable index of the state of stimulus information in STM. It also reinforces the idea that sustained activity need not be the neural basis for the STR of information (LaRocque *et al.*, 2013; Lewis-Peacock and Postle, 2012; Stokes and Duncan, 2014). Second, and more broadly, it raises concerns about the practice of defining functional localizers in cognitive neuroimaging. The Lewis-Peacock and Postle (2012) data demonstrate empirically a point that has been made, either explicitly or implicitly, in many recent discussions of MVPA (e.g., Haxby *et al.*, 2001; Haynes and Rees, 2006; Kriegeskorte, Goebel, and Bandettini, 2006; Norman *et al.*, 2006; Pereira, Mitchell, and Botvinick, 2009), as well as of reverse inference (Poldrack, 2006), which is that one cannot reliably infer the active representation of information by simply inspecting the level of signal intensity in a particular region of the brain. A reason for this is that neural representations, widely assumed to be high-dimensional and anatomically distributed, are almost guaranteed to be poorly characterized by the essentially one-dimensional time-varying signal from an ROI. Stated differently, interpretation of time-varying signal from an ROI requires the assumption that locally homogeneous activity (often on the order of a square centimeter, or more) can be construed as supporting a single mental function, and as doing so independent of other brain areas (for more elaboration of this argument, see Lewis-Peacock and Postle, 2012; Riggall and Postle, 2012). Because these latter assumptions are almost certainly not true under most conditions, it follows that elements within a functional ROI defined with univariate statistics are certain to be involved in many more functions than just the one that the experimenters had in mind when they set out to define this "functionally specific ROI." Similarly, the empirical results of applications of MVPA to multiunit extracellular recordings from the monkey (e.g., Crowe, Averbeck, and Chafee, 2010; Meyers *et al.*, 2008; Stokes and Duncan, 2014) indicate that caution should be taken in inferring the function of activity in individual neurons that may have been defined as having "selective" properties.

## Limitations and Outstanding Questions

This final section of this chapter is organized by themes under which are reviewed caveats that need to accompany some of the arguments made earlier in this chapter, as well as some future directions that MVPA-based working memory research might take.

### Necessity

Successful MVPA decoding means that patterns of activity are reliably different in two or more stimulus conditions, but it does not necessarily follow from this that a region from which one can decode is necessary for the active representation of that information. An alternative possibility is that the differential patterns observed in the area in question may be "echoes" of the critical stimulus-representing activity that is occurring elsewhere in the brain. This may explain the seeming contradiction of the lack of stimulus specificity of the FFA as demonstrated by MVPA of activity from this region (Haxby *et al.*, 2001) versus the relative specificity of perceptual deficits that arise from damage to (as reviewed, for example, by Farah, 1990) or stimulation of (e.g., Parvizi *et al.*, 2012) this region. That is, it is possible that the ability to predict from FFA signal whether the stimulus being viewed is a cat, a bottle, or a chair (Haxby *et al.*, 2001) may be due to the fact that differential levels of activity from the regions whose activity *is* necessary for perceiving stimuli from these categories also bias the state of activity in the FFA.

Another illustration of this idea that relates to the AMI/UMI distinction comes from Peters and colleagues (2012), who have argued for a distinction between *search templates* that are held in working memory to guide a visual search (and are analogous to the AMIs emphasized in this chapter) and *accessory memory items* that can be simultaneously held in working memory, but are irrelevant to the search (analogous to UMIs, e.g., Olivers *et al.*, 2011). In an fMRI study of visual search from a rapid serial visual presentation of superimposed face and house stimuli, they were able to decode the category of the UMI, during the rapid serial visual presentation (RSVP) stream, from 17 discrete regions that were located in all four lobes of the brain and in neostriatum, in both hemispheres (Peters, Roelfsema, and Goebel, 2012). Although it is possible that subjects solved their task by maintaining 17 discrete "copies" of the UMI, a more likely account is that the category-discriminating activity of some of these regions was a byproduct of task-critical neural representation occurring elsewhere. Note that one cannot appeal to anatomically distributed regions for this particular argument, because the "roaming searchlight" technique used to identify these areas only used signal arising locally within the area covered by the searchlight at any single point in the procedure. This question of the "aperture" of MVPA is addressed again later in this section.

If successful decoding of information need not imply that the region in question is representing that information in a meaningful way, what about the converse? Can one posit that successful MVPA decoding is a necessary, if not sufficient, condition for determining that a region contributes to the representation of a particular stimulus or category of information? In a strict sense, the answer has to be "no," because failure to decode stimulus (or category) identity is a failure to reject the null hypothesis. However, questions such as this can sometimes be profitably reframed in terms of sensitivity.

## Sensitivity

We cannot definitively rule out the possibility that, for example, the failure of Riggall and Postle (2012) to decode the remembered direction of motion from PFC was due to PFC representing this information at a spatial scale too fine-grained for fMRI to detect, or in a neural code to which fMRI is insensitive (e.g., oscillatory synchrony; Salazar *et al.*, 2012). Having acknowledged this inherent limitation of interpreting negative findings with MVPA, however, it is also important to acknowledge that MVPA methods are unequivocally much more sensitive than univariate methods. Sticking with STM for motion, there is no univariate method (e.g., comparing intensity of BOLD evoked response from area MT and/or other regions; "fMRI adaptation"; etc.) that would allow one to reliably predict the remembered direction of motion on a particular set of trials. Thus, although there are legitimate concerns that one can raise about over-interpreting, say, a failure to decode motion direction from PFC, this does not alter the fact that such a conclusion can be drawn with higher confidence than can be the conclusion from elevated BOLD signal in PFC that this activity corresponds to the active representation of stimulus information. This is the reason that multivariate patterns boast, almost as a rule, quantitatively better specificity than do voxels defined by univariate contrasts.

### Localized versus anatomically distributed

One curious fact about MVPA is that one of the more common procedures by which it is applied to neuroimaging datasets is via the so-called roaming searchlight approach. This is implemented by defining a sphere with a given volume (e.g., a radius of 6 mm; Peters, Roelfsema, and Goebel, 2012), locating it on a particular voxel, and assessing multivariate changes within the voxels in the sphere as a function of task condition. The sphere is then moved by one voxel and the process repeated, iteratively across every voxel in the dataset. I say "curious," because this procedure imposes strict localizationist constraints on a method inherently well suited to detect neural representations that are anatomically broadly distributed. Thus, if a particular representation depended on functional connectivity between distal regions of, say, parietal and temporal cortex, a searchlight analysis would not detect this representation. A practical reason for implementing a roaming searchlight is that it avoids some of the complications associated with whole-brain classification. These include concerns about overfitting the model solution if every gray matter voxel is included in the analysis, or about introducing bias via the feature-selection step that one implements to select just a subset of voxels over which to perform MVPA. Some of these concerns are currently being addressed by applying sparse machine-learning methods to MVPA[7] (for an overview of machine-learning approaches to MVPA, see Pereira, Mitchell, and Botvinick, 2009). For the purposes of this chapter, I will sum up this section by observing that an important goal for future cognitive neuroscience research is developing a better understanding of how the constraints of different implementations of MVPA can limit, or bias, what a particular analysis is telling us about the neural representation of information. This will allow researchers to implement the MVPA procedure that is best suited for the scientific question being addressed.

## Conclusion

This chapter has summarized how a relatively recent methodological development, the introduction of MVPA to the analysis of neuroimaging datasets, has led to new insights about the neural bases of the STR of information. It may be that the sustained, elevated signal that has long been accepted as the neural correlate of STM relates to processes being carried out in "real time," but not to the storage, per se, of information. An important next step in validating this idea is to assess what was previously referred to as the "gold standard" of evidence for STR, the sensitivity of particular regions to the amount of information being held in STM (i.e., "load sensitivity"). Initial data from our laboratory indicate that this, too, is not a reliable indicator of storage (Emrich *et al.*, 2013). Although this possibility may seem to fly in the face of "everything that we know" about STM, there are precedents for it in the literature. For example, it is widely accepted that the oscillation of circuits in sensory systems in the alpha band is a mechanism for suppressing the function of those circuits (e.g., Buzsaki, 2006). The finding of load sensitivity of delay-period alpha-band power in verbal STM has therefore been interpreted as evidence for (stimulus-nonspecific) inhibition increasing as a function of load (Jensen *et al.*, 2002). More recently, it has been suggested that the load-dependent changes in the "contralateral delay activity"

(CDA) that are often interpreted as a neural correlate of storage in visual STM (e.g., Reinhart *et al.*, 2012; Vogel and Machizawa, 2004) may also reflect changes in the dynamics of alpha-band oscillations (van Dijk *et al.*, 2010). By this view, the CDA would be a byproduct of general state changes in the visual system, rather than an index of storage, per se.

An additional literature that is implicated in the results and ideas reviewed here is that of extracellular recordings from awake, behaving monkeys performing tests of working memory and STM. Here, too, the recent application of multivariate methods has begun to challenge traditional assumptions about the function of sustained, elevated firing rates. For example, Meyers *et al.* (2008) have shown with MVPA that the representation of stimulus category information in a delayed-match-to-category task "is coded by a nonstationary pattern of activity that changes over the course of a trial with individual neurons [in inferior temporal cortex and PFC] containing information on much shorter time scales than the population as a whole" (p. 1407). That is, this information does not seem to be carried in the sustained activity of individual neurons. A similar principle has been reported for the representation of spatial information in parietal cortex (Crowe, Averbeck, and Chafee, 2010).

These are exciting times to be studying the neural and cognitive bases of working and short-term memory, and MVPA techniques are among the many recent methodological innovations that hold promise for important discoveries in the coming years.

## Acknowledgments

I thank Drs. Mark Stokes and Jarrod Lewis-Peacock for helpful comments on an earlier draft of this chapter. This work was supported by NIH grant MH064498.

## Notes

1   To be sure, connectivity analyses are increasingly common in the neuroimaging literature. Many studies employing such analyses, however, nonetheless draw on assumptions of signal intensity and modularity. It is also the case that MVPA can be applied in a manner that makes the assumption of modularity. This is addressed in the section on *Implications and practical considerations*.

2   As an aside, it is worthy of note that although MVPA has been applied successfully to sensory processing in topographically organized cortex (e.g., as in the decoding of orientation (Harrison and Tong, 2009; Serences *et al.*, 2009), it has also been successfully applied to "higher-level" processing in polymodal cortex. Thus, for example, MVPA has demonstrated contextual reinstatement during episodic memory retrieval (Polyn *et al.*, 2005), the recognition of individual faces (Kriegeskorte *et al.*, 2007), and neural correlates of free choice (Soon *et al.*, 2008), all entailing the decoding of information from polymodal temporal, parietal, and/or frontal cortex.

3   All the while acknowledging, of course, that the blood-oxygen-level-dependent (BOLD) signal reflects a hemodynamic response to the cellular activity that we really care about.

4   Behavioral data from Oberauer (2005) and from LaRocque *et al.* (2013) indicate that subjects remove items from the focus of attention even during the second delay period of this multi-step task, when they know that $p = 0.5$ that the uncued memory item will be cued by the second retrocue.

5  Note that in a subsequent study from this group, Lepsien, Thornton, and Nobre (2011) observed that delay-period signal in ROIs "preferentially responsive to face or scene stimuli" – in fusiform and parahippocampal gyri, respectively – was not sensitive to memory load, leading them to call into question the role of these regions in STM maintenance, per se.

6  Here again I'll note that this author is among the many, many, cognitive neuroscientists who have published studies applying this logic (e.g., Postle, 2006b; Postle, Druzgal, and D'Esposito, 2003; Postle and Hamidi, 2007). Thus, I want to make clear that my intent here is not to create the impression that the two groups whose papers are being examined here are in any way noteworthy for applying the signal-intensity assumption in their neuroimaging research. It is simply the case that their papers have high thematic overlap with those of Lewis-Peacock *et al.* (2012) and LaRocque *et al.* (2013), which form the backbone of this chapter.

7  A complication with applying sparse machine-learning techniques to neuroimaging datasets, in turn, is that the weighting of features (for fMRI, voxels) that satisfy sparcity goals of a particular algorithm may produce a solution that distorts the "true" anatomical distribution of information in the brain. That is, care must be taken when interpreting the anatomical distribution of "importance maps" that result from MVPA.

# References

Bisley, J., Zaksas, D., Droll, J.A., and Pasternak, T. (2004). Activity of neurons in cortical area MT during a memory for motion task. *Journal of Neurophysiology*, 91, 286–300.

Bullmore, E., and Sporns, O. (2009). Complex brain networks: graph theoretical analysis of structural and functional systems. *Nature Reviews Neuroscience*, 10, 186–198.

Buzsaki, G. (2006). *Rhythms of the Brain*. New York, NY: Oxford University Press.

Christophel, T.B., Hebart, M.N., and Haynes, J.-D. (2012). Decoding the contents of visual short-term memory from human visual and parietal cortex. *Journal of Neuroscience*, 32, 2983–12989.

Cohen, M.X. (2011). It's about time. *Frontiers in Human Neuroscience*, 5. doi: 10.3389/fnhum.2011.00002.

Courtney, S.M., Ungerleider, L.G., Keil, K., and Haxby, J. (1996). Object and spatial visual working memory activate separate neural systems in human cortex. *Cerebral Cortex*, 6, 39–49.

Courtney, S.M., Ungerleider, L.G., Keil, K., and Haxby, J.V. (1997). Transient and sustained activity in a distributed neural system for human working memory. *Nature*, 386, 608–611.

Cowan, N. (1988). Evolving conceptions of memory storage, selective attention, and their mutual constraints within the human information processing system. *Psychological Bulletin*, 104, 163–171.

Crowe, D.A., Averbeck, B.B., and Chafee, M.V. (2010). Rapid sequences of population activity patterns dynamically encode task-critical spatial information in parietal cortex. *Journal of Neuroscience*, 30, 11640–11653.

D'Esposito, M., Ballard, D., Aguirre, G.K., and Zarahn, E. (1998). Human prefrontal cortex is not specific for working memory: a functional MRI study. *NeuroImage*, 8, 274–282.

Emrich, S.M., Riggall, A.C., LaRocque, J.J., and Postle, B.R. (2013). Distributed patterns of activity in sensory cortex reflect the precision of multiple items maintained in visual short-term memory. *The Journal of Neuroscience*, 33, 6516–6523.

Farah, M.J. (1990). *Visual Agnosia*. Cambridge, MA: MIT Press.

Freedman, D.J., and Assad, J. (2006). Experience-dependent representation of visual categories in parietal cortex. *Nature*, 443, 85–88.

Friston, K.J., Holmes, A.P., Worsley, K.J., *et al.* (1995). Statistical parametric maps in functional imaging: a general linear approach. *Human Brain Mapping*, 2, 189–210.

Fuentemilla, L., Penny, W.D., Cashdollar, N., *et al.* (2010). Theta-coupled periodic replay in working memory. *Current Biology*, 20, 606–612.

Fuster, J.M., and Alexander, G.E. (1971). Neuron activity related to short-term memory. *Science*, 173, 652–654.

Gnadt, J.W., and Andersen, R.A. (1988). Memory related motor planning activity in posterior parietal cortex of macaque. *Experimental Brain Research*, 70, 216–220.

Griffin, I.C., and Nobre, A.C. (2003). Orienting attention to locations in internal representations. *Journal of Cognitive Neuroscience*, 15, 1176–1194.

Harrison, S.A., and Tong, F. (2009). Decoding reveals the contents of visual working memory in early visual areas. *Nature*, 458, 632–635.

Haxby, J.V., Gobini, M.I., Furey, M.L., *et al.* (2001). Distributed and overlapping representatinons of faces and objects in ventral temporal cortex. *Science*, 293, 2425–2430.

Haynes, J.-D., and Rees, G. (2006). Decoding mental states from brain activity in humans. *Nature Reviews Neuroscience*, 7, 523–534.

Hebb, D.O. (1949). *The Organization of Behavior: A Neuropsychological Theory*. New York, NY: John Wiley & Sons, Inc.

Jensen, O., Gelfand, J., Kounios, J., and Lisman, J.E. (2002). Oscillations in the alpha band (9–12 Hz) increase with memory load during retention in a short-term memory task. *Cerebral Cortex* 12, 877–882.

Jha, A., and McCarthy, G. (2000). The influence of memory load upon delay interval activity in a working memory task: an event-related functional MRI study. *Journal of Cognitive Neuroscience*, 12 (suppl. 2), 90–105.

Jonides, J., Smith, E. Koeppe, R., *et al.* (1993). Spatial working memory in humans as revealed by PET. *Nature*, 363, 623–625.

Kanwisher, N., McDermott, J. and Chun, M.M. (1997). The fusiform face area: a module in human extrastriate cortex specialized for face perception. *Journal of Neuroscience*, 17, 4302–4311.

Kriegeskorte, N., Formisano, E., Sorger, B., and Goebel, R. (2007). Individual faces elicit distinct response patterns in human anterior temporal cortex. *Proceedings of the National Academy of Sciences of the USA*, 104, 20600–20605.

Kriegeskorte, N., Goebel, R., and Bandettini, P.A. (2006). Information-based functional brain mapping. *Proceedings of the National Academy of Sciences of the USA*, 103, 3863–3868.

LaRocque, J.J., Lewis-Peacock, J.A. Drysdale, A., *et al.* (2013). Decoding attended information in short-term memory: an EEG study. *Journal of Cognitive Neuroscience*, 25, 127–142.

Lebedev, M.A., Messinger, A., Kralik, J.D., and Wise, S.P. (2004). Representation of attended versus remembered locations in prefrontal cortex. *PLoS Biology*, 2, 1919–1935.

Lepsien, J., and Nobre, A.C. (2007). Attentional modulation of object representations in working memory. *Neuropsychologia*, 17, 2072–2083.

Lepsien, J., Thornton, I., and Nobre, A.C. (2011). Attention and short-term memory: Crossroads. *Neuropsychologia*, 49, 1569–1577.

Leung, H.-C., Seelig, D., and Gore, J.C. (2004). The effect of memory load on cortical activity in the spatial working memory circuit. *Cognitive, Affective, and Behavioral Neuroscience*, 4, 553–563.

Lewis-Peacock, J.A., Drysdale, A., Oberauer, K., and Postle, B.R. (2012). Neural evidence for a distinction between short-term memory and the focus of attention. *Journal of Cognitive Neuroscience*, 23, 61–79.

Lewis-Peacock, J.A., and Postle, B R. (2008). Temporary activation of long-term memory supports working memory. *Journal of Neuroscience*, 28, 8765–8771.

Lewis-Peacock, J.A., and Postle, B.R. (2012). Decoding the internal focus of attention. *Neuropsychologia*, 50, 470–478.

Linden, D.E.J., Oosterhof N.N., Klein C., and Downing, P.E. (2012). Mapping brain activation and information during category-specific visual working memory. *Journal of Neurophysiology*, 107, 628–639.

McElree, B. (2001). Working memory and focal attention. *Journal of Experimental Psychology: Learning, Memory, and Cognition*, 27, 817–835.

Meyers, E.M., Freedman, D.J. Kreiman, G., *et al.* (2008). Dynamic population coding of category information in inferior temporal and prefrontal cortex. *Journal of Neurophysiology*, 100, 1407–1419.

Nakamura, K., and Kubota, K. (1995). Mnemonic firing of neurons in the monkey temporal pole during a visual recognition memory task. *Journal of Neurophysiology*, 74, 162–178.

Nee, D.E., and Jonides, J. (2008). Neural correlates of access to short-term memory. *Proceedings of the National Academy of Sciences of the USA*, 105, 14228–14233.

Nee, D.E., and Jonides, J. (2011). Dissociable contributions of prefrontal cortex and the hippocampus to short-term memory: evidence for a 3-state model of memory. *NeuroImage*, 15, 1540–1548.

Nobre, A.C., Coull, J.T., Maquet, P., *et al.* (2004). Orienting attention to locations in perceptual versus mental representations. *Journal of Cognitive Neuroscience*, 16, 363–373.

Nobre, A.C., and Stokes, M.G. (2011). Attention and short-term memory: crossroads. *Neuropsychologia*, 49, 1391–1392.

Norman, K.A., Polyn, S.M., Detre, G.J., and Haxby, J.V. (2006). Beyond mind-reading: multi-voxel pattern analysis of fMRI data. *Trends in Cognitive Sciences*, 10, 424–430.

Oberauer, K. (2002). Access to information in working memory: exploring the focus of attention. *Journal of Experimental Psychology: Learning, Memory, and Cognition*, 28, 411–421.

Oberauer, K. (2005). Control of the contents of working memory: a comparison of two paradigms and two age groups. *Journal of Experimental Psychology: Learning, Memory, and Cognition*, 31, 714–728.

O'Craven, K.M., Downing, P.E., and Kanwisher, N. (1999). fMRI evidence for objects as the units of attentional selection. *Nature*, 401, 584–587.

Olivers, C.N.L., Peters, J., Houtkamp, R., and Roelfsema, P.R. (2011). Different states in visual working memory: when it guides attention and when it does not. *Trends in Cognitive Sciences* 15, 327–334.

Owen, A.M., Stern, C.E., Look, R.B., *et al.* (1998). Functional organization of spatial and nonspatial working memory processing within the human lateral frontal cortex. *Proceedings of the National Academy of Sciences of the USA*, 95, 7721–7726.

Palva, S., and Palva, J.M. (2011). Functional roles of alpha-band phase synchronization in local and large-scale cortical networks. *Frontiers in Psychology*, 2. doi: 10.3389/fpsyg.2011.00204.

Parvizi, J., Jacques, C., Foster, B.L., *et al.* (2012). Electrical stimulation of human fusiform face-selective regions distorts face perception. *Journal of Neuroscience* 3 2, 14915–14920.

Pereira, F., Mitchell, T., and Botvinick, M.M. (2009). Machine learning classifiers and fMRI: a tutorial overview. *NeuroImage*, 45, S199–S209.

Peters, J., Roelfsema, P.R., and Goebel, R. (2012). Task-relevant and accessory items in working memory have opposite effects on activity in extrastriate cortex. *Journal of Neuroscience*, 32, 17003–17011.

Poldrack, R.A. (2006). Can cognitive processes be inferred from neuroimaging data? *Trends in Cognitive Sciences*, 10, 59–63.

Polyn, S.M., Natu, V.S., Cohen, J.D., and Norman, K.A. (2005). Category-specific cortical activity precedes retrieval during memory search. *Science*, 310, 1963–1966.

Postle, B.R. (2006a). Working memory as an emergent property of the mind and brain. *Neuroscience*, 139, 23–38.

Postle, B.R. (2006b). Distraction-spanning sustained activity during delayed recognition of locations. *NeuroImage*, 30, 950–962.

Postle, B.R. (2011). What underlies the ability to guide action with spatial information that is no longer present in the environment? In *Spatial Working Memory* (ed. A. Vandierendonck and A. Szmalec). Hove, UK: Psychology Press, pp. 897–901.

Postle, B.R., Berger, J.S., and D'Esposito, M. (1999). Functional neuroanatomical double dissociation of mnemonic and executive control processes contributing to working memory performance. *Proceedings of the National Academy of Sciences of the USA*, 96, 12959–12964.

Postle, B.R., Druzgal, T.J., and D'Esposito, M. (2003). Seeking the neural substrates of working memory storage. *Cortex*, 39, 927–946.

Postle, B.R., and Hamidi, M. (2007). Nonvisual codes and nonvisual brain areas support visual working memory. *Cerebral Cortex*, 17, 2134–2142.

Ranganath, C., DeGutis, J., and D'Esposito, M. (2004). Category-specific modulation of inferior temporal activity during working memory encoding and maintenance. *Cognitive Brain Research*, 20, 37–45.

Reinhart, R.M., Heitz, R.P., Purcell, B.A., *et al.* (2012). Homologous mechanisms of visuospatial working memory maintenance in macaque and human: properties and sources. *Journal of Neuroscience*, 32, 7711–7722.

Riggall, A.C., and Postle, B.R. (2012). The relation between working memory storage and elevated activity, as measured with fMRI. *Journal of Neuroscience*, 32, 12990–12998.

Salazar, R.F., Dotson, N.M., Bressler, S.L., and Gray, C.M. (2012). Content-specific fronto-parietal synchronization during visual working memory. *Science*, 338, 1097–1100.

Sauseng, P., Klimesch, W., Heise, K.F., *et al.* (2009). Brain oscillatory substrates of visual short-term memory capacity. *Current Biology*, 19, 1846–1852.

Serences, J.T., Ester, E.F., Vogel, E.K., and Awh, E. (2009). Stimulus-specific delay activity in human primary visual cortex. *Psychological Science*, 20, 207–214.

Soon, C.S., Brass, M., Heinze, H.J., and Haynes, J.-D. (2008). Unconscious determinants of free decision in the human brain. *Nature Neuroscience*, 11, 543–545.

Stokes, M., and Duncan, J. (2014). Dynamic brain states for preparatory attention and working memory. In *The Oxford Handbook of Attention* (ed. A.C. Nobre and S. Kastner). Oxford: Oxford University Press, pp. 897–901.

Super, H., Spekreijse, H., and Lamme, V.A.F. (2001). A neural correlate of working memory in the monkey primary visual cortex. *Science*, 293, 120–124.

Suzuki, W.A., Miller, E.K., and Desimone, R. (1997). Object and place memory in the macaque entorhinal cortex. *Journal of Neurophysiology*, 78, 1062–1081.

Swaminathan, S.K., and Freedman, D.J. (2012). Preferential encoding of visual categories in parietal cortex compared with prefrontal cortex. *Nature Neuroscience*, 15, 315–320.

Takeda, K., and Funahashi, S. (2002). Prefrontal task-related activity representing visual cue location or saccade direction in spatial working memory tasks. *Journal of Neurophysiology*, 87, 567–588.

Takeda, K., and Funahashi, S. (2004). Population vector analysis of primate prefrontal activity during spatial working memory. *Cerebral Cortex*, 14, 1328–1339.

Takeda, K., and Funahashi, S. (2007). Relationship between prefrontal task-related activity and information flow during spatial working memory performance. *Cortex*, 43 (1), 38–52.

Todd, J.J., and Marois, R. (2004). Capacity limit of visual short-term memory in human posterior parietal cortex. *Nature*, 428, 751–754.

Tsujimoto, S., and Sawaguchi, T. (2004). Properties of delay-period neuronal activity in the primate prefrontal cortex during memory- and sensory-guided saccade tasks. *European Journal of Neuroscience*, 19 (2), 447–457.

Uhlhaas, P.J., Pipa, G., Lima, B., *et al.* (2009). Neural synchrony in cortical networks: history, concept and current status. *Frontiers in Integrative Neuroscience*, 3. doi: 10.3389/neuro.07.017.2009.

van Dijk, H., van der Werf, J., Mazaheri, A., *et al.* (2010). Modulations of oscillatory activity with amplitude asymmetry can produce cognitively relevant event-related responses. *Proceedings of the National Academy of Sciences of the USA*, 107, 900–905.

Vogel, E.K., and Machizawa, M.G. (2004). Neural activity predicts individual differences in visual working memory capacity. *Nature*, 428, 748–751.

Xu, Y., and Chun, M.M. (2006). Dissociable neural mechanisms supporting visual short-term memory for objects. *Nature*, 440, 91–95.

Zaksas, D., and Pasternak, T. (2006). Directional signals in the prefrontal cortex and in area MT during a working memory for visual motion task. *Journal of Neuroscience*, 26, 11726–11742.

Zarahn, E., Aguirre, G.K., and D'Esposito, M. (1997). A trial-based experimental design for fMRI. *NeuroImage*, 6, 122–138.

Zhou, Y.D., and Fuster, J.M. (1996). Mnemonic neuronal activity in somatosensory cortex. *Proceedings of the National Academy of Sciences of the USA*, 93, 10533–10537.

# 3

# The Outer Limits of Implicit Memory

## Anthony J. Ryals and Joel L. Voss

## Introduction

In this review, we will describe the many, varied, and sometimes surprising reaches of implicit memory – that is, memory that is expressed through behavior without an individual's awareness of its occurrence. Prevalent theorizing about implicit memory tends to characterize it as a tightly limited set of phenomena, including many assumptions regarding how implicit memory concerns only a few types of information, can occur only over a very brief duration, is supported by a relatively restricted collection of brain regions, and can be expressed through only a small number of behaviors. Before describing the much broader "outer limits" of implicit memory, it is informative to speculate about why limited views of implicit memory have become pervasive. We have drawn inspiration from Plato's *Allegory of the Cave*, which paints a vivid picture of a steep underground cavern in which prisoners have been bound to the floor since birth. These prisoners, immobilized by chains, are prevented from moving or turning their heads to view anything other than what appears directly in front of them. The prisoners' concept of reality is based upon shadows cast on the cave wall created by objects passing in front of a fire behind them. The presence of the rich daylight-filled world outside the confines of the cave is unknown to the prisoners. That is, their physical reality is constrained by their inflexible bonds, and this constraint in turn limits their mental reality (Plato, 380 BCE). In a similar fashion, we will argue, over-reliance on conventional paradigms for measuring implicit memory has restricted the view of the full nature and scope of implicit-memory phenomena. Recent methodological and technological advances in cognitive neuroscience have presented the intriguing possibility that the influence of implicit processing on human memory may be far broader than has traditionally been assumed (Dew and Cabeza, 2011; Voss, Lucas, and Paller, 2012; see also Chapter 18).

Current concepts of implicit memory have grown out of a history of findings in cases of neurological impairments, such as those that produce amnesia, that have suggested complex relationships between human memory and conscious awareness (e.g., Scoville and Milner, 1957; Warrington and Weiskrantz, 1968; Weiskrantz and Warrington, 1979). Mental functioning often involves conscious awareness of internal and external states in the present as well as prospection about future states. Likewise,

*The Wiley Handbook on the Cognitive Neuroscience of Memory*, First Edition.
Edited by Donna Rose Addis, Morgan Barense, and Audrey Duarte.
© 2015 John Wiley & Sons, Ltd. Published 2015 by John Wiley & Sons, Ltd.

past experiences can be evoked consciously as explicit memories. However, the level of conscious awareness involved in memory can be variable (e.g., Ebbinghaus, 1885; Tulving, 1985). For example, perhaps an individual is able to recollect the name of a childhood friend and an image of a time they shared in the past. This is an example of a highly conscious memory retrieval event known as a recollection. In a similar manner, upon seeing an old friend, perhaps the individual's experience is limited to fragmented partial information such as the fact that this person's name starts with a "J" (e.g., Koriat *et al.*, 2003). A third possibility, when all recollection fails, is a mere "feeling" that the person is known (e.g., Mandler, 1980, 2008). This feeling of famil-iarity also involves conscious awareness, but to a lesser degree than does recollection. Another possibility, and the primary topic of this chapter, is that memory can occur without an individual's conscious awareness (e.g., Jacoby and Kelley, 1992; Merikle and Reingold, 1991).

Conscious versus non-conscious expressions of memory have often been studied by using different test formats, with "direct" tests used to study conscious memory and "indirect" tests used to study non-conscious memory. In a direct test, individuals are asked to deliberately retrieve information they have previously experienced (e.g., MacLeod and Daniels, 2000; Richardson-Klavehn and Bjork, 1988; Roediger and McDermott, 1993). For instance, as illustrated in Figure 3.1, a direct test of recogni-tion memory might involve first reading a collection of words. Then, the direct test is administered after a short delay. During the direct test, a participant may view the same words again, intermixed with an equal number of words that were not experi-enced during the initial "study" session, and the participant attempts to indicate whether each word is *old* (if it was studied earlier) or if it is *new* (if it appeared for the first time during the test). Other forms of direct tests include free-recall, cued-recall, and the remember/know procedure (e.g., Gardiner, Ramponi, and Richardson-Klavehn, 1998; Tulving, 1985). In contrast, an indirect test does not require explicit retrieval of information from the study session, but rather memory is tested covertly.

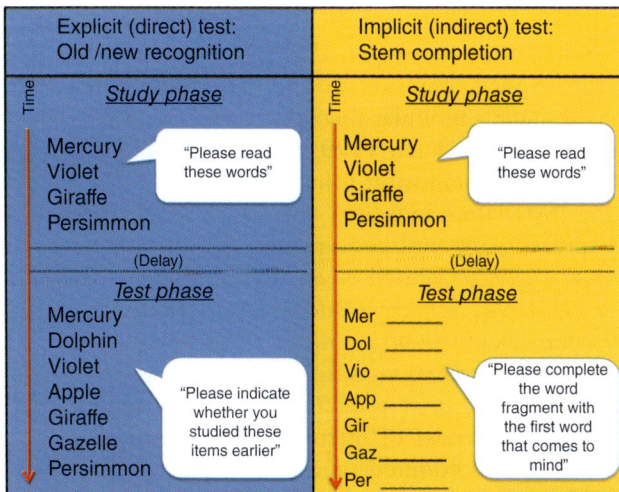

**Figure 3.1**    Example direct and indirect memory test formats. These tests were designed to measure explicit memory and implicit memory, respectively.

For example, participants may be asked to complete word stems with the first word to come to mind, and the participant would be more likely to complete these word stems with a previously viewed word than with another word (e.g., given the stem *vio—*, the participant would be more likely to respond "violet" if it had been viewed earlier than to respond with "violence," "viola," or another similar word). Additional indirect test formats include free-association, category verification, fragment completion, and lexical decision. These tasks measure what are known as *priming* effects. Priming is broadly thought to include any form of influence (positive or negative) on performance due to prior exposure to a stimulus without awareness (e.g., Graf and Schacter ,1985; Schacter, 1992; Tulving and Schacter, 1990). One form of priming is perceptual, such that the influence on memory depends on sensory characteristics of a stimulus. Another form, conceptual priming, occurs when an influence upon memory is based on meaning of a previously experienced stimulus. In addition to testing implicit and explicit memory using direct and indirect methods separately, a third type of test, the process dissociation procedure (PDP) was originally developed in an attempt to tease apart the influence of explicit (controlled) processing from that of implicit (automatic) processing within one experimental framework (e.g., Jacoby, 1991).

Performance on direct versus indirect memory tests has frequently been attributed to distinct memory systems that encompass unique brain regions (e.g., Schacter, 1992). A pervasive distinction has been between explicit and implicit systems (also referred to as declarative and non-declarative systems). Scoville and Milner (1957) demonstrated that a patient known by his initials, H.M., had a profound loss of memory after undergoing removal of his hippocampus and surrounding structures of the medial temporal lobe (MTL). In addition to the disruption of past memories, H.M. also experienced profound anterograde amnesia, which prevented him from forming new explicit memories. In general, patient H.M. failed at direct tests thought to reflect explicit memory. Despite this deficit, H.M. exhibited many instances of preserved implicit learning without awareness when probed using indirect tests. These findings suggested that the MTL is primarily involved in conscious/explicit memory, whereas other brain regions (which were left relatively intact) must be those that support the residual implicit memory capabilities (e.g., Baddeley and Warrington, 1970; Corkin, 1968; Seger, 1994; Shimamura, 1986). By the beginning of the 1980s, the explicit/implicit division based on direct and indirect task performance helped shape a modular theory of memory systems that has persevered for several decades (e.g., Roediger, 1990; Squire, 1987). Accordingly, neuroimaging research using positron emission tomography (PET) and functional magnetic resonance imaging (fMRI) has indicated distinctions between explicit memory and priming in both perceptually and conceptually driven tasks (e.g., Buckner *et al.*, 1995; Cabeza *et al.*, 1997; Gabrieli *et al.*, 1996; Nyberg, Cabeza, and Tulving, 1996; Raichle *et al.*, 1994, Schacter, Buckner, and Koutstaal, 1998). By the late 1990s, cognitive neuroscientists and cognitive psychologists had largely adopted the explicit/implicit memory distinction as follows: explicit or declarative memory (i.e., recall and recognition) is measured using direct tests and depends on MTL structures involved in conscious awareness of memory, whereas implicit or non-declarative memory (i.e, priming, conditioning, and motor learning) is measured through indirect tests and depends on regions outside of MTL which do not support conscious awareness of memory. However, as discussed below, this strong division has recently come under considerable scrutiny in light of evidence that indicates a greater degree of flexibility in the explicit/implicit memory distinction (see also Hannula and Greene, 2012).

Despite the substantial evidence for distinct implicit and explicit memory processes and systems, many of these distinctions may be more apparent than real. In fact, much of the work that has defined the fundamental characteristics of implicit versus explicit memory has done so using fundamentally different experimental paradigms to measure the properties of each (e.g., direct versus indirect tests). Defining properties of implicit and explicit memory based solely on findings using tasks that were designed to have strong differential sensitivity to these properties involves a circularity in reasoning and leaves many of the interesting characteristics of each memory type unexplored (e.g., Voss and Paller, 2007). In other words, if an indirect or implicit task is used to study a memory phenomenon, then by definition, results from this task will likely be categorized as arising from implicit memory. Similarly, if a different memory phenomenon manifests in a direct or explicit task, this phenomenon may be classified as explicit in nature. As we describe below, many surprising characteristics of implicit memory have been discovered by using the full range of cognitive neuroscience techniques available to measure memory-related brain processing during both implicit and explicit memory tests, and by testing memory outside of the standard paradigms that have been used extensively. Indeed, one of the most surprising and potentially transformative ideas to emerge in recent years is that implicit and explicit memory may be based on similar brain mechanisms, and thus be more interrelated than previously appreciated (see also Dew and Cabeza, 2011, 2012).

For the remainder of this review, we will discuss evidence that has overturned long-held beliefs regarding the fundamental properties of implicit memory. Some recent advances have resulted simply by testing memory using new experimental procedures. Moreover, as technical capabilities have advanced in cognitive neuroscience, so has the ability to accurately trace the neural origins of implicit memory that occurs even during explicit testing (i.e., outside of the indirect testing paradigms normally used to measure it). These recent advances suggest a much broader role for implicit memory than previously acknowledged, and a much more complex relationship may exist between implicit and explicit memory than has been previously assumed. In order to understand this complex relationship, it is important to first examine four long-held assumptions about implicit memory. It should be noted that we are not advocating that the traditional beliefs mentioned below should be discounted as *wrong*. Rather, our stance is that, similar to the constraints experienced by the prisoners in Plato's cave (Figure 3.2), what is discovered as a property of memory is constrained and *limited* by the manner in which the discovery is made (i.e., by the test format). These beliefs are commonly incorporated as design features of implicit memory tests, thus helping to perpetuate them as defining features of implicit memory as frequently described in the extant literature.

**Belief 1: Implicit memory manifests through restricted behaviors during indirect testing.** As described above, indirect memory tests have been almost exclusively used to study implicit memory. Furthermore, the influence of implicit memory in these tests is often quite trivial: a small increase or decrease in response time, the slight feeling of preference for a previously seen stimulus, or a small bias to complete a word fragment with one possible ending over another.

**Limitation**: Almost all tests used to measure implicit memory use restricted outcomes such as those mentioned above as dependent measures. Defining an outcome based on

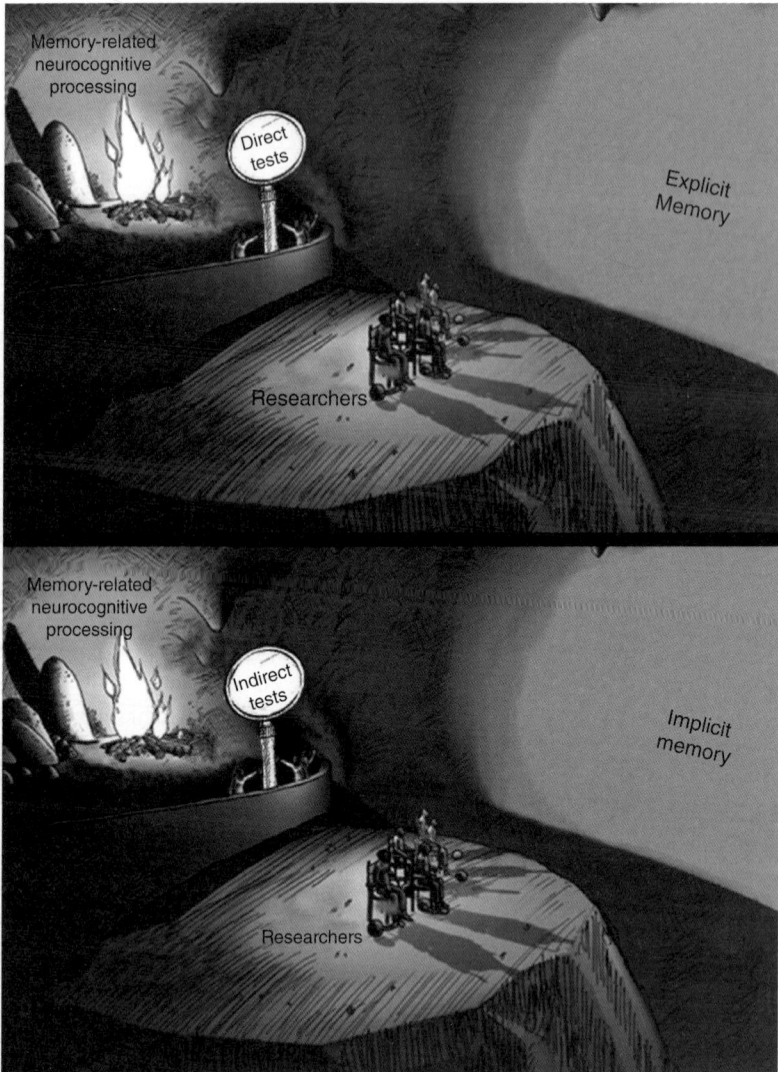

**Figure 3.2** An adaptation of Plato's allegory of the cave, illustrating over-reliance on conventional paradigms for measuring implicit memory. We argue that this has restricted the view of the full nature and scope of implicit-memory phenomena. In this illustration, neurocognitive processing responsible for memory can be characterized as either implicit or explicit depending on the nature of the test format (indirect or direct), which serves as a lens through which experimenters learn about the nature of these memory types.

the type of task used to study it may limit the understanding of the processes involved in producing the outcome.

**Belief 2: Implicit memory concerns only familiar stimuli having pre-existing memory representations.** Implicit memory is almost always studied using words and nameable pictures that have strong pre-existing memory representations. Indeed, it is unclear how word-stem completion and similar kinds of standard indirect-test formats could be performed otherwise.

**Limitation:** This has led most accounts of implicit memory to ignore other types of stimuli, and it is therefore commonly thought that implicit memory can only concern a restricted range of stimulus categories. Thus, the extent to which implicit influences on memory may extend across stimulus qualities is relatively unexplored.

**Belief 3: Implicit memory is short-lived.** Most tests of implicit memory use very short delays. Indeed, standard priming tests (especially semantic priming) incorporate delays of hundreds of milliseconds to several seconds (e.g., Jacoby and Whitehouse 1989).

**Limitation:** Implicit memory has not been routinely tested at delays comparable to those used in many studies of long-term memory, and therefore implicit memory is often considered a very short-lived phenomenon. Different testing circumstances are needed to determine if implicit memory lingers much longer.

**Belief 4: Implicit memory involves processing by only those brain regions that are not involved in explicit memory.** The many dissociations between neural correlates of implicit and explicit memory and reports of preserved implicit memory in cases when explicit memory has been disrupted by MTL damage has led to the belief that implicit memory involves only those brain regions that are not involved in explicit memory.

**Limitation:** Most studies have attempted to identify those conditions in which dissociations between implicit and explicit memory are most likely to occur (e.g., in direct versus indirect tests), thus helping to perpetuate the notion that the brain regions responsible are always distinct. Very few studies have looked for associations, or commonalities, in neural substrates of implicit and explicit memory, and therefore these potential commonalities in relevant functional neuroanatomy are relatively unknown.

Now that we have outlined some of the long-held beliefs regarding the properties of implicit memory and described how these beliefs may have come about via an over-adherence to limited methods for studying implicit memory, we will review some recent evidence showing the ways in which implicit memory stretches beyond the tight boundaries that have been assumed. Our description of these properties of implicit memory is not meant to be exhaustive, but it serves to highlight how recent evidence has warranted a re-evaluation of each of the four beliefs about implicit memory, and it is intended to serve as a starting point for future investigations on the properties of implicit (and explicit) memory.

## Implicit Memory Concerns a Wide Range of Behaviors Measured in a Variety of Tasks

A prime example of how the nature of the memory test can mask influences from implicit memory is the remember/know (R/K) procedure commonly used as a test of explicit memory (Tulving, 1985). In a typical R/K experiment, participants study items (e.g., words, pictures) and then take a recognition test (Figure 3.1), with each old response classified as *remember* (R) or *know* (K). An R response indicates they can remember seeing an item before within the context of the experiment. A K response indicates they merely feel they have experienced an item earlier in the experiment but cannot recollect its prior occurrence. R responses are interpreted as an index of explicit recollection, and K responses are interpreted as an index of an explicit feeling of familiarity. By definition, all expressions of memory fall into either R or K categories (see Yonelinas, 2002, for a review), and there is no attempt to account for any influences of implicit processing. (Likewise, indirect tests do not necessarily allow for influences of explicit processing; e.g., Toth, Reingold, and Jacoby, 1994.)

How might one go about measuring implicit memory during such a test? Voss, Baym, and Paller (2008) reasoned that if implicit memory were to support accurate responses during a recognition memory test, then they would primarily be measureable when subjects did not report R or K (i.e., when explicit memory was not driving the response). They found an interesting pattern simply by including a third response option: G, for *guess* (see also Tunney and Fernie, 2007). By constructing the memory paradigm so as to maximally enhance influences from implicit processing, such as by dividing attention while subjects studied with a secondary task and using nonverbal "kaleidoscope" images as memoranda, Voss, Baym and Paller (2008) found that recognition responses classified by subjects as guesses could nonetheless be highly accurate, reflecting implicit memory. Indeed, in a follow-up event-related brain potential (ERP) study (Voss and Paller, 2009), neural correlates of highly accurate G responses based on implicit memory were distinct from neural correlates of explicit memory signaled by R and K responses. The negative-going ERP deflection occurring between 200 and 400 ms was more negative for correct *guesses* than for new items, and this old/new ERP effect (N300) was quite different from the ERP signatures traditionally attributed to recollection and familiarity. This shows that implicit memory is operative and able to drive behavior even during direct memory tests such as recognition that are generally accepted as pure tests of explicit memory.

Additional support for an implicit ERP signature in an explicit memory task was demonstrated in a study of the word recognition without identification (RWI) paradigm by Ryals *et al.* (2011). In the RWI task, participants viewed lists of regular words during a study phase. At test, they were given twice as many word fragments, half of which corresponded to words they had studied and half of which did not. Ryals *et al.* found that when word identification failed, participants were able to rate fragments of studied words as higher in familiarity than new fragments. As in Voss and Paller (2009), this RWI effect also corresponded to an N300 ERP deflection, with greater negativity for studied than for unstudied fragments. For individuals who did not demonstrate the behavioral RWI effect, no N300 was found. Though RWI itself has traditionally been attributed to familiarity-based recognition that occurs in the absence of recollection, the findings of Ryals and colleagues present an intriguing possibility that RWI may be a form of unconscious recognition which may manifest outside of (or simultaneously with) conscious familiarity, again showing that implicit memory can occur during direct tests of recognition.

## Implicit Memory Can Occur During Recollection Involving Long-term Semantic Memory

Some recent behavioral research has also suggested that implicit information can influence explicit recollection of semantic knowledge. Ryals and Cleary (in preparation) performed a series of experiments using a modified RWI procedure to explore partial recollection as a distinct entity in recognition memory. Ryals and Cleary first had participants study a list of target answers (e.g., "Huxley"), after which they viewed a list of twice as many general-knowledge questions. Half of these general-knowledge questions corresponded to target answers studied earlier while half did not (i.e., the study target "Huxley" corresponded to the test question "What is the last name of the author of *A Brave New World?*"). When prompted with a general-knowledge test question, participants were instructed to provide the correct answer and to also rate the likelihood that they had studied the answer previously, using a 0–10 scale. If unable to answer a test question, they were instructed to provide any partial information about the answer that came to mind. Partial information was defined as the first or last letter of the answer, the number of syllables in the answer, or a word that sounded similar to the answer. When examining trials for test questions that did indeed correspond to studied target answers, the authors discovered dissociations between recollection of the full target answer, partial target recollection, and mere familiarity that occurred in the absence of any recollection. As anticipated, partial target recollection occurred when participants were prompted to provide any fragmentary information about the target answer in the event that full target retrieval failed. However, Ryals and Cleary also found an intriguing and unanticipated finding in these experiments. When unable to fully retrieve a target answer, participants sometimes provided an incorrect answer that they thought was correct. Interestingly this incorrect answer sometimes contained partial information that corresponded to the correct target. For instance, If the incorrect answer to a test question was "Huxley," one participant provided the answer "Hudson" that they assumed was correct, yet they were unaware of the veridical partial information (the correct first two letters) that manifested in their answer. Ryals and Cleary suggested that this manifestation of partial recollection within incorrect answers resulted from fragmentary semantic access occurring outside of conscious awareness. Although it will be important to determine if this fragmentary retrieval extends to episodic as well as semantic memory, the notion of partial retrieval without full-blown awareness is consistent with the proposal that that memory tasks presumed to tap only explicit memory may also capture implicit memory (Voss, Lucas, and Paller, 2012).

## Implicit Memory Can Co-occur with Familiarity and Recollection in Explicit Tasks

Mounting evidence indicates that one ERP signal commonly identified during direct memory tests, the so-called FN400 potential, may in fact reflect implicit memory for conceptual information, therefore indicating that implicit memory is pervasive during explicit memory testing. The FN400 is a mid-frontal old/new effect that occurs between 300 and 500 ms after stimulus presentation, and it is commonly attributed to explicit familiarity memory (e.g., Rugg and Curran, 2007). However, substantial evidence (reviewed in Voss, Lucas, and Paller, 2012) indicates that in fact it is a signature of implicit conceptual information processing that occurs without awareness. For example, Voss and Paller (2006) found evidence that conceptual implicit memory for famous faces elicits a frontal ERP effect that occurs 250–500 ms after stimulus exposure. This frontal ERP effect is such that neurological activity corresponding to primed faces was significantly more positive in amplitude than that corresponding to unprimed faces. The time window in which this effect occurred was consistent with that of the FN400 component typically attributed to explicit familiarity. Furthermore, Voss and Paller found that a later (500–750 ms) effect predicted explicit facial recognition: thus the pattern for implicit perceptual priming and explicit recognition were shown to be spatiotemporally distinct. In a subsequent study, Voss, Schendan, and Paller (2010) found further evidence that the FN400 is linked to conceptual implicit memory for meaningful geometric shapes ("squiggles"). This effect was also shown to be distinct from earlier-occurring perceptual priming as indexed by the P170 component. Based on these and other findings, Voss, Lucas, and Paller (2012) have concluded that conceptual implicit memory processing might be indexed by FN400 potentials, and thus FN400 may not index episodic familiarity as is typically assumed (at least in some circumstances). These potentials appear to selectively associate with conceptual implicit memory during tests designed to tap priming as well as tests designed to measure explicit memory. Furthermore, fMRI data suggest that neural correlates of conceptual implicit memory can occur during explicit memory testing, and are distinct form neural correlates of explicit retrieval of the same information (e.g., Voss, Federmeier, and Paller, 2012). Taken together, this research suggests that conceptual implicit memory processing is pervasive during tests intended to measure familiarity and recollection; it is so pervasive that its neural correlates have been erroneously assigned to those of familiarity. In many circumstances, especially involving common words and nameable images, familiarity and conceptual implicit memory are correlated. Nonetheless, we have shown that they can be disentangled and linked to distinct neural correlates (Paller, Voss, and Boehm, 2007; Voss, Lucas, and Paller, 2012).

## Implicit Memory Concerns Many Stimulus Categories, Including Novel Objects and Words

The preponderance of studies of implicit priming, such as word-stem completion, the lexical decision task, and word-fragment completion, hinge upon the use of word and non-word verbal stimuli (e.g., Gooding, Mayes, and van Eijk, 2000; Rajaram and Roediger, 1993). However, recent research has provided evidence in support of perceptual and conceptual priming across a multitude of stimulus types. For instance, Voss and Paller (2010) found evidence for perceptual priming for novel color kaleidoscope images that possessed no pre-experimental meaning to participants. Voss and Paller observed that the magnitude of this priming effect corresponded to the magnitude of a negative ERP deflection occurring between 100 and 300 ms after stimulus exposure. Importantly, this ERP signature was notably similar to that previously related to implicit recognition (Voss, Baym, and Paller, 2008; Voss and Paller, 2009) rather than that associated with explicit memory expressions such as recollection or familiarity. Likewise, Slotnick and Schacter (2006) found unconscious perceptual priming for novel two-dimensional shapes. Additional evidence for implicit conceptual influences on memory tests has been found using minimalist abstract line drawings (squiggles) (Voss, Federmeier, and Paller, 2012; Voss and Paller, 2007) as well as obscure words which participants rated to have little to no meaning (Voss, Lucas, and

Paller, 2012). Even novel object priming is quite broad and has unexpected properties. Thus it is not only the perceptual features of stimuli that can support implicit memory, but the conceptual features are crucial as well. Although the neural effects of conceptual semantic priming have received some attention using standard priming paradigms (e.g., Heath *et al.*, 2012; Rissman, Eliassen, and Blumstein, 2003), it will be important to examine the role of implicit processes in explicit memory tests using a multitude of stimulus types in order to understand the extent to which similar neural processes are involved in priming irrespective of stimulus format.

## Implicit Memory is not Necessarily Short-Lived

Much of the research examining perceptual priming has used very short delays (e.g., several hundred milliseconds to several minutes) between the brief prime exposure and later presentation of target probes. However, robust priming effects have been demonstrated using delays ranging from minutes (Becker *et al.*, 1997), to days (e.g., Tulving, Schacter, and Stark, 1982), weeks (Mitchell and Brown, 1988), and months after initial exposure to a prime (e.g., Sloman *et al.*, 1988). Mitchell (2006) even demonstrated perceptual priming for novel shapes in a picture fragment identification task that persisted for 17.4 years. This very long-term priming occurred after a single exposure despite some participants forgetting that they had even participated in the initial study. For the most part, the duration of implicit memory has not been adequately tested, as many researchers adhere to standard experimental paradigms that involve short delays between primes and probes. Furthermore, it has been proposed by some that the duration of conceptual implicit memory is much more limited than that of perceptual implicit memory (Neely, 1991; Ochsner, Chiu, and Schacter, 1994; Roediger and Geraci, 2005), yet this question remains understudied. In contrast to this view, our findings mentioned above, that FN400 and fMRI correlates of conceptual implicit memory are found normally during recognition testing, indicates that this type of implicit memory may last for at least as long as explicit memory does – i.e., over the common delays of minutes to days used frequently in studies of this nature.

## Implicit Memory is Supported by a Variety of Brain Regions, Even those that are Strongly Linked to Explicit Memory

The hippocampus is involved in conscious recollection, a prime example of explicit memory. Based on early dissociation findings, hippocampus and surrounding MTL are thought not to support implicit memory (i.e., implicit memory remains relatively intact following their destruction). However, new findings from many groups suggest that hippocampus and other MTL structures also support a wide range of implicit memory phenomena (e.g., Hannula and Greene, 2012; see also Chapter 18). Recent reports have also suggested a role for MTL structures in rapid associative learning and memory. Although associative memory is generally considered as a hallmark of explicit memory (e.g., Graf and Schacter, 1985), newer evidence suggest that brain regions involved in associative memory can nonetheless engage in implicit memory processing. For example, Schapiro, Kustner, and Turk-Browne (2012) recently provided evidence that hippocampus is involved in incidental learning of temporal relationships between visual stimuli independent of behavior and outside conscious awareness of participants. In another example, Wimmer and Shohamy (2012) found that hippocampus is involved in implicitly biasing decisions through a dynamic (yet covert) modulation of value within a network of existing memory representations as a result of new experience. Although destruction of hippocampus and surrounding MTL clearly disrupts explicit memory in amnesic patients, MTL damage also influences implicit expressions of associative memory that can be measured covertly through behaviors such as eye movements (e.g., Hannula and Cohen, 2007, reviewed in Hannula and Greene, 2012).

Another brain region putatively linked primarily to explicit recollection is prefrontal cortex (PFC), which, through its interactions with hippocampus, is thought to build explicit recollective memory (e.g., Kirwan, Wixted, and Squire, 2008; see also Chapter 7). PFC has been traditionally linked to executive function that occurs with awareness. However, recent findings suggest that some prefrontal executive functions, such as inhibitory control, can occur without awareness (e.g., Boy, Husain, and Sumner, 2010; Horga and Maia, 2012; Lau and Passingham, 2007; van Gaal *et al.*, 2008, 2010; van Gaal and Lamme, 2012). Indeed, some recent evidence indicates that memory-based cognitive control can depend on interactions between hippocampus and PFC, yet it can occur without conscious awareness. For instance, Voss *et al.* (2011a, 2011b) found that individuals sometimes backtrack to view recently seen objects for a second time when attempting to memorize arrays of objects, and that this backtracking behavior was associated with hippocampal–prefrontal connectivity. Furthermore, individuals did not report awareness of this backtracking study strategy, providing suggestive preliminary evidence that the prefrontal–MTL interactions that are important for the cognitive control of memory may occur without awareness.

Overall, these findings indicate that implicit memory does not neatly dissociate from explicit memory in terms of the responsible neuroanatomy, and can be supported perhaps by all structures important for memory (see also Chapter 18). These findings are consistent with accounts of the function of brain regions that focus on the nature of the operations that are performed (e.g., associative binding by hippocampus, cognitive control by PFC: see Chapter 7) rather than on the presence of or lack of conscious awareness. Understanding memory function may necessitate studying the mechanisms involved across the spectrum of subjective awareness, rather than dividing memory functions based solely on the subjective status of these operations (e.g., Henke, 2010; Reder, Park, and Kieffaber, 2009; Rose *et al.*, 2011).

## Conclusions

Our review of the outer limits of implicit memory shows that it is far more broad and ubiquitous than is commonly appreciated (Figure 3.3). The research mentioned in this chapter has merely begun to scratch the surface of the possible ways that memory processing can occur without conscious awareness. The more that the outer limits of implicit memory become stretched by cognitive neuroscience and cognitive psychology, the more the strong assumptions regarding divisions between implicit and

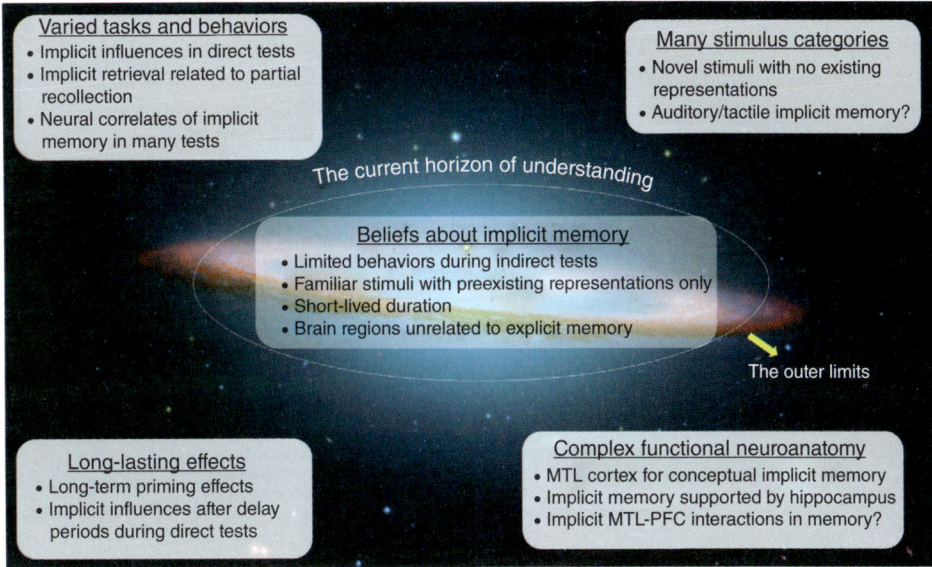

**Figure 3.3** A summary of four beliefs that are at the center of many accounts of implicit memory, and the outer limits that extend these beliefs.

explicit memory are called into question. Dew and Cabeza (2011) offered an excellent case for reconsidering the boundary between explicit and implicit memory. They stated that this boundary, based on traditional dichotomous-systems views, has become insufficient in light of behavioral and neurological evidence from more recent research. These dichotomous views have largely hinged upon dissociating one process from another. That is, the goal of many experimental memory tasks is to isolate processes and demonstrate differences between states in memory. Although important, this approach may largely ignore any potential similarities between memory states. Furthermore, in paradigms relying on dissociations, failures to find desired dissociations may be mistakenly interpreted as null findings. However, failure to find dissociations in these cases may actually be revealing similarities between states indicative of an *association*. In order to understand the relationship between memory and consciousness, Dew and Cabeza stated that there must be an equal focus on studying the interrelatedness (associations) between neurological structures and the functions they give rise to. A key part of this equal focus must involve the acknowledgment that implicit unconscious processing may have substantial influences upon performance and strategy choice in explicit memory tasks and daily cognitive functioning.

Furthermore, it is possible that contributions from specific brain regions (e.g., MTL, PFC) are relatively invariant across different memory circumstances, and that implicit and explicit expressions may vary with factors such as test type, task demands, attention, stimulus modality, and assumptions about computing process estimates (Wang and Yonelinas, 2012a). For example, recent evidence has suggested that the same MTL cortex (perirhinal) region which gives rise to conceptual implicit memory in a priming task also gives rise to explicit familiarity in recognition tasks (Wang and Yonelinas, 2012b). That is not to say that implicit priming and explicit familiarity are the same process, but rather that under certain circumstances, the same brain structure may be associated with different states of awareness of memory.

In summary, there is a very real and pressing need to identify associations as well as dissociations in memory (Stark, 2012). Furthermore, future research will need to ascertain the boundary conditions associated with unconscious influences on memory function. Like the individuals inflexibly bound in Plato's cave, researchers will need to shed the restraints of some traditional assumptions in order to expand the limits of our understanding of implicit and explicit memory phenomena.

# References

Baddeley, A.D., and Warrington, E.K. (1970). Amnesia and the distinction between long- and short-term memory. *Journal of Verbal Learning and Verbal Behavior*, 9 (2), 176–189. doi: 10.1016/S0022-5371(70)80048-2.

Becker, S., Moscovitch, M., Behrmann, M., and Joordens, S. (1997). Long-term semantic priming: a computational account and empirical evidence. *Journal of Experimental Psychology: Learning, Memory, and Cognition*, 23 (5), 1059–1082.

Boy, F., Husain, M , and Sumner, P. (2010). Unconscious inhibition separates two forms of cognitive control. *Proceedings of the National Academy of Sciences of the USA*, 107 (24), 11134–11139. doi: 10.1007/s00221-010-2417-x.

Buckner, R.L., Petersen, S.E., Ojemann, J.G., *et al.* (1995). Functional anatomical studies of explicit and implicit memory retrieval tasks. *Journal of Neuroscience*, 15 (1), 12–29.

Cabeza, R., Kapur, S., Craik, F.I., *et al.* (1997). Functional neuroanatomy of recall and recognition: a PET study of episodic memory. *Journal of Cognitive Neuroscience*, 9 (2), 254–265.

Corkin, S. (1968). Acquisition of motor skill after bilateral medial temporal-lobe excision. *Neuropsychologia*, 6 (3), 255–265.

Dew, I.T., and Cabeza, R. (2011). The porous boundaries between explicit and implicit memory: behavioral and neural evidence. *Annals of the New York Academy of Sciences* 1224 (1), 174–190. doi: 10.1111/j.1749-6632.2010.05946.x.

Dew, I.T., and Cabeza, R. (2012). Implicit contamination extends across multiple methodologies: Implications for fMRI. *Cognitive Neuroscience*, 3 (3–4), 214–215. doi: 10.1080/17588928.2012.689972.

Ebbinghaus, H. (1885). *Über das Gedächtnis* [On Memory]. Leipzig: Duncker und Humblot (English Translation, New York, NY: Dover Press).

Gabrieli, J.D., Desmond, J.E., Demb, J.B., *et al.* (1996). Functional magnetic resonance imaging of semantic memory processes in the frontal lobes. *Psychological Science*, 7 (5), 278–283.

Gardiner, J.M., Ramponi, C., and Richardson-Klavehn, A. (1998). Experiences of remembering, knowing, and guessing. *Consciousness and Cognition*, 7 (1), 1–26.

Gooding, P., Mayes, A., and Van Eijk, R. (2000). A meta-analysis of indirect memory tests for novel material in organic amnesics. *Neuropsychologia*, 38 (5), 666–676. doi: 10.1016/S0028-3932(99)00119-0.

Graf, P., and Schacter, D.L. (1985). Implicit and explicit memory for new associations in normal and amnesic subjects. *Journal of Experimental Psychology: Learning, Memory, and Cognition*, 11 (3), 501–518. doi: 10.1037/0278-7393.11.3.501.

Hannula, D.E., and Greene, A.J. (2012). The hippocampus reevaluated in unconscious learning and memory: at a tipping point? *Frontiers in Human Neuroscience*, 6. doi: 10.3389%2Ffnhum.2012.00080.

Heath, S., McMahon, K., Nickels, L. A., *et al.* (2012). Priming picture naming with a semantic task: an fMRI investigation. *PloS One*, 7 (3), e32809. doi: 10.1371%2Fjournal.pone.0032809.

Henke, K. (2010). A model for memory systems based on processing modes rather than consciousness. *Nature Reviews Neuroscience*, 11 (7), 523–532. doi: 10.1038/nrn2850.

Horga, G., and Maia, T.V. (2012). Conscious and unconscious processes in cognitive control: a theoretical perspective and a novel empirical approach. *Frontiers in Human Neuroscience*, 6. doi: 10.3389/fnhum.2012.00199.

Jacoby, L.L. (1991). A process dissociation framework: separating automatic from intentional uses of memory. *Journal of Memory and Language*, 30 (5), 513–541.

Jacoby, L.L., and Kelley, C.M. (1992). Unconscious influences on memory: dissociations and automaticity. The neuropsychology of consciousness. In *The neuropsychology of consciousness, Foundations of neuropsychology* (ed. A. D. Milner and M. D. Rugg). San Diego, CA: Academic Press.

Jacoby, L.L., and Whitehouse, K. (1989). An illusion of memory: false recognition influenced by unconscious perception. *Journal of Experimental Psychology: General*, 118 (2), 126–135.

Kirwan, C.B., Wixted, J.T., and Squire, L.R. (2008). Activity in the medial temporal lobe predicts memory strength, whereas activity in the prefrontal cortex predicts recollection. *Journal of Neuroscience*, 28 (42), 10541–10548.

Koriat, A., Levy-Sadot, R., Edry, E., and de Marcas, S. (2003). What do we know about what we cannot remember? Accessing the semantic attributes of words that cannot be recalled. *Journal of Experimental Psychology: Learning, Memory, and Cognition*, 29 (6), 1095–1105. doi: 10.1037/0278-7393.29.6.1095.

Lau, H.C., and Passingham, R.E. (2007). Unconscious activation of the cognitive control system in the human prefrontal cortex. *Journal of Neuroscience*, 27 (21), 5805–5811.

MacLeod, C.M., and Daniels, K.A. (2000). Direct versus indirect tests of memory: Directed forgetting meets the generation effect. *Psychonomic Bulletin and Review*, 7 (2), 354–359.

Mandler, G. (1980). Recognizing: the judgment of previous occurrence. *Psychological Review*, 87 (3), 252–271.

Mandler, G. (2008). Familiarity breeds attempts: a critical review of dual-process theories of recognition. *Perspectives on Psychological Science*, 3 (5), 390–399. doi: 10.1111/j.1745-6924. 2008.00087.x.

Merikle, P.M., and Reingold, E.M. (1991). Comparing direct (explicit) and indirect (implicit) measures to study unconscious memory. *Journal of Experimental Psychology: Learning, Memory, and Cognition*, 17 (2), 224–233.

Mitchell, D.B. (2006). Nonconscious priming after 17 years invulnerable implicit memory? *Psychological Science*, 17 (11), 925–929. doi: 10.1111/j.1467-9280.2006.01805.x.

Mitchell, D.B., and Brown, A.S. (1988). Persistent repetition priming in picture naming and its dissociation from recognition memory. *Journal of Experimental Psychology: Learning, Memory, and Cognition*, 14 (2), 213–222. doi: 10.1037/0278-7393.14.2.213.

Neely, J.H. (1991). Semantic priming effects in visual word recognition: a selective review of current findings and theory. In *Basic processes in reading: Visual word recognition* (ed. D. Besner and G. W. Humphreys). Hillsdale, NJ: Erlbaum, pp. 264–336.

Nyberg, L., Cabeza, R., and Tulving, E. (1996). PET studies of encoding and retrieval: the HERA model. *Psychonomic Bulletin and Review*, 3 (2), 135–148. doi: 10.3758/BF03212412.

Ochsner, K.N., Chiu, C.-Y.P., and Schacter, D.L. (1994). Varieties of priming. *Current Opinion in Neurobiology*, 4 (2), 189–194.

Paller, K.A., Voss, J.L., and Boehm, S.G. (2007). Validating neural correlates of familiarity. *Trends in Cognitive Sciences*, 11 (6), 243–250. doi: 10.1016/j.tics.2007.04.002.

Plato (380 BCE). *Plato's The Republic*. Translated by B. Jowett. New York, NY: The Modern Library, 1941.

Raichle, M.E., Fiez, J.A., Videen, T.O., *et al.* (1994). Practice-related changes in human brain functional anatomy during nonmotor learning. *Cerebral Cortex*, 4 (1), 8–26.

Rajaram, S., and Roediger, H.L. (1993). Direct comparison of four implicit memory tests. *Journal of Experimental Psychology: Learning, Memory, and Cognition*, 19 (4), 765–776.

Reder, L.M., Park, H., and Kieffaber, P.D. (2009). Memory systems do not divide on consciousness: reinterpreting memory in terms of activation and binding. *Psychological Bulletin*, 135 (1), 23–49. doi: 10.1037/a0013974.

Richardson-Klavehn, A., and Bjork, R.A. (1988). Measures of memory. *Annual Review of Psychology*, 39 (1), 475–543.

Rissman, J., Eliassen, J.C., and Blumstein, S. (2003). An event-related fMRI investigation of implicit semantic priming. *Journal of Cognitive Neuroscience*, 15, 1160–1175. doi: 10.1162/089892903322598120.

Roediger, H.L. (1990). Implicit memory: retention without remembering. *American Psychologist*, 45 (9), 1043–1056.

Roediger, H.L., and Geraci, L. (2005). Implicit memory tasks in cognitive research. In *Cognitive Methods and Their Application to Clinical Research* (ed. A. Wenzel and D.C. Rubin). Washington, DC: American Psychological Association, pp. 129–151.

Roediger, H.L., and McDermott, K.B. (1993). Implicit memory in normal human subjects. In *Handbook of Neuropsychology*, vol. 8 (ed. F. Boller and J. Grafman). Amsterdam: Elsevier, pp. 63–131.

Rose, M., Haider, H., Salari, N., and Büchel, C. (2011). Functional dissociation of hippocampal mechanism during implicit learning based on the domain of associations. *Journal of Neuroscience*, 31 (39), 13739–13745. doi: 10.1523/JNEUROSCI.3020-11.2011.

Rugg, M.D., and Curran, T. (2007). Event-related potentials and recognition memory. *Trends in Cognitive Sciences*, 11 (6), 251–257. doi: 10.1016/j.tics.2007.04.004.

Ryals, A.J., Yadon, C.A., Nomi, J.S., and Cleary, A.M. (2011). When word identification fails: ERP correlates of recognition without identification and of word identification failure. *Neuropsychologia*, 49 (12), 3224–3237.

Schacter, D.L. (1992). Understanding implicit memory: a cognitive neuroscience approach. *American Psychologist*, 47 (4), 559–569.

Schacter, D.L., Buckner, R.L., and Koutstaal, W. (1998). Memory, consciousness and neuroimaging. *Philosophical Transactions of the Royal Society of London, Series B: Biological Sciences*, 353 (1377), 1861–1878.

Schapiro, A.C., Kustner, L.V., and Turk-Browne, N.B. (2012). Shaping of object representations in the human medial temporal lobe based on temporal regularities. *Current Biology*, 22, 1622–1627. doi: 10.1016/j.cub.2012.06.056.

Scoville, W.B., and Milner, B. (1957). Loss of recent memory after bilateral hippocampal lesions. *Journal of Neurology, Neurosurgery, and Psychiatry*, 20 (1), 11–21. doi: 10.1136/jnnp.20.1.11.

Seger, C.A. (1994). Implicit learning. *Psychological Bulletin*, 115 (2), 163–196.

Shimamura, A.P. (1986). Priming effects in amnesia: Evidence for a dissociable memory function. *Quarterly Journal of Experimental Psychology*, 38 (4), 619–644.

Sloman, S.A., Hayman, C., Ohta, N., *et al.* (1988). Forgetting in primed fragment completion. *Journal of Experimental Psychology: Learning, Memory, and Cognition*, 14 (2), 223–239.

Slotnick, S.D., and Schacter, D.L. (2006). The nature of memory related activity in early visual areas. *Neuropsychologia*, 44 (14), 2874–2886.

Squire, L.R. (1987). *Memory and Brain*. New York, NY: Oxford University Press.

Stark, C.E.L. (2012). It's time to fill gaps left by simple dissociations. *Cognitive Neuroscience*, 3, 215–216. doi: 10.1080/17588928.2012.689967.

Toth, J.P., Reingold, E.M., and Jacoby, L.L. (1994). Toward a redefinition of implicit memory: process dissociations following elaborative processing and self-generation. *Journal of Experimental Psychology: Learning, Memory, and Cognition*, 20 (2), 290–303.

Tulving, E. (1985). Memory and consciousness. *Canadian Psychology/Psychologie Canadienne*, 26 (1), 1–12.

Tulving, E., and Schacter, D.L. (1990). Priming and human memory systems. *Science*, 247 (4940), 301–306.

Tulving, E., Schacter, D.L., and Stark, H.A. (1982). Priming effects in word-fragment completion are independent of recognition memory. *Journal of Experimental Psychology: Learning, Memory, and Cognition*, 8 (4), 336–342.

Tunney, R.J., and Fernie, G. (2007). Repetition priming affects guessing not familiarity. *Behavioral and Brain Functions*, 3 (1), 40. doi: 10.1186/1744-9081-3-40.

van Gaal, S., and Lamme, V.A. (2012). Unconscious high-level information processing implication for neurobiological theories of consciousness. *The Neuroscientist*, 18 (3), 287–301.

van Gaal, S., Ridderinkhof, K.R., Fahrenfort, J.J., *et al.* (2008). Frontal cortex mediates unconsciously triggered inhibitory control. *Journal of Neuroscience*, 28 (32), 8053–8062.

van Gaal, S., Ridderinkhof, K.R., Scholte, H.S., and Lamme, V.A. (2010). Unconscious activation of the prefrontal no-go network. *Journal of Neuroscience*, 30 (11), 4143–4150.

Voss, J.L., Baym, C.L., and Paller, K.A. (2008). Accurate forced-choice recognition without awareness of memory retrieval. *Learning and Memory*, 15 (6), 454–459.

Voss, J.L., Federmeier, K.D., and Paller, K.A. (2012). The potato chip really does look like Elvis! Neural hallmarks of conceptual processing associated with finding novel shapes subjectively meaningful. *Cerebral Cortex*, 22 (10), 2354–2364.

Voss, J.L., Gonsalves, B.D., Federmeier, K.D., *et al.* (2011a). Hippocampal brain-network coordination during volitional exploratory behavior enhances learning. *Nature Neuroscience*, 14 (1), 115–120.

Voss, J.L., Lucas, H.D., and Paller, K.A. (2012). More than a feeling: pervasive influences of memory without awareness of retrieval. *Cognitive Neuroscience*, 3 (3–4), 193–207.

Voss, J.L., and Paller, K.A. (2006). Fluent conceptual processing and explicit memory for faces are electrophysiologically distinct. *Journal of Neuroscience*, 26 (3), 926–933.

Voss, J.L., and Paller, K.A. (2007). Neural correlates of conceptual implicit memory and their contamination of putative neural correlates of explicit memory. *Learning and Memory*, 14 (4), 259–267.

Voss, J.L., and Paller, K.A. (2009). An electrophysiological signature of unconscious recognition memory. *Nature Neuroscience*, 12 (3), 349–355.

Voss, J.L., and Paller, K.A. (2010). Real-time neural signals of perceptual priming with unfamiliar geometric shapes. *Journal of Neuroscience*, 30 (27), 9181–9188.

Voss, J.L., Schendan, H.E., and Paller, K.A. (2010). Finding meaning in novel geometric shapes influences electrophysiological correlates of repetition and dissociates perceptual and conceptual priming. *NeuroImage*, 49 (3), 2879–2889.

Voss, J.L., Warren, D.E., Gonsalves, B.D., *et al.* (2011b). Spontaneous revisitation during visual exploration as a link among strategic behavior, learning, and the hippocampus. *Proceedings of the National Academy of Sciences of the USA*, 108 (31), E402–E409.

Wang, W.-C., and Yonelinas, A.P. (2012a). Familiarity and conceptual implicit memory: Individual differences and neural correlates. *Cognitive Neuroscience* 3 (3), 213–214.

Wang, W.-C., and Yonelinas, A.P. (2012b). Familiarity is related to conceptual implicit memory: An examination of individual differences. *Psychonomic Bulletin and Review* 19 (6), 1154–1164.

Warrington, E.K., and Weiskrantz, L. (1968). New method of testing long-term retention with special reference to amnesic patients. *Nature* 217, 972–974.

Weiskrantz, L., and Warrington, E.K. (1979). Conditioning in amnesic patients. *Neuropsychologia* 17 (2), 187–194.

Wimmer, G.E., and Shohamy, D. (2012). Preference by association: how memory mechanisms in the hippocampus bias decisions. *Science* 338 (6104), 270–273.

Yonelinas, A.P. (2002). The nature of recollection and familiarity: a review of 30 years of research. *Journal of Memory and Language*, 46 (3), 441–517.

# 4

# The Neural Bases of Conceptual Knowledge

## Revisiting a Golden Age Hypothesis in the Era of Cognitive Neuroscience

### Timothy T. Rogers and Christopher R. Cox

## Introduction

In one of Plato's best-known dialogues, Socrates encounters his friend Euthyphro, who has arrived at court to prosecute a case. The charge is manslaughter, and Socrates is shocked to hear that the defendant is Euthyprho's own father. During a recent holiday, one of the workers on the family estate killed a slave; Euthyphro's father had the offender bound, gagged, and turned out of doors while he waited for advice from local wise men on how best to proceed. In the interval, the worker died of exposure in a ditch. Socrates wonders why his friend was moved to prosecute his own father under these circumstances, but Euthyphro expresses no doubts: he is perfectly capable, he asserts, of determining whether or not an act is "pious" (i.e., morally acceptable). Socrates, who has his own legal problems, is eager to learn Euthyphro's secret. "Teach me," he asks, "how I can tell a pious act from an impious one?"

Euthyphro's stumbling responses to this request, and the challenges that Socrates raises at each turn of the argument, constitute one of Western culture's earliest attempts to wrestle with a question that is central to human cognition: When we encounter a new item or event in the world, how do we come to know what kind of thing it is? Though Euthyphro focuses on the concept of piety, Plato's other writings, and the philosophical inquiries to which they gave rise in succeeding centuries, have illustrated the complexities that attend this question applied to essentially any natural language concept: How do we tell which items in our environment are horses, bicycles, trees, lakes, newspapers? How do we tell diamonds from zirconium, or dolphins from sharks, or planets from stars? What makes a lemon a lemon – is it just the color, shape, and sour taste, or is there something deeper? In general, what are the various "kinds of things" that exist in the world? What causes an item or event to be of a particular kind, and how do we figure out which items belong to which kinds? What inferences can we draw about an item or event once we know what kind of thing it is, and how do we draw those inferences?

*The Wiley Handbook on the Cognitive Neuroscience of Memory*, First Edition.
Edited by Donna Rose Addis, Morgan Barense, and Audrey Duarte.
© 2015 John Wiley & Sons, Ltd. Published 2015 by John Wiley & Sons, Ltd.

In cognitive science, these are questions about human conceptual or semantic knowledge – the store of everyday knowledge by which we recognize objects and events, classify them and make inferences about their unspecified properties, and understand and produce statements about them. In the late nineteenth century, the Golden Era of neuropsychological investigation into brain function, there arose in neurological circles a view of conceptual knowledge that owed much to the seventeenth-century Empiricist philosopher John Locke. This view was advanced in various forms by Meynert, Luria, and others, but was very beautifully described by Wernicke in his classic work on aphasia:

> The concept of a rose is composed of a "tactile memory image" – "an image of touch" – in the central projection field of the somesthetic cortex. It is also composed of a visual memory image located in the visual projection field of the cortex. The continuous repetition of similar sensory impressions results in such a firm association between those different memory images that the mere stimulation of one sensory avenue by means of the object is adequate to call up the concept of the object. In some cases, many memory images of different sensory areas and in others only a few correspond to a single concept. However, by the very nature of the object, a firmly associated constellation of such memory images which form the anatomic substrate of each concept is established. This sum total of closely associated memory images must "be aroused into consciousness" for perception not merely of sounds of the corresponding words but also for comprehension of their meaning. Following our anatomic mode of interpretation, we also postulate for this process the existence of anatomic tracts, fibers, connections, or association tracts between the sensory speech center of word-sound-comprehension and those projection fields which participate in the formation of the concept (Eggert, 1977).

Thus Golden Age neurology proposed that several functionally localized modules exist in the brain specialized to encode different kinds of *surface representations* – representations of various sensory and motor states, including spoken or written word forms – and that the meanings arising from perception of a word, object, or event reflect nothing more nor less than the learned associations existing among these surface representations. The Golden Age view has enjoyed a renaissance in contemporary efforts to understand how the brain supports human semantic knowledge, with most scientists currently studying the neural basis of concepts endorsing some variant of this hypothesis. Amongst scientists who are unconcerned about the neural mechanisms that underlie cognition, however, the hypothesis has often been viewed as fundamentally flawed (see papers in Laurence and Margolis, 1999). The effort to reconcile these perspectives is a potent driving force in current research.

This chapter assesses the Golden Age hypothesis from the standpoint of contemporary cognitive neuroscience. We begin by reviewing evidence that has led to widespread support of the central ideas, before considering three different perspectives on a central question for current research: What is the broader architecture of the cortical semantic network? Although the three views have somewhat different roots, we will argue that they are now beginning to converge. In the conclusion, we will summarize what we think this convergence might look like, and consider some current challenges for contemporary theories, some of which date back to issues raised by Plato some 2500 years ago.

## Contemporary Support for the Golden Age Hypothesis

The revival of the Golden Age hypothesis in recent times is due largely to the emergence of neuroimaging technologies that, for the first time, have allowed scientists to test the hypothesis in a fairly straightforward way. In 1995, Martin and colleagues published an influential paper suggesting that retrieval from semantic memory involves the activation of representations identical or intimately related to those evoked by direct perception (Martin *et al.*, 1995). Participants viewed a series of visually presented words and, for each, were asked to retrieve either the item's color or an associated function while their brains were scanned with positron emission tomography (PET). Retrieving the color increased activity in posterior ventral occipital cortex, just anterior to V4 regions that respond to colored stimuli. Retrieving the function caused heightened activation in the middle temporal gyrus (MTG), just anterior to the human analog of area MT, thought to process visually perceived motion. Because the study used words, the patterns did not reflect visual associative learning, as might be the case, for instance, if participants had viewed line drawings of objects. Thus the differences appeared to arise from truly semantic processes – processes that depend on knowledge about the meaning of the presented word. Several studies followed in a similar vein, issuing from a variety of laboratories and using a range of different tasks and behavioral methods, but leading to quite similar conclusions. These studies suggested that word meanings can involve activation of associated motor plans (Hauk, Johnsrude, and Pulvermüller, 2004), sounds (Kellenbach, Brett, and Patterson, 2001), patterns of motion (Chao, Haxby, and Martin, 1999), color (Chao and Martin, 1999), size (Kellenbach, Brett, and Patterson, 2001), and shape (Chao, Haxby, and Martin, 1999; Martin and Chao, 2001).

These observations are grossly consistent with the Golden Age hypothesis, but leave it unclear whether the reported effects play a causal role in underlying conceptual processes. Behavioral research provides some initial evidence that sensory and motor representations do play a causal role in semantic task performance. Perhaps best known in this tradition are studies in "embodied" semantic cognition – the school of thought proposing that words and other symbols have meaning because they are "grounded" in neural representations of bodily sensory and motor states (Barsalou *et al.*, 2003; Glenberg, 2010). On this view, the meaning of a word like "lift," for instance, inheres critically in the comprehender's ability to generate a motor plan and a corresponding somatosensory model corresponding to the act of lifting.

Embodied theorists have devised a variety of ingenious methods for assessing whether the engagement of such "embodied" representations plays a causal role in lexical semantics. In a representative study, participants read sentences and indicated whether they were sensible by manipulating a lever (Glenberg and Kaschak, 2002). Half of the participants indicated "yes" by pushing the lever away from them; the remaining participants indicated "yes" by pulling it toward them. If the sentence implied an outward-directed motion (e.g., "Close the drawer"), participants were faster when pushing the lever to indicate their response. If the sentence implied an inward-directed motion (e.g., "Open the drawer"), the reverse was true. The implication is that, while reading the sentence, participants construct a kind of sub-threshold motor simulation of the actions that the sentence describes. When the action-simulation is consistent with the actual motor response demanded by the overt task, the response is speeded; otherwise it is slowed. Many similar finding have been reported in recent years (Barsalou *et al.*, 2003).

Experimental findings in embodied approaches to meaning are not limited to manipulating motor and somatosensory states. Several experiments have shown that semantic judgments about perceptual properties of familiar objects can likewise be affected by embodied context (Barsalou, 2008). In one such study, participants were given a sentence describing a familiar concept and were asked to make a rapid property attribution judgment. By using different sentence contexts, the experimenters manipulated the implied spatial configuration of the target concept and its relationship to the comprehender. For instance, a sentence such as "Up in the sky there is a duck" implies that the duck is above the observer and has its wings extended, since it is likely flying. In contrast, a sentence such as "Floating on the pond there is a duck" implies that the duck is on a level with the observer and has its wings retracted. After reading such a sentence, participants viewed a property name (e.g., "wings") and had to decide whether the property was true of the item named in the sentence (e.g., the duck). The speed and accuracy of the judgment varied with the spatial configuration and relationships implied by the sentence. When the duck was "overhead" participants were faster to decide that it had wings compared to when the duck was "floating" (Barsalou, 1982). The suggestion is that, in comprehending the sentence, listeners construct a kind of mental simulation that specifies what the target object would look like if the listener were in the situation described by the sentence (for more discussion of mental simulation, see Chapter 14). The features associated with a given concept become more readily retrievable when they are "perceptually" salient in this mental simulation. Thus, under this view, the evoked visual representations, far from being epiphenomenal to meaning retrieval, are an intrinsic part of the meaning.

A few recent studies have directly tested the causal status of sensory-motor representations in word comprehension using transcranial magnetic stimulation (TMS). For instance, Oliveri *et al.* (2004), measured the motor evoked potential (MEP) at the hand by paired-pulse stimulation of M1 while participants orally performed a morphological transformation task (generating a plural or singular form for nouns; generating a tense transformation for verbs). Half of the nouns and half of the verbs had strong action associates, while the remainder did not. The authors found that the MEP was uninfluenced by the grammatical class of the word, but strongly influenced by its meaning, with larger MEPs observed for action-associated words. Thus word meaning appeared to influence the responsiveness of M1 neurons to external stimulation. In a similar vein, Pobric, Jefferies and Lambon Ralph (2010) found that repetitive TMS applied to the inferior parietal cortex, a region thought to contribute to praxis (i.e., knowledge about the actions by which we engage objects), selectively slowed production of tool names – suggesting that praxic representations may contribute to the computation of meaning for tools.

Together, the functional imaging, behavioral, and TMS results provide compelling evidence that nineteenth-century views about the neural bases of conceptual knowledge were at least partially correct: computing the meaning of a given word or image appears to involve activating cortical states identical or intimately related to those that directly encode perceptual, motor, affective, or linguistic experience. Such activation appears to be not merely epiphenomenal but causal, insofar as it influences the speed and accuracy with which semantic judgments are made.

# The Broader Architecture of the Cortical Semantic Network

What are the neural pathways that support associative activation amongst various sensory, motor, and linguistic representations, and what functional properties do these pathways possess? In this section we review three somewhat different answers to this question, and review the motivation and evidence supporting each. We then offer a critical appraisal of the three views taken together, before summarizing the key conclusions.

## The tripartite view: organization by modality and hemisphere

The first proposal derives from classical neurological perspectives on brain function, which have strongly emphasized gross functional dissociations among language, perception, and action following brain injury. Such dissociations provide the basis for the broadest relevant diagnostic categories in neuropsychology – the aphasias, agnosias, and apraxias – which are thought to reflect a coarse partitioning of cognitive function in the brain. In particular, the classical neurological view places language function in left hemisphere perisylvian regions (Mesulam *et al.*, 2003); visual perception of objects in the ventral visual stream along the inferior surface of the temporal lobes, with perhaps greater contribution of the right hemisphere for some visual processes (Farah, 1990); and knowledge about action in the parietal and motor cortices (Goodale and Milner, 1992). Accordingly, such a view suggests a division of the conceptual knowledge network into three subnetworks: a "lexical semantic" system responsible for verbal semantic knowledge, a "visual" or "perceptual" network responsible for nonverbal knowledge about the visual or perceptual properties of objects, and an "action" semantic system that encodes knowledge about how to interact with objects. We will refer to this idea, illustrated in Figure 4.1, as the *tripartite* view.

The proposal that lexical semantics is supported by a left-lateralized subsystem that is somewhat autonomous and separate from visual or action semantics has a long history in neuropsychology, and stems from case studies demonstrating that verbal assessments of everyday knowledge appear to doubly dissociate from visual recognition and action knowledge (Coltheart, 2004; McCarthy and Warrington, 1986). The functional dissociation of lexical and perceptual semantic knowledge has been recently argued by Mesulam and colleagues (2003, 2013), who have conducted extensive case-series analyses of patients with a progressive degenerative disorder that, in clinical assessments, appears to primarily affect language comprehension and production. Some such patients can produce quite fluent speech that is largely devoid of specific content and is accompanied by a profound anomia, but nevertheless perform at or near ceiling on standard clinical tests of visual perception and object recognition. Mesulam (2001) dubbed this pattern fluent primary progressive aphasia (fPPA), and has shown that it is accompanied by gray matter atrophy that appears to be largely left-lateralized. Taking both fluent and dysfluent cases into account, the atrophy in primary progressive aphasia is described as affecting perisylvian regions in the left temporal, parietal, and frontal lobes, consistent with the classical view that these regions form a left-lateralized language network. Moreover, other cases of progressive dementia (see Chapter 20), such as the posterior cortical atrophy observed in rare cases of Alzheimer's disease, can present with the reverse problems – severe difficulties in visual perception and recognition, but with language largely spared (Caine, 2004). Such case-series studies thus reinforce the conclusions derived from single-case studies that lexical and perceptual semantics are functionally independent.

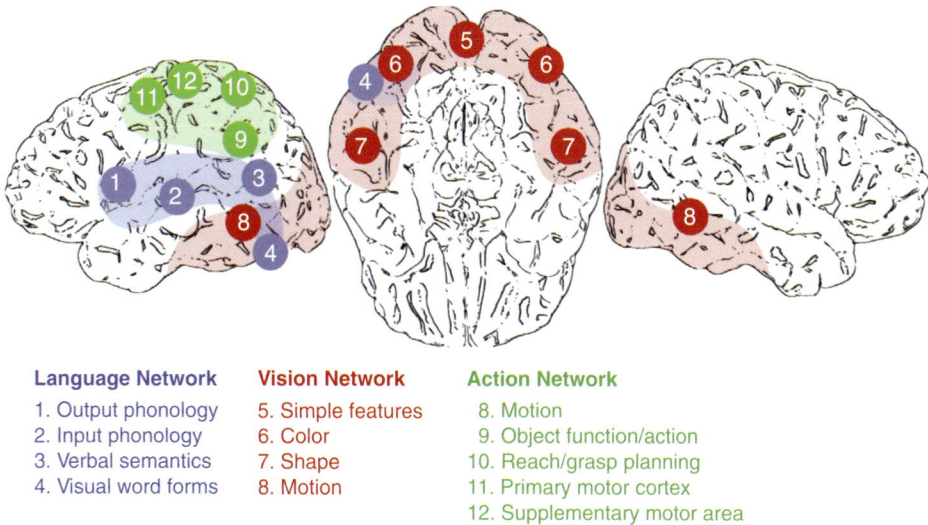

**Language Network**
1. Output phonology
2. Input phonology
3. Verbal semantics
4. Visual word forms

**Vision Network**
5. Simple features
6. Color
7. Shape
8. Motion

**Action Network**
8. Motion
9. Object function/action
10. Reach/grasp planning
11. Primary motor cortex
12. Supplementary motor area

**Figure 4.1** Schematic illustrating the tripartite view. The left hemisphere perisylvian language network (blue) captures both classical and contemporary findings, with input phonology in the superior temporal gyrus (1), output phonology in Broca's area (2), verbal semantics in Wernicke's area (3), and visual word forms in the posterior ventral occipeto-temporal cortex (4). The visual object knowledge-network (red) includes simple visual features in occipital cortex (5), extends bilaterally along the ventral surface of the temporal lobes where color (6) and form (7) representations are thought to reside, and branches up to the human analog of area MT in posterior MTG, which encodes visual motion (8). The action network (green) incorporates the motion-perception region in posterior MTG (8), inferior parietal cortex, which is thought to support object-associated action knowledge (9), the superior parietal cortex, which supports visually-guided action and grasping (10), motor and premotor cortex (11), and the supplementary motor area (12).

The view that action knowledge is functionally independent of visual/perceptual and lexical knowledge also stems largely from neuropsychological dissociations among these abilities (Ochipa, Rothi, and Heilman, 1989). Perhaps most compelling in this literature are the elegant studies of different forms of apraxia conducted by Buxbaum and colleagues (Binkofski and Buxbaum, 2013; Buxbaum, 2001; Buxbaum and Saffran, 2002; Buxbaum, Veramontil, and Schwartz, 2000). Working with large numbers patients with varying etiologies, these authors have identified a variety of qualitatively different disorders of action knowledge. In the case of action disorganization syndrome, patients can often retrieve the characteristic function associated with a single object, but show serious deficits organizing these simple actions into sequences that accomplish a familiar goal, such as wrapping a present or making a cup of tea (Schwartz *et al.*, 1998). In the case of ideational apraxia, even the simple action associations appear to be disrupted, with patients frequently confusing the actions associated with semantically related items (Ochipa, Rothi, and Heilman, 1989). For instance, such patients might mistakenly brush their hair with a toothbrush, or try to write with a paintbrush. Nevertheless such patients typically show a good visual recognition and spared ability to name and verbally describe these items, suggesting that they have impaired knowledge specifically about actions associated with familiar objects. In still other cases, patients may show selective loss or sparing of knowledge about praxis, that is, about the particular motor actions necessary to engage an object in action (Buxbaum, 2001). For instance, such patients might not know to grasp a spoon by the handle.

The neuroanatomical correlates of such deficits have recently been laid bare by lesion-symptom mapping methods, which suggest that impairments to knowledge about object use often arise from damage to regions in the left parietal cortex (Kalénine, Buxbaum, and Coslett, 2010). Visually guided reaching and grasping deficits appear to be associated with damage to more dorsal regions, while loss of knowledge about object-associated action is best predicted by pathology in the left inferior parietal lobe. Such studies thus suggest that there exist at least two dissociable components of the action-knowledge network, differently situated within parietal cortex.

Functional imaging studies lend additional support to this idea. Boronat *et al.* (2005) asked subjects to judge if pairs of items were either (1) manipulated similarly or (2) used for the same purpose. The stimuli were selected so that form and function did not always correspond. For instance, the typewriter and piano engage similar praxis in the service of different functions, while the match and the lighter subserve similar functions but engage different praxis. Both kinds of judgments elicited activation within the posterior parietal cortex relative to a control baseline, but activation elicited by the manipulation judgment was located more superiorly to that elicited by the function judgment – suggesting, in concert with the lesion-overlap data, that praxis and function knowledge may depend upon different subregions of parietal cortex.

Both functional neuroimaging and lesion-overlap data further suggest that regions outside the parietal cortex are involved in representing knowledge about action. One such region is the posterior MTG, which appears to be strongly activated when participants retrieve semantic information about tools or other manipulable objects and when they perceive simple mechanical motion (Chao, Haxby, and Martin, 1999; Martin *et al.*, 1996). In a recent study of patients with impairments in action recognition, lesions in this region were found to correlate with impairment discriminating among semantically related manipulable objects, but not with impairment discriminating objects that engage similar praxis, which tended to correlate instead with pathology in inferior parietal regions (Kalénine, Buxbaum, and Coslett, 2010). Lesion-symptom correlational studies also suggest that pathology in this region predicts deficits in naming highly manipulable objects (Campanella *et al.*, 2010). As noted in the introduction, there are also several studies suggesting that regions in the prefrontal cortex, including the supplementary motor area and premotor cortex, are important for supporting semantic knowledge about actions (Hauk, Johnsrude, and Pulvermüller, 2004). Taken together, these studies suggest the existence of an "action-knowledge" network that includes the left posterior MTG, several regions in the left parietal cortex, and premotor regions of the frontal lobe.

## The many-hubs view: organization by multiple domain-specific convergence zones

A second proposal places emphasis, not on the functional independence of representations in different modalities, but on the different pathways proposed to link various surface representations. The central idea is that there exist in cortex a number of cross-modal "convergence zones," each connecting two or more kinds of modality-specific representations (Damasio, 1989). Mappings among different sensory, motor,

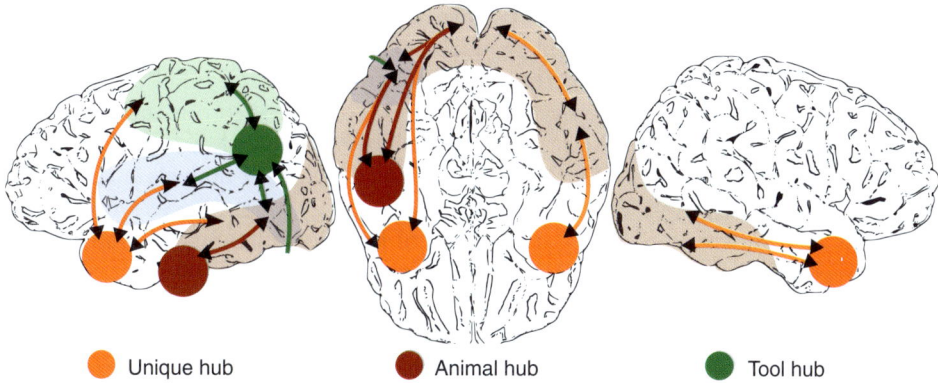

● Unique hub     ● Animal hub     ● Tool hub

**Figure 4.2** Schematic illustrating the many-hubs view. The shading indicates the same modality-specific subnetworks as Figure 4.1. In addition, possible locations of category-specific hubs are shown, including a hub for unique entities in the temporal poles (orange), for animal representations in ventral anterior temporal cortex (red), and for tools/manmade objects in the left posterior MTG/OTP junction (green).

and linguistic representations are encoded by the particular convergence zone that connects these. Thus, for instance, there may exist one convergence zone for connecting visual representations of object shape to representations of action plans; another for connecting the same representations of object shape to visual representations of motion patterns; another for connecting the object shape representations to word-form representations; and so on. We will refer to this idea, illustrated in Figure 4.2, as the *many-hubs* view.

Advocates of the many-hubs view often additionally propose that different convergence zones may be especially important for the representation of different semantic categories. For instance, conceptual knowledge about tools may depend critically on the ability to retrieve information about their praxis from their visual appearance or their names. Knowledge of other categories, such as animals or buildings, may involve little information about praxis. Consequently the convergence zone that maps from visual images and/or words to praxic representations may come to predominantly encode representations of tools (Mahon, Schwarzbach, and Caramazza, 2010). Other regions might come to predominantly encode representations of animals, due to their reliance on motion and perceptual properties (Gainotti *et al.*, 1995; Warrington and Shallice, 1984), or unique entities like Jennifer Anniston or the Eiffel Tower, due to their association with specific contexts and episodes encoded in medial temporal regions (Grabowski *et al.*, 2001). Thus the many-hubs view often goes hand in hand with the hypothesis that the cortical semantic network is partly organized by semantic class, with different cortical regions preferentially involved in the representations of particular concepts.

Evidence for multiple domain-specific hubs stems partly from lesion-overlap studies across groups of patients exhibiting apparent category-specific loss of semantic knowledge. Gainotti (2000) has suggested that greater impairment of knowledge for animals/living things is associated with damage to ventral/inferior temporal cortex bilaterally, all along the rostral–caudal length, though with a greater likelihood of pathology in the left hemisphere. In contrast, a greater impairment of knowledge for manmade objects/tools was likely to be associated with wide-ranging left-hemisphere pathology in the territory of the middle cerebral artery – that is, across frontoparietal regions and curling down around the occipito-temporal-parietal (OTP) junction to the posterior MTG. Other lesion-symptom analyses have fleshed out these observations, suggesting that loss of knowledge about individual people is correlated with pathology in the temporal poles; that loss of knowledge about animals is correlated with specific pathology in the anterior inferior temporal gyrus, the posterior fusiform, and parts of early visual cortex; and that loss of knowledge about tools/manmade objects is correlated with pathology in the vicinity of the OTP junction and posterior MTG (Campanella *et al.*, 2010; Damasio *et al.*, 1996; Rudrauf *et al.*, 2008).

Support for the many-hubs view also stems from functional neuroimaging. For instance, Damasio *et al.* (1996) used PET to measure functional activation elicited by naming pictures of people, animals, and manmade objects, and compared this to the results of a lesion-symptom correlation analysis for the same categories. The imaging analysis both validated and extended the lesion-symptom analysis: greater activation was observed in the left temporal pole for naming people, in the posterior MTG for naming manmade objects, and in the ventral occipitotemporal regions bilaterally for naming animals. The imaging also identified additional category-specific patterns not found in the lesion-symptom analysis, including a region in the anterior part of the left inferior temporal gyrus that appeared to respond more strongly to animals, and another region stretching down inferiorly from the posterior MTG that appeared to respond more strongly to artifacts.

The finding of tool/artifact selective responding in posterior MTG has been reported by several groups, as has the finding of greater activation in the temporal pole for person recognition, relative to object recognition (Gauthier *et al.*, 1997; Gorno-Tempini *et al.*, 2001; Gorno-Tempini and Price, 2001). Reports of animal-selective responding in neuroimaging studies have been somewhat more variable. Several authors have found greater activation for tools/artifacts than for animals/living things in the medial posterior fusiform, and the reverse effect in the lateral aspect of the same region, in studies using both visual images and words (see Chouinard and Goodale, 2010, for review). Others have suggested, from lesion-overlap and functional imaging data, that animal concepts depend preferentially upon aspects of the ventral anterior temporal lobe (ATL), though different studies place the important region either laterally (Tranel, Damasio, and Damasio, 1997) or medially (Moss *et al.*, 2005; Noppeney *et al.*, 2007) in the left hemisphere, or even preferentially in the right hemisphere (Brambati *et al.*, 2006). Several studies have also failed to find any category-specific responding, an issue to which we return below.

## The single-hub view: organization by a bilateral domain-general convergence zone

The third view proposes that communication amongst various sensory, motor, linguistic, and affective representations is mediated, at least in part, by a single domain-general cross-modal "hub" situated bilaterally in the ATL (Patterson, Nestor, and Rogers, 2007). The hub is assumed to contribute to semantic processing for all kinds of concepts and all receptive and expressive modalities, though there may also exist other more direct pathways between various surface representations. This view is illustrated in Figure 4.3.

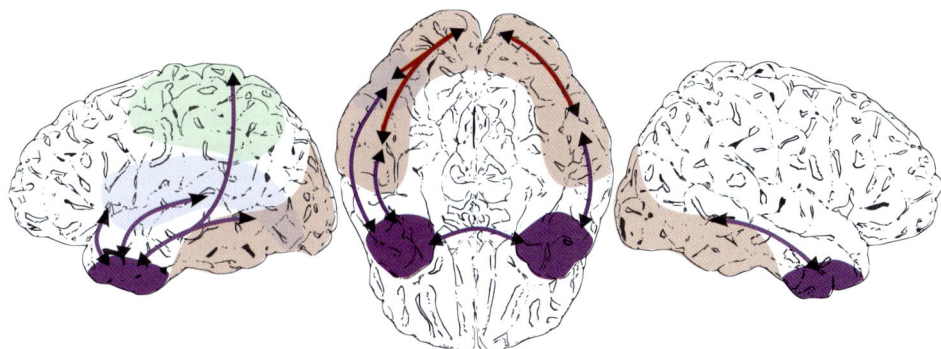

**Figure 4.3** Schematic illustrating the single-hub view. The shading indicates the same modality-specific subnetworks as Figure 4.1. The purple region indicates the hypothesized semantic hub, situated on the ventral surface of the anterior temporal cortex bilaterally. Red arrows indicate incoming visual information.

The single-hub view originated with the study of a neurological syndrome called semantic dementia (SD), a progressive dementing illness that is unique in two respects (see Chapter 20). First, it produces a gradual but remarkably selective dissolution of conceptual knowledge that affects all conceptual domains and all modalities of testing (Hodges *et al.*, 1999). Though such patients typically present with marked anomia and verbal comprehension impairment, their deficits are not purely verbal: they show serious problems discriminating real from chimeric objects (Rogers *et al.*, 2003), recalling the characteristic colors of familiar objects (Rogers, Patterson, and Graham, 2007), matching both words and pictures with their characteristic sounds (Bozeat *et al.*, 2000), sorting words or pictures into semantic categories (Hodges, Graham, and Patterson, 1995), retrieving knowledge about the characteristic praxis, function, and functional associates of common manipulable objects (Hodges *et al.*, 2000), and even recognizing odors (Luzzi *et al.*, 2007). Yet these often profound impairments coexist with otherwise relatively intact cognitive functioning: good performance on tests of episodic memory that do not depend upon intact semantics (such as the delayed Rey figure copy); intact working memory as assessed by forward and backward digit span; largely normal perception and attention; speech that, apart from word-finding difficulties, is fluent and grammatical; and good performance on tests of reasoning and problem solving such as the Raven's progressive matrices (Hodges *et al.*, 1999; Rogers *et al.*, 2006). Patients with SD thus represent the purest form of semantic/conceptual impairment on record.

The second remarkable aspect of SD is the consistency of its neuropathology, which invariably affects the anterior temporal cortices, especially in their lateral and inferior aspects (Acosta-Cabronero *et al.*, 2011; Mummery *et al.*, 2000). In about two-thirds of the patients, the structural pathology appears to be more pronounced in the left hemisphere, but both hemispheres are hypometabolic in the disorder. The profound semantic impairment is thought to arise from this bilateral pathology, since unilateral damage in similar regions produces much milder patterns of impairment (Schapiro *et al.*, 2013).

Corroborating evidence has amassed in recent years from other methods in cognitive neuroscience. One early puzzle for the single-hub view was that the neuropsychological evidence did not appear to align well with evidence from functional neuroimaging. One reason is likely the predominance of functional magnetic resonance imaging (fMRI) in these studies. fMRI yields especially noisy signal in parts of the brain near the air-filled sinuses, especially the inferior surface of the ATL and the orbitofrontal cortex. Other methods, most notably PET, do not encounter the same problem, and such studies are much more likely to show inferior ATL activation associated with semantic task performance (for review see Visser, Jefferies, and Lambon Ralph, 2010). Recent technical innovations in fMRI have improved the signal-to-noise ratio in problem regions, and where these methods have been applied researchers have observed robust activation in inferior ATL regions associated with semantic task performance (Binney *et al.*, 2010). Thus as the technical limitations of fMRI are being overcome, the literature is coming into better alignment with the neuropsychological evidence.

Other emerging methods have likewise lent support to the single-hub theory. For instance, Chan and colleagues (2011), using intracranial multi-electrode recording in human participants, observed category-selective patterns of activity in ventral anterior temporal regions that differentiated animals from manmade objects across different tasks and modalities. Such results provide strong evidence that ATL regions extract important cross-modal semantic regularities. Studies employing TMS have further suggested that these evoked patterns of activation are not epiphenomenal, but play a causal role in the generation of responses in semantic tasks. Thus unilateral TMS stimulation to the ATL slows performance in tasks that rely on word meaning, such as synonym judgment, but not in comparably difficult tasks that do not rely on word meaning, such as numerical magnitude estimation (Pobric, Jefferies, and Lambon Ralph, 2007). Such effects are observed whether the stimulation is applied to the left or the right ATL, consistent with the view that the hub is bilaterally distributed; and it disrupts performance for living things, manmade objects, and abstract concepts, consistent with the view that the hub supports domain-general processing. This pattern stands in contrast to stimulation of other brain regions such as the left inferior parietal lobe, which can produce category-specific patterns of slowing (Pobric, Jefferies, and Lambon Ralph, 2010).

Finally, simulations with computer models have suggested why the cortical semantic system might adopt such an architecture (Rogers, *et al.* 2004a; Rogers and McClelland, 2004). The key insight is that the various different kinds of sensory, motor, linguistic, and affective representations that constitute important components of the semantic network do not, by and large, capture the core similarities that structure conceptual representations. Items that are similar in kind can nevertheless vary quite substantially in many of their surface details. Light bulbs and pears are similar in shape but are quite different kinds of things; ostriches and hummingbirds differ dramatically in size and in the way that the move, but nevertheless are conceived as quite similar kinds of things; tape and glue do not look similar, nor do they engage similar praxis in their use, but nevertheless we think of them as being similar kinds of things. Such examples seem to indicate that, in addition to representations of the particular surface properties associated with familiar kinds, the semantic system must represent conceptual similarity structure that is not directly reflected in any single representational modality.

The single-hub theory proposes that the functional role of the ATL is to extract this similarity structure. The central idea is that, although conceptual similarity structure may not be perfectly represented in any single representational modality taken on its own, it is apparent in the covariance structure apparent across all the different modalities coded in other parts of the network. A central hub that connects to all the various surface modalities is capable of detecting and exploiting cross-modal correlational structure, and in so doing comes to represent conceptual similarity structure even where this is not directly apparent in any single modality. When an item or the word that denotes it is encountered in the environment, its surface representation activates the corresponding pattern of activation in the hub, which in turn feeds back to other surface representations. Because the hub representations express conceptual similarity structure, acquired knowledge about a given item will tend to generalize to other items that are similar in kind, rather than to perceptually similar but conceptually distinct items – a key function of semantic memory (Rogers and McClelland, 2004).

This proposal also explains a central aspect of knowledge dissolution in SD, which is not random but highly structured. Specifically, memory tends to erode most rapidly for names and other arbitrary properties of items that differentiate them from their conceptual neighbors. For instance, such patients often forget that the zebra has stripes or that the camel has a hump – properties not shared by other four-legged mammals – but rarely forget that the zebra has eyes or that the camel has four legs. Likewise, subordinate names such as "robin" or "dalmatian," which serve to differentiate highly specific categories, are much more vulnerable to the impairment than are more general names. In patients with more severe disease, this pattern can lead to greater comprehension impairments for basic-level terms (e.g., "bird," "car") than for more general labels (e.g., "animal," "vehicle"), even though the latter are generally of lower frequency, are acquired later in development, and are more difficult for healthy controls to process (Rogers and Patterson, 2007). The erosion of knowledge about specific, individuating details has been documented in a wide variety of tasks involving many different modalities of representation, including naming and verbal comprehension, sorting of words and pictures, object recognition, color knowledge, and action (Adlam *et al.*, 2006).

According to the single-hub theory, this pattern arises directly from the fact that the ATL hub encodes conceptual similarity structure, and is a primary vehicle for computing cross-modal inferences. To see this, consider how the semantic system under this view retrieves a name from a visually presented stimulus, such as a picture of a beagle. The stimulus is encoded in a visual representation of shape, which in turn causes a pattern of activation in the hub. The hub feeds activation back to representations of word forms. In order for the word "beagle" to be activated, the pattern in the hub must be nearly identical to the learned pattern for the beagle item, because other conceptually related items (e.g., other dogs) are represented with similar patterns of activity but do not share the same name. Thus the system has learned that it should not activate the "beagle" name for most of the representational neighborhood surrounding the *beagle* representation. In contrast, all of the beagle's conceptual neighbors share the name "dog," so the system should activate this lexical item as long as the pattern encoded in the hub is in the right general neighborhood. Moreover, the system has learned to activate still more general labels (such as "animal"), not just for the various dogs, but for other conceptual neighbors that are more distant still (i.e., all the various animals, which populate a very broad region of the representational space around the *beagle* representation). In other words, specific names (and other properties) can be activated from hub patterns that span a relatively narrow range; intermediate names and properties such as those common to basic-level categories can be activated from a somewhat broader range of the space;

and superordinate properties, such as those common to animals, can be activated from a very broad part of the space (Rogers *et al.*, 2004a).

When the neurons that encode the hub representation die as a consequence of disease, the patterns that arise in response to a stimulus become distorted. Small distortions (due to mild pathology) may prevent the system from occupying the comparatively narrow range of spaces from which highly specific properties can be generated. Larger distortions may prevent the system from even finding the somewhat broader regions from which properties common to basic-level categories can be generated. The patterns would have to be very highly distorted, however, before they fell out of the region from which superordinate properties can be generated. Thus the coarse-to-fine dissolution of semantic knowledge observed in SD arises, on this view, from the fact that the affected areas in inferior ATL encode conceptual similarity structure, and use this structure to activate surface representations of properties associated with familiar items.


# A Critical Appraisal and Comparison of the Three Views

Although the three views we have outlined are not necessarily mutually exclusive, their juxtaposition is illuminating. The empirical phenomena that motivate some perspectives may appear to challenge the underlying motivations for other points of view. Here we briefly consider how the full scope of phenomena reviewed constrains hypotheses about the broader architecture.


## Explaining domain- and modality-general semantic impairments

First, the studies of SD that motivated the single-hub view challenge the tripartite and many-hubs views, which share the contention that there is no "core" conceptual representation in the cortical semantic network that contributes to processing of all kinds of concepts in all modalities of reception and expression. If knowledge is partitioned in a widely distributed network with no common core, it is difficult to understand how the relatively circumscribed pathology in SD produces such a global dissolution of knowledge.

One response to this critique is to observe that, because SD is a progressive dementia, it is difficult to be certain about the exact distribution of pathology throughout cortex. Although the structural and metabolic damage appears to be concentrated within anterior temporal regions, it may be that the pathology is broader in scope but undetectable by neuroimaging methods. On this view, the global and cross-modal semantic impairments in SD are attributable to widespread damage throughout cortex, and not from selective damage to the ATL. There are, however, several compelling lines of evidence from neuropsychology that refute this proposal. First, other forms of frontotemporal dementia that arise from the same disease process, but that mainly spare anterior temporal regions – affecting, for instance, insular or orbitofrontal cortex – produce very different cognitive impairments, with conceptual knowledge largely spared (Hodges *et al.*, 1999; see also Chapter 20). Second, other dementing illnesses such as Alzheimer's disease, in which hypometabolism is very widespread, nevertheless do not produce comparably profound disorders of semantic knowledge (Nestor, Fryer, and Hodges, 2006; Chapter 20).

Third, recent lesion–symptom correlation studies have shown that the best predictor of impaired performance in behavioral assessments of semantic knowledge is the degree of pathology in the ATL, especially on its ventral surface (Mion *et al.*, 2010). Fourth, as previously noted, TMS to the ATL selectively slows semantic processing of both words and pictures, for living, nonliving, and abstract concepts. Thus the cognitive profile that uniquely characterizes SD appears to be caused by bilateral damage to the inferior aspects of the ATL, a profile that according the tripartite or many-hubs views cannot arise from such circumscribed pathology.

## Explaining modality-specific impairments

Of course, it is the converse point – the fact that visual, verbal, and action knowledge appear to be selectively impaired or spared across different patients – that is the primary motivation for the tripartite view. If semantics depends upon a single domain-general cross-modal hub, what accounts for such patterns of impairment? There are at least three responses to this question that are consistent with the single-hub view.

*Modality-specificity arises from uncontrolled confounding factors*  First, patterns of apparent modality-specific impairment can sometimes reflect confounding factors that have gone uncontrolled in the study of patients with more general semantic impairment. SD has been especially useful in illuminating such confounds. When knowledge degrades in this disorder, behavior across many tasks becomes increasingly influenced by modality-specific statistical structure, and less by knowledge about semantic structure. When stimuli are not matched for this statistical structure (for instance, for their orthographic or visual typicality), these factors can produce apparent dissociations across modalities. As one example, the orthographic regularity of targets and distractors can strongly influence word recognition in SD: when targets in a lexical decision task are well-formed (i.e., composed of common letter patterns) and distractors are ill-formed, patients with severe word-comprehension deficits can perform at ceiling discriminating words from nonwords, making it seem as though word recognition is spared when word meaning is impaired. When targets and distractors are matched for orthographic typicality, performance on the same tasks declines in proportion with word comprehension (Rogers *et al.*, 2004b). Likewise, visual object recognition in this disorder is strongly influenced by the degree to which targets and distractors are composed of visually prototypical parts. In a recognition task requiring participants to discriminate real from chimeric animals, SD patients falsely endorsed chimeric items composed of highly prototypical animal parts (e.g., a cow with a horse's head) and rejected real animals that possess atypical parts (e.g., a seahorse). In tests where all real objects are composed of prototypical parts and all distractors contain unusual parts, such patients can appear to have preserved recognition; but the same patients show deficits commensurate with their verbal semantic impairment when the targets and distractors are equally prototypical (Rogers *et al.*, 2004b). Thus sensitivity to typicality or specificity may provide an alternative explanation as to why verbal, visual, and action knowledge may sometimes appear to dissociate: if typicality and specificity across tasks is not controlled, the observed dissociations may arise from such a confound.

Adlam *et al.* (2006) investigated the putative dissociation of lexical semantics from nonverbal semantic knowledge in patients diagnosed with fPPA – the syndrome providing perhaps the strongest support for the view that verbal semantic impairments do not cause visual or action impairments. They examined the performance of seven newly presenting patients, all of whom met the diagnostic clinical criteria for fPPA described by Mesulam (2001), on a battery of verbal and nonverbal tasks that controlled or manipulated the regularity of the surface structure in the test items. Under these conditions, no patient showed the dissociation between verbal and nonverbal tasks expected under the tripartite view. In contrast to the predictions of the tripartite view, performance on verbal and nonverbal assessments of knowledge (including tests of both perceptual and action knowledge) was equally likely to be impaired; all patients showed deficits in at least some nonverbal semantic tasks; and volumetric analyses showed that both verbal and nonverbal semantic tasks were associated with the same distribution of pathology in cortex.

*Modality-specificity arises from damage to the "spokes" rather than the "hub" of the semantic network*  A second possibility is that, where modality-specific patterns of impairment are not attributable to confounding factors, they arise from pathology to the modality-specific parts of the semantic network, or to more direct mappings between these, rather than to the hub. An early demonstration of this possibility was described by Plaut (2002), who proposed a cross-modal system of representation for encoding mappings among words, visual representations, and actions. Within this scheme, Plaut (2002) further proposed a graded anatomical division of labor, such that neurons contribute more strongly to mappings between nearby sensory-motor representations. Thus only the neurons that are roughly equidistant from all surface representations would act as a true cross-modal hub. Neurons closer to the "edges" of the cross-modal region would encode information mainly relevant to computing mappings between pairs of surface representations. Lesions to some parts of the cross-modal representation might selectively impair some cross-modal mappings while leaving others intact, while damage to the central portion of the representation might produce a modality-general impairment. Plaut (2002) used a computational model instantiating these principles to provide a compelling account of optic aphasia, a rare neuropsychological syndrome in which patients are unable to name visually presented objects, despite being able to (a) name them from touch and (b) retrieve their characteristic praxis from vision. This proposal represents an interesting compromise between the single-hub and many-hubs views.

*Phonology is left-lateralized*  A third hypothesis is targeted specifically at explaining why patients with SD so frequently present with profound anomia, while many of their other symptoms are less obviously apparent. In cases where pathology is very strongly left-lateralized, anomia can be quite profound while nonverbal semantic impairment is relatively mild. Indeed, this pattern provides part of the evidence supporting the view that there exists a left-lateralized verbal semantic system (Mesulam et al., 2003). Yet the reverse pattern, in which nonverbal semantic knowledge is seriously compromised with only mild anomia, is essentially never observed in the disorder, even in the minority of cases who present with strongly right-lateralized pathology. Instead, such patients typically show naming and nonverbal comprehension impairments that are about equal (Lambon Ralph et al., 2001).

   To account for this pattern, Lambon Ralph et al. (2001) have proposed that, although the semantic hub is itself bilateral, phonological output representations are largely left-lateralized. Thus the left hemisphere component of the hub may be more effective at driving spoken output. In simulations with a neural network model, the authors showed that this hypothesis nicely explained the relationship between the degree of asymmetry in the neuropathology and the degree of impairment observed in naming versus other semantic task profiles.

## Explaining category-specific patterns of impairment and functional activation

A central motivation for the many-hubs view has been the study of category-specific semantic impairment, where patients appear to have selectively lost knowledge about a particular semantic category such as living things or manmade objects, and accompanying brain imaging studies that appear to show selective engagement of particular cortical networks by items from different semantic categories. These empirical phenomena remain controversial, however, for at least three reasons.

First, the great majority of neuroimaging studies reporting apparent patterns of category-specific activation have employed pictures as stimuli. Such studies are often difficult to interpret because semantic category structure is confounded with many different aspects of visual structure. Line drawings of animals are often visually more complex than line drawings of tools and other manmade objects, while tools and other manmade objects are usually much more commonly encountered in the visual environment (Funnell and Sheridan, 1992; Stewart, Parkin, and Hunkin, 1992). Living and nonliving items may also systematically differ in the information carried across different spatial frequency bands (Coppens and Frisinger, 2005), an important factor for interpreting functional imaging data since visuospatial frequency constrains the anatomy of the visual system. Very few imaging or behavioral studies have taken care to simultaneously control for familiarity, visual complexity, and the nature of the information encoded across different spatial frequencies, and it is not clear whether apparent category-specific patterns in these studies reflect such confounds.

Second, patterns of results in both neuropsychological and neuroimaging studies are known to be strongly influenced by the specificity or precision with which an item must be categorized in a given task. Several studies have suggested that animals from different basic-level categories are more likely to share many properties (such as eyes, legs, the ability to move, and so on) than are manmade objects from different basic-level categories (e.g., cars and boats share few properties apart from the fact that they are vehicles). Thus representations of animals may be somewhat more "crowded" in general than are representations of manmade objects, so that animals are harder to differentiate from their semantic neighbors (Humphreys and Forde, 2001). Such a confound could produce both semantic impairments and patterns of functional activation that seem to be selective to animals. Consistent with this view, Lambon Ralph, Lowe and Rogers (2007) studied seven patients with herpes viral encephalitis, all of whom showed worse performance naming animals than manmade objects equated for frequency, familiarity, and visual complexity. When the same patients were asked to name animals and artifacts at a more precise level of specificity (e.g., "robin" instead of "bird," "ferry" instead of "boat"), the category-specific effect disappeared: the patients were equally impaired for both domains. The authors suggested that this occurred because, when the task requires items to be recognized very precisely, there are many close competitors in both living and nonliving domains. Similar results have been observed in functional imaging studies of categorization at different levels of specificity (Rogers *et al.*, 2005).

One way of bypassing such problems is to assess semantic memory with words rather than pictorial stimuli. Words do not have the same visual confounds as images, and it is much easier to control for other confounding factors such as familiarity (which can be estimated by word-frequency counts in large corpora) and specificity (since each word is intrinsically tied to a particular level of specificity). Although a few studies employing words as stimuli have indeed yielded results consistent with the many-hubs view (e.g., Mahon *et al.*, 2009), such evidence appears to be relatively rare. A meta-analysis focusing exclusively on studies that used well-controlled word stimuli found no significant differences contrasting animals and manmade objects (Binder *et al.*, 2009). Other meta-analyses have failed to find consistent evidence for category-specific activation even when including studies that employed pictorial stimuli (Joseph, 2001). Given these null results and the many potential confounding factors in the existing literature, the importance of category-specificity for theories about the gross architecture of the semantic network remains unclear.

## Conclusions and Open Questions

The preceding review suggests several conclusions about the architecture of the cortical semantic network:

1  Evidence supporting the tripartite view suggests that knowledge about the meanings of words is grounded in distributed subnetworks that encode sensory, motor, and linguistic knowledge, including, though probably not limited to, (1) a frontoparietal network that encodes knowledge about actions, (2) a left perisylvian network that encodes knowledge about word forms, and (3) a bilateral ventral-temporal network that encodes visual knowledge.

2  The single-hub view suggests that these networks communicate with one another through a central bilateral hub in the inferior/ventral aspects of the ATL, which contributes to semantic processing for all kinds of concepts across all modalities of reception and expression.

3  The many-hubs view suggests that modality-specific subnetworks may also communicate through other pathways, and some network subcomponents may contribute more strongly to the representation of particular conceptual domains. In particular, the left posterior MTG/OTP junction may contribute to knowledge of manipulable objects by virtue of their connection to action representations in the parietal network. Other category effects remain controversial.

4  Though the hub is bilateral, modality-specific subnetworks, especially for language though possibly also for action, are probably left-lateralized. Consequently left ATL pathology may produce a greater impact on naming and speech production than on other semantic tasks, and tasks requiring overt or covert naming or reading may more strongly engage left-hemisphere parts of the network.

5  When items must be classified at a very specific or even unique level in a given task, semantic representations in the anterior temporal hub must be specified with great precision. Such tasks will therefore be most sensitive to mild anterior temporal

pathology, and will be most likely to elicit strong anterior temporal activation in neuroimaging studies.

If this view is generally correct, we are left with two remaining issues. The first pertains to questions about semantic access, retrieval, or control. To this point we have written as though processing of a word, image, or other stimulus automatically engages a broad network of associations across other stimulus modalities, with the item's meaning inhering in the total operation of the full network. But this characterization is certainly incorrect: in any given situation, only a restricted part of our full complement of knowledge is ever relevant to the task at hand, and indeed the task itself frequently constrains what information is relevant or important (Barsalou, 1982). Thus most people will generally agree that the ability to produce music is an important feature of a piano, but when helping a friend move, this property seems less salient than the piano's weight. We have focused on the architecture of the cortical network that encodes knowledge about the associations among various kinds of sensory, motor, and linguistic representations, but have not discussed the systems involved in the interrogation of this knowledge base.

A full accounting of this interesting question would require its own review. Here we will briefly note that there is increasing evidence of a role for frontoparietal networks in the "control" of activation in the semantic network (for more discussion of controlled memory retrieval processes, see Chapter 7). Thompson-Schill *et al.* (1997) have shown that the dorsolateral prefrontal cortex becomes more strongly engaged in semantic tasks that require the participant to resolve the competition amongst many potential responses. For instance, when asked to generate the action associated with an object, this region responds more strongly to items for which there are many correct responses (e.g., "computer") than for items for which there is just one (e.g., "paintbrush"). Others have reported similar findings, and there is continuing debate regarding how such patterns are best interpreted (see, e.g., Badre and Wagner, 2002). One hypothesis, in keeping with a broad literature on cognitive control more generally (Cohen, Aston-Jones, and Gilzenrat, 2004), is that representations in prefrontal cortex (and other parts of the executive system) serve to constrain or "guide" the flow of activation in the cortical semantic network, so that only those sensory-motor representations relevant to the task at hand become activated. This view accords well with the early observations of Martin *et al.* (1995) that cortical regions associated with a particular property type (e.g., color, motion) activate more strongly when the participant must retrieve information about the corresponding property.

It also aligns with recent neuropsychological evidence from patients with semantic aphasia (SA) – a form of cross-modal semantic impairment arising from cerebrovascular accidents in left hemisphere frontal and parietal regions (Jefferies and Lambon Ralph, 2006). Semantic impairments in SA differ qualitatively from those observed in SD, and in many cases the differences are consistent with the view that patients with SA are unable to select or resolve the competition amongst various alternative responses. For instance, patients with SA have a harder time understanding words whose meanings vary across linguistic contexts (Hoffman, Rogers, and Lambon Ralph, 2011), benefit from phonological cueing and from other contextual cues that constrain the range of possible responses (Jefferies, Patterson, and Lambon Ralph, 2008), and are less affected by the psycholinguistic factors that strongly influence performance in SD (Jefferies and Lambon Ralph, 2006). These deficits can be caused by damage either to prefrontal or to parietal cortex in the left hemisphere, and the different loci appear to produce remarkably similar impairments, raising the possibility that both frontal and parietal regions operate together as part of a "semantic control" system (Noonan *et al.*, 2010).

The second issue concerns a question hinted at in the introduction: What are we to make of words like "piety," whose meanings are not clearly associated with sensory-motor states? This is a pressing question for any grounded approach to meaning that we will not solve in this chapter. We will note, however, that the neuroanatomical perspective in this review may provide a clue towards the beginnings of an answer. The clue lies in the existence of the ATL hub. Earlier we suggested that such a hub might be needed to represent the conceptual similarity structure that governs generalization, and that is not captured by sensory, motor, or linguistic representations taken independently. Computer simulations have shown that neural networks can acquire knowledge of such structure through learning the associations among many different kinds of properties – but only when the network architecture is *convergent*: there must be a single region that contributes to the representation and processing of all kinds of information across all varieties of inputs and outputs (Rogers and McClelland, 2004). With such a region, the network is capable of detecting patterns of systematic high-order covariation across various inputs and outputs, and of constructing internal representations that efficiently exploit such structure, including representations whose similarities differ substantially from those expressed in each input modality taken independently (Rogers *et al.*, 2004a). Indeed, it has been shown that such an architecture is capable of learning completely abstract relationships – that is, the network can represent items as similar when they relate to other entities in similar ways, even if they share no properties at all in common (Rogers and McClelland, 2008). In contrast, if the same associations among the same properties are encoded across multiple different pathways, the network loses the ability to detect and exploit high-order covariation, and thus fails to acquire representations that express abstract conceptual structure. Such simulations thus suggest that the single-hub architecture may be necessary in order for people to learn abstract conceptual structure. Although this hypothesis provides a promising starting point, it is clear there is a long way to go before we resolve Euthyprho's argument with Socrates.

# References

Acosta-Cabronero, J., Patterson, K., Fryer, T., *et al.* (2011). Atrophy, hypometabolism and white matter abnormalities in semantic dementia tell a coherent story. *Brain*, 134 (7), 2025–2035.

Adlam, A.-L., Patterson, K., Rogers, T.T., *et al.* (2006). Semantic dementia and fluent primary progressive aphasia: two sides of the same coin? *Brain*, 129, 3066–3080.

Badre, D., and Wagner, A. (2002). Semantic retrieval, mnemonic control, and prefrontal cortex. *Behavioral and Cognitive Neuroscience Reviews*, 1 (3), 206–218.

Barsalou, L.W. (1982). Context-independent and context-dependent information in concepts. *Memory and Cognition*, 10, 82–93.

Barsalou, L.W. (2008). Grounded cognition. *Annual Review of Psychology*, 59, 617–645.

Barsalou, L.W., Simmons, W.K., Barbey, A., and Wilson, C.D. (2003). Grounding conceptual knowledge in modality-specific systems. *Trends in Cognitive Sciences*, 7 (2), 84–91.

Binder, J.R., Desai, R.H., Graves, W.W., and Conant, L.L. (2009). Where is the semantic system? A critical review and meta-analysis of 120 functional neuroimaging studies. *Cerebral Cortex*, 19 (12), 2767–2796. doi: 10.1093/cercor/bhp055.

Binkofski, F., and Buxbaum, L.J. (2013). Two action systems in the human brain. *Brain and Language*, 127 (2), 222–229. doi: 10.1016/j.bandl.2012.07.007.

Binney, R.J., Embleton, K.V., Jefferies, E., *et al.* (2010). The ventral and inferolateral aspects of the anterior temporal lobe are crucial in semantic memory: evidence from a novel direct comparison of distortion-corrected fMRI, rTMS, and semantic dementia. *Cerebral Cortex*, 20 (11), 2728–2738. doi: 10.1093/cercor/bhq019.

Boronat, C.B., Buxbaum, L.J., Coslett, H.B., *et al.* (2005) Distinctions between manipulation and function knowledge of objects: evidence from functional magnetic resonance imaging. *Brain Research Cognitive Brain Research*, 23 (2–3), 361–373. doi: 10.1016/j.cogbrainres.2004.11.001.

Bozeat, S., Lambon Ralph, M.A., Patterson, K., *et al.* (2000). Nonverbal semantic impairment in semantic dementia. *Neuropsychologia*, 38, 1207–1215.

Brambati, S.M., Myers, D., Wilson, A., *et al.* (2006). The anatomy of category-specific object naming in neurodegenerative diseases. *Journal of Cognitive Neuroscience*, 18, 1644–53. doi: 10.1162/jocn.2006.18.10.1644.

Buxbaum, L.J. (2001). Ideomotor apraxia: a call to action. *Neurocase*, 7(6), 445–458. doi: 10.1093/neucas/7.6.445.

Buxbaum, L.J., and Saffran, E.M. (2002). Knowledge of object manipulation and object function: dissociations in apraxic and nonapraxic subjects. *Brain and Language*, 82 (2), 179–199.

Buxbaum, L.J., Veramontil, T., and Schwartz, M.F. (2000). Function and manipulation tool knowledge in apraxia: knowing 'what for' but not 'how'. *Neurocase*, 6 (2), 83–97. doi: 10.1080/13554790008402763.

Caine, D. (2004). Posterior cortical atrophy: a review of the literature. *Neurocase*, 10 (5), 382–385. doi: 10.1080/13554790490892239.

Campanella, F., D'Agostini, S., Skrap, M., and Shallice, T. (2010). Naming manipulable objects: anatomy of a category specific effect in left temporal tumours. *Neuropsychologia*, 48 (6), 1583–1597. doi: 10.1016/j.neuropsychologia.2010.02.002.

Chan, A.M., Baker, J.M. Eskandar, E., *et al.* (2011). First-pass selectivity for semantic categories in human anteroventral temporal lobe. *Journal of Neuroscience: the Official Journal of the Society for Neuroscience*, 31 (49), 18119–18129. doi: 10.1523/JNEUROSCI.3122-11.2011.

Chao, L.L., Haxby, J.V., and Martin, A. (1999). Attribute-based neural substrates in temporal cortex for perceiving and knowing about objects. *Nature Neuroscience*, 2 (10), 913–919.

Chao, L.L., and Martin, A. (1999). Cortical regions associated with perceiving, naming, and knowing about colors. *Journal of Cognitive Neuroscience*, 11 (1), 25–35.

Chouinard, P.A., and Goodale, M.A. (2010). Category-specific neural processing for naming pictures of animals and naming pictures of tools: an ALE meta-analysis. *Neuropsychologia*, 48 (2), 409–418. doi: 10.1016/j.neuropsychologia.2009.09.032.

Cohen, J.D., Aston-Jones, G., and Gilzenrat, M.S. (2004). A systems-level perspective on attention and cognitive control. In *Cognitive Neuroscience of Attention* (ed. M.I. Posner). New York, NY: Guilford Press, pp. 71–90.

Coltheart, M. (2004). Are there lexicons? *Quarterly Journal of Experimental Psychology*, 57 (7), 1153–1171.

Coppens, P., and Frisinger, D. (2005). Category-specific naming effect in non-brain-damaged individuals. *Brain and Language*, 94 (1), 61–71. doi: 10.1016/j.bandl.2004.11.008.

Damasio, A.R. (1989). The brain binds entities and events by multiregional activation from convergence zones. *Neural Computation*, 1, 123–132.

Damasio, H., Grabowski, T.J., Tranel, D., and Hichwa, R.D. (1996). A neural basis for lexical retrieval. *Nature*, 380 (6574), 499–505.

Eggert, G. H. (1977). *Wernicke's Works on Aphasia: A Sourcebook and Review*. Vol. 1. The Hague: Mouton.

Farah, M. J. (1990). *Visual Agnosia*. Cambridge, MA: MIT Press.

Funnell, E., and Sheridan, J. (1992). Categories of knowledge? Unfamiliar aspects of living and nonliving things. *Cognitive Neuropsychology*, 9 (2), 135–153. doi: 10.1080/02643299208252056.

Gainotti, G. (2000). What the locus of brain lesion tells us about the nature of the cognitive defect underlying category-specific disorders: a review. *Cortex*, 36 (4), 539–559. doi: 10.1016/S0010-9452(08)70537-9.

Gainotti, G., Silveri, M.C., Daniele, A., and Giustoli, L. (1995). Neuroanatomical correlates of category-specific semantic disorders: a critical survey. *Memory*, 3 (3/4), 247–264.

Gauthier, I., Anderson, A.W. Tarr, M.J., *et al.* (1997). Levels of categorization in visual recognition studied with functional MRI. *Current Biology*, 7, 645–651.

Glenberg, A.M. (2010). Embodiment as a unifying perspective for psychology. *Wiley Interdisciplinary Reviews: Cognitive Science*, 1 (4), 586–596. doi: 10.1002/wcs.55.

Glenberg, A.M., and Kaschak, M.P. (2002). Grounding language in action. *Psychonomic Bulletin and Review*, 9 (3), 558–565. doi: 10.3758/BF03196313.

Goodale, M.A., and Milner, A.D. (1992). Separate visual pathways for perception and action. *Trends in Neurosciences*, 15 (1), 20–25. doi: 10.1016/0166-2236(92)90344-8.

Gorno-Tempini, M., and Price, C. (2001). Identification of famous faces and buildings: a functional neuroimaging study of semantically unique items. *Brain*, 124 (10), 2087–2097.

Gorno-Tempini, M., Price, C., Rudge, P., and Cipolotti, L. (2001). Identification without naming: a functional neuroimaging study of an anomic patient. *Journal of Neurology, Neurosurgery and Psychiatry*, 70 (3), 397–400.

Grabowski, T.J., Damasio, H., Tranel, D., *et al.* (2001). A role for left temporal pole in the retrieval of words for unique entities. *Human Brain Mapping*, 13 (4), 199–212.

Hauk, O., Johnsrude, I., and Pulvermüller, F. (2004). Somatotopic representation of action words in human motor and premotor cortex. *Neuron*, 41 (2), 301–307. doi: 10.1016/S0896-6273(03)00838-9.

Hodges, J.R., Bozeat, S., Patterson, K., and Spatt, J. (2000). The role of conceptual knowledge in object use evidence from semantic dementia. *Brain* 123, 1913–1925.

Hodges, J.R., Garrard, P., Perry, R., *et al.* (1999). The differentiation of semantic dementia and frontal lobe dementia from early Alzheimer's disease: a comparative neuropsychological study. *Neuropsychology*, 13, 31–40.

Hodges, J.R., Graham, N., and Patterson, K. (1995). Charting the progression in semantic dementia: implications for the organisation of semantic memory. *Memory*, 3, 463–495.

Hoffman, P., Rogers, T.T., and Lambon Ralph, M.A. (2011). Semantic diversity accounts for the 'missing' word frequency effect in stroke aphasia: insights using a novel method to quantify contextual variability in meaning. *Journal of Cognitive Neuroscience*, 23 (9), 2432–2446. doi: 10.1162/jocn.2011.21614.

Humphreys, G.W., and Forde, E.M. (2001). Hierarchies, similarity, and interactivity in object-recognition: on the multiplicity of 'category-specific' deficits in neuropsychological populations. *Behavioral and Brain Sciences*, 24 (3), 453–509.

Jefferies, E., and Lambon Ralph, M.A. (2006). Semantic impairment in stroke aphasia versus semantic dementia: a case-series comparison. *Brain* 129, 2132–2147.

Jefferies, E., Patterson, K., and Lambon Ralph, M.A. (2008). Deficits of knowledge versus executive control in semantic cognition: insights from cued naming. *Neuropsychologia*, 46 (2), 649–658. doi: 10.1016/j.neuropsychologia.2007.09.007.

Joseph, J.E. (2001). Functional neuroimaging studies of category specificity in object recognition: a critical review and meta-analysis. *Cognitive, Affective and Behavioral Neuroscience*, 1 (2), 119–136.

Kalénine, S., Buxbaum, L.J., and Coslett, H.B. (2010). Critical brain regions for action recognition: lesion symptom mapping in left hemisphere stroke. *Brain*, 133 (11), 3269–3280. doi: 10.1093/brain/awq210.

Kellenbach, M., Brett, M., and Patterson, K. (2001). Large, colorful or noisy? Attribute- and modality-specific activations during retrieval of perceptual attribute knowledge. *Cognitive, Affective and Behavioral Neuroscience*, 1 (3), 207–221.

Lambon Ralph, M.A., Lowe, C., and Rogers, T.T. (2007). Neural basis of category-specific semantic deficits for living things: evidence from semantic dementia, HSVE and a neural network model. *Brain*, 130, 1127–1137.

Lambon Ralph, M.A., McClelland, J.L. Patterson, K., *et al.* (2001). No right to speak? The relationship between object naming and semantic impairment: neuropsychological evidence and a computational model. *Journal of Cognitive Neuroscience*, 13, 341–356.

Laurence, S., and Margolis, E. (1999). Concepts and cognitive science. In *Concepts: Core Readings* (ed. E. Margolis and S. Laurence). Boston, MA: MIT Press, pp. 3–81.

Luzzi, S., Snowden, J.S., Neary, D., *et al.* (2007). Distinct patterns of olfactory impairment in Alzheimer's disease, semantic dementia, frontotemporal dementia, and corticobasal degeneration. *Neuropsychologia*, 45 (8), 1823–1831. doi: 10.1016/j.neuropsychologia.2006.12.008.

Mahon, B.Z., Anzellotti, S., Schwarzbach, J., *et al.* (2009). Category-specific organization in the human brain does not require visual experience. *Neuron*, 63 (3), 397–405. doi: 10.1016/j.neuron.2009.07.012.

Mahon, B.Z., Schwarzbach, J., and Caramazza, A. (2010). The representation of tools in left parietal cortex is independent of visual experience. *Psychological Science*, 21 (6), 764–771. doi: 10.1177/0956797610370754.

Martin, A., and Chao, L.L. (2001). Semantic memory in the brain: structure and processes. *Current Opinion in Neurobiology*, 11, 194–201.

Martin, A., Haxby, J.V., Lalonde, F.M., *et al.* (1995). Discrete cortical regions associated with knowledge of color and knowledge of action. *Science*, 270, 102–105.

Martin, A., Wiggs, C., Ungerleider, L., and Haxby, J.V. (1996). Neural correlates of category-specific knowledge. *Nature*, 379, 649–652.

McCarthy, R., and Warrington, E.K. (1986). Visual associative agnosia: a clinico-anatomical study of a single case. *Journal of Neurology, Neurosurgery and Psychiatry*, 49, 1233–1240.

Mesulam, M.M. (2001). Primary progressive aphasia. *Annals of Neurology*, 49 (4), 425–432. doi: 10.1002/ana.91.

Mesulam, M.M., Grossman, M., Hillis, A., *et al.* (2003). The core and halo of primary progressive aphasia and semantic dementia. *Annals of Neurology*, 54 (suppl. 5), S11–S14.

Mesulam, M.M., Wieneke, C., Hurley, R., *et al.* (2013). Words and objects at the tip of the left temporal lobe in primary progressive aphasia. *Brain*, 136 (2), 601–618. doi: 10.1093/brain/aws336.

Mion, M., Patterson, K., Acosta-Cabronero, J., *et al.* (2010). What the left and right fusiform gyri tell us about semantic memory. *Brain* 133, 3256–3268.

Moss, H.E., Rodd, J M , Stamatakis, E.A., *et al.* (2005). Anteromedial temporal cortex supports fine grained differentiation among objects. *Cerebral Cortex*, 15, 626–627.

Mummery, C.J., Patterson, K., Price, C.J., *et al.* (2000). A voxel-based morphometry study of semantic dementia: relationship between temporal lobe atrophy and semantic memory. *Annals of Neurology*, 47 (1), 36–45.

Nestor, P.J., Fryer, T.D., and Hodges, J.R. (2006). Declarative memory impairments in Alzheimer's disease and semantic dementia. *NeuroImage*, 30, 1010–1020.

Noonan, K.A., Jefferies, E., Corbett, F., and Lambon Ralph, M.A. (2010). Elucidating the nature of deregulated semantic cognition in semantic aphasia: evidence for the roles of prefrontal and temporo-parietal cortices. *Journal of Cognitive Neuroscience*, 22 (7), 1597–1613.

Noppeney, U., Nagaraja, S.S., Tyler, L.K., *et al.* (2007). Temporal lobe lesions and semantic impairment: a comparison of herpes simplex virus encephalitis and semantic dementia. *Brain*, 130 (4), 1138–1147.

Ochipa, C., Rothi, L.J. and Heilman, K.M. (1989). Ideational apraxia: a deficit in tool selection and use. *Annals of Neurology*, 25 (2), 190–193. doi: 10.1002/ana.410250214.

Oliveri, M., Finocchiaro, C., Shapiro, K., *et al.* (2004). All talk and no action: a transcranial magnetic stimulation study of motor cortex activation during action word production. *Journal of Cognitive Neuroscience*, 16 (3), 374–381. doi: 10.1162/089892904322926719.

Patterson, K., Nestor, P. J., and Rogers, T.T. (2007). Where do you know what you know? The representation of semantic knowledge in the human brain. *Nature Reviews Neuroscience*, 8, 976–987.

Plaut, D.C. (2002). Graded modality-specific specialisation in semantics: a computational account of optic aphasia. *Cognitive Neuropsychology*, 19 (7), 603–639.

Pobric, G., Jefferies, E., and Lambon Ralph, M.A. (2007). Anterior temporal lobes mediate semantic representation: mimicking semantic dementia by using rTMS in normal participants. *Proceedings of the National Academy of Sciences of the USA*, 104 (50), 20137–20141. doi: 10.1073/pnas.0707383104.

Pobric, G., Jefferies, E., and Lambon Ralph, M.A. (2010). Category-specific versus category-general semantic impairment induced by transcranial magnetic stimulation. *Current Biology*, 20 (10), 964–968. doi: 10.1016/j.cub.2010.03.070.

Rogers, T.T., Hocking, J., Mechelli, A., *et al.* (2005). Fusiform activation to animals is driven by the process, not the stimulus. *Journal of Cognitive Neuroscience* (173), 434–445.

Rogers, T.T., Ivanoiu, A., Patterson, K., and Hodges, J.R. (2006). Semantic memory in Alzheimer's disease and the fronto-temporal dementias: a longitudinal study of 236 patients. *Neuropsychology*, 20 (3), 319–335.

Rogers, T.T., Lambon Ralph, M.A., Garrard, P., *et al.* (2004a). The structure and deterioration of semantic memory: a computational and neuropsychological investigation. *Psychological Review*, 111 (1), 205–235.

Rogers, T.T., Lambon Ralph, M.A., Hodges, J.R., and Patterson, K. (2003). Object recognition under semantic impairment: the effects of conceptual regularities on perceptual decisions. *Language and Cognitive Processes*, 18 (5/6), 625–662.

Rogers, T.T., Lambon Ralph, M.A., Hodges, J.R., and Patterson, K. (2004b). Natural selection: the impact of semantic impairment on lexical and object decision. *Cognitive Neuropsychology*, 21 (2–4), 331–352.

Rogers, T.T., and McClelland, J.L. (2004). *Semantic Cognition: A Parallel Distributed Processing Approach*. Cambridge, MA: MIT Press.

Rogers, T.T., and McClelland, J.L. (2008). A Simple model from a powerful framework that spans levels of analysis. *Behavioral and Brain Sciences*, 31, 729–749.

Rogers, T.T., and Patterson, K. (2007). Object categorization: reversals and explanations of the basic-level advantage. *Journal of Experimental Psychology: General*, 136 (3), 451–469.

Rogers, T.T., Patterson, K., and Graham, K. (2007). Colour knowledge in semantic dementia: it's not all black and white. *Neuropsychologia*, 45, 3285–3298.

Rudrauf, D., Mehta, S., Bruss, J., *et al.* (2008). Thresholding lesion overlap difference maps: application to category-related naming and recognition deficits. *NeuroImage*, 41 (3), 970–984.

Schapiro, A.C., McClelland, J.L., Welbourne, S.R., *et al.* (2013). Why bilateral damage is worse than unilateral damage to the brain. *Journal of Cognitive Neuroscience*, 25 (12), 2107–2123.

Schwartz, M.F., Montgomery, M.W., Buxbaum, L.J., *et al.* (1998). Naturalistic action impairment in closed head injury. *Neuropsychology*, 12 (1), 13–28.

Stewart, F., Parkin, A.J., and Hunkin, N.M. (1992). Naming impairments following recovery from herpes simplex encephalitis: category-specific? *Quarterly Journal of Experimental Psychology Section A*, 44 (2), 261–284. doi: 10.1080/02724989243000037.

Thompson Schill, S.L., D'Esposito, M., Aguirre, G.K., and Farah, M.J. (1997). Role of left inferior prefrontal cortex in retrieval of semantic knowledge: a reevaluation. *Proceedings of the National Academy of Sciences of the USA*, 94, 14792–14797.

Tranel, D., Damasio, H. and Damasio, A.R. (1997). A neural basis for the retrieval of conceptual knowledge. *Neuropsychologia*, 35 (10), 1319–1327.

Visser, M., Jefferies, E., and Lambon Ralph, M.A. (2010). Semantic processing in the anterior temporal lobes: a meta-analysis of the functional neuroimaging literature. *Journal of Cognitive Neuroscience*, 22 (6), 1083–1094.

Warrington, E.K., and Shallice, T. (1984). Category specific semantic impairments. *Brain*, 107, 829–854.

# 5

# Encoding and Retrieval in Episodic Memory

## *Insights from fMRI*

### Michael D. Rugg, Jeffrey D. Johnson, and Melina R. Uncapher

## Introduction

In this chapter we review evidence from functional magnetic resonance imaging (fMRI) studies relevant to the question of how episodic memories are encoded and retrieved, and how encoding and retrieval are related. We outline a theoretical framework that has guided much of the research conducted in these areas in the past few years and provide a selective review of relevant studies, focusing largely on findings pertaining to the cerebral cortex outside the medial temporal lobe (MTL). More exhaustive reviews of this literature can be found in the meta-analyses of Kim (2010, 2011). Detailed discussion of the specific functional roles of the hippocampus and adjacent MTL regions in episodic memory is beyond the scope of the present chapter (see, for example, Davachi, 2006; Diana, Yonelinas, and Ranganath, 2007; Montaldi *et al.*, 2006; Squire, Wixted, and Clark, 2007; see also Chapter 6).

Our use of the term *episodic memory* refers to memories for unique events, that is, events that are individuated by their contexts, such as where you parked your car today rather than yesterday (Tulving, 1983). A key feature of episodic memories is their associational nature, such that different elements of an event are bound together in memory; in the example above, remembering where your car is currently parked depends on retrieval of associations between the act of parking the car, the location of the act, and when it occurred (see Chapter 18). Episodic memory can be contrasted with two other kinds of explicit (conscious) memory in which contextual associations play little or no role. Semantic memory supports general knowledge that is acquired through repeated exposure to the same information in a variety of different contexts, such that the information becomes largely decontextualized (see Chapter 4). Similarly, a sense of familiarity can support simple judgments of recognition memory, but provides no access to contextual or other qualitative information about the prior event (e.g., Yonelinas, 2002).

Before outlining the theoretical framework that links encoding and retrieval, we briefly define what we mean by these terms. *Encoding* refers to the processes that are

*The Wiley Handbook on the Cognitive Neuroscience of Memory*, First Edition.
Edited by Donna Rose Addis, Morgan Barense, and Audrey Duarte.
© 2015 John Wiley & Sons, Ltd. Published 2015 by John Wiley & Sons, Ltd.

engaged when an event is experienced that contribute to the formation of a durable, veridical memory of the event. These processes have been the subject of extensive psychological research, some of which we discuss below. We conceive of encoding as distinct from the cellular and synaptic processes that operate in the minutes and hours after an event has been experienced to stabilize or "consolidate" its memory (Dudai, 2004). Clearly, if these processes are impaired (as in experimental animals administered a protein synthesis inhibitor shortly after a learning experience), a memory will not persist no matter how effectively it was encoded. Other things being equal, though, we assume that the durability of a memory and its resistance to interference are determined to a significant extent by processes active around the time an event is experienced. The findings described below from studies investigating fMRI "subsequent memory effects" provide compelling support for this assumption.

Our use of the term *retrieval* refers to the processes initiated by a retrieval cue that lead to the emergence of a consciously accessible representation of a specific past episode. A retrieval cue might take the form of an external event (as in tests of recognition memory or cued recall) or it might be generated internally (as in free recall). Either way, as we elaborate below, successful retrieval depends critically on how the cue is processed and the relationship between this processing and the processing that was engaged when the event was experienced.

## Theoretical Framework

In this section we outline two theoretical frameworks – one rooted in experimental psychology and the other in neurobiology – that have both been highly influential in guiding ideas about how episodic memory functions. Both frameworks propose that there is an intimate relationship between the processes engaged when an event is experienced and those that are engaged when it is later remembered. Although they come out of different experimental traditions, and are articulated at different levels of explanation, the two frameworks are highly complementary. Integrating the frameworks leads to an account of episodic encoding and retrieval that can be framed at the explanatory level of cognitive neuroscience. The account generates predictions, outlined below in the sections describing studies of encoding and retrieval, that are testable in healthy humans with functional neuroimaging methods such as event-related fMRI.

Experimental psychologists have long investigated the relationship between the encoding and retrieval of episodic information, emphasizing the interdependency of these seemingly distinct mnemonic functions (e.g., Fisher and Craik, 1977; Morris, Bransford, and Franks, 1977; Tulving and Thomson, 1973). One outcome of this line of research has been the principle of transfer-appropriate processing (Morris, Bransford, and Franks 1977). Transfer-appropriate processing (TAP) is predicated on the twin assumptions that memories are represented in terms of the cognitive operations engaged by an event as it is initially processed, and that successful memory retrieval occurs when those earlier operations are recapitulated (Kolers, 1973; for review see Roediger, Gallo, and Geraci, 2002). According to the first of these assumptions, ostensibly the same event will give rise to different memory representations depending on which aspects of the event are emphasized or attended at study. According to the second assumption, the effectiveness of a retrieval cue will depend on the similarity between the processing engaged by the cue and the processing that occurred during encoding: the greater the similarity (the "study–test overlap"), the greater the likelihood of successful retrieval (Roediger and Guynn, 1996; Roediger, Weldon, and Challis, 1989; see Nairne, 2002, for caveats). Thus the question of what constitutes the most effective way of encoding information into memory can be fully addressed only if the retrieval conditions are specified. Similarly, the question of what constitutes an effective retrieval cue can be answered only if the processes engaged during encoding have been defined.

The idea at the core of the TAP principle, namely that retrieval of an episodic memory involves the reinstatement or recapitulation of processes active at the time of encoding, is also found in neurobiologically based models of memory retrieval (e.g., Alvarez and Squire, 1994; Norman and O'Reilly, 2003; Rolls, 2000; Shastri, 2002). According to these models, recollection of a recent event occurs if the pattern of cortical activity elicited by the event when it was initially experienced is reinstated by activation of a hippocampally stored representation of that pattern. Through this mechanism, anatomically distinct cortical regions that were concurrently active during the online processing of an event will also be co-activated during its retrieval, preserving associations between the features of the event that, together, make it distinct from other similar occurrences. In the model of Norman and O'Reilly (2003), for example, memory encoding is a consequence of the formation in the CA3 region of the hippocampus of a sparsely encoded representation of the pattern of cortical activity elicited by an event. Retrieval occurs when this representation is reactivated, which in turn leads to the reinstatement of the pattern of cortical activity encoded in the representation. Crucially, reactivation of the hippocampal representation does not depend on perfect overlap between the originally encoded activity and the activity engendered during a retrieval attempt. Because CA3 is highly effective at "pattern completion" (Marr, 1971; Wallenstein, Hasselmo, and Eichenbaum, 1998), activity that only partially overlaps the encoded information can be sufficient to cause reactivation of the entire representation, and hence reinstatement of the original cortical pattern. Because of this pattern-completion mechanism, memories can be retrieved in response to retrieval cues that elicit activity that only partially resembles the activity elicited by the original event.

The principles of TAP and cortical reinstatement share several key concepts. These include the idea that memory retrieval involves the recapitulation of processes and representations that were active during encoding, and that the likelihood of successful retrieval is a function of the extent to which the processing engaged by a retrieval cue overlaps with that engaged at encoding.

Figure 5.1 illustrates one way in which these ideas can be schematized in terms of large-scale patterns of brain activity. The figure attempts to capture the twin ideas that the retrieval of a prior episode involves reinstatement of the pattern of neural activity engaged during the original experience, and that retrieval cues need only elicit a fraction of the original activity in order to trigger the reinstatement of the entire pattern. The figure also highlights the key role played by the hippocampus in both successful encoding and retrieval. Before discussing empirical findings relevant to this theoretical framework, some caveats and qualifications are in order:

1   Encoding–retrieval overlap is represented in Figure 5.1 in terms of co-activation of cortical regions on a relatively coarse spatial scale, concordant with what can

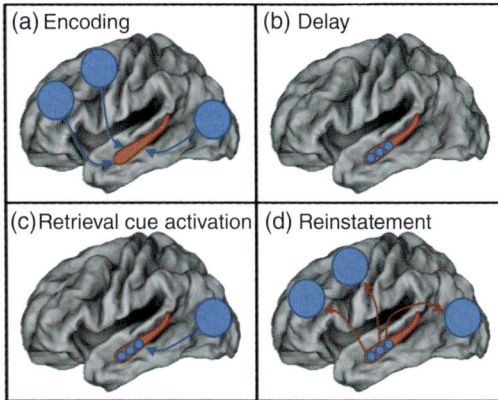

**Figure 5.1** Schematic depiction of the proposed relationship between encoding- and retrieval-related processing in episodic memory. (a) During encoding, presentation of a stimulus event activates a diverse set of cortical regions. The resulting pattern of cortical activity is captured by the hippocampus. (b) Following encoding, the pattern of cortical activity elicited by the event is stored as a memory representation in the hippocampus. (c) Later presentation of a part of the event (the retrieval cue) leads to partial reinstatement of the original pattern of cortical activity, which feeds forward to the hippocampus. (d) Overlap between the activity elicited by the retrieval cue and the stored pattern of activity causes the hippocampal representation to be reactivated, which in turn leads to full reinstatement of the original pattern of cortical activity.

typically be detected with fMRI. Cortical activity can, however, be differentiated on a much more fine-grained spatial scale (ultimately, of course, to the level of individual or small populations of neurons), and with respect to its temporal as well as its spatial properties. For example, online processing of two different faces is differentiated not so much by activity in distinct cortical regions, but by differences in the patterning of activity within a common region. Thus, the task of the hippocampus, or any other structure whose function is to capture and later reinstate patterns of activity associated with the processing of an event, is considerably more complex than simply registering which cortical areas were co-activated by the event.

2    Figure 5.1 is far from being a complete specification of the component processes underlying successful retrieval. Indeed, if this were all that there was, it is unclear how we would be able to distinguish between the perception of an event and our later memory of it (although see Johnson, Hashtroudi, and Lindsay, 1993). Furthermore, if episodic retrieval were elicited every time there was overlap between current and past processing, we would be in a state of almost continuous retrieval. This would be highly maladaptive: it is not helpful when struggling to park your car to be distracted by a vivid recollection of the last time you parked in the same lot. As was noted by Tulving (1983), these and related considerations suggest that episodic retrieval is subject to some kind of control mechanism. Tulving proposed that stimulus events are processed as retrieval cues only when an individual adopts a specific cognitive state, which he termed retrieval mode (see Chapter 1). According to this proposal, depending on whether or not retrieval mode is engaged, the same stimulus event will be processed either as an episodic

retrieval cue or with respect to its online significance. It is currently unclear how this and related ideas about retrieval processing (Rugg and Wilding, 2000) should be incorporated into the framework outlined in Figure 5.1.

3   The framework outlined in Figure 5.1 implies that retrieval consists of little more than the "replaying" of the processing engaged by the original experience. If this were so, then recollection would be "all or nothing"; either everything that was registered in the brain as an event unfolded would be retrieved, or nothing would be. Moreover, memories would be largely veridical. Clearly, neither of these scenarios is accurate. Memories are a very imperfect mirror of experience: they are invariably partial, and often highly distorted, records of the original event (e.g., Bartlett, 1932; Loftus and Palmer, 1974; Schacter, 2002; see also Chapter 8). Among the many factors contributing to this imperfect relation between an event and our later memory of it, two stand out. First, the different features of an event are not equally likely to be successfully encoded. Other things being equal, those aspects of the event that are attended to the most fully are most likely to be later remembered (see below, and Moscovitch, 1992). Second, there is a wealth of evidence that episodic retrieval is a constructive process, in which retrieved information is combined with other knowledge about the event and the result interpreted in light of current expectations and biases (e.g., Bransford and Franks, 1971; Brewer, 1987; Brewer and Treyens, 1981; Schacter, Norman, and Koutstaal, 1998). Thus, retrieved episodic information may only partially determine the content of the resulting memory representation. Together, these two factors will act to reduce the amount of overlap between encoding- and retrieval-related neural activity to well below the 100% illustrated in Figure 5.1. Specifically, as we discuss below, cortical activity elicited during an event by attended information is more likely to be incorporated into the resulting hippocampal representation than is the activity elicited by unattended information. And the constructive nature of memory retrieval means that retrieval-related neural activity will reflect not only the reinstatement of activity elicited at encoding, but also any non-episodic information that was incorporated into the memory representation.

## Empirical Findings

### Encoding

Studies of memory encoding were among some of the first attempts to use functional neuroimaging – then in the form of positron emission tomography (PET) – to study the neural correlates of cognitive processing (e.g., Kapur *et al.*, 1994). Early studies, either with PET or with fMRI, employed "blocked" experimental designs and operationalized the neural correlates of encoding in terms of comparisons between different study tasks that yielded relatively good versus relatively poor levels of memory performance. These studies identified several brain regions, including the prefrontal cortex and, less consistently, the MTL, where elevated activity appeared to be associated with more effective encoding (see Rugg, Otten, and Henson, 2002 for a review of this early literature). Blocked design and task-based approaches to the study of encoding suffer from a number of problems, however. First, there is the difficulty of identifying effects that are tied specifically to differential encoding activity rather than to other cognitive operations also modulated by the task manipulation. A second problem is that in task-based designs, encoding is manipulated through qualitative changes in the cognitive processes engaged by study tasks. Thus, task-based designs cannot address the question of what modulates the efficacy of encoding of stimulus events that seemingly engage the same cognitive processes as they are experienced.

An alternative approach to the study of encoding is to identify brain regions where within-task item-related activity predicts successful memory on a later retrieval test. Such "subsequent memory" comparisons, which were originally developed in the context of event-related potential (ERP) research (Rugg *et al.*, 1995; Sanquist *et al.*, 1980), identify activity at the time of encoding that is in some sense "predictive" of later memory performance (such activity is referred to as a "subsequent memory effect"). The subsequent memory procedure is now near-ubiquitous in fMRI studies of memory encoding.

The logic of the subsequent memory procedure is straightforward: (1) brain activity elicited by a series of study items is acquired; (2) memory for the study items is later tested; (3) the brain activity that was elicited at study is "backsorted" according to performance on the subsequent memory test. Differences in the activity elicited by subsequently remembered and subsequently forgotten items are taken to be correlates of differences in the efficacy of encoding, and regions exhibiting these differences are regarded as candidate loci of operations supporting successful encoding. These differences can take one of two forms: contrasts can be employed that identify regions where the activity elicited by study items that go on to be successfully remembered is greater than it is for items that subsequently fail to be remembered. The result of such a contrast is what is typically meant by the term subsequent memory effect. Here, we also use the term "positive" subsequent memory effect, to distinguish these effects from "negative" subsequent memory effects, when remembered study items elicit *less* activity than items that fail to be accurately remembered.

## Positive subsequent memory effects

As was discussed above, according to the TAP principle episodic encoding is a "byproduct" of online processing. Therefore, no cognitive system is expected to be uniquely dedicated to memory encoding, and encoding-related cortical activity should be evident in the same regions that support the cognitive operations engaged during a given study task. In other words, cortical subsequent memory effects should vary in their locations according to the processes engaged during study. By contrast, given the centrality of the role of the hippocampus in capturing the patterns of cortical activity elicited by events as they are experienced, hippocampal subsequent memory effects should be evident regardless of the nature of the study processing. As described below, fMRI evidence supports these two predictions.

In a study by Otten and Rugg (2001), for example, subjects were cued on a trial-by-trial basis to make either a semantic (living/nonliving) or a phonological (odd/even number of syllables) judgment on a series of study words. For both tasks, items that were recognized with high confidence on a memory test undertaken some 15 minutes later elicited greater cortical activity during study than items that failed to be recognized. As is illustrated in Figure 5.2, the loci of these subsequent memory effects differed according to the study task. Whereas the effects associated with the semantic task were found primarily in medial and left inferior frontal cortex, effects for the

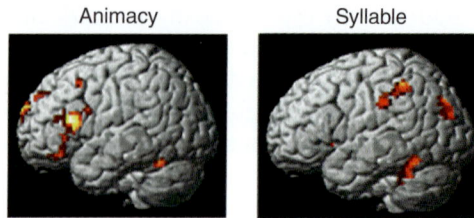

**Figure 5.2**   Data from Otten and Rugg (2001) illustrating the subsequent memory effects associated with words subjected to animacy judgments (left) and syllable judgments (right).

syllable task predominated in posterior cortical regions (see Otten, Henson, and Rugg, 2002; and Park, Uncapher, and Rugg, 2008, for similar findings). Importantly, and in accordance with the TAP principle, the subsequent memory effects overlapped with regions selectively engaged by each study task (as identified by contrasting the activity elicited by all items belonging to each task).

Evidence in support of the TAP principle is not confined to experiments where study processing was varied through a task manipulation. For example, Gottlieb and colleagues investigated the subsequent memory effects elicited during the encoding of pairs of study items that comprised a picture of an object and its name, presented either visually or auditorily (Gottlieb, Uncapher, and Rugg, 2010; see also Gottlieb *et al.*, 2012). The requirement on the subsequent memory test was to discriminate between studied and unstudied pictures and, for each picture judged as studied, to indicate whether its name had been presented visually or auditorily. It was thus possible to contrast the activity elicited on auditory and visual study trials according to whether successful recognition of the picture was accompanied by accurate memory for the modality of its name. Unsurprisingly, contrasts between the two classes of study trial revealed widespread regions where activity was either visually or auditorily selective. Crucially, modality-selective subsequent memory effects were evident in a subset of the same regions (Figure 5.3). As is evident from the figure, visually selective subsequent effects were identified in ventral temporal cortex whereas auditorily selective effects were evident in the superior temporal sulcus. Analogous findings were reported by Park and Rugg (2011) for the encoding of word–word and picture–picture associations.

Other findings in support of the TAP principle come from studies reporting dissociable subsequent memory effects for the different contextual features of a single study episode. In Uncapher, Otten, and Rugg (2006), subjects were scanned while they studied words presented in one of four possible locations and in one of four possible colors. A subsequent memory test required the subjects to discriminate studied from unstudied items and, for each recognized item, to recall the color and location in which it had been studied. Using as a baseline the study activity elicited by items that were later recognized but for which neither color nor location information were correctly recalled ("recognition-only" items), we investigated whether successful retrieval of either of the two contextual features was associated with distinct subsequent memory effects. In addition, we asked whether there were any brain regions where subsequent memory effects were specific for study items for which both features were later retrieved. The key findings are illustrated in Figure 5.4. Relative to items attracting recognition-only judgments, study items for which location was accurately

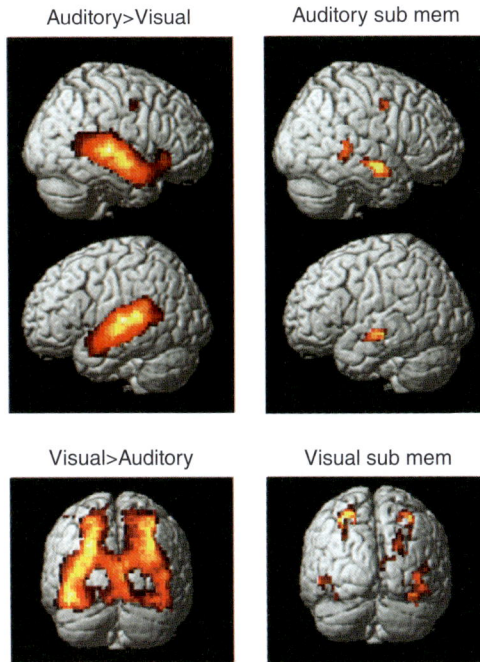

**Figure 5.3** Data from Gottlieb, Uncapher, and Rugg (2010). Left: outcome of the contrasts between study trials containing auditorily or visually presented words. Right: regions where subsequent memory effects for auditory (upper) or visual (lower) study trials overlapped with the relevant contrast between the two classes of study trial.

remembered elicited additional activity in retrosplenial cortex, whereas items whose color was remembered elicited greater study activity in posterior inferior temporal cortex. These regions have been implicated previously in the processing of location information and color knowledge respectively (Chao and Martin, 1999; Frings *et al.*, 2006; Kellenbach, Brett, and Patterson, 2001).

Figure 5.4 also illustrates a region – the right intraparietal sulcus (IPS) – where subsequent memory effects were uniquely associated with items for which both features were remembered on the later test. These effects indicate that conjoint encoding of the two features was not simply the result of the concurrent engagement of processes supporting memory for each feature alone. Rather, it appears that conjoint encoding engaged processes that operated across color and location information, perhaps binding the two features into a single perceptual representation (Cusack, 2005; Humphreys, 1998; for review, see Robertson, 2003). Uncapher, Otten, and Rugg (2006) suggested that the IPS subsequent memory effect in Figure 5.4 might reflect the benefit of allocating attention at the "object level" rather than to individual features of a stimulus event, allowing the features to be integrated in a unified perceptual representation, and hence more likely to be incorporated into a cohesive memory representation.

In a follow-up study we investigated whether the encoding of a contextual feature is sensitive to whether it is explicitly attended to during study (Uncapher and Rugg, 2009). Subjects were required to selectively attend either to color or to location information

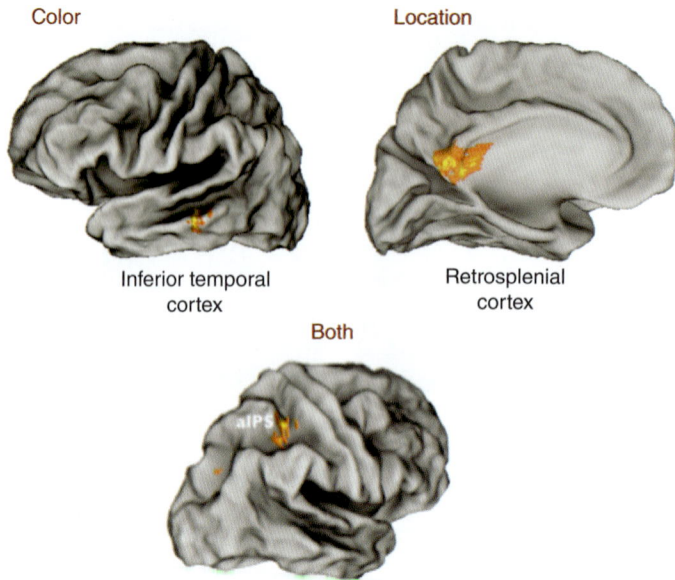

**Figure 5.4**   Data from Uncapher, Otten, and Rugg (2006) illustrating feature-selective and multi-featural subsequent memory effects. Top panel: subsequent memory effects (relative to correctly recognized study words for which no contextual feature could be accurately recalled) associated with accurate memory for the location (left) and color (right) of the study word. Bottom panel: subsequent memory effects in the right intraparietal sulcus (IPS) uniquely associated with accurate memory for both color and location.

(so  as to detect infrequent "targets" defined by a specific color or location, depending on the task) while incidentally encoding pictures of objects. If, as we had previously argued (Uncapher, Otten, and Rugg, 2006), feature-selective subsequent memory effects reflect the benefit to encoding that accrues when a feature is strongly attended, the effects should be greater when the feature was task-relevant (and hence attended) than when it was not. As is illustrated in Figure 5.5, this prediction was borne out.

As was outlined earlier, the hippocampus is held to be responsible for encoding the patterns of cortical activity engaged during the online processing of an event. Since attention modulates both the magnitude of cortical activity (Corbetta *et al.*, 1990) and the likelihood of later successful memory (e.g., Chun and Turk-Browne, 2007), we conjectured that hippocampal activity, like activity in the cortex, should be attentionally modulated. As can be seen in Figure 5.5, a region in the hippocampus did indeed respond selectively to the attended rather than the unattended feature. This finding suggests that one mechanism by which attention influences encoding is through the modulation of cortical–hippocampal interactions.

The findings reviewed in this section provide strong evidence for a central tenet of TAP – namely, that encoding is a "byproduct" of online processing. The findings suggest that the distinction between processes supporting the online processing of an event, and those supporting its encoding into memory, are not honored at the cortical level. Rather, cortical subsequent memory effects appear to reflect the amount of attentional resources allocated to (or, perhaps, captured by) a particular feature of an

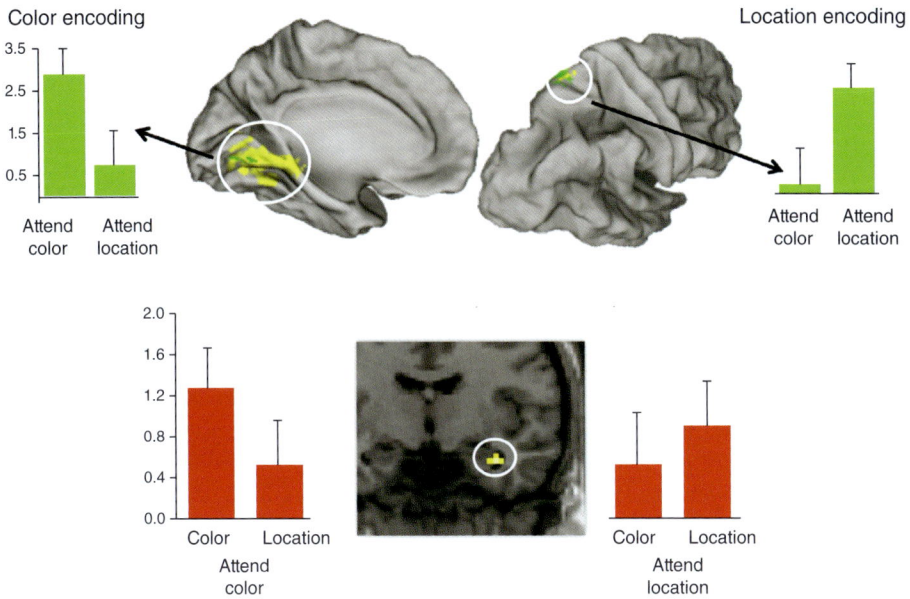

**Figure 5.5** Data from Uncapher and Rugg (2009). Upper: regions where color- (left) and location-selective (right) subsequent memory effects were modulated by the direction of attention. Lower: right hippocampal region where color and location subsequent memory effects were reciprocally modulated by attention.

event and, consequently, the likelihood that the cortical activity engaged by the processing of that feature will form part of a hippocampally mediated, offline representation of the event.

## Negative subsequent memory effects

As was noted earlier, "positive" subsequent memory effects can be accompanied by so-called "negative" effects, when later forgotten study events elicit higher activity than do events that are later remembered (Otten and Rugg, 2001; Wagner and Davachi, 2001). Negative effects are typically found in regions belonging to what is often referred to as the "default mode network": posterior and frontal midline cortex, along with inferior parietal and dorsolateral prefrontal regions. The default mode network is so named because its constituent regions exhibit higher activity during task-independent periods (sometimes referred to as a "resting" state) than when an externally imposed task is being performed (Shulman *et al.*, 1997; for reviews, see Buckner, Andrews-Hanna, and Schacter, 2008; and Gusnard and Raichle, 2001).

From the time they were first identified, it has been proposed that negative subsequent memory effects reflect competition for cognitive resources between study events and elements of the internal and external environment, such as task-irrelevant thoughts or stimulus features (e.g., Wagner and Davachi, 2001). Such a view is in keeping with the notion that default mode activity reflects the allocation of processing resources toward internal cognitive events at the expense of events originating from the environment (such as the study events in an encoding experiment). Relatively little research, however, has been directed toward a more mechanistic understanding of these effects, or to attempts to dissociate them anatomically.

Cabeza (2008) suggested that negative subsequent memory effects may reflect an encoding impairment caused by the reflexive ("bottom-up") capture of attention by task-irrelevant information. This suggestion received support from a review of studies reporting subsequent memory effects in lateral parietal cortex (Uncapher and Wagner, 2009), a region heavily implicated in the control of attention (Corbetta, Patel, and Shulman, 2008). Uncapher and Wagner reported that negative subsequent memory effects are localized exclusively to ventral parietal cortex, with the majority of the effects falling in the vicinity of the temporoparietal junction (TPJ), a region held to be a key component of a network mediating the bottom-up capture of attention (Corbetta, Patel, and Shulman, 2008). Negative subsequent memory effects were also evident, however, in the adjacent angular gyrus, a component of the default mode network (Buckner, Andrews-Hanna, and Schacter, 2008). These observations suggest that negative subsequent memory effects are unlikely to reflect the modulation of a single, functionally homogeneous network. Rather, the loci of the effects suggest that there are at least two mechanisms by which encoding can be impaired: attentional capture and the failure to disengage fully from "default" (task-independent) cognitive processing.

In a test of the attentional capture hypothesis, Uncapher, Hutchinson, and Wagner (2011) manipulated top-down and bottom-up attention within a subsequent memory paradigm using a Posner cueing procedure. Subjects were cued on a trial-by-trial basis to focus their attention on one of two locations, in anticipation of an upcoming study item. The majority of the items (82%) appeared in the cued location, forcing items appearing in the uncued location to gain attention through a "bottom-up" re-orienting process (Posner, 1980). Thus, bottom-up attention effects could be identified by contrasting activity elicited by objects appearing in uncued relative to cued locations, a contrast that revealed robust effects in the TPJ bilaterally. Crucially, negative subsequent memory effects associated with correctly cued study items overlapped these attentional effects, strongly supporting the proposal that negative subsequent memory effects in this region reflect impairment of encoding arising from the capture of attention by task-irrelevant input. The nature of this input – for example, whether it can take the form of both internal and external events – remains to be characterized.

## Retrieval

In this section we review evidence for the existence of a network of "core" regions where activity is enhanced when a retrieval cue elicits recollection of a prior event. We then go on to discuss studies addressing the question of whether any neural correlates of recollection are content-sensitive and whether, as would be predicted from the theoretical framework outlined previously, these correlates reflect reinstatement of activity elicited during encoding. We focus on effects associated with successful recollection, making only passing reference to work on retrieval cue or post-retrieval processing (Rugg and Wilding, 2000). Thus, we concentrate on studies contrasting activity elicited by retrieval cues (mainly, but not exclusively, recognition memory test items) according to whether the cues were or were not associated with recollection of details of the study episode, as this is operationalized either by successful retrieval of contextual (source) information or by phenomenal report (a "remember" judgment).

As in the case of studies of encoding, the earliest functional neuroimaging studies of retrieval (see Rugg, Otten, and Henson, 2002, for review) employed blocked designs and hence did not directly contrast activity elicited by recollected and unrecollected test items. Two of the earliest event-related studies were those of Henson *et al.* (1999) and Eldridge *et al.* (2000). In both studies the authors employed the remember/know (R/K) test procedure and contrasted the activity elicited by correctly recognized items according to whether the items were endorsed as recollected or as familiar only. Among the regions where activity was enhanced for recollected items were the hippocampus, the posterior cingulate, and lateral parietal cortex. Numerous subsequent studies employing either variants of the R/K procedure or tests of source memory reported similar results, and also identified regions additional to those reported in the early studies. Although the findings across individual studies differ in detail, the consensus is that successful recollection is consistently associated with enhanced activity in the MTL, especially the hippocampus and parahippocampal cortex, along with retrosplenial, posterior cingulate, medial prefrontal, and ventral posterior parietal cortex (angular gyrus) (Figure 5.6).

We (Hayama, Vilberg, and Rugg, 2012; Johnson and Rugg, 2007; Rugg and Vilberg, 2013) have proposed that these regions form part of a "core" recollection network engaged when recollection is successful regardless of how memory is cued, or the nature of the recollected content. Consistent with this proposal, the same regions identified as recollection-sensitive in studies employing variants of recognition memory tests have also been identified in studies of cued recall (e.g., Hayama, Vilberg, and Rugg, 2012; Okada, Vilberg, and Rugg, 2012; Schott *et al.*, 2005), a memory test held to rely heavily on recollection. In a recent study from our laboratory, cued recall and source memory tests were employed in combination (Hayama, Vilberg, and Rugg, 2012). Subjects first studied a series of words presented on the left or right side of a display monitor. Test items comprised three-letter word stems, with the requirement

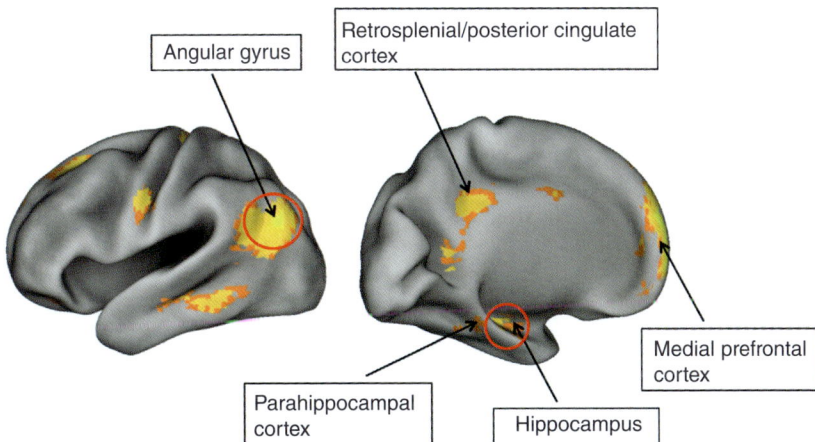

**Figure 5.6** The putative core recollection network. The outcome of the contrast between correctly recognized test words endorsed as "remember" or "know" in an unpublished study (*n* = 19) by Wang and Rugg. The words had been studied either as pictures or as words in the context of two different encoding tasks. Illustrated are regions where recollection was associated with enhanced activity at test regardless of the encoding condition.

to use each stem to recall a studied word. When recall was successful, the word was to be named along with its study location. When recall failed, the first word brought to mind by the cue was to be named. Relative to stems that elicited unsuccessful recall, stems associated with successful recall elicited enhanced activity in all of the components of the putative "core" recollection network. Importantly, recall effects in three of the regions belonging to the network – left ventral parietal, retrosplenial, and parahippocampal cortex – were enhanced when the associated source memory judgment was accurate rather than inaccurate, suggesting that these regions were responding to the amount of information recollected rather than to its content.

The functional significance of recollection-related activity in the different regions constituting the putative core network remains to be established. It seems unlikely to be a coincidence, however, that each of the cortical components of the network exhibits structural and functional connectivity with the hippocampus (Aggleton, 2012). As was discussed previously, the hippocampus is held to play a pivotal role in episodic memory by virtue of its capacity to store patterns of cortical activity elicited during the online processing of an event (and hence to encode associations between the different components of the event) and later, in response to an appropriate retrieval cue, to reinstate those patterns. Therefore it is unsurprising that the hippocampus becomes active when a retrieval cue elicits successful recollection.

The functional roles of other regions of the putative recollection network remain to be established. Because of the density of its connections with the hippocampus, and the memory impairments that accompany lesions to the region, retrosplenial cortex has been proposed to be a component of an "extended hippocampal system" (Aggleton, 2012). Recent evidence suggests that, like parahippocampal cortex, both this region and the medial prefrontal cortex (mPFC, which shares connections with the hippocampus and parahippocampal and retrosplenial cortices; Aggleton, 2012) play a role in the processing of contextual information (Kveraga *et al.*, 2011).

Unlike retrosplenial cortex and mPFC, there is little evidence other than that from neuroimaging studies to implicate the angular gyrus in episodic memory. Evidence from functional connectivity and diffusion-tensor imaging (DTI) tractography studies indicates that this region is interconnected with the hippocampus and with parahippocampal and retrosplenial/posterior cingulate cortices (Sestieri *et al.*, 2011; Uddin *et al.*, 2010), suggesting that it might be part of a common functional network. On the basis of fMRI findings, several proposals have been advanced regarding the functional significance of recollection-related activity in the angular gyrus. According to one idea (Cabeza, Ciaramelli, and Moscovitch, 2012), the sensitivity of the region to recollection reflects its role in "bottom-up" attentional re-orienting. By this account, recollection is a salient internal event that triggers the re-direction of attention from a retrieval cue toward the contents of retrieval (as was noted earlier, however, bottom-up attention has usually been linked with the TPJ rather than the angular gyrus). We (Vilberg and Rugg, 2008) have proposed that the angular gyrus might contribute to the representation of recollected information, perhaps acting as a component of the "episodic buffer" posited to act as an interface between episodic memory and executive processes (Baddeley, 2000). A related proposal is that the region acts as a "convergence zone," binding the different features of an episode into an integrated representation (Shimamura, 2011).

In our view, there are two findings that favor a representational rather than an attentional account of recollection-related activity in the angular gyrus. First, recollection-related activity in the region covaries with the amount of information retrieved, whether operationalized by subjective report (Vilberg and Rugg, 2007), an encoding manipulation (Vilberg and Rugg, 2009), or confidence of source memory judgments (Yu, Johnson, and Rugg, 2012). Whereas this result is clearly consistent with the proposal that the angular gyrus contributes to the representation of recollected information, it is less obvious how it can be reconciled with the idea that the region supports a re-orienting process triggered by the occurrence of recollection (the attentional account). The second finding comes from a recent study that investigated the time-course of recollection-related activity (Vilberg and Rugg, 2012). In this study, subjects first studied a series of word–picture pairs. Test items comprised studied and unstudied words under the requirement to retrieve the picture associated with each studied word, and to hold it in mind until cued to make one of three possible judgments about the picture. Crucially, the period over which the retrieved picture had to be maintained varied unpredictably between 2 and 8 seconds. The key contrast was between activity elicited by studied test words according to whether their associates were successfully versus unsuccessfully retrieved. As is illustrated in Figure 5.7,

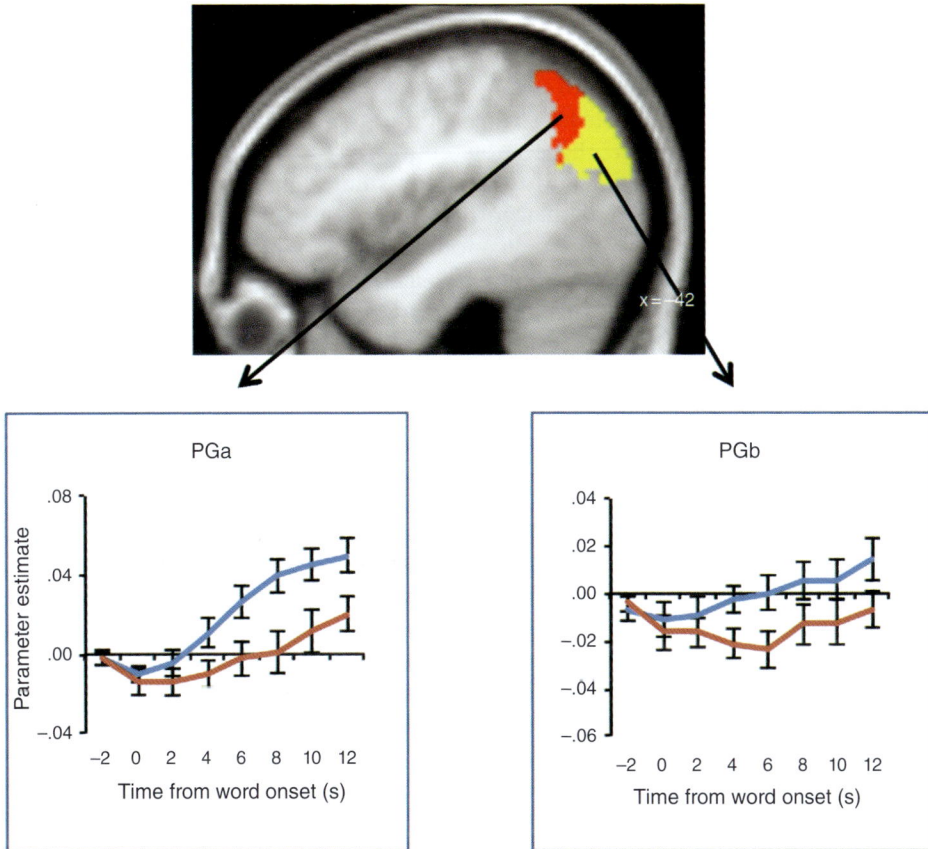

**Figure 5.7** Data from Vilberg and Rugg (2012) illustrating sustained recollection-related activity in the left anterior (PGa) and posterior (PGb) angular gyrus. Blue line: time-course of activity associated with test words eliciting successful recollection of the pictures with which they were paired at study. Red line: activity elicited by test words that failed to elicit successful recollection.

recollection-related activity in the angular gyrus was sustained across the delay interval, as would be expected of a region contributing to the representation of the recollected information. Interestingly, a different pattern was observed in the hippocampus and other members of the putative recollection network. Here, recollection-related activity was transient and unaffected by the delay manipulation. This finding is consistent with a role for these regions in the reinstatement of episodic information, but not in its maintenance.

In summary, although the functional roles of its different components remain to be elucidated, current evidence suggests that successful recollection is associated with the engagement of a network of regions that are largely insensitive to how recollection is cued, or to the nature of the recollected information. We assume that the network interacts with content-sensitive cortical regions (see below) to instantiate consciously accessible episodic representations.

## Content-sensitive recollection effects

In addition to the generic recollection effects discussed above, fMRI studies have also identified neural correlates of recollection that vary according to the content of the retrieved episode. These studies were largely motivated by the prediction of overlap between patterns of neural activity elicited during the encoding of an event and its subsequent recollection (see the section entitled *Theoretical framework*, above). Consistent with this prediction, in several early studies employing blocked experimental designs it was reported that cortical regions where activity differed while encoding one stimulus class rather than another were also differentially active during later memory tests for the stimuli (e.g., Nyberg *et al.*, 2000; Vaidya *et al.*, 2002). However, whereas the findings from these studies are consistent with the cortical reinstatement hypothesis, they are inconclusive because of the possibility that the content-sensitive retrieval effects reflected processes engaged prior to rather than after successful retrieval (cf. Polyn *et al.*, 2005).

Findings from event-related fMRI studies provide stronger evidence for overlap between encoding- and recollection-related activity (e.g., Gottfried *et al.*, 2004; Kahn, Davachi, and Wagner, 2004; Skinner, Grady, and Fernandes, 2010; Wheeler, Petersen, and Buckner, 2000; Woodruff *et al.*, 2005; for review, see Danker and Anderson, 2010). However, in several of these studies the critical items were presented on multiple study trials, raising the possibility that the effects reflect a form of learning distinct from that supporting memory for unique events. Furthermore, evidence of overlap between encoding and recollection effects in the majority of these studies was in the form of a single association (i.e., only one class of study items was employed, precluding the demonstration of recollection effects that dissociated according to recollected content), raising the possibility that the findings reflected content-independent differences in the activity elicited by recollected and unrecollected test items. Two studies employing trial-unique study presentations reported the more compelling pattern of a crossover interaction in the engagement of different cortical regions according to the nature of the recollected information (Kahn, Davachi, and Wagner, 2004; Woodruff *et al.*, 2005). However, in neither study was encoding-related activity obtained. Instead, both studies identified content-sensitive recollection effects in regions that had been reported in prior studies to exhibit material-specific activity.

A study from our laboratory subjected the cortical reinstatement hypothesis to a more stringent test (Johnson and Rugg, 2007). In one encoding condition, words were superimposed on landscape scenes under the requirement to imagine where in the scene the object denoted by the word might be found. In the other condition, words were presented against a blank background with the requirement to covertly generate a sentence that incorporated the word. Memory for the words was later tested with the R/K procedure, allowing identification of test items that were accompanied by recollection of qualitative details about the study episode. fMRI data were acquired during both the study and test phases, permitting a direct comparison between encoding- and retrieval-related neural activity. Unsurprisingly, the two classes of study trial elicited very different patterns of neural activity. A subset of the regions where study activity differed across the encoding tasks also exhibited differential activity at test, with the activity varying according to the encoding history of the recollected words (see Figure 5.8). The overlap between content-sensitive neural activity at encoding and test constitutes evidence that the pattern of cortical activity engaged during encoding was partially reinstated during retrieval. It is currently unclear why reinstatement was evident in only some of the regions active during encoding, and what factors determine the regions where reinstatement effects are evident.

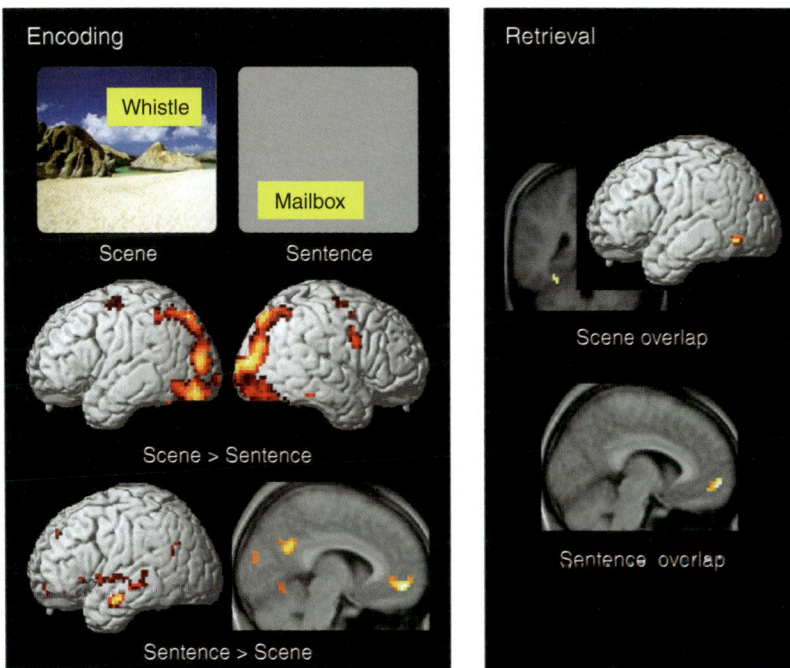

**Figure 5.8**   Data from Johnson and Rugg (2007). (Left) Regions where activity differed during the encoding of words in the scene task compared to the sentence-generation task. (Right) Regions where recollection-related activity (defined by the contrast between items endorsed as "remember" versus "know") was both greater for words studied in one of the encoding tasks than in the other, and also overlapped with the corresponding contrast between the two encoding tasks.

Reinstatement of encoding-related activity during episodic retrieval has also been investigated using multi-voxel pattern analysis, or MVPA (Johnson *et al.*, 2009; Kuhl *et al.*, 2011; Kuhl, Bainbridge, and Chun, 2012; McDuff, Frankel, and Norman, 2009; for reviews, see Rissman and Wagner, 2012; see also Chapters 1, 2, and 6). This method allows assessment of the similarity between patterns of fMRI activity distributed across a population of voxels even when effects at the single-voxel level are not statistically significant or spatially contiguous. In one common implementation of MVPA, a pattern classifier is "trained" to optimally discriminate between the patterns of activity associated with different classes of experimental trials in a predefined population of voxels (Norman *et al.*, 2006). The classifier can then be applied to a new sample of trials to assess the degree to which the new trials contain similarly distinct patterns of activity across the same voxels. This approach lends itself naturally to the investigation of cortical reinstatement: if retrieval is associated with the reinstatement of patterns of activity elicited during encoding, a classifier trained to discriminate between different classes of study trials should also be able to discriminate between the retrieval activity elicited by test items belonging to the different study conditions.

Johnson *et al.* (2009) employed this logic to investigate the relationship between the reinstatement of study activity and the subjective experiences of recollection and familiarity. Subjects studied words in one of three tasks: imagining an artist drawing the object denoted by a study word, generating different functions for the object, or covertly pronouncing the word backwards (also see McDuff, Frankel, and Norman, 2009). In the subsequent memory test, the requirement was either to endorse the word as recollected (a remember response), or if recollection failed, to judge using a four-point confidence scale (from confident old to confident new) whether the word had been studied. Using the fMRI data from the study phase, a classifier was trained to distinguish between patterns of activity associated with the three study tasks. The classifier was then employed to categorize data from the test phase, and the classifier's accuracy in identifying the study task associated with each test item served as an index of the extent to which encoding-related neural activity was reinstated. Consistent with our previous results (Johnson and Rugg, 2007), robust reinstatement effects were evident for correctly recognized test words endorsed as being recollected. Importantly, however, reinstatement was not exclusively associated with recollection. Reinstatement was also evident (albeit more weakly and in fewer cortical regions) for unrecollected words that were endorsed as having been studied with high confidence. These findings may constitute evidence for a recollection signal that varies continuously in strength (Wixted, 2007; Wixted and Mickes, 2010). By this account, the relationship between the phenomenological experience of recollection and the retrieval of qualitative information about a study episode (as indexed by cortical reinstatement) is not one-to-one. Rather, the "strength" of recollection must exceed some criterion level to elicit a "remember" judgment.

In two more recent studies, Kuhl and colleagues (2011, 2012) used MVPA to investigate the relationship between cortical reinstatement and recollection. These authors were interested in how successful retrieval of a "targeted" episode is influenced by reinstatement of activity associated with another "competing" study episode. Subjects undertook a paired-associate learning task in which, over the course of the experiment, words switched associations between two different classes of images (faces and scenes). Memory was later probed for the more recently learned associate while a pattern classifier was used to assess the relative levels of reinstatement of face and scene content. In both studies, the ability to recollect details about the more recent memory was inversely related to classifier accuracy for the originally learned class of associate, suggesting that neural activity for the competing episode was reinstated (also see Öztekin and Badre, 2011). In the second study, Kuhl, Bainbridge, and Chun (2012) extended the previous results by demonstrating that concurrent reinstatement of "competing" study episodes was accompanied by activity in anterior cingulate cortex, perhaps reflecting the engagement of control processes that served to resolve the interference between the two concurrently activated memory representations.

A more recent study still (Ritchey *et al.*, 2013) constitutes an interesting advance over the reinstatement studies reviewed above. In the prior studies, reinstatement effects were investigated by contrasting activity that was common to a set of test items that shared a similar encoding history (e.g., items that had been paired with scenes, as opposed to sentences in the study of Johnson and Rugg, 2007). Ritchey and colleagues addressed the question of whether cortical reinstatement effects could be detected at the level of individual items (see also Staresina *et al.*, 2012; Xue *et al.*, 2010). Subjects studied a series of trial-unique scenes, and subsequently discriminated between studied and new items using the same test procedure that was employed by Johnson *et al.* (2009; see above). The across-voxel similarity in the patterns of activity elicited by each scene during the study and test phases was computed in numerous regions of interest that extended over much of the cortex. In several of these regions the similarity index was greater for individual scenes that were recollected or confidently endorsed as old than it was for scenes misclassified as new. Furthermore, the amount of study–test similarity correlated positively with hippocampal activity. These findings provide additional support for the idea that episodic retrieval involves the hippocampally mediated reinstatement of patterns of activity elicited when the retrieved event was originally experienced (Figure 5.1).

We conclude this section by mentioning an outstanding issue concerning the findings described above. The issue arises because of the relatively poor temporal resolution of the fMRI blood-oxygen-level-dependent (BOLD) signal. As a consequence, it is difficult to specify the onset of recollection-related BOLD responses with sufficient accuracy to rule out two alternative accounts of the reinstatement effects we have described above. Whereas we (along with other researchers) have assumed that these effects directly reflect the consequences of successful recollection, it is also possible that the effects reflect processes operating "pre-" or "post-" retrieval. According to the first of these accounts, the reinstatement effects reflect the benefit to retrieval that comes from a high level of processing overlap between study processing and the processing accorded a retrieval cue (cf. Morris *et al.*, 1977). Thus, effects held to reflect the reinstatement of encoded content actually come about because of the relationship between cue processing and the likelihood of successful retrieval. By the second account, reinstatement effects reflect not the initial retrieval of episodic information, but its downstream elaboration and maintenance. Adjudicating between our preferred account and these two alternatives will benefit from the employment of methods – such as ERPs and magnetoencephalography (MEG) – with higher temporal resolution than fMRI (see Johnson and Rugg, 2007, for an initial step in this direction).

## Concluding Comments

The findings from fMRI studies of episodic encoding and retrieval are remarkably congruent with the two major theoretical frameworks – TAP and cortical reinstatement – outlined at the beginning of the chapter. In keeping with those frameworks, there is little evidence for a specialized encoding network at the cortical level: instead, the enhancement of cortical activity associated with successful encoding (subsequent memory effects) is found in some of the same regions that are engaged by the online processing demands of the study event, and these effects are accompanied by enhanced activity in the hippocampus. By contrast, successful recollection is associated with engagement not only of the hippocampus and a subset of the cortical regions that were active during encoding, but also with other regions – including ventral posterior parietal cortex – where activity is enhanced regardless of the nature of the retrieved content.

These findings shed significant light on the cognitive neuroscience of encoding, retrieval, and their interrelationship, while leaving many questions unresolved. Perhaps the most intriguing of these concerns how the information represented in distributed patterns of "reinstated" cortical activity becomes bound into a coherent, consciously accessible representation of a prior experience. We conjecture that the answer to this question will be more apparent when there is a fuller understanding of the functions of the generic recollection network illustrated in Figure 5.6.

## Acknowledgments

Preparation of this chapter, and much of the research described in it, was supported by NIMH grants R01MH072966 and R01MH074528.

## References

Aggleton, J.P. (2012). Multiple anatomical systems embedded within the primate medial temporal lobe: implications for hippocampal function. *Neuroscience and Biobehavioral Reviews*, 36 (7), 1579–1596.

Alvarez, P., and Squire, L.R. (1994). Memory consolidation and the medial temporal lobe: a simple network model. *Proceedings of the National Academy of Sciences of the USA*, 91 (15), 7041–7045.

Baddeley, A. (2000). The episodic buffer: a new component of working memory? *Trends in Cognitive Sciences*, 4 (11), 417–423.

Bartlett, F.C. (1932). *Remembering: A Study in Experimental and Social Psychology*. Cambridge: Cambridge University Press.

Bransford, J.D., and Franks, J.J. (1971). The abstraction of linguistic ideas. *Cognitive Psychology* 2 (4), 331–350.

Brewer, W. (1987). Schemas versus mental models in human memory. In *Modelling Cognition* (ed. P. Morris). Chichester, UK: John Wiley & Sons, Ltd, pp. 187–197.

Brewer, W.F., and Treyens, J.C. (1981). Role of schemata in memory for places. *Cognitive Psychology*, 13 (2), 207–230.

Buckner, R.L., Andrews-Hanna, J.R., and Schacter, D.L. (2008). The brain's default network. *Annals of the New York Academy of Sciences*, 1124 (1), 1–38.

Cabeza, R. (2008). Role of parietal regions in episodic memory retrieval: the dual attentional processes hypothesis. *Neuropsychologia*, 46 (7), 1813–1827.

Cabeza, R., Ciaramelli, E., and Moscovitch, M. (2012). Cognitive contributions of the ventral parietal cortex: an integrative theoretical account. *Trends in Cognitive Sciences*, 16 (6), 338–352.

Chao, L.L., and Martin, A. (1999). Cortical regions associated with perceiving, naming, and knowing about colors. *Journal of Cognitive Neuroscience*, 11 (1), 25–35.

Chun, M.M., and Turk-Browne, N.B. (2007). Interactions between attention and memory. *Current pinion in Neurobiology*, 17 (2), 177–184.

Corbetta, M., Miezin, F.M., Dobmeyer, S., *et al.* (1990). Attentional modulation of neural processing of shape, color, and velocity in humans. *Science*, 248 (4962), 1556–1559.

Corbetta, M., Patel, G., and Shulman, G.L. (2008). The reorienting system of the human brain: from environment to theory of mind. *Neuron*, 58 (3), 306–324.

Cusack, R. (2005). The intraparietal sulcus and perceptual organization. *Journal of Cognitive Neuroscience*, 17 (4), 641–651.

Danker, J.F., and Anderson, J.R. (2010). The ghosts of brain states past: remembering reactivates the brain regions engaged during encoding. *Psychological Bulletin*, 136 (1), 87–102.

Davachi, L. (2006). Item, context and relational episodic encoding in humans. *Current Opinion in Neurobiology*, 16 (6), 693–700.

Diana, R.A., Yonelinas, A.P., and Ranganath, C. (2007). Imaging recollection and familiarity in the medial temporal lobe: a three-component model. *Trends in Cognitive Sciences*, 11 (9), 379–386.

Dudai, Y. (2004). The neurobiology of consolidations, or, how stable is the engram? *Annual Review of Psychology*, 55, 51–86.

Eldridge, L.L., Knowlton, B.J., Furmanski, C.S., *et al.* (2000). Remembering episodes: a selective role for the hippocampus during retrieval. *Nature Neuroscience*, 3 (11), 1149–1152.

Fisher, R.P., and Craik, F.I. (1977). Interaction between encoding and retrieval operations in cued recall. *Journal of Experimental Psychology: Human Learning and Memory*, 3 (6), 701–711.

Frings, L., Wagner, K., Quiske, A., *et al.* (2006). Precuneus is involved in allocentric spatial location encoding and recognition. *Experimental Brain Research*, 173 (4), 661–672.

Gottfried, J.A., Smith, A.P., Rugg, M.D. and Dolan, R.J. (2004). Remembrance of odors past: human olfactory cortex in cross-modal recognition memory. *Neuron*, 42 (4), 687–695.

Gottlieb, L.J., Uncapher, M.R., and Rugg, M.D. (2010). Dissociation of the neural correlates of visual and auditory contextual encoding. *Neuropsychologia*, 48 (1), 137–144.

Gottlieb, L.J., Wong, J., de Chastelaine, M., and Rugg, M.D. (2012). Neural correlates of the encoding of multimodal contextual features. *Learning and Memory*, 19 (12), 605–614.

Gusnard, D.A., and Raichle, M.E. (2001). Searching for a baseline: functional imaging and the resting human brain. *Nature Reviews Neuroscience*, 2 (10), 685–694.

Hayama, H.R., Vilberg, K.L., and Rugg, M.D. (2012). Overlap between the neural correlates of cued recall and source memory: evidence for a generic recollection network? *Journal of Cognitive Neuroscience*, 24 (5), 1127–1137.

Henson, R.N., Rugg, M., Shallice, T., *et al.* (1999). Recollection and familiarity in recognition memory: an event-related functional magnetic resonance imaging study. *Journal of Neuroscience*, 19 (10), 3962–3972.

Humphreys, G.W. (1998). Neural representation of objects in space: a dual coding account. *Philosophical Transactions of the Royal Society of London, Series B: Biological Sciences*, 353 (1373), 1341–1351.

Johnson, J.D., McDuff, S.G., Rugg, M.D., and Norman, K.A. (2009). Recollection, familiarity, and cortical reinstatement: a multivoxel pattern analysis. *Neuron*, 63 (5), 697–708.

Johnson, J.D., and Rugg, M.D. (2007). Recollection and the reinstatement of encoding-related cortical activity. *Cerebral Cortex*, 17 (11), 2507–2515.

Johnson, M.K., Hashtroudi, S., and Lindsay, D.S. (1993). Source monitoring. *Psychological Bulletin*, 114 (1), 3–26.

Kahn, I., Davachi, L., and Wagner, A.D. (2004). Functional-neuroanatomic correlates of recollection: implications for models of recognition memory. *Journal of Neuroscience*, 24 (17), 4172–4180.

Kapur, S., Craik, F., Tulving, E., *et al.* (1994). Neuroanatomical correlates of encoding in episodic memory: levels of processing effect. *Proceedings of the National Academy of Sciences of the USA*, 91 (6), 2008–2011.

Kellenbach, M.L., Brett, M., and Patterson, K. (2001). Large, colorful, or noisy? Attribute- and modality-specific activations during retrieval of perceptual attribute knowledge. *Cognitive, Affective, and Behavioral Neuroscience*, 1 (3), 207–221.

Kim, H. (2010). Dissociating the roles of the default-mode, dorsal, and ventral networks in episodic memory retrieval. *NeuroImage*, 50 (4), 1648–1657.

Kim, H. (2011). Neural activity that predicts subsequent memory and forgetting: a meta-analysis of 74 fMRI studies. *NeuroImage*, 54 (3), 2446–2461.

Kolers, P.A. (1973). Remembering operations. *Memory and Cognition*, 1 (3), 347–355.

Kuhl, B.A., Bainbridge, W.A., and Chun, M.M. (2012). Neural reactivation reveals mechanisms for updating memory. *Journal of Neuroscience*, 32 (10), 3453–3461.

Kuhl, B.A., Rissman, J., Chun, M.M., and Wagner, A.D. (2011). Fidelity of neural reactivation reveals competition between memories. *Proceedings of the National Academy of Sciences of the USA*, 108 (14), 5903–5908.

Kveraga, K., Ghuman, A.S., Kassam, K.S., *et al.* (2011). Early onset of neural synchronization in the contextual associations network. *Proceedings of the National Academy of Sciences of the USA*, 108 (8), 3389–3394.

Loftus, E.F., and Palmer, J.C. (1974). Reconstruction of automobile destruction: an example of the interaction between language and memory. *Journal of Verbal Learning and Verbal Behavior*, 13 (5), 585–589.

Marr, D. (1971). Simple memory: a theory for archicortex. *Philosophical Transactions of the Royal Society of London, Series B: Biological Sciences*, 262 (841), 23–81.

McDuff, S.G., Frankel, H.C. and Norman, K.A. (2009). Multivoxel pattern analysis reveals increased memory targeting and reduced use of retrieved details during single-agenda source monitoring. *Journal of Neuroscience*, 29 (2), 508–516.

Montaldi, D., Spencer, T.J., Roberts, N., and Mayes, A.R. (2006). The neural system that mediates familiarity memory. *Hippocampus*, 16 (5), 504–520.

Morris, C.D., Bransford, J.D., and Franks, J.J. (1977). Levels of processing versus transfer appropriate processing. *Journal of Verbal Learning and Verbal Behavior*, 16 (5), 519–533.

Moscovitch, M. (1992). Memory and working with memory: a component process model based on modules and central systems. *Journal of Cognitive Neuroscience*, 4, 257–267.

Nairne, J.S. (2002). The myth of the encoding–retrieval match. *Memory*, 10 (5–6), 389–395.

Norman, K.A., and O'Reilly, R.C. (2003). Modeling hippocampal and neocortical contributions to recognition memory: a complementary-learning-systems approach. *Psychological Review*, 110 (4), 611–646.

Norman, K.A., Polyn, S.M., Detre, G.J., and Haxby, J.V. (2006). Beyond mind-reading: multivoxel pattern analysis of fMRI data. *Trends in Cognitive Sciences*, 10 (9), 424–430.

Nyberg, L., Habib, R., McIntosh, A.R., and Tulving, E. (2000). Reactivation of encoding-related brain activity during memory retrieval. *Proceedings of the National Academy of Sciences of the USA*, 97 (20), 11120–11124.

Okada, K., Vilberg, K.L., and Rugg, M.D. (2012). Comparison of the neural correlates of retrieval success in tests of cued recall and recognition memory. *Human Brain Mapping*, 33 (3), 523–533.

Otten, L.J., Henson, R.N., and Rugg, M.D. (2002). State-related and item-related neural correlates of successful memory encoding. *Nature Neuroscience*, 5 (12), 1339–1344.

Otten, L.J., and Rugg, M.D. (2001). Task-dependency of the neural correlates of episodic encoding as measured by fMRI. *Cerebral Cortex*, 11 (12), 1150–1160.

Öztekin, I., and Badre, D. (2011). Distributed patterns of brain activity that lead to forgetting. *Frontiers in Human Neuroscience*, 5. doi: 10.3389/fnhum.2011.00086.

Park, H., and Rugg, M.D. (2011). Neural correlates of encoding within- and across-domain inter-item associations. *Journal of Cognitive Neuroscience*, 23 (9), 2533–2543.

Park, H., Uncapher, M.R., and Rugg, M.D. (2008). Effects of study task on the neural correlates of source encoding. *Learning and Memory*, 15 (6), 417–425.

Polyn, S.M., Natu, V.S., Cohen, J.D., and Norman, K.A. (2005). Category-specific cortical activity precedes retrieval during memory search. *Science*, 310 (5756), 1963–1966.

Posner, M.I. (1980). Orienting of attention. *Quarterly Journal of Experimental Psychology*, 32 (1), 3–25.

Rissman, J., and Wagner, A.D. (2012). Distributed representations in memory: insights from functional brain imaging. *Annual Review of Psychology*, 63, 101–128.

Ritchey, M., Wing, E.A., LaBar, K.S., and Cabeza, R. (2013). Neural similarity between encoding and retrieval is related to memory via hippocampal interactions. *Cerebral Cortex*, 23(12), 2818–2828. doi: 10.1093/cercor/bhs258.

Robertson, L.C. (2003). Binding, spatial attention and perceptual awareness. *Nature Reviews Neuroscience*, 4 (2), 93–102.

Roediger, H., and Guynn, M. (1996). Retrieval processes. In *Human Memory* (ed. E. Bjork and R. Bjork). San Diego, CA: Academic Press, pp. 197–236.

Roediger, H., Weldon, M., and Challis, B. (1989). Explaining dissociations between implicit and explicit measures of retention: a processing account. In *Varieties of Memory and Consciousness: Essays in Honor of Endel Tulving* (ed. H. Roediger and F.I.M. Craik). Hillsdale, NJ: Erlbaum, pp. 3–41.

Roediger, H.L., Gallo, D.A., and Geraci, L. (2002). Processing approaches to cognition: the impetus from the levels-of-processing framework. *Memory*, 10 (5–6), 319–332.

Rolls, E.T. (2000). Memory systems in the brain. *Annual Review of Psychology*, 51 (1), 599–630.

Rugg, M.D., Cox, C.J., Doyle, M.C., and Wells, T. (1995). Event-related potentials and the recollection of low and high frequency words. *Neuropsychologia*, 33 (4), 471–484.

Rugg, M.D., Otten, L.J., and Henson, R.N.A. (2002). The neural basis of episodic memory: evidence from functional neuroimaging. *Philosophical Transactions of the Royal Society of London, Series B: Biological Sciences*, 357 (1424), 1097–1110.

Rugg, M.D., and Vilberg, K.L. (2013). Brain networks underlying episodic memory retrieval. *Current Opinion in Neurobiology*, 23 (2), 255–260.

Rugg, M.D., and Wilding, E.L. (2000). Retrieval processing and episodic memory. *Trends in Cognitive Sciences*, 4 (3), 108–115.

Sanquist, T.F., Rohrbaugh, J.W., Syndulko, K., and Lindsley, D.B. (1980). Electrocortical signs of levels of processing: perceptual analysis and recognition memory. *Psychophysiology*, 17 (6), 568–576.

Schacter, D.L. (2002). *The Seven Sins of Memory: How the Mind Forgets and Remembers*. New York, NY: Houghton Mifflin.

Schacter, D.L., Norman, K.A., and Koutstaal, W. (1998). The cognitive neuroscience of constructive memory. *Annual Review of Psychology*, 49, 289–318.

Schott, B.H., Henson, R.N., Richardson-Klavehn, A., *et al.* (2005). Redefining implicit and explicit memory: the functional neuroanatomy of priming, remembering, and control of retrieval. *Proceedings of the National Academy of Sciences of the USA*, 102 (4), 1257–1262.

Sestieri, C., Corbetta, M., Romani, G.L., and Shulman, G.L. (2011). Episodic memory retrieval, parietal cortex, and the default mode network: functional and topographic analyses. *Journal of Neuroscience*, 31 (12), 4407–4420.

Shastri, L. (2002). Episodic memory and cortico-hippocampal interactions. *Trends in Cognitive Sciences*, 6 (4), 162–168.

Shimamura, A.P. (2011). Episodic retrieval and the cortical binding of relational activity. *Cognitive, Affective, and Behavioral Neuroscience*, 11 (3), 277–291.

Shulman, G.L., Fiez, J.A., Corbetta, M., *et al.* (1997). Common blood flow changes across visual tasks: II. Decreases in cerebral cortex. *Journal of Cognitive Neuroscience*, 9 (5), 648–663.

Skinner, E.I., Grady, C.L., and Fernandes, M.A. (2010). Reactivation of context-specific brain regions during retrieval. *Neuropsychologia*, 48 (1), 156–164.

Squire, L.R., Wixted, J.T., and Clark, R.E. (2007). Recognition memory and the medial temporal lobe: a new perspective. *Nature Reviews Neuroscience*, 8 (11), 872–883.

Staresina, B.P., Henson, R.N., Kriegeskorte, N., and Alink, A. (2012). Episodic reinstatement in the medial temporal lobe. *Journal of Neuroscience*, 32 (50), 18150–18156.

Tulving, E. (1983). *Elements of Episodic Memory*. New York, NY: Oxford University Press.

Tulving, E., and Thomson, D.M. (1973). Encoding specificity and retrieval processes in episodic memory. *Psychological Review*, 80 (5), 352–373.

Uddin, L.Q., Supekar, K., Amin, H., *et al.* (2010). Dissociable connectivity within human angular gyrus and intraparietal sulcus: evidence from functional and structural connectivity. *Cerebral Cortex*, 20 (11), 2636–2646.

Uncapher, M.R., Hutchinson, J.B., and Wagner, A.D. (2011). Dissociable effects of top-down and bottom-up attention during episodic encoding. *Journal of Neuroscience*, 31 (35), 12613–12628.

Uncapher, M.R., Otten, L.J., and Rugg, M.D. (2006). Episodic encoding is more than the sum of its parts: an fMRI investigation of multifeatural contextual encoding. *Neuron*, 52 (3), 547–556.

Uncapher, M.R., and Rugg, M.D. (2009). Selecting for memory? The influence of selective attention on the mnemonic binding of contextual information. *Journal of Neuroscience*, 29 (25), 8270–8279.

Uncapher, M.R., and Wagner, A.D. (2009). Posterior parietal cortex and episodic encoding: insights from fMRI subsequent memory effects and dual-attention theory. *Neurobiology of Learning and Memory*, 91 (2), 139–154.

Vaidya, C.J., Zhao, M., Desmond, J.E., and Gabrieli, J.D. (2002). Evidence for cortical encoding specificity in episodic memory: memory-induced re-activation of picture processing areas. *Neuropsychologia*, 40 (12), 2136–2143.

Vilberg, K.L., and Rugg, M.D. (2007). Dissociation of the neural correlates of recognition memory according to familiarity, recollection, and amount of recollected information. *Neuropsychologia*, 45 (10), 2216–2225.

Vilberg, K.L., and Rugg, M.D. (2008). Memory retrieval and the parietal cortex: a review of evidence from a dual-process perspective. *Neuropsychologia*, 46 (7), 1787–1799.

Vilberg, K.L., and Rugg, M.D. (2009). Functional significance of retrieval-related activity in lateral parietal cortex: evidence from fMRI and ERPs. *Human Brain Mapping*, 30 (5), 1490–1501.

Vilberg, K.L., and Rugg, M.D. (2012). The neural correlates of recollection: transient versus sustained fMRI effects. *Journal of Neuroscience*, 32 (45), 15679–15687.

Wagner, A.D., and Davachi, L. (2001). Cognitive neuroscience: forgetting of things past. *Current Biology*, 11 (23), 964–967.

Wallenstein, G.V., Hasselmo, M.E., and Eichenbaum, H. (1998). The hippocampus as an associator of discontiguous events. *Trends in Neurosciences*, 21 (8), 317–323.

Wheeler, M.E., Petersen, S.E., and Buckner, R.L. (2000). Memory's echo: vivid remembering reactivates sensory-specific cortex. *Proceedings of the National Academy of Sciences of the USA*, 97 (20), 11125–11129.

Wixted, J.T. (2007). Dual-process theory and signal-detection theory of recognition memory. *Psychological Review*, 114 (1), 152–176.

Wixted, J.T., and Mickes, L. (2010). A continuous dual-process model of remember/know judgments. *Psychological Review*, 117 (4), 1025.

Woodruff, C.C., Johnson, J.D., Uncapher, M.R., and Rugg, M.D. (2005). Content-specificity of the neural correlates of recollection. *Neuropsychologia*, 43 (7), 1022–1032.

Xue, G., Dong, Q., Chen, C., *et al.* (2010). Greater neural pattern similarity across repetitions is associated with better memory. *Science*, 330 (6000), 97–101.

Yonelinas, A.P. (2002). The nature of recollection and familiarity: a review of 30 years of research. *Journal of Memory and Language*, 46 (3), 441–517.

Yu, S.S., Johnson, J.D. and Rugg, M.D. (2012). Dissociation of recollection-related neural activity in ventral lateral parietal cortex. *Cognitive Neuroscience*, 3 (3–4), 142–149.

# 6

# Medial Temporal Lobe Subregional Function in Human Episodic Memory
## *Insights from High-Resolution fMRI*
### Jackson C. Liang and Alison R. Preston

## Introduction

Episodic memory fundamentally shapes human behavior, allowing us to draw upon past experience to inform current decisions and make predictions about upcoming events. For decades, research has documented the critical role of the medial temporal lobe (MTL) in episodic memory (Eichenbaum and Cohen, 2001). While the link between MTL function and episodic memory is beyond debate, a recent focus has centered on characterizing the contributions of specific MTL substructures to episodic memory formation and retrieval (see Chapter 5).

The MTL (Figure 6.1a) comprises a heterogeneous group of structures, each with a unique cellular organization and pattern of anatomical connectivity. The subregions of the MTL include the hippocampus, which itself comprises the dentate gyrus (DG), the cornu ammonis (CA) fields, and the subiculum, as well as the surrounding entorhinal (ERC), perirhinal (PRC), and parahippocampal (PHC) cortices (Figure 6.1b). Several theoretical perspectives propose that anatomical differences between MTL subregions give rise to unique functional roles in episodic memory (Davachi, 2006; Diana, Yonelinas, and Ranganath, 2007; McClelland, McNaughton, and O'Reilly, 1995; O'Reilly and Rudy, 2001). However, testing how MTL subregions contribute to human memory function poses a unique challenge for cognitive neuroscience research. Individuals with MTL lesions typically have damage that affects several MTL subregions, spanning both hippocampus and surrounding MTL cortices. Even those individuals with restricted hippocampal lesions have damage to multiple hippocampal subregions. Therefore, while the neuropsychological study of MTL patients has taught us a great deal about the essential nature of the region for episodic memory, it is limited in its ability to discern the functional roles of individual human MTL subregions. Similarly, because MTL subregions are relatively small and adjacent, standard approaches to functional magnetic resonance imaging (fMRI) that use voxel dimensions greater than 3 mm cannot resolve signal originating from a particular MTL subfield. Testing

*The Wiley Handbook on the Cognitive Neuroscience of Memory*, First Edition.
Edited by Donna Rose Addis, Morgan Barense, and Audrey Duarte.
© 2015 John Wiley & Sons, Ltd. Published 2015 by John Wiley & Sons, Ltd.

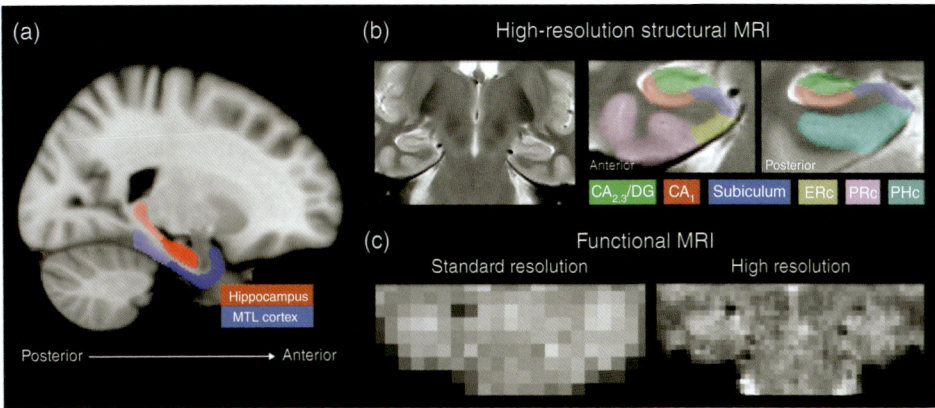

**Figure 6.1** High-resolution fMRI of human MTL subregions. (a) Sagittal brain slice depicting the location of the hippocampus (in red) and surrounding MTL cortex (in blue). Dark gradation indicates the anterior portions of the hippocampus and MTL cortex, while light gradation depicts the corresponding posterior regions. (b) Structural images collected using high-resolution MRI in the coronal plane, perpendicular to the anterior–posterior MTL axis. Anterior and posterior segments show demarcation of anatomical MTL regions of interest (ROIs) including hippocampal subfields DG/CA2/CA3, CA1, and subiculum and MTL cortical subregions ERC, PRC and PHC. (c) Left panel shows a standard-resolution fMRI image acquired using a functional sequence (3.75 × 3.75 × 3.6 mm voxels); right panel shows a high-resolution fMRI image acquired using a GRAPPA-EPI sequence (1.5 mm isotropic voxels).

the predictions of anatomically based models of MTL function in the human brain thus requires a spatial resolution beyond the limits of neuropsychological study and standard functional neuroimaging methods.

Over the last decade, implementation of high-resolution functional magnetic resonance imaging (hr-fMRI) has opened the door for investigation of MTL subregional function in humans. In this chapter, we review the technical aspects of hr-fMRI as applied to the study of the human MTL and discuss two core topics that have dominated research in this area: (1) functional dissociations between hippocampus and surrounding MTL cortices based on episodic memory content, and (2) functional distinctions between the components of the hippocampal circuit. We also discuss new multivariate pattern-information analysis techniques, which examine distributed patterns of activation in contrast to average responses pooled across an entire region. Such techniques, when combined with hr-fMRI, have the power to provide new insights into the function of MTL subregions. We end by discussing challenges for hr-fMRI of the human MTL and suggest future directions that could improve our ability to answer questions about the role of this region in episodic memory.

## What is High Resolution When it Comes to Human MTL Imaging?

Standard fMRI methods typically employ inplane resolutions of $\geq 3 \times 3$ mm (Figure 6.1c). At this spatial resolution, precise identification of distinct hippocampal subfields is not possible, and the ability to differentiate activation arising from the ERC and PRC is also limited. A little over a decade ago, two research groups

(Small *et al.*, 2000a, 2000b; Zeineh, Engel, and Bookheimer, 2000) developed techniques that enabled data acquisition from human MTL with enhanced spatial resolution ($< 2 \times 2$ mm inplane resolution) that when combined with specialized data analysis procedures afford localization of blood-oxygen-level-dependent (BOLD) signals to individual MTL subregions (Figure 6.1c). Such reduced voxel sizes not only improve the ability to distinguish anatomical boundaries between regions, but also reduce partial volume effects that may mask activations of interest (Bellgowan *et al.*, 2006).

These initial studies, and several that followed them, acquired functional images in the oblique coronal plane (inplane), perpendicular to the long axis of the hippocampus, with a larger voxel dimension in the anterior–posterior direction (thruplane; e.g., $1.6 \times 3 \times 1.6$ mm; Zeineh, Engel, and Bookheimer, 2000). By increasing spatial resolution in the coronal plane, these methods maximize the ability to identify key anatomical landmarks (Amaral and Insausti, 1990; Duvernoy, 1998; Insausti *et al.*, 1998; Pruessner *et al.*, 2000, 2002) that distinguish the boundaries between MTL subregions in the human brain. More recent studies (Bakker *et al.*, 2008; Hassabis *et al.*, 2009) have advanced acquisition methods further, allowing for isotropic voxel dimensions at the resolution of $1.5$ mm$^3$. In all cases, hr-fMRI methods enable segmentation of the human hippocampus into the subiculum, CA1, and a combined DG/CA2/CA3 region (these subfields cannot be accurately differentiated even using current hr-fMRI methods; Figure 6.1b). These high-resolution acquisition techniques also afford more accurate segmentation of parahippocampal gyrus into the ERC, PRC, and PHC subregions, and more recently have been used to differentiate medial and lateral regions within ERC (Schultz, Sommer, and Peters, 2012).

To preserve spatial resolution, hr-fMRI studies of MTL function typically forgo or apply only minimal smoothing, to minimize blurring of anatomical boundaries between regions. Several hr-fMRI studies have also refrained from conducting voxel-level group analyses, because of the inherent challenges of registering small MTL subregions across participants; instead, these studies employ anatomically based region-of-interest (ROI) analyses in the native space of individual participants. In this approach, the functional time-series is co-registered to an even higher-resolution structural image (e.g., $0.4 \times 3 \times 0.4$ mm) at the level of individual participants. Anatomical MTL subregions are then defined on the high-resolution structural image separately for each participant (Figure 6.1b), and task-related activation is extracted from each voxel within a region and averaged across all voxels in a given ROI. While this method avoids the potential issues of across-participant registration, it may also demonstrate reduced detection sensitivity, as voxels that are nonresponsive to the task are included in the averaging. To increase detection sensitivity, some studies first identify task-activated voxels within anatomical regions with a contrast orthogonal to the main question of interest and then perform selective averaging, assessing effects of interest on those task-activated voxels only. However, both of these ROI methods preclude detection of heterogeneous responses that may be present within individual MTL subregions, as an average response is calculated across all selected voxels in a region. If different voxels within a region have distinct response profiles, selective averaging further limits detection sensitivity.

In the past few years, several advances have been made in cross-participant registration techniques (Avants *et al.*, 2011; Ekstrom *et al.*, 2009; Yassa and Stark, 2009) that allow for reliable voxel-level analyses at the group level. These techniques employ fully deformable nonlinear registration algorithms to warp each participant's anatomical and functional images to a template image (either a target participant's brain or a study-specific group template) using each participant's anatomically defined MTL subregions as a guide. After cross-participant registration, second-level group analyses can be used to identify activation patterns that are consistent across the group. One previously successful approach to cross-participant analyses relies on computational unfolding of MTL images into two-dimensional flat maps (Ekstrom *et al.*, 2009; Zeineh *et al.*, 2003). However, the unfolding operation can be prone to error that results in large spatial distortions, leading to inaccurate labeling of subregions after warping. Label-guided alignment approaches result in more accurate correspondence of MTL subregions across subjects and higher statistical sensitivity than standard methods (Yassa and Stark, 2009). Importantly, these methods also permit visualization of the topographic distribution of activation both within and across MTL subfields.

## Anatomically Derived Theories of MTL Subregional Function

Before delving into the empirical work using hr-fMRI to study human MTL function, it is important to consider the theoretical frameworks that guide such research. Leading models of MTL function in episodic memory (Davachi, 2006; Diana, Yonelinas, and Ranganath, 2007; Eichenbaum, Yonelinas, and Ranganath, 2007; Knierim, Lee, and Hargreaves, 2006; Manns and Eichenbaum, 2006; McClelland, McNaughton, and O'Reilly, 1995; Norman and O'Reilly, 2003) derive many of their predictions from the anatomical organization of the region, with the putative function of each MTL subregion being linked to the nature of its inputs, outputs, and internal circuitry (Figure 6.2). In the case of MTL cortex, PRC receives predominant input from unimodal visual association areas in ventral temporal cortex, while PHC receives input from posterior visual association areas in parietal cortex as well as auditory and somatosensory information (Jones and Powell, 1970; Suzuki and Amaral, 1994; Van Hoesen and Pandya, 1975; Van Hoesen, Pandya, and Butters, 1975). This pattern of extrinsic connectivity with neocortex suggests that episodic memory encoding and retrieval may differentially recruit PRC and PHC depending on the nature of event content, with PRC supporting memory for visual objects and PHC supporting memory for visuospatial information. An influential extension of this view suggests that PRC mediates memory for individual items experienced within single episodes (the "what"), while PHC mediates memory for the context in which those items were experienced (the "where") (Davachi, 2006; Diana, Yonelinas, and Ranganath, 2007; Eichenbaum, Yonelinas, and Ranganath, 2007).

Moreover, PRC and PHC provide the respective inputs to the lateral and medial ERC in the rodent brain (Figure 6.2, dark blue arrows) (Burwell, 2000; Van Hoesen and Pandya, 1975), suggesting that the segregation of mnemonic content would also be reflected in different regions of the ERC (Knierim, Lee, and Hargreaves, 2006; Manns and Eichenbaum, 2006). While PRC and PHC projections remain segregated within ERC, parallel inputs from lateral and medial ERC converge onto the same subsets of DG granule cells and CA3 pyramidal cells in the rodent hippocampus (Figure 6.2, light blue arrows) (Canto, Wouterlood, and Witter, 2008). DG in turn

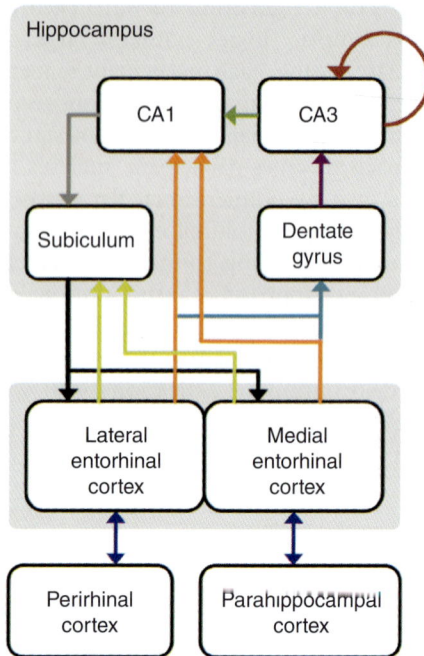

**Figure 6.2** Schematic diagram of connectivity between MTL cortex and hippocampal subfields. See text for detailed description of circuitry. Although not pictured, subiculum also receives direct input from PRC and PHC.

projects to CA3 via the mossy fiber pathway (Figure 6.2, purple arrow) (Witter *et al.*, 2000). Projections from CA3 pyramidal cells include collaterals to other CA3 pyramidal cells comprising an extensive system of associational connections within the region (Figure 6.2, brown arrow). The convergence of inputs from lateral and medial ERC, as well as CA3 collateral connections, potentially distinguishes the putative function of the DG and CA3 from that of MTL cortical regions, with these hippocampal regions playing a domain-general role in episodic memory by binding disparate inputs from PRC and PHC into cohesive memory representations for long-term storage, i.e., binding the "what" happened to the "where" it happened (Diana, Yonelinas, and Ranganath, 2007; Eichenbaum *et al.*, 2007).

Whereas mnemonic processing in MTL cortical regions would be distinguished by their selective responses to specific forms of event content, hippocampal memory traces would reflect the arbitrary relationships among multimodal event elements as well as associations between those elements and the context of their occurrence ("what happened where") (Eichenbaum and Cohen, 2001; Morris *et al.*, 2003). Importantly, the sparse connectivity between DG and CA3 is thought to magnify distinctions between overlapping patterns of cortical input elicited by highly similar events, a process termed *pattern separation* (McClelland, McNaughton and O'Reilly, 1995; O'Reilly and Rudy, 2001). Pattern separation is thought to result in separable memory traces for highly similar events that reduce the likelihood that memories would interfere with one another. CA3 circuitry is also hypothesized to support reactivation of stored memories from partial cues through recurrent excitation, a processed termed *pattern completion* (McClelland, McNaughton and O'Reilly, 1995; O'Reilly and Rudy, 2001). While DG and CA3 likely make distinct contributions to pattern separation and pattern completion, hr-fMRI methods to date have not reliably distinguished between either of these subfields or between the adjacent CA2 region. Thus, the majority of hr-fMRI studies commonly define a single region that encompasses all these structures, which is typically referred to as DG/CA2/CA3.

Further along in the hippocampal circuit, CA3 provides a major input to CA1 (Figure 6.2, green arrow), which also receives direct input from ERC (Figure 6.2, orange arrows). Notably, whereas the projections from lateral and medial ERC converge on the same cells in DG and CA3, they target distinct groups of cells in CA1 and subiculum (Canto, Wouterlood and Witter, 2008; Witter, Van Hoesen, and Amaral, 1989). The differences in ERC connectivity between hippocampal subfields suggests that while different forms of event content may evoke similar response patterns in DG and CA3, the responses of CA1 and subiculum may be heterogeneous with respect to different types of memory content, with different cells mediating memory for different kinds of content. Moreover, the convergence of inputs from CA3 and segregated sensory information from lateral and medial ERC in CA1 suggests that the CA1 hippocampal subregion compares memory-based output from CA3 pattern completion mechanisms to incoming sensory information from ERC to detect deviations between current events and stored memories (Hasselmo and Schnell, 1994; Kumaran and Maguire, 2007; Lisman and Otmakhova, 2001; Vinogradova, 2001). When current experience violates expectations cued from memory, this CA1 comparator mechanism is thought to drive new encoding processes that form a new memory trace or update existing memories to account for new information.

The subiculum, the final structure in the hippocampal circuit, receives highly processed input from CA1 (Figure 6.2, gray arrow) as well as direct inputs from ERC (Figure 6.2, gold arrows), PRC, and PHC. As the output structure of the hippocampus, the role of subiculum may be to distribute highly processed input from the CA fields to the neocortical regions from which the input originated (Kloosterman, Witter, and Van Haeften, 2003). For example, information about reinstated memories resulting from CA3 pattern completion would reach the subiculum via CA1; via back-projections to PRC and PHC (Figure 6.2, black arrows), subiculum could then facilitate reinstatement of the content-specific neocortical patterns active during initial learning. It is important to note that much of what we know about the structure and connectivity of the MTL region is based on the rodent brain, in particular the distinction between medial and lateral ERC, and it remains to be seen whether such distinctions translate to the human brain.

In addition to these hypothesized functional differences between hippocampal subfields, there has been renewed interest in functional differences along the anterior–posterior axis of the hippocampus (Poppenk *et al.*, 2013). Animal research has shown that the anatomical connectivity and function of the ventral (anterior in the human) and dorsal (posterior in the human) hippocampus are distinct. In the rodent brain, the higher density of neuromodulatory inputs to ventral hippocampus relative to the dorsal hippocampus (Gage and Thompson, 1980; Verney *et al.*, 1985) suggests that this region represents the behavioral salience of incoming information to guide memory formation regardless of content type (Fanselow and Dong, 2010; Moser and Moser, 1998). In contrast, animal lesion studies suggest that posterior hippocampus may be selectively involved in spatial learning tasks (Moser, Moser, and Andersen, 1993;

Moser *et al.*, 1995). Episodic memory representations in the human brain might also reflect such anatomical and functional differences along the anterior–posterior hippo-campal axis, with the posterior hippocampus playing a predominant role in mediating memory for information about the spatial context of individual events.

Collectively, these anatomical considerations provide an important theoretical framework motivating the body of studies using hr-fMRI to study human MTL function. In each of the following sections, we consider how hr-fMRI has informed these influential theories of MTL subregional function, beginning with empirical work on content representation in the human MTL.

## Empirical Evidence for Content-Based Dissociations between Human MTL Subregions

Several neuropsychological (Barense *et al.*, 2005; Barense, Gaffan, and Graham, 2007; Bohbot *et al.*, 1998; Epstein *et al.*, 2001; Lee *et al.*, 2005a, 2005b) and standard-resolution neuroimaging studies in humans (Awipi and Davachi, 2008; Lee, Scahill, and Graham, 2008; Pihlajamaki *et al.*, 2004; Sommer *et al.*, 2005) have revealed functional differences between PRC and PHC along visual object and visuospatial domains respectively, as predicted by anatomically based theories (see also Chapter 10). However, other evidence suggests that processing of specific forms of event content is distributed across subregional boundaries. For instance, PRC responses have been observed during encoding of objects, faces, and scenes (Buffalo, Bellgowan, and Martin, 2006) and during binding of items to their specific features (Haskins *et al.*, 2008; Staresina and Davachi, 2006, 2008). Similarly, mnemonic responses in PHC have also been demonstrated for multiple forms of event content including spatial and nonspatial contextual information (Aminoff, Gronau, and Bar, 2007; Bar and Aminoff, 2003; Bar, Aminoff, and Ishai, 2008; Litman, Awipi, and Davachi, 2009).

These findings thus suggest two distinct possibilities for the nature of content representation in PRC and PHC: one consisting of well-defined PRC and PHC functional modules exhibiting preferential responding to specific event content, and an alternative possibility with PRC and PHC processing and representing multiple forms of event content. High-resolution fMRI provides additional empirical leverage to distinguish between these opposing possibilities by enabling more precise delineation of the boundaries between MTL cortical regions – in particular PRC from ERC – as well as unambiguous discrimination between MTL cortex and hippocampus.

Similarly, by delineating activation patterns arising from individual hippocampal subregions, hr-fMRI may resolve conflicting views of hippocampal function that alternately suggest processing in this region is either content-general (Awipi and Davachi, 2008; Davachi, 2006; Diana, Yonelinas, and Ranganath, 2007; Knierim, Lee, and Hargreaves, 2006; Manns and Eichenbaum, 2006; Staresina and Davachi, 2008) or specialized for spatial memory (Bird and Burgess, 2008; Kumaran and Maguire, 2005; Taylor, Henson, and Graham, 2007). One intriguing possibility suggested by the anatomical data is that distinct hippocampal regions, either individual subregions or different regions along the anterior–posterior hippocampal axis, may show dissociable response patterns with respect to representation of different forms of event content.

In an initial hr-fMRI study examining content-sensitivity in MTL regions (Preston *et al.*, 2010), participants performed an incidental target detection task during the presentation of trial-unique, novel face and scene stimuli intermixed with highly familiar faces and scenes. Consistent with its proposed role in visuospatial processing, PHC responses were greater for novel scene trials relative to novel face trials. Moreover, greater activation in PHC scene-selective voxels was associated with enhanced subsequent scene memory. In contrast, PRC showed a pattern of novelty-based responding that was similar for faces and scenes. Moreover, the magnitude of novelty-based responses in face-sensitive and scene-sensitive voxels in PRC and subiculum correlated with later memory performance for each respective form of event content. While these findings are consistent with a content-specific role for PHC in episodic encoding, they suggest that mnemonic processes in PRC and subiculum are generalized across different forms of event content (see also Dudukovic *et al.*, 2011).

Notably, exploration of content-sensitive responses in ERC was limited in these initial hr-fMRI reports, with minimal task-related activation observed in either study. Animal work suggests, however, that ERC plays a key role in episodic encoding and retrieval, with the lateral ERC mediating memory for object-related information and the medial ERC mediating spatial memory (Knierim, Lee, and Hargreaves, 2006; Manns and Eichenbaum, 2006). Recent hr-fMRI work has examined these hypothesized dissociations in content representation between the lateral and medial ERC, finding enhanced modulation of lateral ERC activation during face retrieval, in contrast to enhanced medial ERC activation during the retrieval of spatial information.

New perspectives on content representation in the MTL have arisen from the application of multivariate pattern-information analyses to hr-fMRI data. Standard univariate fMRI analyses compare the mean response of a group of contiguous voxels across experimental conditions to isolate individual voxels or regions that show a statistically significant response to the experimental conditions of interest. To increase statistical sensitivity, univariate approaches may include spatial averaging across multiple voxels (e.g., a mean response to faces and a mean response to scenes within a specific anatomical ROI, as illustrated by the bar chart in Figure 6.3a). Although this approach reduces noise inherent in all fMRI acquisitions, it also reduces sensitivity by blurring out fine-grained spatial patterns that might discriminate between experimental conditions (Kriegeskorte and Bandetti, 2007). Instead, multivariate pattern-information approaches enhance detection sensitivity by looking at the contribution of multiple voxels, treating the pattern of response across all voxels within a region as a combinatorial code related to distinct mental operations (e.g., encoding faces versus encoding scenes; see Chapters 1 and 2 for more discussion of multivariate pattern-information techniques).

One such technique is multi-voxel pattern analysis (MVPA; Haynes and Rees, 2006; Norman *et al.*, 2006). Whereas univariate approaches use multiple regression to predict the activity of individual voxels based on the experimental condition, classification-based MVPA uses multiple regression to predict the experimental condition based on the activity of multiple voxels. In this approach, a machine-learning algorithm called a neural classifier is trained to distinguish brain patterns based on condition (e.g., whether the participant is encoding a face or a scene) using a subset of data. The trained classifier is then tested on previously unseen data (Figure 6.3b). Only if the experimental conditions are represented by distinct spatial patterns will final classifier predictions be accurate.

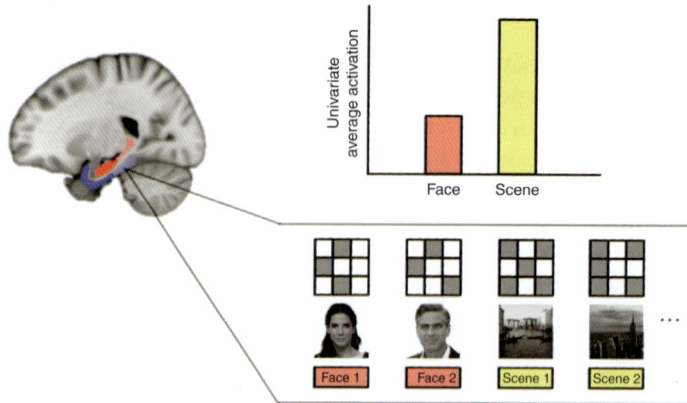

**Figure 6.3** Univariate and multivariate approaches for fMRI analysis. While standard univariate analyses (a) average across multiple voxels, multivariate approaches consider the contribution of multiple voxels, examining the pattern of response across all voxels within a region. Multivariate approaches include multi-voxel pattern analysis (b) and representational similarity analysis (c), the latter which makes use of multidimensional scaling (d).

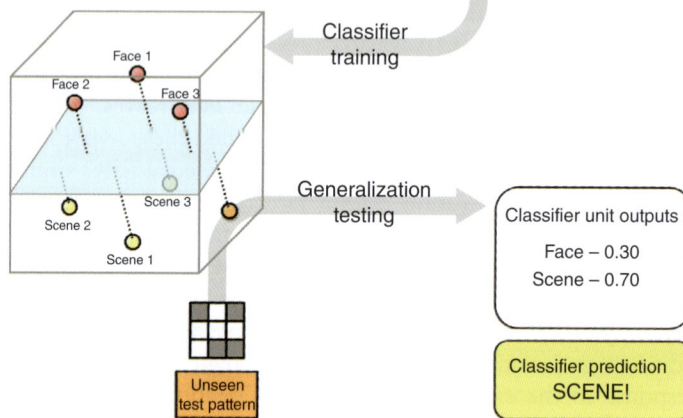

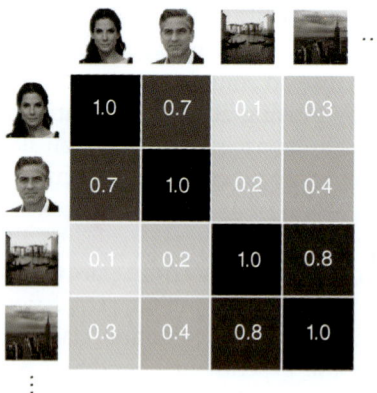

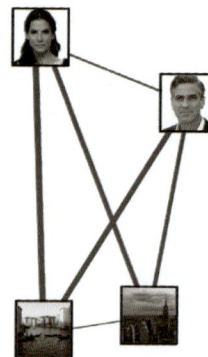

A related approach is representational similarity analysis (RSA; Kriegeskorte and Bandettini, 2007; Kriegeskorte, Mur and Bandettini, 2008) which does not use neural classifiers but rather examines the similarity structure (through correlation) between the multi-voxel patterns elicited by experimental conditions (Figure 6.3c). RSA assumes that if two stimuli (e.g., two different faces) are represented similarly in the brain, there should be enhanced similarity between the multi-voxel patterns evoked by the two stimuli (i.e., a higher correlation value). Conversely, distinct mental representations would be reflected by dissimilar multi-voxel patterns. Representational similarity matrices can be visualized using multidimensional scaling (MDS), where stimuli evoking similar voxel patterns are plotted closer together in representational space, while stimuli evoking dissimilar voxel patterns are plotted further apart (Figure 6.3d).

To date, two hr-fMRI studies have employed MVPA methods to examine content-based differences in MTL subregional representation. In the first study (Diana, Yonelinas, and Ranganath, 2008), participants viewed images in blocks composed of different forms of visual content (objects, scenes, faces, toys, and abstract shapes). While patterns of activation in PRC and hippocampus did not contain sufficient information to classify the different content types, PHC demonstrated accurate classification performance across all stimulus types tha included visual objects and faces. However, univariate analyses of PHC responses revealed a selective response to scenes. These findings highlight that univariate and multivariate approaches to fMRI data analyses index different aspects of the neural code, and further indicate that the scene-selectivity of PHC responses observed in previous studies, both standard- and high-resolution, do not convey the full nature of content representation in PHC.

A second hr-fMRI study (Liang, Wagner, and Preston, 2012) extended this work by demonstrating robust coding of many forms of event content in both PRC and PHC using both MVPA and RSA. In this study, participants incidentally encoded visual (faces, scenes, visual words) and auditory (environmental sounds, spoken words) stimuli. As in prior research, the univariate response in PRC was maximal for faces, while PHC showed a scene-selective pattern of response. However, these PRC and PHC effects were accompanied by greater consistency between multi-voxel patterns evoked by faces and scenes in both regions, and in the case of PHC, auditory stimuli as well. Importantly, the distinct representation of face, scene, and auditory content in PHC was most prominent at the most posterior aspect, counter to the prediction from standard-resolution univariate analyses (e.g., Epstein and Kanwisher, 1998; Staresina, Duncan, and Davachi, 2011) that this posterior aspect should be the most scene-selective region of PHC. Moreover, the distinctive representation of faces and auditory content was observed in PHC despite the absence of an above-baseline response for these stimuli in the univariate analyses, further emphasizing the enhanced sensitivity of multivariate methods to representational content in MTL regions.

Liang, Wagner, and Preston (2012) also observed different patterns of content-based responding across the anterior–posterior axis of the hippocampus. Mean univariate responses in anterior hippocampus were above baseline for all content classes. However, the spatial pattern of response in this region did not discriminate between different forms of event content. In contrast, posterior hippocampus showed a distributed coding of scene content that was distinct from other forms of content. These findings are consistent with the anatomically based view that anterior and posterior hippocampus serve different functions with respect to episodic memory. Anterior hippocampal signals may convey the behavioral salience of stimuli (e.g., that a stimulus is novel or rewarding) regardless of the perceptual form of the stimulus, while posterior hippocampus may play a predominant role in representing spatial memory content (see also Hassabis *et al.*, 2009).

Another means of assessing MTL content representation is to assess how specific regions within the MTL communicate with one another – a method known as *functional connectivity* (see also Chapter 13). Recent hr-fMRI studies indexing connectivity within the MTL circuit provide convergent evidence for functional differences along the anterior–posterior hippocampal axis, particularly in CA1 and subiculum (Libby *et al.*, 2012). This work revealed that anterior regions of CA1 and subiculum show predominant connectivity with PRC regions, while posterior CA1 and subiculum show greater connectivity to PHC. Such differences in anterior–posterior hippocampal connectivity with cortex were notably absent in the DG/CA2/CA3. These findings provide the first evidence that, in the human brain, PRC and PHC communicate with distinct regions of CA1 and subiculum, whereas PRC and PHC communicate with DG/CA2/CA3 in a similar manner. In particular, these connectivity findings suggest that distinct coding of spatial content in posterior hippocampus observed using MVPA approaches (Hassabis *et al.*, 2009; Liang, Wagner, and Preston, 2012) may primarily reflect CA1 and subiculum representations derived from PHC input.

One issue surrounding high-resolution MVPA studies of MTL content representation (Diana, Yonelinas, and Ranganath, 2008; Hassabis *et al.*, 2009; Liang, Wagner, and Preston, 2012) is the lack of a direct link between distributed patterns of activation and behavioral measures of memory performance. It is therefore unclear whether the distributed representations of event content observed in PRC, PHC, and posterior hippocampus observed in these studies are related to successful encoding of specific types of stimuli. Recent hr-fMRI evidence suggests that distributed hippocampal activation patterns distinguish individual episodic memories during vivid recall (Chadwick *et al.*, 2010; Chadwick, Hassabis, and Maguire, 2011). Moreover, patterns of hippocampal activation elicited by individual complex scenes have been used to decode participants' choice behavior in a perceptual decision-making task (Bonnici *et al.*, 2012b), further linking distributed hippocampal representations to behavior. Future hr-fMRI work will be necessary to determine whether similar relationships between distributed MTL representations and memory performance are true for a diversity of event content beyond the spatial domain.

## Differentiation of Function between Hippocampal Subfields

In addition to providing key insights into the nature of content representation in the hippocampus and MTL cortex, hr-fMRI studies have played in important role in delineating the specific processes and computations that are supported by individual hippocampal subregions. To date, studies of hippocampal subregional function have focused on three core topics: (1) the differential role of hippocampal subregions in encoding and retrieval processing, (2) hippocampal subregional computations that support pattern separation and pattern completion, and (3) the proposed comparator function of the CA1 field of the hippocampus.

## Hippocampal subregional contributions to episodic encoding and retrieval

One of the earliest hr-fMRI studies of the MTL demonstrated a dissociation of encoding and retrieval operations between hippocampal subfields (Zeineh *et al.*, 2003). While DG/CA2/CA3 was engaged during encoding of face–name pairs, subiculum was engaged during retrieval of learned associations (Figure 6.4a). Similarly, several follow-up studies found that DG/CA2/CA3 encoding responses were greater for remembered than for forgotten events (Eldridge *et al.*, 2005; Suthana *et al.* 2009, 2011) even when memory was tested after a long delay (Carr *et al.*, 2010). In contrast, responses in CA1 and subiculum were associated with success effects at the time of retrieval (Eldridge *et al.*, 2005; Viskontas *et al.*, 2009). Based on these findings, the authors hypothesized that the input structures of the hippocampus, DG/CA2/CA3,

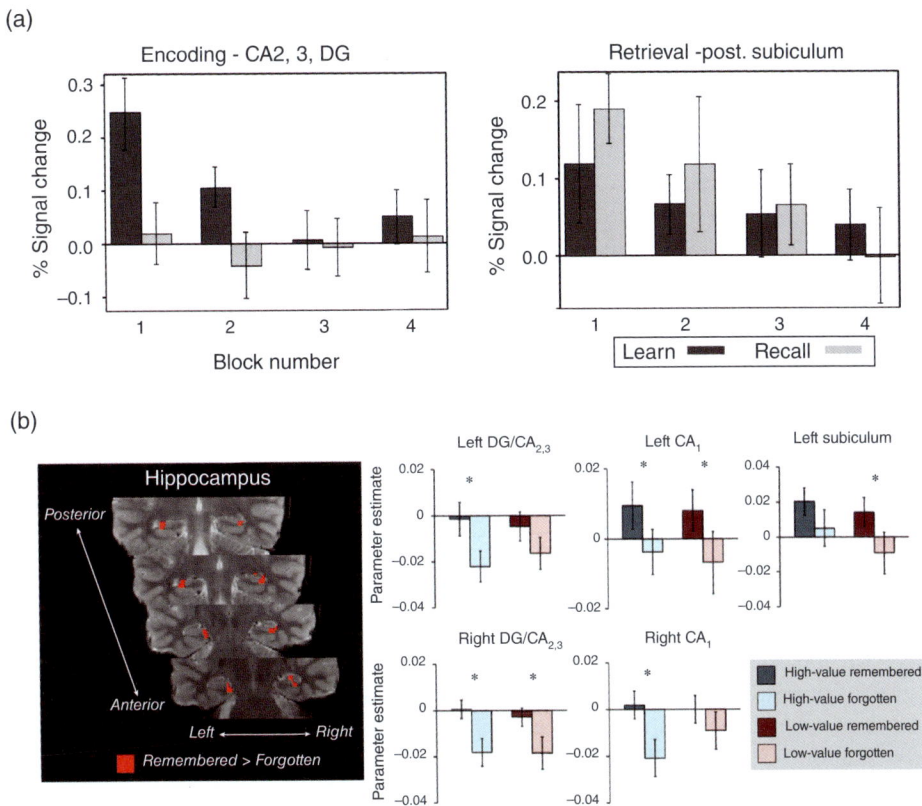

**Figure 6.4** Encoding and retrieval effects in hippocampal subfields. (a) Encoding- and retrieval-related activation in hippocampus for face–name paired associates. Percent signal change is plotted for each of four alternating encoding and recall blocks in DG/CA2/CA3 (left) and posterior subiculum (right). Adapted with permission from Zeineh *et al.* (2003). (b) Encoding activation in hippocampus during paired associate encoding under conditions of high and low reward. Voxels within the hippocampus demonstrating subsequent memory effects are displayed in red (left). Bar graphs (right) depict encoding activation in DG/CA2/CA3, CA1, and subiculum for high-value remembered trials (dark blue), high-value forgotten trials (light blue), low-value remembered trials (red), and low-value forgotten pairs (pink). Adapted with permission from Wolosin, Zeithamova, and Preston (2012).

are predominantly engaged during new event encoding, whereas the output structures of the hippocampus, the CA1 and subiculum, subserve the successful retrieval of memories (see Olsen *et al.*, 2009, for supporting evidence from a delayed-match-to-sample paradigm).

However, in contrast to these studies, anatomical models of hippocampal function emphasize that individual subfields play important roles during both encoding and retrieval and may transiently switch between states (Colgin *et al.*, 2009; Hasselmo and Schnell, 1994; Hasselmo, Schnell, and Barkai, 1995; Meeter, Murre, and Talamini, 2004). Indeed, other hr-fMRI studies have shown encoding and retrieval processes that are localized to multiple hippocampal subfields. During incidental encoding, subiculum activation was modulated by the novelty of the presented item (Bakker *et al.*, 2008), with the degree of novelty-related modulation predicting later memory (Preston *et al.*, 2010). Furthermore, an hr-fMRI study examining the effect of reward on encoding responses in MTL subregions found that encoding activation was related to later memory in all hippocampal subfields (Figure 6.4b; Wolosin, Zeithamova, and Preston, 2012). Similarly, several studies have shown retrieval success effects throughout the hippocampal circuit (Chen *et al.*, 2011; Suzuki, Johnson, and Rugg, 2011). Together, these recent experiments illustrate that encoding and retrieval processes are not restricted to specific hippocampal subfields as suggested by earlier studies. However, further work is required to determine whether subfields might perform specific aspects of encoding and retrieval, such as encoding of the environment during spatial navigation (Suthana *et al.*, 2009) or of salience cues encountered during novel events (Wolosin, Zeithamova and Preston, 2012).

## Pattern separation and completion

Another central focus of hr-fMRI studies in humans has sought to characterize hippocampal subregional responses elicited by highly overlapping perceptual inputs to determine their putative roles in pattern separation and pattern completion. Convergent electrophysiological research in rodents has shown that DG responses exhibit the greatest differentiation between highly overlapping input patterns, indicating this region's key role in pattern separation (Leutgeb *et al.*, 2007). In turn, the role of CA3 and CA1 in pattern separation and pattern completion is thought to vary based on the degree of overlap between inputs representing past and present experiences, with the CA3 responding in a nonlinear manner to pattern overlap and the CA1 responding in a linear fashion (Guzowski, Knierim, and Moser, 2004; Lee, Rao, and Knierim, 2004; Leutgeb *et al.*, 2004; Vazdarjanova and Guzowski, 2004). For example, a low degree of overlap between input patterns leads to a novel pattern of response in CA3 (i.e., pattern separation), whereas higher degrees of overlap between input patterns elicits reinstatement of a previously established CA3 response (i.e., pattern completion).

In the first hr-fMRI study to demonstrate pattern separation and pattern completion biases in human hippocampal subfields (Bakker *et al.*, 2008), participants viewed a sequential presentation of visual objects that contained novel objects seen for the first time, identical repetitions of previously presented objects, and novel lure items that were perceptually similar to previously presented objects. This approach relies on an effect known as *repetition suppression*, in which MTL regions show a reduced BOLD response to previously viewed stimuli when they are later shown again. The authors hypothesized that regions biased toward pattern completion would automatically reinstate the representation of a previously viewed object when presented with its corresponding perceptual lure, and thus show similar responses to both repeated and lure objects. In contrast, regions biased toward pattern separation would differentiate the lures from previously presented highly similar objects and treat them as novel, thus showing greater activation for both novel and lure trials relative to repeated objects. The results showed a pattern of activation in CA1 and subiculum consistent with pattern completion, whose response was reduced for both repeated and lure items. In contrast, responses in DG/CA2/CA3 showed a pattern separation bias, successfully differentiating lure trials from similar, familiar objects (for related hr-fMRI findings isolated to the entire hippocampal region see Johnson, Muftuler, and Rugg, 2008).

To address predictions from rodent models that the balance between pattern separation and completion in different hippocampal subregions may depend on the overlap between present input and past experience, a subsequent experiment used two types of perceptual lures that had either high or low degrees of perceptual similarity to previously presented objects (Lacy *et al.*, 2011). Consistent with prior findings, responses in DG/CA2/CA3 demonstrated a pattern separation bias, with the level of bias being similar for high- and low-similarity lures. In contrast, CA1 responses showed a graded response that depended on the degree of similarity between lures and familiar objects. These data converge with rodent research to suggest that human DG/CA2/CA3 shows a nonlinear response to overlapping patterns, while human CA1 responses are more linear in nature. However, future experiments that provide more quantitative manipulations of stimulus similarity across several levels of similarity will be required before making strong claims regarding the nature of pattern separation and completion biases in the human hippocampus. Notably, when the same stimuli and presentation procedures were combined with an intentional task focus, which required participants to identify each object as novel, repeated, or lure, dissociations between hippocampal subfields were not apparent (Kirwan and Stark, 2007). These divergent findings suggest that mnemonic demands have a major influence on processing in the hippocampus (see also Dudukovic and Wagner, 2007; Duncan, Curtis, and Davachi, 2009; Kumaran and Maguire, 2009), with task goals impacting the bias to form new memory representations versus retrieving existing ones. Future hr-fMRI studies are needed that directly address how goal states influence the computational properties of hippocampal subregions and, in particular, the trade-off between pattern separation and pattern completion.

One could also argue that paradigms manipulating visual similarity between individual objects as a means to study hippocampal pattern separation and completion biases do not assess the true nature of overlapping episodic memories. Using videos depicting real-world actions performed by individuals in different contexts, Chadwick *et al.* (2010) showed that the distributed pattern of hippocampal activation evoked during vivid recall distinguished between individual memories. However, because the episodes portrayed in the videos did not share common features, this study did not directly address how the hippocampus codes highly overlapping episodic memories. In a second study (Chadwick, Hassabis and Maguire, 2011), the videos were constructed from two realistic action sequences filmed on a "green screen" background that were superimposed on the same two spatial contexts, resulting in four video clips with highly overlapping features. Hippocampal activation patterns were distinct during recollection of each individual video, providing evidence for pattern-separated hippocampal representations depicting highly overlapping episodic information.

While these studies did not attempt to differentiate individual hippocampal subfields, the combination of these naturalistic stimuli, multivariate analysis methods, and quantitative manipulations of event similarity would be well suited to address critical questions of pattern separation and completion biases in individual MTL subregions. To date, only one published report has used multivariate classification to test for hippocampal subregional differences in pattern separation and completion biases, finding evidence for pattern completion in both CA1 and CA3 (Bonnici *et al.*, 2012a). Future high-resolution studies combining both univariate and multivariate methods will be necessary to determine how these results line up with prior work associating CA3 predominately with pattern separation.

## Hippocampus as a comparator

Several mnemonic processes, including pattern separation and pattern completion, require a comparison of the similarity between new events and existing memory representations. This comparator function is thought to elicit encoding processes when present events deviate from predictions derived from reinstated memory representations, and it has been hypothesized to rely on the CA1 subfield of the hippocampus (Hasselmo and Schnell, 1994; Kumaran and Maguire, 2007; Lisman and Otmakhova, 2001; Vinogradova, 2001). Two recent hr-fMRI studies (Chen *et al.*, 2011; Duncan *et al.*, 2012) tested this hypothesis by examining hippocampal subfield responses to memory probes that matched or did not match previously studied events. In one experiment (Chen *et al.*, 2011), participants studied associations between faces and houses prior to fMRI scanning. During the scanned retrieval phase, one member of the studied face–house pairs was presented at the beginning of the trial. During a delay period, participants were instructed to recall the stimulus paired with the cue image. At the end of the trial, participants judged whether a probe image was the correct paired associate (a match) or a familiar image from another studied face–house pair (a mismatch). For correctly judged probe items, CA1 showed greater activation for mismatch probes compared to match probe items, consistent with a comparator signal that detects deviations from cued expectations. However, this pattern of CA1 response was only observed for house probes that were preceded by face cues, suggesting that CA1 may specifically serve as a comparator in the spatial domain.

In a second study, participants studied three-dimensional room layouts prior to hr-fMRI scanning (Duncan *et al.*, 2012). During a scanned recognition phase, participants viewed studied rooms that contained changes in layout and/or pieces of furniture. Within the hippocampus, only CA1 responses demonstrated sensitivity to changes in studied images, with a graded pattern of response based on the number of changes. This graded pattern of CA1 response was observed irrespective of which dimension of change participants were instructed to pay attention to ("layout" or "furniture"), suggesting that the putative CA1 comparator response is automatic and does not depend on extrinsic task goals. While these studies provide compelling evidence that CA1 serves mnemonic comparator, further work is needed to determine how such automatic CA1 responses relate to successful encoding of new episodic information.

# Limitations and Future Directions for High-Resolution fMRI of Human MTL

While hr-fMRI has advantages over standard approaches to brain imaging, it does have limitations. Notably, many of the studies reviewed here employ coronal acquisitions with a large thruplane resolution (3 mm or more). Such acquisition parameters maximize resolution in the inplane direction, in which distinguishing anatomical landmarks are most evident, while minimizing repetition time. However, because the anatomical landmarks that define individual MTL subregions shift gradually along the anterior–posterior MTL axis, large thruplane dimensions may prevent precise localization of activation when voxels include signal from multiple subfields. For this reason, some hr-fMRI studies opt not to make strong claims about individual subfields, and prefer to treat the hippocampus as an entire region (e.g., Suzuki, Johnson and Rugg, 2011).

Current high-resolution methods are also limited in their ability to resolve CA2, CA3, and DG as separate regions, with virtually all current hr-fMRI studies treating these as a single region despite their dramatic differences in connectivity and structure. Recently, one hr-fMRI study reported functional differences between DG and other hippocampal subfields (Bonnici *et al.*, 2012a), made possible through structural acquisitions with higher thruplane resolution than previous studies (0.5 mm). While this procedure undoubtedly benefits from the use of anatomical landmarks visible only in the sagittal plane, some caution is warranted. First, the inplane resolution is somewhat lower than what has been reported in other hr-fMRI studies (0.53 versus 0.43 mm), thus losing detail in the plane most commonly used to segment hippocampal subfields. Second, the resolution of the underlying functional data (1.5 mm³) is no different from prior studies, and thus the ability to distinguish signal arising from DG and each of the CA fields in the functional data remains unchanged. For this reason, strong claims about dissociable responses in DG and CA3, for example, likely cannot be made based on such data.

Finally, the effort to test theories concerning small substructures is hampered by signal dropout and geometric distortion in functional acquisitions that are not present in structural images. Such distortion and dropout is particularly evident in anterior MTL regions. Distortion increases the likelihood that signal will be errantly displaced from a hippocampal subfield to one of its neighbors. Although such distortion can be corrected using field maps, the low spatial resolution of standard field maps precludes correction of detailed structures such as the hippocampal subfields. Efforts are currently under way to integrate higher-resolution field maps into imaging analyses, but these maps require additional acquisition time and may provide limited benefits.

Recent technical developments, such as human 7 T imaging and multiband parallel imaging techniques (Moeller *et al.*, 2010), may further enhance spatial resolution, allowing us to move beyond current limitations. In particular, multiband parallel imaging techniques dramatically increase the number of slices that can be collected at a single time-point. Increasing spatial resolution beyond 1.5 mm³ will enable finer distinctions between hippocampal subfields or subregions of ERC, while also providing more detailed patterns of activation that can be leveraged using multivariate analysis techniques. Lowering the sampling rate to 1 second (or less) will also provide richer datasets for functional connectivity analyses. Finally, these new acquisition techniques permit increased coverage beyond the MTL, while maintaining high spatial and temporal resolution, thus permitting novel investigations of how MTL subregions interact with memory centers in the frontal and parietal cortices.

## Concluding Remarks

High-resolution fMRI is an essential technique for evaluating theories of MTL function that had previously been tested only in animals. The combination of hr-fMRI and multivariate pattern-information analysis techniques, in particular, has substantially advanced our understanding of how memory is represented in MTL subregions, allowing for greater parity and convergence with animal studies. High-resolution fMRI techniques also have increasing translational relevance. Many of the paradigms described in this review are being applied to clinical populations with neurological and psychiatric disorders associated with memory impairment (e.g., Gaisler-Salomon *et al.*, 2009; Schobel *et al.*, 2009; Suthana *et al.*, 2009; Yassa *et al.*, 2010), providing further insight into the relationship between pathological changes to MTL subregions and disease processes that affect memory. New technical developments are likely to advance the field further, affording greater leverage to characterize the critical MTL computations and representations that underlie episodic memory.

## References

Amaral, D. G., and Insausti, R. (1990). Hippocampal formation. In *The Human Nervous System* (ed. G. Paxinos). San Diego, CA: Academic Press, pp. /11–55.

Aminoff, E., Gronau, N., and Bar, M. (2007). The parahippocampal cortex mediates spatial and nonspatial associations. *Cerebral Cortex*, 17 (7), 1493–1503. doi: 10.1093/cercor/bhl078.

Avants, B.B., Tustison, N.J., Song, G., *et al.* (2011). A reproducible evaluation of ANTs similarity metric performance in brain image registration. *NeuroImage*, 54 (3), 2033–2044. doi: 10.1016/j.neuroimage.2010.09.025.

Awipi, T., and Davachi, L. (2008). Content-specific source encoding in the human medial temporal lobe. *Journal of Experimental Psychology: Learning, Memory, and Cognition*, 34 (4), 769–779. doi: 10.1037/0278-7393.34.4.769.

Bakker, A., Kirwan, C.B., Miller, M., and Stark, C.E. (2008). Pattern separation in the human hippocampal CA3 and dentate gyrus. *Science*, 319 (5870), 1640–1642. doi: 10.1126/science.1152882.

Bar, M., and Aminoff, E. (2003). Cortical analysis of visual context. *Neuron*, 38 (2), 347–358.

Bar, M., Aminoff, E., and Ishai, A. (2008). Famous faces activate contextual associations in the parahippocampal cortex. *Cerebral Cortex*, 18 (6), 1233–1238.

Barense, M.D., Bussey, T.J., Lee, A.C., *et al.* (2005). Functional specialization in the human medial temporal lobe. *Journal of Neuroscience*, 25 (44), 10239–10246. doi: 10.1523/JNEUROSCI.2704-05.2005.

Barense, M.D., Gaffan, D., and Graham, K.S. (2007). The human medial temporal lobe processes online representations of complex objects. *Neuropsychologia*, 45 (13), 2963–2974. doi: 10.1016/j.neuropsychologia.2007.05.023.

Bellgowan, P.S., Bandettini, P.A., van Gelderen, P., *et al.* (2006). Improved BOLD detection in the medial temporal region using parallel imaging and voxel volume reduction. *NeuroImage*, 29 (4), 1244–12251. doi: 10.1016/j.neuroimage.2005.08.042.

Bird, C.M., and Burgess, N. (2008). The hippocampus and memory: insights from spatial processing. *Nature Reviews Neuroscience*, 9 (3), 182–194. doi: 10.1038/nrn2335.

Bohbot, V.D., Kalina, M., Stepankova, K., *et al.* (1998). Spatial memory deficits in patients with lesions to the right hippocampus and to the right parahippocampal cortex. *Neuropsychologia*, 36 (11), 1217–1238.

Bonnici, H.M., Chadwick, M.J., Kumaran, D., *et al.* (2012a). Multi-voxel pattern analysis in human hippocampal subfields. *Frontiers in Human Neuroscience*, 6, 290.

Bonnici, H.M., Kumaran, D., Chadwick, M.J., *et al.* (2012b). Decoding representations of scenes in the medial temporal lobes. *Hippocampus*, 22 (5), 1143–1153. doi: 10.1002/hipo.20960.

Buffalo, E.A., Bellgowan, P.S., and Martin, A. (2006). Distinct roles for medial temporal lobe structures in memory for objects and their locations. *Learning and Memory*, 13 (5), 638–643. doi: 10.1101/lm.251906.

Burwell, R.D. (2000). The parahippocampal region: corticocortical connectivity. *Annals of the New York Academy of Sciences*, 911, 25–42.

Canto, C.B., Wouterlood, F.G., and Witter, M.P. (2008). What does the anatomical organization of the entorhinal cortex tell us? *Neural Plasticity*, 2008, 1–18.

Carr, V.A., Viskontas, I.V., Engel, S.A., and Knowlton, B.J. (2010). Neural activity in the hippocampus and perirhinal cortex during encoding is associated with the durability of episodic memory. *Journal of Cognitive Neuroscience*, 22 (11), 2652–2662. doi: 10.1162/jocn.2009.21381.

Chadwick, M.J., Hassabis, D., and Maguire, E.A. (2011). Decoding overlapping memories in the medial temporal lobes using high-resolution fMRI. *Learning and Memory*, 18 (12), 742–746. doi: 10.1101/lm.023671.111.

Chadwick, M.J., Hassabis, D., Weiskopf, N., and Maguire, E.A. (2010). Decoding individual episodic memory traces in the human hippocampus. *Current Biology*, 20 (6), 544–547. doi: 10.1016/j.cub.2010.01.053.

Chen, J., Olsen, R.K., Preston, A.R., *et al.* (2011). Associative retrieval processes in the human medial temporal lobe: hippocampal retrieval success and CA1 mismatch detection. *Learning and Memory*, 18 (8), 523–528. doi: 10.1101/lm.2135211.

Colgin, L.L., Denninger, T., Fyhn, M., *et al.* (2009). Frequency of gamma oscillations routes flow of information in the hippocampus. *Nature*, 462 (7271), 353–357. doi: 10.1038/nature08573.

Davachi, L. (2006). Item, context and relational episodic encoding in humans. *Current Opinion in Neurobiology*, 16 (6), 693–700. doi: 10.1016/j.conb.2006.10.012.

Diana, R.A., Yonelinas, A.P., and Ranganath, C. (2007). Imaging recollection and familiarity in the medial temporal lobe: a three-component model. *Trends in Cognitive Sciences*, 11 (9), 379–386.

Diana, R.A., Yonelinas, A.P., and Ranganath, C. (2008). High-resolution multi-voxel pattern analysis of category selectivity in the medial temporal lobes. *Hippocampus*, 18 (6), 536–541. doi: 10.1002/hipo.20433.

Dudukovic, N.M., Preston, A.R., Archie, J.J., *et al.* (2011). High-resolution fMRI reveals match enhancement and attentional modulation in the human medial-temporal lobe. *Journal of Cognitive Neuroscience*, 23 (3), 670–682. doi: 10.1162/jocn.2010.21509.

Dudukovic, N.M., and Wagner, A.D. (2007). Goal-dependent modulation of declarative memory: neural correlates of temporal recency decisions and novelty detection. *Neuropsychologia*, 45 (11), 2608–2620.

Duncan, K., Curtis, C., and Davachi, L. (2009). Distinct memory signatures in the hippocampus: intentional States distinguish match and mismatch enhancement signals. *Journal of Neuroscience*, 29 (1), 131–139.

Duncan, K., Ketz, N., Inati, S.J., and Davachi, L. (2012). Evidence for area CA1 as a match/mismatch detector: a high-resolution fMRI study of the human hippocampus. *Hippocampus*, 22 (3), 389–398. doi: 10.1002/hipo.20933.

Duvernoy, H.M. (1998). *The Human Hippocampus*. New York, NY: Springer.

Eichenbaum, H., and Cohen, N.J. (2001). *From Conditioning to Conscious Recollection: Memory Systems of the Brain*. New York, NY: Oxford University Press.

Eichenbaum, H., Yonelinas, A.P., and Ranganath, C. (2007). The medial temporal lobe and recognition memory. *Annual Review of Neuroscience*, 30, 123–152. doi: 10.1146/annurev.neuro.30.051606.094328.

Ekstrom, A.D., Bazih, A.J., Suthana, N.A., *et al.* (2009). Advances in high-resolution imaging and computational unfolding of the human hippocampus. *NeuroImage*, 47 (1), 42–49. doi: 10.1016/j.neuroimage.2009.03.017.

Eldridge, L.L., Engel, S.., Zeineh, M.M., *et al.* (2005). A dissociation of encoding and retrieval processes in the human hippocampus. *Journal of Neuroscience*, 25 (13), 3280–3286. doi: 10.1523/JNEUROSCI.3420-04.2005.

Epstein, R., Deyoe, E.A., Press, D Z., *et al.* (2001). Neuropsychological evidence for a topographical learning mechanism in parahippocampal cortex. *Cognitive Neuropsychology*, 18 (6), 481–508. doi: 10.1080/02643290125929.

Epstein, R., and Kanwisher. N. (1998). A cortical representation of the local visual environment. *Nature*, 392, 598–601.

Fanselow, M.S., and Dong, H.W. (2010). Are the dorsal and ventral hippocampus functionally distinct structures? *Neuron*, 65 (1), 7–19. doi: 10.1016/j.neuron.2009.11.031.

Gage, F.H., and Thompson, R.G. (1980). Differential distribution of norepinephrine and serotonin along the dorsal–ventral axis of the hippocampal formation. *Brain Research Bulletin*, 5 (6), 771–773.

Gaisler-Salomon, I., Schobel, S.A., Small, S.A., and Rayport, S. (2009). How high-resolution basal-state functional imaging can guide the development of new pharmacotherapies for schizophrenia. *Schizophrenia Bulletin*, 35 (6), 1037–1044. doi: 10.1093/schbul/sbp114.

Guzowski, J.F., Knierim, J.J., and Moser, E.I. (2004). Ensemble dynamics of hippocampal regions CA3 and CA1. *Neuron*, 44 (1), 581–584. doi: 10.1016/j.neuron.2004.11.003.

Haskins, A.L., Yonelinas, A.P., Quamme, J.R., and Ranganath. C. (2008). Perirhinal cortex supports encoding and familiarity-based recognition of novel associations. *Neuron*, 59 (4), 554–560.

Hassabis, D., Chu, C., Rees, G., *et al.* (2009). Decoding neuronal ensembles in the human hippocampus. *Current Biology*, 19 (7), 546–554. doi: 10.1016/j.cub.2009.02.033.

Hasselmo, M.E., and Schnell, E. (1994). Laminar selectivity of the cholinergic suppression of synaptic transmission in rat hippocampal region CA1: computational modeling and brain slice physiology. *Journal of Neuroscience* 14 (6), 3898–3914.

Hasselmo, M.E., Schnell, E., and Barkai, E. (1995). Dynamics of learning and recall at excitatory recurrent synapses and cholinergic modulation in rat hippocampal region CA3. *Journal of Neuroscience*, 15 (7), 5249–5262.

Haynes, J.D., and Rees, G. (2006). Decoding mental states from brain activity in humans. *Nature Reviews Neuroscience*, 7 (7), 523–534.

Insausti, R., Insausti, A.M., Sobreviela, M.T., *et al.* (1998). Human medial temporal lobe in aging: anatomical basis of memory preservation. *Microscopy Research and Technique*, 43 (1), 8–15.

Johnson, J.D., Muftuler, L.T., and Rugg, M.D. (2008). Multiple repetitions reveal functionally and anatomically distinct patterns of hippocampal activity during continuous recognition memory. *Hippocampus*, 18 (10), 975–980. doi: 10.1002/hipo.20456.

Jones, E.G., and Powell, T.P. (1970). An anatomical study of converging sensory pathways within the cerebral cortex of the monkey. *Brain* 93 (4), 793–820.

Kirwan, C.B., and Stark, C.E. (2007). Overcoming interference: an fMRI investigation of pattern separation in the medial temporal lobe. *Learning and Memory*, 14 (9), 625–633. doi: 10.1101/lm.663507.

Kloosterman, F., Witter, M.P., and Van Haeften, T. (2003). Topographical and laminar organization of subicular projections to the parahippocampal region of the rat. *Journal of Comparative Neurology*, 455 (2), 156–171. doi: 10.1002/cne.10472.

Knierim, J.J., Lee, I., and Hargreaves, E.L. (2006). Hippocampal place cells: parallel input streams, subregional processing, and implications for episodic memory. *Hippocampus*, 16 (9), 755–64. doi: 10.1002/hipo.20203.

Kriegeskorte, N., and Bandettini, P. (2007). Combining the tools: activation- and information-based fMRI analysis. *NeuroImage*, 38 (4), 666–668. doi: 10.1016/j.neuroimage.2007.06.030.

Kriegeskorte, N., Mur, M., and Bandettini, P. (2008). Representational similarity analysis – connecting the branches of systems neuroscience. *Frontiers in Systems Neuroscience*, 2, 4. doi: 10.3389/neuro.06.004.2008.

Kumaran, D., and Maguire, E.A. (2005). The human hippocampus: cognitive maps or relational memory? *Journal of Neuroscience*, 25 (31), 7254–7259.

Kumaran, D., and Maguire, E.A. (2007). Which computational mechanisms operate in the hippocampus during novelty detection? *Hippocampus*, 17 (9), 735–748.

Kumaran, D., and Maguire, E.A. (2009). Novelty signals: a window into hippocampal information processing. *Trends in Cognitive Sciences* 13 (2), 47–54.

Lacy, J.W., Yassa, M.A., Stark, S.M., *et al.* (2011). Distinct pattern separation related transfer functions in human CA3/dentate and CA1 revealed using high-resolution fMRI and variable mnemonic similarity. *Learning and Memory*, 18 (1), 15–18. doi: 10.1101/lm.1971111.

Lee, A.C., Buckley, M.J., Pegman, S.J., *et al.* (2005a). Specialization in the medial temporal lobe for processing of objects and scenes. *Hippocampus*, 15 (6), 782–797. doi: 10.1002/hipo.20101.

Lee, A.C., Bussey, T.J., Murray, E.A., *et al.* (2005b). Perceptual deficits in amnesia: challenging the medial temporal lobe "mnemonic" view. *Neuropsychologia*, 43 (1), 1–11. doi: 10.1016/j.neuropsychologia.2004.07.017.

Lee, A.C., Scahill, V.L., and Graham, K.S. (2008). Activating the medial temporal lobe during oddity judgment for faces and scenes. *Cerebral Cortex*, 18 (3), 683–696. doi: 10.1093/cercor/bhm104.

Lee, I., Rao, G., and Knierim, J.J. (2004). A double dissociation between hippocampal subfields: differential time course of CA3 and CA1 place cells for processing changed environments. *Neuron*, 42 (5), 803–815. doi: 10.1016/j.neuron.2004.05.010.

Leutgeb, J.K., Leutgeb, S., Moser, M.B., and Moser, E.I. (2007). Pattern separation in the dentate gyrus and CA3 of the hippocampus. *Science*, 315 (5814), 961–6. doi: 10.1126/science.1135801.

Leutgeb, S., Leutgeb, J.K., Treves, A., *et al.* (2004). Distinct ensemble codes in hippocampal areas CA3 and CA1. *Science*, 305 (5688), 1295–1298.

Liang, J.C., Wagner, A.D., and Preston, A.R. (2012). Content representation in the human medial temporal lobe. *Cerebral Cortex*, 23 (1), 80–96. doi: 10.1093/cercor/bhr379.

Libby, L.A., Ekstrom, A.D., Ragland, J.D., and Ranganath, C. (2012). Differential connectivity of perirhinal and parahippocampal cortices within human hippocampal subregions revealed by high-resolution functional imaging. *Journal of Neuroscience*, 32 (19), 6550–6560. doi: 10.1523/JNEUROSCI.3711-11.2012.

Lisman, J.E., and Otmakhova, N.A. (2001). Storage, recall, and novelty detection of sequences by the hippocampus: elaborating on the SOCRATIC model to account for normal and aberrant effects of dopamine. *Hippocampus*, 11 (5), 551–568. doi: 10.1002/hipo.1071.

Litman, L., Awipi, T., and Davachi, L. (2009). Category-specificity in the human medial temporal lobe cortex. *Hippocampus*, 19 (3), 308–319. doi: 10.1002/hipo.20515.

Manns, J.R., and Eichenbaum, H. (2006). Evolution of declarative memory. *Hippocampus*, 16 (9), 795–808. doi: 10.1002/hipo.20205.

McClelland, J.L., McNaughton, B.L., and O'Reilly, R.C. (1995). Why there are complementary learning systems in the hippocampus and neocortex: Insights from the successes and failures of connectionist models of learning and memory. *Psychological Review*, 102, 419–457.

Meeter, M., Murre, J.M., and Talamini, L.M. (2004). Mode shifting between storage and recall based on novelty detection in oscillating hippocampal circuits. *Hippocampus*, 14 (6), 722–741.

Moeller, S., Yacoub, E., Olman, C.A., *et al.* (2010). Multiband multislice GE-EPI at 7 tesla, with 16-fold acceleration using partial parallel imaging with application to high spatial and temporal whole-brain fMRI. *Magnetic Resonance in Medicine*, 63 (5), 1144–1153. doi: 10.1002/mrm.22361.

Morris, R.G., Moser, E.I., Riedel, G., *et al.* (2003). Elements of a neurobiological theory of the hippocampus: the role of activity-dependent synaptic plasticity in memory. *Philosophical Transactions of the Royal Society of London, Series B: Biological Sciences*, 358 (1432), 773–786. doi: 10.1098/rstb.2002.1264.

Moser, E., Moser, M.B., and Andersen, P. (1993). Spatial learning impairment parallels the magnitude of dorsal hippocampal lesions, but is hardly present following ventral lesions. *Journal of Neuroscience*, 13 (9), 3916–3925.

Moser, M.B., and Moser, E.I. (1998). Functional differentiation in the hippocampus. *Hippocampus*, 8 (6), 608–619. doi: 10.1002/(SICI)1098-1063(1998)8:6&lt;608::AID-HIPO3&gt;3.0.CO;2-7.

Moser, M.B., Moser, E.I., Forrest, E., *et al.* (1995). Spatial learning with a minislab in the dorsal hippocampus. *Proceedings of the National Academy of Sciences of the USA*, 92 (21), 9697–96701.

Norman, K.A., and O'Reilly, R.C. (2003). Modeling hippocampal and neocortical contributions to recognition memory: a complementary-learning-systems approach. *Psychology Review*, 110 (4), 611–646.

Norman, K.A., Polyn, S.M., Detre, G.J., and Haxby, J.V. (2006). Beyond mind-reading: multi-voxel pattern analysis of fMRI data. *Trends in Cognitive Sciences*, 10 (9), 424–430. doi: 10.1016/j.tics.2006.07.005.

O'Reilly, R.C., and Rudy, J.W. (2001). Conjunctive representations in learning and memory: principles of cortical and hippocampal function. *Psychology Review*, 108 (2), 311–345.

Olsen, R.K., Nichols, E.A., Chen, J., *et al.* (2009). Performance-related sustained and anticipatory activity in human medial temporal lobe during delayed match-to-sample. *Journal of Neuroscience*, 29 (38), 11880–11890. doi: 10.1523/JNEUROSCI.2245-09.2009.

Pihlajamaki, M., Tanila, H. Kononen, M., *et al.* (2004). Visual presentation of novel objects and new spatial arrangements of objects differentially activates the medial temporal lobe subareas in humans. *European Journal of Neuroscience*, 19 (7), 1939–1949. doi: 10.1111/j.1460-9568.2004.03282.x.

Poppenk, J., Evensmoen, H.R., Moscovitch, M., and Nadel, L. (2013). Long-axis specialization of the human hippocampus. *Trends in Cognitive Sciences*, 17 (5), 230–240.

Preston, A.R., Bornstein, A.M., Hutchinson, J.B., *et al.* (2010). High-resolution fMRI of content-sensitive subsequent memory responses in human medial temporal lobe. *Journal of Cognitive Neuroscience*, 22 (1), 156–173. doi: 10.1162/jocn.2009.21195.

Pruessner, J.C., Köhler, S., Crane, J., *et al.* (2002). Volumetry of temporopolar, perirhinal, entorhinal and parahippocampal cortex from high-resolution MR images: considering the variability of the collateral sulcus. *Cerebral Cortex*, 12 (12), 1342–1353.

Pruessner, J.C., Li, L.M., Serles, W., *et al.* (2000). Volumetry of hippocampus and amygdala with high-resolution MRI and three-dimensional analysis software: minimizing the discrepancies between laboratories. *Cerebral Cortex*, 10 (4), 433–442.

Schobel, S.A., Lewandowski, N.M., Corcoran, C.M., *et al.* (2009). Differential targeting of the CA1 subfield of the hippocampal formation by schizophrenia and related psychotic disorders. *Archives of General Psychiatry*, 66 (9), 938–946. doi: 10.1001/archgenpsychiatry.2009.115.

Schultz, H., Sommer, T., and Peters, J. (2012). Direct evidence for domain-sensitive functional subregions in human entorhinal cortex. *Journal of Neuroscience*, 32 (14), 4716–4723. doi: 10.1523/JNEUROSCI.5126-11.2012.

Small, S.A., Nava, A.S., Perera, G.M., *et al.* (2000a). Evaluating the function of hippocampal subregions with high-resolution MRI in Alzheimer's disease and aging. *Microscopy Research and Technique*, 51 (1), 101–108. doi: 10.1002/1097-0029(20001001)51:1<101::AID-JEMT11>3.0.CO;2-H.

Small, S.A., Wu, E.X., Bartsch, D., *et al.* (2000b). Imaging physiologic dysfunction of individual hippocampal subregions in humans and genetically modified mice. *Neuron*, 28 (3), 653–664.

Sommer, T., Rose, M., Glascher, J., *et al.* (2005). Dissociable contributions within the medial temporal lobe to encoding of object-location associations. *Learning and Memory*, 12 (3), 343–351. doi: 10.1101/lm.90405.

Staresina, B.P., and Davachi, L. (2006). Differential encoding mechanisms for subsequent associative recognition and free recall. *Journal of Neuroscience*, 26 (36), 9162–9172. doi: 26/36/9162 [pii]10.1523/JNEUROSCI.2877-06.2006.

Staresina, B.P., and Davachi, L. (2008). Selective and shared contributions of the hippocampus and perirhinal cortex to episodic item and associative encoding. *Journal of Cognitive Neuroscience*, 20 (8), 1478–1489. doi: 10.1162/jocn.2008.20104.

Staresina, B.P., Duncan, K.D., and Davachi, L. (2011). Perirhinal and parahippocampal cortices differentially contribute to later recollection of object- and scene-related event details. *Journal of Neuroscience*, 31 (24), 8739–8747. doi: 10.1523/JNEUROSCI.4978-10.2011.

Suthana, N., Ekstrom, A.D., Moshirvaziri, S., *et al.* (2009). Human hippocampal CA1 involvement during allocentric encoding of spatial information. *Journal of Neuroscience*, 29 (34), 10512–10519. doi: 10.1523/JNEUROSCI.0621-09.2009.

Suthana, N., Ekstrom, A., Moshirvaziri, S., *et al.* (2011). Dissociations within human hippocampal subregions during encoding and retrieval of spatial information. *Hippocampus* 21 (7), 694–701. doi: 10.1002/hipo.20833.

Suzuki, M., Johnson, J.D., and Rugg, M.D. (2011). Recollection-related hippocampal activity during continuous recognition: a high-resolution fMRI study. *Hippocampus*, 21 (6), 575–583. doi: 10.1002/hipo.20781.

Suzuki, W.A., and Amaral, D.G. (1994). Perirhinal and parahippocampal cortices of the macaque monkey: cortical afferents. *Journal of Comparative Neurology*, 350 (4), 497–533.

Taylor, K.J., Henson, R.N., and Graham, K.S. (2007). Recognition memory for faces and scenes in amnesia: dissociable roles of medial temporal lobe structures. *Neuropsychologia*, 45 (11), 2428–2438. doi: 10.1016/j.neuropsychologia.2007.04.004.

Van Hoesen, G., and Pandya, D.N. (1975). Some connections of the entorhinal (area 28) and perirhinal (area 35) cortices of the rhesus monkey. I. Temporal lobe afferents. *Brain Research*, 95, 1–24.

Van Hoesen, G., Pandya, D.N., and Butters, N. (1975). Some connections of the entorhinal (area 28) and perirhinal (area 35) cortices of the rhesus monkey. II. *Frontal lobe afferents. Brain Research*, 95 (1), 25–38.

Vazdarjanova, A., and Guzowski, J.F. (2004). Differences in hippocampal neuronal population responses to modifications of an environmental context: evidence for distinct, yet complementary, functions of CA3 and CA1 ensembles. *Journal of Neuroscience*, 24 (29), 6489–6496.

Verney, C., Baulac, M., Berger, B., *et al.* (1985). Morphological evidence for a dopaminergic terminal field in the hippocampal formation of young and adult rat. *Neuroscience*, 14 (4), 1039–1052.

Vinogradova, O.S. (2001). Hippocampus as comparator: role of the two input and two output systems of the hippocampus in selection and registration of information. *Hippocampus*, 11 (5), 578–98. doi: 10.1002/hipo.1073.

Viskontas, I.V., Carr, V.A., Engel, S.A., and Knowlton. B.J. (2009). The neural correlates of recollection: hippocampal activation declines as episodic memory fades. *Hippocampus*, 19 (3), 265–272. doi: 10.1002/hipo.20503.

Witter, M.P., Naber, P.A., van Haeften, T., *et al.* (2000). Cortico-hippocampal communication by way of parallel parahippocampal-subicular pathways. *Hippocampus*, 10 (4), 398–410. doi: 10.1002/1098-1063(2000)10:4<398::AID-HIPO6>3.0.CO;2-K.

Witter, M.P., Van Hoesen, G.W., and Amaral, D.G. (1989). Topographical organization of the entorhinal projection to the dentate gyrus of the monkey. *Journal of Neuroscience*, 9, 216–228.

Wolosin, S.M., Zeithamova, D., and Preston, A.R. (2012). Reward modulation of hippocampal subfield activation during successful associative encoding and retrieval. *Journal of Cognitive Neuroscience* 24 (7), 1532–1547. doi: 10.1162/jocn_a_00237.

Yassa, M.A., and Stark, C.E. (2009). A quantitative evaluation of cross-participant registration techniques for MRI studies of the medial temporal lobe. *NeuroImage*, 44 (2), 319–327.

Yassa, M.A., Stark, S.M., Bakker, A., *et al.* (2010). High-resolution structural and functional MRI of hippocampal CA3 and dentate gyrus in patients with amnestic mild cognitive impairment. *NeuroImage*, 51 (3), 1242–1252. doi: 10.1016/j.neuroimage.2010.03.040.

Zeineh, M.M., Engel, S.A., and Bookheimer, S.Y. (2000). Application of cortical unfolding techniques to functional MRI of the human hippocampal region. *NeuroImage*, 11, 668–683.

Zeineh, M.M., Engel, S.A., Thompson, P.M., and Bookheimer, S.Y. (2003). Dynamics of the hippocampus during encoding and retrieval of face–name pairs. *Science*, 299 (5606), 577–580. doi: 10.1126/science.1077775.

# 7

# Memory Retrieval and the Functional Organization of Frontal Cortex

### Erika Nyhus and David Badre

## Introduction

To be adaptive, the long-term memory system must support retrieval of previously stored knowledge that has high utility given our current task and goals. In this framing, the problem of memory retrieval concerns balancing the recovery of useful information on the one hand against the inherent costs associated with retrieval itself (Anderson and Milson, 1989). Central to striking this balance is cognitive control function (sometimes called executive function), or the ability to leverage abstract goals and contextual representations in order to adaptively influence retrieval and memory-based performance.

The prefrontal cortex (PFC) is necessary for cognitive control function, including during the cognitive control of memory. Whereas damage to medial temporal lobe (MTL) structures produces amnesia that catastrophically impairs the encoding of new information and retrieval of recently encoded information (Scoville and Milner, 1957), damage to the PFC results in more subtle memory deficits (Moscovitch, 1992; Stuss and Alexander, 2005). For example, PFC patients are impaired in contexts that require retrieval of specific information (i.e., source memory tasks; Janowsky et al., 1989; Swick, Senkfor, and Van Petten, 2006), reliance on retrieval strategies (Moscovitch and Melo, 1997), overcoming interference (Moscovitch, 1982; Squire, 1982; Winocur, Kinsbourne, and Moscovitch, 1981), ordering information at retrieval (Shimamura, Janowsky, and Squire, 1990), or retrieval with limited cue support (e.g., free recall; Janowsky, Shimamura, and Squire, 1989; Jetter et al., 1986; Stuss et al. 1994). Neuroimaging studies have similarly implicated PFC in relation to specific manipulations of cognitive control at retrieval (Badre and Wagner, 2007; Fletcher and Henson, 2001; Rugg and Wilding, 2000). Thus, PFC is a crucial component of the system that supports cognitive control of memory.

In general, the mechanism of cognitive control can be described in terms of a process of guided activation (Miller and Cohen, 2001), wherein contextual or goal information is maintained in working memory and thereby has the opportunity to provide a top-down influence on processing elsewhere. Nevertheless, a central debate

*The Wiley Handbook on the Cognitive Neuroscience of Memory*, First Edition.
Edited by Donna Rose Addis, Morgan Barense, and Audrey Duarte.
© 2015 John Wiley & Sons, Ltd. Published 2015 by John Wiley & Sons, Ltd.

in the study of cognitive control concerns whether cognitive control is a unitary process or involves a diverse set of functionally distinguishable control processes (e.g., Cooper, 2010).

Mirroring the debate about the componentiality of cognitive control, the PFC is likely not a functionally homogeneous structure supporting a unitary executive, but may contain distinct subsystems that support different forms of cognitive control. Neuroimaging studies have provided the primary evidence in favor of functional dissociations in PFC (Badre and Wagner, 2007; Simons and Spiers, 2003; Spaniol *et al.*, 2009). Though debate still exists as to whether there are undifferentiated "multiple-demand zones" within the PFC – such as within the mid-dorsolateral PFC (Duncan, 2010) – it seems now widely accepted that functional distinctions likely exist, such as between ventral and dorsal lateral PFC (Petrides, 2002; Simons and Spiers, 2003), rostral versus caudal PFC (Buckner, 2003; Race, Shanker, and Wagner, 2008), left versus right lateral PFC (Nolde, Johnson, and Raye, 1998; Tulving *et al.*, 1994), and lateral PFC versus medial and subcortical systems (Kuhl *et al.*, 2008; Scimeca and Badre, 2012). Considerable controversy remains, however, regarding the validity of these distinctions and how to map them onto both individual experimental tasks and real-world behavior.

The cognitive control of memory is also likely componential, emerging from a set of interacting component processes. For example, cognitive control has the opportunity to influence retrieval performance in several ways, ranging from processes that structure inputs to the memory system (e.g., cue elaboration) to output control that monitors the outcome of retrieval and selects which representations are permitted to influence decision and action (Benjamin, 2007; see also Chapter 5). These and other distinct memory control processes could likewise be supported by different brain systems. Though research has only begun to refine understanding of these mechanisms and their neural correlates, several distinctions have been proposed regarding differential control processing in the PFC (e.g., Badre and Wagner, 2007; Nyberg, Cabeza, and Tulving, 1996; Simons and Spiers, 2003; Spaniol *et al.*, 2009; Tulving *et al.*, 1994).

Here we will focus on an example of functional specification within PFC related to cognitive control of memory retrieval. We will discuss the hypothetical specialization within ventrolateral PFC (vlPFC) between controlled retrieval and post-retrieval selection/monitoring operations. We will conclude by broadening the discussion of this distinction to consider the participation of these PFC subregions within distinct larger-scale functional networks.

## Venterolateral PFC and the Two-Process Model

The left vlPFC refers to the broad region of lateral frontal cortex that is ventral to the inferior frontal sulcus and rostral to premotor cortex (Figure 7.1). Investigation of the function of this region has long provided the strongest evidence in favor of functional specialization within PFC, from the classic studies of language impairment by Paul Broca (e.g., Broca, 1861) to early functional magnetic resonance imaging (fMRI) studies that distinguished subregions within left vlPFC related to the domain of verbal processing (e.g., the semantic versus phonological distinction; Poldrack

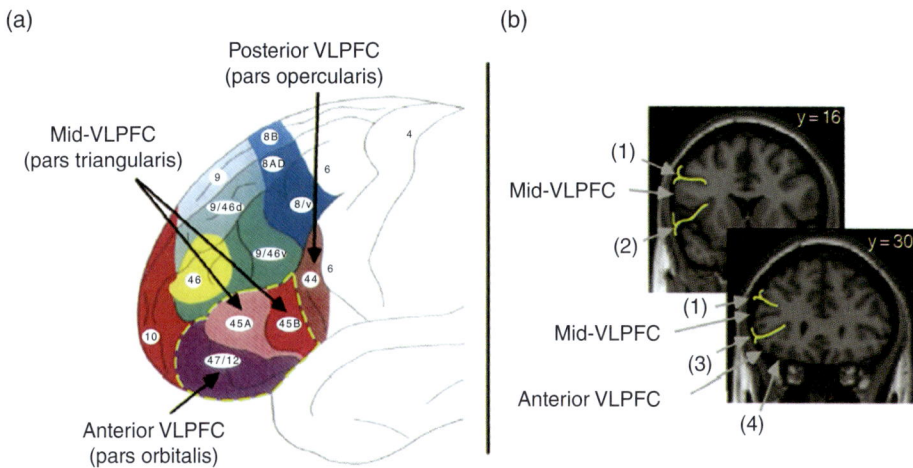

**Figure 7.1**    Anatomical divisions of vlPFC. (a) Schematic representation of the cytoarchitectonic divisions of the lateral PFC (adapted from Petrides and Pandya, 2002). Labels highlight the anterior vlPFC (pars orbitalis (~ Brodmann area [BA] 47)) and mid-vlPFC (pars triangularis (~ BA 45)). (b) Coronal slices from the Montreal Neurological Institute (MNI) canonical brain depict the anatomical boundaries that define mid-vlPFC and anterior vlPFC (reprinted with permission from Badre and Wagner, 2007). Labeled anatomical boundaries are (1) inferior frontal sulcus, (2) insular sulcus, (3) horizontal ramus of the lateral fissure, and (4) orbital gyrus.

*et al.*, 1999). More recent work has focused on functional distinctions within this region as they relate to the cognitive control of memory. Specifically, recent work in our lab and in others has focused on a distinction between controlled retrieval, supported by anterior vlPFC, and post-retrieval selection, supported by mid-vlPFC (Badre and Wagner, 2007). Here, we will consider the evidence for and against this potential distinction within left vlPFC.

To illustrate the distinction at the process level between controlled retrieval and selection, it is helpful to consider the analogy of searching for specific information on the Internet. For example, consider that you wish to find information about our lab. First, you need to "hit" our link from the broad, latent associative structure of the web. To do this, you devise a particular keyword to put in your web browser. Of course, some keywords will be more effective than others. For example, searching for "Badre lab" is likely to produce our lab's website as the top link. However, a less effective search, such as "science lab," would make it unlikely that you would find the link to our lab without a prohibitive cost in browsing time. Similar to this example, controlled retrieval refers to strategically guiding the activation of task-relevant information from its latent state. In human memory, controlled retrieval can progress by focusing on or elaborating effective cues and thereby increasing the likelihood that task-relevant information is activated from memory. From this perspective, one means of manipulating controlled retrieval experimentally is to reduce the strength of association between salient cues and target knowledge that would support automatic, cue-driven retrieval. In these cases, a top-down influence can aid in activating relevant knowledge from memory.

Importantly, however, it is very difficult to devise even a pair of keywords in a search engine that produce only a single web link. (In fact, it is rare enough that there is a hobby called "Googlewhacking", whereby people try to achieve fame by finding pairs of keywords that produce only one hit through Google™.) Thus, once we retrieve information into our browser, we "browse" or further select the links we want from this limited retrieved set. Though human memory is different in important ways from the Internet, it is a similarly vast, associative structure that uses a form of priority, such as previous co-occurrence, to rank the likelihood that a given representation will be retrieved given a particular cue (Anderson and Milson, 1989; Griffiths, Steyvers, and Firl, 2007). But, as on the Internet, this associative structure ensures that multiple representations will be retrieved given any cue, and that the highest-ranked representation may not be the one that is needed, given current goals and decision criteria. Thus, it is adaptive if a controlled retrieval system is complemented by an output control system that maintains current decision criteria and selects relevant items from among competitors in working memory. The process of selecting from among retrieved information is termed post-retrieval selection. From this perspective, manipulations of response or decision criteria or varying the degree of competition among retrieved representations should affect post-retrieval selection.

Multiple lines of evidence support the involvement of left vlPFC in the cognitive control of memory. Functional neuroimaging studies, including using fMRI and positron emission tomography (PET), have repeatedly demonstrated greater activation in vlPFC under conditions of effortful or goal-directed retrieval, such as controlling phonological and semantic representations (e.g., Gold *et al.*, 2005), retrieving items with weak versus strong cue support (e.g., Badre *et al.*, 2005), overcoming proactive interference (e.g., Öztekin and Badre, 2011), and active inhibition of memories (e.g., Anderson *et al.*, 2004). Moreover, disruption of vlPFC due to neurological damage or disease decreased patients' ability to select among competing information (Metzler, 2001; Thompson-Schill *et al.*, 1998). Similarly, intraoperative stimulation (Klein *et al.*, 1997) or application of transcranial magnetic stimulation (Devlin, Matthews, and Rushworth, 2003; Gough, Nobre, and Devlin, 2005) disrupts performance when participants are required to retrieve semantic information. Thus, in broad terms, vlPFC makes a necessary contribution to cognitive control of memory retrieval. However, an ongoing debate concerns the precise nature of vlPFC contributions to memory retrieval, and its functional organization in support of cognitive control.

Drawing on a wide range of declarative memory paradigms, including tests of both semantic and episodic memory, as well as retrieval during action selection, such as task switching, Badre and Wagner (2007) proposed that distinct subdivisions of the rostral left vlPFC support distinct controlled retrieval and post-retrieval selection processes, associated with the inferior frontal gyrus (IFG) pars orbitalis (~ Brodmann area [BA] 47) and pars triangularis (~ BA 45), respectively. These subregions were termed anterior vlPFC and mid-vlPFC, respectively (Figure 7.1). We now briefly summarize the evidence that supports this distinction.

The two-process model proposes that anterior vlPFC is activated when memory must be searched in a goal-directed manner (i.e., controlled retrieval; Badre and Wagner, 2007). Accordingly, when bottom-up cues are insufficient to elicit activation of target knowledge (i.e., automatic retrieval), demands on controlled retrieval processes increase. Control can aid retrieval in these contexts by elaborating cues or generating retrieval plans that structure the input to the retrieval system and so make it more likely that relevant information will be retrieved. Consistent with this hypothesis, anterior vlPFC is consistently activated during semantic retrieval tasks in which the association between available cues and target knowledge is weak. For example, deciding that "candle" is semantically related to "flame" is easier and requires less controlled retrieval than deciding that "candle" is related to "halo," because the association between candle and halo is weak relative to the association between candle and flame. Thus, experiments that manipulate associative strength, based either on pre-experimental norms (Badre *et al.*, 2005; Wagner *et al.*, 2001) or on associations learned during the experimental session (Danker, Gunn, and Anderson, 2008), consistently show greater activation in anterior vlPFC under weak relative to strong associative strength conditions (Figure 7.2). In a way similar to high cue–target association strength, anterior vlPFC shows repetition suppression effects accompanying the increased semantic fluency that follows repetition of an item during a semantic memory task, even when the decision/response level effects are not repeated (Race, Shanker, and Wagner, 2008).

According to the two-process model, mid-vlPFC is activated under conditions in which multiple items are retrieved from memory, but only a subset must be selected for further processing (i.e., post-retrieval selection; Badre and Wagner, 2007). As described above, automatic and controlled retrieval processes can result in the recovery of multiple representations. Thus, post-retrieval selection is needed to resolve competition

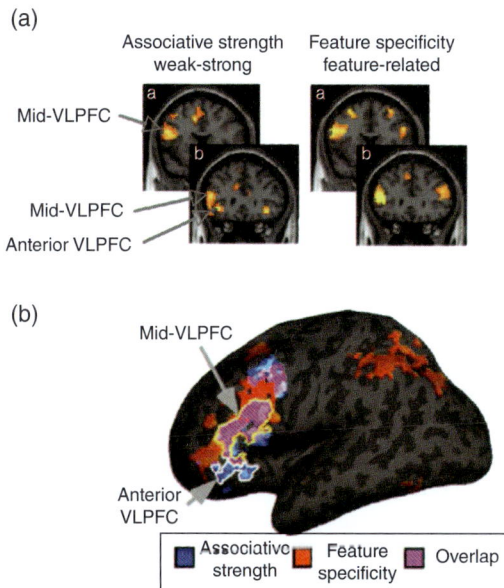

**Figure 7.2**    Results from manipulations of control during semantic retrieval provide evidence for the two-process model (reprinted with permission from Badre *et al.*, 2005). (a) Contrasts of weak relative to strong associative strength (associative strength) ($p < 0.001$) and decisions of item similarity based on features (e.g., color) relative to general semantic relatedness (feature specificity) ($p < 0.001$). (b) Contrasts of associative strength (blue) and feature specificity (red) and their overlap (purple) are rendered on an inflated MNI canonical surface. Anterior vlPFC was sensitive to associative strength, whereas mid-vlPFC was sensitive to both associative strength and feature specificity.

among the multiple retrieved representations, and to permit selected representations
to guide decision and action.

Support for mid-vlPFC and post-retrieval selection comes from several sources.
First, mid-vlPFC shows greater activation when participants are asked to decide if two
items (e.g., "apple" and "blood") are similar along a particular dimension, such
as color, relative to deciding whether they are generally semantically related to
one another regardless of dimension (feature specificity effect) (Badre *et al.*, 2005;
Thompson-Schill *et al.*, 1997) (Figure 7.2). This difference is thought to arise because
making the decision along a particular task-relevant dimension requires focusing
attention only on the retrieved details relevant to the decision and ignoring any other
properties. Notably, anterior vlPFC does not show a difference between specific and
general decision conditions (Badre *et al.*, 2005).

Proactive interference (PI) occurs when a prior learned association automatically
elicits retrieval of information that competes with a current retrieval task (Anderson
and Neely, 1996; Postman and Underwood, 1973). PI during short-term item
recognition has consistently been associated with increased activation in mid-vlPFC
(Badre and Wagner, 2005; Postle and Brush, 2004; Postle, Brush, and Nick, 2004).
PI during short-term item recognition does not consistently produce activation
increases in anterior vlPFC. However, as discussed below, other manipulations of
PI have been associated with anterior vlPFC activation (Öztekin and Badre, 2011).

During lexical decision, an unexpected target produces an interference effect above
a neutral baseline. This interference effect is thought to be due to competition between information retrieved during preparation for the target and the information that
must be retrieved upon encountering the unexpected target. Competition of this type
during lexical decision is associated with increased activation in mid-vlPFC. By contrast, anterior vlPFC shows priming effects consistent with the reduced retrieval
demands (Gold *et al.*, 2006). Thus, across these examples, it appears that mid-vlPFC
is critical under conditions of competition, presumably when there is a demand to
select relevant information for further processing. By contrast, anterior vlPFC is not
consistently activated under these circumstances.

Importantly, attempts to directly dissociate anterior and mid-vlPFC are complicated
by the fact that, akin to our Internet search analogy, any process of retrieval, be it
controlled or automatic, holds the potential for competition. Thus, similar to anterior
vlPFC, mid-vlPFC often shows increased activation under conditions requiring
controlled retrieval (Badre *et al.*, 2005; Wagner *et al.*, 2001). And so, though single
dissociations are sometimes observed (e.g., Danker, Gunn, and Anderson, 2008), double dissociations are less common. However, if one pits competition against associative
strength, it is possible to dissociate these regions. For example, when the number of
retrieval cues is small (low overall retrieval) but associative strength is weak, there will
be more demands on controlled retrieval than selection. By contrast, when the number
of retrieval cues is large (high overall retrieval) but associative strength is high, this puts
greater demands on selection than controlled retrieval. Consistent with this prediction,
Badre *et al.* (2005) directly pitted number of available retrieval cues against associative
strength and produced activation in anterior vlPFC but not mid-vlPFC. Thus, crossing
the number of retrieval cues (i.e., increasing retrieval demands) with associative
strength dissociates anterior from mid-vlPFC; and when this is taken together with the
feature specificity effect described above, this produces a region-by-effect interaction,
dissociating anterior and mid-vlPFC (Badre and Wagner, 2007).

In summary, there is evidence both across and within studies for dissociable functions between anterior vlPFC and mid-vlPFC during cognitive control of memory, and these functions can be characterized as controlled retrieval and post-retrieval selection respectively. Nevertheless, there have been challenges to the two-process model. These have included formal theoretical arguments about whether two processes are required to achieve controlled retrieval and selection functions, as opposed to a single-process model that can support both functions (Danker, Gunn, and Anderson, 2008; Thompson-Schill and Botvinick, 2006). These models make clear that a single process could achieve these two functions. However, it would seem difficult for a single-process model to account for the empirical dissociation between these processes. There has also been some debate about the nature of the relationship between anterior vlPFC and controlled retrieval, and whether the manipulation of associative strength actually reflects the domain of information being retrieved, such as retrieval of abstract semantics (Goldberg *et al.*, 2007). Again, however, a strictly domain-based account appears too difficult to reconcile with the broader data supporting the controlled retrieval hypothesis, such as the observation of activation in anterior vlPFC when retrieving weak, arbitrary paired associations (Danker, Gunn, and Anderson, 2008).

However, recent years have produced a potentially important challenge to the characterization of post-retrieval selection and its hypothesized relationship with competition. First, Öztekin and Badre (2011) manipulated competition using a release-from-PI paradigm in which competition was quantified for each trial using multi-voxel pattern analysis (MVPA; for more discussion of this method, see Chapters 1, 2, and 6). This procedure estimated the degree to which competing information was active during each memory decision, as reflected in the distributed fMRI activation in lateral temporal cortex. Importantly, these MVPA indices are correlated with behavioral PI effects and forgetting in memory. However, activation in anterior vlPFC, rather than mid-vlPFC, varied with PI conditions. Moreover, a mediation analysis showed that activation in anterior vlPFC mediated the relationship between the MVPA indices and behavioral PI. In other words, anterior vlPFC was associated with competition resolution in this task.

Second, Snyder, Banich, and Munakata (2011) used a latent semantic analysis procedure to independently characterize the cue–target association strength and competition of target words during a verb generation task. Latent semantic analysis evaluates large bodies of texts to build a multidimensional semantic space in which every word can be plotted in terms of its meaning and its similarity to other words' meanings. Any word can be coded both in terms of its distance from another word in the space (i.e., association strength) and its neighborhood density (i.e., competition: how many words cluster closely around that word in the space). Behaviorally, these two demands are separable, consistent with the concept of distinct controlled retrieval and selection processes (Snyder *et al.*, 2010). However, regions of interest (ROIs) in both anterior and mid-vlPFC showed additive activation changes to both manipulations. Thus, again, a more formal definition of competition in memory found sensitivity to this manipulation within anterior vlPFC, suggesting that this factor alone cannot account for the previously observed dissociation.

The Öztekin and Badre (2011) and Snyder, Banich, and Munakata (2011) results call into question the concept of competition during memory retrieval as being a clear distinguishing factor between anterior vlPFC and mid-vlPFC. Reconciling these findings with the empirical dissociations observed elsewhere will be important for understanding both the function of vlPFC and the factors that affect cognitive control of memory. For example, in Snyder, Banich, and Munakata (2011), competition arose from within the distributed, semantic structure of long-term memory itself. By contrast, prior studies of post-retrieval selection that show selective mid-vlPFC activation have directly or indirectly manipulated control over the decision criteria required to make a response based on retrieved information. Indeed, repeating a concept produces repetition suppression in anterior vlPFC, even when the decision that is made about that concept changes (e.g., categorization based on size versus material type; Race, Shanker, and Wagner, 2008). By contrast, repetition suppression in mid-vlPFC requires both repetition of the concept and the decision (Race, Shanker, and Wagner, 2008). Consistent with peri- and post-retrieval processing, these distinct repetition effects are separable in time, as assessed with electroencephalography (EEG) (Race, Badre, and Wagner, 2010). Hence, as opposed to the presence or absence of competition, the critical factor governing the involvement of anterior vlPFC versus mid-vlPFC may be the locus of competition, either in working memory or in long-term memory, and the mechanisms that are deployed to resolve that competition. Future studies will be required to separate competition from decision manipulations in order to further understand the distinctions between anterior and mid-vlPFC during control of memory.

## Separable Functional Frontal Networks

Importantly, subregions of the PFC do not function in isolation. Rather they are participants in larger association networks that dynamically produce controlled behavior. In recent years, functional connectivity analysis of fMRI data (fcMRI) has begun to characterize the networks of regions that may functionally affiliate during particular cognitive or motor tasks or as a consequence of spontaneous activity during rest (Fox and Raichle, 2007; see also Chapter 1). During rest, fcMRI has taken advantage of large samples and datasets in order to parcellate the cortex into different regional groupings that correlate in the low-frequency components of their signal (Buckner, 2010). Among other factors, these low-frequency correlations may reflect the presence of polysynaptic pathways connecting brain regions. Therefore, fcMRI, even at rest, can provide evidence for the presence of functional brain networks. However, given that other factors beyond fixed anatomy likely contribute to these correlations, one should be cautious in assuming that the precise boundaries found at rest will remain fixed across task manipulations. Nevertheless, these networks can provide a helpful guide for generating hypotheses to be tested in task data. Moreover, it may be informative to consider the degree to which the regional distinctions drawn in PFC during control of memory – such as between controlled retrieval and post-retrieval selection – might reflect differences across these broader functional networks.

Of particular relevance to the present discussion, fcMRI across different analysis methods has consistently suggested that roughly ventral versus dorsal frontal regions participate in separable functional networks (Dosenbach *et al.*, 2007; Vincent *et al.*, 2008; Yeo *et al.*, 2011; Figure 7.3A). First, a dorsal frontoparietal network has been repeatedly observed that includes regions of dorsolateral PFC (dlPFC) and posterior parietal cortex, along the intraparietal sulcus. Second, vlPFC and orbital frontal cortex consistently correlate with a network that includes medial and lateral temporal regions, including hippocampus. This latter network includes many of the regions observed previously in the "default-mode" network (Raichle *et al.*, 2001). However, the division between these two networks is not clearly between the inferior and middle frontal gyrus, which are often labeled vlPFC and dlPFC respectively. Rather, the caudal and dorsal portions of the inferior frontal gyrus cluster with the dorsal frontoparietal control network, whereas the rostral and ventral portions of inferior frontal gyrus cluster separately. And, as can be observed in Figure 7.3a, prior definitions of anterior and mid-vlPFC differentially fall on these separate networks, in that anterior vlPFC consistently falls in the ventral network, whereas mid-vlPFC falls on both or strictly on the dorsal network. This pattern raises the prospect that the observed difference between anterior vlPFC and mid-vlPFC may be reflective of a broader distinction among functional networks (Figure 7.3b).

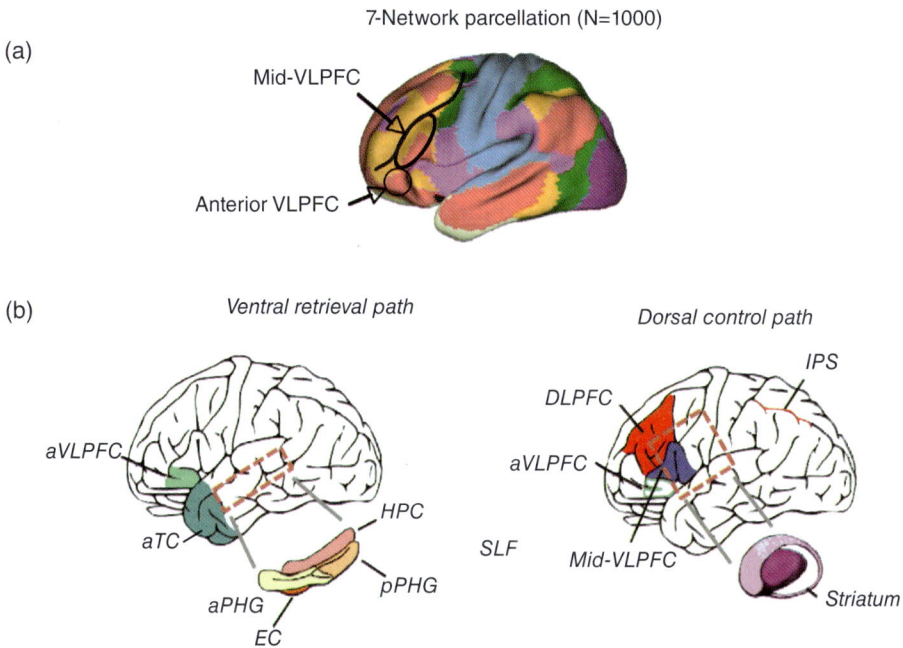

**Figure 7.3** Schematic representation of separable controlled retrieval and post-retrieval control networks. (a) Seven-network cluster in a sample of 1000 participants (reprinted with permission from Yeo *et al.*, 2011) with locations of inferior frontal sulcus (thick line), and anterior and mid-vlPFC regions (circles), indicated. Note that these are approximate locations for illustrative purposes and have not been established formally. Anterior vlPFC falls within the ventral network (red), whereas mid-vlPFC falls on both the dorsal control network (orange) and the ventral network (red) or strictly on the former. (b) Proposed distinction between the ventral controlled retrieval network and the dorsal frontoparietal post-retrieval control network. The ventral controlled retrieval network includes anterior vlPFC (aVLPFC), anterior temporal cortex (aTC), anterior parahippocampal gyrus (aPHG), and hippocampus (HPC), whereas the dorsal frontoparietal post-retrieval control network includes dorsolateral PFC (DLPFC), and inferior parietal lobes (IPS). Other abbreviations: EC, entorhinal cortex; pPHG, posterior parahippocampal gyrus.

Our lab recently tested this hypothesis by analyzing functional connectivity during an episodic memory retrieval task (Barredo, Öztekin, and Badre, 2013).
Participants performed a single-agenda source monitoring or exclusion task (Jacoby,
1991). Specifically, at encoding participants performed one of two semantic
decisions with words (size or organic). Then, at test, they verified whether they had
performed a target source task with each word, indicating yes or no. Importantly,
we assume that any evidence of an item being old drives a tendency to endorse the
item. Thus, these "incongruent" items, in which the correct response for the source
decision is "no" despite the studied items themselves being familiar to the subject,
produce decision or response-level conflict in order to either reject the evidence of
oldness as not diagnostic for the source decision and/or to override the positive
response. This conflict is evident in increased reaction time (RT) and errors for
these incongruent items relative to congruent items (which were seen with the
target source task and entail a "yes" response). Beyond congruency, we also manipulated the association strength between item cues and target source information by
varying repetition during encoding. A single encounter with an item at encoding
should produce a weaker memory trace associating that item with its source task
compared to multiple repetitions. So greater controlled retrieval should be required
on weak associative strength trials.

Importantly, controlled retrieval is only affected by associative strength, and is
insensitive to congruency. This is because congruency does not affect the likelihood
of retrieval, but concerns how remembered information is related to the current
response criteria. By contrast, post-retrieval decision processes will show an interaction between strength and congruency, wherein strong items are easier to endorse
than weak items for congruent trials, but strong items are harder to reject than
weak items for incongruent trials. Therefore, regions showing a main effect of
associative strength without an interaction with congruency may be sensitive to
retrieval, whereas regions showing a strength-by-congruency interaction are sensitive
to post-retrieval factors.

Using this logic, we observed evidence that anterior vlPFC is a member of a ventral
retrieval pathway whereas mid-vlPFC affiliates with the dorsal frontoparietal control
system (see Figure 7.3b). Specifically, we observed that anterior vlPFC and other
regions along the ventral pathway, such as anterior temporal cortex, anterior parahippocampal gyrus, and hippocampus, showed effects of controlled retrieval that did not
interact with congruency. Functional connectivity analysis of these functionally
defined seeds confirmed that they were members of a common correlated network,
specifically correlating more with one another than with regions outside of the
network. By contrast, mid-vlPFC showed an interaction between strength and congruency in the univariate analysis and was functionally connected to dlPFC and
inferior parietal regions that are members of the frontoparietal post-retrieval control
network (Dosenbach *et al.*, 2007; Vincent *et al.*, 2008; Yeo *et al.*, 2011). Mid-vlPFC
did not correlate with the ventral retrieval network. Notably, in addition to coupling
with the ventral retrieval pathway, anterior vlPFC also correlated with mid-vlPFC
and the dorsal frontoparietal post-retrieval control network (Figure 7.4). This finding
potentially suggests that anterior vlPFC acts as a hub, coordinating processing between the ventral controlled retrieval system and the dorsal post-retrieval control
system. But the precise functional significance of this observation is an important
question for future work.

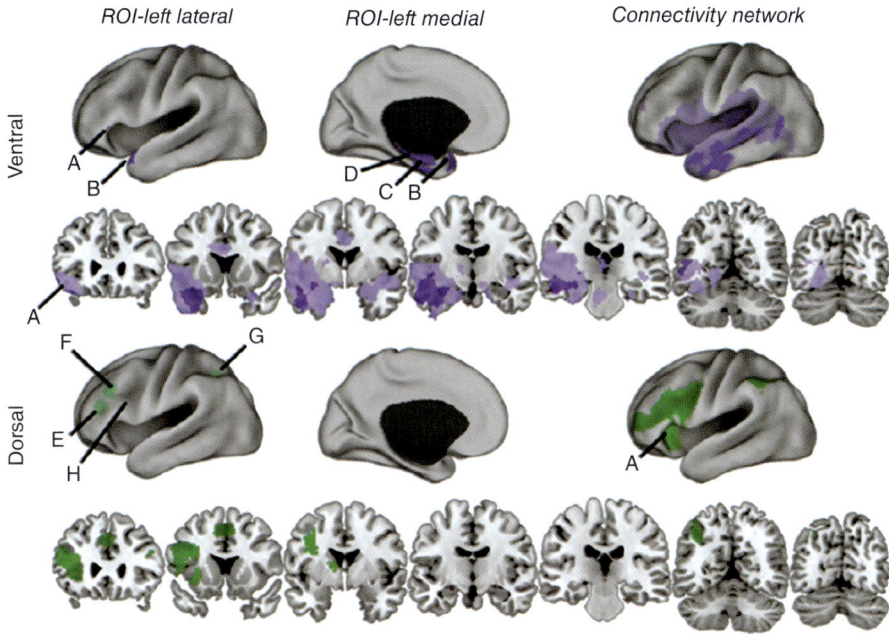

**Figure 7.4**   Functional connectivity along the ventral controlled retrieval network and the dorsal frontoparietal post-retrieval control network (reprinted with permission from Barredo, Oztekin, and Badre, 2013). Anterior vlPFC functionally couples with aTC, aPHG, and HPC (purple, top). Mid-vlPFC functionally couples with dlPFC, IPS, inferior temporal gyrus (ITG), and basal ganglia (green, bottom). Comparison across networks illustrates that the overlap between frontoparietal control network and retrieval network is primarily limited to aVLPFC. All contrasts are valid ìANDî conjunctions from false discovery rate (FDR)-corrected seed maps thresholded at $p < 0.05$. Some of the major structures functionally coupling with various seeds are labeled as follows: (A) aVLPFC, (B) aTC, (C) aPHG, (D) HPC, (E) lateral PFC (PFCl), (F) lateral posterior PFC (PFClp), (G) IPS, and (H) mid-vlPFC. Note that mid-vlPFC lies within the sulcus and cannot be seen in lateral view; approximate location only is marked.

These results provide a broader context for the previous distinctions between anterior vlPFC and mid-vlPFC. Specifically, prior work has defined vlPFC synonymously with the inferior frontal gyrus and has drawn distinctions – such as between anterior vlPFC and mid-vlPFC – within this anatomically defined region. However, as noted above, the functional boundary between these networks may not be at the inferior frontal sulcus. Rather the dorsal frontoparietal post-retrieval control system includes the middle frontal gyrus and the caudal and dorsal portion of the inferior frontal gyrus. Thus, purely as a matter of location within the inferior frontal gyrus, prior definitions of anterior vlPFC are more likely to fall on the ventral controlled retrieval network, and definitions of mid-vlPFC are more likely to fall on the frontoparietal post-retrieval control network or to be on the border of both retrieval and post-retrieval control networks.

In this regard, it is notable that tasks previously observed to activate dlPFC are those that manipulate post-retrieval monitoring (Rugg, Otten, and Henson, 2002; Rugg and Wilding, 2000), active inhibition of memories (Anderson *et al.*, 2004;

Butler and James, 2010; Depue, Curran, and Banich, 2007; Kuhl *et al.*, 2008), and relational operations within working memory (Blumenfeld and Ranganath, 2007; Fletcher *et al.*, 1998). Based on the operational definitions of these functions used in the literature, it is difficult to draw a clear process distinction between these post-retrieval/decision-level functions and the concept of post-retrieval selection outlined above. It is possible that such distinctions exist and there is further functional specialization between mid-vlPFC and dlPFC. However, another possibility raised by the connectivity analysis is that this process similarity reflects the fact that mid-vlPFC should be functionally grouped with this broader dorsal network. Hence, at least one key functional neuroanatomic distinction in control of memory is between (1) processes affecting retrieval directly (controlled retrieval) that are supported by a ventral retrieval network and (2) processes operating post-retrieval to align remembered information with current task goals and decision criteria that are supported by a more dorsal frontoparietal network.

## Transient Dynamics within Frontal Networks

In the previous sections, we have described a distinction between control processes that operate to influence retrieval itself versus those that operate post-retrieval to align retrieval with task goals and decision criteria. Evidence from fMRI has suggested that this distinction is supported by distinct neuroanatomical subsystems. The temporal resolution afforded by EEG has provided complementary evidence for this distinction (for more on EEG, see Chapter 16). First, these peri- and post-retrieval processes should be distinguishable temporally. Event-related potential (ERP) studies have shown early posterior (~400 ms post-stimulus onset) and late right frontal (~1000 ms post-stimulus onset) differences between correctly recognized old and new items ("old/new effects") during source retrieval (Allan, Wilding, and Rugg, 1998; Wilding and Rugg, 1996), supporting the presence of multiple temporal components during retrieval. Race, Badre, and Wagner (2010) more directly related early and late ERP components to retrieval and post-retrieval decision and response processes. Participants were asked to make semantic decisions about presented items. Items were repeated during the experiment, sometimes with the same decision and sometimes with a different decision, allowing item-semantic priming to be separated from decision-related priming effects. In ERP, the item priming occurred at an earlier stage than the decision priming, consistent with modulation of early retrieval processes versus late decision processes. Thus, the ERP data are largely consistent with two temporally distinguishable components related to retrieval versus post-retrieval decision or monitoring demands. However, given recent insights regarding the importance of at least two broad functional networks to controlled retrieval and selection, data from EEG can also address the nature of neural dynamics within the networks described above.

Although functional connectivity indicates anatomical connections between frontal and posterior brain regions, the mechanism by which these brain regions dynamically interact during declarative memory retrieval has not been specified. It has been proposed that neural oscillations provide the means by which brain areas interact to perform cognitive tasks (Başar and Schürmann, 2001; Miller and Wilson, 2008; Varela *et al.*, 2001; see also Chapter 2). Fluctuations in postsynaptic potentials produce local oscillations. In addition, oscillators in one brain region can phase synchronize with oscillators in another region through long-range connections. A mechanism for interaction for both local populations of neurons and large neural assemblies is through phase synchronization of oscillations (Miller and Wilson, 2008; Varela *et al.*, 2001). As neurons oscillate, they effectively open and close their window to both send and receive information (Buzsáki and Draguhn, 2004; Womelsdorf *et al.*, 2007). For information to be transferred from one neuronal group to another, the sending neuron must be excitable at the same time that the receiving group is excitable. This requires the coupling of oscillations between sending and receiving neurons through phase synchronization (Fries, 2005). This pattern of neural interaction allows for efficient neural communication through the transient coupling of synchronously firing neurons forming functional neural networks.

There is convincing evidence that neural rhythms contribute to memory retrieval. During episodic retrieval, a number of EEG studies have found greater theta power for hits than for correct rejections. Moreover, differences in theta power distinguish individual differences in episodic memory retrieval performance (reviewed in Nyhus and Curran, 2010). We recently proposed that theta oscillations represent interactions between brain systems for the control of episodic retrieval (Nyhus and Curran, 2010). This hypothesis was initially motivated by studies attempting to localize the sources of theta oscillations during episodic retrieval. In general, theta power increases are frequently observed in frontal scalp locations during successful episodic retrieval, and in frontal and posterior scalp locations for retrieval of specific details of the study episode.

To test whether theta oscillations are related to the control of memory retrieval, we conducted three EEG experiments during which subjects performed a source retrieval task (Nyhus, 2010). Results showed right frontal theta power that was greater for old than new words. In addition, theta coherence between right frontal and left parietal channels was greater for old than new words, for incorrect than correct memory judgments, and for low-confidence than high-confidence response (Figure 7.5). Post-retrieval monitoring demands should be greater when decisions are uncertain, which is more likely for incorrect than correct memory judgments and for low- than high-confidence responses. Therefore, these results suggest that transient theta interactions in a frontoparietal network are involved in the monitoring of episodic memory.

Although these results suggest that theta oscillations are important for communication among brain regions in a post-retrieval control network, future research is needed to localize the source of these effects, and to determine the frequency of communication among the controlled retrieval and post-retrieval control networks. For example, though there are no data on the oscillatory correlates of controlled retrieval as distinct from selection, it is notable that semantic retrieval, which is particularly dependent on anterior vlPFC, has been associated with alpha rather than theta band oscillations. Due to their spatial and temporal limitations, EEG and fMRI methods alone are not sufficient to identify the relationship between oscillations and specific functional networks involved in memory retrieval. Future research simultaneously recording EEG and fMRI is necessary to examine the relationship between oscillatory effects and the functional networks identified with fMRI in declarative memory retrieval.

(a)

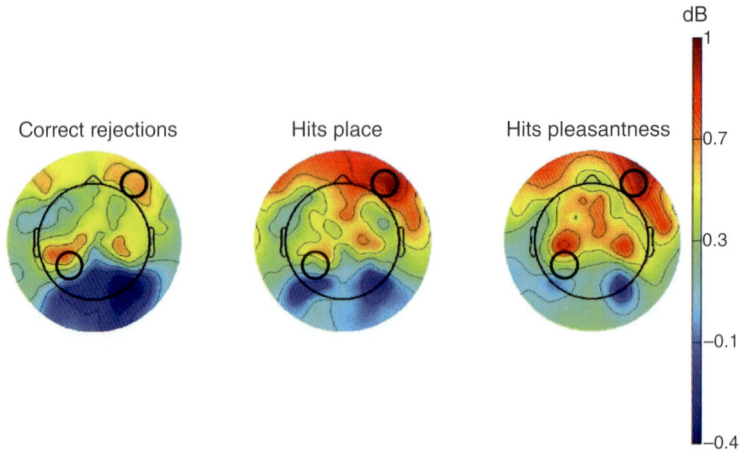

(b)

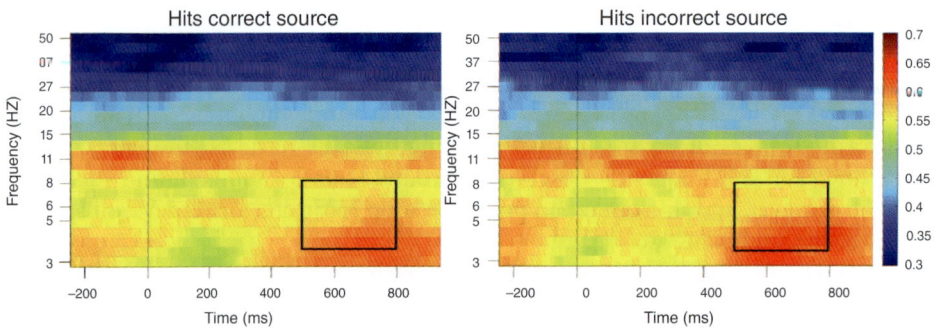

**Figure 7.5** Theta effects during a source retrieval task (reprinted with permission from Nyhus, 2010). (a) Theta power across all channels from 500 to 800 ms. Black circles mark the approximate locations of analyzed channels in right frontal (channel 1) and left parietal (channel 53) brain regions. Color scale: decibel change from pre-stimulus baseline. (b) Theta coherence for all frequencies across one right frontal channel (channel 1) and one left parietal channel (channel 53). Highlighted is theta coherence from 500 to 800 ms. Color scale: magnitude of cross-coherence from 0 to 1, with 0 indicating absence of synchronization and 1 indicating perfect synchronization for each frequency at each time-point.

# Conclusion

In order to deal effectively with our environment, declarative memory systems have developed to adaptively retrieve information that is relevant while outweighing the costs of retrieval. Although information can be automatically retrieved, cognitive control of declarative memory retrieval is important for adaptive retrieval. Here, we have highlighted one functional distinction in the cognitive control of memory that appears to receive support from multiple methods: controlled retrieval versus post-retrieval selection.

As described above, evidence suggests that a ventral retrieval pathway that includes the anterior vlPFC biases memory retrieval when memories are not readily accessible. A more dorsal network that includes mid-vlPFC and potentially dlPFC aligns what has been retrieved with task goals by selecting appropriate representations, setting decision criteria, and monitoring the outcome of retrieval. These associated networks likely coordinate their activity via oscillations, such as in the theta band for post-retrieval control, the dynamics of which are largely unknown.

Though progress has been made in understanding how the brain controls memory retrieval, a number of fundamental questions remain to be addressed. For example, how are memory control strategies learned, evaluated, and adjusted? What are the neural mechanisms by which PFC can increase the likelihood of retrieval or select relevant items from working memory? How does anterior vlPFC "know" that memory strength is weak and so it is necessary to guide retrieval? Of course, satisfying answers to these questions must be provided without recourse to a "homunculus" or little man in the head who just performs these functions. Rather, formal theoretical and computational models that can incorporate findings from neuroscience data are required. Thus, in our view, considerable progress on these questions will be made by extending existing models of cognitive control to the domain of memory.

# References

Allan, K., Wilding, E.L., and Rugg, M.D. (1998). Electrophysiological evidence for dissociable processes contributing to recollection. *Acta Psychologica*, 98 (2–3), 231–52. doi: 10.1016/S0001-6918(97)00044-9.

Anderson, J.R., and Milson, R. (1989). Human memory: an adaptive perspective. *Psychological Review*, 96 (4), 703–719. doi: 10.1037/0033-295X.96.4.703.

Anderson, M.C., and Neely, J.H. (1996). Interference and inhibition in memory retrieval. In *Memory. Handbook of Perception and Cognition* (ed. E. L. Bjork and R. A. Bjork). San Diego, CA: Academic Press, pp. 237–313.

Anderson, M.C., Ochsner, K.N., Kuhl, B., *et al.* (2004). Neural systems underlying the suppression of unwanted memories. *Science*, 303 (5655), 232–235. doi: 10.1126/science.1089504.

Badre, D., Poldrack, R.A. Pare-Blagoev, E.J., *et al.* (2005). Dissociable controlled retrieval and generalized selection mechanisms in ventrolateral prefrontal cortex. *Neuron*, 47 (6), 907–918. doi: 10.1016/j.neuron.2005.07.023.

Badre, D., and Wagner, A.D. (2005). Frontal lobe mechanisms that resolve proactive interference. *Cerebral Cortex*, 15 (12), 2003–2012. doi: 10.1093/cercor/bhi075.

Badre, D., and Wagner, A.D. (2007). Left ventrolateral prefrontal cortex and the cognitive control of memory. *Neuropsychologia* 45 (13), 2883–2901. doi: 10.1016/j.neuropsychologia.2007.06.015.

Barredo, J., Öztekin, I., and Badre, D. (2013). Ventral fronto-temporal pathway supporting cognitive control of episodic memory retrieval. *Cerebral Cortex*, published online October 31, 2013. doi:10.1093/cercor/bht291.

Başar, E., and Schürmann, M. (2001). Toward new theories of brain function and brain dynamics. *International Journal of Psychophysiology*, 39 (2–3), 87–89.

Benjamin, A.S. (2007). Memory is more than just remembering: strategic control of encoding, accessing memory, and making decisions. In *The Psychology of Learning and Motivation, Volume 48: Skill and Strategy in Memory Use* (ed. A. S. Benjamin and B. H. Ross). New York, NY: Elsevier, pp. 175–223.

Blumenfeld, R.S., and Ranganath, C. (2007). Prefrontal cortex and long-term memory encoding: an integrative review of findings from neuropsychology and neuroimaging. *Neuroscientist*, 13 (3), 280–291. doi: 10.1177/1073858407299290.

Broca, P. (1861). Remarques sur le siège de la faculté du langage articulé, suivies d'une observation d'aphémie (perte de la parole). *Bulletin de la Société Anatomique de Paris*, 36, 330–357.

Buckner, R.L. (2003). Functional-anatomic correlates of control processes in memory. *Journal of Neuroscience*, 23 (10), 3999–4004. doi: 10.1523/JNEUROSCI.2625-04.2004.

Buckner, R.L. (2010). Human functional connectivity: new tools, unresolved questions. *Proceedings of the National Academy of Sciences of the USA*, 107 (24), 10769–10770. doi: 10.1073/pnas.1005987107.

Butler, A.J., and James, K.H. (2010). The neural correlates of attempting to suppress negative versus neutral memories. *Cognitive, Affective, and Behavioral Neuroscience*, 10 (2), 182–194. doi: 10.3758/CABN.10.2.182.

Buzsáki, G., and Draguhn, A. (2004). Neuronal oscillations in cortical networks. *Science*, 304 (5679), 1926–1929. doi: 10.1126/science.1099745.

Cooper, R.P. (2010). Cognitive control: componential or emergent? *Topics in Cognitive Science*, 2, 598–613. doi: 10.1111/j.1756-8765.2010.01110.x.

Danker, J.F., Gunn, P., and Anderson, J.R. (2008). A rational account of memory predicts left prefrontal activation during controlled retrieval. *Cerebral Cortex*, 18 (11), 2674–2685. doi: 10.1093/cercor/bhn027.

Depue, B.E., Curran, T., and Banich, M.T. (2007). Prefrontal regions orchestrate suppression of emotional memories via a two-phase process. *Science*, 317 (5835), 215–219. doi: 10.1126/science.1139560.

Devlin, J.T., Matthews, P.M., and Rushworth, M.F. (2003). Semantic processing in the left inferior prefrontal cortex: a combined functional magnetic resonance imaging and tran-scranial magnetic stimulation study. *Journal of Cognitive Neuroscience*, 15 (1), 71–84. doi: 10.1162/089892903321107837.

Dosenbach, N.U., Fair, D.A., Miezin, F.M., *et al.* (2007). Distinct brain networks for adaptive and stable task control in humans. *Proceedings of the National Academy of Sciences of the USA*, 104 (26), 11073–11078. doi: 10.1073/pnas.0704320104

Duncan, J. (2010). The multiple-demand (MD) system of the primate brain: mental programs for intelligent behaviour. *Trends in Cognitive Sciences*, 14 (4), 172–179. doi: 10.1016/j.tics.2010.01.004.

Fletcher, P.C., and Henson, R.N. (2001). Frontal lobes and human memory: insights from functional neuroimaging. *Brain*, 124 (5), 849–881. doi: 10.1093/brain/124.5.849.

Fletcher, P.C., Shallice, T., Frith, C.D., *et al.* (1998). The functional roles of prefrontal cortex in episodic memory. II. Retrieval. *Brain*, 121 (7), 1249–1256. doi: 10.1093/brain/121.7.1249.

Fox, M.D., and Raichle, M.E. (2007). Spontaneous fluctuations in brain activity observed with functional magnetic resonance imaging. *Nature Reviews Neuroscience*, 8 (9), 700–711. doi: 10.1038/nrn2201.

Fries, P. (2005). A mechanism for cognitive dynamics: neuronal communication through neuronal coherence. *Trends in Cognitive Sciences*, 9 (10), 474–480. doi: 10.1016/j.tics.2005.08.011.

Gold, B.T., Balota, D.A., Jones, S.J., *et al.* (2006). Dissociation of automatic and strategic lexical-semantics: functional magnetic resonance imaging evidence for differing roles of multiple frontotemporal regions. *Journal of Neuroscience*, 26 (24), 6523–6532. doi: 10.1523/JNEUROSCI.0808-06.2006.

Gold, B.T., Balota, D.A., Kirchhoff, B.A., and Buckner, R.L. (2005). Common and dissociable activation patterns sssociated with controlled semantic and phonological processing: evidence from fMRI adaptation. *Cerebral Cortex*, 15 (9), 1438–1450. doi: 10.1093/cercor/bhi024.

Goldberg, R.F., Perfetti, C.A., Fiez, J.A., and Schneider, W. (2007). Selective retrieval of abstract semantic knowledge in left prefrontal cortex. *Journal of Neuroscience*, 27 (14), 3790–3798. doi: 10.1523/JNEUROSCI.2381-06.2007.

Gough, P.M., Nobre, A.C., and Devlin, J.T. (2005). Dissociating linguistic processes in the left inferior frontal cortex with transcranial magnetic stimulation. *Journal of Neuroscience*, 25 (35), 8010–8016. doi: 10.1523/JNEUROSCI.2307-05.2005.

Griffiths, T.L., Steyvers, M., and Firl, A. (2007). Google and the mind: predicting fluency with PageRank. *Psychological Science*, 18, 1069–1076. doi: 10.1111/j.1467-9280.2007.02027.x.

Jacoby, L.L. (1991). A process dissociation framework: separating automatic from intentional uses of memory. *Journal of Memory and Language*, 30, 513–541. doi: 10.1016/0749-596X(91)90025-F.

Janowsky, J.S., Shimamura, A.P., Kritchevsky, M., and Squire, L.R. (1989). Cognitive impairment following frontal lobe damage and its relevance to human amnesia. *Behavioral Neuroscience*, 103 (3), 548–560. doi: 10.1037/0735-7044.103.3.548.

Janowsky, J.S., Shimamura, A.P., and Squire, L.R. (1989). Source memory impairment in patients with frontal lobe lesions. *Neuropsychologia*, 27 (8), 1043–1056. doi: 10.1016/0028-3932(89)90184-X.

Jetter, W., Poser, U., Freeman, R.B., Jr., and Markowitsch, H.J. (1986). A verbal long term memory deficit in frontal lobe damaged patients. *Cortex*, 22 (2), 229–242.

Klein, D., Olivier, A., Milner, B., *et al.* (1997). Obligatory role of the LIFG in synonym generation: evidence from PET and cortical stimulation. *Neuroreport*, 8 (15), 3275–3279. doi: 10.1097/00001756-199710200-00017.

Kuhl, B.A., Kahn, I., Dudukovic, N.M., and Wagner, A.D. (2008). Overcoming suppression in order to remember: contributions from anterior cingulate and ventrolateral prefrontal cortex. *Cognitive, Affective and Behavioral Neuroscience*, 8 (2), 211–221. doi: 10.3758/CABN.8.2.211.

Metzler, C. (2001). Effects of left frontal lesions on the selection of context-appropriate meanings. *Neuropsychology*, 15 (3), 315–328. doi: 10.1037/0894-4105.15.3.315.

Miller, E.K., and Cohen, J.D. (2001). An integrative theory of prefrontal cortex function. *Annual Review of Neuroscience*, 24, 167–202. doi: 10.1146/annurev.neuro.24.1.167.

Miller, E.K., and Wilson, M.A. (2008). All my circuits: using multiple electrodes to understand functioning neural networks. *Neuron*, 60 (3), 483–488. doi: 10.1016/j.neuron.2008.10.033.

Moscovitch, M. (1982). Multiple dissociations of function in the amnesic syndrome. In *Human Memory and Amnesia* (ed. L S. Cermak). Hillsdale, NJ: Erlbaum, pp. 337–370.

Moscovitch, M. (1992). Memory and working-with-memory: a component process model based on modules and central systems. *Journal of Cognitive Neuroscience*, 4 (3), 257–267. doi: 10.1162/jocn.1992.4.3.257.

Moscovitch, M., and Melo, B. (1997). Strategic retrieval and the frontal lobes: evidence from confabulation and amnesia. *Neuropsychologia* 35 (7), 1017–34. doi: 10.1016/S0028-3932(97)00028-6.

Nolde, S.F., Johnson, M.K., and Raye, C.L. (1998). The role of prefrontal cortex during tests of episodic memory. *Trends in Cognitive Sciences*, 2 (10), 399–406. doi: 10.1016/S1364-6613(98)01233-9.

Nyberg, L., Cabeza, R., and Tulving, E. (1996). PET studies of encoding and retrieval: the HERA model. *Psychonomic Bulletin and Review*, 3 (2), 135–148. doi: 10.3758/BF03212412.

Nyhus, E. (2010). Theta oscillations in top-down control of episodic memory retrieval. Doctoral dissertation, Psychology, University of Colorado at Boulder, Boulder, CO.

Nyhus, E., and Curran, T. (2010). Functional role of gamma and theta oscillations in episodic memory. *Neuroscience and Biobehavioral Reviews*, 34 (7), 1023–1035. doi: 10.1016/j.neubiorev.2009.12.014.

Öztekin, I., and Badre, D. (2011) Distributed patterns of brain activity that lead to forgetting. *Frontiers in Human Neuroscience*, 5, 86. doi: 10.3389/fnhum.2011.00086.

Petrides, M. (2002). The mid-ventrolateral prefrontal cortex and active mnemonic retrieval. *Neurobiology of Learning and Memory*, 78 (3), 528–538. doi: 10.1006/nlme.2002.4107.

Petrides, M., and Pandya, D.N. (2002). Comparative cytoarchitectonic analysis of the human and the macaque ventrolateral prefrontal cortex and corticocortical connection patterns in the monkey. *European Journal of Neuroscience*, 16 (2), 291–310.

Poldrack, R.A., Wagner, A.D., Prull, M.W., *et al.* (1999). Functional specialization for semantic and phonological processing in the left inferior prefrontal cortex. *NeuroImage*, 10 (1), 15–35. doi: 10.1006/nimg.1999.0441.

Postle, B.R., and Brush, L.N. (2004). The neural bases of the effects of item-nonspecific proactive interference in working memory. *Cognitive, Affective and Behavioral Neuroscience*, 4 (3), 379–392. doi: 10.3758/CABN.4.3.379.

Postle, B.R., Brush, L.N., and Nick, A.M. (2004). Prefrontal cortex and the mediation of proactive interference in working memory. *Cognitive, Affective and Behavioral Neuroscience*, 4 (4), 600–608. doi: 10.3758/CABN.4.4.600.

Postman, L., and Underwood, B.J. (1973). Critical issues in interference theory. *Memory and Cognition*, 1, 19–40. doi: 10.3758/BF03198064.

Race, E.A., Badre, D., and Wagner, A.D. (2010). Multiple forms of learning yield temporally distinct electrophysiological repetition effects. *Cerebral Cortex*, 20 (7), 1726–1738. doi: 10.1093/cercor/bhp233.

Race, E.A., Shanker, S., and Wagner, A.D. (2008). Neural priming in human frontal cortex: multiple forms of learning reduce demands on the prefrontal executive system. *Journal of Cognitive Neuroscience*, 21 (9), 1766–1781. doi: 10.1162/jocn.2009.21132.

Raichle, M.E., MacLeod, A.M. Snyder, A.Z., et al. (2001). A default mode of brain function. *Proceedings of the National Academy of Sciences of the USA*, 98 (2), 676–682. doi: 10.1016/j.neuroimage.2007.02.041.

Rugg, M.D., Otten, L.J., and Henson, R.N. (2002). The neural basis of episodic memory: evidence from functional neuroimaging. *Philosophical Transactions of the Royal Society of London, Series B: Biological Sciences*, 357 (1424), 1097–1110. doi: 10.1098/rstb.2002.1102.

Rugg, M.D., and Wilding, E.L. (2000). Retrieval processing and episodic memory. *Trends in Cognitive Sciences*, 4 (3), 108–115. doi: 10.1016/S1364-6613(00)01445-5.

Scimeca, J.M., and Badre, D. (2012). Striatal contributions to declarative memory retrieval. *Neuron*, 75 (3), 380–392. doi: 10.1016/j.neuron.2012.07.014.

Scoville, W.B., and Milner, B. (1957). Loss of recent memory after bilateral hippocampal lesions. *Journal of Neurology, Neurosurgery, and Psychiatry*, 20 (1), 11–21. doi: 10.1136/jnnp.20.1.11.

Shimamura, A.P., Janowsky, J.S., and Squire, L.R. (1990). Memory for the temporal order of events in patients with frontal lobe lesions and amnesic patients. *Neuropsychologia*, 28 (8), 803–813.

Simons, J.S., and Spiers, H.J. (2003). Prefrontal and medial temporal lobe interactions in long-term memory. *Nature Reviews Neuroscience*, 4 (8), 637–648. doi: 10.1038/nrn1178.

Snyder, H.R., Banich, M.T., and Munakata, Y. (2011). Choosing our words: retrieval and selection processes recruit shared neural substrates in left ventrolateral prefrontal cortex. *Journal of Cognitive Neuroscience*, 23 (11), 3470–3482. doi: 10.1162/jocn_a_00023.

Snyder, H.R., Hutchison, N., Nyhus, E., et al. (2010). Neural inhibition enables selection during language processing. *Proceedings of the National Academy of Sciences of the USA*, 107 (38), 16483–16488. doi: 10.1073/pnas.1002291107/-/DCSupplemental.

Spaniol, J., Davidson, P.S., Kim, A.S., et al. (2009). Event-related fMRI studies of episodic encoding and retrieval: meta-analyses using activation likelihood estimation. *Neuropsychologia*, 47 (8–9), 1765–1779. doi: 10.1016/j.neuropsychologia.2009.02.028.

Squire, L.R. (1982). The neuropsychology of human-memory. *Annual Review of Neuroscience*, 5, 241–273. doi: 10.1146/annurev.ne.05.030182.001325.

Stuss, D.T., and Alexander, M.P. (2005). Does damage to the frontal lobes produce impairment in memory? *Current Directions in Psychological Science*, 14 (2), 84–88. doi: 10.1111/j.0963-7214.2005.00340.x.

Stuss, D.T., Alexander, M.P. Palumbo, C.L., et al. (1994). Organizational strategies of patients with unilateral or bilateral frontal lobe injury in word list learning tasks. *Neuropsychologia*, 8 (3), 355–373.

Swick, D., Senkfor, A.J., and Van Petten, C. (2006). Source memory retrieval is affected by aging and prefrontal lesions: behavioral and ERP evidence. *Brain Rsearch*, 1107 (1), 161–176. doi: 10.1016/j.brainres.2006.06.013.

Thompson-Schill, S.L., and Botvinick, M.M. (2006). Resolving conflict: a response to Martin and Cheng (2006). *Psychonomic Bulletin and Review* 13 (3), 402–408; discussion 409–11. doi: 10.3758/BF03193860.

Thompson-Schill, S.L., D'Esposito, M., Aguirre, G.K., and Farah, M.J. (1997). Role of left inferior prefrontal cortex in retrieval of semantic knowledge: a reevaluation. *Proceedings of the National Academy of Sciences of the USA*, 94 (26), 14792–14797.

Thompson-Schill, S.L., Swick, D. Farah, M.J., *et al.* (1998). Verb generation in patients with focal frontal lesions: a neuropsychological test of neuroimaging findings. *Proceedings of the National Academy of Sciences of the USA*, 95 (26), 15855–15860. doi: 10.1073/pnas.95.26.15855

Tulving, E., Kapur, S., Craik, F.I., *et al.* (1994). Hemispheric encoding/retrieval asymmetry in episodic memory: positron emission tomography findings. *Proceedings of the National Academy of Sciences of the USA*, 91 (6), 2016–2020. doi: 10.1073/pnas.91.6.2016.

Varela, F., Lachaux, J.P., Rodriguez, E., and Martinerie, J. (2001). The brainweb: phase synchronization and large-scale integration. *Nature Reviews Neuroscience*, 2 (4), 229–239. doi: 10.1038/35067550.

Vincent, J.L., Kahn, I. Snyder, A.Z., *et al.* (2008). Evidence for a frontoparietal control system revealed by intrinsic functional connectivity. *Journal of Neurophysiology*, 100 (6), 3328–3342. doi: 10.1152/jn.90355.2008.

Wagner, A.D., Maril, A., Bjork, R.A., and Schacter, D.L. (2001). Prefrontal contributions to executive control: fMRI evidence for functional distinctions within lateral Prefrontal cortex. *NeuroImage*, 14 (6), 1337–1347. doi: 10.1006/nimg.2001.0936.

Wilding, E.L., and Rugg, M.D. (1996). An event-related potential study of recognition memory with and without retrieval of source. *Brain*, 119 (3), 889–905. doi: 10.1093/brain/119.3.889.

Winocur, G., Kinsbourne, M., and Moscovitch, M. (1981). The effect of cueing on release from proactive-interference in Korsakoff amnesic patients. *Journal of Experimental Psychology: Human Learning and Memory*, 7 (1), 56–65.

Womelsdorf, T., Schoffelen, J.M., Oostenveld, R., *et al.* (2007). Modulation of neuronal interactions through neuronal synchronization. *Science*, 316 (5831), 1609–1612. doi: 10.1126/science.1139597.

Yeo, B.T., Krienen, F.M., Sepulcre, J., *et al.* (2011). The organization of the human cerebral cortex estimated by intrinsic functional connectivity. *Journal of Neurophysiology*, 106 (3), 1125–1165. doi: 10.1152/jn.00338.2011.

# 8

# Functional Neuroimaging
# of False Memories

## Nancy A. Dennis, Caitlin R. Bowman, and
## Indira C. Turney

## Introduction

Our memories are far from perfect. In fact we are prone to memory distortions that often render even the most vivid retrieval of past events inaccurate. One such example of the fallible nature of memory is that of *false memories*. A false memory refers to the situation in which we generate a memory of a past experience when in fact no such event occurred. Examples include remembering you took out the trash, when in fact you did not; remembering that you were told to pick up apples and bananas from the grocery store, when in fact oranges and pears were the to-be-purchased fruits; and believing you met a new acquaintance in one setting (e.g., a holiday party) when in fact you met him or her in another (e.g., a work seminar). Critical to the definition of false memory is that when making such an error of commission, an individual sincerely believes that the misremembered event actually occurred in the past. Often the false memory is not completely without precedence: on many occasions an event highly related to that which is falsely retrieved actually did occur; in other instances an individual may retrieve the correct event but misremember the source of the event (i.e., the time or place the event occurred). Given these similarities in phenomenology, true and false memories are often very difficult to differentiate.

Because of the overlap in the behavioral characteristics of true and false memories, and their high rate of occurrence in memory tests throughout the lifespan (McCabe *et al.*, 2009), the study of false memories represents a critical area of memory research. They have traditionally been examined using a variety of behavioral paradigms, but recent advances in neuroimaging have allowed for the use of positron emission tomography (PET), functional magnetic resonance imaging (fMRI), and event-related potentials (ERPs) to elucidate the specific brain regions that support both true and false memories, as well as to identify a neural signature that differentiates the two types of memories. In this chapter we will briefly review findings from studies employing the most commonly utilized false memory paradigms in neuroimaging research. Within this review we will highlight neural processes that are common to true and false memories as well as those that distinguish between the two types of

*The Wiley Handbook on the Cognitive Neuroscience of Memory*, First Edition.
Edited by Donna Rose Addis, Morgan Barense, and Audrey Duarte.
© 2015 John Wiley & Sons, Ltd. Published 2015 by John Wiley & Sons, Ltd.

memory processes. The review will include retrieval-related studies and encoding studies, and will conclude with a look at developmental studies of false memories.

## False Memory Paradigms

While a wide variety of experimental paradigms have been developed to study false memories (for a review, see Brainerd and Reyna, 2005), only a small number have been adapted for use in neuroimaging. Those that have been so adapted focus on ensuring that the experimental paradigm produces a sufficient number of false memories in order to estimate a reliable neural signal. Accordingly, many false memory paradigms explicitly manipulate the relatedness between study and test items in order to produce ample false memories. The most widely used example is the Deese–Roediger–McDermott (DRM) paradigm (Deese, 1959; Roediger and McDermott, 1995). In the typical DRM paradigm, participants are presented with lists of words in which all the items in a given list are semantically related to an item that is not presented (the critical lure). For example, the words *bed, rest, awake, tired, dream, wake, snooze, blanket, doze, slumber, snore, nap, peace, yawn*, and *drowsy* are all related to the critical related word, *sleep*. Though *sleep* is not presented in the original list of studied words, individuals tend to recall and/or recognize the critical lure at both a rate and confidence level similar to that associated with retrieval of the studied items (Roediger and McDermott, 1995). Due to the fact that the traditional DRM paradigm converges on one related word, thereby requiring long lists to be used in order to identify a single false memory, variations on the paradigm have been used in neuroimaging studies. One common variation includes using conceptual lists where a subset of the category exemplars are presented during study (e.g., farm animals: *chicken, sheep, pig, goat*) and several others are used as related lures at retrieval (e.g., *horse, cow*).

In addition to manipulating the semantic relatedness amongst items, many researchers have also used manipulations of perceptual relatedness to measure neural processes underlying false memories. Most neuroimaging studies utilizing this technique employ one of two major variations: categorized pictures (e.g., Gutchess and Schacter, 2012) or computer-generated abstract shapes (e.g., Slotnick and Schacter, 2004). In the categorical version of the paradigm, participants are presented with pictures of multiple exemplars from various categories during encoding (e.g., multiple exemplars of "chair"). During retrieval, target items are intermixed with related lures (category exemplars that were not presented at encoding) and unrelated lures (new items whose category was not presented during encoding). The use of computer-generated shapes works in a similar manner, whereby related lures are shapes that share perceptual overlap with a target while unrelated lures are more distinct.

A second major category of experimental paradigms designed to examine the neural basis of false memories is what we will label source-misattribution paradigms (i.e., imagery, misinformation, and source memory paradigms). In these paradigms, false memories are associated with incorrect memory for the original presentation, or source, of information. For example, in a typical imagery paradigm participants are provided with a list of items to study. While half of the items are accompanied by a pictorial representation of the item, the other half are presented only in word form and the participants are asked to think about or imagine the item. At retrieval, memory is tested for which items were actually accompanied by a visual representation. False memories occur when participants believe that a presented word was accompanied by a visual representation, when in fact the participant had been asked to imagine the item. In the misinformation paradigm, participants are presented with an episode during an initial study phase (e.g., vignettes depicting a car accident). Following this initial presentation, information about the episode is presented again, with alterations (e.g., with a yield sign inserted in the vignette instead of the original stop sign). The new or altered information presented during this second phase is what is referred to as "misinformation." At test, participants are asked to remember the original scenario of events. False memories occur when the misinformation is retrieved instead (e.g., remembering a yield sign instead of a stop sign). Finally, in source memory paradigms, false memories occur when, at retrieval, participants associate memory for one item with the source of a different item.

# Neuroimaging of False Memories

Traditionally, false memories stemming from semantic or perceptual relatedness have been considered to be theoretically and qualitatively distinct from those stemming from source-misattribution paradigms (e.g., Brainerd and Reyna, 2005; Stark, Okado, and Loftus, 2010). In particular, related false memories are posited to occur due to retrieval of the shared semantic or perceptual gist across both targets and lures. On the other hand, false memories stemming from misattribution paradigms include information that has been explicitly presented or referenced during encoding. As such, imagery and misinformation paradigms often cite source confusion and misattribution (Johnson, Hashtroudi, and Lindsay, 1993) as the underlying mechanism supporting false memories and focus on the examination of neural processes during the study phase to help explain the occurrence of false memories (see also *Encoding studies* section, below). Despite differences in methodology and theoretical cause of false memories across both relatedness and source-misattribution paradigms, similar findings have been observed at retrieval.

## Retrieval studies

By evoking a strong theme across encoded items, the DRM paradigm (and its variants) and perceptual false memory paradigms examine false memories associated with recognition responses to critical, or related, lures. Importantly, these critical lures share the same gist (i.e., semantic, conceptual meaning) or common features with items that were presented during encoding. As such, it is not surprising that the two paradigms exhibit highly similar findings, both with respect to commonalities in neural activity mediating true and false memories and with respect to neural correlates that differentiate based on the veracity of the memory.

*Common neural processing*   One of the most ubiquitous findings generated from false memory studies is the considerable overlap in the neural networks mediating both true and false memories (Figure 8.1). Specifically, overlapping neural activity has

(a)

Schacter et al., 1997

(b)

Atkins & Reuter-Lorenz, 2011

(c)

Gutchess & Schacter, 2012

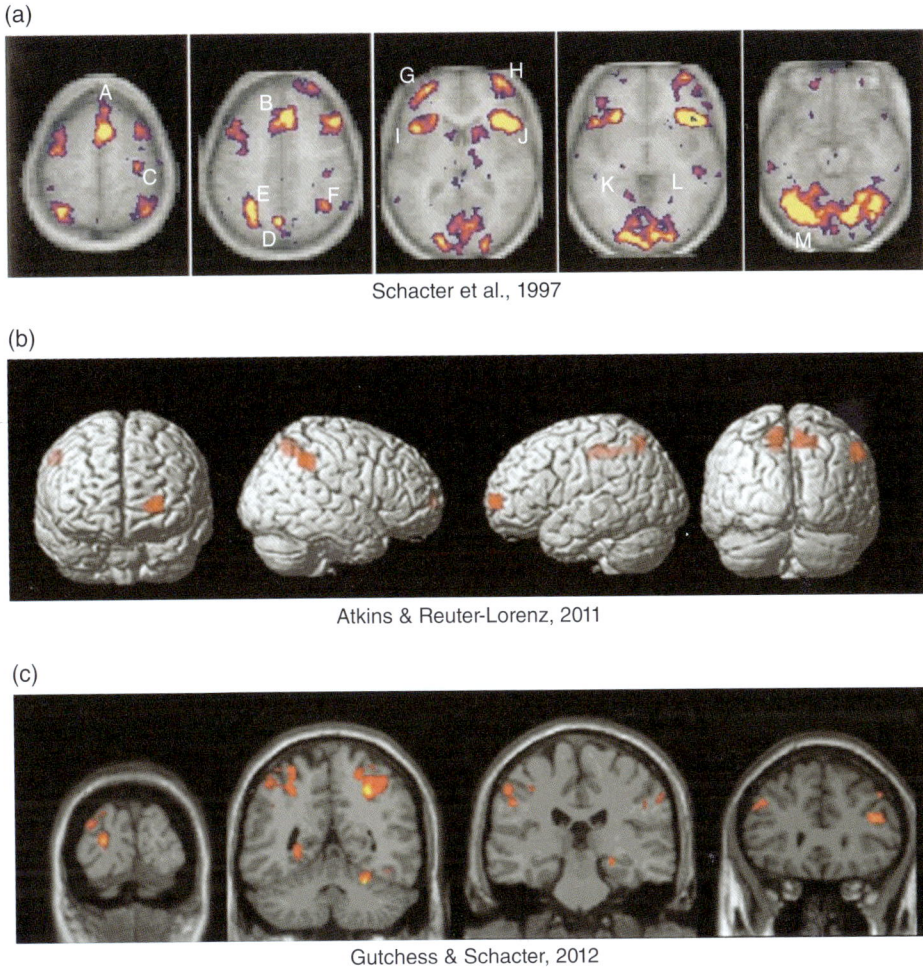

**Figure 8.1**  Results from relatedness paradigms showing common neural activity for true and false memories throughout frontal, parietal, temporal, and occipital cortices: (a) adapted from Schacter *et al.*, 1997; (b) adapted from Atkins and Reuter-Lorenz, 2011; (c) adapted from Gutchess and Schacter, 2012.

been found in bilateral frontal and parietal regions (Atkins and Reuter-Lorenz, 2011; Cabeza *et al.*, 2001; Dennis, Bowman, and Vandekar, 2012; Garoff-Eaton, Kensinger, and Schacter, 2007; Garoff-Eaton, Slotnick, and Schacter, 2006; Iidaka *et al.*, 2012; Kahn, Davachi, and Wagner, 2004; Schacter *et al.*, 1996, 1997; Slotnick and Schacter, 2004; Okado and Stark, 2003; von Zerssen *et al.*, 2001), bilateral caudate and insula (Stark, Okado, and Loftus, 2010; von Zerssen *et al.*, 2001), lateral temporal cortex (Cabeza *et al.*, 2001; Garoff-Eaton, Slotnick, and Schacter, 2006; Schacter *et al.*, 1996; Stark, Okado, and Loftus, 2010), occipital cortex (Dennis, Bowman, and Vandekar, 2012; Garoff-Eaton, Slotnick, and Schacter, 2006; Iidaka *et al.*, 2012; Schacter *et al.*, 1997; Slotnick and Schacter, 2004; Stark, Okado, and Loftus, 2010; von Zerssen *et al.*, 2001), and hippocampus/parahippocampal gyrus (PHG[1] Cabeza *et al.*, 2001; Dennis, Bowman, and Vandekar, 2012; Garoff-Eaton, Slotnick, and Schacter, 2006; Gutchess and Schacter, 2012; Kahn, Davachi, and Wagner, 2004; Schacter *et al.*, 1996, 1997; Slotnick and Schacter, 2004; Stark, Okado, and Loftus, 2010; von Zerssen *et al.*, 2001). This widespread overlap in neural activity mediating both true and false memories has been attributed to several factors, including the fact that targets and related lures share similar properties (e.g., Garoff-Eaton, Slotnick, and Schacter, 2006), the engagement of highly similar retrieval-related evaluation and monitoring processes (e.g., Atkins and Reuter-Lorenz, 2011), retrieval of contextual information (e.g., Okado and Stark, 2003), and evidence that both types of memories are supported by above-threshold familiarity processing (e.g., Kahn, Davachi, and Wagner, 2004).

While stimulus properties common to both targets and lures can include many features, in the case of relatedness paradigms these shared features often include a shared semantic meaning and/or perceptual similarity. By virtue of this similarity between targets and related lures, these stimuli are likely to evoke comparable retrieval-related activity within brain regions mediating both perceptual and semantic processing. Similar perceptual processing in late visual cortices (Brodmann areas [BA] 19 and 37) has been suggested to reflect processing that contributes to the conscious experience of memory, which is independent of true "oldness" (Slotnick and Schacter, 2004). Others have suggested that such processing is likely to reflect successful retrieval of the general properties of originally studied items such as shape and color (Garoff-Eaton, Slotnick, and Schacter, 2006) or those involving the semantic label or general category (e.g., fruit, bird) to which the item belongs. As such, common activity in semantic processing regions, such as left temporal gyrus and dorsolateral prefrontal cortex (PFC), has often been interpreted as retrieval of these semantic labels (Dennis, Kim, and Cabeza, 2008; Garoff-Eaton, Kensinger, and Schacter, 2007; Kim and Cabeza, 2007a; von Zerssen *et al.*, 2001).

Common activity in frontal regions has also been associated with retrieval effort and monitoring processes, presumed to operate independently of retrieval success (e.g., Atkins and Reuter-Lorenz, 2011). In this way, it is unsurprising that such activity underlies both true and false memory retrieval, as these processes support decision making, not necessarily the accuracy of a given decision or memory. Similarly, common activity in the precuneus and lateral parietal cortex is interpreted as reflecting general "recovery operations" (Cabeza *et al.*, 2001) or the general feeling of oldness (Atkins and Reuter-Lorenz, 2011) that also occurs independent of retrieval accuracy. Taken together, the results of studies that report common activity between true and false memories emphasize that activity across several different brain regions can reflect language, perceptual, and monitoring processes that are independent of the encoding history of the stimuli.

*Distinct neural processing*   Despite finding such a large degree of overlap in neural recruitment, many studies also find differences in the level of neural engagement within regions mediating true and false memories. One of the most notable differences is that of increased activity in sensory cortices associated with true compared to false memories (Figure 8.2) (Abe *et al.*, 2008; Atkins and Reuter-Lorenz, 2011; Cabeza *et al.*, 2001; Dennis, Bowman, and Vandekar, 2012; Moritz *et al.*, 2006; Schacter *et al.*, 1996; Slotnick and Schacter, 2004). Greater engagement of sensory processing regions for true compared to false retrieval has most often been interpreted

(a)

Slotnick & Schacter (2004)

(b)

Stark et al. (2010)

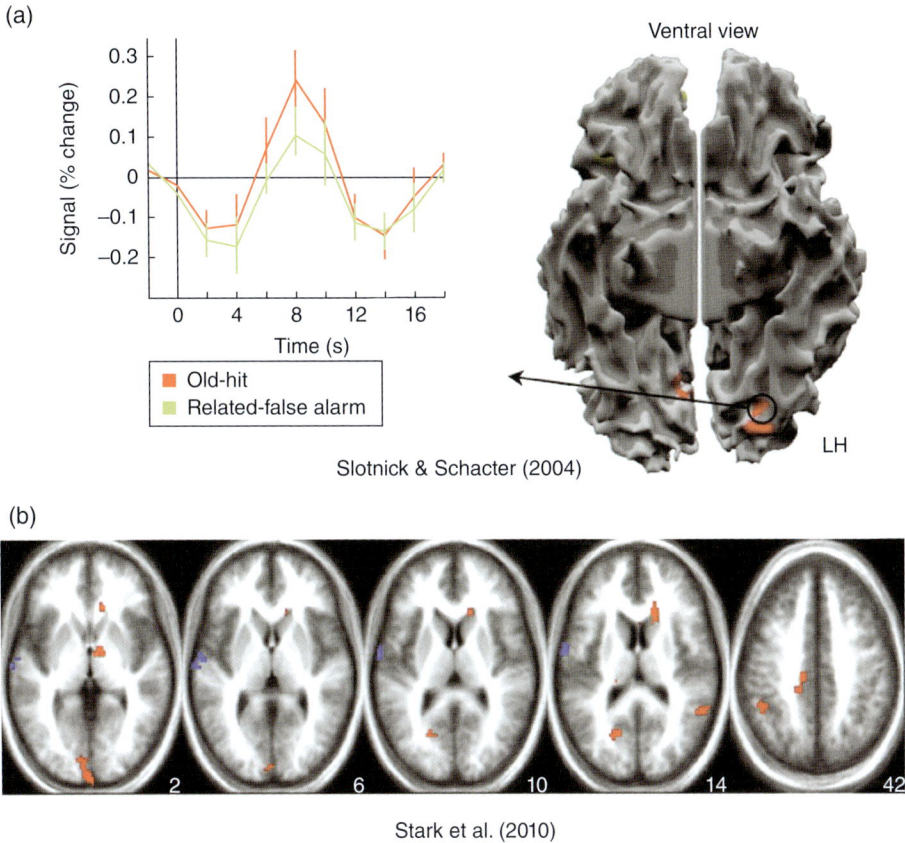

**Figure 8.2**　Activity supporting the sensory reactivation theory. (a) True recognition shows significantly greater activation in early visual cortex (BA 17/18) compared to false recognition (adapted from Slotnick and Schacter, 2004); (b) Regions showing a difference in activity for true versus false memory (red) include early visual cortical regions (BA 17/18) and striate cortex (adapted from Stark, Okado, and Loftus, 2010).

with respect to the "sensory reactivation hypothesis." Founded in behavioral research that found true memories to be associated with more sensory and perceptual details than false memories (e.g., Marche, Brainerd, and Reyna, 2010; Mather, Henkel, and Johnson, 1997; Norman and Schacter, 1997), the theory posits that by virtue of having been presented previously, true memories will elicit reactivation of the encoding episode in sensory regions that were involved in their initial encoding – a finding that has been observed across several traditional memory studies (e.g., Vaidya *et al.*, 2002; Wheeler, Petersen, and Buckner, 2000). Having never been presented previously, false memories will not be accompanied by this heightened sensory signal. For example, in one of the earliest imaging studies of false memories, Schacter and colleagues (1996) utilized a verbal encoding task to present related words at study. While participants exhibited a highly similar network for both true and false memories, greater activity for true retrieval was found in the temporal–parietal junction, a region associated with auditory processing. Researchers interpreted this finding as reflecting participants' retrieval of the auditory or phonological aspects of the item's presentation during the study phase. Several ERP studies have also observed differential activity over posterior cortices for true and false memories, supporting different amounts of sensory processing for true compared to false memories (Curran *et al.*, 2001; Fabiani, Stadler, and Wessels, 2000; Nessler and Mecklinger, 2003; Nessler, Mecklinger, and Penney, 2001; Walla *et al.*, 2000).

Recent findings from perceptual studies have both supported and expanded this earlier work, by showing not only increased activity in visual cortices for true memories, but also a dissociation between memory accuracy and recruitment of early versus late visual processing regions. Specifically, research has shown that activity in early visual processing regions (i.e., BA 17 and 18) distinguishes between true and false memories, while, as noted above, activity in late visual cortex (i.e., BA 19 and 37) is commonly active for true and false memories (Dennis, Bowman, and Vandekar, 2012; Slotnick and Schacter, 2004). While both early and late visual cortex are associated with object perception and identification, early visual cortex has been associated with recapitulation of a sensory signature (Buckner and Wheeler, 2001; Rugg and Wilding, 2000; Vaidya *et al.*, 2002) and late visual cortex has been linked to retrieval of general object identity and meaning (Vaidya *et al.*, 2002; Wheeler and Buckner, 2003; Wheeler, Petersen, and Buckner, 2000). Thus, with respect to true and false memories, common activity has been interpreted as reflecting retrieval of common perceptual details and conscious processing of an item as "old," whereas activity in early visual cortex has been interpreted as reflecting retrieval of perceptual and sensory details associated with the encoding episode (Dennis, Bowman, and Vandekar, 2012; Slotnick and Schacter, 2004; Stark, Okado, and Loftus, 2010).

Despite strong evidence supporting the sensory reactivation hypothesis, not all perceptual false memory studies find this dissociation (Garoff-Eaton, Slotnick, and Schacter, 2006; Gutchess and Schacter, 2012). For example, a recent study by Gutchess and Schacter (2012) found that as the gist representation was strengthened at encoding, the false-alarm rate increased, as did activation in both the hippocampus and in early and late visual processing regions (BA 17 and 37). The authors interpreted this increase in early and late visual cortex as indicative of a role for gist in sensory reactivation, suggesting that increased gist during false memories may reflect the retrieval of prototypical features shared by new and old items. Interestingly, high levels of gist had the opposite effect for true memories, such that increasing gist led to reduced visual activity, which the authors interpreted as reflecting the fact that true memories rely on parsing individual perceptual features and that this may be best supported under low gist conditions.

Consistent with findings from relatedness paradigms, several source-misattribution studies have found support for the sensory reactivation hypothesis, observing greater activity in sensory cortices for true compared to false retrieval (Fabiani, Stadler, and Wessels, 2000; Gonsalves *et al.*, 2004; Gonsalves and Paller, 2000; Kensinger and Schacter, 2006; Okado and Stark, 2003; Stark, Okado, and Loftus, 2010). For example, Okado and Stark (2003) also observed greater activity in several regions of visual cortices including right middle occipital cortex, left cuneus, left lingual gyrus, left fusiform gyrus for true compared to false memories. The authors concluded that this increase reflected the retrieval of item details associated with those items physically presented during encoding as opposed to items only imagined. More recently the same group also showed support for the sensory reactivation hypothesis using a misinformation paradigm (Figure 8.2) (Stark, Okado, and Loftus, 2010). Specifically, researchers found that true memories of the original, visually presented event were accompanied by greater activation in early visual cortex (BA 17/18) compared to false memories of the auditorily presented misinformation. Interestingly, when the presentation of auditory misinformation led to a false recollection, participants' false retrieval was accompanied by greater activity in left superior temporal gyrus (i.e., auditory cortex, BA 22/42) than if the misinformation was correctly rejected. In both studies the authors attributed this increase in sensory cortex activity for true memories to the retrieval of sensory information associated with the original information presentation.

While the low spatial resolution afforded by ERP studies cannot differentiate between early and late visual processing, Gonsalves and Paller (2000) found that true memories exhibited greater processing in posterior sensory cortices, showing enhanced positivity in the 900–1200 ms window for true compared to false memories. The authors suggested that this difference may reflect the retrieval of visual details, which was greater for true memories and linked to the information encountered and stored at encoding. Fabiani and colleagues (2000) also saw differential activity across posterior electrode sites for true compared to false memories. In accord with the sensory reactivation theory, the authors concluded that increased positivity for true memories represented retrieval of the memory trace formed during encoding, whereas the absence of activity for false memories correctly indicated the absence of a sensory signature.

A second region that has been shown to differentiate true and false memories is the medial temporal lobe (MTL). While common activity in MTL regions has been identified (see above), several studies find that the MTL only supports retrieval of true memories or shows greater activity for true compared to false memories (Cabeza *et al.*, 2001; Dennis, Bowman, and Vandekar, 2012; Dennis, Kim, and Cabeza, 2008; Giovanello *et al.*, 2009; Kahn, Davachi, and Wagner, 2004; Kensinger and Schacter, 2006; Kim and Cabeza, 2007a; Paz-Alonso *et al.*, 2008). In several studies researchers have suggested that greater MTL activation for true memories reflects greater recovery of sensory details associated with true memories (Cabeza *et al.*, 2001; Kahn, Davachi, and Wagner, 2004; Okado and Stark, 2003), whereas others have suggested that this neural increase reflects the role of the hippocampus in binding together true details from past events (Kensinger and Schacter, 2006), or recollection processes (Dennis, Bowman, and Vandekar, 2012; Kim and Cabeza, 2007a). Considered with the fact that some studies find no MTL differences for true and false memories (Schacter *et al.*, 1997; Slotnick and Schacter, 2004; Stark, Okado, and Loftus, 2010), a satisfying theory regarding the role of the MTL in false memories may not be currently attainable, but several studies have tried to offer an explanation for the mixed results. For example, Cabeza and colleagues (2001) found that the anterior hippocampus exhibited similar activation for both true and false retrieval, whereas the posterior PHG showed greater activity for true retrieval (Figure 8.3). They suggested that activity in anterior regions reflects recovery of semantic information that supports both types of memories, whereas posterior PHG, by virtue of its connectivity with sensory cortices, reflects retrieval of sensory information specific to true memories.

Recently our lab found a similar mix of MTL results, observing common anterior hippocampus/PHG activity for both types of memories and greater right hippocampal

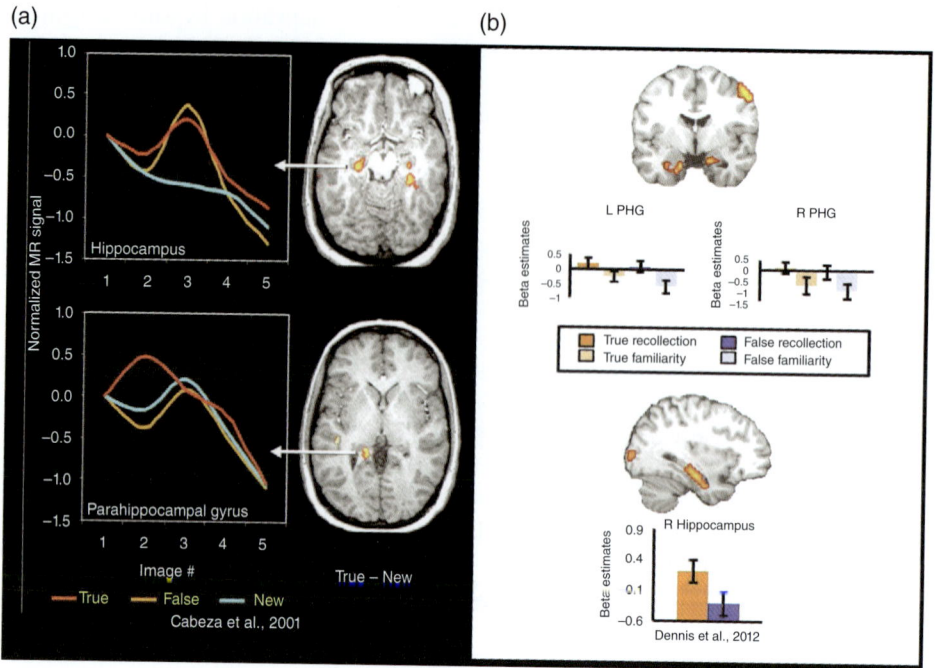

**Figure 8.3** MTL activity during true and false memories. (a) The left anterior hippocampus shows common activity for both true and false compared to new items (upper panel), whereas the left posterior PHG shows increased activity only for true memories (lower panel) (adapted from Cabeza *et al.*, 2001; Copyright (2001) National Academy of Sciences of the USA. Reproduced with permission). (b) Activity in bilateral anterior PHG shows common activity for true and false recollection (upper panel), whereas activity in right hippocampus shows greater activity for true compared to false recollection (lower panel) (adapted from Dennis, Bowman, and Vandekar, 2012. Reproduced with permission of Elsevier).

activity for true compared to false recollection (Figure 8.3) (Dennis, Bowman, and Vandekar, 2012). Our results suggest that even though the MTL mediates retrieval processes leading to both true and false recollection, the hippocampus proper has the ability to distinguish between detailed recollection of true and erroneous events. We suggested that increased hippocampal activity may represent more details retrieved for true memories or the accurate reconstruction/binding of details supporting true recollection of past experiences. Furthermore, even though anterior MTL regions were commonly active in both true and false recollection, connectivity maps showed differential engagement of frontal, parietal, and occipital cortices for each type of memory. Specifically, true recollection was associated with functional connectivity within a more inferior network (including fusiform gyrus, hippocampus, middle temporal gyrus), whereas false recollection engaged a more superior network (including superior parietal, superior frontal gyrus, posterior cingulate cortex). We interpreted these differences as indicating that true recollection is driven by bottom-up integration of information from sensory input and item retrieval whereas false recollection is driven by top-down attention control processes. Thus, even though a given MTL region may mediate both types of memories, the processing involved may reflect subtle differences in the cognitive operations associated with true and false memories.

While differential activity in sensory cortices and the MTL has been the focus of analyses distinguishing true from false memories, increased activity in the prefrontal cortex has been shown to differentiate related false memories. Specifically, a number of studies have reported increased activity in bilateral prefrontal cortices for false compared to true memories (Cabeza *et al.*, 2001; Garoff-Eaton, Kensinger, and Schacter, 2007; Kensinger and Schacter, 2006; Kim and Cabeza, 2007a; Kubota *et al.*, 2006; Okado and Stark, 2003; Schacter *et al.*, 1996, 1997; Slotnick and Schacter, 2004). Studies have attributed increased PFC activity to monitoring, reconstructive processes, and semantic elaboration – with the interpretation dependent upon the specific locus of PFC activation. For example, in a DRM task, Schacter and colleagues (1996) found right dorsolateral/anterior PFC to be more active during false compared to true recognition. Given the role of this region in retrieval monitoring (e.g., Fletcher, Shallice, and Dolan, 1998; Henson, Shallice, and Dolan, 1999), the authors concluded that the activation may reflect the need for increased retrieval monitoring and evaluation associated with the strong familiarity evoked by the false memory. In an imagery study by Okado and Stark (2003), increased PFC activity for false memories was localized to the right anterior cingulate gyrus. Given the role of the anterior cingulate in response competition and conflict (Kerns *et al.*, 2004), the authors concluded that this reflects the increased effort involved in incorrectly endorsing an imagined item as "seen." ERP studies also support the conclusion that frontal regions may distinguish between true and false memories, and be engaged in greater monitoring and evaluation associated with false retrieval (Curran *et al.*, 2001; Fabiani, Stadler, and Wessels, 2000; Goldmann *et al.*, 2003; Nessler, Mecklinger, and Penney, 2001; Wiese and Daum, 2006). For example, Nessler and Mecklinger (2003) observed that ERPs were more positive at frontal locations for false than true recognition across short retention delays (40 s versus 80 s). They suggested that this may reflect participants' greater focus on related lures leading to false recollection in long delays compared to familiarity discrimination during short delays.

Others have interpreted increased activity in PFC as reflecting semantic elaboration underlying false memories (Cabeza *et al.*, 2001; Garoff-Eaton, Kensinger, and Schacter, 2007; Kubota *et al.*, 2006). For example, Garoff-Eaton and colleagues (2007) found increased activity in left inferior, middle, and medial frontal gyrus for false retrieval associated with lures that were conceptually related to encoded items (e.g., *silver, bronze*), but not when the lure was perceptually related to encoded items (e.g., *bell, tell*). Given that both types of false memories should require equivalent monitoring and evaluation, they attributed the increased left prefrontal activity to the retrieval of both conceptual information that pertained to item meaning and the semantic gist associated with studied items that also pertained to the related lures (see also evidence from encoding studies below). The idea that false memories are mediated by either familiarity or the gist representation associated with the encoding theme is a conclusion reached in several neuroimaging studies (Dennis, Kim, and Cabeza, 2008; Duarte, Graham, and Henson, 2010; Garoff-Eaton, Kensinger, and Schacter, 2007; Kim and Cabeza, 2007a, 2007b; Moritz *et al.*, 2006). This theory is supported not only by the above-mentioned increased false memory activity in left prefrontal cortices, but also by false memory activity in regions outside prefrontal cortex that are also associated with semantic processing. For example, in a semantic relatedness study, Moritz *et al.* (2006) found that, compared to true memories, false memories for critical lures were associated with activation in left inferior temporal lobe, a region associated with general semantic processing (for a review, see Saumier and Chertkow, 2002; Wise and Price, 2006). The authors proposed that such activity may reflect semantic gist processing or the spreading of activation in semantic networks. Taken together, results suggest that when critical lures are semantically or perceptually related to study items, the semantic gist may evoke a sense of familiarity that is strong enough to form the basis of a false memory. Such a conclusion was posited by Kim and Cabeza (2007a), who found frontoparietal activity to mediate high-confidence false memories. Given the role of frontal and parietal cortex in familiarity (Cansino et al., 2002; Yonelinas et al., 2005), the authors concluded that a strong feeling of familiarity underlies false memories associated with critical lures that match the gist trace evoked during encoding (e.g., categorical information relating items). A similar familiarity argument is also made in support of unrelated lures as well (see Duarte, Graham, and Henson, 2010).

## Encoding studies

While most studies examining the neural correlates of false memories have focused on the retrieval phase, it has been well argued that encoding processes also contribute to false memories. However, it is relatively difficult, from a methodological perspective, to design a study that isolates the neural processes that contribute to the formation of a false memory. For example, in the relatedness paradigms it is suggested that false memories arise from gist that is built up across many trials (see Brainerd and Reyna, 2002), and so activity on any given trial may only partially contribute to a false memory. Similarly, in misinformation paradigms false memories may arise due to processing during either the original or the misinformation phase. Thus, the practice of isolating a *single* time-point during encoding that would create a false memory is a difficult, and often unattainable, endeavor. Despite this challenge, a handful of studies have examined the influence of encoding processes on the formation of false memories (Baym and Gonsalves, 2010; Gonsalves et al., 2004; Gonsalves and Paller, 2000; Kensinger and Schacter, 2005; Kim and Cabeza, 2007b; Kubota et al., 2006; Okado and Stark, 2005) and have attempted to elucidate the cognitive and neural processes that underlie the formation of false memories.

Misinformation studies overcome the issue of localizing encoding-related false memory activity by defining true memories as those consistent with the original event phase, whereas false memories arise when information from the secondary event phase is remembered as if it were presented during the original event. Perhaps unsurprisingly, evidence from misinformation studies suggests that if an individual is presented with two sources of information, the information that receives the greater amount of neural processing (either original/true information or secondary/false information) is that which is most likely to be remembered (Baym and Gonsalves, 2010; Gonsalves et al., 2004; Okado and Stark, 2005; Stark, Okado, and Loftus, 2010). For example, Okado and Stark (2005) found that encoding activity in the left hippocampus and perirhinal cortex was greater for true than for false memories in the original encoding phase, yet during the presentation of misinformation, activity in this region was greater for false than for true memories. The authors concluded that, given the role of the hippocampus in the encoding of source information (Davachi, Mitchell, and Wagner, 2003), greater contextual processing in this region during encoding reflected which information would be ultimately bound to the encoding episode. Consistent with the above evidence, studies have also found that the degree of visual imagery engaged during encoding leads to subsequent false memories in reality-monitoring paradigms (Aminoff, Schacter, and Bar, 2008; Gonsalves *et al.*, 2004; Kensinger and Schacter, 2005). For example, Gonsalves and colleagues (2004) found that greater engagement of precuneus, right inferior parietal cortex, and anterior cingulate during imagery trials led to subsequent false memories (i.e., participants believing to have viewed the item during encoding) (see also Gonsalves and Paller, 2000, for ERP evidence). Citing the role of these regions in visual imagery tasks (e.g., Ishai, Ungerleider, and Haxby, 2000; Kosslyn and Thompson, 2000), the authors concluded that the enhanced visual imagery during encoding led to inaccurate memories. Taken together, these results suggest that false memories may be dependent on activation associated with both the presentation of the true information and the presentation of the misinformation episode.

The engagement of sensory cortices during encoding has also been investigated in relatedness studies. For example, in a modified DRM paradigm, Kim and Cabeza (2007b) used an encoding trial composed of four related items (e.g., chick, sheep, pig, goat) to examine encoding activity leading to subsequent true and false memories. By presenting all related items on a single trial, the authors attempted to capture that elusive single time-point when a false memory of related information would occur during study. They found that while regions involved in semantic elaboration (left ventro- and dorsomedial PFC) and conscious item processing (bilateral occipito-temporal and occiptotparietal cortex) were involved in both true and false memory formation. True memory formation showed greater activity in left posterior PHG and early visual cortex (BA 18/17) (Figure 8.4). Thus, results suggest that encoding of specific perceptual information supports subsequent true memories. Using a perceptual relatedness paradigm, Garoff-Eaton and colleagues (2006) found a dissociation in sensory processing for the encoding of false memories. Specifically, while right fusiform cortex was engaged for subsequent true memories, the left fusiform was engaged for both subsequent true memories and trials leading to the endorsement of similar lure items. Thus, the authors concluded that right fusiform supports encoding of visual details specific to an individual item, whereas left fusiform encodes more general perceptual information. The foregoing results suggest that false memory formation is a byproduct of elaborative semantic and visual processing, whereas the formation of true memories is also based on the encoding of sensory details and raw memory traces.

Overall, results suggest that encoding-related processing contributes to false memories in several ways. With respect to the encoding of item-specific details, and consistent with the sensory reactivation theory, findings suggest that encoding of detailed sensory information associated with true events supports subsequent veridical memories and lower occurrences of false memories. Secondly, greater processing of misinformation or greater engagement in imagery during the study phase will ultimately lead to a strong memory trace that is likely to be misidentified as part of the true memory in subsequent memory tests. With regard to related false memories, results suggest that processes which support true memories, such as elaborative semantic processing and encoding of gist, also form the foundation of subsequent false memories.

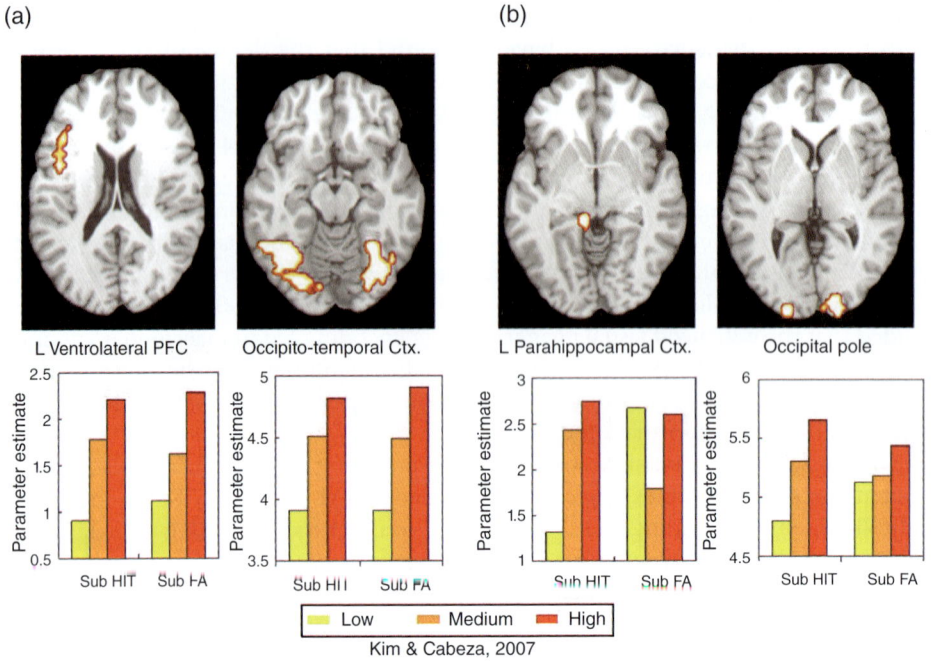

**Figure 8.4** Common and distinct activity at encoding that predicts subsequent true and false memories. (a) Activity in left ventrolateral PFC and occipitotemporal cortex shows a similar pattern of activity for subsequent true and false memories. (b) Activity in left PHG and occipital pole shows increased activity for subsequent true memories, but not for subsequent false memories (adapted from Kim and Cabeza, 2007b. Reproduced with permission of Oxford University Press).

## Unrelated false memory studies

While the foregoing results illustrate the neural mechanisms involved in related false memories and false memories that arise due to a targeted encoding manipulation, sometimes false memories arise that are unrelated to information presented at encoding. Often labeled as "unrelated false memories," these false memories are interesting because there is seemingly no basis for the formation of the memory. Due to the difficult nature of obtaining a sufficient number of unrelated false memories for imaging analysis, very few neuroimaging studies have investigated the neural basis for these false memories (Duarte, Graham, and Henson, 2010; Garoff-Eaton, Slotnick, and Schacter, 2006; Iidaka *et al.*, 2012). Consequently, given the small number of studies and variety in methods and analyses used, there has been little consensus about the underlying neural process supporting such memories.

Garoff-Eaton and colleagues (2006) were the first to directly explore the neural basis of unrelated false memories and did so by using the abstract shape paradigm (described above). They found that the left superior and middle temporal gyri were more active for unrelated false recognitions than for either true or related false recognitions. The authors concluded that, given the role of these brain regions in mediating language processing, unrelated false recognition may arise as participants misattribute a verbal tag generated at encoding to an unrelated item generated during retrieval. While a number of studies have shown that false memories arise from a reliance on verbal and semantic information as opposed to sensory information, it is unclear why the verbal labeling strategy would lead to unrelated and not related false recognitions, as it has in other studies (Cabeza *et al.*, 2001; Dennis, Kim, and Cabeza, 2007, 2008; Garoff-Eaton, Slotnick, and Schacter, 2006; Schacter *et al.*, 1996). Interestingly, no region exhibited overlap between unrelated and related false recognition and true recognition. The authors concluded that these two types of false memories do not share overlapping cognitive processes.

Unlike the study by Garoff-Eaton *et al.* (2006), a study by Duarte, Graham, and Henson (2010) found considerable overlap in the neural correlates mediating true and false memories, even when lures were unrelated line drawings. Specifically, overlap was seen in medial parietal, middle frontal, and lateral temporal regions. The authors attributed this activity to common familiarity processing shared by true and false recognition. One region that did distinguish between true and false memories was the anterior MTL. While the anterior MTL has been associated with common activity in previous studies (e.g., Cabeza *et al.*, 2001; Dennis, Bowman, and Vandekar, 2012), the authors suggested that this overlap was driven by semantic and/or perceptual similarities between old and new items that was not present amongst the unrelated items in their study. Given that the study did not include related lures, a conclusion cannot be drawn with respect to similarities between related and unrelated false memories.

Lastly, Iidaka and colleagues (2012) examined related and unrelated false memories of faces. They found that regions including left superior and inferior parietal, left inferior frontal gyrus, and early visual cortex (BA 18) supported unrelated false recognitions compared to unrelated correct rejections. However, several of these regions (including left superior parietal and left inferior frontal gyrus) were also active for related false recognition. Thus, without any direct comparisons or conjunction analyses, it is unclear the extent to which this activity is unique to unrelated false memory or is part of a network that reflects more general processes involved in false memories.

While it is difficult to draw general conclusions as to the neural basis of unrelated false memories from such a small sample of studies, data from both Duarte and colleagues (2010) and Iidaka and colleagues (2012) suggest that, like related false memories, the cognitive process mediating false memories to unrelated items may be similar to those underlying true memories. Specifically, results across all false memory paradigms suggest that the processes involved in memory retrieval are not based on the veridicality of the memory itself, but reflect the search and monitoring/evaluation process of stored representations.

## Developmental studies

While the study of the neural basis of false memories is itself a relatively new endeavor, research is relatively limited with respect to developmental differences. Behavioral research has shown that developmental differences in false memories depend on the type of false memory being measured. For example, while both children and older adults are more susceptible to misinformation and source misattribution than are young adults, false memories stemming from semantic and perceptual relatedness increase from childhood to adulthood, and throughout aging (see Brainerd and Reyna, 2005; Brainerd, Reyna, and Ceci, 2008). Though these age differences have been examined broadly at a behavioral level, only one study to date has examined the neural basis of false memories in children (Paz-Alonso *et al.*, 2008), and only a handful of neuroimaging studies have investigated the question in older adults (Dennis, Bowman, and Peterson, 2014; Dennis, Kim, and Cabeza, 2007, 2008; Duarte, Graham, and Henson, 2010; Giovanello *et al.*, 2009; Gutchess, Ieuji, and Federmeier, 2007).

Using the DRM paradigm, Paz-Alonso and colleagues (2008) found significant developmental differences across frontal, parietal, and MTL regions mediating both true and false memories. Specifically, while the anterior MTL and the parietal cortex failed to distinguish between true and false memories in young children (8-year-olds), they showed a graded response distinguishing veridicality across older children (12-year-olds) and adults. With respect to false memories, researchers found that the left ventrolateral PFC exhibited increased activity for hits and related false memories in adults but not in children (ages 8 and 12). The authors suggested that this developmental change is indicative of more elaborate semantic processing with age. Similarly, evidence from aging studies has suggested that older adults (> 60 years old) exhibit a greater reliance on semantic processing than do younger adults, and it is proposed that this increase may underlie increases in semantic false memories across the lifespan (Dennis, Kim, and Cabeza, 2007, 2008).

With respect to false memories and aging, neuroimaging data has supported findings from behavioral studies showing age-related reductions in recollection processing associated with true memories and age-related reliance on gist and/or familiarity processing supporting both true and false memories (e.g., Balota *et al.*, 1999; Koutstaal and Schacter, 1997; Spencer and Raz, 1995; Tun *et al.*, 1998). Specifically, false memory studies have observed age deficits in neural activity mediating true recollection in both the MTL (Dennis, Kim, and Cabeza, 2007, 2008; Duarte, Graham, and Henson, 2010) and the visual cortex (Dennis, Bowman, and Peterson, 2014; Dennis, Kim, and Cabeza, 2007; Duarte, Graham, and Henson, 2010; see also Gutchess, Ieuji, and Federmeier, 2007, for ERP evidence). In addition to overall decreases in visual activity, visual processing regions that differentiate true from false memories in young adults (i.e., fusiform gyrus, early visual cortex) have not exhibited the same differentiation in aging (Figure 8.5) (Dennis, Bowman, and Peterson, 2014; Duarte, Graham, and Henson, 2010; Gutchess, Ieuji, and Federmeier, 2007). Taken together, these results support the theory that an age-related deficit in processing veridical information, and differentiating between studied and unstudied information within sensory cortices, contributes to age-related increases in false memories.

As noted, the prevailing finding in aging research is an age-related shift from recollection to familiarity and gist processing. False memory research has found that this shift in processing is associated with both true and false memories (Dennis, Bowman, and Peterson, 2014; Dennis, Kim, and Cabeza, 2007, 2008; Duarte, Graham, and Henson, 2010; Giovanello *et al.*, 2009). For example, using both semantic and perceptual related paradigms, Dennis and colleagues (Dennis, Bowman, and Peterson, 2014; Dennis, Kim, and Cabeza, 2007, 2008) have found both true and false memories to be mediated by the middle and superior temporal gyri, regions involved in semantic and gist processing (Saumier and Chertkow, 2002; Simons *et al.*, 2005). Giovanello and colleagues (2009) also found age-related increases in familiarity

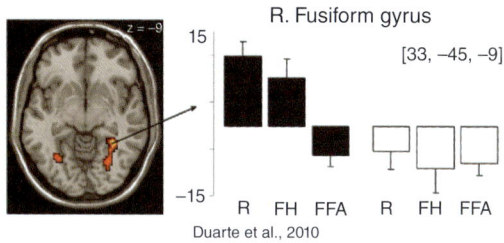

R. Fusiform gyrus

[33, −45, −9]

Duarte et al., 2010

**Figure 8.5** Age-related dedifferentiation in visual processing regions. Young adults (black bars) show increased activity in the right fusiform gyrus for true recollection (R) and true familiarity (FH) compared to familiar false alarms (FFA) while older adults (white bars) do not show differentiation between true and false memories (adapted from Duarte, Graham, and Henson, 2010).

processing within right PHG supporting false memories. Duarte, Graham, and Henson (2010) found that both recollection and familiarity-related activity actually showed evidence of age-related deficits, concluding that the similarities in familiarity processing and reduced differentiation between true and false memories led to increased false memories in older adults. Taken together, the results suggest that older adults encode information in a less detailed fashion and thus do not have those details available to them at retrieval, thereby making the representation of true and false memories more similar.

## Conclusions and Future Directions

Overall, neuroimaging studies have shown that, by and large, the neural correlates that mediate retrieval of false memories overlap with those supporting true memory retrieval. Taking into account the commonalities that often exist between targets and related lures, as well as the reconstructive nature of memory retrieval, this is not a surprising finding. Specifically, the results suggest that retrieval of common object properties such as semantic label or context elicit similar processing across true and false memories. In addition, the same evaluation and monitoring processes that are involved in identifying true memories are also active when retrieving false memories. Despite such significant overlap, neural differences with respect to the veridicality of memories do emerge. These differences are most commonly reported as greater MTL and visual cortex activity for true relative to false memories, and greater activity in frontal cortices for false relative to true memories. Greater activity for true compared to false memories in visual cortices (and other sensory processing regions) has been interpreted with respect to the sensory reactivation hypothesis. The idea that true memories are accompanied by the retrieval of greater sensory details compared to false memories may also underlie the finding across several studies that MTL activity is greater for true compared to false memories. Several interpretations regarding increased PFC activity for false memories have also been offered, including a greater reliance on gist and familiarity processes as well as greater monitoring associated with making what may be a more difficult memory decision.

Unfortunately, despite the observed differences between true and false memories, no neural signal or pattern of activation has shown itself to be a reliable neural marker of either true or false memory across all studies. Sensory reactivation, while replicated across several studies, is not ubiquitous. Nor is increased frontal activity supporting false memories. While differences in methodologies and stimuli can account for some variations in the data, these discrepancies require further investigation. Future research should focus not only on replications of current findings, controlling both for stimuli content and methodological differences, but also on analyzing patterns of brain activity and use of effective connectivity methods. One promising line of research, specifically with regard to elucidating the role of the MTL in false memories, involves high-resolution fMRI and multi-voxel pattern analysis (see Chapter 6 for more discussion of these techniques). In particular, recent work by Yassa and colleagues (Lacy *et al.*, 2011; Yassa and Stark, 2008, 2011; Yassa *et al.*, 2011) suggests that different subregions within the MTL respond differentially to true and false memories, possible accounting for the mix of results observed using traditional fMRI methods.

In addition to understanding the neural basis of false memories during retrieval studies, it is widely accepted that encoding processes also contribute to the occurrence of false memories. However, pinpointing the neural processes that lead to subsequent false memories has been challenging. With respect to relatedness studies, results have suggested that subsequent false memories are associated with familiarity and gist processing during encoding, whereas false memories stemming from imagery and misinformation are associated with enhanced processing of the misinformation as compared to details associated with the true encoding event. To this end, encoding evidence also supports the sensory reactivation theory, finding that subsequent true memories are associated with greater initial sensory processing, and that greater engagement of sensory processing during encoding reduces subsequent false memories.

A third important finding from neuroimaging research has been that fact that the neural correlates mediating false memories differ across the lifespan. Mirroring previously observed age-related differences in episodic memory (see Chapters 17 and 18), false memory studies also find age-related deficits in neural processing mediating true memories, including deficits in sensory-related processing during both encoding and retrieval. Age-related deficits in processing details of episodic memories may lead to a degraded representation of the event, thereby making an individual vulnerable to false memories. Supporting the idea of dedifferentiation in aging, true as well as false memories in older adults have been shown to be mediated by both gist and familiarity processing.

While the current research represents a solid start to understanding the neural basis of false memories, more research is needed. For example, despite finding increased frontal activity for false memories, research to date has not identified a biomarker or neural signal clearly differentiating false from true memories. In addition, while a number of studies have found that true memories elicit greater activity in sensory regions, possibly reflecting reactivation of sensory details from study, the exact location of this activity has differed from study to study, and no study has directly tested the reactivation theory, comparing encoding and retrieval activity. Finally, despite the large number of neuroimaging studies, very few studies have directly linked their results to theories of false memories – e.g., source monitoring theory (Johnson, Hashtroudi, and Lindsay, 1993), activation monitoring theory (Roediger and McDermott, 1995), and fuzzy trace theory (Brainerd and Reyna, 2002). In the same vein, the foregoing theories of false memory were originally developed to account for behavioral data, and thus do not include hypotheses and predictions regarding neural activations. Future neuroimaging research should do more than simply report results, but should attempt to couch its findings in terms of behavioral theories. Moreover, behavioral theories should be expanded to generate testable neural predictions.

# Acknowledgments

This research was supported by a National Science Foundation (NSF) Grant BCS1025709 awarded to N.A.D. and was conducted while N.A.D. was an AFAR Research Grant recipient from the American Federation for Aging Research. We wish to thank Avery Rizio and Kristina Peterson for helpful comments through the writing process.

# Note

1 This may underestimate the overlap in medial temporal lobe (MTL) regions, as the specific analyses reported across several studies precluded us from drawing definitive conclusions.

# References

Abe, N., Okuda, J., Suzuki, M., *et al.* (2008). Neural correlates of true memory, false memory, and deception. *Cerebral Cortex*, 18 (12), 2811–2819.

Aminoff, E., Schacter, D.L., and Bar, M. (2008). The cortical underpinnings of context-based memory distortion. *Journal of Cognitive Neuroscience*, 20 (12), 2226–2237. doi: 10.1162/jocn.2008.20156.

Atkins, A.S., and Reuter-Lorenz, P.A. (2011). Neural mechanisms of semantic interference and false recognition in short-term memory. *NeuroImage*, 56 (3), 1726–1734. doi: 10.1016/j.neuroimage.2011.02.048.

Balota, D.A., Cortese, M.J., Duchek, J.M., *et al.* (1999). Veridical and false memories in healthy older adults and in dementia of the Alzheimer's Type. *Cognitive Neuropsychology*, 16, 361–384.

Baym, C.L., and Gonsalves, B.D. (2010). Comparison of neural activity that leads to true memories, false memories, and forgetting: an fMRI study of the misinformation effect. *Cognitive, Affective and Behavioral Neuroscience*, 10 (3), 339–348. doi: 10.3758/CABN.10.3.339.

Brainerd, C.J., and Reyna, V.F. (2002). Fuzzy-trace theory and false memory. *Current Directions in Psychological Science*, 11, 164–169.

Brainerd, C.J., and Reyna, V.F. (2005). *The Science of False Memory*. Oxford Psychological Series. Oxford: Oxford University Press.

Brainerd, C.J., Reyna, V.F., and Ceci, S.J. (2008). Developmental reversals in false memory: a review of data and theory. *Psychological Bulletin*, 134 (3), 343–382.

Buckner, R.L., and Wheeler, M.E. (2001). The cognitive neuroscience of remembering. *Nature Reviews Neuroscience*, 2 (9), 624–634.

Cabeza, R., Rao, S.M., Wagner, A.D., *et al.* (2001). Can medial temporal lobe regions distinguish true from false? An event-related functional MRI study of veridical and illusory recognition memory. *Proceedings of the National Academy of Sciences of the USA*, 98 (8), 4805–4810.

Cansino, S., Maquet, P., Dolan, R.J., and Rugg, M.D. (2002). Brain activity underlying encoding and retrieval of source memory. *Cerebral Cortex*, 12 (10), 1048–1056.

Curran, T., Schacter, D.L., Johnson, M.K., and Spinks, R. (2001). Brain potentials reflect behavioral differences in true and false recognition. *Journal of Cognitive Neuroscience*, 13 (2), 201–216.

Davachi, L., Mitchell, J.P., and Wagner, A.D. (2003). Multiple routes to memory: distinct medial temporal lobe processes build item and source memories. *Proceedings of the National Academy of Sciences of the USA*, 100 (4), 2157–2162.

Deese, J. (1959). On the prediction of occurrence of particular verbal intrusions in immediate recall. *Journal of Experimental Psychology*, 58 (1), 17–22.

Dennis, N.A., Bowman, C.R., and Peterson, K.P. (2014). Age-related differences in the neural correlates mediating false recollection. *Neurobiology of Aging*, 35 (2), 395–407. doi: 10.1016/j.neurobiolaging.2013.08.019.

Dennis, N.A., Bowman, C.R., and Vandekar, S.N. (2012). True and phantom recollection: an fMRI investigation of similar and distinct neural correlates and connectivity. *NeuroImage*, 59 (3), 2982–2993. doi: 10.1016/j.neuroimage.2011.09.079.

Dennis, N.A., Kim, H., and Cabeza, R. (2007). Effects of aging on the neural correlates of true and false memory formation. *Neuropsychologia*, 45, 3157–3166.

Dennis, N.A., Kim, H., and Cabeza, R. (2008). Age-related differences in brain activity during true and false memory retrieval. *Journal of Cognitive Neuroscience*, 20 (8), 1390–1402.

Duarte, A., Graham, K.S., and Henson, R.N. (2010). Age-related changes in neural activity associated with familiarity, recollection and false recognition. *Neurobiology of Aging*, 31 (10), 1814–1830.

Fabiani, M., Stadler, M.A., and Wessels, P.M. (2000). True but not false memories produce a sensory signature in human lateralized brain potentials. *Journal of Cognitive Neuroscience*, 12 (6), 941–949.

Fletcher, P.C., Shallice, T., and Dolan, R.J. (1998). The functional roles of prefrontal cortex in episodic memory. I. Encoding. *Brain*, 121 (7), 1239–1248.

Garoff-Eaton, R.J., Kensinger, E.A., and Schacter, D.L. (2007). The neural correlates of conceptual and perceptual false recognition. *Learning and Memory*, 14 (10), 684–692.

Garoff-Eaton, R.J., Slotnick, S.D., and Schacter, D.L. (2006). Not all false memories are created equal: the neural basis of false recognition. *Cerebral Cortex*, 16 (11), 1645–1652.

Giovanello, K.S., Kensinger, E.A., Wong, A.T., and Schacter, D.L. (2009). Age-related neural changes during memory conjunction errors. *Journal of Cognitive Neuroscience*, 22 (7), 1348–1361.

Goldmann, R.E., Sullivan, A.L., Droller, D.B., *et al.* (2003). Late frontal brain potentials distinguish true and false recognition. *Neuroreport*, 14 (13), 1717–1720. doi: 10.1097/01. wnr.0000087908.78892.23.

Gonsalves, B., and Paller, K.A. (2000). Neural events that underlie remembering something that never happened. *Nature Neuroscience*, 3 (12), 1316–1321.

Gonsalves, B., Reber, P.J., Gitelman, D.R., *et al.* (2004). Neural evidence that vivid imagining can lead to false remembering. *Psychological Science*, 15 (10), 655–660.

Gutchess, A.H., Ieuji, Y., and Federmeier, K.D. (2007). Event-related potentials reveal age differences in the encoding and recognition of scenes. *Journal of Cognitive Neuroscience*, 19 (7), 1089–1103. doi: 10.1162/jocn.2007.19.7.1089.

Gutchess, A.H., and Schacter, D.L. (2012). The neural correlates of gist-based true and false recognition. *NeuroImage*, 59 (4), 3418–3426. doi: 10.1016/j.neuroimage.2011.11.078.

Henson, R.N., Shallice, T., and Dolan, R.J. (1999). Right prefrontal cortex and episodic memory retrieval: a functional MRI test of the monitoring hypothesis. *Brain*, 122 (7), 1367–1381.

Iidaka, T., Harada, T., Kawaguchi, J., and Sadato, N. (2012). Neuroanatomical substrates involved in true and false memories for face. *NeuroImage*, 62 (1), 167–176. doi: 10.1016/j.neuroimage.2012.04.044.

Ishai, A., Ungerleider, L.G., and Haxby, J.V. (2000). Distributed neural systems for the generation of visual images. *Neuron*, 28 (3), 979–990.

Johnson, M.K., Hashtroudi, S., and Lindsay, D.S. (1993). Source monitoring. *Psychological Bulletin*, 114 (1), 3–28.

Kahn, I., Davachi, L., and Wagner, A.D. (2004). Functional-neuroanatomic correlates of recollection: implications for models of recognition memory. *Journal of Neuroscience*, 24 (17), 4172–4180.

Kensinger, E.A., and Schacter, D.L. (2005). Emotional content and reality-monitoring ability: fMRI evidence for the influences of encoding processes. *Neuropsychologia*, 43 (10), 1429–1443.

Kensinger, E.A., and Schacter, D.L. (2006). Amygdala activity is associated with the successful encoding of item, but not source, information for positive and negative stimuli. *Journal of Neuroscience*, 26 (9), 2564–2570.

Kerns, J.G., Cohen, J.D., MacDonald, A.W., III, *et al.* (2004). Anterior cingulate conflict monitoring and adjustments in control. *Science*, 303 (5660), 1023–1026.

Kim, H.K., and Cabeza, R. (2007a). Trusting our memories: dissociating the neural correlates of confidence in veridical and illusory memories. *Journal of Neuroscience*, 27, 12190–12197.

Kim, H.K., and Cabeza, R. (2007b). Differential contributions of prefrontal, medial temporal, and sensory-perceptual regions to true and false memory formation. *Cerebral Cortex*, 17, 2143–2150.

Kosslyn, S.M., and Thompson, W.L. (2000). Neural systems activated during visual mental imagery. In *Brain Mapping: The Systems* (ed. A. W. Toga and J. C. Mazziotta). San Diego, CA: Academic Press, pp. 535–560.

Koutstaal, W., and Schacter, D.L. (1997). Gist-based false recognition of pictures in older and younger adults. *Journal of Memory and Language*, 37, 555–583.

Kubota, Y., Toichi, M., Shimizu, M., *et al.* (2006). Prefrontal hemodynamic activity predicts false memory: a near-infrared spectroscopy study. *NeuroImage*, 31 (4), 1783–1789. doi: 10.1016/j.neuroimage.2006.02.003.

Lacy, J.W., Yassa, M.A., Stark, S.M., *et al.* (2011). Distinct pattern separation related transfer functions in human CA3/dentate and CA1 revealed using high-resolution fMRI and variable mnemonic similarity. *Learning and Memory*, 18 (1), 15–18. doi: 10.1101/lm.1971111.

Marche, T.A., Brainerd, C.J., and Reyna, V.F. (2010). Distinguishing true from false memories in forensic contexts: can phenomenology tell us what is real. *Applied Cognitive Psychology*, 24 (8), 1168–1182.

Mather, M., Henkel, L.A., and Johnson, M.K. (1997). Evaluating characteristics of false memories: remember/know judgments and memory characteristics questionnaire compared. *Memory and Cognition*, 25 (6), 826–837.

McCabe, D.P., Roediger, H.L., McDaniel, M.A., and Balota, D.A. (2009). Aging reduces veridical remembering but increases false remembering: neuropsychological test correlates of remember–know judgments. *Neuropsychologia*, 47 (11), 2164–2173. doi: 10.1016/j.neuropsychologia.2008.11.025.

Moritz, S., Glascher, J., Sommer, T., *et al.* (2006). Neural correlates of memory confidence. *NeuroImage*, 33 (4), 1188–1193. doi: 10.1016/j.neuroimage.2006.08.003.

Nessler, D., and Mecklinger, A. (2003). ERP correlates of true and false recognition after different retention delays: stimulus- and response-related processes. *Psychophysiology*, 40 (1), 146–159.

Nessler, D., Mecklinger, A., and Penney, T.B. (2001). Event related brain potentials and illusory memories: the effects of differential encoding. *Cognitive Brain Research*, 10 (3), 283–301.

Norman, K.A., and Schacter, D.L. (1997). False recognition in younger and older adults: exploring the characteristics of illusory memories. *Memory and Cognition*, 25 (6), 838–848.

Okado, Y., and Stark, C. (2003). Neural processing associated with true and false memory retrieval. *Cognitive, Affectective and Behavioural Neuroscience*, 3 (4), 323–334.

Okado, Y., and Stark, C.E. (2005). Neural activity during encoding predicts false memories created by misinformation. *Learning and Memory*, 12 (1), 3–11. doi: 10.1101/lm.87605.

Paz-Alonso, P.M., Ghetti, S., Donohue, S.E., *et al.* (2008). Neurodevelopmental correlates of true and false recognition. *Cerebral Cortex*, 18 (9), 2208–2216.

Roediger, H.L., and McDermott, K.B. (1995). Creating false memories: remembering words not presented in lists. *Journal of Experimental Psychology: Learning, Memory, and Cognition*, 21, 8033–8014.

Rugg, M.D., and Wilding, E.L. (2000). Retrieval processing and episodic memory. *Trends in Cognitive Sciences*, 4 (3), 108–115.

Saumier, D., and Chertkow, H. (2002). Semantic memory. *Current Neurology and Neuroscience Reports*, 2 (6), 516–522.

Schacter, D.L., Buckner, R.L., Koutstaal, W., *et al.* (1997). Late onset of anterior prefrontal activity during true and false recognition: an event-related fMRI study. *NeuroImage*, 6 (4), 259–269.

Schacter, D.L., Reiman, E., Curran, T., *et al.* (1996). Neuroanatomical correlates of veridical and illusory recognition memory: evidence from positron emission tomography. *Neuron*, 17 (2), 267–274.

Simons, J.S., Verfaellie, M., Hodges, J.R., *et al.* (2005). Failing to get the gist: reduced false recognition of semantic associates in semantic dementia. *Neuropsychology*, 19 (3), 353–361.

Slotnick, S.D., and Schacter, D.L. (2004). A sensory signature that distinguishes true from false memories. *Nature Neuroscience*, 7 (6), 664–672.

Spencer, W.D., and Raz, N. (1995). Differential effects of aging on memory for content and context: a meta-analysis. *Psychology and Aging*, 10 (4), 527–539.

Stark, C.E., Okado, Y., and Loftus, E.F. (2010). Imaging the reconstruction of true and false memories using sensory reactivation and the misinformation paradigms. *Learning and Memory*, 17 (10), 485–488. doi: 10.1101/lm.1845710.

Tun, P.A., Wingfield, A., Rosen, M.J., and Blanchard, L. (1998). Response latencies for false memories: gist-based processes in normal aging. *Psychology and Aging*, 13 (2), 230–241.

Vaidya, C.J., Zhao, M., Desmond, J.E., and Gabrieli, J.D. (2002). Evidence for cortical encoding specificity in episodic memory: memory-induced re-activation of picture processing areas. *Neuropsychologia*, 40 (12), 2136–2143.

von Zerssen, G.C., Mecklinger, A., Opitz, B., and von Cramon, D.Y. (2001). Conscious recollection and illusory recognition: an event-related fMRI study. *European Journal of Neuroscience*, 13 (11), 2148–2156.

Walla, P., Endl, W., Lindinger, G., *et al.* (2000). False recognition in a verbal memory task: an event-related potential study. *Cognitive Brain Research*, 9 (1), 41–44.

Wheeler, M.E., and Buckner, R.L. (2003). Functional dissociation among components of remembering: control, perceived oldness, and content. *Journal of Neuroscience*, 23 (9), 3869–3880.

Wheeler, M.E., Petersen, S.E., and Buckner, R.L. (2000). Memory's echo: vivid remembering reactivates sensory-specific cortex. *Proceedings of the National Academy of Sciences of the USA*, 97 (20), 11125–11129.

Wiese, H., and Daum, I. (2006). Frontal positivity discriminates true from false recognition. *Brain Research*, 1075 (1), 183–192. doi: 10.1016/j.brainres.2005.12.117.

Wise, R.J.S., and Price, C.J. (2006). Functional imaging of language. In *Handbook of Functional Neuroimaging of Cognition*, 2nd edn (ed. R. Cabeza and A. Kingstone). Cambridge, MA: MIT Press, pp. 191–228.

Yassa, M.A., Lacy, J.W., Stark, S.M., *et al.* (2011). Pattern separation deficits associated with increased hippocampal CA3 and dentate gyrus activity in nondemented older adults. *Hippocampus*, 21 (9), 968–979. doi: 10.1002/hipo.20808.

Yassa, M.A., and Stark, C.E. (2008). Multiple signals of recognition memory in the medial temporal lobe. *Hippocampus*, 18 (9), 945–954. doi: 10.1002/hipo.20452.

Yassa, M.A., and Stark, C.E.L. (2011). Pattern separation in the hippocampus. *Trends in Neurosciences*, 34 (10), 515–525. doi: 10.1016/j.tins.2011.06.006.

Yonelinas, A.P., Otten, L.J., Shaw, K.N., and Rugg, M.D. (2005). Separating the brain regions involved in recollection and familiarity in recognition memory. *Journal of Neuroscience*, 25 (11), 3002–3008.

# 9

# Déjà Vu

## *A Window into Understanding the Cognitive Neuroscience of Familiarity*

### Chris B. Martin, Chris M. Fiacconi, and Stefan Köhler

## Recognition Memory and the Medial Temporal Lobes

The ability to distinguish between new and previously encountered aspects of the environment is of critical benefit to adaptive human behavior. We constantly take advantage of this ability in everyday life, such as when we greet a colleague at the shopping mall, but not the strangers that we pass. Recognition of prior occurrence is widely accepted to be supported by two phenomenologically distinct processes: recollection and familiarity. Recollection involves the detailed recovery of contextual, associative details about an episode in which a stimulus was previously encountered. For example, while at the grocery store, you may recognize the woman in the check-out line next to your own and be able to recall the fact that you met her while at a dinner last Saturday. Familiarity, by contrast, supports item recognition in the absence of the retrieval of any contextual information regarding a prior stimulus encounter. It can vary in strength from a weak intuition to a strong sense of belief that the current stimulus has been previously encountered. For example, for the individual you met in the grocery store, you may simply feel a compelling sense that she is familiar and you have encountered her before.

Extant research on recognition memory has primarily focused on dissociating the cognitive and neural mechanisms of familiarity from those that support recollection. Toward this end, several recognition memory paradigms have been developed to probe and quantify these processes, including the remember/know (R/K) procedure, the analysis of receiver operating characteristics of confidence-based recognition decisions, the process dissociation procedure, and response deadline manipulations (see Yonelinas, 2002, for review). Findings from such research have fueled ongoing debates regarding the extent to which familiarity and recollection represent functionally distinct cognitive processes, and whether they are supported by different brain structures, specifically within the medial temporal lobes (MTL; see Chapter 6 for a review of MTL anatomy).

*The Wiley Handbook on the Cognitive Neuroscience of Memory*, First Edition.
Edited by Donna Rose Addis, Morgan Barense, and Audrey Duarte.
© 2015 John Wiley & Sons, Ltd. Published 2015 by John Wiley & Sons, Ltd.

Beginning with Scoville and Milner's (1957) seminal work on patient H.M., findings obtained from neuropsychological investigations, functional magnetic resonance imaging (fMRI) in healthy humans, and lesion research in nonhuman species, indicate that the MTL forms a critical node or bottleneck for recognition memory. However, a consensus as to how to characterize the exact functional contributions of MTL structures is still lacking. An influential view that has gained considerable support is that the hippocampus (HC) plays a specific role in the encoding and subsequent recovery of contextual information about a prior stimulus encounter, whereas perirhinal cortex (PRC) supports item recognition based on the familiarity of the stimulus itself (Aggleton and Brown, 1999; see Montaldi and Mayes, 2010; Ranganath, 2010, for recent reviews).

While the evidence remains controversial (Wixted and Squire, 2011), a substantial number of findings from research in patients with selective HC lesions support dual-process models by revealing selective recollection impairments that leave familiarity intact (Aggleton *et al.*, 2005; Bowles *et al.*, 2010; Jäger *et al.*, 2009; Mayes *et al.*, 2002; Turriziani *et al.*, 2008; Vargha-Khadem *et al.*, 1997; see also Chapter 1). Differences related to lesion extent and documentation, the selection of patients, and overall memory impairment have been suggested to account for findings in patients in whom these impairments were not selective (for discussion, see Bowles *et al.*, 2010; Holdstock *et al.*, 2008).

Familiarity assessment has been the subject of considerably less research in cognitive neuroscience than processes related to the recovery of contextual details. In fact, neuropsychological research has only recently revealed that the assessment of familiarity can be selectively impaired after systemic (Cohn, Moscovitch, and Davidson, 2010; Davidson *et al.*, 2006) or focal brain lesions in the temporal or frontal cortex (Aly *et al.*, 2011; Bowles *et al.*, 2007; Martin *et al.*, 2011). In the current chapter, we will review promising new research that speaks to our understanding of the cognitive and neural mechanisms that support familiarity-based recognition by focusing specifically on the phenomenon of déjà vu.

## Déjà Vu: Some Basic Considerations

Defined as "any subjectively inappropriate impression of familiarity of a present experience with an undefined past" (Neppe, 1983), déjà vu experiences have intrigued researchers for well over a century. One critical aspect of this experience, captured with the notion of "undefined past," is that the sense of familiarity is not accompanied by the successful recollection of information pertaining to a relevant prior episode; this can be seen as an absence of "source memory" (Mitchell and Johnson, 2009). Not every impression of familiarity without episodic recollection, however, amounts to a déjà vu experience. Rather, déjà vu experiences represent instances in which familiarity is perceived with a subjective sense of inappropriateness, that is, a sense that the current environment or situation should in fact not feel familiar. It is this incongruence, which can be seen as a signal of memory conflict, that places déjà vu experiences among the most fascinating and striking phenomenological expressions of human memory.

Although déjà vu has captured the allure of popular culture in many domains (e.g., literature, film, music), the scientific investigation of the phenomenon has begun only recently, and consequently our understanding of the underlying cognitive and neural mechanisms remains relatively poor. Research progress into the nature of déjà vu has been hampered by many factors, including its typically brief duration and spontaneous occurrence, the varying operational definitions employed by different researchers, and a historical lack of experimental paradigms to elicit the phenomenon in a noninvasive manner in the psychological laboratory. Accordingly, the bulk of what is known about déjà vu in healthy individuals has come from survey-based research employing questionnaires and diary studies. Despite these limitations, promising new research has begun to shed light on both déjà vu and related feelings of familiarity. Here, we will review the empirical inroads gleaned from cognitive research conducted with healthy individuals and clinical research in the context of temporal lobe epilepsy (TLE), respectively.

## Studies of Déjà Vu in Healthy Individuals

Most research conducted in healthy individuals has focused on retrospective or prospective reports of spontaneously occurring déjà vu in daily life. Numerous demographic factors and psychological variables have been identified that modulate the incidence and frequency of déjà vu experience in the population at large, and it is clear that there is considerable variability in this regard. An in-depth review of related research is beyond the scope of this chapter but has been extensively covered in a recent monograph (Brown, 2004). Of particular interest to the current review, research has also started to address the neural basis of inter-individual differences in the incidence of déjà vu in healthy individuals. Specifically, Brazdil *et al.* (2012) examined variability in brain morphology on structural magnetic resonance images in relation to the frequency of déjà vu experiences in a large sample of 113 healthy participants. Interestingly, self-reported frequency of déjà vu experiences was negatively correlated with gray matter volume in MTL structures across individuals. However, the extent to which this relationship specifically holds for PRC remains to be determined. From the perspective of the dual-process model of recognition memory, it will be important to examine in future research the differential contribution of morphological variability in different MTL structures to déjà vu experiences in a more precise manner.

In another approach, researchers have also started to develop behavioral paradigms that aim to elicit feelings of déjà vu in the psychological laboratory, and thus bring this phenomenon into the realm of controlled experimental investigation (Brown and Marsh, 2008, 2009; Cleary, Ryals, and Nomi, 2009; Cleary *et al.*, 2012). Brown and Marsh conducted research to test the hypothesis that déjà vu experiences may occur when an initial encounter with a particular environment results in the more fluent processing of that environment in a subsequent encounter, while no pertinent contextual information about the initial presentation can be recovered (Brown and Marsh, 2008, 2010). This account was addressed in a study in which participants engaged in shallow (i.e., nonsemantic) processing of scenes from their home campus, and scenes from an unfamiliar campus that they had never visited in a study phase. One week later, they were presented with both old and new scenes and were asked to rate the likelihood that they had actually visited the location depicted by each scene. It was found that the prior presentation of a scene from an unfamiliar campus increased the likelihood that participants claimed to have visited that location. Furthermore, following the rating task, participants were asked to describe their subjective experience throughout the experimental session. On the basis of these open-ended subjective reports, the authors classified experiences according to whether they fulfilled criteria of déjà vu, and reported that nearly half of the participants commented on experiencing déjà vu or "something very similar to it" (Brown and Marsh, 2008, p. 190). In related research that was based on a similar rationale, Brown and Marsh (2009) also found that participants endorsed the presence of experimentally induced déjà vu in a targeted questionnaire that was administered after completing a priming experiment with abstract symbols. Participants were presented with a series of unfamiliar symbols and asked to judge whether they had ever encountered the symbols prior to the experiment. Each target item was primed by a brief presentation (35 ms) of the identical symbol, a different symbol, or no symbol at all. The authors found that a given symbol was more likely to be judged as having been encountered previously when it followed identity priming (see also Jacoby and Whitehouse, 1989). In this study, 50% of participants reported experiencing déjà vu during the experiment.

Cleary and colleagues (2009, 2012) developed another behavioral paradigm designed to elicit feelings of déjà vu, taking into consideration that such feelings most typically pertain to entire scenes. They presented participants with a series of linedrawn visual scenes that were associated with simple labels for study. In a subsequent test phase, participants were presented with a series of novel scenes that did or did not resemble the studied scenes with respect to their spatial configuration. For each new scene, participants were asked to name the study scene that most closely resembled the currently presented new scene, to rate its familiarity, and to indicate whether they experienced déjà vu. Prior to testing, Cleary, Ryals, and Nomi (2009) provided participants with a definition of déjà vu as "experiencing a vivid feeling that you have previously experienced something, even when you know that you haven't" – a definition that closely resembles the one proposed by Neppe (1983). New scenes for which the label of the corresponding scene at study could not be identified were found to be rated as more familiar and more likely to elicit feelings of déjà vu when they were configurally similar to the scenes that had initially been studied. In a follow-up study, this basic procedure was also employed in a 3D virtual-reality setting in which participants could actively explore each scene at study, and thus were immersed in a richer visual environment (Cleary *et al.*, 2012). This time, the test phase also included the presentation of the original scenes (Experiment 2) and required participants to judge whether each scene was old or new. Critically, the authors found that old scenes incorrectly labeled as "new" were more likely to elicit feelings of déjà vu than new scenes that were configurally similar to those scenes presented at study and that were correctly judged to be unfamiliar. In addition, accurately judged new scenes that were configurally similar to studied scenes were more likely to elicit feelings of déjà vu than accurately judged new configurally dissimilar scenes. Given that in all three aforementioned conditions, participants classified the test scene as "new," the authors suggested that any accompanying feelings of déjà vu might truly reflect familiarity together with a sense of inappropriateness. Thus, Cleary and colleagues concluded that a high degree of configural similarity between the present environment and past environments can indeed trigger a déjà-vu-like experience.

The research reviewed represents an admirable first step towards understanding the cognitive mechanisms involved in a phenomenon that is extremely difficult to study in the laboratory. At present, however, it still remains somewhat difficult to discern whether the experiences participants reported in these studies reflect true instances of déjà vu, or whether they merely reflect a sense of familiarity (that could be true or false) in the absence of recollection. This issue is important because déjà vu, by its very definition (Brown, 2004; Neppe, 1983), also involves the sense that the perceived familiarity is inappropriate. We recognize that participants were carefully instructed about the formal definition of déjà vu in some of this research (e.g., Cleary *et al.*, 2012) before they offered any reports. However, as other others have argued (Illman *et al.*, 2012b), such a set-up is likely going to create specific demand characteristics, in particular when déjà vu is probed on a trial-by-trial basis (Cleary, Ryals, and Nomi, 2009, Cleary *et al.*, 2012); such probing can introduce a confirmation bias in which participants assume that déjà vu should occur on at least a subset of trials. A confirmation bias is of particular concern when experiments aim to elicit experiences that are rather rare in daily life, a feature that characterizes déjà vu in almost all healthy individuals who report it (e.g., Warren-Gash and Zeman, 2014). In future research, objective markers of memory conflict, which could be obtained with neuroimaging methods in combination with the paradigms developed to elicit déjà vu in the laboratory, may provide means to ascertain the validity of experimentally induced déjà vu with more certainty. Moreover, such research will also be instrumental for understanding the contributions of specific MTL structures to any experimentally induced déjà vu experiences.

## Déjà Vu in Temporal Lobe Epilepsy

Déjà vu experiences have also attracted some interest in the clinical neurological literature, primarily in epilepsy (Gloor, 1990; Spatt, 2002). It is well known that déjà vu experiences are symptomatic of the aura of simple and complex partial seizures in a subset of TLE patients. In these ictal events, déjà vu is usually felt as a vivid and compelling mnemonic experience with a subjective sense that the feeling of familiarity is inappropriate. Given these characteristics, the scientific investigation of déjà vu in TLE can offer unique insight into the neural mechanisms that mediate familiarity assessment, and how they interact with other memory and cognitive control processes. Here, we review research on déjà vu in TLE that speaks to these issues with a focus on phenomenology, localization, and behavioral correlates.

### Phenomenology

Descriptions of déjà vu are often provided spontaneously by TLE patients when reporting their subjective experiences during the aura of their seizures in a clinical interview. Phenomenological descriptions provided by such patients suggest that ictal déjà vu is neither evoked by, nor bound to, specific stimuli in the immediate environment, a point that was previously emphasized by O'Connor and Moulin (2008). For example, one patient included in our recent investigation of déjà vu in TLE (Martin *et al.*, 2012) described her experience as follows: "It's highly visual. Things will suddenly become very familiar. There isn't a progression from vaguely to highly familiar; it's just highly familiar. It's initially object-specific, but when I focus my attention on something else it too becomes familiar. I will even search the room for something that isn't familiar but everything seems to be so." This account illustrates that déjà vu is initially experienced for whatever object or scene that is at the focus of attention at the moment of seizure onset, but readily spreads to other aspects of the environment as the seizure progresses.

Given that the mechanism of elicitation appears to be different in spontaneously occurring and ictal déjà vu, one may wonder whether the subjective phenomenology in terms of mnemonic experience is indeed the same (see also Adachi *et al.*, 2010). Spontaneous reports are often consistent with the formal definition of the phenomenon without any prior provision of related criteria (e.g., Martin *et al.*, 2012; O'Connor and Moulin, 2008). For example, one TLE patient whom we recently examined offered the following description of déjà vu at the onset of his seizures: "It's a really strange feeling. I'll feel like I've been somewhere before – like I'm looking at a snapshot of a scene that I've seen previously. The strange bit is that I also know that I have not been to that place before." This account was similar in spirit to the descriptions provided by six other patients included in that experimental study (Martin *et al.*, 2012). Generally, the experience was described as consisting of strong feelings of familiarity for the immediate visual environment that persist for only a few seconds and that are accompanied by a conflicting sense that they are inappropriate. Similar experiences in other modalities were rarely reported in this sample (audition – two individuals, taste – one individual). To the extent that similar characteristics have also been reported in retrospective studies of healthy individuals (Brown, 2004), we believe that the study of déjà vu in TLE patients can inform our understanding of the phenomenon more broadly; it offers a unique opportunity to gain better insight into its neural mechanisms, and its relation to familiarity and recollection, as probed in cognitive experiments.

When considering research on déjà vu in TLE, it should be kept in mind that clinical neurology has historically made reference to this phenomenon sometimes with other, often less specific terms (e.g., dreamy state). Accordingly, in this literature déjà vu has not always been distinguished clearly from other experiential phenomena that can accompany seizures originating in the temporal lobes (see Illman *et al.*, 2012a, for discussion). In this context, it is worth noting that déjà vu experiences are typically described as being static in their phenomenology in that they only pertain to the environment currently perceived. There are other mnemonic experiences that are more dynamic in nature and that may be considered to be pathological states of recollection. Such experiences have been referred to as déjà vécu in research on TLE and other neurological conditions, and relate to the progression of sequences of events (Moulin *et al.*, 2005). Whether the presence of déjà vécu is related to other structural brain abnormalities than déjà vu is an issue that, to our knowledge, has not been addressed in any systematic manner as of yet. Despite this challenge, however, several research findings on relatively well-defined déjà vu experiences in TLE patients point to a surprisingly consistent picture concerning the neuroanatomical basis of this specific phenomenon in the MTL.

## Neural correlates

Research addressing the neural correlates of déjà vu in TLE has generally been conducted with one of two experimental approaches. The first, and historically most widely employed approach in clinical settings, has been to evoke déjà vu through electrical intracranial stimulation of cortical tissue pre-surgically or intraoperatively. With the second approach, researchers have compared TLE patients with and without déjà vu with respect to distinct seizure characteristics that manifest in ictal scalp or intracranial electrical recordings, and/or neuroimaging measures of lasting differences in brain morphology or focal brain metabolism. Modern epilepsy research that has attempted to localize mnemonic experiential phenomena accompanying seizures in TLE based on stimulation or ictal EEG recordings has primarily, although not exclusively, linked them to the MTL (Bancaud *et al.*, 1994; Gloor *et al.*, 1982; Vignal *et al.*, 2007; Weinand *et al.*, 1994). Several studies conducted with intracranial EEG recordings, for example, have demonstrated that seizure activity that is associated with mnemonic experiential phenomena, including déjà vu, is more consistently localized to medial than lateral temporal lobe structures (Gil-Nagel and Risinger, 1997; Vignal *et al.*, 2007; Weinand *et al.*, 1994). Gloor *et al.* (1982) reported similar findings using stereotactically implanted depth electrodes to stimulate the MTL and lateral temporal lobes in 35 TLE patients, four of whom experienced déjà vu with their seizures. In the TLE patients whose seizures were accompanied by déjà vu, virtually all evoked déjà vu experiences were obtained through stimulation of the MTL, including the amygdala, but rarely from stimulation of the lateral temporal lobes.

Evidence from other studies conducted in TLE patients suggests that, within the MTL, déjà vu may be specifically associated with activity in extra-hippocampal structures in the anterior parahippocampal region (i.e., PRC and entorhinal cortex, ERC; Bartolomei *et al.*, 2004; Guedj *et al.*, 2010). Such findings are of particular relevance to the dual-process model of MTL organization that has been advocated by Aggleton and Brown (1999) and others. Bartolomei *et al.* (2004) employed intracranial cortical stimulation to examine the role of specific MTL structures in the genesis of déjà vu experiences. Through the use of surgically implanted depth electrodes, they targeted the amygdala, anterior HC, and PRC and ERC (collectively referred to as rhinal cortex). Stimulation applied to rhinal cortex manifested in phenomenological impressions of déjà vu in 11% of all stimulations. Comparison of effects for ERC and PRC revealed that stimulation of ERC was more frequently associated with déjà vu and PRC with the recovery of specific visual memories regarding distinct, frequently encountered objects. By contrast, only 2.2% of stimulations of the amygdala and 2.1% in the anterior HC yielded déjà vu. More recently, data that link déjà vu to processes in rhinal cortex have also been reported by Guedj *et al.* (2010) based on an examination of interictal brain metabolism. The authors conducted an 18-FDG-PET investigation that directly compared lasting, interictal glucose metabolic abnormalities in unilateral TLE patients, with and without déjà vu, and healthy control participants. The results revealed more pronounced hypometabolism in ipsilateral rhinal cortex of those patients whose seizures were typically accompanied by déjà vu as compared to those who did not experience déjà vu with their seizures. No differences were found between the patient groups with respect to metabolic activity in either the HC or amygdala. The only other structure that exhibited such differences was a region in the ipsilateral lateral superior temporal gyrus. Compared to healthy control participants, both patient groups did show hypometabolism in ipsilateral HC. This finding suggests that lasting functional changes in the hippocampus can be detected in the context of TLE with déjà vu, but may not be uniquely associated with the generation of these experiences. That MTL structures other than rhinal cortices also play a role once the seizure has been triggered is suggested by additional evidence from studies that have focused on the synchronization of intracranial electroencephalography (EEG) signals in the MTL in relation to déjà vu (Bartolomei *et al.*, 2012; see also Barbeau *et al.*, 2005).

Taken together, the evidence reviewed regarding the localization of déjà vu in TLE primarily links the phenomenon to rhinal cortex, as opposed to other MTL structures such as the HC or amygdala. Considered in relation to the cognitive neuroscience literature of recognition memory reviewed previously, these findings point to overlap concerning the neural mechanism of familiarity. The dual-process model of recognition memory represents a theoretical framework within which déjà vu experiences in TLE can be readily interpreted to the extent that an erroneous familiarity signal that arises from seizure activity in PRC is at the core of the déjà vu experience. We note that this account, in and of itself, does not offer any explanation as to why the familiarity experience in déjà vu is experienced as subjectively inappropriate. We will return to this point after reviewing research on the behavioral correlates of the presence of déjà vu in TLE.

## Behavioral correlates

The presence of interictal hypometabolism in rhinal cortex that was found to be uniquely associated with the presence of déjà vu in TLE patients (Guedj *et al.*, 2010) raises the interesting question as to whether unique interictal behavioral impairments might also be present in this group. Based on the dual-process model of MTL organization, one might predict that any such lasting impairments would be reflected in selective familiarity impairments on recognition memory tasks that probe familiarity and recollection separately. Although mild memory impairments in pre-surgical patients with TLE are well documented in general, this specific issue has received surprisingly little empirical investigation in the neuropsychological literature so far.

In our own work, we initially became interested in examining déjà vu in TLE within the dual-process model framework following research we undertook on a single case, patient N.B., whom we tested post-surgically. Prior to surgical intervention, this individual suffered from intractable TLE caused by a circumscribed ganglioglioma in the left amygdala. Interestingly, the aura of her complex partial seizures was frequently accompanied by phenomenological feelings of déjà vu. To control these seizures, N.B. underwent a rare surgical resection that targeted anterior regions of lateral and medial temporal cortex in the left hemisphere. Critically, her resection included large portions of PRC and ERC, but spared the HC; the extent of the resection was quantified in our laboratory using magnetic resonance (MR) volumetry, which confirmed intact structural integrity of the HC. In our post-surgical examination of N.B.'s recognition memory performance, we discovered that her ability to discriminate between previously studied and novel stimuli was selectively impaired when based on familiarity assessment. In four different experiments, conducted with three different methodological approaches to probe familiarity and recollection for verbal materials (R/K paradigm, receiver operating characteristics of confidence-based recognition decisions, and a response deadline procedure), we showed that N.B. exhibited impairments in familiarity assessment with preserved recollection (Bowles *et al.*, 2007). Evidence from an fMRI study also suggested that, despite impoverished inputs from PRC and ERC, N.B.'s left HC showed clear signs of functional integrity, as reflected in novelty responses that were comparable to those we observed in control participants (Bowles *et al.*, 2011). Although this study provided critical new support for the dual-process model of MTL organization, the suggested link between déjà vu and selective familiarity impairments must be considered indirect, given that N.B. no longer experienced seizures at the time we revealed her memory impairments.

In research that has focused on behavioral correlates of déjà vu and other mnemonic phenomena in association with TLE pre-surgically, one study failed to identify any significant differences between patients whose seizures were or were not accompanied by the phenomenon (Vederman *et al.*, 2010). In this investigation, however, memory performance was evaluated using standard neuropsychological tests with verbal materials only. Thus the authors could not examine familiarity assessment, specifically. Moreover, memory was tested with verbal stimuli presented in the auditory modality. Such an arrangement may not be optimal to reveal behavioral correlates of a phenomenon that is predominantly visual in nature. Interictal behavioral deficits that are unique to TLE patients with déjà vu may only be revealed through the use of memory tasks that probe recognition memory for visual stimuli in particular.

In recent research conducted in our own laboratory, we employed experimental tasks of visual recognition memory to examine whether the presence of ictal déjà vu in TLE is indeed associated with selective impairments when judgments are based on familiarity assessment (Martin *et al.*, 2012). Toward this end, we compared two groups of pre-surgical patients with intractable unilateral TLE; patients in the first group ($n = 7$) consistently experienced déjà vu as part of their seizures (TLE+) while individuals in the second group ($n = 6$) had never experienced any mnemonic phenomenon during their seizures (TLE−). Semi-structured interviews confirmed that ictal déjà vu in TLE+ patients could indeed be characterized as feelings of familiarity for the immediate visual environment that were experienced as subjectively inappropriate. We conducted two experiments that involved the presentation of novel complex visual scenes in a study phase and a requirement to make recognition judgments in a subsequent test phase. The scenes employed were sampled from a set of discrete categories (i.e., three types of rooms) so as to prevent memory discrimination based on gist and so as to encourage reliance on perceptual characteristics of objects that differed across scene exemplars. Using an R/K procedure (Tulving, 1985), we first sought to determine whether impairments in unilateral TLE with déjà vu would be selective for familiarity assessment and would spare recollection when these processes were probed with meta-memory judgments in the test phase ("How do you know that this scene was presented previously?"). In a second experiment, we used a variant of the process dissociation procedure developed by Jacoby and colleagues (i.e., an exclusion task), to probe the interplay between familiarity and recollection when they were placed in opposition by way of experimental manipulation (see Yonelinas and Jacoby, 2012, for review). Specifically, this experiment allowed us to determine whether TLE patients with déjà vu could still engage recollection processes successfully when it was necessary to counteract feelings of familiarity. To get at this issue, participants were first presented with a set of scenes in a study phase. In the subsequent test phase they were presented with a mixed list of previously studied and novel items. Critically, all of the novel lures were also repeated at various delays during the test phase, with participants being asked to endorse only items as old that had indeed been encountered during the study phase rather than as repeated lures during the test phase (Jennings and Jacoby, 1997). Inasmuch as repetition of lures at test will generate a sense of familiarity for these items, accurate exclusion of these items from "old" responses is thought to rely on recollection of contextual detail.

Results from the R/K task for categorized visual scenes revealed evidence for impairments that were limited to familiarity-based assessment in the TLE+ patient group. These impairments were reflected in reduced accuracy of discrimination and reflected increased false-alarm rates as well as increased "miss" responses for old items. We also observed a strikingly selective pattern of impairments in TLE+ patients with the exclusion task. Despite displaying recognition impairments that affected the ability to discriminate between previously studied and novel stimuli, TLE+ patients showed evidence of a spared ability to counter feelings of familiarity for repeated lures, presumably based on intact recollection. The selective deficits observed in these patients contrasted with the broader pattern of recognition memory impairments in the TLE– patient group. Specifically, these individuals showed deficits that affected both recollection and familiarity in the R/K paradigm; it also affected the ability to counter familiarity in the exclusion task by way of recollection. Interestingly this behavioral pattern across patient groups paralleled noticeable differences in ipsilesional MTL volumes. Volumetric measures of T1-weighted anatomical MR images revealed that ipsilateral MTL structures were overall less affected in TLE+ than in TLE– patients, with hints of more focal volume reductions in the rhinal cortices of patients who displayed déjà vu in their seizure profile (i.e., TLE+).

To our knowledge, the findings reported in Martin *et al.* (2012) represent the first demonstration of an empirical link between déjà vu and behavioral indices of familiarity assessment on experimental tasks of recognition memory. This link is suggestive of a shared neural mechanism that is common to feelings of familiarity in ictal déjà vu and feelings of familiarity outside of the ictal context (see Spatt, 2002, for related discussion). We will consider the nature of this proposed shared mechanism as part of our concluding section.

## Implications and Conclusions

Taken together, the research reviewed reveals interesting links between the phenomenon of déjà vu, the assessment of familiarity, and the functional organization of the human MTL. Specifically, convergent evidence obtained from cortical stimulation (Bartolomei *et al.*, 2004), functional neuroimaging (Guedj *et al.*, 2010), and neuropsychological studies (Martin *et al.*, 2012) that have focused on déjà vu in TLE suggests that the phenomenon is associated with processes in rhinal cortex, with some evidence pointing specifically to ERC (Bartolomei *et al.*, 2004). These findings converge with those from neuropsychological studies in patients with temporal lobe lesions and fMRI research with healthy individuals, which have implicated rhinal cortex as integral for the assessment of familiarity in experimental recognition memory tasks (for reviews, see Eichenbaum, Yonelinas, and Ranganath, 2007; Montaldi and Mayes, 2010; Ranganath, 2010). Recent investigations conducted in our own laboratory have directly bridged these fields of research by revealing that déjà vu in the context of TLE is indeed associated with selective deficits at the level of familiarity in visual recognition memory tasks (Martin *et al.*, 2012).

### Mechanisms of déjà vu in perirhinal cortex

As discussed, numerous fMRI studies have previously implicated PRC in familiarity assessment on recognition memory tasks in healthy individuals (for review, Montaldi and Mayes, 2010; Ranganath, 2010; see also Chapter 1). A substantial body of data obtained with electrophysiological recordings in nonhuman species has also shown that PRC supports the discrimination of novel from familiar objects (for reviews, see Brown, Warburton, and Aggleton, 2010; Brown and Xiang, 1998). In both the fMRI blood-oxygen-level-dependent (BOLD) response and in electrophysiological recordings, old items previously encountered in the experimental setting are typically associated with a reduced PRC response relative to novel stimuli. It may seem curious, then, that TLE+ patients experience feelings of familiarity, rather than novelty, in association with electrical discharge during the aura of their seizures. However, it must be kept in mind that activity during the aura of TLE seizures is typically reflected in patterns of electrical discharge that consists of an abnormal rhythmic response, which differs considerably from typical neuronal spiking responses in relation to the processing of specific stimuli (e.g., Vignal *et al.*, 2007; Gloor *et al.*, 1982). Such discharge can be expected to interfere with the normal response that would otherwise signal stimulus novelty. In other words, acute seizure activity in PRC may introduce a bias in the electrophysiological response pattern that shifts it away from any expression of novelty.

While ictal déjà vu experiences are characterized by a false sense of familiarity that could be likened to a "false alarm" memory decision, the interictal familiarity impairments we reported for TLE+ patients in Martin *et al.* (2012) reflected not only an increase in false alarms, but also a decrease in the hit rate for familiarity-based responses. This interictal pattern can be understood if one considers that there was no acute seizure discharge at the time the memory decisions were being made. A significant body of research on TLE suggests that the majority of patients with complex partial seizures do have lasting structural abnormalities in epileptogenic regions that can interfere with normal cognitive functioning, even in the absence of acute seizures (Bell *et al.*, 2011). The functional consequences of lasting structural abnormalities, whether gross or subtle, are unlikely to manifest in exactly the same manner as those associated with acute seizure activity. Thus, while seizure discharge in rhinal tissue seems to generate acute subjective feelings of familiarity, the interictal manifestation of the corresponding structural and/or metabolic abnormalities could be a noisy memory signal that leads to an impoverished ability to discriminate between old and new items based on familiarity. A considerable body of work indicates that familiarity-based memory decisions rely on a signal-detection mechanism for discrimination of two item distributions on a continuous dimension of memory strength (for review, see Yonelinas and Parks, 2007). If this signal is noisy, performance can be affected by an increase in false alarms as well as a decrease in hits on familiarity-based recognition decisions.

In ictal déjà vu, the eliciting stimulus can be readily identified as the epileptic discharge that occurs during an aura of complex partial seizures, and the experienced sense of familiarity reflects a direct consequence of this abnormal rhythmic neuronal activity. Déjà vu experiences in healthy individuals may also rely on familiarity signals generated in the rhinal cortices. As discussed in our review, however, empirical evidence that speaks to neural mechanisms in healthy individuals is sparse (but see Brazdil *et al.*, 2012). The presumed rhinal signals during déjà vu in healthy individuals would not be the outcome of endogenous neural activity, but would typically be triggered by some external stimulus in the environment (see Brown, 2004, for diary-based documentation). To the extent that déjà vu experiences elicited with memory paradigms in the laboratory offer any guidance, the evidence reviewed suggests that the similarity between the stimulus that triggers déjà vu and stimuli that were encountered previously plays an important role (Brown and Marsh, 2009; Cleary, Ryals, and Nomi, 2009). The evidence obtained with such laboratory paradigms, although limited, as discussed, hints that similarity at the level of objects and/or the level of spatial configurations in scenes could be "driving" the experience.

## Déjà vu as a conflict between competing medial temporal lobe memory signals

In daily life, it is quite common to experience feelings of familiarity that are unaccompanied by the recollection of any specific preceding encounter with the stimulus in question. As noted, déjà vu experiences differ from such situations in that they are also characterized by a subjective sense of inappropriateness. Inasmuch as the familiarity signal in déjà vu is tied specifically to processes and computations in rhinal cortices, it is possible that processes in other MTL structures play a role in invoking this sense of inappropriateness (for related proposals, see Gloor, 1990; Spatt, 2002). A structure of particular relevance is the HC. The fact that TLE patients who experience déjà vu during their seizures, and who appear to have spared hippocampal functioning, exhibit a preserved ability both to make accurate recollection-based recognition responses and to counteract familiarity signals with recovery of contextual information in an exclusion task can be seen as consistent with such an account (Martin *et al.*, 2012).

In terms of precise mechanisms, the sense of inappropriateness during déjà vu could rely on the rapid generation of a match–mismatch signal in the HC that indexes violations of contextually based expectations (Köhler *et al.*, 2005; Kumaran and Maguire, 2006, 2007). Findings from a number of studies provide evidence for contextually based novelty signals in the HC (for reviews, see Kumaran and Maguire, 2007; Ranganath and Rainer, 2003). For example, Köhler *et al.* (2005) used fMRI to examine the role of different MTL structures in novelty detection. Participants were familiarized with a series of pairs of objects in varying spatial configurations, and were subsequently asked to detect changes in the pairings, or the locations in which objects had been presented during familiarization. It was found that parts of the HC responded to both types of contextual novelty. More recent research has also directly demonstrated that the HC generates these contextual novelty signals in sequences of events when expectations about upcoming items can be generated and, critically, when these expectations are indeed violated (Duncan *et al.*, 2012; Kumaran and Maguire, 2006, 2007). In this research, it has been shown that hippocampal match–mismatch signals can be observed for violations that pertain to the temporal sequencing as well as to spatial characteristics of events. It is typically assumed that the generation of match–mismatch signals critically depends on the presence of overlap between novel sensory inputs and stored representations. In other words, some aspect of the current environment has to match with stored information about the same or similar previously encountered environments, so as to elicit a match–mismatch signal of this nature.

In spontaneously occurring déjà vu in healthy individuals, such match–mismatch signals would denote the violation of an expectation that was derived from pertinent stored information retrieved in response to specific environmental or situational cues that define the context. We note that, within such a model, the retrieval of stored information that allows for the generation of an expectation would not necessarily occur at the level of conscious mnemonic experience; rather, it may simply reflect pattern completion at the level of hippocampal activity. Further, it has been suggested that this information would not have to be episodic but could in fact capture more abstract (i.e., semantic) characteristics that hold for the current general situation. In other words, the match component may not be associated with conscious recollection from episodic memory. However, the mismatch signal would be consciously perceived as novelty and inform the impression that the concurrently experienced familiarity signal (generated in PRC) is "wrong" (i.e., subjectively inappropriate). Although clearly speculative, an account of déjà vu with reference to contextually based mismatch signals is also in line with the idea that feelings of familiarity are generally more striking under conditions in which expectations are violated than when they are not (Whittlesea and Williams, 1998). People are more likely to experience a sense of familiarity when encountering their "butcher on the bus" than when seeing him in the butcher shop (Mandler, 1980).

We hasten to add that it is possible that processes other than the hippocampal computation of contextual novelty could lead to the sense that a presently experienced impression of familiarity is wrong – in the aura of seizures as well as in spontaneously occurring déjà vu in healthy individuals. Processes that are supported by prefrontal cortex, for example, may also play a role (see Chapter 7 for a review of prefrontal contributions to retrieval); it is well established that prefrontal regions support evaluative monitoring processes that guide memory decisions and help to avoid memory errors (see Schacter and Slotnick, 2004, for review), some of them operating on a very fast timescale (Gilboa *et al.*, 2009). These processes include evaluation of affective signals and more deliberate processes akin to deductive reasoning. A challenging goal for future research is to systematically investigate whether and how hippocampal and prefrontal processes interact in producing the sense of inappropriateness that accompanies familiarity in déjà vu.

### Distinct familiarity signals for different visual stimulus categories in the medial temporal lobes?

As alluded to previously, whether the feelings of familiarity for current visual input that are experienced during déjà vu can be best characterized as pertaining to individual objects within the present environment, or visual scenes in their entirety (e.g., spatial layout) remains an unresolved issue. Retrospective, questionnaire-based data regarding the qualitative characteristics of spontaneously occurring déjà vu in healthy individuals have been interpreted to suggest that the familiarity at the core of the experience typically extends to the entire immediate visual environment (Brown, 1994, as cited in Brown, 2004). Interestingly, however, anecdotal observations provided by some TLE patients whose seizures are accompanied by déjà vu suggest that the experienced familiarity may start as an item-specific impression that evolves into one that encompasses the entire environment (Martin *et al.*, 2012; O'Connor and Moulin, 2008). Whether familiarity during déjà vu pertains specifically to items or scenes is an issue that is also relevant for understanding the neural mechanisms underlying the phenomenon, specifically its familiarity component.

It has been argued, based on observations from neurophysiological, lesion, and neuroimaging research, that familiarity signals generated in PRC are closely tied to visual object processing in the ventral visual pathway (e.g., Graham, Barense, and Lee, 2010; Murray, Bussey, and Saksida, 2007; see also Chapter 10). It may seem curious, then, that déjà vu is experienced with respect to entire scenes, and that the familiarity impairments we have reported in TLE patients with déjà vu are evident in the context of memory decisions for complex visual scenes (Martin *et al.*, 2012). However, given that four of the seven patients examined indicated that their typical déjà vu experience during seizures is initially item-specific, these data do not necessarily argue against the notion that familiarity assessment in PRC is object-based. One possible scenario is that seizure activity originating in PRC spreads to other MTL structures, namely the parahippocampal cortex (PHC). Findings from research based on intraoperative stimulation of the rhinal cortices suggests that stimulations triggering déjà vu are indeed associated with synchronized changes in other MTL structures (Bartolomei *et al.*, 2012). Parahippocampal cortex, which is situated adjacent to PRC and covers the more posterior aspects of the collateral sulcus, has been shown to be critical for representing the spatial layout of visual scenes and the sense of space that can be conveyed by large scale objects in the environment, such as buildings (Aguirre, Zarahn, and D'Esposito, 1998; Epstein and Kanwisher, 1998; Mullally and Maguire, 2011; Troiani *et al.*, 2012). Recent evidence from our laboratory suggests that PHC may also play an important role in the assessment of familiarity for such stimuli (Martin *et al.*, 2013). In a study conducted in healthy individuals, we employed multi-voxel pattern analyses of fMRI data to compare patterns of activity in various MTL structures that are associated with the subjectively perceived familiarity of faces, chairs, and buildings. Most pertinent to the current discussion, familiarity signals for buildings were revealed in PHC but not in PRC, as reflected in the observation that distributed patterns of activation in PHC reliably distinguished between familiar and novel buildings in the absence of recollection. At present it is unknown whether similar familiarity signals can be observed for entire scenes in PHC. Based on our current understanding, we would predict this to be the case. In déjà vu, a shift from object-based to scene-based familiarity may be associated with differential involvement of PRC and PHC, respectively. At present it is unknown whether déjà vu experiences, in TLE patients or in healthy individuals, can also originate with activity in PHC.

## Summary

In conclusion, the research reviewed in this chapter suggests that current models of recognition memory and MTL organization provide a powerful framework to advance our understanding of one of the most fascinating, yet elusive, expressions of human memory. We have summarized how attempts to elicit déjà vu in the cognitive laboratory with experimental manipulations of memory have provided promising first evidence that points to possible underlying cognitive mechanisms. In reviewing this work, we have also highlighted the methodological and interpretive challenges that researchers face when aiming to understand a phenomenon that reflects, at its core, the subjective interpretation of a mnemonic state that is fleeting and relatively rare in daily life. A parallel empirical approach to elucidate the cognitive and neural mechanisms of this phenomenon has involved the examination of behavioral and neural markers of déjà vu in individuals who regularly experience déjà vu in the context of TLE. A comparison of memory performance between such individuals and others who do not experience déjà vu as part of their seizures has revealed a direct link between MTL mechanisms of déjà vu and familiarity assessment on experimental tasks of recognition memory.

The theoretical account we have proposed here characterizes déjà vu as a conflict between a familiarity signal that is generated in PRC and a contextually based novelty signal that is computed in the HC.

# References

Adachi, N., Akanuma, N., Ito, M., *et al.* (2010). Two forms of déjà vu experiences in patients with epilepsy. *Epilepsy and Behavior*, 18 (3), 218–222. doi: 10.1016/j.yebeh.2010.02.016.

Aggleton, J.P., and Brown, M.W. (1999). Episodic memory, amnesia, and the hippocampal anterior thalamic axis. *Behavioral and Brain Sciences*, 22 (3), 425–444. doi: 10.1017/S0140525X99002034.

Aggleton, J.P., Vann, S.D., Denby, C., *et al.* (2005). Sparing of the familiarity component of recognition memory in a patient with hippocampal pathology. *Neuropsychologia*, 43 (12), 1810–1823. doi: 10.1016/j.neuropsychologia.2005.01.019.

Aguirre, G.K., Zarahn, E., and D'Esposito, M. (1998). An area within human ventral cortex sensitive to building stimuli: evidence and implications. *Neuron*, 21 (2), 373–383. doi: 10.1016/S0896-6273(00)80546-2.

Aly, M., Yonelinas, A.P., Kishiyama, M.M., and Knight, R.T. (2011). Damage to the lateral prefrontal cortex impairs familiarity but not recollection. *Behavioral Brain Research*, 225 (1), 297–304. doi: 10.1016/j.bbr.2011.07.043.

Bancaud, J., Brunet-Bourgin, F., Chauvel, P., and Halgren, E. (1994). Anatomical origin of déjà vu and vivid memories in human temporal lobe epilepsy. *Brain*, 117 (1), 71–90. doi: 10.1093/brain/117.1.71.

Barbeau, E., Wendling, F., Régis, J., *et al.* (2005). Recollection of vivid memories after perirhinal region stimulations: synchronization in the theta range of spatially distributed brain areas. *Neuropsychologia*, 43 (9), 1329–1337. doi: 10.1016/j.neuropsychologia.2004.11.025.

Bartolomei, F., Barbeau, E., Gavaret, M., *et al.* (2004). Cortical stimulation study of the role of rhinal cortex in déjà vu and reminiscence of memories. *Neurology*, 63 (5), 858–864. doi: 10.1212/01.WNL.0000137037.56916.3F.

Bartolomei, F., Barbeau, E.J., Nguyen, T., *et al.* (2012). Rhinal-hippocampal interactions during déjà vu. *Clinical Neurophysiology*, 123 (3), 489–495. doi: 10.1016/j.clinph.2011.08.012.

Bell, B., Lin, J.J., Seidenberg, M., and Hermann, B. (2011). The neurobiology of cognitive disorders in temporal lobe epilepsy. *Nature Reviews Neurology*, 7 (3), 154–164. doi: 10.1038/nrneurol.2011.3.

Bowles, B., Crupi, C., Mirsattari, S.M., *et al.* (2007). Impaired familiarity with preserved recollection after anterior temporal-lobe resection that spares the hippocampus. *Proceedings of the National Academy of Sciences of the USA*, 104 (41), 16382–16387. doi: 10.1073/pnas.0705273104.

Bowles, B., Crupi, C., Pigott, S., *et al.* (2010). Double dissociation of selective recollection and familiarity impairments following two different surgical treatments for temporal-lobe epilepsy. *Neuropsychologia*, 48 (9), 2640–2647. doi: 10.1016/j.neuropsychologia.2010.05.010.

Bowles, B., O'Neil, E.B., Mirsattari, S.M., *et al.* (2011). Preserved hippocampal novelty responses following anterior temporal-lobe resection that impairs familiarity but spares recollection. *Hippocampus*, 21 (8), 847–854. doi: 10.1002/hipo.20800.

Brazdil, M., Marecek, R., Urbanek, T., *et al.* (2012). Unveiling the mystery of déjà vu: the structural anatomy of déjà vu. *Cortex*, 48 (9), 1240–1243. doi: 10.1016/j.cortex.2012.03.004.

Brown, A.S. (2004). *The Déjà Vu Experience*. New York, NY: Psychology Press.

Brown, A.S., and Marsh, E.J. (2008). Evoking false beliefs about autobiographical experience. *Psychonomic Bulletin and Review*, 15 (1), 186–190. doi: 10.3758/PBR.15.1.186.

Brown, A.S., and Marsh, E.J. (2009). Creating illusions of past encounter through brief exposure. *Psychological Science*, 20 (5), 534–538. doi: 10.1111/j.1467-9280.2009.02337.x.

Brown, A. S., and Marsh, E.J. (2010). Digging into déjà vu: recent research findings on possible mechanisms. In *The Psychology of Learning and Motivation* (ed. B. H. Ross). Burlington, MA: Academic Press, pp. 33–62.

Brown, M.W., Warburton, E.C., and Aggleton, J.P. (2010). Recognition memory: material, processes, and substrates. *Hippocampus*, 20 (11), 1228–1244. doi: 10.1002/hipo.20858.

Brown, M.W., and Xiang, J.Z. (1998). Recognition memory: neuronal substrates of the judgement of prior occurrence. *Progress in Neurobiology*, 55 (2), 149–189.

Cleary, A.M., Brown, A.S., Sawyer, B.D., *et al.* (2012). Familiarity from the configuration of objects in 3-dimensional space and its relation to déjà vu: A virtual reality investigation. *Consciousness and Cognition*, 21 (2), 969–975. doi: 10.1016/j.concog.2011.12.010.

Cleary, A.M., Ryals, A.J., and Nomi, J.S. (2009). Can déjà vu result from similarity to a prior experience? Support for the similarity hypothesis of déjà vu. *Psychonomic Bulletin and Review*, 16 (6), 1082–1088. doi: 10.3758/PBR.16.6.1082.

Cohn, M., Moscovitch, M., and Davidson, P.S. (2010). Double dissociation between familiarity and recollection in Parkinson's disease as a function of encoding tasks. *Neuropsychologia*, 48 (14), 4142–4147. doi: 10.1016/j.neuropsychologia.2010.10.013.

Davidson, P.S., Anaki, D., Saint-Cyr, J.A., *et al.* (2006). Exploring the recognition memory deficit in Parkinson's disease: estimates of recollection versus familiarity. *Brain*, 129 (7), 1768–1779. doi: 10.1093/brain/awl115.

Duncan, K., Ketz, N., Inati, S.J., and Davachi, L. (2012). Evidence for area CA1 as a match/mismatch detector: a high-resolution fMRI study of the human hippocampus. *Hippocampus*, 22 (3), 389–398. doi: 10.1002/hipo.20933.

Eichenbaum, H., Yonelinas, A.P., and Ranganath, C. (2007). The medial temporal lobe and recognition memory. *Annual Review of Neuroscience*, 30, 123–152. doi: 10.1146/annurev.neuro.30.051606.094328.

Epstein, R.A., and Kanwisher, N. (1998). A cortical representation of the local visual environment. *Nature*, 392 (6676), 598–601. doi: 10.1038/33402.

Gil-Nagel, A., and Risinger, M.W. (1997). Ictal semiology in hippocampal versus extrahippocampal temporal lobe epilepsy. *Brain*, 120 (1), 183–192.

Gilboa, A., Alain, C., He, Y., *et al.* (2009). Ventromedial prefrontal cortex lesions produce early functional alterations during remote memory retrieval. *Journal of Neuroscience*, 29 (15), 4871–4881. doi: 10.1523/JNEUROSCI.5210-08.2009.

Gloor, P. (1990). Experiential phenomena of temporal lobe epilepsy: facts and hypotheses. *Brain*, 113 (6), 1673–94.

Gloor, P., Olivier, A., Quesney, L., *et al.* (1982). The role of limbic system in experiential phenomena of temporal lobe epilepsy. *Annals of Neurology*, 12 (2), 129–144.

Graham, K., Barense, M.D., and Lee, A.C. (2010). Going beyond LTM in the MTL: a synthesis of neuropsychological and neuroimaging findings on the role of the medial temporal lobe in memory and perception. *Neuropsychologia*, 48 (4), 831–853, doi: 10.1016/j.neuropsychologia.2010.01.001.

Guedj, E., Aubert, S., McConigal, A., *et al.* (2010). Déjà vu in temporal lobe epilepsy: metabolic pattern of cortical involvement in patients with normal brain MRI. *Neuropsychologia*, 48 (7), 2174–2181. doi: 10.1016/j.neuropsychologia.2010.04.009.

Holdstock, J.S., Parslow, D.M., Morris, R.G., *et al.* (2008). Two case studies illustrating how relatively selective hippocampal lesions in humans can have quite different effects on memory. *Hippocampus*, 18 (7), 679–691. doi: 10.1002/hipo.20427.

Illman, N.A., Butler, C.R., Souchay, C., and Moulin, C.J. (2012a). Déjà experiences in temporal lobe epilepsy. *Epilepsy Research and Treatment*, 2012, 1–15. doi: 10.1155/2012/539567.

Illman, N.A., Moulin, C.J., O'Connor, A.R., and Chauvel, P. (2012b). Déjà vu experiences in epilepsy: contributions from memory research. In *Epilepsy and Memory* (ed. A. Zeman, N. Kapur, and M. Jones-Gotman). Oxford: Oxford University Press, pp. 118–138.

Jacoby, L.L., and Whitehouse, K. (1989). An illusion of memory: false recognition influenced by unconcsious perception. *Journal of Experimental Psychology: General*, 118 (2), 126–135. doi: 10.1037/0096-3445.118.2.126.

Jäger, T., Szabo, K., Griebe, M., *et al.* (2009). Selective disruption of hippocampus-mediated recognition memory processes after episodes of transient global amnesia. *Neuropsychologia*, 47 (1), 70–76. doi: 10.1016/j.neuropsychologia.2008.08.019.

Jennings, J., and Jacoby, L. (1997). An opposition procedure for detecting age-related deficits in recollection: telling effects of repetition. *Psychology and Aging*, 12 (2), 352–361.

Köhler, S., Danckert, S., Gati, J.S., and Menon, R.S. (2005). Novelty responses to relational and non-relational information in the hippocampus and the parahippocampal region: a comparison based on event-related fMRI. *Hippocampus*, 15 (6), 763–774. doi: 10.1002/hipo.20098.

Kumaran, D., and Maguire, E.A. (2006). An unexpected sequence of events: mismatch detection in the human hippocampus. *PLoS Biology*, 4 (12), e424. doi: 10.1371/journal.pbio.0040424.

Kumaran, D., and Maguire, E.A. (2007). Match mismatch processes underlie human hippo-campal responses to associative novelty. *Journal of Neuroscience*, 27 (52), 14365–14374. doi: 10.1523/JNEUROSCI.1677-07.2007.

Kumaran, D., and Maguire, E.A. (2007). Which computational mechanisms operate in the hippo-campus during novelty detection? *Hippocampus*, 17 (9), 735–748, doi: 10.1002/hipo.20326.

Mandler, G. (1980). Recognizing: the judgment of previous occurrence. *Psychological Review*, 87, 252–271.

Martin, C.B., Bowles, B., Mirsattari, S.M., and Köhler, S. (2011). Selective familiarity deficits after left anterior temporal-lobe removal with hippocampal sparing are material specific. *Neuropsychologia*, 49 (7), 1870–1878. doi: 10.1016/j.neuropsychologia.2011.03.012.

Martin, C.B., McLean, D.A., O'Neil, E.B., and Köhler, S. (2013). Distinct familiarity-based response patterns for faces and buildings in perirhinal and parahippocampal cortex. *Journal of Neuroscience*, 33 (26), 10915–10923. doi: 10.1523/JNEUROSCI.0126-13.2013.

Martin, C.B., Mirsattari, S.M., Pruessner, J.C., *et al.* (2012). Déjà vu in unilateral temporal-lobe epilepsy is associated with selective familiarity impairments on experimental tasks of recognition memory. *Neuropsychologia*, 50 (13), 2981–2991. doi: 10.1016/j.neuropsychologia.2012.07.030.

Mayes, A.R., Holdstock, J.S., Isaac, C.L., *et al.* (2002). Relative sparing of item recognition memory in a patient with adult-onset damage limited to the hippocampus. *Hippocampus*, 12 (3), 325–340. doi: 10.1002/hipo.1111.

Mitchell, K.J., and Johnson, M.K. (2009). Source monitoring 15 years later: what have we learned from fMRI about the neural mechanisms of source memory? *Psychological Bulletin*, 135 (4), 638–677. doi: 10.1037/a0015849.

Montaldi, D., and Mayes, A.R. (2010). The role of recollection and familiarity in the functional differentiation of the medial temporal lobes. *Hippocampus*, 20 (11), 1291–1314. doi: 10.1002/hipo.20853.

Moulin, C.J., Conway, M.A., Thompson, R.G., James, N., and Jones, R.W. (2005). Disordered memory awareness: recollective confabulation in two cases of persistent déjà vecu. *Neuropsychologia*, 43 (9), 1362–1378.

Mullally, S.L., and Maguire, E.A. (2011). A new role for the parahippocampal cortex in representing space. *Journal of Neuroscience*, 31 (20), 7441–7449. doi: 10.1523/JNEUROSCI.0267-11.2011.

Murray, E.A., Bussey, T.J., and Saksida, L.M. (2007). Visual perception and memory: a new view of medial temporal lobe function in primates and rodents. *Annual Review of Neuroscience*, 30, 99–122. doi: 10.1146/annurev.neuro.29.051605.113046.

Neppe, V.M. (1983). The concept of déjà vu. *Parapsychological Journal of South Africa*, 4, 1–10.

O'Connor, A.R., and Moulin, C.J. (2008). The persistence of erroneous familiarity in an epi-leptic male: challenging perceptual theories of déjà vu activation. *Brain and Cognition*, 68 (2), 144–147. doi: 10.1016/j.bandc.2008.03.007.

Ranganath, C. (2010). A unified framework for the functional organization of the medial temporal lobes and the phenomenology of episodic memory. *Hippocampus*, 20 (11), 1263–1290. doi: 10.1002/hipo.20852.

Ranganath, C. and Rainer, C. (2003). Neural mechanisms for detecting and remembering novel events. *Nature Reviews Neuroscience*, 4 (3), 193–202. doi: 10.1038/nrn1052

Schacter, D.L., and Slotnick, S.D. (2004). The cognitive neuroscience of memory distortion. *Neuron*, 44 (1), 149–160. doi: 10.1016/j.neuron.2004.08.017.

Scoville, W.B., and Milner, B. (1957). Loss of recent memory after bilateral hippocampal lesions. *Journal of Neurology, Neurosurgery, and Psychiatry*, 20 (1), 11–21. doi: 10.1136/jnnp.20.1.11.

Spatt, J. (2002). Déjà vu: possible parahippocampal mechanisms. *Journal of Neuropsychiatry, and Clinical Neuroscience*, 14 (1), 7–10. doi: 10.1038/nrn2154.

Troiani, V., Stigliani, A., Smith, M.E., Epstein, R.A. (2012). Multiple object properties drive scene-selective regions. *Cerebral Cortex*. doi: 10.1093/cercor/bhs364.

Tulving, E. (1985). Memory and consciousness. *Canadian Psychology/Psychologie Canadienne*, 26 (1), 1–12. doi: 10.1037/h0080017.

Turriziani, P., Serra, L., Fadda, E., *et al.* (2008). Recollection and familiarity in hippocampal amnesia. *Hippocampus*, 18 (5), 469–480. doi: 10.1002/hipo.20412.

Vargha-Khadem, F., Gadian, D.G., Watkins, K.E., *et al.* (1997). Differential effects of early hippocampal pathology on episodic and semantic memory. *Science*, 277 (5324), 376–380. doi: 10.1126/science.277.5324.376.

Vederman, A.C., Holtzer, R., Zimmerman, M.E., *et al.* (2010). Ictal mnemestic aura and verbal memory function. *Epilepsy and Behavior*, 17 (4), 474–477. doi: 10.1016/j.yebeh.2010.01.018.

Vignal, J., Maillard, L., McGonigal, A., Chauvel, P. (2007). The dreamy state: hallucinations of autobiographical memory evoked by temporal lobe stimulations and seizure. *Brain*, 130 (1), 88–99. doi: 10.1093/brain/awl329.

Warren-Gash, C. and Zeman, A. (2014). Is there anything distinctive about epileptic deja vu? *Journal of Neurology, Neurosurgery, and Psychiatry*, 85, 143–147. doi: 10.1136/jnnp-2012-303520.

Weinand, M.E., Hermann, B., Wyler, A.R., *et al.* (1994). Long-term subdural strip electro-corticographic monitoring of ictal déjà vu. *Epilepsia*, 35 (5), 1054–1059. doi: 10.1111/j.1528-1157.1994.tb02554.x.

Whittlesea, B.W., and Williams, L.D. (1998). Why do strangers feel familiar, but friends don't? A discrepancy-attribution account of feelings of familiarity. *Acta Psychologica*, 98 (2), 141–165.

Wixted, J.T., and Squire, L.R. (2011). The medial temporal lobe and the attributes of memory. *Trends in Cognitive Sciences*, 15 (5), 210–217. doi: 10.1016/j.tics.2011.03.005.

Yonelinas, A.P. (2002). The nature of recollection and familiarity: a review of 30 years of research. *Journal of Memory and Language*, 46 (3), 441–517. doi: 10.1006/jmla.2002.2864.

Yonelinas, A.P., and Jacoby, L.L. (2012). The process-dissociation approach two decades later: convergence, boundary conditions, and new directions. *Memory and Cognition*, 40 (5), 663–680. doi: 10.3758/s13421-012-0205-5.

Yonelinas, A.P., and Parks, C.M. (2007). Receiver operating characteristics (ROCs) in recognition memory: a review. *Psychological Bulletin*, 133 (5), 800–832. doi: 10.1037/0033-2909.133.5.800.

# 10

# Medial Temporal Lobe Contributions to Memory and Perception

## *Evidence from Amnesia*

## Danielle Douglas and Andy Lee

## Introduction

The medial temporal lobe (MTL) has been thought to be involved in memory formation ever since patient H.M. underwent a bilateral resection of this area to control his intractable seizures. The removal of his MTL left patient H.M. unable to create new, consciously accessible, "declarative" memories, a condition known as anterograde amnesia (Scoville and Milner, 1957). Additionally, Scoville and Milner (1957) found that the severity of a given patient's amnesia was positively correlated to the amount of damage to the hippocampal complex, a finding which was later extended to the whole MTL in nonhuman primates (Zola-Morgan, Squire, and Ramus, 1994). Therefore, the structures that comprise the MTL were first conceptualized as subserving a general MTL declarative memory system, with all structures within this heterogeneous area operating in unison to support the formation of long-term memories (Squire, 1982). It is now nearly ubiquitously accepted that structures of the MTL play an essential role in some types of memory formation (Voss and Paller, 2010). However, the cognitive and neural processes underlying memory formations, and how each MTL structure supports these processes, remains a point of strong contention in the field.

Although there are still proponents of a unitary declarative memory system (Squire, Stark, and Clark, 2004; Squire and Wixted, 2011; Squire, Wixted, and Clark, 2007), most accounts of the role of the MTL focus on possible delineations between the functions of its various regions in their service of long-term declarative encoding. For example, the dual-process model of memory posits that the MTL supports one of two interrelated but separable functions: recollection and familiarity (Aggleton and Brown, 1999; Brown and Aggleton, 2001; Brown, Warburton, and Aggleton, 2010). Recollection, defined as the ability to recall source information related to a specific event, is thought to necessitate the hippocampus (HC) and its most intimately connected regions, such as the anterior thalamic nuclei. Familiarity,

*The Wiley Handbook on the Cognitive Neuroscience of Memory*, First Edition.
Edited by Donna Rose Addis, Morgan Barense, and Audrey Duarte.
© 2015 John Wiley & Sons, Ltd. Published 2015 by John Wiley & Sons, Ltd.

the feeling of having encountered an item in the past, is purportedly dependent on the perirhinal cortex (PRC) and the heavily connected medial dorsal thalamus.

A related but different model, the convergence, recollection and familiarity theory (CRAFT; Montaldi and Mayes, 2010), emphasizes that recollection is supported by the HC via pattern separation (Norman and O'Reilly, 2003), by which differences between neuronal codes are amplified to emphasize differences between stimuli. This computation is qualitatively different from that of the PRC and parahippocampal cortex (PHC), which support familiarity. CRAFT further supposes that the PRC supports object/item familiarity whereas the PHC supports contextual familiarity. Similarly, the complementary learning systems is a proposed network model in which item familiarity depends on a measure of representation "sharpness" in the PRC, in addition to pattern-separation-based recollection in the HC (Norman, 2010).

In contrast, informational accounts of MTL function stipulate that the engagement of different areas within this region is better characterized by what type of information is being processed (e.g., items, contexts, item/context associations) rather than the processes themselves. Both the item-context (Davachi, 2006) and binding-in-context (BIC; Eichenbaum, Yonelinas, and Ranganath, 2007; Ranganath, 2010) theories of MTL function conceptualize the role of the PRC as encoding and later retrieving information about items, while the HC binds this item-specific information with contextual information stored in the PHC as relational associations (see Chapter 18 for more discussion of relational memory processes). Because of these roles, the different areas will be differentially related to familiarity and recollection, but this relationship is secondary to the stimulus-dependent engagement of the area. These theories predict that deficits for object recognition will be found with PRC damage, whereas HC damage will result in reduced performance on spatial memory tasks. Differences between these informational theories lie within their definition of context: the item-context account refers only to spatial context, whereas the BIC account also includes temporal, semantic, and emotional contexts (Diana, Yonelinas, and Ranganath, 2007).

Although models of MTL function have predominantly focused on the role of this region in long-term declarative memory, a growing body of evidence suggests that the MTL is crucial for solving problems that do not depend on long-term memory (LTM), such as oddity judgments (see below), for which it is not necessary to hold information in memory to resolve the task as the stimuli are presented simultaneously (for reviews, see Graham, Barense, and Lee, 2010; Baxter, 2009). Findings such as these suggest that the MTL is necessary for some types of perception, and perhaps working memory, in addition to LTM. The aforementioned mnemonic accounts of MTL function either account insufficiently for this new evidence, or require unparsimonious additions to existing models.

Novel theoretical viewpoints are necessary, therefore, to provide a framework in which both mnemonic and visual discrimination data can be interpreted. One such viewpoint is a representational account of MTL function. Like informational accounts, representational theories propose that the recruitment of a given MTL structure is stimulus-dependent. They diverge, however, in that the informational accounts emphasize mnemonic processing of these stimuli, whereas the representational theories assert that this stimulus-dependent engagement will occur regardless of the cognitive process involved (Murray, Bussey, and Saksida, 2007; Saksida and Bussey, 2010). Therefore, representational views integrate evidence for long-term mnemonic specializations within the MTL with the more recent demonstrations of functions beyond LTM (e.g., perception, working memory), thereby shifting the theoretical focus away from the MTL as an exclusive LTM system. A representational account proposes that, instead of being specialized for memory per se, some structures in the MTL process representations of high-level stimuli (e.g., objects, scenes), which can be called upon for perceptual or mnemonic purposes.

The remainder of this chapter will discuss a representational understanding of MTL processing in further detail. A brief description of relevant MTL anatomy will first be provided, followed by a synopsis of the animal work that formed the foundation of this viewpoint. Convergent research in human amnesic patients will then be discussed. Finally, we will discuss the implications of such a model for our understanding of how the brain supports memory, and, by extension, why damage to the MTL renders individuals susceptible to memory impairments.

## Neuroanatomy of the MTL

The MTL is composed of several heterogeneous, yet highly interconnected regions which are organized in a hierarchical fashion (Lavenex and Amaral, 2000). The major afferents between these regions are from the PHC and PRC to entorhinal cortex (ERC), from ERC to HC, with the HC projecting back to all of these structures via the ERC, forming a loop (Figure 10.1; see also Chapter 6).

Situated in the rhinal sulcus, the PRC occupies the anterior portion of the inferior medial temporal gyrus (Brodmann areas [BA] 35 and 36; Amaral, Insausti, and Cowan, 1987; Insausti, Amaral, and Cowan, 1987; Suzuki *et al.*, 1993). The PRC is contiguous with what is classically considered the ventral visual stream (VVS) or "what" stream, which projects from the striate cortex to the inferior temporal structures TEO and TE. The VVS is widely believed to be important for object perception (Amaral, Insausti, and Cowan, 1987; Insausti, Amaral, and Cowan, 1987; Ungerleider and Mishkin, 1982), and is also organized hierarchically: anterior regions respond to conjunctions of features that are neuronally represented in posterior regions (Desimone and Ungerleider, 1989). The PRC receives the majority of its inputs from these adjacent visual cortical areas, as well as the PHC. Other diverse polymodal areas (orbitofrontal, cingulate cortex, and dorsal superior temporal sulcus) and primary sensory areas (somatosensory, auditory) also converge in the PRC.

The PHC (areas TH and TF) also receives major inputs from TE and TEO, in addition to the parietal cortex (Amaral, Insausti, and Cowan, 1987), which is considered the terminus of the dorsal "where/how" visual stream (DVS), necessary for

**Figure 10.1** A simplified illustration of connections within the medial temporal lobe (MTL). The perirhinal cortex (PRC) and parahippocampal cortex (PHC) share efferent and afferent connections with each other and the entorhinal cortex (ERC). The ERC projects to the hippocampus (HC), which in turn projects into the ERC.

encoding spatial locations of objects as well the objects' utility (Goodale and Milner, 1992; Ungerleider and Mishkin, 1982). This structure also receives projections from polymodal cortices such as the superior temporal sulcus and retrosplenial cortex, and interacts with HC via the PRC and ERC (Lavenex, Suzuki, and Amaral, 2004).

The ERC (BA 28, 34), which sits medially and superiorly to the PRC, is heavily and reciprocally connected with both this region and the PHC (Insausti, Amaral, and Cowan, 1987). The HC, as referred to here, comprises CA fields 1, 2, and 3, subiculum, and dentate gyrus. The ERC is the source of projections that constitute the perforant path, the major source of incoming innervation to the HC via synapses in the dentate gyrus. Lying at the peak of the MTL hierarchy, the HC projects back to the PRC via the lateral ERC and to the PHC via the medial ERC, forming two primary, unidirectional loops of information flow (Amaral and Lavanex, 2007).

## What Nonhuman Primate Lesion Studies Can Tell Us About MTL Function

The curious neuropsychological profile of patient H.M. (Scoville and Milner, 1957) initiated a surge of interest in the neuroanatomical substrates of long-term memory. Because of the difficulties and limitations associated with studying human patients, nonhuman primate models (predominantly macaque monkeys) were employed in an attempt to elucidate the crucial structures involved in global amnesia. The delayed non-match-to-sample task (DNMS) was designed to tap into object recognition (Mishkin, 1978), a type of explicit memory impaired in human amnesic patients (Parkin and Leng, 1993). Briefly, the DNMS task begins with an encoding phase: an everyday object is placed over a small well, in which there is a food reward. This object must be displaced to access the food reward, after which there is a delay. In the following retrieval phase, two objects – the object shown during the previous trial and a novel object – are each placed over a well. The food reward is now located only under the new object so that, across trials, normal animals learn to select the novel object during the retrieval phase.

Early object-recognition studies using macaques demonstrated that ablations of the HC and amygdala together, but not alone, produced severe impairments on the DNMS (Mishkin, 1978) and these areas were proposed to comprise the core of the declarative memory system (Squire and Zola-Morgan, 1991). However, it was later realized that the combined ablations necessary to produce the most dramatic deficits also damaged the underlying rhinal cortex: aspirations of the amygdala damage the anterior rhinal cortex, and those of the HC damage the posterior rhinal cortex (Buckley, 2005; Horel, Voytko, and Salsbury, 1984). Follow-up investigations have demonstrated that selective PRC ablations are sufficient in re-creating deficits on DNMS performance that are equally severe as, or more severe than, those reported with any other combination of lesions (Meunier *et al.*, 1993). Furthermore, when methodological advances allowed for more selective lesions to the HC and amygdala, while sparing the rhinal cortex, these lesions were found to have no effect on DNMS performance (Baxter and Murray, 2001; Murray and Mishkin, 1998).

In a study by Meunier *et al.* (1993), it was found that PRC lesions induced deficits that were mild during the shortest delay between encoding and retrieval phases

(10 seconds), and became progressively more severe as the delay was increased (maximum 120 seconds). This seemed to suggest intact perceptual processing of items, and impaired recognition of those items as memory demands increased with longer delays. Thus, the PRC was highlighted as a crucial structure for object recognition, while seemingly unnecessary for object perception (Meunier *et al.*, 1993; Gaffan and Murray, 1992; Zola-Morgan *et al.*, 1993).

In later studies, however, PRC ablations were shown to impair performance on tasks with no obvious memory component. For example, deficits were shown on zero-second delay trials in a DNMS task, as well as concurrent object discrimination tasks in which the animal chooses between two simultaneously presented objects, one that has been rewarded throughout the task and one that has not (Buckley and Gaffan, 1997, 1998b; Buckley, Gaffan, and Murray, 1997; Eacott, Gaffan, and Murray, 1994). This led to the suggestion that the PRC may, in fact, be crucial for object perception as well as recognition. In contrast to previous DNMS research in which simultaneous and short-delay matching deficits were not observed (e.g., Gaffan and Murray, 1992; Meunier *et al.*, 1993; Zola-Morgan *et al.*, 1993), these studies employed computer-generated two-dimensional "objects" as their stimuli (a small typographic symbol superimposed on a larger typographic symbol, each of a different color) and additionally, the stimulus sets across trials were much larger. Thus, it was suggested that these differences between stimulus sets contributed to contradictory findings across studies (Eacott, Gaffan, and Murray, 1994). Particularly, performance seemed to worsen with increases in perceptual demand. For example, Buckley and Gaffan (1997) demonstrated that PRC-lesioned monkeys performed normally on concurrent discriminations with small numbers of foil objects, but were impaired on larger sets. Similarly, while these monkeys were able to discriminate between simultaneously presented objects from one viewpoint, varying the viewpoint resulted in impairments (Buckley and Gaffan, 1998a, 1998b). Although these tasks required the animal to learn across a number of trials, the results suggested that it was the variation in perceptual elements of the stimuli, and not mnemonic load, that elicited a need for the PRC.

A follow-up study by Buckley *et al.* (2001) employed a paradigm in which the monkey was rewarded for choosing the odd one out from a group of simultaneously presented stimuli. In each trial, six objects were presented simultaneously on-screen, and the monkey was rewarded for choosing the image of the object (target) that was different from all of the others (foils) by touching it. Two conditions were employed: one of low perceptual demand, in which a single feature (e.g., color or shape) could be used to discriminate between the target and foils, and one of high perceptual demand, in which the foil objects were presented from different viewpoints and thus could not be distinguished from the target object based on any single feature. PRC-lesioned monkeys performed normally on the former task but were impaired on the latter, suggesting that PRC ablations produce deficits only when object-level representations, comprising unique conjunctions of lower-level features making up an object, are necessary to solve a task (i.e., object discrimination). These results agree with previous findings that macaques are unimpaired on simultaneous presentation tasks when single features can be used to discriminate between stimuli (e.g., Gaffan and Murray, 1992; Zola-Morgan *et al.*, 1993), suggesting that the deficits in high perceptual demand oddity judgments are a result of an inability to represent feature conjunctions.

Proponents of a purely mnemonic role for the PRC argue that the perceptual deficits found in the aforementioned studies can be ascribed to inadvertent damage of the nearby VVS structures TE and/or TEO (Buffalo *et al.*, 1998, 1999, 2000). For example, one re-analysis of previous ablation studies demonstrated a stronger correlation between concurrent discrimination errors and extent of TE damage, compared to the correlation between concurrent discrimination errors and PRC damage (Buffalo *et al.*, 1998). However, this is unlikely to account for the monkey oddity data: Buckley *et al.* (2001) found that monkeys with PRC damage performed normally on two control oddity tasks in which a single feature (color or shape) distinguished the target from foils, but demonstrated impairments when these features were shared across objects. Although the discrimination of single-feature differences was just as difficult for controls as the conjunctive oddity task, these lower-level features have previously been shown to be represented in TE and TEO (Tanaka, 1996). Moreover, single-feature perceptual deficits resulting from ablations to TE/TEO have been dissociated from feature-conjunctive perceptual deficits associated with ablations to the PRC (Buckley, Gaffan, and Murray, 1997). These findings suggest that any inadvertent damage to adjacent structures did not significantly impact task performance.

Results from work with nonhuman primates seem to suggest, therefore, that the destruction of the PRC eliminates the ability to represent object feature conjunctions, regardless of whether this conjunction is needed to solve a perceptual or mnemonic task. When stimulus sets have many features in common across targets and foils, this inability results in difficulty resolving feature ambiguity (FA) among stimuli. FA is a property resulting from a given feature being rewarded when present in a target object but unrewarded when present in the foil object (Figure 10.2). To investigate the possibility that the PRC is critical for resolving FA, Bussey, Saksida, and Murray (2002) administered a two-choice concurrent discrimination learning task to monkeys with selective PRC damage, in which three levels of FA between target and foil objects were presented: minimum (no features in common), intermediate (half of the features in common), and maximum (all features in common). Note that the maximum FA condition could only be solved by representing both features together, as each individual feature was equally represented across target and foil stimuli. Consistent with a feature-conjunctive role of the PRC, lesioned monkeys were unimpaired on the minimum FA condition, moderately impaired on the intermediate FA condition, and severely impaired on the maximum FA condition. Similarly, these monkeys demonstrated intact concurrent discriminations of pairs of images that had been morphed to provide low FA, but were impaired when the targets and foils shared a greater degree of features with one another (Bussey, Saksida, and Murray, 2003).

These demonstrations of the importance of the PRC for object processing led Murray and Bussey (1999) to propose that the PRC is, in fact, an extension of the VVS hierarchy. Specifically, this theory states that visual representations become hierarchically more complex as one moves rostrally through the VVS, so that each area subsumes the features represented in the more caudal area (Bussey and Saksida, 2002; Bussey, Saksida, and Murray, 2005; Murray and Bussey, 1999; Murray, Bussey, and Saksida, 2007; Saksida and Bussey, 2010). Proponents of this view conceptualize the PRC as the apex of the ventral visual "what" stream of object recognition, necessary for representing object-level feature conjunctions (Figure 10.3). The PRC therefore represents complex conjunctions of simpler visual features (pattern, shape, color), which are themselves represented in more caudal areas such as V4 and TE/TEO (Tanaka, 1996). Thus, when representation of more than one feature is required, whether in the context of a perceptual or a mnemonic task, ablations to the PRC will

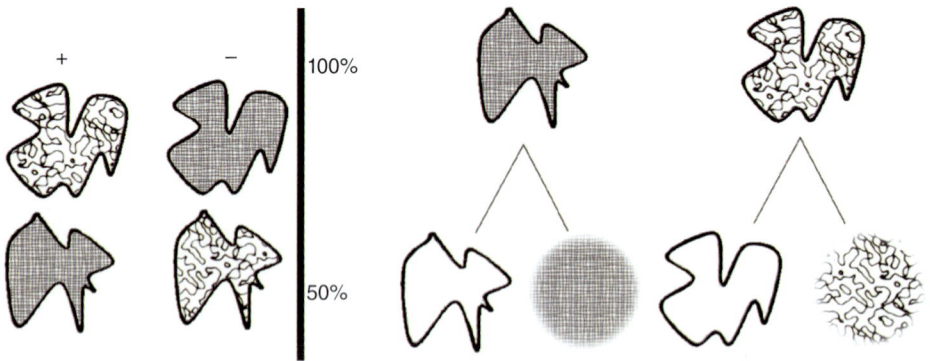

**Figure 10.2** An illustration of maximal feature ambiguity (FA). Objects that are always rewarded (+) and never rewarded (−) comprise two features each. These individual features are equally represented across rewarded and unrewarded objects. This ensures that one can only resolve the task based on feature conjunctions at the object level (100% rewarded), as the individual features are only rewarded 50% of the time.

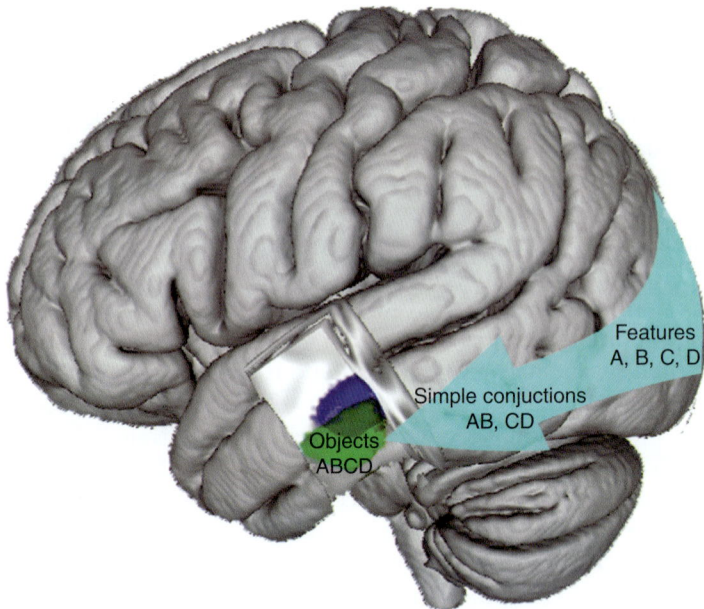

**Figure 10.3** Depiction of the ventral visual stream (VVS, light blue arrow), extended into the medial temporal lobe (MTL) on a model of the brain in which a section of the MTL is cut out to reveal the PRC (green) and HC (blue) that underlie the cortical surface. While classical models of MTL function propose an anatomical segregation of mnemonic and perceptual processes, the representational-hierarchical model presumes that both of these cognitive abilities rely on representations throughout the VVS. As one moves from caudal to rostral areas, the representations become more complex, subsuming those directly posterior to them, so that PRC represents object-level conjunctions (ABCD) of features represented in adjacent TE/TEO (AB, CD), whereas the HC binds these objects in spatial relationships with one another. Figure adapted from Barense *et al.* (2012a).

impair performance. In other words, the theory hypothesizes that engagement of these various areas does not depend entirely on the process involved (perception versus LTM) but instead upon the level of representation required (simple versus conjunctive).

From this perspective, failed attempts to find an effect of PRC lesion on perceptual processing may be explained by a lack of FA in tasks employing small set sizes (e.g., Gaffan and Murray, 1992), or stimuli that vary vastly from one another (e.g., Suzuki *et al.*, 1993). These types of stimulus sets tend to have fewer features in common across stimuli, and therefore may not adequately tax conjunctive representations and mask high-level perceptual deficits. Thus, it seems that differences in degrees of FA in stimulus sets may explain the conflicting findings of perceptual impairment in the PRC ablation literature.

## The Hippocampus and Perception

If the PRC is involved in object perception, as the nonhuman primate literature suggests, could other regions of the MTL be important for some types of perception as well? There is a large amount of data implicating the HC in spatial memory. For example, single cell recording in the rat HC has shown that some HC neurons fire only to a particular spatial location ("place cells"; O'Keefe and Dostrovsky, 1971), which led to the proposal that this structure comprises a cognitive map of the animal's external environment (O'Keefe and Nadel, 1978). In the same vein, neuronal recordings have demonstrated HC cells that signal location (Hori *et al.*, 2003; Ono *et al.*, 1991, 1993) and spatial view information (Robertson, Rolls, and Georges-François, 1998; Rolls, 1999; Rolls, Robertson, and Georges-François, 1997) in monkeys, as well as in humans (Ekstrom *et al.*, 2003). Additionally, HC damage has been demonstrated to impair some forms of spatial memory in both monkeys (Hampton, Hampstead, and Murray, 2004; Lavenex, Amaral, and Lavenex, 2006; Murray, Baxter, and Gaffan, 1998) and humans (Bird and Burgess, 2008; Bohbot *et al.*, 1998; Burgess, 2002; Feigenbaum and Morris, 2004; Holdstock *et al.*, 2000b; King *et al.*, 2002; Maguire, Nannery, and Spiers, 2006; Rosenbaum *et al.*, 2000, 2005; Spiers *et al.*, 2001; Taylor, Henson, and Graham, 2007), and these findings are further bolstered by functional neuroimaging studies showing human HC involvement in spatial navigation (Ghaem *et al.*, 1997; Hassabis *et al.*, 2009; Iglói *et al.*, 2010; Maguire, Frackowiak, and Frith, 1997; Maguire *et al.*, 1998; Morgan *et al.*, 2011; Spiers and Maguire, 2006, 2007).

Though the above studies are highly suggestive of a crucial role for the HC in some types of spatial cognition, this role has primarily been investigated within the mnemonic domain. More recently, studies with human participants have suggested the importance of the HC for spatial perception (see next section) and taking these findings into account, the representational-hierarchical model has been broadened in order to incorporate a role for the HC in representing spatial stimuli. Anatomically, the HC receives convergent inputs from both the VVS-associated PRC and from the DVS-associated PHC, placing it in an ideal position to integrate both object and spatial information. Thus, similar to the conjunctive nature of PRC object representations, the HC is thought to represent conjunctions of scene elements to support high-level spatial perception (Lee, Yeung and Barense, 2012; Murray, Bussey, and Saksida, 2007; Saksida and Bussey, 2010).

Hints of the HC being important in spatial perceptual processes exist in the animal literature as well. McTighe *et al.* (2009) tested the ability of rats with dorsal HC lesions to perform a touchscreen pattern separation task in which two boxes within an array of boxes were illuminated at one of three distances from each other (close, intermediate, or far). They found that the lesioned animals were impaired at discriminating the location of the rewarded box, but only when the rewarded box was close to the unrewarded box, suggesting that the perceptual properties of the stimulus were essential to detecting an effect of lesion. Thus, evidence from rodent work also suggests that the HC may play a role in spatial perception.

## Evidence from Neuropsychological Studies in Humans

Since the original study of patient H.M. and other similar cases by Scoville and Milner (1957) there have been a large number of investigations examining the cognitive profiles of patients with MTL damage. Notably, the vast majority of these investigations report that MTL-damaged patients perform within the normal range on a number of perceptual tasks (for a comprehensive review see Lee, Barense, and Graham, 2005). There are, however, several gross limitations to these assessments that must be borne in mind while evaluating the literature on the perceptual abilities of MTL-damaged patients. First, visual perception was often not assessed directly, but rather inferred by the finding that MTL-damaged patients demonstrated normal motor and perceptual learning (e.g., Donovan, 1985; Manns and Squire, 2001; but see Chun and Phelps, 1999). Additionally, many of the standard neuropsychological perceptual tasks used may not have necessitated the PRC as they did not require conjunctive feature representations, either because fairly simple stimuli were employed (e.g., comparing circles to ellipses; Sidman, Stoddard, and Mohr, 1968), or complex stimuli were used in tasks that could be solved via serial feature processing (e.g., copying the Rey-Osterrieth figure; Beatty *et al.*, 1987). Moreover, the occasional reports of perceptual difficulties in MTL-damaged patients (e.g., Benson, Marsden, and Meadows, 1974) were dismissed as due to cortical damage beyond the MTL.

Three initial studies that specifically investigated the role of the PRC in MTL-damaged patients found no evidence for a perceptual deficit (Buffalo, Reber, and Squire, 1998; Holdstock *et al.*, 2000a; Stark and Squire, 2000). Two employed a match-to-sample task in an attempt to dissociate perception from memory by varying the delay between initial exposure to target stimuli and subsequent reintroduction of those stimuli along with foils (Buffalo, Reber, and Squire, 1998; Holdstock *et al.*, 2000a). Contradicting evidence from the animal literature (e.g., Eacott, Gaffan, and Murray, 1994), they reported normal performance at the zero-second delay, but reduced accuracy at longer delays. A third investigation employed the oddity tasks used on macaques by Buckley *et al.* (2001) to assess the effect of PRC damage in human patients (Stark and Squire, 2000). While Buckley *et al.* (2001) reported monkeys with PRC ablations to be unimpaired on simple single-feature discriminations and impaired on conjunctive feature discriminations with faces and objects, Stark and Squire (2000) found MTL patients to be unimpaired on both types of tasks. Thus, data from these three studies suggested that the role of the PRC must be different between macaques and humans, as it is crucial for perception in the former (e.g., Buckley and Gaffan, 1998b; Buckley *et al.*, 2001; Bussey, Saksida, and Murray, 2002) but only for memory in the latter.

These initial studies, however, suffered from several limitations: the match-to-sample task involved stimuli composed of two-dimensional abstract symbols of various colors, shapes, and lines (Buffalo, Reber, and Squire, 1998; Holdstock *et al.*, 2000a), whereas Stark and Squire (2000) used a limited number of faces and objects (i.e., sets of 10) in their study. As a result, the stimulus sets employed in these early investigations were likely to have a low degree of FA. Since the representational-hierarchical model argues that the PRC is critical for representing object-level feature conjunctions, it may not be surprising, therefore, that these studies failed to demonstrate perceptual deficits in their patients with MTL damage.

Three key studies in 2005 addressed these concerns and extended their investigations of perceptual processing in the PRC to the HC and its role in spatial cognition (Barense *et al.*, 2005; Lee, *et al.*, 2005a, 2005b). Because of the location of the PRC, individuals with isolated and selective lesions of this area are extraordinarily rare (Lee *et al.*, 2006). Therefore, to elucidate the contribution of the PRC and HC to a given task, these experimenters contrasted the performance of amnesic patients with widespread MTL damage that included the PRC (MTL patients) to another group of amnesic patients with damage circumscribed to the HC (HC patients).

In one of these studies, Barense *et al.* (2005) investigated the effect of FA on amnesic individuals with PRC damage via a two-choice concurrent discrimination task. Similar to the task employed by Bussey, Saksida, and Murray (2002) with monkeys, participants were presented with pairs of novel (barcodes, blobs) and real-world (bugs, beasts) objects, and were rewarded for selecting the (arbitrarily designated) target stimulus with a pleasant, high-pitched tone (Figure 10.4). Within each category (except beasts), three levels of FA between targets and foils were presented: minimum (no features in common), intermediate (one of two features in common), and maximum (both features in common). The beast discrimination test consisted of only minimum and maximum ambiguity conditions. In all stimulus sets, the trials with maximum FA could only be solved by representing a conjunction of both features of a given object. Consistent with findings from monkeys (Bussey, Saksida, and Murray, 2002), MTL patients showed deficits for maximum but not minimum feature overlap when compared to HC patients and healthy controls (except for bugs, on which MTL patients were impaired on all levels). Additionally, because the number of features within a condition was inversely related to the amount of FA, these deficits were not dependent on mnemonic load. These findings support a role for the human PRC in processing object-level feature conjunctions and demonstrate that FA is an important factor in PRC-dependent object recognition deficits. It is important to note, however, that the paradigm used by Barense *et al.* (2005) was mnemonic in nature (participants had to learn and remember the rewarded item in each stimulus pair) and thus does not allow one to ascribe the observed effects to a perceptual deficit alone.

To minimize mnemonic load, and to extend investigations to the HC, Lee *et al.* (2005b) employed a simultaneous matching task in which patients were asked to choose one of two real-world morphed objects, faces, scenes, or colors that most closely matched an exemplar stimulus that was always present (Lee *et al.*, 2005b; Figure 10.5). Targets and foils were morphed to varying degrees to produce five levels of overlapping features ranging from low (0–9%), to high (40–49%). Patients with

**Figure 10.4**  Blob pairs illustrating minimal and maximal feature ambiguity (FA), as employed in Barense *et al.* (2005). Blobs that are unrewarded (−) are in the left column and those that are rewarded (+) are in the right column. Figure adapted from Lee, Barense, and Graham, 2005. Reproduced with permission of Taylor and Francis.

selective HC damage were impaired on scene discrimination alone, whereas those with larger MTL lesions were impaired on this task when scenes and faces were presented. Thus, in addition to support for a role of the PRC in object perception, these findings are suggestive of a role of the HC in scene perception.

To further investigate the role of the MTL in high-level perception, Lee *et al.* (2005a) employed a face oddity task (here with three foils), as well as a scene oddity task designed to tap into high-level spatial representation. In the scene oddity task, patients were asked to choose the different room from four simultaneously presented images of virtual scenes. A viewpoint manipulation was added to each task in which the distractors were either taken from the same viewpoint, or from a different viewpoint. Presenting objects from different viewpoints necessitates the use of complex, conjunctive representations to discriminate between the target stimulus and distractors. Thus there were four tasks: face same views, face different views, scene same views, and scene different views (Figure 10.6). HC patients were impaired on scene different views only, whereas MTL patients were impaired on both scene different views and face different views but unimpaired on either same-views task. Lee *et al.* (2005a) also administered a set of tasks similar to those of Stark and Squire (2000), but presenting 20 (instead of 10) study items, as item set size is a crucial factor in detecting PRC deficits (Buckley and Gaffan, 1997). In contrast to Stark and Squire (2000), and in line with evidence from the macaque literature, MTL patients were impaired on object and face tasks, but not color discrimination. Moreover, all of these patients

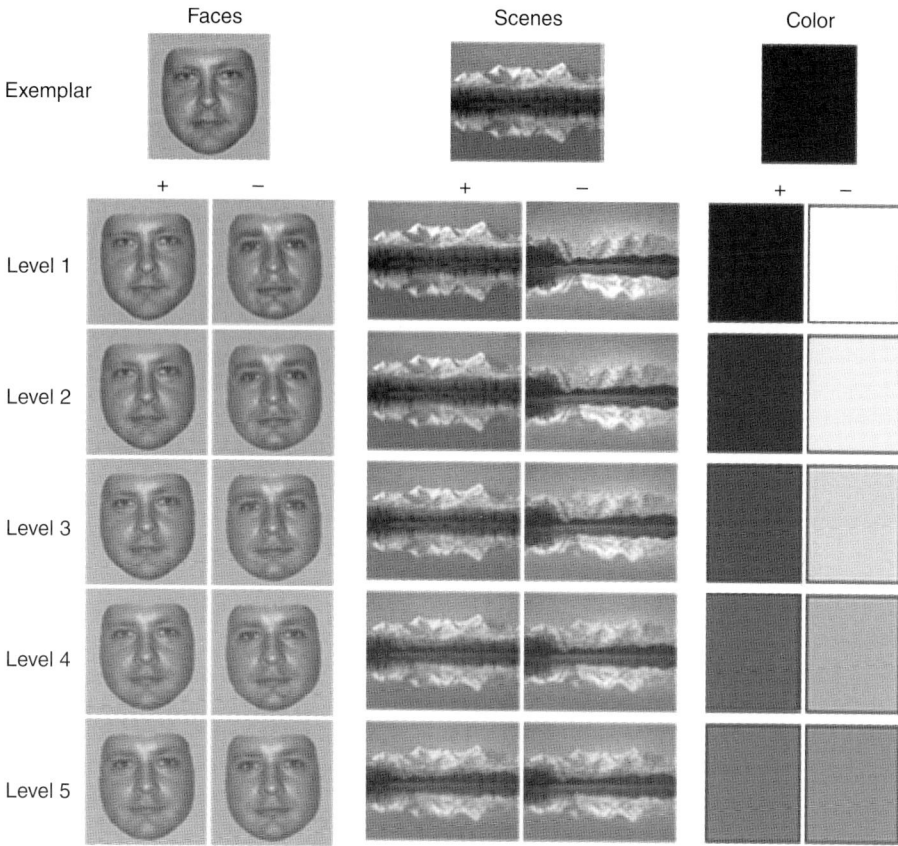

**Figure 10.5** Exemplars and stimulus pairs for the face, scene, and object conditions of the simultaneous match-to-sample task (Lee *et al.*, 2005b). Participants chose the stimulus that most closely matched the exemplar, which remained on screen with the pairs (rewarded stimuli in the left column). Pairs are each a morphed composite of the exemplar stimulus and an unrewarded stimulus.

performed normally on a battery of classic neuropsychological tests of visual perception, which agrees with the previous neuropsychological literature and suggests that these tests do not tap into the types of high-level visual impairments that MTL-damaged patients seem to display. Thus, in line with the predictions of the representational-hierarchical model, PRC damage impaired the perception of objects when conjunctive relationships between the objects' lower-level features were emphasized, whereas HC damage impaired the perception of scenes when conjunctive relationships between the scenes' lower-level features were emphasized.

Because of the rarity of selective PRC lesions, the above studies on MTL-damaged amnesic patients only provide a single dissociation between patients with large MTL lesions (impairment on both complex object and scene tasks) and those with selective HC lesions (impairment on complex scene tasks only). However, in their early stages of progression, semantic dementia (SD), a progressive condition associated with the gradual cross-modal loss of semantic knowledge (Hodges *et al.*, 1992; Snowden, Goulding and Neary, 1989) more heavily degrades the PRC than other MTL structures

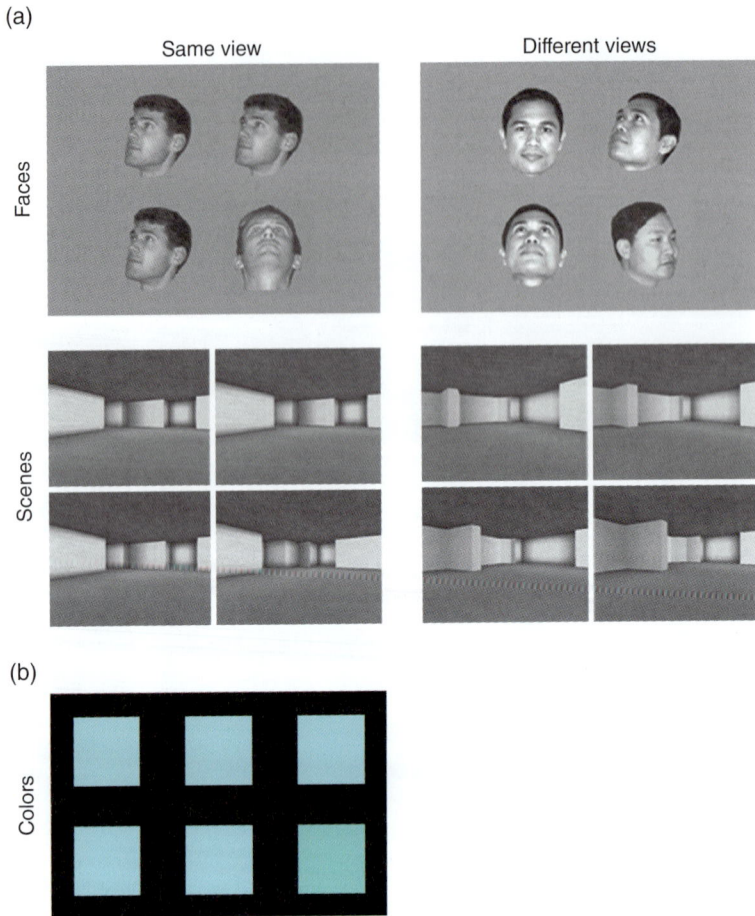

**Figure 10.6** Representative trial displays of (a) same-view and different-view oddity task for the face and scene categories, as well as (b) the color control condition (Lee *et al.*, 2005a). Participants chose the stimulus that was the odd one out (correct answer is located in bottom right corner).

(e.g., HC), whereas Alzheimer's disease (AD) damages the HC more than PRC (Davies *et al.*, 2004). While neither disease is selective to one region, the skew of damage in each case allows for a potential double dissociation in PRC- and HC-related deficits. Thus, SD and AD patients were tested using the face and scene oddity tasks, with same-and different-view foils (Lee *et al.*, 2006), as in Lee *et al.* (2005a). In another study, Lee *et al.* (2007) administered a mnemonic version of the face, scene, and object morph tasks used in Lee *et al.* (2005b) (the task was identical to that described previously except that the exemplar image was not presented simultaneously on each trial). As predicted, AD patients were selectively impaired on the different-views scene task and highly morphed scene discrimination, whereas SD patients were selectively impaired on the different-views face task and highly morphed object discrimination. Similarly, a recent investigation demonstrated that SD patients were impaired on an object discrimination task with a high degree of FA (Barense *et al.*, 2010b).

These results provide strikingly convergent evidence for specialization of the PRC and HC for scene and face processing, respectively.

## Addressing Criticisms of a Perceptual Role for MTL Regions

Several alternative interpretations for the above amnesic deficits have been proposed that would allow for one to maintain a purely memory-based understanding of MTL functioning. First, it has been suggested that a deficit of encoding into LTM in patient groups could have caused group differences in some of the studies discussed above (e.g., Levy, Shrager, and Squire, 2005; see also Knutson, Hopkins, and Squire, 2012). For example, in Lee *et al.* (2005b), although each trial was unique, the same exemplars were used to create the stimuli across trials within each condition, and thus repeated exposure to them could have improved control group performance on subsequent trials (Shrager *et al.*, 2006; Kim *et al.*, 2011). In favor of this interpretation, one study found that HC damage only impaired performance when replicating the discrimination task of Lee *et al.* (2005b) exactly, but not when unique exemplars were used to create the stimuli on each trial (Kim *et al.*, 2011). It is important to note, however, that control group performance in Lee and colleagues (2005b) actually worsened across time, suggesting that control participants' intact learning was in fact detrimental, and not beneficial, to task performance. Additionally, in both studies with trial-unique stimuli (Kim *et al.*, 2011; Lee *et al.*, 2005b), significant differences between patients and controls were evident even in the earliest trials, and these deficits did not worsen incrementally across the experiment. Thus, it is difficult to reconcile these patterns of results with a learning impairment explanation of MTL patient's deficits. Finally, MTL patients have also demonstrated deficits on other types of tasks using trial-unique stimuli (e.g., Barense *et al.*, 2012b; Lee *et al.*, 2005a, 2006; Lee and Rudebeck, 2010). Thus, the LTM impairments of MTL-damaged patients are unlikely to account for their deficits on visual discrimination tasks.

Another possible interpretation of visual discrimination impairments in amnesic patients, which is consistent with a purely mnemonic role for the MTL, is that the simultaneous presentation of multiple stimuli in the tasks on which patients have demonstrated deficits may confound perceptual difficulties with working memory impairments (Ranganath and Blumenfeld, 2005). Recent evidence from neuroimaging (Cashdollar *et al.*, 2009; Hannula and Ranganath, 2008; Ranganath and D'Esposito, 2001; Stern *et al.*, 2001) and neuropsychological studies (Bird *et al.*, 2010; Hannula, Tranel, and Cohen, 2006; Hartley *et al.*, 2007; Olson *et al.*, 2006a, 2006b; Ryan and Cohen, 2004; Warren *et al.*, 2010) suggests that the MTL plays an important role in some kinds of working memory. Thus, patient deficits on oddity and concurrent discrimination tasks may, in fact, reflect a primary problem with working memory.

Notably, a role for the MTL in supporting working memory is consistent with the representational-hierarchical model, which proposes that representations can be recruited irrespective of the cognitive process at hand (e.g., perception versus memory). Nevertheless, two recent studies have employed paradigms that rule out impaired working memory as the sole contributor to visual discrimination deficits in patients with MTL damage. The first (Lee and Rudebeck, 2010) tracked participants' eye movements while they were presented with a single line-drawn object (Williams and Tarr, 1997) and made a judgment of whether this object was possible (structurally coherent) or impossible (structurally incoherent; Figure 10.7). Compared to controls, the MTL patient with PRC damage was impaired on the possible/impossible judgments, and fixated for less time on the structurally incoherent region during incorrect judgments, strongly suggesting abnormal perceptual processing of the object. Due to the complexity of the stimuli, however, there remained the possibility that a representational degradation across a given trial could explain the deficits.

In response to such concerns, Barense *et al.* (2012b) employed a classic "figure-ground" perceptual task with MTL and HC patients. In this task, participants were asked to indicate which part of a simple two-part stimulus was perceived as the "figure" (i.e., the portion of the display that appeared to stand out as having a definite shape and seemed closer than the other regions), the other part thus being perceived as the background that seemed to continue behind the figures (Peterson and Gibson, 1994; Figure 10.8). Four types of stimuli were presented, containing: (1) a familiar contour, comprising a configuration of simple parts, (2) parts of a familiar contour rearranged, (3) a familiar contour inverted, (4) parts of a familiar contour rearranged and inverted. Previous studies have demonstrated that the familiarity of the shape of the black/white portion of the stimulus influences the likelihood of that portion being identified as the figure (e.g., a portion resembling an everyday object is more likely to be considered the figure; Peterson and Gibson, 1994). Barense *et al.* (2012b) found that, compared to controls, MTL patients assigned the label of "figure" to the familiar contour less often than controls, and to the rearranged elements (lines and angles) that made up that familiar contour more often than controls, thus eliminating the figure assignment effect of whole-contour familiarity. Inverting the elements in the stimulus attenuated this element-driven figure-assignment effect, suggesting that MTL patients are unable to differentiate between the familiar contour and the familiar elements (lines and angles) that made up that contour. This deficit is thought to be driven by the patients' inability to represent the elements of the contour conjunctively to make up a whole, a process that is suggested to be dependent on the PRC.

Together, the findings of Lee and Rudebeck (2010) and Barense *et al.* (2012b) comprise the most direct evidence for a role of the PRC in perceptual processes per se, as both used stimuli that were trial-unique, novel, and presented alone. Thus, object processing deficits were found with tasks that did not involve simultaneous

(a)                                          (b)

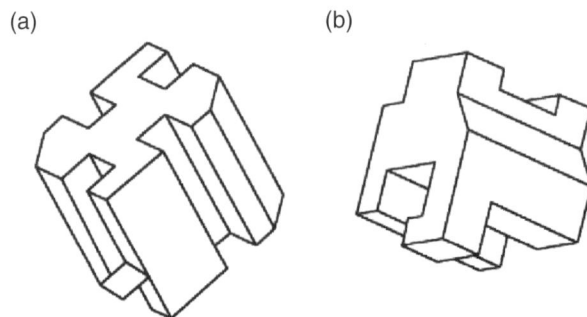

**Figure 10.7** Representative trials from the possible/impossible judgment task (Lee and Rudebeck, 2010), showing (a) impossible and (b) possible objects.

**Figure 10.8** Representative stimuli from the figure/ground judgment task (Barense *et al.*, 2012b). Here the familiar contour is of a pineapple, in white.

presentation of multiple objects, further evincing a role for the PRC in the ability to process complex objects.

Finally, it has been proposed that damage to posterior VVS regions might be responsible for the perceptual deficits demonstrated in patients with MTL damage (Suzuki, 2009). This, however, is unlikely for several reasons. First, studies employing qualitative visual ratings of hardcopy magnetic resonance imaging (MRI) scans reported that the mean lateral temporal lobe volumes of the patients in question (those with both selective HC damage and larger MTL lesions) were not significantly different from controls (Lee *et al.*, 2005b). Second, thorough reassessments of lesion extent via volumetric analyses of structural MRI for two patients who have consistently demonstrated high-level perceptual deficits (e.g., Barense, Gaffan, and Graham, 2007; Barense *et al.*, 2012a, 2012b; Lee and Rudebeck, 2010; Lee *et al.*, 2005a) confirmed that there was only a selective HC lesion in one case, and no significant damage to the posterior fusiform gyrus or posterior lateral temporal cortex bilaterally, nor to the anterior fusiform gyrus or anterior lateral temporal cortex in the left hemisphere in the second patient with a larger MTL lesion (Lee and Rudebeck, 2010). Third, both voxel-based morphometry and diffuser tensor imaging techniques revealed normal ranges of white matter connectivity within regions typically associated with visual processing, and functional MRI (fMRI) revealed normal resting state connectivity in these areas (Rudebeck, Filippini, and Lee, 2013), as well as normal activation of extrastriate areas associated with the perception of objects, faces and scenes (Lee and Rudebeck, 2010). Fourth, MTL patients perform normally on difficult color and size discriminations shown to be impaired in monkeys with TE/TEO lesions (Buckley, Gaffan, and Murray, 1997). Finally, convergent evidence from fMRI of neurologically intact individuals demonstrates that PRC activity is associated with concurrent discrimination of real-world (Devlin and Price, 2007; Lee, Scahill, and Graham, 2008; Barense, Henson, and Graham, 2011) and novel objects (Barense *et al.*, 2010a) requiring viewpoint-invariant representations, whereas HC activity is associated with concurrent discrimination of virtual scenes requiring viewpoint-invariant representations (Barense *et al.*, 2010a; Lee, Scahill, and Graham, 2008). Thus, all available evidence suggests that damage beyond the MTL cannot explain the high-level perceptual deficits found in MTL patients.

In summary, findings from humans largely parallel those in the animal literature: when a problem requires that a conjunction of object features be represented, PRC damage will result in deficits on the task; whereas when a problem requires a conjunction of scene features to be represented, HC damage will result in deficits on the task (Table 10.1). These results follow the prediction of the representational-hierarchical model that MTL structure engagement will be stimulus-dependent, regardless of cognitive process engaged.

## Implications of the MTL's Involvement in Perception

As described above, there is a growing body of literature suggesting that the role of the MTL is not limited to the mnemonic domain, but also extends to perception. The representational-hierarchical model eschews traditional assumptions that these cognitive processes are anatomically segregated, and instead proposes that they rely upon common neural representations.

If MTL damage leads to a fundamental problem of representation, why then are the most obvious deficits found in the mnemonic domain? Classically, MTL memory impairments are thought to be the result of incomplete consolidation: a memory trace is not properly stored in LTM and thus decays. Within the representational-hierarchical framework, one might expect that inadequate perceptual representations hasten this decay. Another possibility is that MTL damage makes one more susceptible to adequately stored but irrelevant memories (Warrington and Weiskrantz, 1970). For instance, in the context of an old/new judgment for an object, compromised object-level representations due to PRC damage necessitate familiarity judgments based on each of the individual features making up the object. When one is exposed to numerous objects sharing a high degree of features, each feature quickly becomes familiar, leading to an inability to distinguish between objects that have been seen before and objects never seen before that share previously seen features. Thus, MTL damage results in difficulties distinguishing between new and old objects because of interference from previously encountered but irrelevant features (e.g., Cowell, Bussey, and Saksida, 2010; Saksida and Bussey, 2010).

In support of this idea, a recent study found that object recognition memory deficits in PRC-damaged rodents can be corrected if visual interference prior to memory retrieval is eliminated (McTighe *et al.*, 2010). Similarly, recognition deficits can be worsened if perceptually similar interference is introduced before recognition memory is tested (Bartko *et al.*, 2010). A recent study by Barense *et al.* (2012a) has provided similar support, in the domain of perception. Amnesic, MTL-damaged patients were administered a perceptual discrimination task in which they were instructed to

**Table 10.1** Findings of perceptual impairments from previous studies examining patient groups with MTL abnormalities.

| Study | Task | Patients | Performance results | | | | | | |
|---|---|---|---|---|---|---|---|---|---|
| | | | Novel objects | Familiar objects | Faces | Scenes | Color | Shape | Size |
| Barense et al., 2005 | Concurrent discrimination, min. FA | MTL | ○ | ○* | — | — | — | — | — |
| | | HPC | ○ | ○ | — | — | — | — | — |
| | Concurrent discrimination, max. FA | MTL | ● | ● | — | — | — | — | — |
| | | HPC | ○ | ○ | — | — | ○ | — | — |
| Lee et al., 2005b | Simultaneous match to sample, morphed | MTL | — | ○ | ● | ● | ○ | — | — |
| | | HPC | — | ○ | ○ | ○ | ○ | — | ○ |
| Lee et al., 2005a | Oddity discrimination, same views | MTL | — | — | ○ | ○ | ○ | ○ | ○ |
| | | HPC | — | — | ○ | ● | ○ | ○ | ○ |
| | Oddity discrimination, different views | MTL | ● | ○ | ● | ● | — | — | — |
| | | HPC | ○ | — | ○ | ○ | — | — | — |
| Lee et al., 2006 | Oddity discrimination, same views | SD | — | — | ○ | ● | — | — | — |
| | | AD | — | — | ● | ○ | — | — | — |
| | Oddity discrimination, different views | SD | — | — | ○ | ● | — | — | — |
| | | AD | — | — | ● | ○ | — | — | — |
| Lee et al., 2007 | Simultaneous match to sample | SD | ○ | ○ | ● | ● | ○ | — | — |
| | | AD | ○ | ○ | ○ | ○ | ○ | — | — |
| Barense et al., 2007 | Oddity discrimination, min. FA | MTL | ○ | ○ | — | — | — | — | — |
| | | HPC | ○ | ● | — | — | ○ | — | ○ |
| | Oddity discrimination, max. FA | MTL | ● | ● | — | — | — | — | ○ |
| | | HPC | ○ | ○ | — | — | — | — | — |

(Continued)

**Table 10.1**  (*Cotinued*)

| Study | Task | Patients | Performance results | | | | | | |
|---|---|---|---|---|---|---|---|---|---|
| | | | *Novel objects* | *Familiar objects* | *Faces* | *Scenes* | *Color* | *Shape* | *Size* |
| Barense *et al.*, 2010b | Concurrent discrimination, min. FA | SD | ○ | ○ | — | — | ○ | — | ○ |
| | Concurrent discrimination, max. FA | SD | ○ | ● | — | — | ○ | — | ○ |
| | Oddity discrimination, min. FA | SD | ○ | ○ | — | — | — | — | — |
| | Oddity discrimination, max. FA | SD | ● | ● | — | — | — | — | — |
| Lee & Rudebeck, 2010 | Impossible/possible judgment | MTL | ● | — | — | — | — | — | — |
| | | HPC | ○ | — | — | — | — | — | — |
| Barense *et al.*, 2012b | Figure/ground judgment | MTL | ● | ○ | — | — | — | — | — |
| | | HPC | ○ | ○ | — | — | — | — | — |
| Barense *et al.*, 2012a | Concurrent matching, low interference | MTL | ○ | — | — | — | — | — | — |
| | | HPC | ○ | — | — | — | — | — | — |
| | Concurrent matching, high interference | MTL | ● | — | — | — | — | — | — |
| | | HPC | ○ | — | — | — | — | — | — |

*Note:* ● impaired performance; ○ normal performance; — not tested; * Normal performance on beasts and impairment on bugs.
AD, Alzheimer's disease group; FA, feature ambiguity; HPC, hippocampal lesion group; MTL, medial temporal lobe lesion group; SD, semantic dementia group; min., minimum; max., maximum.

determine whether two simultaneously presented trial-unique novel objects (blobs) that shared numerous features (e.g., high FA) were identical. These key trials were either presented in low-interference blocks, in which filler trials consisted of discriminations between real-world objects that shared few features with the stimuli in the key trials, or in high-interference blocks, in which filler trials involved discriminating between blobs that shared numerous features with the stimuli in the key trials. Critically, MTL patients were impaired on key trials presented within the latter but not the former blocks. Thus, intact memories of the high-interference filler trial stimuli impaired performance on the key discrimination trials, implying that impoverished object representations render MTL patients unable to overcome feature-level interference (Baxter, 2012). Extended outside of the laboratory, one might expect that MTL damage induces amnesia because the vast majority of everyday experiences rely on the perception of high-level conjunctions to represent an event in a place and time.

It is important to highlight that some predictions of the representational-hierarchical model remain unexplored or not yet precisely defined. For example, though the HC seems to be involved in highly conjunctive spatial representations, it remains to be seen how representations intersect with other types of information (e.g., temporal) that are also HC-dependent. Additionally, how compromised visual representations are related to verbal memory impairments that are often present in amnesia, such as story recall, is unclear. Given the multimodal nature of both the HC and PRC, and the mnemonic impairments of amnesic patients, the representation of nonvisual constructs within the MTL remains an open question for future research.

# References

Aggleton, J.P., and Brown, M.W. (1999). Episodic memory, amnesia, and the hippocampal–anterior thalamic axis. *Behavioral and Brain Sciences*, 22 (3), 425–444. doi: 10.1017/S0140525X99002034.

Amaral, D.G., Insausti, R., and Cowan, W.M. (1987). The entorhinal cortex of the monkey: I. Cytoarchitectonic organization. *Journal of Comparative Neurology*, 264 (3), 326–355. doi: 10.1002/cne.902640305.

Amaral, D., and Lavenex, P. (2007). Hippocampal neuroanatomy. In *The Hippocampus Book* (ed. P. Andersen, R. Morris, D. Amaral, T. Bliss, and J. O'Keefe). Oxford: Oxford University Press, pp. 37–114.

Barense, M.D., Bussey, T.J., Lee, A.C.H., *et al.* (2005). Functional specialization in the human medial temporal lobe. *Journal of Neuroscience*, 25 (44), 10239–10246. doi: 10.1523/JNEUROSCI.2704-05.2005.

Barense, M.D., Gaffan, D., and Graham, K.S. (2007). The human medial temporal lobe processes online representations of complex objects. *Neuropsychologia*, 45 (13), 2963–2974. doi: 10.1016/j.neuropsychologia.2007.05.023.

Barense, M.D., Groen, I.I.A., Lee, A.C.H., *et al.* (2012a). Intact memory for irrelevant information impairs perception in amnesia. *Neuron*, 75 (1), 157–167. doi: 10.1016/j.neuron.2012.05.014.

Barense, M.D., Henson, R.N.A., and Graham, K.S. (2011). Perception and conception: temporal lobe activity during complex discriminations of familiar and novel faces and objects. *Journal of Cognitive Neuroscience*, 23 (10), 3052–3067. 10.1162/jocn_a_00010.

Barense, M.D., Henson, R.N.A., Lee, A.C.H., and Graham, K.S. (2010a). Medial temporal lobe activity during complex discrimination of faces, objects, and scenes: effects of viewpoint. *Hippocampus*, 20 (3), 389–401. doi: 10.1002/hipo.20641.

Barense, M.D., Ngo, J.K.W., Hung, L.H.T., and Peterson, M.A. (2012b). Interactions of memory and perception in amnesia: the figure-ground perspective. *Cerebral Cortex*, 22 (11), 2680–2691. doi: 10.1093/cercor/bhr347.

Barense, M.D., Rogers, T.T., Bussey, T.J., *et al.* (2010b). Influence of conceptual knowledge on visual object discrimination: insights from semantic dementia and MTL amnesia. *Cerebral Cortex*, 20 (11), 2568–2582. doi: 10.1093/cercor/bhq004.

Bartko, S.J., Cowell, R.A., Winters, B.D., *et al.* (2010). Heightened susceptibility to interference in an animal model of amnesia: impairment in encoding, storage, retrieval – or all three? *Neuropsychologia*, 48 (10), 2987–2997. doi: 10.1016/j.neuropsychologia.2010.06.007.

Baxter, M.G. (2009). Involvement of medial temporal lobe structures in memory and perception. *Neuron*, 61 (5), 667–677. doi: 10.1016/j.neuron.2009.02.007.

Baxter, M.G. (2012). It's all coming back to me now: perception and memory in amnesia. *Neuron*, 75 (1), 8–10. doi: 10.1016/j.neuron.2012.06.019.

Baxter, M.G., and Murray, E.A. (2001). Effects of hippocampal lesions on delayed nonmatching-to-sample in monkeys: a reply to Zola and Squire (2001). *Hippocampus*, 11 (3), 201–203. doi: 10.1002/hipo.1037.

Beatty, W.W., Salmon, D.P. Bernstein, N., and Butters, N. (1987). Remote memory in a patient with amnesia due to hypoxia. *Psychological Medicine*, 17, 657–665. doi: 10.1017/S0033291700025897.

Benson, D.F., Marsden, C.D., and Meadows, J.C. (1974) The amnesic syndrome of posterior cerebral artery occlusion. *Acta Neurologica Scandinavica*, 50 (2), 133–145. doi: 10.1111/j.1600-0404.1974.tb02767.x

Bird, C.M., and Burgess, N. (2008). The hippocampus and memory: insights from spatial processing. *Nature Reviews Neuroscience*, 9 (3), 182–194. doi: 10.1038/nrn2335.

Bird, C.M., Chan, D., Hartley, T., *et al.* (2010). Topographical short-term memory differentiates Alzheimer's disease from frontotemporal lobar degeneration. *Hippocampus*, 20 (10), 1154–1169. doi: 10.1002/hipo.20715.

Bohbot, V.D., Kalina, M., Stepankova, K., *et al.* (1998). Spatial memory deficits in patients with lesions to the right hippocampus and to the right parahippocampal cortex. *Neuropsychologia*, 36 (11), 1217–1238. doi: 10.1016/S0028-3932(97)00161-9.

Brown, M.W., and Aggleton, J.P. (2001). Recognition memory: what are the roles of the perirhinal cortex and hippocampus? *Nature Reviews Neuroscience*, 2 (1), 61–62. doi: 10.1038/35049064.

Brown, M.W., Warburton, E.C., and Aggleton, J.P. (2010). Recognition memory: material, processes, and substrates. *Hippocampus*, 20 (11), 1228–1244. doi: 10.1002/hipo.20858.

Buckley, M.J. (2005). The role of the perirhinal cortex and hippocampus in learning, memory, and perception. *Quarterly Journal of Experimental Psychology Section B: Comparative and Physiological Psychology*, 58 (3–4), 246–268. doi: 10.1080/02724990444000186.

Buckley, M.J., Booth, M.C.A., Rolls, E.T., and Gaffan, D. (2001). Selective perceptual impairments after perirhinal cortex ablation. *Journal of Neuroscience*, 21 (24), 9824–9836.

Buckley, M.J., and Gaffan, D. (1997). Impairment of visual object-discrimination learning after perirhinal cortex ablation. *Behavioral Neuroscience*, 111 (3), 467–475. doi: 10.1037/0735-7044.111.3.467.

Buckley, M.J., and Gaffan, D. (1998a). Learning and transfer of object-reward associations and the role of the perirhinal cortex. *Behavioral Neuroscience*, 112 (1), 15–23. doi: 10.1037//0735-7044.112.1.15.

Buckley, M.J., and Gaffan, D. (1998b). Perirhinal cortex ablation impairs visual object identification. *Journal of Neuroscience*, 18 (6), 2268–2275.

Buckley, M.J., Gaffan, D., and Murray, E.A. (1997). Functional double dissociation between two inferior temporal cortical areas: perirhinal cortex versus middle temporal gyrus. *Journal of Neurophysiology*, 77 (2), 587–598.

Buffalo, E.A., Ramus, S.J., Clark, R.E., *et al.* (1999). Dissociation between the effects of damage to perirhinal cortex and area TE. *Learning and Memory*, 6 (6), 572–599. doi: 10.1101/lm.6.6.572.

Buffalo, E.A., Ramus, S.J., Squire, L.R., and Zola, S.M. (2000). Perception and recognition memory in monkeys following lesions of area TE and perirhinal cortex. *Learning and Memory*, 7 (6), 375–382. doi: 10.1101/lm.32100.

Buffalo, E.A., Reber, P.J., and Squire, L.R. (1998a). The human perirhinal cortex and recognition memory. *Hippocampus*, 8 (4), 330–339. doi: 10.1002/(SICI)1098-1063(1998)8, 4<330::AID-HIPO3>3.0.CO;2-L.

Buffalo, E.A., Stefanacci, L., Squire, L.R., and Zola, S.M. (1998b). A reexamination of the concurrent discrimination learning task: the importance of anterior inferotemporal cortex, area TE. *Behavioral Neuroscience*, 112 (1), 3–14.

Burgess, N. (2002). The hippocampus, space, and viewpoints in episodic memory. *Quarterly Journal of Experimental Psychology Section A: Human Experimental Psychology*, 55 (4), 1057–1080. doi: 10.1080/02724980244000224.

Bussey, T.J., and Saksida, L.M. (2002). The organization of visual object representations: a connectionist model of effects of lesions in perirhinal cortex. *European Journal of Neuroscience*, 15 (2), 355–364. doi: 10.1046/j.0953-816x.2001.01850.x.

Bussey, T.J., Saksida, L.M., and Murray, E.A. (2002). Perirhinal cortex resolves feature ambiguity in complex visual discriminations. *European Journal of Neuroscience*, 15 (2), 365–374. doi: 10.1046/j.0953-816x.2001.01851.x.

Bussey, T.J., Saksida, L.M., and Murray, E.A. (2003). Impairments in visual discrimination after perirhinal cortex lesions: testing 'declarative' vs. 'perceptual-mnemonic' views of perirhinal cortex function. *European Journal of Neuroscience*, 17 (3), 649–660. doi: 10.1046/j.1460-9568.2003.02475.x.

Bussey, T.J., Saksida, L.M., and Murray, E.A. (2005). The perceptual-mnemonic/feature conjunction model of perirhinal cortex function. *Quarterly Journal of Experimental Psychology Section B: Comparative and Physiological Psychology*, 58 (3–4), 269–282. doi: 10.1080/02724990544000004.

Cashdollar, N., Malecki, U., Rugg-Gunn, F.J., *et al.* (2009). Hippocampus-dependent and -independent theta-networks of active maintenance. *Proceedings of the National Academy of Sciences of the USA*, 106 (48), 20493–20498. doi: 10.1073/pnas.0904823106.

Cowell, R.A., Bussey, T.J., and Saksida, L.M. (2010). Functional dissociations within the ventral object processing pathway: cognitive modules or a hierarchical continuum? *Journal of Cognitive Neuroscience*, 22 (11), 2460–2479. doi: 10.1162/jocn.2009.21373.

Chun, M.M., and Phelps, E.A. (1999). Memory deficits for implicit contextual information in amnesic subjects with hippocampal damage. *Nature Neuroscience*, 2 (9), 844–847. doi: 10.1038/12222.

Davachi, L. (2006). Item, context and relational episodic encoding in humans. *Current Opinion in Neurobiology*, 16 (6), 693–700. doi: 10.1016/j.conb.2006.10.012.

Davies, R.R., Graham, K.S., Xuereb, J.H., *et al.* (2004). The human perirhinal cortex and semantic memory. *European Journal of Neuroscience*, 20 (9), 2441–2446. doi: 10.1111/j.1460-9568.2004.03710.x.

Desimone, R., and Ungerleider, L.G. (1989). Neural mechanisms of visual processing in monkeys. In *Handbook of Neuropsychology*, Vol. 2 (ed. F. Boller and J. Grafman). New York, NY: Elsevier, pp. 267–299.

Devlin, J.T., and Price, C.J. (2007). Perirhinal contributions to human visual perception. *Current Biology*, 17 (17), 1484–1488. doi: 10.1016/j.cub.2007.07.066

Diana, R.A., Yonelinas, A.P., and Ranganath, C. (2007). Imaging recollection and familiarity in the medial temporal lobe: a three-component model. *Trends in Cognitive Sciences*, 11 (9), 379–386. doi: 10.1016/j.tics.2007.08.001.

Donovan, G.P. (1985). Preserved and impaired information processing systems in human bitemporal amnesiacs and their infrahuman analogues: role of hippocampectomy. *Journal of Mind and Behavior*, 6 (4), 515–552.

Eacott, M.J., Gaffan, D., and Murray, E.A. (1994). Preserved recognition memory for small sets, and impaired stimulus identification for large sets, following rhinal cortex ablations in monkeys. *European Journal of Neuroscience*, 6 (9), 1466–1478. doi: 10.1111/j.1460-9568.1994.tb01008.x

Eichenbaum, H., Yonelinas, A.P., and Ranganath, C. (2007). The medial temporal lobe and recognition memory. *Annual Reviews in Neuroscience*, 30, 123–152. doi: 10.1146/annurev.neuro.30.051606.094328.

Ekstrom, A.D., Kahana, M.J., Caplan, J.B., *et al.* (2003). Cellular networks underlying human spatial navigation. *Nature*, 425 (6954), 184–188. doi: 10.1038/nature01964.

Feigenbaum, J.D., and Morris, R.G. (2004). Allocentric versus egocentric spatial memory after unilateral temporal lobectomy in humans. *Neuropsychology*, 18 (3), 462–472. doi: 10.1037/0894-4105.18.3.462.

Gaffan, D., and Murray, E.A. (1992). Monkeys (*Macaca fascicularis*) with rhinal cortex ablations succeed in object discrimination learning despite 24-hr intertrial intervals and fail at matching to sample despite double sample presentations. *Behavioral Neuroscience*, 106 (1), 30–38. doi: 10.1037/0735-7044.106.1.30.

Ghaem, O., Mellet, E., Crivello, F., *et al.* (1997). Mental navigation along memorized routes activates the hippocampus, precuneus, and insula. *Neuroreport*, 8 (3), 739–744. doi: 10.1097/00001756-199702100-00032.

Goodale, M.A., and Milner, D. (1992). Separate visual pathways for perception and action. *Trends in Neurosciences*, 15 (1), 20–25. doi: 10.1097/00001756-199702100-00032.

Graham, K.S., Barense, M.D., and Lee, A.C.H. (2010). Going beyond LTM in the MTL: a synthesis of neuropsychological and neuroimaging findings on the role of the medial temporal lobe in memory and perception. *Neuropsychologia*, 48 (4), 831–853. doi: 10.1016/j.neuropsychologia.2010.01.001.

Hampton, R.R., Hampstead, B.M., and Murray, E.A. (2004). Selective hippocampal damage in rhesus monkeys impairs spatial memory in an open-field test. *Hippocampus*, 14 (7), 808–818. doi: 10.1002/hipo.10217.

Hannula, D.E., and Ranganath, C. (2008). Medial temporal lobe activity predicts successful relational memory binding. *Journal of Neuroscience*, 28 (1), 116–124. doi: 10.1523/JNEUROSCI.3086-07.2008.

Hannula, D.E., Tranel, D., and Cohen, N.J. (2006). The long and the short of it: relational memory impairments in amnesia, even at short lags. *Journal of Neuroscience* 26 (32), 8352–8359. doi: 10.1523/JNEUROSCI.5222-05.2006.

Hartley, T., Bird, C.M., Chan, D., *et al.* (2007). The hippocampus is required for short-term topographical memory in humans. *Hippocampus*, 17 (1), 34–48. doi: 10.1002/hipo.20240.

Hassabis, D., Chu, C., Rees, G., *et al.* (2009). Decoding neuronal ensembles in the human hippocampus. *Current Biology*, 19 (7), 546–554. doi: 10.1016/j.cub.2009.02.033.

Hodges, J.R., Patterson, K., Oxbury, S., and Funnell, E. (1992). Semantic dementia progressive fluent aphasia with temporal lobe atrophy. *Brain*, 115 (6), 1783–1806.

Holdstock, J.S., Gutnikov, S.A., Gaffan, D., and Mayes, A.R. (2000a). Perceptual and mnemonic matching-to-sample in humans: contributions of the hippocampus, perirhinal and other medial temporal lobe cortices. *Cortex*, 36 (3), 301–322. doi: 10.1016/S0010-9452(08)70843-8.

Holdstock, J.S., Mayes, A.R., Cezayirli, E., *et al.* (2000b). A comparison of egocentric and allocentric spatial memory in a patient with selective hippocampal damage. *Neuropsychologia*, 38 (4), 410–425. doi: 10.1016/S0028-3932(99)00099-8.

Horel, J.A., Voytko, M.L., and Salsbury, K.G. (1984). Visual learning suppressed by cooling the temporal pole. *Behavioral Neuroscience*, 98 (2), 310–324. doi:10.1037//0735-7044.98.2.310.

Hori, E., Tabuchi, E., Matsumura, N., *et al.* (2003). Representation of place by monkey hippocampal neurons in real and virtual translocation. *Hippocampus*, 13 (2), 190–196. doi: 10.1002/hipo.10062.

Iglói, K., Doeller, C.F., Berthoz, A., *et al.* (2010). Lateralized human hippocampal activity predicts navigation based on sequence or place memory. *Proceedings of the National Academy of Sciences of the USA*, 107 (32), 14466–14471. doi: 10.1073/pnas.1004243107.

Insausti, R., Amaral, D.G., and Cowan, W.M. (1987). The entorhinal cortex of the monkey: II. Cortical afferents. *Journal of Comparative Neurology*, 264 (3), 356–395. doi: 10.1002/cne.902640306.

Kim, S., Jeneson, A., van der Horst, A.S., *et al.* (2011). Memory, visual discrimination performance, and the human hippocampus. *Journal of Neuroscience*, 31 (7), 2624–2629. doi: 10.1523/JNEUROSCI.5954-10.2011.

King, J.A., Burgess, N., Hartley, T., *et al.* (2002). Human hippocampus and viewpoint dependence in spatial memory. *Hippocampus*, 12 (6), 811–820. doi: 10.1002/hipo.10070.

Knutson, A.R., Hopkins, R.O., and Squire, L.R. (2012). Visual discrimination performance, memory, and medial temporal lobe function. *Proceedings of the National Academy of Sciences of the USA*, 107 (32), 13106–13111. doi: 10.1073/pnas.1208876109.

Lavenex, P., and Amaral, D.G. (2000). Hippocampal–neocortical interaction: a hierarchy of associativity. *Hippocampus*, 10 (4), 420–430. doi: 10.1002/1098-1063(2000)10:4<420::AID-HIPO8>3.0.CO;2-5.

Lavenex, P., Amaral, D.G., and Lavenex, P. (2006). Hippocampal lesion prevents spatial relational learning in adult macaque monkeys. *Journal of Neuroscience*, 26 (17), 4546–4558. doi: 10.1523/JNEUROSCI.5412-05.2006.

Lavenex, P., Suzuki, W.A., and Amaral, D.G. (2004). Perirhinal and parahippocampal cortices of the macaque monkey: intrinsic projections and interconnections. *Journal of Comparative Neurology*, 472 (3), 371–394. doi: 10.1002/cne.20079.

Lee, A.C.H., Barense, M.D., and Graham, K.S. (2005). The contribution of the human medial temporal lobe to perception: bridging the gap between animal and human studies. *Quarterly Journal of Experimental Psychology Section B: Comparative and Physiological Psychology*, 58 (3–4), 300–325. doi: 10.1080/02724990444000168.

Lee, A.C.H., Buckley, M.J., Gaffan, D., *et al.* (2006). Differentiating the Roles of the hippocampus and perirhinal cortex in processes beyond long-term declarative memory: a double dissociation in dementia. *Journal of Neuroscience*, 26 (19), 5198–5203. doi: 10.1523/JNEUROSCI.3157-05.2006.

Lee, A.C.H., Buckley, M.J., Pegman, S.J., *et al.* (2005a). Specialization in the medial temporal lobe for processing of objects and scenes. *Hippocampus*, 15 (6), 782–797. doi: 10.1002/hipo.20101.

Lee, A.C.H., Bussey, T.J., Murray, E.A., *et al.* (2005b). Perceptual deficits in amnesia: challenging the medial temporal lobe 'mnemonic' view. *Neuropsychologia*, 43 (1), 1–11. doi: 10.1016/j.neuropsychologia.2004.07.017.

Lee, A.C.H., Levi, N., Davies, R.R., *et al.* (2007). Differing profiles of face and scene discrimination deficits in semantic dementia and Alzheimer's disease. *Neuropsychologia*, 45 (9), 2135–2146. doi: 10.1016/j.neuropsychologia.2007.01.010.

Lee, A.C.H., and Rudebeck, S.R. (2010). Human medial temporal lobe damage can disrupt the perception of single objects. *Journal of Neuroscience*, 30 (19), 6588–6594. doi: 10.1523/JNEUROSCI.0116-10.2010.

Lee, A.C.H., Scahill, V.L., and Graham, K.S. (2008). Activating the medial temporal lobe during oddity judgment for faces and scenes. *Cerebral Cortex*, 18 (3), 683–696. doi: 10.1093/cercor/bhm104.

Lee, A.C.H., Yeung, L.K., and Barense, M.D. (2012). The hippocampus and visual perception. *Frontiers in Human Neuroscience*, 6, 91. doi: 10.3389/fnhum.2012.00091.

Levy, D.A., Shrager, Y., and Squire, L.R. (2005). Intact visual discrimination of complex and feature-ambiguous stimuli in the absence of perirhinal cortex. *Learning and Memory*, 12 (1), 61–66. doi: 10.1101/lm.84405.

Maguire, E.A., Burgess, N., Donnett, J.G., *et al.* (1998). Knowing where and getting there: a human navigation network. *Science*, 280 (5365), 921–924. doi: 10.1126/science.280.5365.921.

Maguire, E.A., Frackowiak, R.S., and Frith, C.D. (1997). Recalling routes around London: activation of the right hippocampus in taxi drivers. *Journal of Neuroscience*, 17 (18), 7103–7110.

Maguire, E.A., Nannery, R., and Spiers, H.J. (2006). Navigation around London by a taxi driver with bilateral hippocampal lesions. *Brain*, 129 (11), 2894–2907. doi: 10.1093/brain/awl286.

Manns, J.R., and Squire, L.R. (2001). Perceptual learning, awareness, and the hippocampus. *Hippocampus*, 11 (6), 776–782. doi: 10.1002/hipo.1093.

McTighe, S.M., Cowell, R.A., Winters, B.D., *et al.* (2010). Paradoxical false memory for objects after brain damage. *Science*, 330 (6009), 1408–1410. doi: 10.1126/science.1194780.

McTighe, S.M., Mar, A.C., Romberg, C., *et al.* (2009). A new touchscreen test of pattern separation: effect of hippocampal lesions. *Neuroreport*, 20 (9), 881–885. doi: 10.1097/WNR.0b013e32832c5eb2.

Meunier, M., Bachevalier, J., Mishkin, M., and Murray, E.A. (1993). Effects on visual recognition of combined and separate ablations of the entorhinal and perirhinal cortex in rhesus monkeys. *Journal of Neuroscience*, 13 (12), 5418–5432.

Mishkin, M. (1978). Memory in monkeys severely impaired by combined but not by separate removal of amygdala and hippocampus. *Nature*, 273, 297–298. doi: 10.1038/273297a0.

Montaldi, D.D., and Mayes, A.R. (2010). The role of recollection and familiarity in the functional differentiation of the medial temporal lobes. *Hippocampus*, 20 (11), 1291–1314. doi: 10.1002/hipo.20853.

Morgan, L.K., Macevoy, S.P., Aguirre, G.K., and Epstein, A. (2011). Distances between real-world locations are represented in the human hippocampus. *Journal of Neuroscience*, 31 (4), 1238–1245. doi: 10.1523/JNEUROSCI.4667-10.2011.

Murray, E.A., Baxter, M.G., and Gaffan, D. (1998). Monkeys with rhinal cortex damage or neurotoxic hippocampal lesions are impaired on spatial scene learning and object reversals. *Behavioral Neuroscience*, 112 (6), 1291–1303. doi: 10.1037/0735-7044.112.6.1291.

Murray, E.A., and Bussey, T.J. (1999). Perceptual-mnemonic functions of the perirhinal cortex. *Trends in Cognitive Sciences*, 3 (4), 142–151.

Murray, E.A., Bussey, T.J., and Saksida, L.M. (2007). Visual perception and memory: a new view of medial temporal lobe function in primates and rodents. *Annual Review of Neuroscience*, 30, 99–122. doi: 10.1146/annurev.neuro.29.051605.113046.

Murray, E.A., and Mishkin, M. (1998). Object recognition and location memory in monkeys with excitotoxic lesions of the amygdala and hippocampus. *Journal of Neuroscience*, 18 (16), 6568–6582.

Norman, K.A. (2010). How hippocampus and cortex contribute to recognition memory: revisiting the complementary learning systems model. *Hippocampus*, 20 (11), 1217–1227. doi: 10.1002/hipo.20855.

Norman, K.A. and O'Reilly, R.C. (2003). Modeling hippocampal and neocortical contributions to recognition memory: a complementary-learning-systems approach. *Psychological Review*, 110 (4), 611–646. doi: 10.1037/0033-295X.110.4.611.

O'Keefe, J., and Dostrovsky, J. (1971). The hippocampus as a spatial map: preliminary evidence from unit activity in the freely-moving rat. *Brain Research*, 34, 171–175. doi: 10.1016/0006-8993(71)90358-1

O'Keefe, J., and Nadel, L. (1978). *The Hippocampus as a Cognitive Map*. Oxford: Clarendon Press.

Olson, I.R., Moore, K.S., Stark, M., and Chatterjee, A. (2006a). Visual working memory is impaired when the medial temporal lobe is damaged. *Journal of Cognitive Neuroscience*, 18 (7), 1087–1097. doi: 10.1162/jocn.2006.18.7.1087.

Olson, I.R., Page, K., Moore, K.S., *et al.* (2006b). Working memory for conjunctions relies on the medial temporal lobe. *Journal of Neuroscience*, 26 (17), 4596–4601. doi: 10.1523/JNEUROSCI.1923-05.2006.

Ono, T., Nakamura, K., Fukuda, M., and Tamura, R. (1991). Place recognition responses of neurons in monkey hippocampus. *Neuroscience Letters*, 121 (1), 194–198. doi: 10.1016/0304-3940(91)90683-K.

Ono, T., Nakamura, K., Nishijo, H., and Eifuku, S. (1993). Monkey hippocampal neurons related to spatial and nonspatial functions. *Journal of Neurophysiology*, 70 (4), 1516–1529.

Parkin, A.J., and Leng, N.R.C. (1993). *Neuropsychology of the Amnesic Syndrome*. Hillsdale, NJ: Erlbaum.

Peterson, M.A. and Gibson, B.S. (1994). Object recognition contributions to figure-ground organization: operations on outlines and subjective contours. *Perception and Psychophysics*, 56 (5), 551–564. doi: 10.3758/BF03206951.

Ranganath, C. (2010). A unified framework for the functional organization of the medial temporal lobes and the phenomenology of episodic memory. *Hippocampus*, 20 (11), 1263–1290. doi: 10.1002/hipo.20852.

Ranganath, C., and Blumenfeld, R.S. (2005). Doubts about double dissociations between short- and long-term memory. *Trends in Cognitive Sciences*, 9 (8), 374–380. doi: 10.1016/j.tics.2005.06.009.

Ranganath, C., and D'Esposito, M. (2001). Medial temporal lobe activity associated with active maintenance of novel information. *Neuron*, 31 (5), 865–873. doi: 10.1016/S0896-6273(01)00411-1.

Robertson, R.G., Rolls, E.T., and Georges-François, P. (1998). Spatial view cells in the primate hippocampus: effects of removal of view details. *Journal of Neurophysiology*, 79, 1145–1156. doi: 10.1093/cercor/9.3.197.

Rolls, E.T. (1999). Spatial view cells and the representation of place in the primate hippo-campus. *Hippocampus*, 9 (3), 467–480. doi: 10.1002/(SICI)1098-1063(1999)9:4<467::AID-HIPO13>3.0.CO;2-F.

Rolls, E.T., Robertson, R.G., and Georges-François, P. (1997). Spatial view cells in the primate hippocampus. *European Journal of Neuroscience*, 9 (8), 1789–1794. doi: 10.1111/j.1460-9568.1997.tb01538.x.

Rosenbaum, R.S., Köhler, S., Schacter, D.L., *et al.* (2005). The case of K.C.: contributions of a memory-impaired person to memory theory. *Neuropsychologia*, 43 (7), 989–1021. doi: 10.1016/j.neuropsychologia.2004.10.007.

Rosenbaum, R.S., Priselac, S., Köhler, S., *et al.* (2000). Remote spatial memory in an amnesic person with extensive bilateral hippocampal lesions. *Nature Neuroscience*, 3 (10), 1044–1048. doi: 10.1038/79867.

Rudebeck, S.R., Filippini, N., and Lee, A.C.H. (2013). Can complex visual discrimination deficits in amnesia be attributed to the medial temporal lobe? An investigation into the effects of medial temporal lobe damage on brain connectivity. *Hippocampus*, 23 (1), 7–13. doi: 10.1002/hipo.22056.

Ryan, J.D., and Cohen, N.J. (2004). Processing and short-term retention of relational information in amnesia. *Neuropsychologia*, 42 (4), 497–511. doi: 10.1016/j.neuropsychologia.2003.08.011.

Saksida, L.M., and Bussey, T. J. (2010). The representational-hierarchical view of amnesia: translation from animal to human. *Neuropsychologia*, 48 (8), 2370–2384. doi: 10.1016/j.neuropsychologia.2010.02.026.

Scoville, W.B., and Milner, B. (1957). Loss of recent memory after bilateral hippocampal lesions. *Journal of Neurology, Neurosurgery, and Psychiatry*, 20 (1), 11–21. doi: 10.1136/jnnp.20.1.11.

Shrager, Y., Gold, J.J., Hopkins, R.O., and Squire, L.R. (2006). Intact visual perception in memory-impaired patients with medial temporal lobe lesions. *Journal of Neuroscience*, 26 (8), 2235–2240. doi: 10.1523/JNEUROSCI.4792-05.2006

Sidman, M., Stoddard, L.T., and Mohr, J.P. (1968). Some additional quantitative observations of immediate memory in a patient with bilateral hippocampal lesions. *Neuropsychologia*, 6 (3), 245–254. doi: 10.1016/0028-3932(68)90023-7.

Snowden, J.S., Goulding, P.J., and Neary, D. (1989). Semantic dementia: a form of circumscribed cerebral atrophy. *Behavioural Neurology*, 2 (3), 167–182.

Spiers, H. J., Burgess, N., Hartley, T., *et al.* (2001). Bilateral hippocampal pathology impairs topographical and episodic memory but not visual pattern matching. *Hippocampus*, 11 (6), 715–725. doi: 10.1002/hipo.1087.

Spiers, H. J., and Maguire, E.A. (2006). Thoughts, behaviour, and brain dynamics during navigation in the real world. *NeuroImage*, 31 (4), 1826–1840. doi: 10.1016/j.neuroimage.2006.01.037.

Spiers, H. J., and Maguire, E.A. (2007). A navigational guidance system in the human brain. *Hippocampus*, 17 (8), 618–626. doi: 10.1002/hipo.20298.

Squire, L.R. (1982). The neuropsychology of human memory. *Annual Review of Neuroscience*, 5, 241–273. doi: 10.1146/annurev.ne.05.030182.001325.

Squire, L.R., Stark, C.E.L., and Clark, R.E. (2004). The medial temporal lobe. *Annual Review of Neuroscience*, 27, 279–306. doi: 10.1146/annurev.neuro.27.070203.144130.

Squire, L.R., and Wixted, J.T. (2011). The cognitive neuroscience of human memory since H.M. *Annual Review of Neuroscience*, 34, 259–288. doi: 10.1146/annurev-neuro-061010-113720.

Squire, L.R., Wixted, J.T., and Clark, R.E. (2007). Recognition memory and the medial temporal lobe: a new perspective. *Nature Reviews Neuroscience*, 8 (11), 872–883. doi: 10.1038/nrn2154.

Squire, L.R., and Zola-Morgan, S.M. (1991). The medial temporal lobe memory system. *Science*, 253 (5026), 1380–1386. doi: 10.1126/science.1896849.

Stark, C.E.L., and Squire, L.R. (2000). Intact visual perceptual discrimination in humans in the absence of perirhinal cortex. *Learning and Memory*, 7 (5), 273–278. doi: 10.1101/lm.35000.

Stern, C.E., Sherman, S.J., Kirchhoff, B.A., and Hasselmo, M.E. (2001). Medial temporal and prefrontal contributions to working memory tasks with novel and familiar stimuli. *Hippocampus*, 11 (4), 337–346. doi: 10.1002/hipo.1048.

Suzuki, W.A. (2009). Perception and the medial temporal lobe: evaluating the current evidence. *Neuron*, 61 (5), 657–666. doi: 10.1016/j.neuron.2009.02.008.

Suzuki, W.A., Zola-Morgan, S.M., Squire, L.R., and Amaral, D.G. (1993). Lesions of the perirhinal and parahippocampal cortices in the monkey produce long-lasting memory impairment in the visual and tactual modalities. *Journal of Neuroscience*, 13 (6), 2430–2451.

Tanaka, K. (1996). Inferotemporal cortex and object vision. *Annual Review of Neuroscience*, 19, 109–139. doi: 10.1146/annurev.ne.19.030196.000545.

Taylor, K.J., Henson, R.N.A., and Graham, K.S. (2007). Recognition memory for faces and scenes in amnesia: dissociable roles of medial temporal lobe structures. *Neuropsychologia*, 45 (11), 2428–2438. doi: 10.1016/j.neuropsychologia.2007.04.004.

Ungerleider, L.G., and Mishkin, M. (1982). Two cortical visual streams. In *Analysis of Visual Behavior* (ed. D. Ingle, M. Goodale, and R. Mansfield). Cambridge, MA: MIT Press, pp. 549–586.

Voss, J.L., and Paller, K.A. (2010). Bridging divergent neural models of recognition memory: introduction to the special issue and commentary on key issues. *Hippocampus*, 20 (11), 1171–1177. doi: 10.1002/hipo.20851.

Warren, D. E., Duff, M.C., Tranel, D., and Cohen, N.J. (2010). Medial temporal lobe damage impairs representation of simple stimuli. *Frontiers in Human Neuroscience*, 4, 35. doi: 10.3389/fnhum.2010.00035.

Warrington, E.K., and Weiskrantz, L. (1970). Amnesic syndrome: consolidation or retrieval? *Nature*, 228, 628–630. doi: 10.1038/228628a0.

Williams, P., and Tarr, M.J. (1997). Structural processing and implicit memory for possible and impossible figures. *Journal of Experimental Psychology: Learning, Memory, and Cognition*, 23 (6), 1344–1361. doi: 10.1037/0278-7393.23.6.1344.

Zola-Morgan, S.M., Squire, L.R., Clower, R.P., and Rempel, N.L. (1993). Damage to the perirhinal cortex exacerbates memory impairment following lesions to the hippocampal formation. *Journal of Neuroscience*, 13 (1), 251–265.

Zola-Morgan, S.M., Squire, L.R., and Ramus, S.J. (1994). Severity of memory impairment in monkeys as a function of locus and extent of damage within the medial temporal lobe memory system. *Hippocampus*, 4 (4), 483–495. doi: 10.1002/hipo.450040410.

11

# The Memory Function of Sleep
## *How the Sleeping Brain Promotes Learning*
### Alexis M. Chambers and Jessica D. Payne

## Introduction

Why do we sleep? Philosophers have pondered this question for centuries, yet despite decades of research scientists are still striving for an answer. Our understanding of sleep has certainly evolved since the great minds of Plato or Aristotle, who conceived of sleep as resulting from physiological processes such as the digestion of food (Barbera, 2008). Beginning in the late nineteenth century, empirical studies of the time-course of memory inadvertently pointed toward a special role of sleep in reducing forgetting, but the implications of such findings were initially ignored (Ebbinghaus, 1885). Even when such findings were later seriously considered, sleep was proposed to play only a passive role in reducing memory interference from external, competing stimuli (Jenkins and Dallenbach, 1924; Van Ormer, 1933). Fortunately, technological advances such as the electroencephalogram (EEG) led to the blossoming of more objective sleep research (Dement and Vaughan, 2000), allowing scientists to better understand this unique feature of life, including its active role in memory formation and the specific neural processes underlying this function (See *How the sleeping brain impacts memory*, below).

### Sleep stages

The technological advances that led to the first all-night sleep recording in 1953 resulted in the classification of the various stages of sleep still recognized today. Electrical signals from the brain (electroencephalogram; EEG), eyes (electrooculogram; EOG), and muscles (electromyogram; EMG), collectively making up the polysomnograph (PSG) recording, revealed highly similar patterns of electrical activity in the brain across individuals as they slept. It soon became clear that this pattern included several distinct sleep stages. The first type of sleep became known as NREM or non-rapid-eye-movement sleep and included four stages (1, 2, 3, and 4) demarking progressively deepening stages of sleep. The second type of sleep, REM or rapid-eye-movement sleep, could also be broken down into two different types, known as tonic and phasic

*The Wiley Handbook on the Cognitive Neuroscience of Memory*, First Edition.
Edited by Donna Rose Addis, Morgan Barense, and Audrey Duarte.
© 2015 John Wiley & Sons, Ltd. Published 2015 by John Wiley & Sons, Ltd.

events. Tonic REM was characterized by a lack of eye movements and reduced muscle tone, while phasic REM was characterized by rapid eye movements and minor muscle twitches (Carskadon and Dement, 1989).

Early observations of such recordings allowed researchers to map out the typical night of sleep, which is similar across individuals. At sleep onset, the brain first advances consecutively through stages 1–4. Stages 3 and 4 together comprise slow-wave sleep (SWS), which is the deepest state during the sleep cycle and is characterized by high-amplitude, low-frequency EEG patterns. The brain then shifts to REM sleep, which is characterized by low-amplitude, high-frequency EEG patterns, periodic rapid eye movements (REMs), and a drastic reduction in muscle tone. Interestingly, the EEG patterns during REM sleep look very similar to patterns obtained during wakefulness, which is why the measurement of eye movements and muscle tone is required to confidently differentiate REM sleep from wakefulness; the EEG alone is often not sufficient. Following REM sleep, the brain then cycles back through all the stages, repeating this cycle about every 90 minutes throughout the night. However, the distribution of these stages across a night of sleep is not entirely even. The first half of the night contains a majority of the night's SWS, whereas the amount of REM in the second half of the night is nearly doubled from the first (Figure 11.1; Payne, 2011).

It should also be noted that, as of 2007, the American Academy of Sleep Medicine (AASM) has recommended an alteration to these customary sleep stages. According to this change, stage 1 and 2 remain the same, but are referred to as stages N1 and N2, respectively. However, stages 3 and 4, which were once distinct, are combined into a single stage, noted as N3. Finally, REM sleep is simply referred to as stage R (Iber *et al.*, 2007). Although these changes are recommended and are taught to those currently learning sleep scoring, some researchers still prefer to use the previous method of sleep scoring.

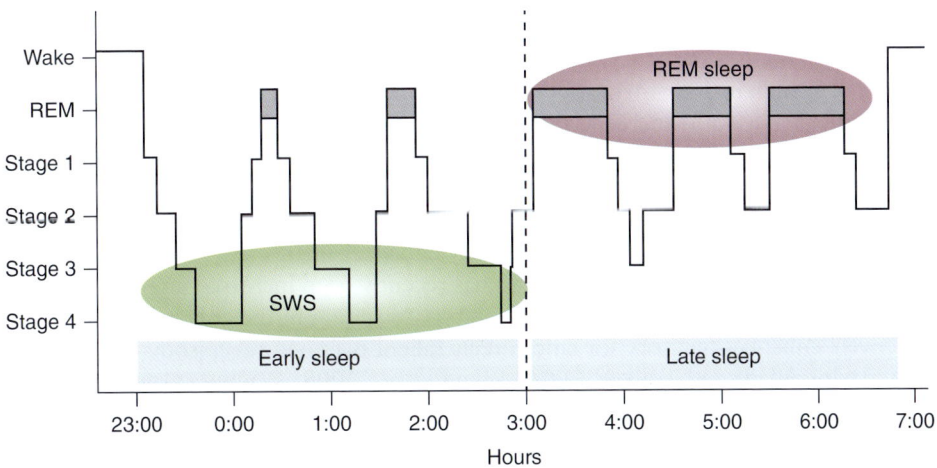

**Figure 11.1** Histogram depicting a typical night of sleep. Source: Payne (2011). Reproduced with permission of Elsevier.

## Stages and types of memory

Although scientists have not yet been able to answer the question of why we sleep, one proposed function of sleep is its close relationship with memory processes. Indeed, sleep after learning has been shown to enhance many forms of memory (Stickgold, 2005) at various stages of memory processing (Walker and Stickgold, 2006).

Like sleep, memory processing can be broken down into various stages. The first is encoding, which occurs when new information or experiences are initially acquired and transformed into mental representations in the brain. The next stage, consolidation, gradually stabilizes these representations over hours, days, and even years, making them resistant to interference from other competing information. Some have proposed that this second stage be further broken down into two substages: stabilization and enhancement (Walker and Stickgold, 2006), while others argue that the consolidation process also involves qualitative changes or transformations in memory representations (for review see Payne, 2011; Payne and Kensinger, 2010). If encoding and consolidation are successfully completed, the third stage can be carried out, which involves retrieval, or accessing the stored memory for later use (see Chapter 5).

Memories can also be broken down into different unique categories or types, differing in their time-course, capacity, and the type of information processed. Distinctions between the various categories of memory arose from neuropsychological studies, often investigating brain lesions and amnesia (Squire, 1986). Since this chapter will focus on long-term memory, it is critical to understand the distinction between declarative or explicit memory and non-declarative or implicit memory, which differ largely on the level of conscious awareness devoted to processing. Declarative memories are those for which we have conscious awareness, while non-declarative memories are acquired below such awareness (Schacter, 1987). Further, declarative memories come in two types: episodic and semantic. Episodic memories are those memories that concern specific life events or episodes, and contain temporal and spatial information, such as the memory of the details surrounding your first kiss. Alternatively, semantic memories concern facts and general knowledge acquired throughout our lives, but lack distinct temporal or spatial information, such as knowing that the capital of France is Paris, but being unable to remember the exact event in which you learned this information (see Chapter 4). On the other hand, non-declarative memories encompass procedural memories, which include memories for performing skills that often cannot be verbally expressed, such as knowing how to ride a bike (see Chapter 3).

A further distinction is that between neutral and emotional memories. Emotional memories are those that have an emotionally salient component, whether positive or negative (Hamann, 2001; Kensinger, 2009; see also Chapter 19). There is a large body of research indicating that emotional saliency enhances memories (Lang, Dhillon, and Dong, 1995; Ochsner, 2000), and there has recently been increased attention paid to this fact within the sleep and memory literature, resulting in the conclusion that sleep selectively enhances memory for emotionally salient over neutral episodic information (Hu, Stylos-Allan, and Walker, 2006; Payne *et al.*, 2008; Wagner, Gais, and Born, 2001). Although these memories often fall under the umbrella of episodic memories, we will treat them as their own category for the purpose of this chapter.

These various types of memory are not only dissociated by the content or level of consciousness associated with them, but they can also be distinguished by the different neural systems that promote them. For instance, declarative memories rely heavily on the medial temporal lobe and the hippocampus (Moscovitch *et al.*, 2005). Evidence supporting this relationship comes from patients with selective hippocampal damage, such as the famous patient H.M. who could not form new episodic memories due to the surgical removal of his bilateral hippocampus to control his severe epilepsy (Scoville and Milner, 1957). He could, however, form new procedural memories (Corkin, 1968), which are supported by areas of the neocortex and subcortical structures such as the basal ganglia (Moscovitch *et al.*, 2005). Finally, there is evidence that emotional memories are supported by activation of the amygdala, a subcortical structure adjacent to the hippocampus that is important for processing emotion (Hamann, 2001; McGaugh, 2004). In fact, this close proximity to the hippocampus is believed to be a crucial factor for the effects of the amygdala on emotional memory formation, due to the ease with which these structures can interact (Hamann *et al.*, 2002; Kensinger and Schacter, 2006). There is evidence that each type of memory is uniquely impacted by neural processing during sleep.

## Sleep Enhances Declarative Memories

The notion that sleep enhances memories began in the early 1900s. In one early study very reminiscent of methods still currently used in the field, G. E. Muller's student Rosa Heine (1914) had four subjects study lists of nonsense syllables and tested their memory for these syllables after a 24-hour delay. The key aspect of her method was that learning of the lists could take place either before a night of sleep or before a day of wake. Thus, learning the syllables could be followed very closely by nocturnal sleep and then a day of wake, or could be followed by many hours of wake and then a night of sleep. The difference between the two conditions was how long after learning the subject went to sleep. Heine found that learning the lists just before sleep resulted in significantly better memory of the syllables during the test than when learning occurred before a period of wake. Although these pointed toward the critical impact of sleep soon after learning, it was generally concluded at the time that sleep was merely shielding the individual from "the interference, inhibition, or obliteration of the old by the new" (Jenkins and Dallenbach, 1924, p. 612; see Van Ormer, 1933 for a review). This view was held even despite the fact that Heine's study allowed both groups to receive approximately equal amounts of waking time and thus should have equated interference across the groups.

However, research on this topic later expanded and matured, resulting in an extended understanding of the cognitive and neural mechanisms acting on declarative memories during sleep and leading to a wealth of literature on the matter. These recent studies have incorporated safeguards for the methodological problems of their predecessors. For instance, while Heine's (1914) work investigated performance of only a handful of subjects, did not control for circadian influences, and did not regulate testing times for all subjects within the same group, current studies have consistently increased sample sizes, utilized control groups, and standardized data collection methods.

### Sleep and memory for verbal stimuli

Like Heine's (1914) study, which used nonsense syllables, modern sleep studies have also investigated memory for verbal stimuli. However, instead of nonsense syllables, current studies commonly test memory for words, or pairs of words. Such studies generally show that sleep enhances memory for words or word pairs more so than an equivalent time spent awake (Lahl *et al.*, 2008; Payne *et al.*, 2012; Plihal and Born, 1997; Tucker *et al.*, 2006), and this effect has been replicated using various methodologies.

In one of these studies, Plihal and Born (1997) investigated whether specific sleep stages might be particularly important for memory improvements in word-pair learning. They required participants to learn pairs of words, and immediately tested them on these pairs by giving them the first word and asking them to fill in the missing word of the pair. Participants were tested on these pairs until they could remember 60% of the pairs. Following this immediate test, they underwent three hours of sleep or three hours of wake, and were then retested.

Most important to their design, this three-hour interval could occur over either the first three hours of nocturnal sleep or the last three hours. In the first case, termed "early" sleep, participants learned the task prior to bedtime and were awoken after three hours of sleep for testing. In the latter case, termed "late" sleep, participants slept for three hours, were awoken to learn the task, and then received another three hours of sleep before being awoken and tested for the final time. Such a design is often employed to better separate the effects of the different types of sleep on such tasks. As mentioned, the first half of the night is dominated by SWS, while the second half of the night contains more REM, thus allowing researchers to better investigate the contributions of these specific stages to performance. The authors found that those who underwent three hours of early sleep improved their recall of the pairs above the immediate test performance significantly more than those who underwent three hours of wake or three hours of late sleep, suggesting that SWS played an important role in performance improvements.

This effect has also been found with a nap paradigm. In such a model, participants are compared by the presence or absence of a nap, usually during the early afternoon and lasting less than an hour. Tucker and colleagues (2006) found that a short nap of about 47 minutes during a six-hour interval between learning and recall testing of a list of word pairs significantly improved memory relative to baseline testing. This effect was not seen in those who did not nap during this interval. Importantly, such a short nap prevented participants from obtaining any sign of REM sleep, restricting the sleep associated with these improvements only to NREM stages, a finding consistent with that of Plihal and Born (1997).

However, it is interesting that many studies of this type fail to find significant correlations between performance and specific sleep stages. Tucker *et al.* (2006) did not obtain such a relationship, nor did Lahl and colleagues (2008), who reproduced the sleep-dependent memory effect for words with a 25- and even a 6-minute nap. They did, however, find that the amount of time it took to fall asleep impacted the performance enhancement afforded by sleep, such that those who fell asleep faster benefited more from the shorter naps. Such a finding suggests that getting at least some amount of sleep after learning, especially directly after learning, is sufficient for memory improvements.

However, similar to problems faced by researchers during Heine's time, some critics still argue that sleep could simply be protecting memories from interfering stimuli, since there is relatively little processing of outside information during sleep (see Ellenbogen, Payne, and Stickgold, 2006; Wixted, 2004, for different opinions on the matter). Recent studies have challenged this assumption by manipulating characteristics of the learned material, and altering the way in which sleep impacts memory. For instance, Payne *et al.* (2012) required participants to study pairs of words that were either semantically related or unrelated before a 12-hour delay that contained either sleep or wake. They found that participants who slept or stayed awake during the delay recalled the lists containing related words equally well. However, while participants who stayed awake had much more difficulty remembering the lists containing unrelated words, those who slept remembered the pairs on this list just as well as those on the related word lists (Figure 11.2). If sleep was acting to simply buffer memories from interfering information, it would be expected that the sleep and wake groups would differ on memory for both types of word pairs, not just one.

Payne *et al.* (2012) also used this paradigm with two other groups of participants. These subjects underwent a 24-hour delay between studying the word pairs and final testing. Thus, participants received both a period of wake and a period of sleep before final testing, but half of participants obtained sleep shortly after the study phase, while the other half studied the words and then slept only after a full day awake. Related to performance after only a 30-minute delay and after the 12-hour delays, they found that the number of the unrelated word pairs forgotten over the wake portion of the 24-hour delay was doubled when this portion came before sleep as opposed to following sleep. However, the amount of forgetting occurring over the sleep portion of the 24 hours was the same irrespective of its relationship to the wake portion. This finding is important because, if sleep were simply shielding against interference, the amount of forgetting over the waking portion of the delay would be the same, regardless of whether wake preceded or followed sleep. Yet forgetting was increased over the wake period when sleep was delayed after learning (Figure 11.3). This suggests that, rather

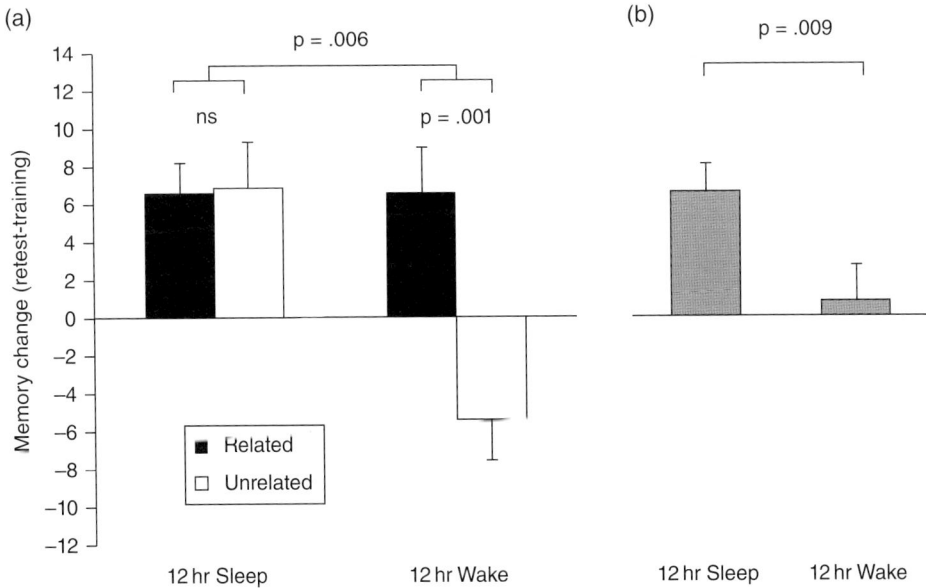

**Figure 11.2** (a) Recall performance for related (black) and unrelated (white) word pairs after a 12-hour consolidation period containing a period of sleep or wake. (b) Recall performance irrespective of word pair type. Source: Payne *et al.* (2012). Reproduced with permission of the authors.

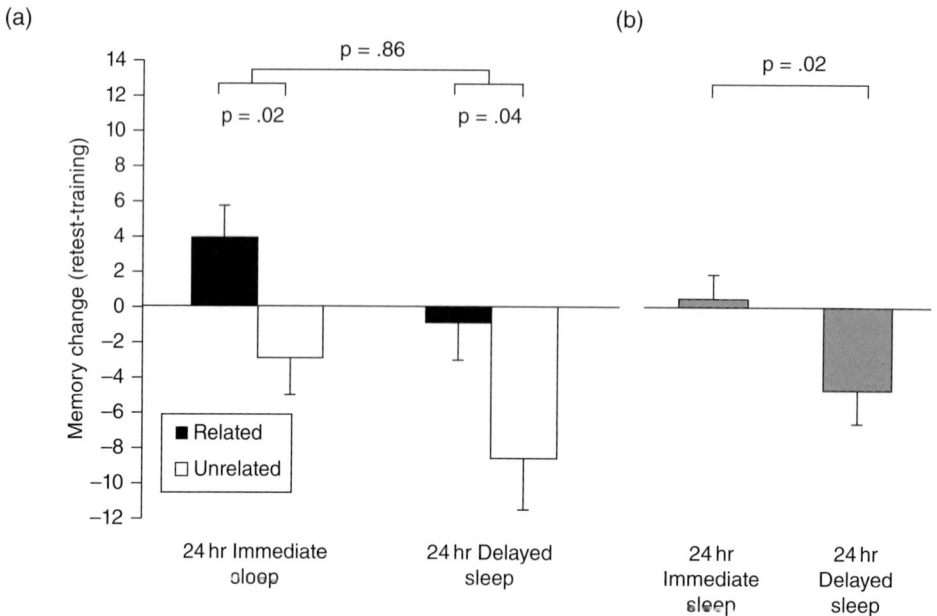

**Figure 11.3** (A) Recall performance for related (black) and unrelated (white) word pairs after a 24-hour consolidation period containing an immediate period of sleep or sleep after a day of wake. (B) Recall performance irrespective of word pair type. Source: Payne *et al.* (2012). Reproduced with permission of the authors.

than protecting against interference, sleep may actually work to stabilize memories, providing the most benefit when it closely follows learning (Payne *et al.*, 2012).

## Sleep and memory for picture stimuli

The impact of sleep on the ability to remember picture stimuli has also been a topic of interest in the sleep and memory literature. This line of study commonly employs methods similar to those used to investigate memory for verbal stimuli, and comparable effects of sleep on memory have been obtained between the two classes of stimuli. For example, to examine memory for image–location pairings, Talamini and colleagues (2008) placed pictures of different faces in various locations on a computer screen and had participants learn these face–location pairings (Figure 11.4). They were tested on these pairings after a brief 10-minute interval, as well as after a 12-hour delay containing either a night of sleep or a day of wake. They found that those who slept forgot significantly fewer of the pairings than those who remained awake. Similar to methods of Payne and colleagues (2012), two additional groups had a 24-hour delay between the learning and final testing sessions. One group obtained sleep during the first portion of this delay, while the other obtained sleep only after a full day of wake. Like Payne *et al.* (2012), Talamini *et al.* found that significant forgetting occurred in those subjects who remained awake for an entire day before sleeping, but not for those who slept first (Figure 11.5). Again, given that both groups received the same amount of sleep and wake before testing, a passive role of sleep in preventing interference can be

**Figure 11.4** Example of the face–location association task. Participants are taught the appropriate location for each presented face by using a joystick to move each face, initially presented at the center of the screen, to one of the eight peripheral locations when indicated by a green circle. Source: Talamini *et al.* (2008). Reproduced with permission of Cold Spring Harbor Laboratory Press.

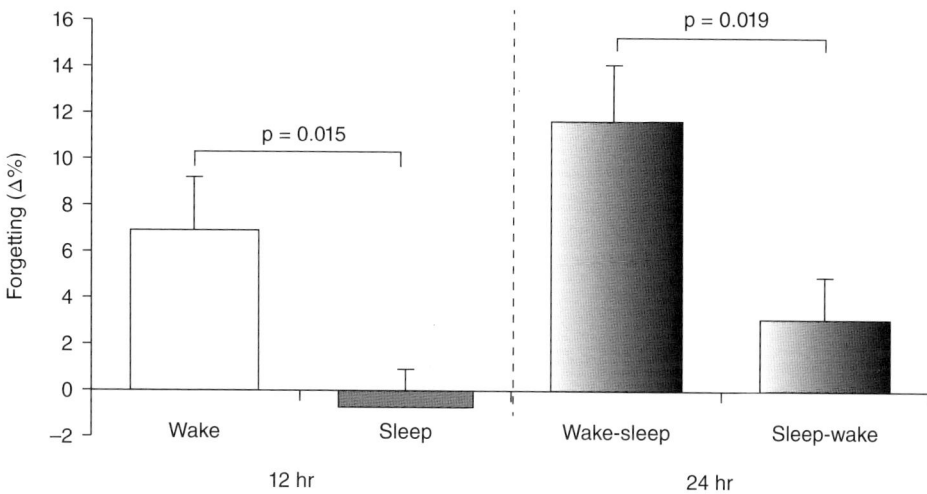

**Figure 11.5** Amount of forgetting occurring across the 12-hour groups containing either a period of wake or a period of sleep, and the 24-hour groups containing either wake before sleep or sleep before wake. Source: Talamini *et al.* (2008). Reproduced with permission of Cold Spring Harbor Laboratory Press.

ruled out. Clearly, sleeping soon after learning affords a greater benefit to memory than if sleep is delayed.

Some studies have shown that this positive impact of sleep after learning can have long-term effects on memory, resulting from the reorganization of the memory trace within the brain. For example, Takashima and colleagues (2006) had subjects memorize a set of images depicting large-scale spatial layouts of natural landscapes and then nap for roughly 90 minutes. Participants then memorized a new set of the pictures before taking a recognition test of all the pictures they had studied. They found that the amount of SWS obtained during this nap was positively associated with recognition performance on only those items studied before the nap, suggesting an enhancing effect of this sleep stage on memory consolidation that is consistent with previous findings for verbal stimuli (Plihal and Born, 1997). Most importantly, however, Takashima *et al.* (2006) also found that this relationship between SWS and memory performance was still evident 30 days after the original learning period, implying a long-term benefit of sleeping after learning. Thus, like studies investigating verbal stimuli, sleep confers an improvement on memory for pictures, an advantage that is not likely due to the reduction of interference and one that lasts long after initial testing.

## Sleep and spatial memory

The common denominator among the types of learning emphasized in the previous two sections is their reliance on the hippocampus. As previously discussed, the hippocampus is important for the support of episodic memories. Interestingly, episodes in our lives are uniquely defined by the space in which they occur, and the hippocampus is also critical for spatial learning, such as learning the layout of a new college campus. It may come as no surprise that research has reflected sleep's enhancing impact on spatial memory as well.

Using their "early/late" sleep paradigm, Plihal and Born (1999a) found that sleep enhanced performance on a mental rotation task. This task required participants to imagine standing in a given location, such as a balcony of a museum, and to visualize 10 objects placed in various locations around them. After a retention interval filled with three hours of early sleep, late sleep, early wake, or late wake, subjects were asked to imagine turning 90 degrees to the right of where they were "standing" during the first session and indicate where all 10 of the objects were after this movement. Those who had received the first three hours of sleep during the interval were more accurate at locating the 10 objects than those in any of the other groups. Because this sleep interval contained more SWS than any other type of sleep, these findings also suggest that this stage plays an important role in processing this type of declarative memory.

Neuroimaging studies have since corroborated this finding. Research investigating regional cerebral blood flow (rCBF) has found that there is a change in the activity of the hippocampus during periods of sleep following spatial learning. Peigneux and colleagues (2004) measured rCBF while training groups of participants on navigating a virtual town as well as during a subsequent period of sleep. Another group of participants did not train on the navigation task, but were likewise scanned during sleep. They found that those who learned the task exhibited a greater activation of the right hippocampus and parahippocampal areas during SWS as compared to wakefulness or REM sleep. There was also significantly more activation in these areas during stage 2 sleep as compared to wakefulness. Further, this activation was also greater than activations previously found during sleep following the learning of a procedural task (Maquet et al., 2000), which indicates that this effect is task-specific. Most critically, however, Peigneux et al. (2004) found that this increase in activation during SWS was positively correlated with later performance on the navigation task. In other words, those with greater activation during SWS performed better on subsequent trials of the task following this period of sleep. Similarly, Rasch and colleagues (2007) found that reintroducing an odor that was originally presented during acquisition of an object–location association task during subsequent SWS resulted in better memory for the object–location pairings than when no odor was presented. They also found activity in the hippocampus to be increased during these SWS odor re-exposures. Overall, these results suggest that SWS is important for spatial learning, and that there is a physiological mechanism during this state involving activity of the hippocampus that may support this effect.

## Summary

Collectively, these investigations have led to a large body of evidence supporting sleep's positive effects on the declarative memory system. Improving upon sleep studies from the early 1900s, current studies have found a significant role for sleep in forming memories for previously encountered word pairs, scenes, and locations – all types of memories that are particularly dependent on the hippocampus. Such information comes from a wide variety of methodologies, including early/late nocturnal sleep paradigms, nap studies, and research focused on extended delays. Such research has led to stronger arguments against an interference account and has targeted SWS as an important stage for declarative memory improvements across all discussed stimuli domains. However, there may also be a role for the timing of sleep after learning, as delaying sleep too long in humans can lead to decreased performance on both verbal and picture memory tasks, even after sleep is finally achieved (Payne *et al.*, 2012; Talamini *et al.*, 2008). Thus, the amount, timing, and type of sleep are important factors to consider when acquiring a range of new declarative memories.

## Sleep Enhances Emotional Memories

Related to the impact sleep has on declarative memories is the effect of sleep on emotional memories (see Chapter 19 for more discussion of emotional memory). As mentioned, these memories are often episodic in nature. However, they are special in that they carry an emotional undertone, which differentiates them from neutral episodic memories. This emotional content can afford a memory benefit on its own, but when added to sleep, this benefit is compounded.

### Sleep and memory for emotional verbal stimuli

One of the first studies to investigate this impact of sleep on emotional memory used written descriptions as study material. Specifically, Wagner, Gais, and Born (2001) had people read and memorize descriptions of either emotional (e.g., someone committing a murder) or neutral (e.g., sculpture manufacturing) content for a later memory test. They further combined the study of this material with the early/late sleep design discussed earlier so that participants received either three hours of sleep early or late in the night after studying the descriptions. Two control groups remained awake during these intervals. They found that those who received late night sleep after learning these descriptions remembered significantly more of the emotional descriptions than the neutral ones, and this performance was far better compared to those who received early night sleep, early night wake, or late night wake. Since REM sleep dominates late in the night, these results suggest that this stage of sleep may be particularly important for emotional memory consolidation.

However, this differentiation between performance in the early and late sleep groups did not remain for a long-term memory test. Four years after this study was conducted, Wagner and colleagues (2006) contacted the original participants to determine the strength of the remaining memory for the descriptions studied. They found that those who slept after originally learning the descriptions, regardless of whether the sleep occurred over the first half of the night or the second, remembered significantly more of the emotional descriptions than those who remained awake after learning. This was in contrast to memory performance for the neutral descriptions, which was not different between the sleep and wake groups. At first glance, it would appear that specific sleep stages might not be important for emotional memory, at least not in the long run. However, as Wagner and colleagues (2006) point out, those in the early sleep group who originally did not show a similar enhancement of emotional memory as those in the late sleep group actually received the second REM-rich half of the night of sleep after the original memory test when they were allowed to return to sleep. The authors suggest that this might have allowed the memory trace to undergo appropriate selective consolidation processes during the ensuing REM period, and the impact of this occurrence was simply not evident until later testing. Thus sleep, and specifically REM sleep, appears to aid emotional memories, an effect which lasts for years to come.

## Sleep and memory for emotional picture stimuli

Similar results of sleep on memory have been obtained for emotional pictorial stimuli as well. For example, Hu, Stylos-Allan, and Walker (2006) required participants to study lists of pictures that were either emotionally arousing or neutral for a later recognition test. Pictures were taken from the International Affective Picture System (IAPS; Lang, Bradley, and Cuthbert, 2008), a widely used database of emotional and neutral pictures with standardized arousal and valence ratings. After a night of sleep or a day filled with wake, participants were tested for their memory of the pictures using the remember/know (R/K) paradigm (see Chapters 1 and 9). This method requires participants to make one of three memory responses. A "remember" response indicates a vivid memory of the stimulus, complete with contextual details. A "know" response, on the other hand, indicates familiarity of the stimulus without the ability to retrieve contextual details about its original presentation. Finally, a "new" response would be given to an item not seen previously.

The authors found that sleep only offered a benefit to memory for the emotionally arousing pictures given "know" responses. In other words, participants who slept were more likely to remember the emotional than the neutral pictures on the basis of familiarity. In contrast, those who remained awake during the retention interval did not remember emotionally arousing pictures any better than neutral ones. Although there was no memory benefit for "remember" judgments in those who slept, there was an increase in conservative responding, as measured by the calculation of response bias C, within this response category only after sleep, especially for emotionally arousing pictures. This finding suggests that sleep may have increased confidence in these judgments, allowing for better differentiation of these items.

However, others have also found that an entire night of sleep is not necessary for emotional memory enhancements. For example, Nishida and colleagues (2009) found an enhancement of memory for emotional pictures after just a 90-minute nap. In their study, participants encoded separate sets of emotional and neutral IAPS pictures both four hours and 15 minutes prior to a memory test for both sets. Those in the sleep group obtained a 90-minute nap in the time between the encoding of the two lists, meaning that only the list encoded four hours prior to the test underwent a consolidation period filled with sleep in this group. The authors found that those in the nap group exhibited improved memory for the emotional pictures encoded before the nap as compared to those encoded after the nap. Those who did not nap did not show this same memory difference. Further, they found that the amount of REM obtained during the nap, along with theta activity during this stage, was positively correlated with this emotional memory improvement, supporting previous findings that suggest an important role for this specific stage on emotional memory processing for both picture and verbal stimuli (Payne, Chambers, and Kensinger, 2012; Wagner, Gais and Born, 2001).

Interestingly, sleep has also been shown to impact memory for specific components of these pictures, rather than for the images in their entirety. Payne and colleagues (2008) found this to be the case in their study, which used pictures edited to contain negative or neutral objects placed on neutral backgrounds to investigate memory for these separate components (Figure 11.6). Similar to the methods of Hu, Stylos-Allan,

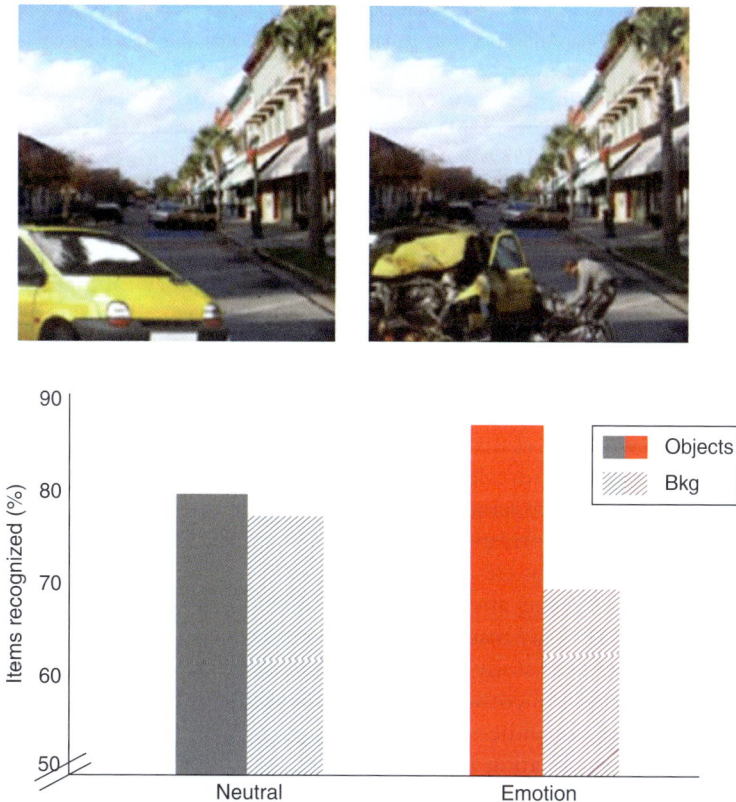

**Figure 11.6** Examples of stimuli from the trade-off task (upper panel). In the neutral example on the left, an intact car is placed on a neutral avenue background. In the negative example on the right, a wrecked car is placed on the same background. The recognition data (lower panel) show evidence of the trade-off whereby negative objects are remembered better than neutral ones, but at the expense of the memory for their backgrounds (Bkg). Source: *Current Directions in Psychological Science* (2010), 19, 292.

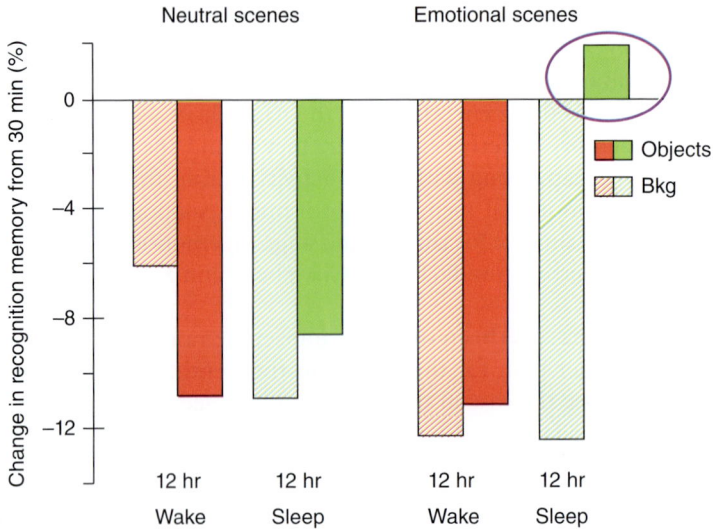

**Figure 11.7** Differences in memory performance for emotional and neutral scene components between 30-minute and 12-hour delays that spanned sleep or wake. Memory for objects and backgrounds (Bkg) generally decayed over time for both the wake and sleep groups, except for emotional objects, which were facilitated by sleep above 30-minute performance levels. Source: *Current Directions in Psychological Science* (2010), 19, 293.

and Walker (2006), participants encoded these scenes in their entirety (although a memory test was not expected in this case), and their memory for pictures was later tested after either a period of nocturnal sleep, or equivalent time of daytime wakefulness. However, contrary to the methods of Hu and colleagues, Payne *et al.* (2008) did not test memory for the pictures in their entirety. They separated the objects from their respective backgrounds and tested recognition memory for these components separately with new components intermixed (i.e., foils). Control groups tested only 30 minutes after encoding revealed that an overall trade-off occurred, whereby negative foreground objects were remembered better than neutral ones, but at the expense of the memory for their corresponding neutral backgrounds. Critically, they found that this result was actually enhanced after a period of sleep, revealing a boost in memory for negative objects above levels seen in the control groups (Figure 11.7). Conversely, a period of wake resulted in a general decay of memory for the separate components. A subsequent study revealed that this selective enhancement in memory for the negative objects was correlated with the amount of REM sleep obtained during the night (Payne, Chambers, and Kensinger, 2012). Thus, these results point toward a selective consolidation function of sleep, and REM sleep in particular, that works to pick out and enhance the most important parts of a scene. This function may have evolutionary significance, because it allows the enhancement of those emotional components of memories that might be critical to future survival, such as remembering a snake to be avoided later.

More recently, this increased memory for the emotionally salient object of the encountered scene has also been shown to correspond to changes in brain activity and connectivity. In a subsequent study, Payne and Kensinger (2011), using the same methods described above, also obtained functional magnetic resonance imaging (fMRI) scanning during retrieval testing. They found that brain activity related to successful recognition of the negative objects reflected activation of a more dispersed area of brain regions after wake, but a more limited area of activation after sleep. Furthermore, the amygdala, important for emotional processing (Hamann *et al.*, 2002), was shown to have stronger connectivity with the hippocampus and ventromedial prefrontal cortex during retrieval of these emotional objects after sleep. These results not only supplement the results of Payne *et al.* (2008) with a specific underlying neural mechanism responsible for the obtained memory enhancement, but also reveal that learning-dependent neural functioning can be greatly altered after just one night of sleep.

Other studies have further found that neural differences between sleep and wake subjects can persist as long as six months after learning. In one collection of such studies, Sterpenich and colleagues (2007, 2009) had participants encode IAPS pictures before either a night of sleep or sleep deprivation. These subjects were tested for recognition memory three days later as well as six months later while undergoing fMRI scanning. They found that after three days, those in the sleep group displayed greater activity in the hippocampus and medial prefrontal cortex than those in the wake group when recognizing emotional pictures as compared to neutral ones (Sterpenich *et al.*, 2007). At testing six months later, however, they found that this pattern of activation in response to emotional picture retrieval in the sleep group had shifted to areas of the medial frontal, parietal, and occipital cortices, as well as the amygdala (Sterpenich *et al.*, 2009). These results suggest that sleep helps to better consolidate emotional memories for long-term use by transferring them to different brain regions, and, along with the long-term memory-enhancing effect of initial sleep found by Wagner and colleagues (2006), highlight the importance of sleeping after encoding various types of emotional memories to ensure that these memories can be readily retrieved later.

## Summary

Sleeping after encoding emotional information allows this newly acquired knowledge to be better consolidated for future use. This finding has been made clear through the use of various methodologies, including early/late sleep paradigms, nap designs, brain imaging techniques, and a host of different written and picture stimuli. Contrary to the general declarative memories discussed in the previous section that were particularly aided by SWS, there is evidence that emotional memories may be supported by REM sleep, a finding likely caused by the increased activity between the emotional and memory centers of the brain during this stage (see *How the sleeping brain impacts memory*, below, for more detail). Indeed, research has revealed that sleep's positive effects on such memories have an underlying neural basis, including stronger connectivity between crucial memory structures following sleep, as well as a greater refinement of the circuitry activated when retrieving memories. However, such neural changes are not restricted to the time period immediately following sleep, but continue to progress over a period of months to years after acquisition, keeping memories strong and available for long-term use. Thus, sleeping after learning new emotional information allows the brain to better organize and consolidate this information than a comparable period of wake, allowing this information to be readily used years later when it may be crucial to our survival.

## Sleep Enhances Procedural Memories

Sleep has also been shown to enhance a variety of procedural memories. These are memories that do not require conscious thought to acquire or access, and are not easily verbalized. Through the use of an assortment of tasks, including texture discrimination, sequence learning, reaction time, and tracing tasks, it has become increasingly clear that task characteristics and individual differences impact sleep-dependent processing of this class of memory.

### Sleep and texture-discrimination performance

One of the more popular procedural tasks used in this line of research is the texture-discrimination task (Figure 11.8). In this task, participants are required to view a briefly presented image consisting of a central target letter (either T or L) and peripheral array of three diagonal bars, all placed against a background of horizontal bars (Figure 11.8a, b). This stimulus is then replaced by a mask consisting of randomly oriented Vs to replace, or "mask," the image of the stimulus on the retina (Figure 11.8c). The participant is then asked to indicate which letter was presented at the center of the original stimulus and the orientation of the diagonal bars in the periphery. Performance on this task at the end of a learning session is compared to performance after a delay, such as after sleep, to investigate improvements that occurred after this passage of time. Numerous studies have found evidence that sleep aids performance on this task (Gais *et al.*, 2000; Karni *et al.*, 1994; Stickgold *et al.*, 2000).

However, there has been some controversy as to which sleep stage may actually contribute to these gains in performance on the texture-discrimination task. Gais and colleagues (2000) combined this task with an early/late sleep paradigm to investigate the contribution of SWS or REM to performance improvements after sleep. They found that those who received "early" sleep benefited from an increase in performance on this task while those in the "late" sleep or wake groups did not. Thus, their results appear to suggest that SWS is particularly important for this task. However, Karni and colleagues (1994) used a sleep deprivation paradigm in which participants were selectively deprived of SWS or REM, or were allowed to sleep the full night, and found that REM may be important for the task. Specifically, those who were REM-deprived were significantly hindered on their ability to perform the task, while those who were

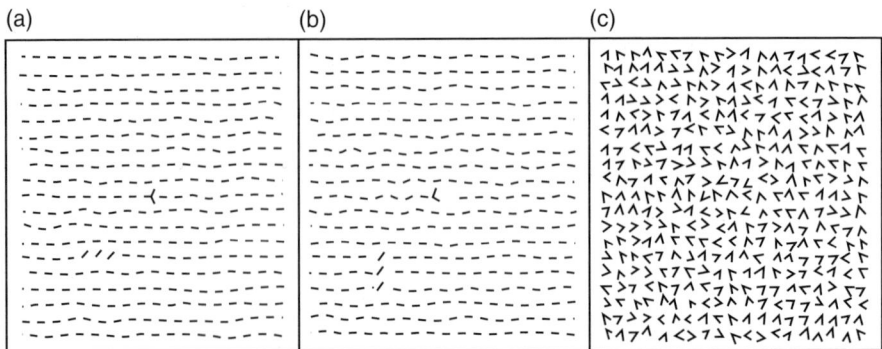

**Figure 11.8**  Examples of the texture-discrimination task stimuli. Source: Payne (2011). Reproduced with permission of Elsevier.

deprived of SWS did not experience any deficit compared to those allowed to sleep normally. Interestingly, a third study by Stickgold and colleagues (2000) provides evidence that both Gais *et al.* (2000) and Karni *et al.* (1994) may be correct. They found that improvement in this task after a night of sleep was correlated with the amount of SWS in the first quarter of the night and REM in the fourth quarter of the night, though these two measures were not correlated with each other. Similarly, using an additional group of participants in their study, Gais and colleagues (2000) found that a full night of sleep led to an improvement that was three times greater than those who obtained only "early" night sleep. Thus, it appears that both SWS and REM are important, and the key may be to have both of these in succession throughout the night for performance increases on this task (Giuditta *et al.*, 1995; Stickgold *et al.*, 2000).

## Sleep and finger-tapping performance

Another popular task for investigating how sleep affects procedural skill learning is the finger-tapping task. This widely used task requires participants to repeatedly type a sequence of five numbers on a computer keyboard using their non-dominant hand. Participants spend 30 seconds typing the sequence, followed by 30 seconds of rest. The goal is to repeat the sequence as quickly and accurately as possible during this 30-second typing block. Enhancements are explored by comparing the speed and accuracy of the sequences during training to that after a delay. Performance on this task improves after practice, but also after the simple passage of time. Many studies have found that when this delay contains sleep, performance improvements are far greater than if the delay contains a period of wake (Walker *et al.*, 2002, 2003). Further, there is evidence that the extent of the improvement seen on this task may be related to task difficulty, so that the more difficult this task is made, the more sleep appears to lead to increased performance (Kuriyama, Stickgold, and Walker, 2004).

Contrary to findings for the texture-discrimination task, improvements on the finger-tapping task after sleep are not related to REM or SWS. Instead, Walker and colleagues (2002) found that sleep-dependent improvements for this particular task were positively correlated with the amount of time spent in NREM stage 2 sleep, indicating a special role for this stage in task improvements. These sleep-dependent performance improvements are also associated with changes in neurophysiology. For example, in an fMRI study of post-sleep brain changes during the finger-tapping task, Fischer and colleagues (2005) found that after a night of sleep, retrieval was associated with decreased fMRI activity in a number of brain areas associated with the task, including the premotor and somatosensory cortices. This decrease was not seen in those who had been sleep-deprived after task acquisition. This finding suggests that task performance may become relatively more automatic after consolidation during sleep than after wake. Therefore, finger-tapping skills are enhanced by sleep, and specifically stage 2 sleep, a state that appears to impact the way in which the brain processes the execution of such a task.

## Task complexity and individual differences

As evidenced by the previously discussed studies, it is difficult to pinpoint a specific sleep stage that is implicated in procedural skill improvements. Recently, studies have investigated further why such discrepancies have been found within this class of memory. One suggestion is that the type of skill being learned may impact which sleep parameters are implicated in procedural skill improvement (Fogel and Smith, 2011; Smith, 2001). For instance, it has been documented that more complex tasks seem to benefit from REM sleep (Maquet *et al.*, 2000; Peigneux *et al.*, 2003), while simple tasks appear to benefit from stage 2 sleep (Fogel and Smith, 2006). Peigneux and colleagues (2003) trained participants on a serial reaction time task (SRTT) that required them to follow a sequence on a computer screen with matching keyboard presses as fast and accurately as possible. Unbeknownst to the participants, these sequences could either be random or possess an underlying pattern, making learning more complex. They found that brain activity in the cuneus, as measured by rCBF, increased more during REM sleep in those who had performed the SRTT with an imbedded patterned sequence than in those who had performed a random sequence. Further, these increases in brain activity were positively related to performance prior to the sleep session for those learning patterned sequences. Thus, due to the differences between those learning the complex (patterned) and simple (random) version of this sequence task, the findings point toward a role for REM sleep in processing more intricate procedural skills.

Conversely, simple procedural tasks like the finger-tapping task previously described, as well as the mirror tracing task, pursuit rotor task, and even simple games, appear to benefit from stage 2 sleep, and more specifically sleep spindle activity (a burst of oscillatory activity prominent during NREM stage 2 sleep) (Fogel and Smith, 2006; Tamaki *et al.*, 2008). In the mirror-tracing task, participants are required to trace the outline of a shape, such as a star or human figure, using only the reflection of the image provided by a mirror. Performance on this task can be assessed by quantifying the number of mistakes (deviations from the line), time spent making these mistakes, and the time it takes to trace the entire figure (Plihal and Born, 1997). Performance on this task is particularly promoted by a period of post-learning sleep (Plihal and Born, 1997).

Using the mirror-tracing task, Tamaki and collegues (2008) compared sleep spindles during a night of sleep following training with those during a night that did not follow training. They found that sleep spindles had higher amplitudes and duration after the training session as compared to the non-training condition, but only for fast spindle activity in the 13–16 Hz range occurring over posterior sites. Further, there was a positive relationship between performance improvements seen after sleep and the duration, density, and amplitude of these fast spindles during the post-learning night. Such relationships were not found for slow spindle activity in the 10–13 Hz range occurring over anterior sites. These results suggest that acquiring this simple mirror-tracing skill is related to sleep spindle activity, and particularly fast spindle activity. Likewise, Fogel and Smith (2006) found that after training on four simple tasks including the pursuit rotor task (described below), a simple tracing task, the ball-and-cup game, and Operation, participants received more stage 2 sleep as well as an increased amount and density of sleep spindles. These increases were accompanied by improved post-sleep performance on all but the tracing task. Together, these studies provide evidence for an important contribution of stage 2 and sleep spindles to learning simple procedural skills.

Along with skill complexity, another factor that appears to impact how sleep influences procedural performance is the initial ability of the learner (Fogel and Smith, 2011; Peters, Smith, and Smith, 2007). After a baseline night of sleep, Peters and colleagues (2007) trained participants on the pursuit rotor task, which requires the learner to use a stylus to follow or "pursue" a target as it moves quickly around a rectangle. Performance is measured by how long participants are able to accurately track the target. Sleep was then monitored during the following night and performance was tested on the same task one week later. Using performance during the training phase of the task, the authors split the participants based on ability so that there were low- and high-performance groups. They found that for those in the high-performance group, density of sleep spindles increased in the night after training and this was related to retest performance. However, for the low-performance group, it was the change in REM density from the pre- to post-training night that was related to subsequent retest performance. Thus, these findings suggest that individual differences in initial task ability may impact what feature of sleep is related to increasing performance, with REM acting to increase weak skills whereas sleep spindles work to improve skills that are already well developed.

## Summary

It is clear that sleep positively impacts procedural memory. However, while previous sections were able to converge on a particular sleep stage that could be responsible for memory improvements, procedural memories have not allowed such a clear-cut finding. This complexity is because sleep's effects on learning depend upon a number of factors, such as the type of task being performed and the pre-existing skills of the learner. The former is exemplified by evidence that learning an intricate task is improved by REM, while stage 2 sleep and related sleep spindles have been implicated in learning simple tasks. Evidence for the latter has been supplied by studies showing that REM sleep is related to improvement of poor performers while stage 2 is related to improvement of high performers. Thus, it is obvious that procedural memories are benefited by sleep after learning, but the way sleep aids such memories depends on the situation that surrounds learning.

# How the Sleeping Brain Impacts Memory

Based upon the studies discussed in the previous sections, it is clear that sleep does have a strong influence on memory, but the question still remains of exactly *how* such a marked impact on various memory systems is afforded by sleep. While the answer to this question is not yet known, a number of mechanisms likely work in tandem to create the effects seen in the aforementioned studies. These studies pointed toward the contribution of specific sleep stages to memory improvements. However, it is important to note that this may be an oversimplification of how exactly sleep has its impact on memory. There are a number of unique physiological processes occurring during different sleep stages which may better account for these effects, including varying activation patterns, electrophysiological signatures, and neurochemical composition of the brain.

## Brain activation during sleep

A variety of positron emission tomography (PET) studies have investigated rCBF during various stages of sleep and wake, and have found drastic differences in brain activation profiles between these states. One such study had participants sleep in a PET scanner to compare rCBF during wake, SWS, and REM sleep (Braun *et al.*, 1997). They found that during SWS there was an overall deactivation of the brain compared to wakefulness, including areas of the midbrain, limbic areas, and higher cortical areas such as the dorsolateral prefrontal cortex (dlPFC). In contrast, during REM sleep there were increases in general brain activation over that seen in SWS. Specifically, these increases were evident in the brainstem, basal ganglia, hippocampus, and nearby limbic areas, as well as in cortical areas. Interestingly, these levels were comparable to, or even greater than, levels seen during wakefulness. Others have corroborated this evidence for increased activity of such structures during REM, especially for the amygdala, hippocampus, and cortex. Indeed, this activation pattern may underlie REM sleep's role in emotional memory enhancements, as these regions are important for processing such memories (Maquet *et al.*, 1996). Further, there is a common finding among these studies that the activity of the executive processes associated with dlPFC is reduced in REM sleep, which may, in conjunction with increased activity of the emotional regions of the brain, contribute to the peculiar, disjointed, and emotional content of dreams (Braun *et al.*, 1997; Maquet *et al.*, 1996; Stickgold *et al.*, 2001).

## The electrophysiology of sleep

Just as there are different neural activation profiles associated with different stages of sleep, so too are there different neural electrical signals which distinguish one stage of sleep from another, and these unique characteristics may hold an important key for each stage's impact on memory. For instance, SWS is associated with an assortment of specific electrophysiological characteristics arising both from cortical structures and from the hippocampus. These features include slow, low-frequency (0.8 Hz) EEG activity known as slow oscillations, higher-frequency (12–15 Hz) sleep spindles, and extremely high-frequency (200 Hz) bursts of activity within the hippocampus known as sharp wave ripples (De Gennaro and Ferrara, 2003; Siapas and Wilson, 1998; Steriade, Nunez, and Amzica, 1993). All of these signatures have been implicated in learning. For example, sleep spindles have been implicated in assimilating new and old information (Tamminen *et al.*, 2010) and have been proposed to play a role in long-term potentiation (LTP), a process of brain plasticity thought to be important for learning (Rosanova and Ulrich, 2005). Additionally, slow oscillations have been suggested to power sleep-dependent hippocampal reactivation of memories that gradually transfer these traces to cortical long-term storage (Wagner and Born, 2008). Further, both slow oscillation amplitude and sleep spindles have been seen to increase during sleep following a period of learning, for both declarative (Gais *et al.*, 2002; Mölle *et al.*, 2009) and procedural tasks (Fogel and Smith, 2006; Huber *et al.*, 2004). Thus, these unique features of SWS, instead of SWS as a whole, could be responsible for a variety of memory enhancements, likely by working to transfer information into long-term storage (Born and Wilhelm, 2012).

Similar to SWS, key electrophysiological characteristics of REM can also be identified that may be sufficient for memory enhancements. For instance, evidence has begun to point toward an important role for REM theta EEG rhythms (4–7 Hz) in memory improvements for a variety of tasks (Fogel, Smith, and Cote, 2007; Jones and Wilson, 2005; Nishida *et al.*, 2009). Specifically, Fogel, Smith, and Cote (2007) had participants train on a word-associates task for a later memory test before undergoing a night of PSG-recorded sleep. A week later, participants again trained and were tested on the word pairs learned during the first session. The authors found participants to exhibit increased theta rhythms during REM after learning the word pairs as compared to a baseline night in which no learning took place. Further, the authors found that

REM sigma rhythms (12–16 Hz) were also increased after learning. Although REM is typically related to emotional and procedural memory, the contribution of such REM signatures to this declarative task highlights the importance of looking beyond simple sleep stages to the mechanisms that may be driving these effects. Theta in particular has been previously implicated in hippocampal LTP (Larson, Wong, and Lynch, 1986) and thus may provide a more specific sleep-dependent mechanism for memory formation at the neural level, as opposed to attributing memory effects to a broad sleep stage per se. This feature of REM has also been related to other hippocampus-dependent memories, such as those involving emotional content (Nishida *et al.*, 2009) and spatial learning tasks (Jones and Wilson, 2005).

## Changes in neurochemicals during sleep

It has further been suggested that the chemical milieu of the sleeping brain may have an extensive impact on how the brain processes information during sleep. NREM and REM sleep can be differentiated by their varying profiles of neurotransmitter and neuro-hormone composition. For example, while NREM sleep is characterized by reductions in aminergic (norepinephrine, NE; serotonin, 5-HT) and cholinergic (acetylcholine, ACh) inputs from waking levels, REM sleep exhibits an even further reduction in amin-ergic tone, but an increase in ACh that is near or above levels seen at waking (Stickgold *et al.*, 2001). Critically, some of these neurochemicals have been explicitly implicated in declarative memory enhancements. For example, when levels of ACh are experimentally increased during "early" sleep dominated by SWS, the typical performance enhance-ments on a word-associates tasks observed after this portion of the night are diminished (Gais and Born, 2004). Alternatively, elevated ACh has been shown to play an important facilitative role in emotional memory formation, especially because of its interaction with the amygdala (McGaugh, 2004). These features of ACh may explain why SWS appears to aid declarative memory when ACh levels are low, and REM appears to aid emotional memories when ACh levels are high.

Further, the glucocorticoid cortisol, a stress hormone arising from the activation of the hypothalamic–pituitary–adrenal (HPA) axis, has been shown to display significant circadian variation and has been implicated in memory processing. Specifically, although excessive elevations of cortisol hinder both LTP and declarative memory, moderate elevations enhance LTP and declarative memory (de Kloet, Oitzl, and Joëls, 1999; Payne *et al.*, 2004). Further, receptors for this hormone are densely located within the hippocampus, which serves as an important element of the negative feedback loop for the HPA axis (de Kloet, Oitzl, and Joëls, 1999; Sapolsky, 2004). Cortisol is lowest in the beginning of the night when SWS is more prevalent, but increases occur throughout the night with peaks that track periods of REM until it is at its highest upon awakening (Dallman, Bhatnagar, and Viau, 2000; Fries, Dettenborn, and Kirschbaum, 2009; Wagner and Born, 2008).

Not surprisingly, cortisol has been found to have a significant interaction with sleep-dependent learning. For example, Plihal and Born (1999b) found that increasing cortisol levels during the early SWS-dominated portion of the night led to performance impairments on a subsequent word-associates memory test, but not a mirror-tracing test. These results are crucial for understanding how sleep can optimize memory via cortisol. A low glucocorticoid environment, such as that observed during SWS, appears to be necessary for enhancements of declarative memories that rely on the hippocampus, like the word associates task. Conversely, procedural memories that are independent of the hippocampus, like the mirror-tracing task, are unaffected by glucocorticoids and can thus be optimized without difficulty under the elevated cortisol concentrations of REM sleep. This finding provides yet another example of the way physiological characteristics of the sleeping brain, as opposed to specific stages of sleep per se, can give rise to memory enhancements. However, it is important not to overly attribute such enhancements to any one of the physiological features discussed, as they likely all work concurrently to provide the optimal processing atmosphere for various memory systems at different phases of sleep.

## Summary

Many studies show a relationship between memory enhancements and specific stages of sleep. However, as described in this section, there are numerous neural events occurring in tandem with such stages that also affect memory performance. For example, effects of REM sleep on memory could be caused by a multitude of the changes seen in brain physiology during this stage, including increases in activation of pertinent brain structures, theta rhythms, ACh, and cortisol. Similarly, the brain structure deactivations, slow oscillations, spindles, sharp wave ripples, decreases in ACh, or decreases in cortisol seen during SWS could individually or collectively have an impact on the memory enhancements found to be related to SWS. Thus, while findings from the sleep and memory literature often point toward an entire stage of sleep as having a relationship to memory improvements, it is also important to consider the neural mechanisms associated with these stages that may be more directly involved in memory consolidation.

## Conclusions

Sleep plays a critical role in memory processing. The dynamic environment of the sleeping brain provides the means necessary for enhancing a variety of different memory systems, including declarative, procedural, and emotional memories. While SWS has been largely associated with declarative memory performance and REM sleep has been related to improvements in procedural and emotional memory domains, there are also many learning tasks that do not fit such a mold. Further, it is also important to remember that many of the mentioned memory enhancements may be the result of the neural environment, including the physical, electrical, and chemical aspects of the sleeping brain that generate and underlie these dynamic stages of sleep. Although there is still much to learn about why we spend a third of our lives in such a vulnerable state, it seems very clear that sleep is critical for memory and learning.

## References

Barbera, J. (2008). Sleep and dreaming in Greek and Roman philosophy. *Sleep Medicine*, 9 (8), 906–910. doi: 10.1016/j.sleep.2007.10.010.

Born, J., and Wilhelm, I. (2012). System consolidation of memory during sleep. *Psychological Research*, 76 (2), 192–203. doi: 10.1007/s00426-011-0335-6.

Braun, A.R., Balkin, T.J., Wesenten, N.J., *et al.* (1997). Regional cerebral blood flow throughout the sleep–wake cycle: an $H_2^{15}O$ PET study. *Brain*, 120 (7), 1173–1197. doi: 10.1093/brain/120.7.1173

Carskadon, M.A., and Dement, W.C. (1989). Normal human sleep: an overview. In *Principles and Practice of Sleep Medicine* (ed. M.H. Kryger, T. Roth, and W.C. Dement). Philadelphia: W.B. Saunders, pp. 3–13.

Corkin, S. (1968). Acquisition of motor skill after bilateral medial temporal-lobe excision. *Neuropsychologia*, 6 (3), 255–265. doi: 10.1016/0028-3932(68)90024-9.

Dallman, M.F., Bhatnagar, S., and Viau, V. (2000). Hypothalamo-pituitary adrenal axis. In *Encyclopedia of Stress* (ed. G. Fink). San Diego: Academic Press, pp. 468–477.

De Gennaro, L., and Ferrara, M. (2003). Sleep spindles: an overview. *Sleep Medicine Reviews*, 7 (5), 423–440. doi: 10.1053/smrv.2002.0252.

de Kloet, E.R., Oitzl, M.S., and Joëls, M. (1999). Stress and cognition: are corticosteroids good or bad guys? *Trends in Neurosciences*, 22 (10), 422–426. doi: 10.1016/S0166-2236(99)01438-1.

Dement, W.C., and Vaughan, C. (2000). *The Promise of Sleep: A Pioneer in Sleep Medicine Explores the Vital Connection Between Health Happiness and a Good Night's Sleep*. New York, NY: Random House.

Ebbinghaus, H. (1885). *Über das Gedächtnis: Untersuchungen zur experimentellen Psychologie*. Leipzig: Duncker & Humblot.

Ellenbogen, J.M., Payne, J.D., and Stickgold, R.R. (2006). The role of sleep in declarative memory consolidation: passive, permissive, active or none? *Current Opinion in Neurobiology*, 16 (6), 716–722. doi: 10.1016/j.conb.2006.10.006.

Fischer, S., Nitschke, M.F., Melchert, U.H., *et al.* (2005). Motor memory consolidation in sleep shapes more effective neuronal representations. *Journal of Neuroscience*, 25 (49), 11248–11255. doi: 10.1523/JNEUROSCI.1743-05.2005.

Fogel, S.M., and Smith, C.T. (2006). Learning-dependent changes in sleep spindles and stage 2 sleep. *Journal of Sleep Research*, 15 (3), 250–255. doi: 10.1111/j.1365-2869.2006.00522.x.

Fogel, S.M., and Smith, C.T. (2011). The function of the sleep spindle: a physiological index of intelligence and a mechanism for sleep-dependent memory consolidation. *Neuroscience and Behavioral Reviews*, 35 (5), 1154–1165. doi: 10.1016/j.neubiorev.2010.12.003.

Fogel, S.M., Smith, C.T., and Cote, K.A. (2007). Dissociable learning-dependent changes in REM and non-REM sleep in declarative and procedural memory systems. *Behavioural Brain Research*, 180 (1), 48–61. doi: 10.1016/j.bbr.2007.02.037.

Fries, E., Dettenborn, L., and Kirschbaum, C. (2009). The cortisol awakening response (CAR): facts and future directions. *International Journal of Psychophysiology*, 72 (1), 67–73. doi: 10.1016/j.ijpsycho.2008.03.014.

Gais, S., and Born, J. (2004). Declarative memory consolidation: mechanisms acting during human sleep. *Learning and Memory*, 11 (6), 679–685. doi: 10.1101/lm.80504.

Gais, S., Mölle, M., Helms, K., and Born, J. (2002). Learning-dependent increases in sleep spindle density. *Journal of Neuroscience*, 22 (15), 6830–6834. doi: 0270-6474/02/226830-05$15.00/0.

Gais, S., Plihal, W., Wagner, U., and Born, J. (2000). Early sleep triggers memory for early visual discrimination skills. *Nature Neuroscience*, 3 (12), 1335–1339.

Giuditta, A., Ambrosini, M.V., Montagnese, P., *et al.* (1995). The sequential hypothesis of the function of sleep. *Behavioural Brain Research*, 69 (1), 157–166. doi: 10.1016/0166-4328(95)00012-I.

Hamann, S. (2001). Cognitive and neural mechanisms of emotional memory. *Trends in Cognitive Sciences*, 5 (9), 394–400. doi: 10.1016/S1364-6613(00)01707-1.

Hamann, S.B., Ely, T.D., Hoffman, J.M., and Kilts, C.D. (2002). Ecstasy and agony: activation of human amygdala in positive and negative emotion. *Psychological Science*, 13 (2), 135–141. doi: 10.1111/1467-9280.00425.

Heine, R. (1914). Über Wiedererkennen und rückwirkende Hemmung. *Zeitschrift für Psychologie mit Zeitschrift für angewandte Psychologie* 68, 161–236.

Hu, P., Stylos-Allan, M., and Walker, M.P. (2006). Sleep facilitates consolidation of emotional declarative memory. *Psychological Science*, 17 (10), 891–898. doi: 10.1111/j.1467-9280.2006.01799.x.

Huber, R., Ghilardi, M.F., Massimini, M., and Tononi, G. (2004). Local sleep and learning. *Nature*, 430 (6995), 78–81. doi: 10.1038/nature02663.

Iber, C., Ancoli-Israel, S., Chesson, A.L., and Quan, S.F., eds. (2007). *The AASM Manual for the Scoring of Sleep and Associated Events: Rules, Terminology, and Technical Specifications.* Westchester, IL: American Academy of Sleep Medicine.

Jenkins, J.G. and Dallenbach, K.M. (1924). Obliviscence during sleep and waking. *American Journal of Psychology*, 35 (4), 605–612. doi: 10.2307/1414040.

Jones, M.W., and Wilson, M.A. (2005). Phase precession of medial prefrontal cortical activity relative to the hippocampal theta rhythm. *Hippocampus*, 15 (7), 867–873. doi: 10.1002/hipo.20119.

Karni, A., Tanne, D., Rubenstein, B.S., *et al.* (1994). Dependence on REM sleep of overnight improvement of a perceptual skill. *Science*, 265 (5172), 679–682. doi: 10.1126/science.8036518.

Kensinger, E.A. (2009). Phases of influence: how emotion modulates the formation and retrieval of declarative memories. In *The Cognitive Neurosciences*, 4th edn (ed. M.S. Gazzaniga). Cambridge, MA: MIT Press, pp. 725–737.

Kensinger, E.A., and Schacter, D.L. (2006). Amygdala activity is associated with the successful encoding of item, but not source, information for positive and negative stimuli. *Journal of Neuroscience*, 26 (9), 2564–2570. doi: 10.1523/JNEUROSCI.5241-05.2006.

Kuriyama, K., Stickgold, R., and Walker, M.P. (2004). Sleep-dependent learning and motor-skill complexity. *Learning and Memory*, 11 (6), 705–713. doi: 10.1101/lm.76304.

Lahl, O., Wispel, C., Willigens, B., and Pietrowsky, R. (2008). An ultra short episode of sleep is sufficient to promote declarative memory performance. *Journal of Sleep Research*, 17 (1), 3–10. doi: 10.1111/j.1365-2869.2008.00622.x.

Lang, A., Dhillon, K., and Dong, Q. (1995). The effects of emotional arousal and valence on television viewers' cognitive capacity and memory. *Journal of Broadcasting and Electronic Media*, 39 (9), 313–327.

Lang, P.J., Bradley, M.M., and Cuthbert, B.N. (2008). *International Affective Picture System (IAPS): Affective Ratings of Pictures and Instruction Manual, Technical Report A-8.* Gainesville, FL: University of Florida.

Larson, J., Wong, D., and Lynch, G. (1986). Patterned stimulation at the theta frequency is optimal for the induction of hippocampal long-term potentiation. *Brain Research*, 368 (2), 347–350. doi: 10.1016/0006-8993(86)90579-2.

Maquet, P., Laureys, S., Peigneux, P., *et al.* (2000). Experience-dependent changes in cerebral activation during human REM sleep. *Nature Neuroscience*, 3 (8), 831–836. doi: 10.1038/77744.

Maquet, P., Peters, J.M., Aerts, J., *et al.* (1996). Functional neuroanatomy of human rapid-eye-movement sleep and dreaming. *Nature*, 383 (6596), 163–166. doi: 10.1038/383163a0.

McGaugh, J.L. (2004). The amygdala modulates the consolidation of memories of emotionally arousing experiences. *Annual Review of Neuroscience*, 27, 1–28. doi: 10.1146/annurev.neuro.27.070203.144157.

Mölle, M., Eschenko, O., Gais, S., *et al.* (2009). The influence of learning on sleep slow oscillations and associated spindles and ripples in humans and rats. *European Journal of Neuroscience*, 29 (5), 1071–1081. doi: 10.1111/j.1460-9568.2009.06654.x.

Moscovitch, M., Rosenbaum. R.S., Gilboa, A., *et al.* (2005). Functional neuroanatomy of remote episodic, semantic and spatial memory: a unified account based on multiple trace theory. *Journal of Anatomy*, 207 (1), 35–66. doi: 10.1111/j.1469-7580.2005.00421.x.

Nishida, M., Pearsall, J., Buckner, R.L., and Walker, M.P. (2009). REM sleep, prefrontal theta, and the consolidation of human emotional memory. *Cerebral Cortex*, 19 (5), 1158–1166. doi: 10.1093/cercor/bhn155.

Ochsner, K.N. (2000). Are affective events richly recollected or simply familiar? The experience and process of recognizing feelings past. *Journal of Experimental Psychology: General*, 129 (2), 242–261. doi: 10.1037//0096-3445.129.2.242.

Payne, J.D. (2011). Learning, memory, and sleep in humans. *Sleep Medicine Clinics*, 6 (1), 15–30. doi: 10.1016/j.jsmc.2010.12.005.

Payne, J.D., Chambers, A.M., and Kensinger, E.A. (2012). Sleep promotes lasting changes in selective memory for emotional scenes. *Frontiers in Integrative Neuroscience*, 6, 108. doi: 10.3389/fnint.2012.00108

Payne, J.D., and Kensinger, E.A. (2010). Sleep's role in the consolidation of emotional episodic memories. *Current Directions in Psychological Science*, 19 (5), 290–295. doi: 10.1177/0963721410383978.

Payne, J.D., and Kensinger, E.A. (2011). Sleep leads to changes in the emotional memory trace: evidence from fMRI. *Journal of Cognitive Neuroscience*, 23 (6), 1285–1297. doi: 10.1162/jocn.2010.21526.

Payne, J.D., Nadel, L., Britton, W.B., and Jacobs, W.J. (2004). The biopsychology of trauma and memory. In *Memory and Emotion* (ed. D. Reisberg and P. Hertel). New York, NY: Oxford University Press, pp. 76–128.

Payne, J.D., Stickgold, R., Swanberg, K., and Kensinger, E.A. (2008). Sleep preferentially enhances memory for emotional components of scenes. *Psychological Science*, 19 (8), 781–788. doi: 10.1111/j.1467-9280.2008.02157.x.

Payne, J.D., Tucker, M.A., Ellenbogen, J.M., *et al.* (2012). Memory for semantically related and unrelated declarative information: the benefit of sleep, the cost of wake. *PLoS ONE*, 7 (3), e33079. doi: 10.1371/journal.pone.0033079.

Peigneux, P., Laureys, S., Fuchs, S., *et al.* (2003). Learned material content and acquisition level modulate cerebral reactivation during posttraining rapid-eye-movements sleep. *NeuroImage*, 20 (1), 125–134. doi: 10.1016/S1053-8119(03)00278-7.

Peigneux, P., Laureys, S., Fuchs, S., *et al.* (2004). Are spatial memories strengthened in the human hippocampus during slow wave sleep? *Neuron*, 44 (3), 535–545. doi: 10.1016/j.neuron.2004.10.007.

Peters, K.R., Smith, V., and Smith, C.T. (2007). Changes in sleep architecture following motor learning depend on initial skill level. *Journal of Cognitive Neuroscience*, 19 (5), 817–829. doi: 10.1162/jocn.2007.19.5.817.

Plihal, W., and Born, J. (1997). Effects of early and late nocturnal sleep on declarative and procedural memory. *Journal of Cognitive Neuroscience*, 9 (4), 534. doi: 10.1162/jocn.1997.9.4.534.

Plihal, W., and Born, J. (1999a). Effects of early and late nocturnal sleep on priming and spatial memory. *Psychophysiology*, 36 (5), 571–582. doi: 10.1017/S0048577299971536.

Plihal, W., and Born, J. (1999b). Memory consolidation in human sleep depends on inhibition of glucocorticoid release. *Neuroreport*, 10 (13), 2741–2747. doi: 10.1097/00001756-19 9909090-00009.

Rasch, B., Buchel, C., Gais, S., and Born, J. (2007). Odor cues during slow-wave sleep prompt declarative memory consolidation. *Science*, 315 (5817), 1426–1429. doi: 10.1126/science.1138581.

Rosanova, M., and Ulrich, D. (2005). Pattern-specific associative long-term potentiation induced by a sleep spindle-related spike train. *Journal of Neuroscience*, 25 (41), 9398–9405. doi: 10.1523/JNEUROSCI.2149-05.2005.

Sapolsky, R.M. (2004). Stressed-out memories. *Scientific American Mind*, 14, 28–33.

Schacter, D.L. (1987). Implicit memory: history and current status. *Journal of Experimental Psychology: Learning, Memory, and Cognition*, 13, 501–518. doi: 10.1037//0278-7393.13.3.501.

Scoville, W.B., and Milner, B. (1957). Loss of recent memory after bilateral hippocampal lesions. *Journal of Neurology, Neurosurgery, and Psychiatry,* 20 (1), 11–21. doi: 10.1136/jnnp.20.1.11.

Siapas, A.G., and Wilson, M.A. (1998). Coordinated interactions between hippocampal ripples and cortical spindles during slow-wave sleep. *Neuron,* 21 (5), 1123–1128. doi: 10.1016/S0896-6273(00)80629-7.

Smith, C. (2001). Sleep states and memory processes in humans: procedural versus declarative memory systems. *Sleep Medicine Reviews,* 5 (6), 491–506. doi: 10.1053/smrv.2001.0164.

Squire, L.R. (1986). Mechanisms of memory. *Science,* 232 (4758), 1612–1619. doi: 10.1126/science.3086978.

Steriade, M., Nunez, A., and Amzica, F. (1993). A novel slow (<1 Hz) oscillation of neocortical neurons in vivo: depolarizing and hyperpolarizing components. *Journal of Neuroscience,* 13 (8), 3252–3265.

Sterpenich, V., Albouy, G., Boly, M., *et al.* (2007). Sleep related hippocampo-cortical interplay during emotional memory recollection. *PLoS Biology,* 5 (11), e282. doi: 10.1371/journal.pbio.0050282.

Sterpenich, V., Albouy, G., Darsaud, A., *et al.* (2009). Sleep promotes the neural reorganization of remote emotional memory. *Journal of Neuroscience,* 29 (16), 5143–5152. doi: 10.1523/JNEUROSCI.0561-09.2009.

Stickgold, R. (2005). Sleep-dependent memory consolidation. *Nature,* 437 (7063), 1272–1278. doi: 10.1038/nature04286.

Stickgold, R., Hobson, J.A., Fosse, R., and Fosse, M. (2001). Sleep, learning, and dreams: off-line memory reprocessing. *Science,* 294 (5544), 1052–1057. doi: 10.1126/science.1063530.

Stickgold, R., Whidbee, D., Schirmer, B., *et al.* (2000). Visual discrimination task improvement: a multi-step process occurring during sleep. *Journal of Cognitive Neuroscience,* 12 (2), 246–254. doi: 10.1162/089892900562075.

Takashima, A., Petersson, K.M., Rutters, F., *et al.* (2006). Declarative memory consolidation in humans: a prospective functional magnetic resonance imaging study. *Proceedings of the National Academy of Sciences of the USA,* 103 (3), 756–761. doi: 10.1073/pnas.0507774103.

Talamini, L.M., Nieuwenhuis, I.L.C., Takashima, A., and Jensen, O. (2008). Sleep directly following learning benefits consolidation of spatial associative memory. *Learning and Memory,* 15 (4), 233–237. doi: 10.1101/lm.771608.

Tamaki, M., Matsuoka, T., Nittono, H., and Hori, T. (2008). Fast sleep spindle (13–15 Hz) activity correlates with sleep-dependent improvement in visuomotor performance. *Sleep,* 31 (2), 204–211.

Tamminen, J., Payne, J.D., Stickgold, R., *et al.* (2010). Sleep spindle activity is associated with the integration of new memories and existing knowledge. *Journal of Neuroscience,* 30 (43), 14356–14360. doi: 10.1523/JNEUROSCI.3028-10.2010.

Tucker, M.A., Hirota, Y., Wamsley, E.J., *et al.* (2006). A Daytime nap containing solely non-REM sleep enhances declarative but not procedural memory. *Neurobiology of Learning and Memory,* 86 (2), 241–247. doi: 10.1016/j.nlm.2006.03.005.

Van Ormer, E.B. (1933). Sleep and retention. *Psychological Bulletin,* 30 (6), 415–439. doi: 10.1037/h0071478.

Wagner, U., and Born, J. (2008). Memory consolidation during sleep: interactive effects of sleep stages and HPA regulation. *Stress,* 11 (1), 28–41. doi: 10.1080/10253890701408822.

Wagner, U., Gais, S. and Born, J. (2001). Emotional memory formation is enhanced across sleep intervals with high amounts of rapid eye movement sleep. *Learning and Memory,* 8 (2), 112–119. doi: 10.1101/lm.36801.

Wagner, U., Hallschmid, M., Rasch, B., and Born, J. (2006). Brief sleep after learning keeps emotional memories alive for years. *Biological Psychiatry,* 60 (7), 788–790. doi: 10.1016/j.biopsych.2006.03.061.

Walker, M.P., Brakefield, T., Morgan, A., *et al.* (2002). Practice with sleep makes perfect: sleep-dependent motor skill learning. *Neuron*, 35 (1), 205–211. doi: 10.1016/S0896-6273(02)00746-8.

Walker, M.P., Brakefield, T., Seidman, J., *et al.* (2003). Sleep and the time course of motor skill learning. *Learning and Memory*, 10 (4), 275–284. doi: 10.1101/lm.58503.

Walker, M.P., and Stickgold, R. (2006). Sleep, memory, and plasticity. *Annual Review of Psychology*, 57, 139–166. doi: 10.1146/annurev.psych.56.091103.070307.

Wixted, J.T. (2004). The psychology and neuroscience of forgetting. *Annual Review of Psychology*, 55, 235–269. doi: 10.1146/annurev.psych.55.090902.141555.

# 12

# Memory Reconsolidation

## Almut Hupbach, Rebecca Gomez, and Lynn Nadel

## Introduction

Memory reconsolidation, in contrast to its older relative, memory consolidation, has only recently emerged as a topic of interest in neuroscience. Both refer to stabilization processes, with consolidation referring to the initial fixation of a memory, and reconsolidation referring to the re-fixation of a reactivated memory. Reconsolidation, though utilizing some of the same cellular and molecular mechanisms, is not just a recapitulation of memory consolidation. Most of the work on consolidation and reconsolidation has been conducted in animals (mainly rats), and the study of human memory reconsolidation, which is the focus of the chapter, is still in its early stages. We start with a brief introduction to consolidation, followed by a description of animal studies on reconsolidation, before outlining in detail what we know about the conditions triggering modification of established long-term memories in humans. We end with a discussion of what we consider important avenues for future studies of human memory reconsolidation.

## Memory Consolidation

Over 100 years ago, Müller and Pilzecker (1900) presented the first set of systematic empirical studies on post-encoding memory stabilization processes. They showed that shortly after initial acquisition, memories are easily disrupted by the presentation and encoding of new information, but that over time, memories become increasingly less vulnerable to retroactive interference. They concluded that the encoding of a memory initiates a gradual memory stabilization process, a process they labeled *memory consolidation*. Since its original introduction, memory consolidation has been extensively researched, especially in animal models, and we now know a great deal about its cellular and molecular underpinnings, its behavioral consequences, and agents than can impair and enhance it (for a review, see Dudai, 2004). Critically, memory consolidation depends on the synthesis of new proteins. If protein synthesis is inhibited, the long-term storage of memories is impaired. Inherent in the consolidation notion is the idea that as time progresses, a memory becomes increasingly stable until it is no

*The Wiley Handbook on the Cognitive Neuroscience of Memory*, First Edition.
Edited by Donna Rose Addis, Morgan Barense, and Audrey Duarte.

longer susceptible to amnesic or memory-enhancing agents. At this time, the memory is considered to be fixed, or in other words, consolidated. On this view, any failure to recall a memory after the consolidation window has closed must reflect a retrieval difficulty.

## Retrieval-Induced Amnesia and the Case for Reconsolidation

Over the years, several investigators have questioned this one-time, post-acquisition window for memory "fixation," and have argued on theoretical and empirical grounds that memory consolidation is not a process that is specific to the initial formation of a memory, but that instead, every time a memory is retrieved, it re-enters a vulnerable state requiring restabilization for the memory to survive (for excellent reviews of the history of consolidation and reconsolidation research, see Dudai, 2004; Riccio, Millin, and Bogart, 2006). Indeed, according to Spear and Mueller (1984, p. 114):

> the term "consolidation" has been used conventionally in reference to the acquisition, input, initial storage, and learning of new associations, memories, episodes, and so forth. We shall argue that a similar or identical process can be anticipated to operate whenever a memory is retrieved, or, more generally, made active.

Empirically, Misanin, Miller, and Lewis (1968) showed that in rats, electroconvulsive shock (ECS) administered 24 hours after Pavlovian fear conditioning caused fear memory loss when the ECS was preceded by a brief exposure to the conditioned stimulus (CS+), presumably because the CS exposure had made the memory active. Importantly, this amnesic effect was similar to the one observed when ECS was given immediately after original fear conditioning (see Lewis, Bregman, and Mahan, 1972, for similar effects in an appetitive memory task). Notwithstanding these early demonstrations of reactivation-induced memory instability, very little attention was given to these effects for 25 years. They were reintroduced in a study aimed at shedding light on the cellular events underlying reconsolidation (Przybyslawski and Sara, 1997). The glutamate receptor subtype N-methyl-D-aspartate (NMDA) is critically involved in triggering long-term synaptic changes underlying memory formation. Przybyslawski and Sara demonstrated that reactivation of a well-established spatial memory made it NMDA-dependent once again. When rats were systemically injected with the NMDA-receptor antagonist MK-801 immediately following a retrieval trial, and memory was tested 24 hours later, performance was significantly impaired. Importantly, there was a temporal gradient of memory vulnerability post reactivation. If the injection was administered two or more hours after retrieval, instead of immediately, performance was unaffected. This study provided evidence that retrieval reintroduces vulnerability to a memory, and that this vulnerability, much like the fragility of a memory during consolidation, is time-limited. To our knowledge, Przybyslawski and Sara were the first to use the term *memory reconsolidation* to describe their empirical findings.

It was not until three years later that the concept of reconsolidation made a breakthrough in the neuroscience community more broadly, and it has been the subject of attention and intense debate ever since. In 2000, Sara (2000a, 2000b) published two theoretical papers on reconsolidation, and Nader, Schafe, and LeDoux (2000) reported an empirical study in *Nature* that captured the interest of many neuroscientists.

What made their study special is that instead of using systemic NMDA injections, Nader *et al.* directly injected the protein-synthesis inhibitor anisomycin into the basolateral nuclei of the amygdala after retrieval of a fear memory. Specifically, rats initially received a pairing of a tone and a foot shock. Twenty-four hours later, half of the animals were again exposed to the tone, which elicited freezing (i.e., a conditioned fear response) and thus acted as a reminder. Immediately after the tone, rats received injections of anisomycin or a vehicle into the basolateral amygdala. Twenty-four hours later rats that had received the anisomycin injection showed less freezing than the vehicle-injected rats, and, importantly, less freezing than rats that had not been exposed to the reminder tone before the drug was given. Nader *et al.* also confirmed Przybyslawski and Sara's (1997) earlier finding of a temporal gradient of reconsolidation. Injection of anisomycin had no detrimental effects on memory when given six hours after reactivation of the fear memory. Nader *et al.* thus showed that reactivation of the fear memory returned it to a state of transient fragility requiring de-novo protein synthesis for restabilization in the basolateral amygdala.

## Reconsolidation and a Recovered Memory Model

Why has the demonstration of retrieval-induced fragility of a supposedly consolidated memory trace been so revolutionary? Such findings seem to contradict a major tenet of the consolidation theory: the idea that memories, once consolidated, should be immune to subsequent disruption. Reconsolidation implies a more dynamic view of memory, one in which the vulnerability of a trace is determined less by the age of the memory than by its active versus inactive state (Figure 12.1).

This view is not new. It was first described by Lewis (1979), and later revitalized by Nader, Schafe, and LeDoux (2000). Since then, reconsolidation effects have been seen in hundreds of studies using a variety of species, tasks, and amnesic agents. It has been shown that memories can be strengthened, weakened or erased, or even updated, depending on the type of memory, its strength, the timing and method of reactivation, and the experiences encountered at reactivation (for reviews, see e.g.,

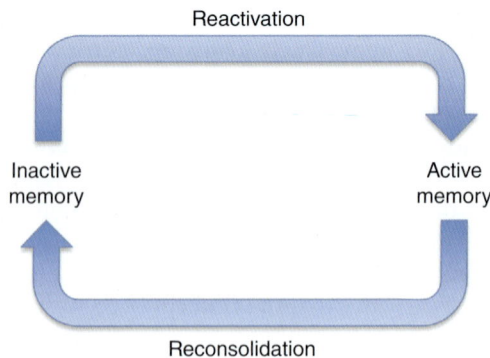

**Figure 12.1** Memory model proposed by Lewis (1979) and specified by Nader *et al.* (2000) to incorporate a reconsolidation process (adapted from Nader, Schafe, and LeDoux, 2000).

Besnard, Caboche, and Serge, 2012; Nader and Einarsson, 2010; Nader and Hardt, 2009). While consolidation and reconsolidation share many cellular substrates, several double dissociations have been reported, emphasizing the distinctiveness of these processes (Dudai, 2004; Tronson and Taylor, 2007). For instance, consolidation of contextual fear memories is critically dependent upon brain-derived neurotrophic factor (BDNF) but not upon the transcription factor Zif268, whereas the opposite is true for the reconsolidation of those memories (Lee, Everitt, and Thomas, 2004). On a functional level, it has been proposed that reconsolidation is more about updating than weakening or strengthening (Lee, 2009; Finnie and Nader, 2012).

Memory reconsolidation has also been demonstrated for a wide variety of tasks and memory systems, but it is not a ubiquitous phenomenon, and several boundary conditions have been identified (e.g., Nader and Einarsson, 2010). For instance, post-reactivation administration of amnesic agents does not impact strong memories (Suzuki *et al.*, 2004; Wang, de Oliveira Alvares, and Nader, 2009), remote memories (Milekic and Alberini, 2002; Suzuki *et al.*, 2004; but see Frankland *et al.*, 2006), and fear memories that were indirectly rather than directly reactivated (Pedeira, Perez-Cuesta, and Maldonado, 2004). However, some of these findings remain controversial, and as Nader and Einarsson (2010) point out, the absence of systematic parametric study of boundary conditions makes it difficult to determine whether reconsolidation is merely harder to induce under these circumstances, or whether memory reconsolidation is prevented altogether.

## Criteria for Reconsolidation

In order to infer from an empirical study that a certain intervention has specifically affected the reconsolidation process, it has to meet at least the following three criteria:

1  The intervention affects only memories that had recently been reactivated.
2  It affects long-term retention but not short-term retrieval, thus reflecting the fact that reconsolidation takes time.
3  Its effects are not transient, but persist over time (or at least until another round of destabilization occurs).

## The Study of Memory Reconsolidation in Humans

Memory reconsolidation is difficult to study in humans because the invasive methods used in animal studies are not available. Human studies have either relied on retroactive interference, similar to the early investigations by Müller and Pilzecker (1900), or they have used acceptable pharmacological interventions or behavioral interventions that cause an endogenous physiological response assumed to affect memory performance. We will first discuss interference-based approaches and then move on to physiological approaches. Finally, we will describe the first clinical applications that have been developed based on reconsolidation findings.

# Interference-Based Paradigms

Table 12.1 summarizes the different interference-based paradigms that have been developed to study memory reconsolidation in humans. The general procedure can be described as follows (illustrated in Figure 12.2). First, participants encode some information. After a delay during which the memory has time to consolidate, the memory is either reactivated or it is not, and some new material is presented that could potentially interfere with the previously learned information. After another delay, during which the memory has time to restabilize or reconsolidate, retrieval of the original information is assessed.

**Table 12.1**   Human memory reconsolidation: interference-based paradigms (detailed explanations in text).

| Experimental paradigm | Reactivation | Interference | Finding | Reference |
|---|---|---|---|---|
| Procedural memory (finger-tapping sequence) | Briefly execute old sequence | Learning new sequence | Recall performance impairment for old sequence after delay (accuracy) | Walker *et al.* (2003) |
| Episodic memory (object-learning paradigm) | Reminder question and continuous re-exposure to training context (experimenter and spatial context) | Learning new object set | Intrusion of new set into memory of old set (recall and source memory judgments) | Hupbach *et al.* (2007, 2008, 2009, 2011) |
| Episodic memory (paired associate learning: cue-response syllables) | Brief re-exposure to training context (music, image, light) and presentation of one of the cues from list 1 | Learning new list of cue-response syllables | Impaired recall of list 1 (Forcato *et al.* 2007, 2009); incorporation of new syllables into former memory upon verbal instruction (Forcato *et al.* 2010) | Forcato *et al.* (2007, 2009, 2010, 2011) |
| Autobiographical memory | Recall of autobiographical events | Memorize unrelated story | Impaired recall of neutral (but not emotional) events | Schwabe and Wolf (2009) |
| Fear conditioning (mild shock contingent upon presentation of specific color plate) | Several CS presentations 10 minutes before extinction training | Extinction training | Long-lasting depletion of fear response (galvanic skin response) | Schiller *et al.* (2010) |

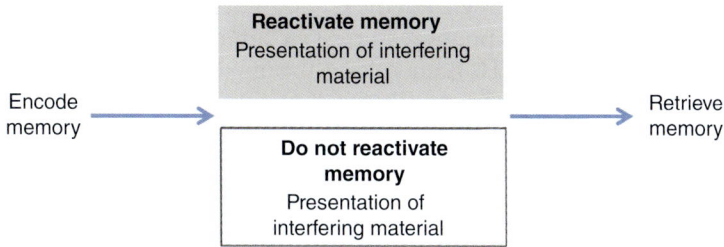

**Figure 12.2** Interference-based approach to study memory reconsolidation in humans.

## Procedural memory

The first experimental demonstration of renewed trace fragility after retrieval in humans came from Walker *et al.* (2003). They trained participants on a finger-tapping sequence (sequence 1: 4–1–3–2–4). Twenty-four hours later, participants learned a second sequence (sequence 2: 2–3–1–4–2). Immediately before sequence 2 learning, some participants were asked to briefly rehearse sequence 1 that they had learned the day before. When memory was tested in a third session after another 24-hour delay, sequence 1 memory accuracy was significantly impaired in the rehearsal group, both in comparison to this group's performance during rehearsal on day 2 and in comparison to a group that had not rehearsed sequence 1 before learning sequence 2. Learning of sequence 2 was comparable in both groups. In order to ensure that sequence 2 learning after rehearsal specifically affected reconsolidation rather than immediate retrieval processes, another group was asked to recall sequence 1 immediately after sequence 2 learning on day 2. This group showed no decline in performance. Thus, similar to the behavioral reconsolidation effects demonstrated in animals, Walker *et al.* showed that human procedural memory undergoes a phase of restabilization after reactivation.

## Episodic memory

Several labs have asked whether reconsolidation also applies to episodic memories, that is, memories for experiences and events that can be consciously retrieved and that capture not only the content but also the temporal and spatial circumstances of their occurrence (e.g., Tulving, 1984).

*Paired-associate learning* Forcato and colleagues (2007) trained participants to memorize two different lists of cue–syllable pairs on two separate days. For each of the learning sessions, a unique context was created: in each session, a specific color of light was projected onto a large screen behind the computer monitor, a specific image was displayed on the monitor's background, and specific music was played through earphones. For some participants, learning of list 2 on day 2 was preceded by a reminder, which consisted of a brief re-exposure to the specific list 1 learning context and the presentation of one of the list 1 cues without its associated syllable or time to retrieve the associate. When asked to retrieve list 1 on day 3, reminded participants showed list 1 memory impairments (increased error rates), suggesting that list 2 learning negatively impacted the reconsolidation of list 1. The same effect was observed when list 2 was presented up to six hours after the reminder, but not when it was presented after a 10-hour delay, showing that the instability that is triggered by the reminder is transient. In a follow-up study, Forcato *et al.* (2009) showed that the structure of the reminder had a significant influence on whether list 1 was affected by list 2. Reconsolidation was only observed when the reminder consisted of the context reminder plus the presentation of one of the list 1 cues. When the associated syllable was presented in addition to the cue, memory for list 1 was not impaired in the final memory test. Forcato *et al.* concluded that the presentation of the response prevents reconsolidation because it reinforces the reactivated memory instead of creating a mismatch between what is expected and what is experienced, a mismatch that seems to be essential for triggering the reconsolidation process (cf. Lee, 2009; Morris *et al.*, 2006). Thus, the reminder structure plays an important role in the triggering of reconsolidation and in the outcome of the reconsolidation process (see also Hupbach *et al.*, 2008; Schiller *et al.*, 2010; Suzuki *et al.*, 2004). Moreover, Forcato and colleagues showed that the incorporation of list 2 into list 1 is contingent on a verbal instruction (Forcato *et al.*, 2010; for discussion see *Object learning*, below), and that repeated reminding without list 2 learning strengthens list 1 memory (Forcato, Rodríguez, and Pedreira, 2011). Taken together, these studies by Forcato and colleagues have shown that learning a second list can trigger memory impairment for the first list, when list 2 learning follows shortly after the reactivation of list 1.

*Object learning* Contemporaneously with Forcato and colleagues, we developed an object-learning paradigm to study reconsolidation in human episodic memory (Hupbach *et al.*, 2007; for procedure, see Figure 12.3). We asked participants to memorize a set of 20 objects. Objects were shown and placed, one after the other, in a distinctive blue basket. Participants were asked to name and remember each object. Immediately after presentation of the entire set, memory was assessed, and training was repeated until participants could remember at least 17 of the 20 objects, or until they had completed four learning trials. Forty-eight hours later (session 2), participants were either reminded of the first learning episode or not, and then learned a second set of 20 unrelated objects. Participants in the reminder group returned to the

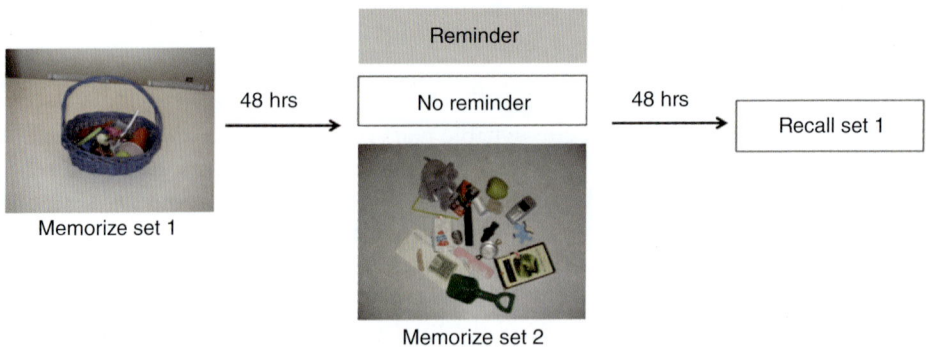

**Figure 12.3** Experimental design of Hupbach *et al.* (2007).

same room, where they worked with the same experimenter. Additionally, they were shown the blue basket again and were asked to describe the general experimental procedure of session 1. Participants in the no-reminder condition were seen in a different room and a different experimenter administered the second session. Nothing was mentioned about session 1. For all participants, set 2 was presented in a different way than set 1, such that the type of presentation would not itself serve as a reminder. All objects were placed on a table, and participants were instructed to name and remember them. The same learning criterion as in session 1 was used. Again 48 hours later (session 3), memory for set 1 was assessed.

Veridical memory for set 1 objects did not differ between the reminder and the no-reminder group. However, participants in the reminder group erroneously included a significant number of set 2 objects (intrusions) during set 1 recall. This was rarely observed in the no-reminder group (Figure 12.4). Importantly, set 2 memory did not differ between the reminder and the no-reminder groups, neither in the number of set 2 items recalled nor in the level of intrusions from set 1 into set 2 (which were quite low in both groups). This suggests that the intrusion of set 2 items into set 1 recall was not caused by general source confusion.

We confirmed this in a follow-up study (Hupbach, Gomez and Nadel, 2009) in which we used a recognition test and asked participants to indicate for each recognized object whether it stemmed from session 1 or session 2. Again, we found that the reminder caused participants to misattribute set 2 items to set 1.

Moreover, these misattributions were made with high confidence: in the reminder group, participants were as confident about misattributed set 2 items as they were about correctly attributed set 1 and set 2 items, though they were less confident about the few set 1 items that they misattributed to set 2. As expected, the no-reminder group made few misattributions in either direction. These results show that reactivating a memory before presenting new information can trigger integration of the new

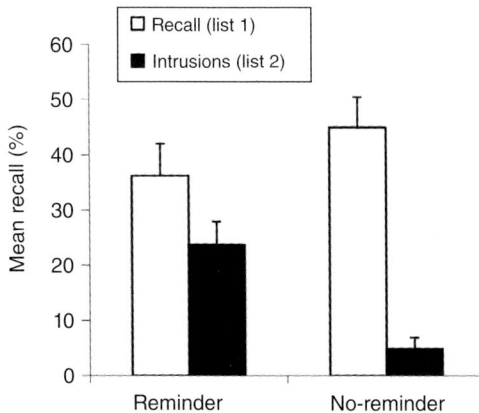

**Figure 12.4** Mean percentage of objects correctly and falsely recalled in the reminder and the no-reminder group. The groups did not differ in the number of items recalled from set 1, but the reminder group showed significantly more intrusions from set 2 into set 1 than the no-reminder group. In all figures, error bars represent standard errors of means. *Note:* Participants were asked to recall objects from set 1. Objects that were falsely recalled from set 2 are labeled as intrusions.

material into the old memory, or in other words, memory updating. This finding fits well with the function of reconsolidation proposed by Lee (2009) and Morris *et al.* (2006), i.e., providing organisms with an adaptive mechanism for ensuring that memories represent the most current state of knowledge.

The study by Forcato *et al.* (2009) described earlier illustrates the importance of the reminder structure for memory reconsolidation effects. In our 2007 study, the reminder consisted of three components: (1) we showed participants the blue basket that was used for set 1 encoding and asked them to describe the general procedure of set 1 learning (reminder question), (2) we performed set 2 learning in the same room in which set 1 learning had taken place (spatial context), and (3) we had the same experimenter from session 1 administer session 2. Are all of these components necessary to trigger reactivation and subsequent memory updating? To address this question we tested three conditions, one for each of the individual reminder components (Hupbach *et al.*, 2008). We found updating only in the spatial context condition. Neither the reminder question nor working with the same experimenter in session 2 triggered intrusions from set 2 into set 1 (Figure 12.5a). However, the individual reminder components might differ in strength, such that the reminder question and experimenter are too weak to reactivate a memory alone, but in combination might be able to do so. Therefore, we tested the three possible two-component combinations (question + experimenter, question + spatial context, experimenter + spatial context). We only observed intrusions in the conditions including spatial context as part of the compound (Figure 12.5b).

At first glance, this special role of spatial context appears to be at odds with the finding by Forcato *et al.* (2009) that a context reminder is insufficient for triggering reconsolidation. However, their context reminder consisted of a specific light and projected image, both briefly presented at the beginning of session 2, but changed before list 2 learning started. In contrast, our context reminder (the testing room) remained stable throughout session 2. That this difference is crucial is further evidenced by our observation that recalling in detail the spatial context in which set 1 was learned while being in a new context, or briefly revisiting the old context before learning set 2 in a new context, does not result in later intrusions (Hupbach *et al.*, 2008).

Why does the spatial context play such a crucial role in memory updating? As stated earlier, the spatial context is one of the defining elements of episodic memories. We have argued that the spatial context provides a scaffold to which experiences can bind (Hupbach *et al.*, 2008). When revisiting an old place, experiences associated with that place are reactivated, which allows them to be updated with anything new in that context. In contrast, when a new place is visited, an entirely new scaffold and event memory are created. Support for these ideas comes from hippocampal place cell recordings in animals. O'Keefe and Dostrovsky (1971) first showed that principal neurons in the rat's hippocampus fire every time the rat occupies a specific place in space. A collection of such place cells in the hippocampus forms the core of a neural system creating "cognitive maps" of the environment (O'Keefe and Nadel, 1978; for an additional discussion of the role of the hippocampus and spatial processing, see Chapter 10). Place cells retain their specific firing "field" when rats return to the same spatial context. When the rat encounters minimal to moderate changes to the environment or what happens in it, place cell firing rates change while the location of the fields remains stable (rate remapping; Leutgeb *et al.*, 2005). However, more dramatic

(a)

(b)

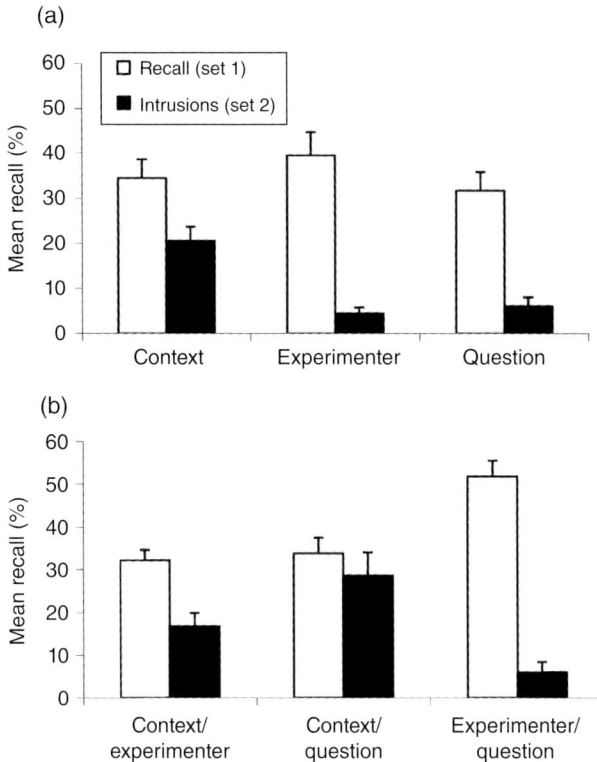

**Figure 12.5** Mean percentage of objects correctly and falsely recalled in the different reminder groups. (a) In each group, only one reminder component was present, i.e., either the spatial context, the experimenter, or the reminder question. (b) In each of the three groups, two different reminder components were combined.

changes of the environment or experience therein cause complete place cell remapping, that is, different cell assemblies represent old places (global remapping; e.g., Wills *et al.*, 2005). In other words, an entirely new cognitive map is created, one that minimizes overlap with the previous map. With regard to our reconsolidation findings, we hypothesize that when new information is learned in the old context, something like rate remapping occurs such that the existing representation is modified. When the new information is learned in a new context, global remapping occurs instead, creating a new and unrelated memory representation.

Up until this point our studies had all been carried out in a rather unfamiliar environment (an unfamiliar lab space in an otherwise familiar building). We wondered if familiarity with a context would modulate its reminder function. Highly familiar contexts are not very diagnostic for specific episodes, as they are associated with a variety of different episodes (everyday activities, but also more unique events such as a birthday party), and we speculated that they might not trigger memory updating. We studied this question empirically in five-year-old children, because context familiarity can be easily manipulated in this age group (Hupbach, Gomez, and Nadel, 2011). The first experiment was carried out in an unfamiliar environment (using rooms in a daycare center that were not part of the children's daily routine). As in our study with

(a)                                              (b)

Unfamiliar context                              Familiar context

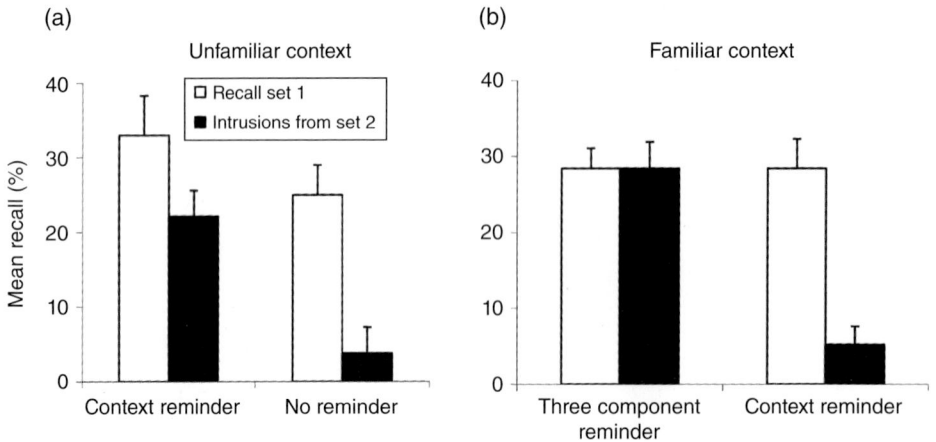

**Figure 12.6**  Mean percentage of objects correctly and falsely recalled by five-year-olds in (a) the context-reminder and no-reminder groups in an *unfamiliar spatial context*, and (b) in the context-reminder and three-component reminder groups in a *familiar spatial context*. Spatial context triggered intrusions from set 2 into set 1 only in unfamiliar, but not in familiar contexts. In familiar contexts, the experimenter and the reminder question caused intrusions.

adults, we found intrusions from set 2 into set 1 in the group that learned set 2 in the same context as set 1 (i.e., context- dependent updating), but significantly fewer intrusions in the group that learned set 2 in a different context (Figure 12.6a). In the crucial second experiment, we tested children at home, in the same place on all three days, such that all children received a context reminder in session 2. In one of the experimental groups, a reminder question was asked and the same experimenter administered sessions 1 and 2, whereas in the other group, the experimenter changed for session 2 and no reminder question was asked. If spatial context initiates updating in a familiar context, then both groups should show intrusions from set 2 into set 1. We observed intrusions when the same experimenter and the reminder question were part of session 2, but not when the spatial context was the only reminder (Figure 12.6b). This result shows that the spatial context loses its reminding power when the context is highly familiar.

*Autobiographical memory*  Our results, and the work of Forcato's group, show that episodic memories can be reactivated and subsequently modified by new learning. What about memory for more personal experiences? Schwabe and Wolf (2009) asked whether new learning can impact the reconsolidation of autobiographical memories (see Chapter 13 for more discussion of autobiographical memory). Instead of asking people to first encode a specific memory, they cued participants with positive, negative, and neutral adjectives (e.g., happy, sad, busy) and instructed them to recall a unique autobiographical memory for each adjective. Participants were instructed to report only memories that had happened at least 24 hours but not more than two weeks ago. Immediately after the reactivation, some participants memorized Bartlett's (1932) "War of ghosts" story. One week later, participants were cued with the memory titles they had produced during the first session and were instructed to again recall as many details of the events as possible. New learning (the "ghosts" story) impaired memory for the neutral events: participants who read the story after reactivating their event memories recalled significantly fewer details of their neutral events than control participants. No effects were found for positive or negative event memories. This result suggests that retrieving autobiographical events can negatively affect their future recall when new learning follows retrieval. Importantly, there was no obvious relation between the newly encoded material and the retrieved memories. Because of its importance for everyday life and potential clinical applications, more studies are needed to address the following open questions. Was it indeed the neutral story that interfered with reconsolidation, or did the recall of emotional memories interfere with the reconsolidation of neutral ones? Perhaps the emotional memories appeared more relevant and therefore interfered with the reconsolidation of the neutral ones. What role does the age of memory play in this effect, and how enduring is the impairment? And finally, why are emotional memories immune to these effects on reconsolidation? Is it a matter of storage strength (see e.g., Suzuki *et al.*, 2004; Wang, de Oliveira Alvares, and Nader, 2009)? Although the use of individual autobiographical memories enhances ecological validity, it comes with the price of diminished experimental control over the specific memory content and circumstance of occurrence. One way of combining ecological validity with experimental control might be the use of staged events, as has been done in other memory domains (e.g., weapon-focus effect; Pickel, Ross, and Truelove, 2006).

## Fear conditioning

Several laboratories have studied reconsolidation in human fear conditioning paradigms, with the benefit that comparable studies have been carried out in animals. Many of the human studies involved pharmacological intervention and will be discussed later (see *Pharmacological manipulations*, below). Among the exceptions, Schiller and colleagues (2010) asked whether the presentation of new non-fearful information after reactivation modifies human fear memories such that fearful responses can be extinguished in a long-lasting manner. Schiller *et al.* used a fear conditioning partial reinforcement paradigm: participants were presented with two differently colored squares. The presentation of one of the squares (CS+) was paired with a mild shock to the wrist on about one-third of the trials, whereas the presentation of the other square (unconditioned stimulus, CS–) was never paired with a shock. A day later, participants underwent extinction training, that is, the squares were presented again, but no shock was administered. Importantly, one group received a reminder (single presentation of CS+) 10 minutes before the start of the extinction training. Additionally, two control conditions were implemented. One group received the reminder six hours prior to extinction training such that extinction training happened outside the reconsolidation window, and the other group was not reminded at all. When participants returned on the following day, fearful responses (indicated by increased skin conductance) re-emerged after several CS+ presentations (without shock) in the two control groups, which is the expected outcome of spontaneous recovery after extinction training. Importantly, however, fear did not return in the group that underwent the extinction training within the reconsolidation window. In other words, recovery of fear after extinction can be prevented when the extinction training is preceded by reactivation of the fear memory (see also the recent replication of this finding by Oyarzún *et al.*, 2012, with aversive auditory stimuli as the CS–). Crucially, no reinstatement of fear responses was observed in a follow-up that was conducted a year later with the same group of participants. In a separate experiment, Schiller *et al.* demonstrated that fear depletion through reconsolidation is stimulus-specific: when two differently colored squares were both associated with shock, but only one square was presented during reactivation, only the fear response associated with the reactivated square was erased. This study suggests that purely behavioral modification of fearful memories is possible. This has important implications for the treatment of anxiety disorders and recovery from traumatic experiences, although it should be noted that Soeter and Kindt (2012) failed to replicate Schiller *et al.*'s findings when fear-relevant pictures (e.g., gun) were used as conditioned stimuli.

Most recently, Agren *et al.* (2012) extended Schiller *et al.*'s (2010) findings by showing erasure of the fear memory trace in the amygdala. They used a similar paradigm as Schiller *et al.* by administering a mild shock to establish fear of a CS+ on day 1. On day 2, memory was reactivated via CS+ presentation either six hours or 10 minutes before an extinction manipulation, with the assumption that extinction training would interfere with memory reconsolidation only in the latter group. On day 3 participants underwent a "renewal" session in the scanner, CS+ and CS– were presented, and shock electrodes were applied, but no shocks were delivered. On day 5 participants were given shocks on their own, after which they were re-exposed to the CS+. This allowed Agren *et al.* to assess the extent of return of fear to the CS+ using skin conductance as their response measure, and to relate the extent of fear return to activity in the amygdala on day 3. In the group that received extinction training outside of the reconsolidation window on day 2, fear returned on day 5 (cf. Schiller *et al.*, 2010), and the extent of fear return was positively correlated with the blood-oxygen-level-dependent (BOLD) activity in the basolateral amygdala. Moreover, functional coupling was observed in the structures forming the fear circuit, including parts of the anterior cingulate cortex, the insula, and the hippocampus. In contrast, when extinction training occurred within the reconsolidation window (10 minutes after reactivation), fear did not return, and presentation of the CS+ on day 5 elicited less activity in the amygdala, and less coupling within the previously identified fear circuit.

These results are noteworthy not merely for the light they shed on underlying brain mechanisms of reconsolidation. They also highlight the difference between extinction and reconsolidation. Under normal conditions (i.e., in the absence of the reactivation of a specific memory), extinction proceeds by creating a parallel memory that can subsequently inhibit the "extinguished" response. That is why one sees spontaneous recovery, and renewal, after standard extinction protocols. In the presence of reactivation, however, extinction seems to go beyond this establishment of a competing memory trace to the actual erasure of the previously formed memory. At least that is what the Agren *et al.* (2012) study shows for the fear circuitry engaged by their task.

## Interim summary

All of the studies reviewed above were based on retroactive interference paradigms: after reactivating a remote memory, some new, potentially interfering information is presented, and its impact on the reactivated memory is assessed after a delay during which the memory had time to reconsolidate. It has been demonstrated for a variety of human memory paradigms that reactivation induces a time-dependent fragility during which memories are again susceptible to the influence of new learning. The outcomes of this process differ depending on the targeted memory. In procedural memory (Walker *et al.*, 2003) and in human fear conditioning (Schiller *et al.*, 2010), the common finding is that reactivated memory traces are impaired by the learning of new, related information. In episodic memory, new information can either impair an old trace (Forcato *et al.*, 2007, 2009, 2010, 2011; Schwabe and Wolf, 2009), or it can be integrated into the reactivated memory (Hupbach *et al.*, 2007, 2008, 2009; Hupbach, Gomez, and Nadel, 2011). What determines the direction of influence resulting in impairment, enhancement, or incorporation of new information? Schiller and Phelps (2011) propose that the outcome is dependent upon the relative localization versus distribution of the underlying memory representations. While fear conditioning and procedural memory are supported by rather localized brain systems, episodic memory engages a more dispersed network involving the medial temporal cortex and neocortical areas (for more discussion, see Chapters 5 and 18). They argue that more localized representations lend themselves to effects of behavioral interference in the form of memory impairment, whereas integration of new information into the reactivated memory is more common for distributed memory representations. It would seem important to specify the reasons (computational or otherwise) why localized versus distributed representations elicit these different effects, if this approach is to prove useful.

We have suggested that the outcome might also depend on the degree to which the new information contradicts or potentially complements the reactivated information. In cases where the new information is incompatible with the reactivated memory (e.g., extinction or reversal paradigms, memory for procedures), impairment is observed, whereas in cases of possible complementarity (e.g., episodic memory paradigms where new items can be added to the reactivated memory), integration is the more likely outcome (Hupbach, 2011).

In the following sections we will describe human studies that target the reconsolidation process through physiological manipulations. Instead of organizing these sections with regard to the targeted memory systems, we cluster them by the type of manipulation, that is, administration of pharmacological agents versus subjecting participants to laboratory stress.

## Physiological Manipulations

Several laboratories have tried to impact the reconsolidation process by administering pharmacological agents that are known to affect memory consolidation or by subjecting people to stress, which causes hormonal changes that have consequences for the memory system. These physiological manipulations will be reviewed in the following sections.

## Pharmacological manipulations

Of the drugs used to manipulate memory consolidation and reconsolidation in humans, propranolol has received the most attention.[1] Propranolol is a sympatholytic beta-blocker that is commonly used to treat hypertension, but that has also been shown to influence memory processes in humans and animals through reducing noradrenergic activity in the amygdala (e.g., van Stegeren *et al.*, 2005), with negative consequences especially for the formation of emotional memories (e.g., McGaugh, 2004; Roozendaal *et al.*, 2006). Because of its negative effects on emotional memory consolidation, propranolol is being discussed as a treatment for trauma victims to prevent the development of post-traumatic stress disorder (PTSD), but the empirical evidence for such protective effects remains inconclusive (see e.g., Hoge *et al.*, 2012).

In animals, infusion of propranolol into the amygdala disrupts the reconsolidation of fear memories such that fear expression is diminished long term. The few human studies similarly and consistently report negative consequences of propranolol administration for the reconsolidation of fear memories. Kindt, Soeter, and Vervliet (2009) used a fear-conditioning paradigm similar to Schiller *et al.* (2010; see *Fear conditioning*, above), but instead of using extinction training as a means to disrupt the reactivated memory, Kindt *et al.* studied the effects of propranolol on reconsolidation. During acquisition, they presented two different fear-relevant stimuli (e.g., pictures of spiders), and paired the presentation of one (CS+) with a mild shock to the wrist on 80% of the trials, whereas the presentation of the other stimulus (CS–) was never paired with a shock. Twenty-four hours later, memory was reactivated by presenting the CS+ again, but without the shock. Importantly, 90 minutes before reactivation, participants had either received an oral dose of propranolol or placebo (because of the delayed action of propranolol, administration preceded instead of followed the reactivation). When fear reactivity was assessed 24 hours after reactivation, propranolol had completely eliminated the expression of the fear memory: no differential fear responses were observed for the CS+ and CS– in the propranolol group. The placebo group, in contrast, showed a conditioned fear response contingent upon the presentation of the CS+. Soeter and Kindt (2012) replicated and extended this result by showing that propranolol not only disrupts reconsolidation of the cue-specific fear memory, it also prevents the generalization of the fear memory to other categorically related cues. This is an important finding, especially in light of potential clinical applications for the treatment of anxiety disorders, which are often characterized by fear generalization.

Propranolol studies have been highly publicized because of their potential implications for the treatment of anxiety disorders or for alleviating symptoms of patients suffering from PTSD. However, clinical studies are sparse, perhaps because they face some unique ethical as well as methodological challenges. In the only randomized double-blind study to date, Brunet *et al.* (2008) asked participants suffering from PTSD to retrieve the traumatic event that had caused the distress, followed by the administration of either propranolol or placebo. A week later, participants who had received propranolol showed significantly reduced physiological reactivity (galvanic skin response, heart rate, left corrugator electromyogram) during script-driven imagery of the event. However, sample sizes were small and a pre-assessment of physiological reactivity is missing, which makes it difficult to draw conclusions about memory reconsolidation. In two other studies, Brunet's group asked PTSD patients to write a detailed trauma narrative (Brunet *et al.*, 2011; Poundja *et al.*, 2012). During the following weeks, patients repeatedly read aloud their trauma narratives 90 minutes after propranolol intake. It was observed that PTSD symptoms improved over the course of this treatment. However, since placebo control groups were not included in these studies, it remains unclear whether improvements were caused by repeatedly reactivating the event in a safe environment or whether propranolol specifically affected the reconsolidation of the reactivated traumatic memories (cf. Brunet *et al.*, 2011; Schiller and Phelps., 2011). The therapeutic usefulness of propranolol for the treatment of anxiety disorders and PTSD requires further evaluation in larger-scale randomized placebo-controlled studies.

## Stress

Physiological and psychological stressors cause a set of time-dependent endocrine, nervous, and immune system responses (for a review, see Charmandari, Tsigos, and Chrousos, 2005). Among other effects, stress is accompanied by the release of corti-costeroids such as cortisol from the adrenal gland into the bloodstream (for a review, see Lupien and McEwen, 1997). Cortisol easily crosses the blood–brain barrier and can thus affect brain systems expressing corticosteroid receptors. High concentrations of corticosteroid receptors are found in the amygdala and the hippocampus, two systems critically involved in (emotional) memory processes (de Kloet, Oitzl, and Joëls, 1999; Lupien and McEwen, 1997). Studies assessing the effects of stress on human memory consolidation commonly report that stress selectively enhances the consolidation of emotionally arousing experiences (e.g., Cahill, Gorski, and Le, 2003; Echterhoff and Wolf, 2012), although some studies also report positive effects for neutral memories (e.g., Preuss and Wolf, 2009).

Few studies have looked at the effects of stress on reconsolidation. Schwabe and Wolf (2010) asked how stress affects reconsolidation of autobiographical memories. They used a design similar to the one described above (see *Autobiographical memory*), but the reconsolidation process was interrupted by a socially evaluated cold pressor test instead of having participants learn some new information. Specifically, partici-pants were asked to retrieve several autobiographical memories in response to cue words, and were then asked to submerge their arm in ice water for up to three minutes while the experimenter monitored and videotaped them. Interestingly, the stressor had similar effects as new learning: it reduced recall of details for neutral autobio-graphical events, while it did not affect memory for positive and negative events. That stress seems to negatively impact the reconsolidation of neutral memories is inter-esting, because it contrasts with what has been reported for consolidation, where stress most often enhances memories, especially emotional ones. We have recently found a similar effect of stress using the Trier Social Stress Test (TSST), a stress-inducing procedure giving subjects just minutes to prepare and deliver a five-minute speech in front of judges (Kirschbaum, Pirke, and Hellhammer, 1993). Subjects in our study took the TSST either immediately before, or immediately after, reactivation and set 2 learning (Dongaonkar and Nadel, 2012; Dongaonkar *et al.*, 2013). Intrusions were numerically reduced in the stress-before-reactivation condition and significantly reduced in the stress-after-reactivation manipulation, suggesting a temporal effect of stress on memory updating. The closer the stressful experience is to the onset of memory updating, the greater the impact.

The findings just discussed contrast with a recent reconsolidation study by Coccoz, Maldonado and Delorenzi (2011), who found that cold pressor stress enhanced memory for neutral content (pairs of syllables). In contrast to Schwabe and Wolf (2010), who asked participants to consciously retrieve the memory before the stressor, Coccoz *et al.* repeated parts of the original learning procedure as a reminder before the stressor (similar to the Forcato *et al.*, 2007, study described in *Paired-associate learning*, above). Additionally, differences in the stress-inducing procedure might account for the discrepant findings. Schwabe and Wolf, as well as Dongaonkar *et al.* (2013), used stress protocols that contain a psychological component, whereas Coccoz *et al.* used a purely physiological stressor. It seems reasonable to assume that public speaking in front of an audience, as requested from participants in TSST, or being videotaped while submerging your arm in ice water, is accompanied by feelings of embarrassment and perceived threat to self-image, which might cause lingering rumination and distraction even after the stress procedure is over. Those psychological after-effects might contribute to the memory impairment seen in the studies by Schwabe and Wolf as well as Dongaonkar *et al.*

## Summary and Future Directions

In contrast to the numerous reconsolidation studies in the animal domain, human studies still lag behind. However, in recent years, several paradigms and manipulations have been developed that allow for the study of reconsolidation in human memory. This research has shown that memories for episodes and procedures, as well as fear memories, can be modified when new information is presented or when stress or pharmacological agents are administered shortly after memory reactivation. The direction of influence (enhancement, impairment, or incorporation of new information) seems to be dependent upon the specific brain regions involved (Schiller and Phelps, 2011), the emotionality of the material (Schwabe and Wolf, 2010), and the relationship between the reactivated memory and the new information (Hupbach, 2011).

Despite these findings, a number of questions remain unanswered. For instance, it remains to be determined which components of a memory are intrinsically stable and immune to modifications (e.g., spatial context information) and which components are flexible and modifiable through reconsolidation. Additionally, controlled clinical studies are needed to assess whether the principles of memory reconsolidation can be used to develop interventions for patients with anxiety disorders and PTSD. A detailed theoretical account of the mechanisms involved in human memory reconsolidation is also missing. One recent step in this direction is the attempt to explain the mechanisms underlying reconsolidation in our object-learning paradigm with the temporal context model (Sederberg *et al.*, 2011). While this computational memory model nicely replicates our basic updating effect, it is, at least in its current form, not able to differentiate between individual reminders and thus cannot account for the special role of spatial context for the updating effect (Hupbach, Gomez, and Nadel, 2011). In addition to a description of the cognitive mechanisms, future studies need to elucidate the neurophysiological underpinnings of human memory reconsolidation. We, and others, have begun investigating brain activation patterns during reactivation and later retrieval using fMRI. In time we can hope to understand not only the behavioral and cognitive dynamics of memory malleability, but also the neural substrates of the reconsolidation process.

## Notes

1   One exception is a recent study by the Forcato group (Rodríguez *et al.*, 2013), in which clonazepam (a benzodiazepine that modulates the effects of GABA in the brain) administered after reactivation enhances later retrieval in the paired-associates paradigm (see *Paired-associate learning*, above).

## References

Agren, T., Engman, J., Frick, A., *et al.* (2012). Disruption of reconsolidation erases a fear memory trace in the human amygdala. *Science*, 337 (6101), 1550–1552.

Bartlett, F.C. (1932). *Remembering: A Study in Experimental and Social Psychology*. Cambridge: Cambridge University Press.

Besnard, A., Caboche, J., and Laroche, S. (2012). Reconsolidation of memory: a decade of debate. *Progress in Neurobiology*, 99, 61–80.

Brunet, A., Orr, S.P., Tremblay, J., *et al.* (2008). Effect of post-retrieval propranolol on psychophysiologic responding during subsequent script-driven traumatic imagery in post-traumatic stress disorder. *Journal of Psychiatric Research*, 42 (6), 503–506.

Brunet, A., Poundja, J., Tremblay, J., *et al.* (2011). Trauma reactivation under the influence of propranolol decreases posttraumatic stress symptoms and disorder: 3 open-label trials. *Journal of Clinical Psychopharmacology*, 31 (4), 547–550.

Cahill, L., Gorski, L., and Le, K. (2003). Enhanced human memory consolidation with post-learning stress: interaction with the degree of arousal at encoding. *Learning and Memory*, 10 (4), 270–274.

Charmandari, E., Tsigos, C., and Chrousos, G. (2005). Endocrinology of the stress response 1. *Annual Review Physiology*, 67, 259–284.

Coccoz, V., Maldonado, H., and Delorenzi, A. (2011). The enhancement of reconsolidation with a naturalistic mild stressor improves the expression of a declarative memory in humans. *Neuroscience*, 185, 61–72.

de Kloet, E.R., Oitzl, M.S., and Joëls, M. (1999). Stress and cognition: are corticosteroids good or bad guys? *Trends in Neurosciences*, 22 (10), 422–426.

Dongaonkar, B., Hupbach, A., Gomez, R., and Nadel, L. (2013). Effects of stress in episodic memory updating. *Psychopharmacology*, 226, 769–779.

Dongaonkar, B., and Nadel, L. (2012). Effects of stress in episodic memory updating. Poster presented at the International Conference on Frontiers in Stress and Cognition: From Molecules to Behavior. Ascona, Switzerland, September 2012.

Dudai, Y. (2004). The neurobiology of consolidations, or, how stable is the engram? *Annual Review Psychology*, 55, 51–86.

Echterhoff, G., and Wolf, O.T. (2012). The stressed eyewitness: the interaction of thematic arousal and post-event stress in memory for central and peripheral event information. *Frontiers in Integrative Neuroscience*, 6, 57. doi: 10.3389/fnint.2012.00057.

Finnie, P.S., and Nader, K. (2012). The role of metaplasticity mechanisms in regulating memory destabilization and reconsolidation. *Neuroscience and Biobehavioral Reviews*, 36 (7), 1667–1707.

Forcato, C., Argibay, P., Pedreira, M., and Maldonado, H. (2009). Human reconsolidation does not always occur when a memory is retrieved: the relevance of the reminder structure. *Neurobiology of Learning and Memory*, 91 (1), 50–57.

Forcato, C., Burgos, V.L., Argibay, P.F., *et al.* (2007). Reconsolidation of declarative memory in humans. *Learning and Memory*, 14 (4), 295–303.

Forcato, C., Rodríguez, M.L., and Pedreira, M.E. (2011). Repeated labilization-reconsolidation processes strengthen declarative memory in humans. *PloS One*, 6 (8), e23305.

Forcato, C., Rodríguez, M.L., Pedreira, M.E., and Maldonado, H. (2010). Reconsolidation in humans opens up declarative memory to the entrance of new information. *Neurobiology of Learning and Memory*, 93 (1), 77–84.

Frankland, P.W., Ding, H.-K., Takahashi, E., *et al.* (2006). Stability of recent and remote contextual fear memory. *Learning and Memory*, 13 (4), 451–457.

Hoge, E.A., Worthington, J.J. Nagurney, J.T., *et al.* (2012). Effect of acute posttrauma propranolol on PTSD outcome and physiological responses during script-driven imagery. *CNS Neuroscience and Therapeutics*, 18 (1), 21–27.

Hupbach, A. (2011). The specific outcomes of reactivation-induced memory changes depend on the degree of competition between old and new information. *Frontiers in Behavioral Neuroscience*, 5, 33. doi: 10.3389/fnbeh.2011.00033.

Hupbach, A., Gomez, R., Hardt, O., and Nadel, L. (2007). Reconsolidation of episodic memories: a subtle reminder triggers integration of new information. *Learning and Memory*, 14 (1–2), 47–53.

Hupbach, A., Gomez, R., and Nadel, L. (2009). Episodic memory reconsolidation: updating or source confusion? *Memory*, 17 (5), 502–510.

Hupbach, A., Gomez, R., and Nadel, L. (2011). Episodic memory updating: the role of context familiarity. *Psychonomic Bulletin and Review*, 18 (4), 787–797.

Hupbach, A., Hardt, O., Gomez, R., and Nadel, L. (2008). The dynamics of memory: context-dependent updating. *Learning and Memory*, 15 (8), 574–579.

Kindt, M., Soeter, M., and Vervliet, B. (2009). Beyond extinction: erasing human fear responses and preventing the return of fear. *Nature Neuroscience*, 12 (3), 256–258.

Kirschbaum, C., Pirke, K.-M., and Hellhammer, D.H. (1993). The 'Trier Social Stress Test': a tool for investigating psychobiological stress responses in a laboratory setting. *Neuropsychobiology*, 28 (1–2), 76–81.

Lee, J.L. (2009). Reconsolidation: maintaining memory relevance. *Trends in Neurosciences*, 32 (8), 413–420.

Lee, J.L., Everitt, B.J., and Thomas, K.L. (2004). Independent cellular processes for hippocampal memory consolidation and reconsolidation. *Science*, 304 (5672), 839–843.

Leutgeb, S., Leutgeb, J.K., Barnes, C.A., *et al.* (2005) Independent codes for spatial and episodic memory in hippocampal neuronal ensembles. *Science*, 309(5734), 619–623.

Lewis, D.J. (1979). Psychobiology of active and inactive memory. *Psychological Bulletin*, 86 (5), 1054.

Lewis, D.J., Bregman, N.J., and Mahan, J.J. (1972). Cue-dependent amnesia in rats. *Journal of Comparative and Physiological Psychology*, 81 (2), 243.

Lupien, S.J., and McEwen, B.S. (1997). The acute effects of corticosteroids on cognition: integration of animal and human model studies. *Brain Research Reviews*, 24 (1), 1–27.

McGaugh, J.L. (2004). The amygdala modulates the consolidation of memories of emotionally arousing experiences. *Annual Review Neuroscience*, 27, 1–28.

Milekic, M.H., and Alberini, C.M. (2002). Temporally graded requirement for protein synthesis following memory reactivation. *Neuron*, 36 (3), 521–525.

Misanin, J.R., Miller, R.R., and Lewis, D.J. (1968). Retrograde amnesia produced by electroconvulsive shock after reactivation of a consolidated memory trace. *Science*, 160 (3827), 554–555.

Morris, R.G., Inglis, J., Ainge, J.A., *et al.* (2006). Memory reconsolidation: sensitivity of spatial memory to inhibition of protein synthesis in dorsal hippocampus during encoding and retrieval. *Neuron*, 50 (3), 479–489.

Müller G.E., and Pilzecker, A. (1900) Experimentelle Beiträge zur Lehre vom Gedächtnis. *Zeitschrift für Psychologie. Ergänzungsband*, 1, 1–300.

Nader, K., and Einarsson, E.Ö. (2010). Memory reconsolidation: an update. *Annals of the New York Academy of Sciences*, 1191 (1), 27–41.

Nader, K., and Hardt, O. (2009). A single standard for memory: the case for reconsolidation. *Nature Reviews Neuroscience*, 10 (3), 224–234.

Nader, K., Schafe, G.E., and LeDoux, J.E. (2000). Fear memories require protein synthesis in the amygdala for reconsolidation after retrieval. *Nature*, 406 (6797), 722–726.

O'Keefe, J., and Dostrovsky, J. (1971). The hippocampus as a spatial map: preliminary evidence from unit activity in the freely-moving rat. *Brain Research*, 34, 171–175. doi: 10.1016/0006-8993(71)90358-1.

O'Keefe, J. and Nadel, L. (1978). *The Hippocampus as a Cognitive Map*. Oxford: Clarendon Press.

Oyarzún, J.P., Lopez-Barroso, D., Fuentemilla, L., *et al.* (2012). Updating fearful memories with extinction training during reconsolidation: a human study using auditory aversive stimuli. *PloS One*, 7 (6), e38849.

Pedreira, M.E., Pérez-Cuesta, L.M., and Maldonado, H. (2004). Mismatch between what is expected and what actually occurs triggers memory reconsolidation or extinction. *Learning and Memory*, 11 (5), 579–585.

Pickel, K.L., Ross, S.J., and Truelove, R.S. (2006). Overcoming weapon focus. *Applied Cognitive Psychology*, 20, 871–893.

Poundja, J., Sanche, S., Tremblay, J. and Brunet, A. (2012). Trauma reactivation under the influence of propranolol: an examination of clinical predictors. *European Journal of Psychotraumatology*, 3, 15470. doi: 10.3402/ejpt.v3i0.15470.

Preuss, D., and Wolf, O.T. (2009). Post-learning psychosocial stress enhances consolidation of neutral stimuli. *Neurobiology of Learning and Memory*, 92 (3), 318–326.

Przybyslawski, J., and Sara, S.J. (1997). Reconsolidation of memory after its reactivation. *Behavioural Brain Research*, 84 (1), 241–246.

Riccio, D.C., Millin, P.M., and Bogart, A.R. (2006). Reconsolidation: a brief history, a retrieval view, and some recent issues. *Learning and Memory*, 13 (5), 536–544.

Rodríguez, M.L., Campos, J., Forcato, C., *et al.* (2013). Enhancing a declarative memory in humans: the effect of clonazepam on reconsolidation. *Neuropharmacology*, 64, 432–442.

Roozendaal, B., Okuda, S., De Quervain, D.-F., and McGaugh, J. (2006). Glucocorticoids interact with emotion-induced noradrenergic activation in influencing different memory functions. *Neuroscience*, 138 (3), 901–910.

Sara, S.J. (2000a). Commentary. Reconsolidation: strengthening the shaky trace through retrieval. *Nature Reviews Neuroscience*, 1 (3), 212–213.

Sara, S.J. (2000b). Retrieval and reconsolidation: toward a neurobiology of remembering. *Learning and Memory*, 7 (2), 73–84.

Schiller D., Monfils, M., Raio, C.M., *et al.* (2010). Preventing the return of fear in humans using reconsolidation update mechanisms. *Nature*, 463, 49–53.

Schiller, D., and Phelps, E.A. (2011). Does reconsolidation occur in humans? *Frontiers in Behavioral Neuroscience*, 5, 24. doi: 10.3389/fnbeh.2011.00024.

Schwabe, L., and Wolf, O.T. (2009). New episodic learning interferes with the reconsolidation of autobiographical memories. *PloS One* 4 (10), e7519.

Schwabe, L., and Wolf, O.T. (2010). Stress impairs the reconsolidation of autobiographical memories. *Neurobiology of Learning and Memory*, 94 (2), 153–157.

Sederberg, P.B., Gershman, S.J., Polyn, S.M., and Norman, K.A. (2011). Human memory reconsolidation can be explained using the temporal context model. *Psychonomic Bulletin and Review*, 18 (3), 455–468.

Soeter, M., and Kindt, M. (2012). Stimulation of the noradrenergic system during memory formation impairs extinction learning but not the disruption of reconsolidation. *Neuropsychopharmacology*, 37 (5), 1204–1215.

Spear, N.E., and Mueller, C.W. (1984). Consolidation as a function of retrieval. In *Memory Consolidation: Psychobiology of Cognition* (ed. H. Weingartner and E.S. Parker). Hillsdale, NJ: Erlbaum, pp. 111–147.

Suzuki, A., Josselyn, S.A., Frankland, P.W., *et al.* (2004). Memory reconsolidation and extinction have distinct temporal and biochemical signatures. *Journal of Neuroscience*, 24 (20), 4787–4795.

Tronson, N.C., and Taylor, J.R. (2007). Molecular mechanisms of memory reconsolidation. *Nature Reviews Neuroscience*, 8 (4), 262–275.

Tulving, E. (1984). Precis of elements of episodic memory. *Behavioral and Brain Sciences*, 7 (2), 223–268.

van Stegeren, A.H., Goekoop, R., Everaerd, W., *et al.* (2005). Noradrenaline mediates amygdala activation in men and women during encoding of emotional material. *NeuroImage*, 24 (3), 898–909.

Walker, M.P., Brakefield, T., Hobson, J.A., and Stickgold, R. (2003). Dissociable stages of human memory consolidation and reconsolidation. *Nature*, 425 (6958), 616–620.

Wang, S.-H., de Oliveira Alvares, L., and Nader, K. (2009). Cellular and systems mechanisms of memory strength as a constraint on auditory fear reconsolidation. *Nature Neuroscience*, 12 (7), 905–912.

Wills, T.J., Lever, C., Cacucci, F., *et al.* (2005). Attractor dynamics in the hippocampal representation of the local environment. *Science*, 308 (5723), 873–876.

# 13

# Neural Correlates of Autobiographical Memory
## *Methodological Considerations*
### Peggy L. St. Jacques and Felipe De Brigard

## Introduction

Autobiographical memory (AM) refers to the retrieval of memories from the personal past. It encompasses multiple processes and neural systems (Conway and Pleydell-Pearce, 2000; Rubin, 2006) often difficult to capture in a single study. AM retrieval typically involves complex retrieval processes, semantic content, personal significance, subjective re-experience, spatiotemporal context, emotion, social interactions, and varying levels of specificity, remoteness, and rehearsal. These qualities make personal memories important and relevant for the future, but also difficult to investigate with traditional laboratory materials (Cabeza and St. Jacques, 2007; St. Jacques and Cabeza, 2012). Neuroimaging studies of AM were much slower to develop compared to similar studies on laboratory memory. For example, an early review of neuroimaging studies of AM reported 11 studies (Maguire, 2001), whereas another review of 275 studies of imaging of cognition included over 50 studies on laboratory memory (Cabeza and Nyberg, 2000). One reason for the relatively slower development of neuroimaging studies of AM is that their inherent complexity can be challenging within the controlled and rigorous scanning environment, and such studies were often criticized by other cognitive neuroscientists as a "waste of time" (see Maguire, 2012). Fortunately, the development of novel techniques and methodologies that capture this inherent complexity, along with the increasing viewpoint that such studies can offer valuable insight into memory and other related processes (Cabeza and St. Jacques, 2007; Gilboa, 2004; Maguire, 2001, 2012; McDermott, Szpunar, and Christ, 2009; Spreng, Mar, and Kim, 2009), has led to a rise in the number of functional neuroimaging studies of AM. Such studies are important because they are generally more ecologically valid (Neisser, 1978), they contribute to the understanding of neural correlates of processes that are difficult to study using laboratory memory stimuli (Cabeza and St. Jacques, 2007; Gilboa *et al.*, 2004; St. Jacques and Cabeza, 2012), and they can inform theories of AM (St. Jacques, 2012).

In this chapter we review innovative methods and analysis techniques that have allowed neuroscientists to overcome some of the challenges of AM research, as well as

*The Wiley Handbook on the Cognitive Neuroscience of Memory*, First Edition.
Edited by Donna Rose Addis, Morgan Barense, and Audrey Duarte.
© 2015 John Wiley & Sons, Ltd. Published 2015 by John Wiley & Sons, Ltd.

how the findings from such studies can provide a unique perspective on cognitive neuroscience. The primary focus of the current chapter is on functional MRI (fMRI), the methodology of choice for the majority of neuroimaging studies in AM, but positron emission tomography (PET) and event-related potential (ERP) studies are mentioned where relevant. Additionally, we focus on neuroimaging studies of primarily healthy young adults. Topics will include an overview of the neural correlates supporting AM retrieval, the methods of eliciting AMs within the rigorous scanning environment, analysis methods, and future methodological directions in this field. Throughout the chapter we will discuss some of the challenges of functional neuroimaging methods that are particularly relevant to AM.

# Neural Correlates Supporting Autobiographical Memory Retrieval

Recalling memories from our personal past involves a distributed set of primarily left-lateralized brain regions (Maguire, 2001), although not all studies show this pattern (Addis *et al.*, 2012; for review see Svoboda, McKinnon, and Levine, 2006). Functional neuroimaging studies have identified a number of regions that are frequently involved during AM retrieval, including the medial and lateral prefrontal cortices (PFC), lateral and medial temporal lobes (MTL; hippocampus, parahippocampal gyrus), ventral parietal cortex, and posterior cingulate cortex (Cabeza and St. Jacques, 2007; McDermott, Szpunar, and Christ, 2009; Spreng, Mar, and Kim, 2009; Svoboda, McKinnon, and Levine, 2006). The typical neural regions involved during AM are sometimes referred to as the "AM retrieval network" or even the "core network" because of their frequency and evidence for interactions among many of these regions. However, it would be more appropriate to consider AM retrieval as involving the interaction among multiple neural networks or systems (Fuster, 2009; Rubin, 2006; also see Svoboda, McKinnon, and Levine, 2006), and some functional neuroimaging studies have employed analysis techniques that allow the examination of the co-activation and interaction among these large-scale networks during AM retrieval (Andrews-Hanna *et al.*, 2010; Spreng *et al.*, 2010; St. Jacques, Kragel, and Rubin, 2011; see Figure 13.1).

One of the primary networks recruited during AM retrieval overlaps with the default network (Figure 13.1), a set of brain regions that are co-active during passive resting states (Raichle *et al.*, 2001). The default network is composed of two subnetworks: (1) a medial PFC network that includes dorsal medial PFC, posterior cingulate, and ventral parietal cortices (Andrews-Hanna *et al.*, 2010; Buckner, Andrews-Hanna, and Schacter, 2008), and (2) an MTL network that comprises hippocampal, ventral medial PFC, retrosplenial, and ventral parietal cortices (Andrews-Hanna *et al.*, 2010; Kahn *et al.*, 2008; Vincent *et al.*, 2006). The medial PFC network is recruited to a greater extent when making decisions that are self-referential versus decisions that are not (Andrews-Hanna *et al.*, 2010), and anterior midline regions overlapping with this network are associated with self-referential processes during AM retrieval (Muscatell, Addis, and Kensinger, 2010; Rabin *et al.*, 2010; Spreng and Grady, 2010; St. Jacques *et al.*, 2011b). In contrast, the MTL network has been linked to constructing a scene based on memory (Andrews-Hanna *et al.*, 2010). Regions within the MTL network, such as

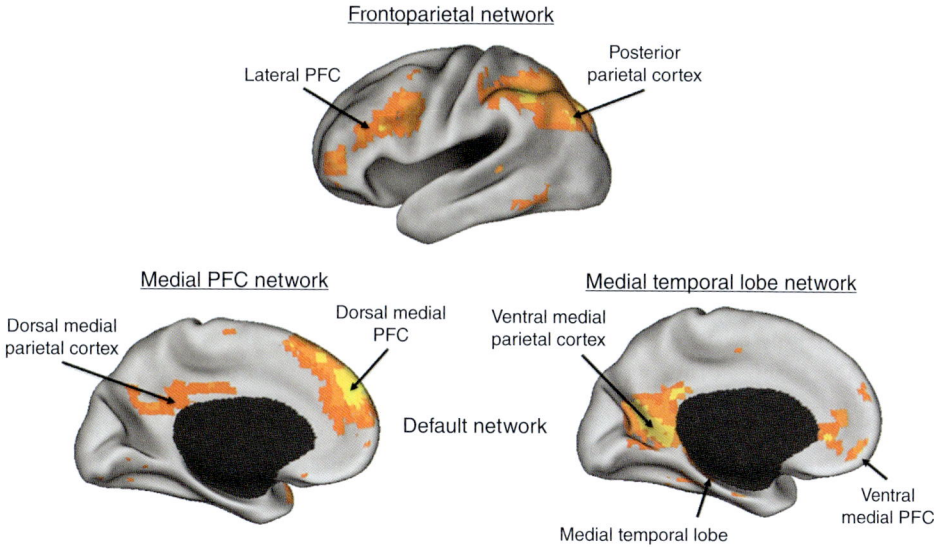

**Figure 13.1**   Large-scale networks contributing to autobiographical memory (AM). PFC, prefrontal cortex.

the hippocampus, are associated with recollection processes during memory retrieval (Diana, Yonelinas, and Ranganath, 2007), and activity within many of the regions comprising the MTL network is frequently correlated with detailed recall and subjective recollection during AM retrieval (Addis *et al.*, 2004b; Daselaar *et al.*, 2008).

The frontoparietal or central executive network (Figure 13.1) is another important neural network involved in AM retrieval. It includes lateral PFC, anterior cingulate, and inferior parietal cortices and is associated with adapative cognitive control processes (Dosenbach *et al.*, 2007; Seeley *et al.*, 2007; Vincent *et al.*, 2008). Frontal and parietal components of this network are engaged during controlled operations that act on memory (Cabeza *et al.*, 2008; Moscovitch and Winocur, 2002). The link between memory search and controlled retrieval processes in AM was based on evidence from an early PET study that found activation in lateral PFC regions when comparing AM to semantic memory (Conway *et al.*, 1999) and has since been supported by subsequent studies (Maguire, 2001; Svoboda, McKinnon, and Levine, 2006). The lateral PFC activity elicited during AM retrieval is predominantly left-lateralized (Maguire, 2001; Svoboda, McKinnon, and Levine, 2006), which is thought to reflect the contribution of complex strategic retrieval processes and the contribution of semantic information during retrieval (Conway, Pleydell-Pearce, and Whitecross, 2001; Conway *et al.*, 1999; Denkova *et al.*, 2006; for review see Svoboda, McKinnon, and Levine, 2006). Consistent with these early observations, St. Jacques, Kragel, and Rubin (2011) found that AM retrieval involved recruitment of a left-lateralized frontoparietal network, suggesting that engagement of this network during AM retrieval is less bilateral than that observed during resting state or in other cognitive tasks.

The neural networks that contribute to AM retrieval may also support tasks relying on similar processes, such as episodic future and counterfactual thinking, perspective taking, and mental navigation. In a meta-analysis of neuroimaging studies including AM, Spreng, Mar, and Kim (2009) observed overlap among neural regions supporting AM, prospection, theory of mind, and the default network (Spreng and Grady, 2010). The remarkable similarity between the neural correlates supporting AM and simulation has led many researchers to suggest that there are common mechanisms underlying both abilities, such as self-projection (Buckner and Carroll, 2007), scene construction (Hassabis and Maguire, 2007), and recombination of episodic components of memory (Schacter, Addis, and Buckner, 2007; see also Chapter 14). Additionally, the frontoparietal network recruited during AM retrieval is also frequently engaged during tasks that involve cognitive control and decision making (e.g., Dosenbach *et al.*, 2007). Subtle differences in these networks may emerge depending on context. For example, St. Jacques, Kragel, and Rubin (2011) observed that recruitment of the frontoparietal network was isolated to the initial search and construction of AM retrieval, whereas default network activation extended into the elaboration period. Using dynamic causal modeling (Friston, Harrison, and Penny, 2003), St. Jacques, Kragel, and Rubin found that the medial PFC network was integral to driving the interaction among these networks. Additionally, memory accessibility and recollection uniquely altered connectivity between these neural networks. Recollection modulated the influence of the medial PFC on the MTL network during elaboration, suggesting that greater connectivity among subsystems of the default network supports greater re-experience. In contrast, memory accessibility modulated the influence of frontoparietal and MTL networks on the medial PFC network, suggesting that the ease of retrieval involves greater fluency among the multiple networks contributing to AM. Examination of the recruitment of particular neural networks, their interaction, and modulation by behavior may help to further distinguish AM retrieval from other similar tasks (e.g., Spreng *et al.*, 2010).

## Eliciting Autobiographical Memories in the Scanning Environment

There are multiple ways to elicit AM in the scanning environment, which differ according to how well control is exerted over the phenomenological properties of memory retrieval while also maintaining ecological validity (Cabeza and St. Jacques, 2007; Maguire, 2001; Svoboda, McKinnon, and Levine, 2006). It is difficult to determine the retrieval cues that will be effective in eliciting AMs without also interfering with the properties of the retrieved memory during scanning and, consequently, subsequent interpretations of brain activations (Cabeza and St. Jacques, 2007). Here we discuss the four main methods that have been used to query AM in the scanning environment: generic cues, pre-scan interview, independent sources, and prospective (Figure 13.2).

### Generic cues

In the *generic cues* method (Crovitz and Schiffman, 1974), participants are provided with a novel retrieval cue and are asked to retrieve an AM associated with the cue (Figure 13.2a). The generic cues method has generally used verbal cues such as nouns

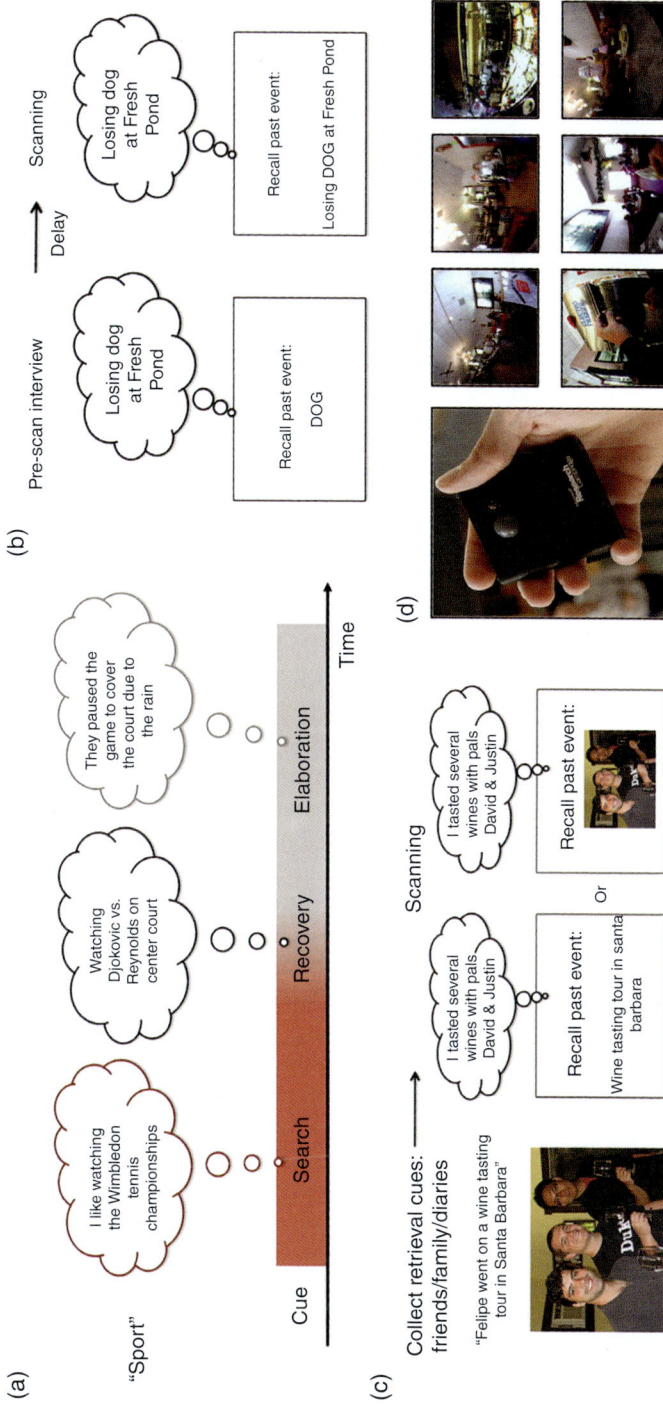

**Figure 13.2** Different methods for eliciting autobiographical memories during functional scanning: (a) generic cues, (b) pre-scan interview, (c) independent sources method, and (d) prospective collection using sensor-based camera.

(e.g., "teapot"; Conway *et al.*, 1999; Graham *et al.*, 2003), emotional words (e.g., "kiss"; Markowitsch *et al.*, 2003; St. Jacques *et al.*, 2011a), or other specialized words (e.g., hockey words; Muscatell, Addis, and Kensinger, 2010). Some studies have also employed odors (Masaoka *et al.*, 2012), pictures (Burianova and Grady, 2007; Burianova, McIntosh, and Grady, 2010; Fitzgerald *et al.*, 2004; Spreng and Grady, 2010; St-Laurent *et al.*, 2011), or musical clips (Ford, Addis, and Giovanello, 2011) as effective cues for eliciting AMs. For example, Ford, Addis, and Giovanello (2011) used musical excerpts to investigate the neural correlates supporting different levels of AM specificity in an unbiased way. During fMRI scanning, participants listened to musical clips and were instructed to press a button indicating the level of specificity of recall from lifetime period (e.g., "when I was in graduate school"), to more general event knowledge for repeated or extended events (e.g., "Christmas day"), and specific events (e.g., "the day I defended my PhD"). They found that more specific events elicited activity in bilateral MTL and medial PFC, whereas less specific events elicited activity in dorsolateral PFC. Thus, the neural correlates supporting AM retrieval differed according to the level of specificity (Addis *et al.*, 2012; Holland, Addis, and Kensinger, 2011).

AMs elicited by generic cues may not always be emotional or significant. However, they are unprepared and can involve a protracted period of retrieval (Figure 13.2a). These features result in two primary advantages of the generic cue method. First, the neural regions supporting memory construction can be investigated (Addis, Wong and Schacter, 2007; Conway, Pleydell-Pearce, and Whitecross, 2001; Daselaar *et al.*, 2008; St. Jacques, Kragel, and Rubin, 2011). For example, Daselaar *et al.* (2008) compared activity related to the search period of AM versus the maintenance/elaboration period. The initial search period was found to engage frontal regions involved in retrieval effort (right lateral PFC) and self-referential processes (medial PFC) but also posterior regions involved in accessing the memory trace (hippocampus, retrosplenial cortex), whereas the later period recruited posterior regions involved in the retrieval of contextual details (visual cortex, precuneus) and frontal regions linked to working memory (left lateral PFC). By segregating the search and elaboration phases of memory construction, the fMRI results show that AM retrieval relies upon separable component processes that come online at different points in time, and which can vary across the lifespan (Addis, Roberts, and Schacter, 2011; St. Jacques, Rubin, and Cabeza, 2012) and in clinical populations (St. Jacques *et al.*, 2011a).

A second advantage of the generic cue method is that online subjective ratings of AM retrieval are more accurate. This is important because phenomenological ratings and other properties of the retrieved memory can be used to examine trial-to-trial fluctuations in behavior as a function of brain activity using parametric analysis (see below). For example, in the aforementioned study using the generic cue method, Daselaar *et al.* (2008) examined activity during search and elaboration phases of AM retrieval that was associated with online ratings of emotion and reliving. They observed that emotion ratings were correlated with early amygdala activity, whereas reliving ratings were correlated with late visual cortex activity. This finding indicates that emotion contributes to AM retrieval even before event-specific memories are completely formed, whereas vividness develops late, as attention is directed to recovered visual images. Similarly, other studies using the generic cue method have observed that the effects of emotion tend to occur earlier (St. Jacques *et al.*, 2011a), whereas the effects associated with vividness occur later (St. Jacques, Kragel, and Rubin, 2011; St. Jacques, Rubin, and Cabeza, 2012).

## Pre-scan interview

In the *pre-scan interview* method (Figure 13.2b), AMs are elicited by cues that refer to specific events (e.g., visiting the London Eye) collected prior to the scanning session (e.g., Addis *et al.*, 2004b; Denkova *et al.*, 2011; Maguire *et al.*, 2001). An advantage of this method is that the memories retrieved in the scanner can be controlled using pre-scan ratings (e.g., age of the memory, emotion, vividness, etc.). For example, Söderlund *et al.* (2012) used this method to pre-select memories of varying remoteness to examine how the connectivity of the hippocampus varied with memory age. Two days before the scanning session, participants were asked to generate, date, and provide titles for events that had occurred in the last week, month, year, and 10 years. During the fMRI scan, participants were presented with the event titles and instructed to retrieve the AM indicated. Similar to previous studies (Cabeza and St. Jacques, 2007; Moscovitch *et al.*, 2005), the hippocampus was active irrespective of the age of the memory. However, the pattern of functional connectivity with the hippocampus and other brain regions differed for AMs that were more recent (1 week to 1 year) versus those that were more remote (10 years). The hippocampus was functionally connected with anterior and posterior midline regions for recent AMs, but not for remote AMs.

Another advantage of the pre-scan interview is that the pre-selected retrieval cues can result in highly specific and accessible memories during scanning. Addis *et al.* (2012) took advantage of this aspect of the pre-scan interview to investigate the neural substrates supporting the two routes to AM retrieval: (1) direct, involving immediate access to a memory via a retrieval cue, and (2) generative retrieval, involving additional strategic retrieval processes to select a specific memory (for review see Conway and Pleydell-Pearce, 2000). One month prior to scanning, participants were asked to retrieve AMs cued using generic cue words (e.g., "dog"). Later, during scanning, participants retrieved an AM elicited by personalized cues from the pre-scan interview ("losing DOG at fresh pond") or generic cues ("event DRESS reminds me of"). Addis and colleagues reasoned that personalized cues should provide more direct access to a specific memory, whereas generic cues would involve more generative retrieval to select a specific memory. There were many similarities in the neural correlates supporting AMs retrieved more directly versus generatively. However, generative retrieval was associated with early recruitment of the lateral PFC, and direct retrieval generally involved stronger activations among regions involved in AM retrieval, such as the posterior and anterior midline.

There are some potential disadvantages to using the pre-scan interview method. During scanning participants may recall the interview session instead of the AM they had originally recalled. Further, retrieving the AM during the interview session could alter its subsequent retrieval during scanning (St. Jacques and Schacter, 2013), and, consequently, the AM actually retrieved during scanning may differ in its content and phenomenological properties. These issues could potentially be attenuated by interposing a substantial time interval between the pre-scan and scanning sessions (e.g., Maguire and Mummery, 1999). In sum, the neural properties supporting AM can differ due to previous retrieval attempts during the pre-scan interview.

## Independent sources method

In the *independent sources* method (Figure 13.2c), cues to elicit AMs are generated by external sources such as friends and family (Gilboa *et al.*, 2004; Rabin *et al.*, 2010; Rabin and Rosenbaum, 2012; Steinvorth, Corkin, and Halgren, 2006). The independent sources method combines some of the advantages of the foregoing two methods, because memories are unrehearsed and can be constrained by gathering additional information from the sources. Additionally, it can provide greater variability in the vividness of memory retrieval, although this could be a disadvantage if participants are unable to remember a large number of events provided by the sources. Gilboa and colleagues (2004) used the independent sources method to investigate the role of the hippocampus in the recall of recent and remote memories that varied in vividness. AMs were elicited by personal photographs that depicted events ranging from childhood to the present collected from friends and relatives of the participants. Participants were asked to recall the event depicted in the photograph during fMRI. Gilboa and colleagues found that the hippocampus was recruited to a greater extent when memories were vividly recalled compared to when they were less vividly recalled, but the extent to which the hippocampus was recruited was not strongly associated with the particular age of the memory.

Similarly, Steinvorth, Corkin, and Halgren (2006) employed the independent sources method to investigate the retrieval processes involved in remembering recent and remote AMs. In this study, personal diaries were also used, and retrieval cues during fMRI scanning consisted of sentences describing personally experienced events. During scanning, participants were asked to search for the described memory and to press a button as soon as they could recall the memory, and then to elaborate upon it. They found that search and elaboration recruited a similar pattern of activation, with involvement of the hippocampus across both retrieval phases irrespective of the age of the memory.

## Prospective method

In the *prospective* method (Figure 13.2d), participants are asked to keep a record of events in their lives to be used as retrieval cues in the scanner (e.g., Cabeza *et al.*, 2004; Levine *et al.*, 2004; St. Jacques *et al.*, 2008). The main advantage of the prospective method is that it allows for the greatest amount of control over the encoding of retrieved memories and can allow verification of retrieval accuracy. For example, St. Jacques *et al.* (2008) used the prospective method to investigate accurate temporal-order memory. Using a digital camera, participants took photos of familiar campus locations in a particular order over a period of several hours, just as a tourist might take photos of landmarks while on vacation. On the following day participants were scanned while making temporal-order judgments concerning pairs of photographs from different locations that varied in the number of photos between them. It was found that accurate temporal-order decisions on pairs of photos with shorter time-lags recruited regions previously associated with recollection (left PFC, parahippocampal gyrus), whereas longer time-lags recruited regions linked to familiarity (right PFC). Use of the prospective method allowed for control over the temporal order of encoding and verification of accuracy, making this study one of the first to examine the neural correlates of temporal order for autobiographical events. Greater control over the properties of memory encoding and accuracy can also allow for careful assessment of impairment in individuals with memory complaints (e.g., Levine *et al.*, 2009).

Until recently, a disadvantage of the prospective method was that recording experiences interfered with the natural encoding of AMs. By using innovative camera technologies that employ sensors and timers to automatically capture hundreds of photographs when worn, it is now possible to prospectively generate idiosyncratic and visually rich retrieval cues which may be more effective in eliciting AMs in the laboratory (e.g., St. Jacques, Conway, and Cabeza, 2010; St. Jacques *et al.*, 2011b). One example of such technology is the SenseCam (also known as ViconRevue), a small wearable digital camera that can automatically trigger thousands of photos in a single day without disrupting the ongoing experience, which differs from other methods using digital cameras to elicit AMs (Cabeza *et al.*, 2004; St. Jacques *et al.*, 2008). Several photographs from a particular event (e.g., eating ice cream) can be consecutively viewed to create a dynamic retrieval cue from the field of view of the wearer (http://www.youtube.com/watch?v=sr1i-sICafs). For example, St. Jacques *et al.* (2011b) used the SenseCam to examine neural differences in self-projection of self versus other perspectives. During functional scanning, participants were shown short event "movies" composed of SenseCam photographs from their own life (self) or another individual's life (other) and were asked to re-experience or understand the self versus other perspectives, respectively. The results showed that projection of self versus other differentially recruited distinct regions of the medial PFC. Projection to the personal past recruited ventral medial PFC, whereas observing another person's perspective recruited dorsal medial PFC, suggesting that the rich sense of re-experience of the personal past is functionally dissociable from similar shifts in perspective that contribute to inference of another person's mental state (also see Rabin *et al.*, 2010; Spreng and Grady, 2010).

## Analysis Methods Relevant to Autobiographical Memory

Most fMRI studies on AM employ a general linear modeling (GLM) approach, as it can be used for several kinds of statistical analysis such as correlations, one- and two-sample *t*-tests, analysis of variance, etc. It is thus frequently utilized to identify brain regions preferentially recruited by a particular task, condition, and/or group – as compared to a contrasting task, condition, and/or group (i.e., subtraction method) – as well as brain regions commonly activated during two or more tasks, conditions and/or groups (i.e., conjunction method). Additionally, researchers capitalize on the fact that AMs vary across subjective (e.g., vividness, valence, etc.) and objective dimensions (e.g., recency/remoteness), which can be analyzed parametrically as predictors shown to modulate activity in different brain regions. Finally, the very complexity of AM has motivated researchers to start employing multivariate approaches in an attempt to understand the relationship between functional brain networks underlying AM. These methods include, but may not be limited to, functional and effective connectivity analyses. These analysis approaches are discussed in turn.

## General linear model

The general linear model (GLM) is a univariate analysis technique that fits a continuous dependent variable – that is, the proxy of neural signal measured by fMRI known as blood-oxygen-level-dependent (BOLD) signal – onto a linear model relating it to one or more continuous or categorical variables, such as reaction times or experimental conditions. Most fMRI researchers in AM use the GLM to determine statistically significant differences in BOLD responses between two or more experimental conditions. More simply, each fMRI dataset could be seen as a matrix of voxels coding for varying levels of BOLD activation for a set time-course. The GLM computes whether the average activation per voxel correlates with the time-course of a particular experimental condition, and whether or not this average statistically differs from the average activation in another condition. Thus, *t*-tests are usually employed to find out whether such differences in activation are statistically significant – a process commonly known as *contrast*. The GLM can also analyze commonalities between conditions, by way of using contrasts in an additive rather than a subtractive manner. Essentially, these *conjunction* analyses examine whether two or more tasks (or groups) engage the same brain regions, by determining whether the same voxels are activated during both tasks (or for both groups) in the absence of any interaction effects (Friston *et al.*, 1999; Nichols *et al.*, 2005).

The first functional neuroimaging studies of AM contrasted autobiographical retrieval tasks with either a resting baseline or a control condition, using the *subtraction* method: the direct comparison of two conditions that are assumed to differ in only the aspect or process being manipulated (i.e., the independent variable). It is thus assumed that the activated voxels that survive this comparison reflect the underlying neural activity of the process of interest. Some of the earliest functional neuroimaging studies actually contrasted AM retrieval against a resting baseline (Andreasen *et al.*, 1995, 1999). For example, Andreasen *et al.* (1995) used PET to examine the neural correlates of AM retrieval versus resting baseline, thought to be an "unfocused" recall of past experiences. The results showed similar activation in the medial PFC and precuneus during focused AM and unfocused memory retrieval occurring during resting baseline. However, it is important to keep in mind the significant overlap between the neural regions associated with AM retrieval and the default network when using resting baseline as a control task. Indeed, in a review of functional neuroimaging studies of AM, Svoboda and colleagues (2006) observed that studies that had employed baseline as a control task were less successful in reporting some of the brain regions that support AM retrieval, such as the medial PFC (Stark and Squire, 2001).

Another strategy is to use a semantic memory task as control (e.g., Conway *et al.*, 1999; Denkova *et al.*, 2006; Graham *et al.*, 2003; Ryan *et al.*, 2001). Following this logic, in an early PET study Conway and collaborators (1999) intended to subtract out the non-autobiographical components of memory retrieval to isolate activations uniquely related to AM (see also Graham *et al.*, 2003). Unfortunately, the use of semantic memory tasks as a control condition for AM could subtract away brain activity that actually supports AM retrieval. For example, an influential theory of AM suggests that semantic memory gates access to autobiographical details (Conway and Pleydell-Pearce, 2000), and there is evidence that AM retrieval involves the integration of both episodic and semantic components in memory (Levine *et al.*, 2002; St. Jacques and Levine, 2007). Moreover, brain regions involved in semantic memory are frequently observed in AM retrieval (for review see Svoboda, McKinnon, and Levine, 2006).

Other studies have attempted to control for visual imagery processes (e.g., Addis *et al.*, 2004b; Gardini *et al.*, 2006) and episodic memory processes (e.g., Cabeza *et al.*, 2004), among other factors. Unfortunately, for complex processes such as those involved in AM, there is really no perfect control condition. Use of the GLM in functional neuroimaging studies of AM is probably most effective when contrasts compare variations within AM, such as recent versus remote AMs (for review see Cabeza and St. Jacques, 2007), episodic AM versus semantic AM (for review see St. Jacques and Cabeza, 2012), direct versus generative retrieval (e.g., Addis *et al.*, 2012; Holland, Addis, and Kensinger, 2011), specific versus general AMs (Ford, Addis, and Giovanello, 2011; Levine *et al.*, 2004; Maguire and Mummery, 1999), etc.

## Parametric approach

Similar to directly contrasting AMs that categorically vary on certain dimensions, the parametric approach examines how AMs vary according to continuous dimensions of AM experience by including additional regressors on variables within the GLM. Parametric modulators can include subjective ratings and other dimensions that are captured online or in a post-scan interview. For example, using a parametric modulation analysis, Addis *et al.* (2004b) observed that activation of the left hippocampus is positively correlated with the level of detail and personal significance, as well as valence, when recency is controlled for. A subsequent study showed that the right frontopolar cortex also co-varies with the amount of detail during both AM and future projection tasks (Addis and Schacter, 2008).

However, the parametric approach should be used with caution. One major issue is that the effects of two phenomenological characteristics that we take to be psychologically distinct may actually be correlated, which means that it may be difficult to interpret whether a parametric effect is unique to a particular regressor. For example, AMs that are more arousing (e.g., Reisberg *et al.*, 1988; Talarico, LaBar, and Rubin, 2004) or positively valenced (e.g., D'Argembeau, Comblain, and Van der Linden, 2003; Destun and Kuiper, 1999; Schaefer and Philippot, 2005) also tend to be more richly recollected. Although it is possible to "control" for the effects of another dimension by including it as a different regressor, a GLM will still have difficultly assigning variance to each regressor when they are highly correlated.

## Multivariate approaches

Multivariate techniques allow for the simultaneous analysis of patterns of co-activation across voxels. One of the most utilized multivariate statistical techniques in neuroimaging research of AM is *partial least squares* analysis (PLS). First introduced to fMRI by McIntosh *et al.* (1996), PLS allows the identification of commonalities or "patterns" of whole-brain activity that correlate with either behaviors or specific aspects of the experimental design (e.g., groups, tasks, conditions). Although several variants of PLS can be used in neuroimaging research (Krishnan *et al.*, 2011), functional neuroimaging studies of AM have used spatiotemporal PLS (ST-PLS) because it permits the identification of cross-correlations between brain activity across multiple time-points and some factor of interest from the experimental design. This temporal dimension of ST-PLS proves advantageous when it comes to studying the neural structures underlying complex cognitive processes that take time, such as those involved in AM. Essentially, ST-PLS takes each participant's fMRI data into a data matrix (or "datamat") and cross-correlates it with a matrix of vectors coding for some factor of the experimental design ("design matrix"). Next, singular value decomposition is used to reveal orthogonal latent variables (LVs) that best account for the covariance. Repeated permutations and bootstrapping are then utilized to calculate the statistical significance of each LV. As such, when a LV reaches statistical significance, it indicates similarities and differences between brain areas underlying two or more design features.

One of the first ST-PLS studies in AM was conducted by Addis and collaborators (2004a). In this study, participants were asked to recall either general or specific AMs, as characterized in Conway's hierarchical AM model (Conway, 1992; Conway and Pleydell-Pearce, 2000). LVs differentiated brain regions preferentially involved during specific (e.g., left precuneus and superior parietal lobe) versus general AM retrieval (e.g., right inferior temporal gyrus and right medial PFC). Importantly, by using ST-PLS analysis, Addis *et al.* (2004a) found that this differential pattern of activity emerged at different times in the trial, with activity in regions associated with general AM peaking earlier (~ 4 seconds after stimulus onset) than those associated with specific AM retrieval (~ 7 seconds). The authors interpreted this finding as lending credence to Conway's model, according to which general AM gates access to information about specific autobiographical events. Levine *et al.* (2004) also employed a PLS analysis in a prospective memory study examining neural regions associated with episodic and semantic components of AM retrieval. This study revealed a LV that differentiated regions uniquely associated with personal episodic information (e.g., medial temporal and posterior cingulate cortices) from general semantic information included in autobiographical remembering (e.g., left temporal and parietal cortices; see also Rajah and McIntosh, 2005).

More recently, PLS analysis in AM research has been employed to explore commonalities and differences between neural processes unique to AM and those engaged during other cognitive tasks, such as prospection, mentalizing, and counterfactual thinking. In addition to the Spreng and Grady (2010) study mentioned above, in which common patterns of brain activity for AM, prospection, and theory of mind were identified, other studies have explored similarities and differences in brain patterns during AM and episodic counterfactual thinking tasks, i.e., in which participants generate alternative ways in which one's past personal events could have occurred but did not (De Brigard and Giovanello, 2012). These studies have shown that episodic counterfactual thinking and AM share a common brain pattern of activation, and that the commonalities between the two vary as a function of how likely participants think it is that the counterfactual event could have occurred (Addis *et al.*, 2009; De Brigard *et al.*, 2013).

Another statistical approach used in AM research is known as *independent component analysis* (ICA; Calhoun *et al.*, 2001). ICA is a data-driven approach that decomposes neural networks via their time-course, and, unlike PLS, the components extracted are not limited to those related to task. While the overlap between components is minimized by ICA, the networks are not necessarily orthogonal as in PLS. Few studies have employed ICA to investigate AM (St. Jacques, Kragel, and Rubin, 2011; also see Botzung *et al.*, 2010). For example, St. Jacques, Kragel, and Rubin (2011) used ICA to examine the large-scale networks contributing to the construction and elaboration of AM. They found that AM retrieval involved functionally dissociable networks including the frontoparietal network, the MTL network and medial PFC network.

Another common approach is to explore functional connectivity, that is, functional relationships among different brain areas engaged during a particular task (Friston *et al.*, 1993; Friston, 1994). As mentioned, AM retrieval involves co-activation of different brain regions. However, mere co-activation does not mean that such regions are functionally, let alone causally, connected. To investigate how different regions cooperate with one another during a particular task, statistical models incorporate information about the time-course and intensity of activations. As such, functional connectivity analyses enable researchers to determine activation synchronicity through time across cross-correlated voxels or regions of interest (ROIs). The resultant pattern of cross-correlations provides an idea of the different brain regions that functionally cooperate during a particular task.

An example of this approach is a study conducted by Greenberg *et al.* (2005), in which, prior to scanning, participants were asked to generate cue words for a number of AMs. During scanning, participants were presented with self-generated word-cues and unrelated words, and they were asked either to retrieve the corresponding AM or else to perform a semantic memory task. Correlational analysis between apriori regions of interest revealed functional connectivity among the amygdala, hippocampus, and right inferior frontal gyrus for the AM task but not for the semantic memory task. In another study, Viard *et al.* (2007) employed targeted correlational analyses to explore patterns of functional connectivity between different brain regions during retrieval of AMs from five lifetime periods in older adults. The analysis revealed strong functional connectivity among left hippocampus, left superior frontal gyrus, bilateral precuneus, and posterior cingulate gyrus across all lifetime periods. More recently, Viard *et al.* (2010) used this same approach to explore the interaction between this network and different retention intervals, revealing that it contributes equally to AM retrieval regardless of the age of the remembered episode – a result that lends credence to the view that the MTL is permanently required to recover episodic AMs irrespective of their remoteness (Nadel and Moscovitch, 1997; Nadel, Campbell, and Ryan, 2007; see also St. Jacques *et al.*, 2011b). Seed-PLS analyses have also been used to study functional connectivity between specific nodes and voxels across the rest of the brain throughout the duration of the event (Addis *et al.*, 2004a; Burianova, McIntosh and Grady, 2010; Söderlund *et al.*, 2012).

One of the limitations of functional connectivity is that it does not provide information about the specific directionality of the functional connections, because it does not make reference to the causal contribution of the neural structures underlying the model. For that reason, researchers have incorporated statistical techniques that allow inference about causal influences among functionally connected neural regions – an approach known as *effective connectivity*. One such technique is structural equation modeling (SEM; Büchel and Friston, 1997; McIntosh and Gonzalez-Lima, 1994), which takes single nodes from the dataset revealed by the connectivity analysis and fits known neuroanatomical constraints onto the correlational model to reveal specific paths that best account for the interregional covariance in the BOLD signal.

Muscatell, Addis, and Kensinger (2010) used this methodology in a study examining differences in effective connectivity depending on the level of self-involvement participants felt toward the remembered AM. Among other findings, their SEM analysis revealed that left hippocampus exerts a positive influence on the medial PFC, which in turn positively influences the amygdala–hippocampal complex, during high self-involvement recollections. However, during low self-involvement recollections, the influence of the medial PFC on the amygdala–hippocampal complex is negative, suggesting that medial PFC and the amygdala–hippocampal complex work together during the retrieval of AMs with high levels of self-involvement, but independently when the level of self-involvement is low. SEM has also been used to examine how the effective connectivity network underlying AM retrieval is altered in patients with hippocampal damage (e.g., Addis, Moscovitch, and McAndrews, 2007; Maguire, Vargha-Khadem, and Mishkin, 2001).

Although we have almost exclusively limited our discussion to PET and fMRI studies, it is worth noting that other techniques have been employed by cognitive neuroscientists studying AM. One such technique is transcranial magnetic stimulation (TMS), whose repetitive use is often employed as a treatment for major depression, typically causing disruption in AM recollection (Burt, Lisanby, and Sackeim, 2002). With the advent of safer and more controlled ways of employing TMS in experimental settings, researchers are starting to use it to examine specific aspects of AM (for a review see Guse, Falkai, and Wobrock, 2010). Intracranial electroencephalography (EEG) has also been employed to explore variations in electrophysiological oscillations during AM. For instance, Steinvorth and colleagues (2010) used intracranial EEG to identify theta, gamma, and delta oscillatory signatures in hippocampal and entorhinal cortex for remote autobiographical recollection, which differed from those evoked by visual imagery and semantic retrieval. No doubt, future research will start incorporating different techniques as they become available.

## Conclusions and Future Directions

Since the mid-1990s, research on functional neuroimaging of AM has come a long way. As Maguire (2012) reminds us, conducting functional neuroimaging studies on AM was initially viewed with skepticism, even disdain. Many thought that such an endeavor would produce essentially uninterpretable data, as it was thought that the complexity of the processes underlying autobiographical recollection would render them unwieldy. Nowadays, however, the consistency and reliability of a growing number of experimental results strongly suggest that functional neuroimaging of AM is a fecund area of investigation, and that its results helps us understand the neural mechanisms responsible for our ordinary experience of remembering the past. Functional neuroimaging evidence has revealed, for instance, that autobiographical recollection involves the interaction of different neural networks, which may depend on the nature of the retrieved memory (Andrews-Hanna *et al.*, 2010; Muscatell, Addis, and Kensinger, 2011; St. Jacques, Kragel, and Rubin, 2011). Additionally, it has also revealed that such networks overlap with the default network (Buckner, Andrews-Hanna, and Schacter, 2008), that they contribute to other cognitive processes such as mentalizing, future and counterfactual thinking (De Brigard *et al.*, 2013), and that, contrary to the classical model of memory consolidation, the hippocampus – and, in general, the MTL – appears to be involved in the retrieval of episodic autobiographical memory regardless of the remoteness of the remembered episode (Söderlund *et al.*, 2012). Additionally, functional neuroimaging studies of AM have also helped to expand the methodological reach and experimental design in research in neuroimaging in general. For instance, many of the studies reviewed above provide evidence demonstrating that it is possible to conduct experiments using ecologically valid stimuli, and that there are several alternatives to manipulate personally relevant stimulus in the scanner without sacrificing experimental control (e.g., St. Jacques *et al.*, 2011b).

Among the most exciting areas of ongoing and future research in functional neuroimaging of AM are studies on involuntary recollection (Berntsen, 1998, 2009). Most of the time, when we remember our personal past, we tend to do so involuntarily, which often results in a vivid recollective experience. However, it is still an open question to what extent the mechanisms of voluntary and involuntary AM retrieval overlap. Using the techniques for functional neuroimaging reviewed above, researchers may be able to shed light on these issues. Equally interesting is the question of the effect of reactivation on the original autobiographical memory (St. Jacques and Schacter, 2013). In one study, Mendelsohn *et al.* (2009) filmed a person during two days. Four months, and then two and a half years later, they tested this person's memory while undergoing fMRI. Their results showed, among other things, that even though the participant tended to incorporate more false details into her recollections as time went by, the AM network tended to correlate more strongly with memory confidence rather than with accuracy (Nadel, Campbell, and Ryan, 2007; Svoboda and Levine, 2009). Given the frequency with which AMs are reactivated in ordinary life, understanding the effects of reactivation on AM and its neural correlates constitutes an exciting avenue for future research (e.g., St. Jacques, Olm, and Schacter, 2013). Finally, another research line that promises important developments in cognitive neuroscience of AM pertains to studies with special populations. The extent to which the neural correlates of AM are altered in pathological aging (see Chapter 20), in individuals with developmental or mood disorders, or in individuals with superior AM (Ally, Hussey, and Donahue, 2012; LePort *et al.*, 2012), to name a few, is still unknown. As a result, functional neuroimaging of autobiographical memory promises to be at the forefront of research in the cognitive neuroscience of memory.

## Acknowledgments

This work was supported by a postdoctoral NRSA AG038079 (P.L.S.).

## References

Addis, D.R., Knapp, K., Roberts, R.P., and Schacter, D.L. (2012). Routes to the past: neural substrates of direct and generative autobiographical memory retrieval. *NeuroImage*, 59 (3), 2908–2922.

Addis, D.R., McIntosh, A.R., Moscovitch, M., *et al.* (2004a). Characterizing spatial and temporal features of autobiographical memory retrieval networks: a partial least squares approach. *NeuroImage*, 23 (4), 1460–1471.

Addis, D.R., Moscovitch, M., Crawley, A.P., and McAndrews, M.P. (2004b). Recollective qualities modulate hippocampal activation during autobiographical memory retrieval. *Hippocampus*, 14 (6), 752–762.

Addis, D.R., Moscovitch, M., and McAndrews, M.P. (2007). Consequences of hippocampal damage across the autobiographical memory retrieval network in patients with left temporal lobe epilepsy. *Brain*, 130, 2327–2342.

Addis, D.R., Pan, L., Vu, M.-A., *et al.* (2009). Constructive episodic simulation of the future and the past: Distinct subsystems of a core brain network mediate imagining and remembering. *Neuropsychologia*, 47 (11), 2222–2238.

Addis, D.R., Roberts, R.P., and Schacter, D.L. (2011). Age-related neural changes in autobiographical remembering and imagining. *Neuropsychologia*, 49 (13), 3656–3669.

Addis, D.R., and Schacter, D. (2008). Effects of detail and temporal distance of past and future events on the engagement of a common neural network. *Hippocampus*, 18, 227–237.

Addis, D.R., Wong A.T., and Schacter, D.L. (2007). Remembering the past and imagining the future: common and distinct neural substrates during event construction and elaboration. *Neuropsychologia*, 45, 1363–1377.

Ally, B.A., Hussey, E.P., and Donahue, M.J. (2013). A case of hyperthymesia: rethinking the role of the amygdala in autobiographical memory. *Neurocase*, 19 (2), 166–181.

Andreasen, N.C., O'Leary, D.S., Cizadlo, T., *et al.* (1995). Remembering the past: two facets of episodic memory explored with positron emission tomography. *American Journal of Psychiatry*, 152 (11), 1576–1585.

Andreasen, N.C., O'Leary, D.S., Paradiso, S., *et al.* (1999). The cerebellum plays a role in conscious episodic memory retrieval. *Human Brain Mapping*, 8 (4), 226–234.

Andrews-Hanna, J.R., Reidler, J.S., Sepulcre, J., *et al.* (2010). Functional–anatomic fractionation of the brain's default network. *Neuron*, 65 (4), 550–562.

Berntsen, D. (1998). Voluntary and involuntary access to autobiographical memory. *Memory*, 6 (2), 113–141.

Berntsen, D. (2009). *Involuntary Autobiographical Memories: An Introduction to the Unbidden Past*. Cambridge: Cambridge University Press.

Botzung, A., LaBar, K.S., Kragel, P., *et al.* (2010). Component neural systems for the creation of emotional memories during free viewing of a complex, real-world event. *Frontiers in Human Neuroscience*, 4, 34. doi: 10.3389/fnhum.2010.00034.

Büchel, C., and Friston, K. (1997). Modulation of connectivity in visual pathways by attention: cortical interactions evaluated with structural equation modelling and fMRI. *Cerebral Cortex*, 7 (8), 768–778.

Buckner, R.L., Andrews-Hanna J.R., and Schacter, D.L. (2008). The brain's default network: anatomy, function, and relevance to disease. *Annals of the New York Academy of Sciences*, 1124 (1), 1–38. doi: 10.1196/annals.1440.011

Buckner, R.L., and Carroll, D.C. (2007). Self-projection and the brain. *Trends in Cognitive Sciences*, 11 (2), 49–57.

Burianova, H., and Grady, C.L. (2007). Common and unique neural activations in autobiographical, episodic, and semantic retrieval. *Journal of Cognitive Neuroscience*, 19 (9), 1520–1534.

Burianova, H., McIntosh, A.R., and Grady, C.L. (2010). A common functional brain network for autobiographical, episodic, and semantic memory retrieval. *NeuroImage*, 49 (1), 865–874.

Burt, T., Lisanby, S.H., and Sackeim, H.A. (2002). Neuropsychiatric applications of transcranial magnetic stimulation: a meta analysis. *International Journal of Neuropsychopharmacology*, 5 (1), 73–103.

Cabeza, R., Ciaramelli, E., Olson, I.R., and Moscovitch, M. (2008). The parietal cortex and episodic memory: an attentional account. *Nature Reviews Neuroscience*, 9 (8), 613–625.

Cabeza, R., and Nyberg, L. (2000). Imaging cognition II. An empirical review of 275 PET and fMRI studies. *Journal of Cognitive Neuroscience*, 12 (1), 1–47.

Cabeza, R., Prince, S.E., Daselaar, S.M., *et al.* (2004). Brain activity during episodic retrieval of autobiographical and laboratory events: an fMRI study using a novel photo paradigm. *Journal of Cognitive Neuroscience*, 16 (9), 1583–1594.

Cabeza, R., and St. Jacques, P. (2007). Functional neuroimaging of autobiographical memory. *Trends in Cognitive Sciences*, 11 (5), 219–227.

Calhoun, V., Adali, T., Pearlson, G., and Pekar, J. (2001). Spatial and temporal independent component analysis of functional MRI data containing a pair of task-related waveforms. *Human Brain Mapping*, 13 (1), 43–53.

Conway, M.A. (1992). A structural model of autobiographical memory. In *Theoretical Perspectives on Autobiographical Memory* (ed. M.A. Conway, D.C. Rubin, H. Spinnler, and W.A. Wagenaar). Dordrecht: Kluwer, pp. 167–193.

Conway, M.A., and Pleydell-Pearce, C.W. (2000). The construction of autobiographical memories in the self-memory system. *Psychological Review*, 107 (2), 261.

Conway, M.A., Pleydell-Pearce, C.W., and Whitecross, S.E. (2001). The neuroanatomy of autobiographical memory: a slow wave cortical potential study of autobiographical memory. *Journal of Memory and Language*, 45, 493–524. doi: 10.1006/jmla.2001.2781

Conway, M.A., Turk, D.J., Miller, S.L., *et al.* (1999). A positron emission tomography (PET) study of autobiographical memory retrieval. *Memory*, 7 (5–6), 679–703.

Crovitz, H.F., and Schiffman, H. (1974). Frequency of episodic memories as a function of their age. *Bulletin of the Psychonomic Society*, 4 (5-B), 517–518.

D'Argembeau, A., Comblain, C., and Van der Linden, M. (2003). Phenomenal characteristics of autobiographical memories for positive, negative, and neutral events. *Applied Cognitive Psychology*, 17 (3), 281–294.

Daselaar, S.M., Rice, H.J., Greenberg, D.L., *et al.* (2008). The spatiotemporal dynamics of autobiographical memory: neural correlates of recall, emotional intensity, and reliving. *Cerebral Cortex*, 18 (1), 217–229.

De Brigard, F., Addis, D. Ford, J., *et al.* (2013). Remembering what could have happened: Neural correlates of episodic counterfactual thinking. *Neuropsychologia*, 51 (12), 2401–2414.

De Brigard, F., and Giovanello, K.S. (2012). Influence of outcome valence in the subjective experience of episodic past, future, and counterfactual thinking. *Consciousness and Cognition*, 21(3), 1085–1096.

Denkova, E., Botzung, A., Scheiber, C., and Manning, L. (2006). Material-independent cerebral network of re-experiencing personal events: Evidence from two parallel fMRI experiments. *Neuroscience Letters*, 407 (1), 32–36.

Denkova, E., Chakrabarty, T., Dolcos, S., and Dolcos, F. (2011). Brain imaging investigation of the neural correlates of emotional autobiographical recollection. *Journal of Visualized Experiments*, (54), e2393. doi: 10.3791/2396.

Destun, L.M., and Kuiper, N.A. (1999). Phenomenal characteristics associated with real and imagined events: the effects of event valence and absorption. *Applied Cognitive Psychology*, 13 (2), 175–186.

Diana, R.A., Yonelinas, A.P., and Ranganath, C. (2007). Imaging recollection and familiarity in the medial temporal lobe: a three-component model. *Trends in Cognitive Sciences*, 11 (9), 379–386.

Dosenbach, N.U., Fair, D.A., Miezin, F.M., *et al.* (2007). Distinct brain networks for adaptive and stable task control in humans. *Proceedings of the National Academy of Sciences of the USA*, 104 (26), 11073–11078.

Fitzgerald, D.A., Posse, S., Moore, G.J., *et al.* (2004). Neural correlates of internally-generated disgust via autobiographical recall: a functional magnetic resonance imaging investigation. *Neuroscience Letters*, 370 (2), 91–96.

Ford, J.H., Addis, D.R., and Giovanello, K.S. (2011). Differential neural activity during search of specific and general autobiographical memories elicited by musical cues. *Neuropsychologia*, 49 (9), 2514–2526.

Friston, K., Jezzard, P., Frackowiak, R., and Turner, R. (1993). Characterizing focal and distributed physiological changes with MRI and PET. In *Functional MRI of the Brain*. Berkeley, CA: Society of Magnetic Resonance in Medicine, pp. 207–216.

Friston, K.J. (1994). Functional and effective connectivity in neuroimaging: a synthesis. *Human Brain Mapping*, 2 (1–2), 56–78.

Friston, K.J., Harrison, L., and Penny, W. (2003). Dynamic causal modelling. *NeuroImage*, 19 (4), 1273–1302.

Friston, K.J., Holmes, A.P., Price, C., *et al.* (1999). Multisubject fMRI studies and conjunction analyses. *NeuroImage*, 10 (4), 385–396.

Fuster, J.M. (2009). Cortex and memory: emergence of a new paradigm. *Journal of Cognitive Neuroscience*, 21 (11), 2047–2072.

Gardini, S., Cornoldi, C., De Beni, R., and Venneri, A. (2006). Left mediotemporal structures mediate the retrieval of episodic autobiographical mental images. *NeuroImage*, 30 (2), 645–655.

Gilboa, A. (2004). Autobiographical and episodic memory: one and the same? Evidence from prefrontal activation in neuroimaging studies. *Neuropsychologia*, 42 (10), 1336–1349.

Gilboa, A., Winocur, G., Grady, C.L., *et al.* (2004). Remembering our past: functional neuroanatomy of recollection of recent and very remote personal events. *Cerebral Cortex*, 14 (11), 1214–1225.

Graham, K.S., Lee, A.C., Brett, M., and Patterson, K. (2003). The neural basis of autobiographical and semantic memory: New evidence from three PET studies. *Cognitive, Affective, and Behavioral Neuroscience*, 3 (3), 234–254.

Greenberg, D.L., Rice, H.J., Cooper, J.J., *et al.* (2005). Co-activation of the amygdala, hippocampus and inferior frontal gyrus during autobiographical memory retrieval. *Neuropsychologia*, 43 (5), 659–674.

Guse, B., Falkai, P., and Wobrock, T. (2010). Cognitive effects of high-frequency repetitive transcranial magnetic stimulation: a systematic review. *Journal of Neural Transmission*, 117 (1), 105–122.

Hassabis, D., and Maguire, E.A. (2007). Deconstructing episodic memory with construction. *Trends in Cognitive Sciences*, 11 (7), 299–306.

Holland, A.C., Addis, D.R., and Kensinger, E.A. (2011). The neural correlates of specific versus general autobiographical memory construction and elaboration. *Neuropsychologia*, 49 (12), 3164–3177.

Kahn, I., Andrews-Hanna, J.R., Vincent, J.L., *et al.* (2008). Distinct cortical anatomy linked to subregions of the medial temporal lobe revealed by intrinsic functional connectivity. *Journal of Neurophysiology*, 100 (1), 129–139.

Krishnan, A., Williams, L.J., McIntosh, A.R., and Abdi, H. (2011). Partial least squares (PLS) methods for neuroimaging: a tutorial and review. *NeuroImage*, 56 (2), 455–475.

LePort, A.K., Mattfeld, A.T., Dickinson-Anson, H., *et al.* (2012). Behavioral and neuroanatomical investigation of highly Superior autobiographical memory (HSAM). *Neurobiology of Learning and Memory*, 98 (1), 78–92.

Levine, B., Svoboda, E., Hay, J.F., *et al.* (2002). Aging and autobiographical memory: dissociating episodic from semantic retrieval. *Psychology and Aging*, 17 (4), 677.

Levine, B., Svoboda, E., Turner, G.R., *et al.* (2009). Behavioral and functional neuroanatomical correlates of anterograde autobiographical memory in isolated retrograde amnesic patient ML. *Neuropsychologia*, 47 (11), 2188–2196.

Levine, B., Turner, G.R.. Tisserand, D., *et al.* (2004). The functional neuroanatomy of episodic and semantic autobiographical remembering: a prospective functional MRI study. *Journal of Cognitive Neuroscience*, 16 (9), 1633–1646.

Maguire, E.A. (2001). Neuroimaging studies of autobiographical event memory. *Philosophical Transactions of the Royal Society of London, Series B: Biological Sciences*, 356 (1413), 1441–1451.

Maguire, E.A. (2012). Studying the freely-behaving brain with fMRI. *NeuroImage*, 62 (2), 1170–1176.

Maguire, E.A., Henson, R.N.A., Mummery, C.J., and Frith, C.D. (2001). Activity in prefrontal cortex, not hippocampus, varies parametrically with the increasing remoteness of memories. *Neuroreport*, 12 (3), 441–444.

Maguire, E.A., and Mummery, C.J. (1999). Differential modulation of a common memory retrieval network revealed by positron emission tomography. *Hippocampus*, 9 (1), 54–61.

Maguire, E.A., Vargha-Khadem, F., and Mishkin, M. (2001). The effects of bilateral hippocampal damage on fMRI regional activations and interactions during memory retrieval. *Brain*, 124 (6), 1156–1170. doi: 10.1093/brain/124.6.1156.

Markowitsch, H.J., Vandekerckhove, M.M., Lanfermann, H., and Russ, M.O. (2003). Engagement of lateral and medial prefrontal areas in the ecphory of sad and happy autobiographical memories. *Cortex*, 39 (4), 643–665.

Masaoka, Y., Sugiyama, H., Katayama, A., *et al.* (2012). Remembering the past with slow breathing associated with activity in the parahippocampus and amygdala. *Neuroscience Letters* 521 (2), 98–103.

McDermott, K.B., Szpunar, K.K., and Christ, S.E. (2009). Laboratory-based and autobiographical retrieval tasks differ substantially in their neural substrates. *Neuropsychologia*, 47 (11), 2290–2298.

McIntosh, A., Bookstein, F., Haxby, J.V., and Grady, C. (1996). Spatial pattern analysis of functional brain images using partial least squares. *NeuroImage*, 3 (3), 143–157.

McIntosh, A., and Gonzalez-Lima, F. (1994). Structural equation modeling and its application to network analysis in functional brain imaging. *Human Brain Mapping*, 2 (1–2), 2–22.

Mendelsohn, A., Furman, O., Navon, I., and Dudai. Y. (2009). Subjective vs. documented reality: A case study of long-term real-life autobiographical memory. *Learning and Memory*, 16 (2), 142–146.

Moscovitch, M., Rosenbaum, R.S., Gilboa, A., *et al.* (2005). Functional neuroanatomy of remote episodic, semantic and spatial memory: a unified account based on multiple trace theory. *Journal of Anatomy*, 207 (1), 35–66.

Moscovitch, M., and Winocur, G. (2002). The frontal cortex and working with memory. In *Principles of Frontal Lobe Function* (ed. D.T. Stuss and R.T. Knight). Oxford: Oxford University Press, pp. 188–209.

Muscatell, K.A., Addis, D.R., and Kensinger, E.A. (2010). Self-involvement modulates the effective connectivity of the autobiographical memory network. *Social, Cognitive and Affective Neuroscience*, 5 (1), 68–76.

Nadel, L., Campbell, J., and Ryan, L. (2007). Autobiographical memory retrieval and hippocampal activation as a function of repetition and the passage of time. *Neural Plasticity*, 2007, 90472. doi: 10.1155/2007/90472.

Nadel, L., and Moscovitch, M. (1997). Memory consolidation, retrograde amnesia and the hippocampal complex. *Current Opinion in Neurobiology*, 7 (2), 217–227.

Neisser, U. (1978). Memory: what are the important questions? In *Practical Aspects of Memory* (ed. M. Gruneberg, P. Morris and R. Sykes). London: Academic Press, pp. 3–24.

Nichols, T., Brett, M., Andersson, J., *et al.* (2005). Valid conjunction inference with the minimum statistic. *NeuroImage*, 25 (3), 653–660.

Rabin, J.S., Gilboa, A., Stuss, D.T., *et al.* (2010). Common and unique neural correlates of autobiographical memory and theory of mind. *Journal of Cognitive Neuroscience*, 22 (6), 1095–1111.

Rabin, J.S., and Rosenbaum, R.S. (2012). Familiarity modulates the functional relationship between theory of mind and autobiographical memory. *NeuroImage*, 62 (1), 520–529.

Raichle, M.E., MacLeod, A.M., Snyder, A.Z., *et al.* (2001). A default mode of brain function. *Proceedings of the National Academy of Sciences of the USA*, 98 (2), 676–682.

Rajah, M.N., and McIntosh, A.R. (2005). Overlap in the functional neural systems involved in semantic and episodic memory retrieval. *Journal of Cognitive Neuroscience*, 17 (3), 470–482.

Reisberg, D., Heuer, F., McLean, J., and O'Shaughnessy, M. (1988). The quantity, not the quality, of affect predicts memory vividness. *Bulletin of the Psychonomic Society*, 26 (2), 100–103.

Rubin, D.C. (2006). The basic-systems model of episodic memory. *Perspectives on Psychological Science*, 1 (4), 277–311.

Ryan, L., Nadel, L., Keil, K., *et al.* (2001). Hippocampal complex and retrieval of recent and very remote autobiographical memories: evidence from functional magnetic resonance imaging in neurologically intact people. *Hippocampus*, 11 (6), 707–714.

Schacter, D.L., Addis, D.R., and Buckner, R.L. (2007). Remembering the past to imagine the future: the prospective brain. *Nature Reviews Neuroscience*, 8 (9), 657–661.

Schaefer, A., and Philippot, P. (2005). Selective effects of emotion on the phenomenal characteristics of autobiographical memories. *Memory*, 13 (2), 148–160.

Seeley, W.W., Menon, V., Schatzberg, A.F., *et al.* (2007). Dissociable intrinsic connectivity networks for salience processing and executive control. *Journal of Neuroscience*, 27 (9), 2349–2356.

Söderlund, H., Moscovitch, M., Kumar, N., *et al.* (2012). As time goes by: hippocampal connectivity changes with remoteness of autobiographical memory retrieval. *Hippocampus*, 22 (4), 670–679.

Spreng, R.N., and Grady, C.L. (2010). Patterns of brain activity supporting autobiographical memory, prospection, and theory of mind, and their relationship to the default mode network. *Journal of Cognitive Neuroscience*, 22 (6), 1112–1123.

Spreng, R.N., Mar, R.A., and Kim, A.S. (2009). The common neural basis of autobiographical memory, prospection, navigation, theory of mind, and the default mode: a quantitative meta-analysis. *Journal of Cognitive Neuroscience*, 21 (3), 489–510.

Spreng, R.N., Stevens, W.D., Chamberlain, J.P., *et al.* (2010). Default network activity, coupled with the frontoparietal control network, supports goal-directed cognition. *NeuroImage*, 53 (1), 303–317.

St. Jacques, P.L. (2012). Functional neuroimaging of autobiographical memory. In *Understanding Autobiographical Memory: Theories and Approaches* (ed. D. Berntsen and D.C. Rubin). Cambridge: Cambridge University Press, pp. 114–138.

St. Jacques, P.L., Botzung, A., Miles, A., and Rubin, D.C. (2011a). Functional neuroimaging of emotionally intense autobiographical memories in post-traumatic stress disorder. *Journal of Psychiatric Research*, 45 (5), 630–637.

St. Jacques, P.L., and Cabeza, R. (2012). Neural basis of autobiographical memory. In *Origins and Development of Recollection: Perspectives from Psychology and Neuroscience* (ed. S. Ghetti and P.J. Bauer). New York, NY: Oxford University Press, pp. 188–218.

St. Jacques, P.L., Conway, M.A., and Cabeza, R. (2011). Gender differences in autobiographical memory for everyday events: retrieval elicited by SenseCam images versus verbal cues. *Memory*, 19 (7), 723–732.

St. Jacques, P.L., Conway, M.A., Lowder, M.W., and Cabeza, R. (2011b). Watching my mind unfold versus yours: an fMRI study using a novel camera technology to examine neural differences in self-projection of self versus other perspectives. *Journal of Cognitive Neuroscience*, 23 (6), 1275–1284.

St. Jacques, P.L., Kragel, P.A., and Rubin, D.C. (2011). Dynamic neural networks supporting memory retrieval. *NeuroImage*, 57 (2), 608–616.

St. Jacques, P.L., and Levine, B. (2007). Ageing and autobiographical memory for emotional and neutral events. *Memory*, 15 (2), 129–144.

St. Jacques, P.L., Olm, C., and Schacter, D.L. (2013). Neural mechanisms of reactivation-induced updating that enhance and distort memory. *Proceedings of the National Academy of Sciences USA*, 110 (49), 19671–19678.

St. Jacques, P.L., Rubin, D.C., and Cabeza, R. (2012). Age-related effects on the neural correlates of autobiographical memory retrieval. *Neurobiology of Aging*, 33 (7), 1298–1310.

St. Jacques, P.L., Rubin, D.C., LaBar, K.S., and Cabeza, R. (2008). The short and long of it: neural correlates of temporal-order memory for autobiographical events. *Journal of Cognitive Neuroscience* 20 (7), 1327–1341.

St. Jacques, P.L., and Schacter, D.L. (2013). Modifying Memory Selectively Enhancing and Updating Personal Memories for a Museum Tour by Reactivating Them. *Psychological Science*, 24 (4), 537–543.

St-Laurent, M., Abdi, H., Burianová, H., and Grady, C.L. (2011). Influence of aging on the neural correlates of autobiographical, episodic, and semantic memory retrieval. *Journal of Cognitive Neuroscience*, 23 (12), 4150–4163.

Stark, C.E., and Squire, L.R. (2001). When zero is not zero: the problem of ambiguous baseline conditions in fMRI. *Proceedings of the National Academy of Sciences of the USA*, 98 (22), 12760–12766.

Steinvorth, S., Corkin, S., and Halgren, E. (2006). Ecphory of autobiographical memories: an fMRI study of recent and remote memory retrieval. *NeuroImage*, 30 (1), 285–298.

Steinvorth, S., Wang, C., Ulbert, I., *et al.* (2010). Human entorhinal gamma and theta oscillations selective for remote autobiographical memory. *Hippocampus*, 20 (1), 166–173.

Svoboda, E., and Levine, B. (2009). The effects of rehearsal on the functional neuroanatomy of episodic autobiographical and semantic remembering: a functional magnetic resonance imaging study. *Journal of Neuroscience*, 29 (10), 3073–3082.

Svoboda, E., McKinnon, M.C., and Levine, B. (2006). The functional neuroanatomy of autobiographical memory: a meta-analysis. *Neuropsychologia*, 44 (12), 2189–2208.

Talarico, J.M., LaBar, K.S., and Rubin, D.C. (2004). Emotional intensity predicts autobiographical memory experience. *Memory and Cognition*, 32 (7), 1118–1132.

Viard, A., Lebreton, K., Chételat, G., *et al.* (2010). Patterns of hippocampal–neocortical inter-actions in the retrieval of episodic autobiographical memories across the entire life-span of aged adults. *Hippocampus*, 20 (1), 153–165.

Viard, A., Piolino, P., Desgranges, B., *et al.* (2007). Hippocampal activation for autobiograph-ical memories over the entire lifetime in healthy aged subjects: an fMRI study. *Cerebral Cortex*, 17 (10), 2453–2467.

Vincent, J.L., Kahn, I., Snyder, A.Z., *et al.* (2008). Evidence for a frontoparietal control system revealed by intrinsic functional connectivity. *Journal of Neurophysiology*, 100 (6), 3328–3342.

Vincent, J.L., Snyder, A.Z., Fox, M.D., *et al.* (2006). Coherent spontaneous activity identifies a hippocampal–parietal memory network. *Journal of Neurophysiology*, 96 (6), 3517–3531.

# 14

# Contributions of Episodic Memory to Imagining the Future

## Victoria C. McLelland, Daniel L. Schacter, and Donna Rose Addis

### Introduction

Most of our thoughts involve consideration of things we have experienced and what we plan to do in the future. We constantly ruminate over the events in our lives, "replaying" them in our minds, analyzing their consequences, imagining new endings, and predicting what will happen in the future. The extent to which this happens tells us how important it is to our survival; it emphasizes that a primary function of the brain is to consider the outcome of what has happened before and use this information to determine future behavior. In this sense, remembering the past and imagining the future are functionally linked.

Recent research has given insight into the relation between remembering and imagining. *Episodic memory*, or memory of events for which the specific time and context are recalled (Tulving, 1972), has been studied in great detail. However, it is only in the last few decades that the similarities between episodic remembering and imagining have been explored in depth. Initial evidence for this link came from studies of patients with damage to brain regions such as the medial temporal lobe and prefrontal cortex (Hassabis *et al.*, 2007; Tulving, 1985; Wheeler, Stuss, and Tulving, 1997). These patients suffered from amnesia and could not remember events from their past, but more surprising was the difficulty they had when asked to imagine their future. These findings suggested that memory and imagination both rely on the ability to mentally project oneself into representations of scenarios outside the present. Neuroimaging research has confirmed this idea, demonstrating that both remembering and imagining activate a common core network that had previously been associated with autobiographical memory retrieval (for a review, see Chapter 13), including the prefrontal cortex, medial temporal lobe, and posterior parietal cortex (Addis, Wong, and Schacter, 2007; Okuda *et al.*, 2003; Schacter, Addis, and Buckner, 2007, 2008; Schacter *et al.*, 2012; Szpunar, Watson, and McDermott, 2007). This network, which is now thought to comprise part of the "default network" due to its activation during rest, is involved in numerous forms of self-projection, including autobiographical memory, imagining the future, and imagining the perspectives of other people (Andrews-Hanna, 2011; Buckner, Andrews-Hanna, and Schacter, 2008).

*The Wiley Handbook on the Cognitive Neuroscience of Memory*, First Edition.
Edited by Donna Rose Addis, Morgan Barense, and Audrey Duarte.
© 2015 John Wiley & Sons, Ltd. Published 2015 by John Wiley & Sons, Ltd.

# Episodic Memory as a Constructive Process

The concept of episodic memory was first described by Endel Tulving (1972). He argued that semantic memory, or general conceptual knowledge not tied to any specific event, exists in contrast with another class of memory: recollection of specific episodes with identifiable spatial and temporal contexts. It is this latter sort of memory that is involved when people remember what it was like to experience things that have happened in their past, such as attending a graduation or wedding, and it is also thought of as being the type required when participants are exposed to various stimuli (e.g., lists of words) and then asked to recall them (though see Gilboa, 2004; McDermott, Szpunar, and Christ, 2009, for a discussion of the neural distinctions between these two types of events). What is common to both of these cases is that during recall, the original episode is to some extent mentally reinstated along with features of its setting. Tulving termed this *episodic memory*, and while he acknowledged that episodic and semantic memory work together, he believed that they could also function independently to a degree that made the distinction one worth considering. Furthermore, he later suggested that episodic memory requires a special sort of consciousness, termed "autonoetic consciousness," which allows a person to have knowledge of the timeline of his or her own life, and the understanding that each event that has been experienced is tied to a "self" whose existence is constant across time (Tulving, 1985). Autonoetic consciousness was thus argued to be necessary for projecting oneself back into specific moments in the past, and therefore for the remembrance of an episodic memory.

Episodic memories can be inaccurate or distorted, which is to say that they tend not to be exact renditions of how the events actually occurred at the time. They may be more like summaries of events that capture the general idea of what happened, often with very vivid perceptual details but with no guarantee of their accuracy (see Chapter 8 for more discussion of memory distortion). Some have proposed that memory distortions result from the *reconstructive* nature of episodic memory: when we recall an episodic memory, we piece together fragments of a scenario and recombine them to form the event (Barclay, 1986; Bartlett, 1932; Neisser, 1986; Schacter, Norman, and Koutstaal, 1998). This form of recall is thought to occur because when an event is experienced, its various elements and features are processed in topographically separate brain regions and this creates a pattern of activity that is distributed across the entire brain. During recall, it is therefore necessary to at least partially restore this pattern, often via the encounter of a cue or fragment of the memory that allows the brain to "complete" the rest of the pattern (Schacter, Norman, and Koutstaal, 1998).

# Memory and Imagination

It has been suggested that the reconstructive nature of memory provides it with a great deal of flexibility (Schacter and Addis, 2007). Bartlett (1932) noticed early on that our ability to form brief mental images allows us flexible use of our memories:

> By the aid of the image ... a man can take out of its setting something that happened a year ago, reinstate it with much if not all of its individuality unimpaired, combine it with something that happened yesterday, and use them both to help him solve a problem with which he is confronted today. (p. 219)

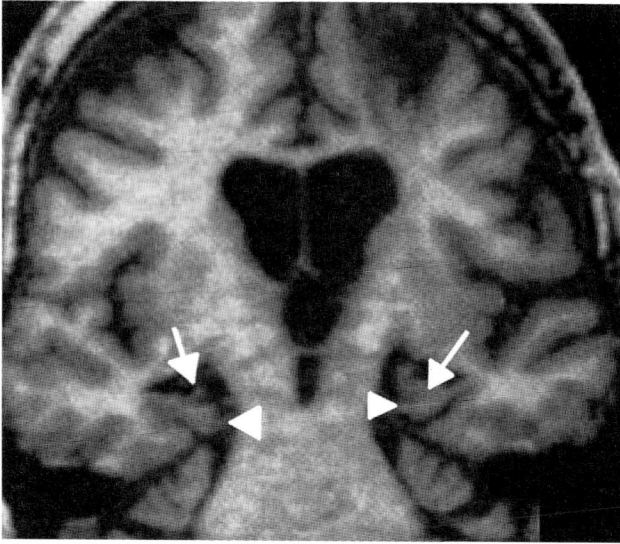

**Figure 14.1**   Magnetic resonance image showing patient K.C.'s severe atrophy of the right and left hippocampus (arrows) and parahippocampal gyri (arrowheads). Adapted from Rosenbaum *et al.* (2000).

The flexibility of our episodic memory system enables us to take details from our past experiences and voluntarily alter or rearrange them to form representations of events that have not yet happened to us (Schacter and Addis, 2007). In other words, our ability to imagine things that might occur in the future is dependent on our capacity to remember the past. When the concept of episodic memory was first developed, its focus was on the domain of remembering past experiences (Tulving, 1972). However, the episodic system has now been reconceptualized as a broader mechanism for simulation of events, with which we can voluntarily re- or pre-experience events in rich detail, and in both the past and the future.

The amnesic patient K.C. (Figure 14.1) is one of the early cases that contributed to this idea (Tulving, 1985). After suffering a head injury in a motorcycle accident, he could not recall a single specific event from his past, and more interestingly described experiencing mental "blankness" when trying to imagine what he might be doing in the future. Despite these deficits, K.C.'s personal semantic memory and general knowledge of the world was intact (Rosenbaum *et al.*, 2005). Observations of this patient prompted Tulving to suggest that the ability to remember episodes from the past is vital for imagining the future. A decade later, it was noted that patients with memory loss following damage to the prefrontal cortex also exhibited a lack of self-concern, limited plans and ambitions for the future, and a reduced desire to daydream and self-reflect (Wheeler, Stuss, and Tulving, 1997). Since these patients also typically retained their semantic knowledge, this finding offered even more support for the idea that in the absence of recollective episodic memory, the ability to mentally travel forward in time is impaired.

Amnesic patient D.B. was reported to show a similar pattern of parallel deficits following cardiac arrest and hypoxic brain damage (Klein, Loftus, and Kihlstrom, 2002).

D.B. showed profound impairment on episodic memory tasks, but his semantic knowledge was mostly spared. Interestingly, on specific measures of temporal awareness, he was unable to provide details about events in his own personal past or future, but he possessed adequate semantic knowledge of both past and future events in the public domain. In concordance with Wheeler, Stuss, and Tulving's (1997) arguments, this suggests that self-referential, episodic mental time travel can be disso- ciated from semantic awareness of general temporal knowledge. Moreover, it suggests that *episodic* memory plays a particularly important role in imagining future *episodes*, but that semantic memory is sufficient to support semantic forms of future thinking (Atance and O'Neill, 2001).

New findings from patients with semantic dementia illustrate, however, that episodic future thinking requires the contribution of both episodic and semantic elements (for a review, see Chapter 20). Semantic dementia patients have anterior temporal lobe damage and corresponding semantic memory deficits, but intact episodic memory (Hodges *et al.*, 1992). Such patients have been shown to recall events from their past in as much detail as controls, but are specifically impaired at imagining detailed future events (Irish *et al.*, 2012). This finding indicates that while access to memories of past events is necessary for episodic future thinking, it is also necessary to draw upon conceptual knowledge when constructing and imagining a new future event, perhaps using this information as an organizational framework in which to place the episodic details. In support of this idea, it has been shown that when participants construct future events, they draw first upon general personal knowledge before accessing specific episodic details from remembered past events (D'Argembeau and Mathy, 2011). Furthermore, imagined episodic future events, particularly those in the distant future, are clustered into broader future event sequences that are often organized around semantic knowledge about personal goals (D'Argembeau and Demblon, 2012).

Other evidence from amnesic patients has specifically implicated the medial temporal lobes in the ability to imagine the future (Hassabis *et al.*, 2007). Five patients with damage restricted to the bilateral hippocampus were asked to imagine future scenarios in response to a verbal cue. Compared to controls, the descriptions of the imagined events generated by the patients were lacking in richness and spatial coherence. Specifically, the details that they did manage to provide seemed fragmented and incom- pletely bound together. It was thus argued that the hippocampus also has a significant role in imagining the future, particularly in binding details together and integrating them into a spatial context.

A variety of other studies have illustrated the close relationship between past and future thought. The developmental trajectories of episodic memory and future thinking are similar, with both emerging gradually at approximately four years of age (Atance and O'Neill, 2005; Suddendorf and Corballis, 1997). This emergence corresponds with the ability of children to imagine themselves taking different per- spectives (Russell, Alexis, and Clayton, 2010). When children are asked to imagine future scenarios and select one of three items that will help them in those scenarios, it is only by five years of age that they are not distracted by items that are seman- tically related to the scenario but in fact unhelpful to them (Atance and Meltzoff, 2005). The ability to accurately describe plans for the next day increases signifi- cantly between the ages of three and five years (Busby and Suddendorf, 2005), and when children are asked what they did yesterday and what they will do tomorrow, the ability to answer the former question predicts the ability to answer the latter (Suddendorf, 2010). This link between the development of memory and imagination further supports the idea of similar underlying processes.

At the other end of the lifespan, a corresponding deterioration is observed for both abilities. Older adults tend to produce significantly fewer episodic details than younger adults both when remembering past events and when imagining future ones, and the number of details generated for past events is significantly correlated with the number of details generated for future ones (Addis, Wong, and Schacter, 2008; Addis *et al.*, 2010). Such parallel declines in past and future are evident when cued with words, and also when asked to imagine events using pictorial cues (Gaesser *et al.*, 2011). Instead of being able to describe vivid visuospatial aspects of the scenes they imagine, older adults are instead more likely to provide semantic or conceptual information that may or may not be relevant to their imagined events. Furthermore, the number of episodic details generated by older adults is highly associated with their scores on a test of relational memory, which, given the role of the hippocampus in relational memory (Konkel and Cohen, 2009), again points to the importance of the medial temporal lobes for imagining the future (Addis, Wong, and Schacter, 2008). When constructing imagined future events, older adults do not show the same level of activity as younger adults in regions known to be important for vivid episodic detail, such as the hippocampus, parahippocampal gyrus, and precuneus (Addis, Roberts, and Schacter, 2011). In contrast, while elaborating on their imagined events, older adults show greater activation than young adults in lateral temporal areas associated with semantic processing (Figure 14.2). When participants rate how much detail they

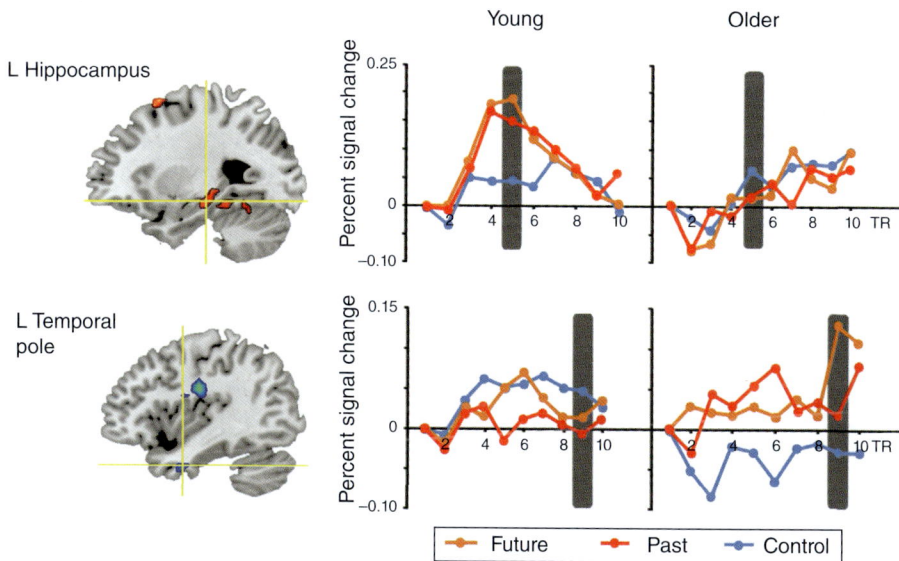

**Figure 14.2**   Percent signal change extracted from regions more active for autobiographical tasks than the control task in young adults, from Addis, Roberts, and Schacter (2011). Young adults engage the left hippocampus more for both future and past events than for the control task, while this effect is not seen in older adults. Conversely, older adults show more activation in the left temporal pole for the autobiographical tasks than for the control task, an effect which is not observed in young adults.

have generated in their imagined events, the detail ratings of young adults are linearly associated with hippocampal activity, while in older adults the ratings correlate with activity in the lateral temporal lobes (Addis, Roberts, and Schacter, 2011). The tendency for older adults to focus on semantic information instead of episodic detail is therefore not only a behavioral phenomenon, but is also reflected in the neural activity underlying older adults' imagined events.

Electrophysiological and neuroimaging studies have investigated the neural networks involved in both remembering the past and imagining the future, and the finding of a common neural network underlying both processes supports the earlier patient data suggesting a relation between them. Electroencephalography (EEG) evidence shows similar significant left frontal activation for the construction of both remembered and imagined events (Conway *et al.*, 2003). PET and fMRI studies have indicated that both remembering and imagining tend to produce similar activation in a core network of regions, including medial prefrontal, medial temporal, and posterior parietal cortices (Addis, Wong, and Schacter, 2007; Hassabis, Kumaran, and Maguire, 2007; Okuda *et al.*, 2003); the widespread nature of this network illustrates the diverse sensory, perceptual, spatiotemporal, and emotional components of these representations. Common network activation points to a similar underlying cognitive process, potentially that mental images acquired in the past and stored in posterior areas are then being reactivated during both remembering and imagining via direction from prefrontal regions (Szpunar, Watson, and McDermott, 2007).

These active regions comprise part of what we now refer to as the *default mode network* (Buckner, Andrews-Hanna, and Schacter, 2008; Raichle *et al.*, 2001), a term derived from the fact that this extensive network is notably active when participants are allowed to mind-wander and are not engaged in an external stimulus-driven task. Meta-analyses have now enabled the parcellation of the default network into subsystems (Andrews-Hanna, 2011; Buckner, Andrews-Hanna, and Schacter, 2008; Kim, 2012): (1) the medial temporal lobe subsystem, supporting memory-related processes including the recall and simulation of episodic events, and consisting of the hippocampus, parahippocampal gyrus, retrosplenial cortex, and ventromedial prefrontal cortex (PFC); as well as (2) the dorsal medial PFC subsystem, supporting inferences about the mental states of the self and others, and consisting of the dorsal medial PFC, temporoparietal junction, lateral temporal cortex, and temporal pole (Andrews-Hanna, 2011). The subsystems both converge on the posterior cingulate cortex and the anterior medial PFC; these two regions serve as hubs linking the subsystems together. Accordingly, the shared neural substrate of remembering and imagining draws on many of these subsystems and hubs.

As a result of the converging evidence linking remembering and imagining, Schacter and Addis formulated their *constructive episodic simulation* hypothesis, which suggests that in order to simulate hypothetical situations, the episodic memory system extracts specific details from past experiences and recombines them in a coherent way (Addis and Schacter, 2012; Schacter and Addis, 2007). This theory fits well with the idea of episodic memory for the past being highly constructive in nature (Bartlett, 1932; Neisser, 1986; Schacter, Norman, and Koutstaal, 1998), with events encoded in a piecemeal fashion instead of as a fixed "instant-replay" style recording. A constructive system is an economical one, as specific details need not be represented in the brain as many times as the person experiences them. The ability to draw on these details in a novel way to imagine future experiences may be simply an adaptive extension of the inherent system design, such that the outcomes of past experiences can flexibly inform choices made about upcoming events.

An alternative hypothesis for the commonality underlying remembering and imagining was proposed by Hassabis and Maguire (2007). They argue that both of these abilities involve the construction of three-dimensional spatial scenes, requiring the mental representation of a location's spatial layout and the insertion of various event elements at various places within it. This *scene construction* hypothesis was based on the known role of the hippocampus in spatial navigation (Maguire *et al.*, 2000), as well as on their findings that patients with hippocampal damage imagine events that are significantly less spatially coherent than the events of normal controls (Hassabis *et al.*, 2007). Their evidence suggests that the role of the hippocampus in imagining the future is in spatially binding the elements of the event into the scene.

The scene construction hypothesis does not necessarily conflict with the constructive episodic simulation hypothesis, as both theories propose that some form of construction is required in remembering and imagining. Rather, it is likely that both theories are correct and complementary, in that episodic details (e.g., people, locations, and objects) are extracted from previous experiences and then re-bound (and in the case of future events, rearranged) into new three-dimensional scenes. Spatial and contextual information therefore provides a vital platform upon which to build these scenarios. It has been found that the familiarity of a simulated event's location determines how vividly and clearly it will be imagined (Arnold, McDermott, and Szpunar, 2011; Szpunar and McDermott, 2008), which is consistent with the idea of the context as a fundamental base for episodic simulation. Furthermore, remembering and imagining events that take place in familiar locations both engage posterior parietal regions (e.g., posterior cingulate cortex and parahippocampal gyrus) significantly more than remembering and imagining events in unfamiliar locations (Szpunar, Chan, and McDermott, 2009). The similar engagement of posterior parietal regions during remembering and imagining might therefore reflect the fact that both tasks typically require the retrieval of familiar locations. Finally, the hippocampus, known for spatial processing, is particularly important for the generation of specific imagined future events, as opposed to general or more abstract imagined future events, perhaps also reflecting the precise spatiotemporal context characterizing events that are highly specific (Addis *et al.*, 2011). All of this evidence supports the idea that contextual information serves as a foundation for episodic processes.

## Differences Between Remembering and Imagining

Remembering and imagining are, of course, not identical processes. We must have some way of distinguishing between experienced and hypothetical events so that we can accurately guide our behavior based on the realities of our environment. In support of this idea, it has been shown that some of the phenomenal characteristics known to accompany the process of remembering the past are slightly different for simulated future events. For example, memories of actual past experiences tend to have significantly more detailed sensory and perceptual features than imagined future events (D'Argembeau and Van der Linden, 2004; Gamboz, Brandimonte, and de Vito, 2010; Johnson and Raye, 1981) and therefore engage visual regions to a greater degree (Addis *et al.*, 2009; Conway *et al.*, 2003; Weiler, Suchan, and Daum, 2010). Real memories also contain more detailed spatial and temporal contextual information, while imagined events are more schematic (Johnson and Raye, 1981). Moreover, the clarity and sensory detail of memories for imagined events dissipates much more rapidly over time as compared to memories of real events (Suengas and Johnson, 1988).

When participants are asked to imagine future events in laboratory-based settings, they are often instructed to generate highly specific scenarios, and in these cases the imagined future events generally take place in precise spatial and temporal contexts (Addis *et al.*, 2011). However, when spontaneous future thoughts are examined instead (i.e., naturally occurring thoughts of the future that were not prompted by some experimental task), they tend to be less specific and more semantic in nature than spontaneous thoughts of the past (Anderson and Dewhurst, 2009). Therefore, naturalistic future thinking seems to be generally more conceptual and less likely to involve specific and detailed episodic scenarios than both laboratory future tasks and thinking about real past experiences. However, it is also noted that repeated rehearsal of apperceptive aspects of both remembered and imagined events (i.e., dwelling on the thoughts and feelings that one would or did have during the event) results in the two types of events being more easily confused (Suengas and Johnson, 1988). More specifically, with this sort of rehearsal that emphasizes emotional components, the sensory and perceptual detail of real memories becomes more difficult to access, while the emotional and cognitive content of the events increases. Consequently, the characteristics that typically distinguish between real and imagined events become less clear. So while remembering and imagining are distinct in many ways, this distinction can be affected by factors such as rehearsal.

Some key differences between remembering and imagining appear to emerge when the event is first being constructed. Both processes involve two phases: (1) the initial construction of an event and (2) the process of mentally elaborating upon it once constructed (Conway *et al.*, 2003). When recalling a memory of a past experience, participants engage in a search process to locate a memory that fits with the provided cue or search criteria, after which the previously experienced representation can be reactivated. In contrast, when imagining a new future event, depending on the task and cue involved, disparate episodic details from multiple memories must be located and then incorporated into the new scenario. Therefore, imagined future events have elements of generation, recombination, and construction that are more intensive than for remembered past events. In an fMRI study, Addis, Wong, and Schacter (2007) had participants indicate with a button-press once a past or future event had been generated, after which they elaborated on the constructed event in as much detail as possible. During initial construction of these events, there was significant differentiation in active regions between past and future. The ventrolateral prefrontal and right frontopolar cortices were more active during construction of future than past events. Furthermore, while the left hippocampus was recruited for construction in both temporal directions, the right hippocampus showed selective engagement for the construction of future events (Addis, Wong, and Schacter, 2007). In contrast, during elaboration, these differences were no longer present and a common core network of

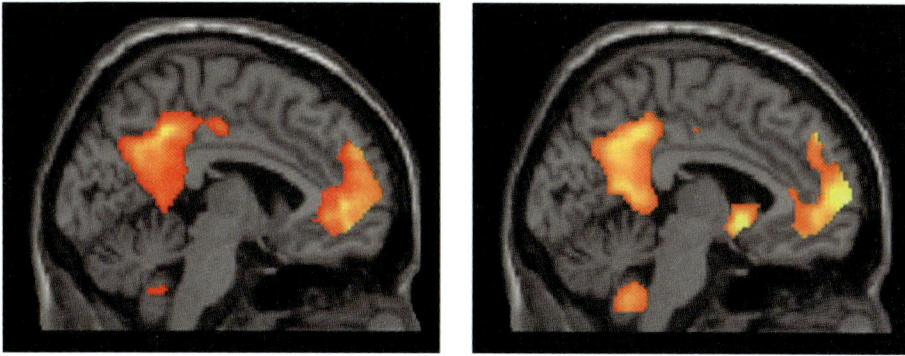

**Figure 14.3**   An illustration of the striking commonalities in left medial prefrontal and parietal activity during the elaboration of past (left) and future (right) events, relative to a control task. Adapted from Addis, Wong, and Schacter (2007).

activation was observed for both remembering the past and imagining the future, including left medial prefrontal cortex and medial posterior regions (Figure 14.3).

When the results of the above study were reanalyzed with respect to the amount of vivid detail generated for each event, the specific contributions of some of these regions to the imagination of future events were clarified (Addis and Schacter, 2008). It was found that during elaboration of future events, activity in the right frontal pole and anterior hippocampus was directly related to the amount of detail in each event, as rated by the participant. Given that frontopolar activation has previously been found to correlate with the degree of intentional thought comprising an imagined event (Okuda *et al.*, 2003), the frontal pole activity in this study may reflect the increased intentional information that accompanies thinking about detailed future plans. The anterior hippocampal activity may come from the creation of multiple new associations between the details that are incorporated and encoded into a coherent event (Giovanello, Schnyer, and Verfaellie, 2009).

## The Hippocampus and Episodic Simulation of the Future

Within the default network's medial temporal lobe (MTL) subsystem, the hippocampus is one of the most fundamental structures for episodic memory. Input to the hippocampus comes from the adjacent perirhinal and parahippocampal cortices, which each integrating information from object- and spatial-related regions in the ventral and dorsal streams, respectively. Given that the hippocampus receives simultaneous input from both of these streams, it is a structure that is anatomically well-placed to integrate visuo-spatial information even further (Lavenex and Amaral, 2000; Squire, Stark, and Clark, 2004). There has been a strong focus on the role of the hippocampus (particularly its posterior extent) in representing spatial information, which may explain the specific involvement of the hippocampus for episodic memory as opposed to semantic or procedural memory, since a defining characteristic of episodic memory is the success-ful reinstatement of an event's initial spatiotemporal context. The hippocampus may act as a sort of cognitive map, storing allocentric representations of space (i.e., in a map-based fashion, regardless of the specific position or perspective of the observer) (O'Keefe and Dostrovsky, 1971; O'Keefe and Nadel, 1978), though others believe that hippocampal involvement in spatial processing is simply one instance of this structure's general function in forming cross-modal associations or arbitrary associations between item or event features (Eichenbaum, 2007; see also Squire, Stark, and Clark, 2004).

The broad connectivity of the hippocampus is thought to allow it to capture and index overall whole-brain patterns of activation that are elicited by the perception or mental representation of an event (Lavenex and Amaral, 2000). Reciprocal connections between the hippocampus and widespread neocortical regions allow a "compressed" representation of the event to be stored in the hippocampus in the form of rapid synaptic changes (McClelland, McNaughton, and O'Reilly, 1995). It has been suggested that what we think of as memory recall involves a recapitulation or reactivation of these previously experienced patterns of activity, resulting in the reinstatement of an earlier mental state. The way in which this occurs may be as a type of pattern completion; if part of the previously elicited pattern of activity is re-encountered, activation may then spread within and from the hippocampus to the remaining components, resulting in the mental recreation of a previous episode (McClelland, McNaughton, and O'Reilly, 1995).

Patient and neuroimaging evidence indicates that the hippocampus may play an important role in imagining the future (Addis and Schacter, 2012; Schacter and Addis, 2009), over and above its already well-established role in remembering the past. A role for the hippocampus in imagining new events is unsurprising, given that a core function of the hippocampus is to bind together disparate features of stimuli and form new associations (Eichenbaum, 2001; Eichenbaum *et al.*, 2012), and these processes are fundamental to the representation of new, multifaceted imagined events. Right hippocampal activity is higher for imagined future events that are later remembered in a cued recall test than for those which are later forgotten, suggesting that hippocampal activity reflects the extent to which the details are successfully bound together and stored in memory (Martin *et al.*, 2011). The amount of recombination and binding required to imagine an event depends largely on how similar it is to previous experiences, and it has been shown that imagined events that are unlikely to occur in real life engage the right anterior hippocampus to a greater extent than more probable events (Weiler, Suchan, and Daum, 2009). The importance of this structure for imagining the future also supports Addis and Schacter's *constructive episodic simulation* hypothesis and Hassabis and Maguire's *scene construction* hypothesis, since an integral part of these ideas is that simulation depends on the binding together of details from previously experienced events into new representations of spatial scenes.

Nonetheless, the role of the hippocampus in imagining the future is currently controversial, due to conflicting evidence for and against the ability of hippocampal amnesic patients to imagine future events. Building on the previously discussed findings reported by Hassabis *et al.* (2007) demonstrating scene construction deficits in hippocampal amnesics, some recent findings have illustrated further that amnesic patients are impaired at episodic simulation of the future (Andelman *et al.*, 2010; Kwan *et al.*, 2010; Race, Keane, and Verfaellie, 2011; Zeman *et al.*, 2012), and that this deficit is in the act of constructing specific episodic scenarios, rather than in simply considering outcomes that might happen in the future (Kwan *et al.*, 2011). In contrast, others report that amnesic patients perform as well as controls on episodic simulation tasks (Hurley, Maguire, and Vargha-Khadem, 2011 [though note that this was a developmental amnesic patient]; Squire *et al.*, 2010).

It has been proposed that the timing of hippocampal damage may affect the extent of the patient's deficit in episodic simulation, such that patients who sustained damage in infancy or early childhood may be less impaired as adults than those whose damage was acquired in adulthood. This idea is based on two lines of evidence. First, developmental amnesic patient Jon, who suffered 50% bilateral loss of his hippocampal tissue perinatally, can imagine future events that are as coherent and detailed as those of control participants (Maguire, Vargha-Khadem, and Hassabis, 2010). Jon's ability to imagine future events is attributed to his residual hippocampal tissue, which is active during autobiographical memory retrieval (Maguire, Vargha-Khadem, and Mishkin, 2001) and scene construction (Mullally, Hassabis, and Maguire, 2012). Second, a group of amnesic children with hippocampal damage resulting from neonatal hypoxia and ischemia were also shown to be unimpaired at imagining fictitious experiences (Cooper *et al.*, 2011), although their later recall of these imagined experiences was significantly worse than that of control children. These two sets of findings have been explained either by potentially active residual hippocampal tissue (as confirmed in patient Jon) or by the reliance on a store of accumulated semantic knowledge which may be able to support scene construction (Addis and Schacter, 2012). This theory of the timing of damage does not explain why patient H.C., another developmental amnesic patient, shows deficits in imagining the future (Kwan *et al.*, 2010), although this result is disputed (Hurley, Maguire, and Vargha-Khadem, 2011).

There are several other factors that may explain the conflicting evidence from amnesic patients, including the way in which simulation ability is measured. The various experiments investigating this issue have used a variety of different tasks. For instance, in the adapted Autobiographical Interview (Addis, Wong, and Schacter, 2008; based on Levine *et al.*, 2002), a single generic cue word is provided and the participant has three minutes to describe as much detail about an imagined event as possible. This task has been used to assess the number of episodic and non-episodic details comprising amnesic patients' future events (Squire *et al.*, 2010). In contrast, the scene construction task (Hassabis *et al.*, 2007) involves provision of the general scenario and the participant is required to build upon the pre-constructed scene, at times receiving prompts about visuospatial information (Berryhill *et al.*, 2010; Hurley, Maguire, and Vargha-Khadem, 2011; Mullally, Hassabis, and Maguire, 2012). The memory and temporal experience questionnaire (Klein, Loftus, and Kihlstrom, 2002) has participants answer questions about their known (semantic) and lived (episodic) past and future (Andelman *et al.*, 2010). The importance of the choice of task is made particularly obvious by the conflicting results found in a single patient: H.C. is unimpaired on the scene construction task (Hurley, Maguire, and Vargha-Khadem, 2011), but significantly impaired on the adapted Autobiographical Interview (Kwan *et al.*, 2010).

The task interacts with patient factors, such as the specific aetiology and nature of the brain damage suffered. Squire *et al.* (2010) argue that many of the patients who have been found to have deficits in imagining the future also have damage to a number of extra-hippocampal regions that could explain their impairment. In support of this claim, damage to regions outside the hippocampus has been shown to affect episodic simulation ability. Patients with damage localized to the posterior parietal cortex or to the prefrontal cortex, and with intact hippocampi, imagine fictitious scenarios in much less detail than controls (Berryhill *et al.*, 2010). Furthermore, it has been shown that semantic dementia patients with atrophy of the anterior temporal lobes, who show deficits in semantic memory but with a relative preservation of episodic memory, are selectively impaired when imagining the future and not when remembering the past (Irish *et al*, 2012). This same pattern of results was also found in two patients with thalamic lesions (Weiler *et al.*, 2011).

Alternatively, deficits in episodic simulation may be explained by broader deficiencies; some amnesic patients, even those with otherwise normal cognitive abilities, may have a general impairment in their capacity to describe their surroundings, even when no mental projection is required and they are simply asked to describe their present situation (Zeman *et al.*, 2012), though others have not found this to be the case (Race, Keane, and Verfaellie, 2011). It has been argued that amnesic patients who are unimpaired at imagining the future are those who do not suffer from complete amnesia; with their relatively preserved remote episodic memory, such patients are able to draw upon a residual store of episodic details and therefore can construct scenarios in the same way as controls (Addis and Schacter, 2012). However, other patients with intact remote episodic memory still show deficits in future thinking (Andelman *et al.*, 2010). It is clear that much further work remains to be done in order to understand the role of the hippocampus in imagining future events.

## Functions of Imagining the Future

According to the constructive episodic simulation hypothesis and related perspectives, the ability to draw on episodic details in a novel way to imagine future experiences is a design feature of episodic memory (Schacter and Addis, 2007; Suddendorf and Corballis, 2007). As noted by Schacter (2012), such a feature must be sufficiently beneficial to the organism that it is worth the associated cost in memory errors that can result from occasionally mistakenly combining those elements. Simulating future events therefore ought to serve important functions for an organism, and several lines of research indicate that this is so.

Conway (2009) suggests that the relationship between remembering and imagining reflects their common purpose: to allow us to maintain goals that refer to time periods extending beyond our immediate circumstances. This idea is based on his experiment in which participants describe as many of their own specific memories as possible for each day prior, up to the point of five days before the present, and then imagine specific upcoming future events in the same manner but in the forward direction in time. The number of specific events listed by participants decreases steadily as time progresses either into the past or into the future, and Conway interprets the range of days on which participants could list multiple specific events to reflect a stable *remembering–imagining window*. This window allows a person to have simultaneous awareness of both recent and approaching events, and it supports the idea that the function of our ability to remember and imagine is to keep a constant and current mental representation of our more immediate goals.

Others have also found that the numbers of remembered and imagined events that had taken or would take place near the present is relatively high, and then decreases linearly with time in both the past and future directions (Spreng and Levine, 2006;

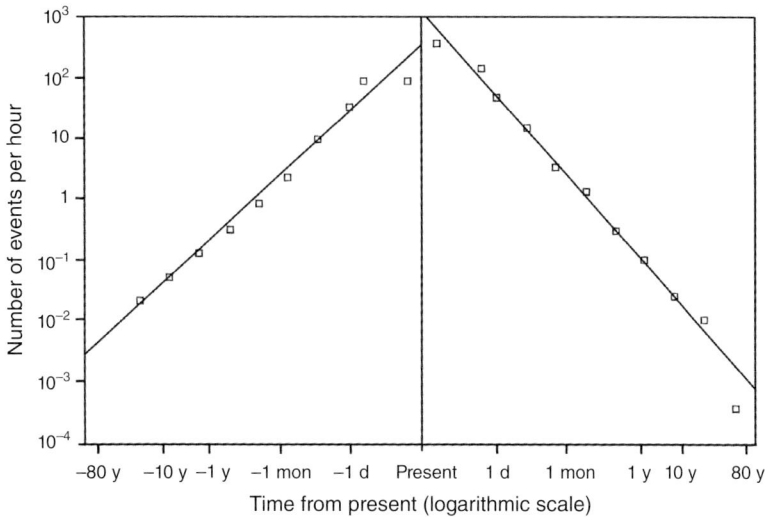

**Figure 14.4**   The temporal distribution of autobiographical event frequency per hour, plotted as a function of time from the present (days, months, years) into the past and future. Reproduced from Spreng and Levine (2006).

Figure 14.4). In addition, temporally close events are more specific, detailed, and vivid than distant ones (Trope and Liberman, 2003), regardless of whether they are remembered in the past or imagined in the future (D'Argembeau and Van der Linden, 2004), although this may be due to difficulty in imagining a clear location in which to set temporally distant future events (Arnold, McDermott, and Szpunar, 2011). Imagining specific personal goals and the steps required to achieve them engages the same default network regions seen when people imagine future events in general (Gerlach *et al.*, 2011; Spreng *et al.*, 2010). Furthermore, imagined future events that are relevant to participants' personal goals engage medial prefrontal and parietal regions of the default mode network more than imagined events that do not relate to their personal goals (D'Argembeau *et al.*, 2010). When asked to imagine and describe the detailed steps required to solve open-ended problems, patients with temporal lobe epilepsy (and the corresponding episodic memory deficits that accompany medial temporal lobe damage) describe fewer relevant steps than controls (Sheldon, McAndrews, and Moscovitch, 2011), suggesting an association between episodic processes and goal-directed problem solving. These findings converge on the idea that the processes of remembering and imagining serve as a way to inform present behavior while maintaining immediate personal aims.

Mental simulation of the future has other adaptive functions in addition to maintaining personal goals. Imagining specific future events reduces temporal discounting, which is the general tendency to assign relatively less value to a large reward in the distant future than to a smaller reward that could be acquired immediately (Benoit, Gilbert, and Burgess, 2011). In other words, imagining the specific act of receiving the large reward in the distant future reduces the tendency to devalue it. Therefore, imagining future events allows a person to make decisions that he or she may not have otherwise made after simply considering the immediate situation, and these decisions are generally found to be ultimately more beneficial. People often have difficulty following through with their good intentions for the future, frequently because their plans are too vague or they are disproportionately influenced by more immediate goals. Planning in advance the exact actions one will take when faced with a specific situation removes the influence of distracting immediate factors on decision making. Deciding to engage in behavior $X$ when in situation $Y$, or forming an "implementation intention" (Gollwitzer, 1999) creates a mental representation of the goal behavior for which recall is triggered by encountering the situation itself. This ease of recall allows the goal-directed behavior to become almost automated and therefore less influenced by distraction. Consequently, the ability to imagine events that might happen in the future allows people to make more advantageous decisions.

At a more basic level, planning for the future has survival value, and the ability to anticipate threats to one's own life was likely a driving evolutionary factor behind the development of a memory system that allows for imagination. Klein, Robertson, and Delton (2010) argue that for this reason, the episodic system is in general even more oriented towards the future than the past, despite the focus of previous research in this area. They suggest that memory performance should therefore be at its optimal level when planning for the future, and especially when considering future scenarios in which survival might be in question. In support of this idea, Klein *et al* showed that when participants consider an event involving camping in the woods and judge the relevance of a list of items to the situation, framing the event in terms of a specific plan for the future results in better memory for the item details than when participants are asked to think of the items in the context of a previous memory of camping in the woods (Klein, Robertson, and Delton, 2010). Object-location memory is also improved when the encoding context calls survival into question, as participants show better memory for the locations of food and animals when asked to imagine the items in a survival scenario, as opposed to when imagining them in a scavenger hunt or hunting contest (Nairne *et al.*, 2012).

A higher-level cognitive role of episodic memory is in maintaining a stable and healthy sense of self, and this function has now been demonstrated to extend to episodic simulation of the future. The ability to remember past autobiographical events, particularly from early adulthood, seems to be vital for preserving a strong identity (Addis and Tippett, 2004). Highly significant memories that are personally meaningful and described as "self-defining" may be particularly important for maintaining identity and for the development of self-worth (Sutin and Robins, 2005). It has now been shown that people have corresponding self-defining imagined future events as well as remembered past events (e.g., "when I get married," or "when I graduate from university"), and these self-defining future events carry significant personal meaning, create a sense of self-continuity, and contribute to self-esteem (D'Argembeau, Lardi, and Van der Linden, 2012). When people imagine episodic events that will happen in their future, these events tend to cluster around time periods in which participants expect to acquire certain future self-images or self-definitions (e.g., "I will be a parent"), suggesting that these episodic future events are tied to semantic representations of the future self (Rathbone, Conway, and Moulin, 2011). Manipulating participants' perceived self-efficacy alters the way in which they imagine future episodic events; those prompted to identify themselves as having high self-efficacy imagine events that are more specific and that contain more positive words (Brown *et al.*, 2012), further illustrating the mutual influence of episodic future thinking and self-related constructs.

Emotional valence significantly affects episodic processes (for a discussion of the influence of emotion on episodic memory, see Chapter 19), including the simulation of future events. For example, most people have an *optimism bias*, or a general tendency to expect that positive things will happen to them in the future, as well as a corresponding inclination to underestimate the likelihood of negative events happening to them personally (Sharot, 2011). When participants imagine future events that have either positive or negative emotional connotations (e.g., "winning an award," or "the end of a romantic relationship"), positive events are perceived as being closer in time to the present than negative ones, and are also rated as eliciting a stronger sense of actually experiencing the event (Sharot *et al.*, 2007). Imagined events that have positive emotional connotations are more likely to be remembered across long delays when participants are asked about them later than are imagined events with negative connotations (Szpunar, Addis, and Schacter, 2012). These tendencies have been shown to be important for maintaining mental health, as the strength of a person's optimism bias is associated with overall wellbeing (Schweizer, Beck-Seyffer, and Schneider, 1999). Optimism bias is also negatively correlated with depressive symptoms, such that people who are more optimistic are less likely to experience symptoms of depression (Strunk, Lopez, and DeRubeis, 2006). The ability to imagine an optimistic future is therefore highly beneficial.

# Summary

It is now firmly established that episodic memory and episodic simulation of the future have much in common. This conclusion is based on evidence that a variety of amnesic patients imagine future events that are less detailed than controls, that the neural bases of remembering and imagining have substantial overlap, and that two processes also share many cognitive features and processes. It is hypothesized that the constructive nature of episodic memory allows for details from past experiences to be rearranged and recombined into mental representations of new scenarios that have not yet occurred (Schacter and Addis, 2007). Despite the similarities between episodic remembering and imagining, it is, however, generally possible to distinguish between events that really happened and those that were simply imagined; real memories tend to contain more vivid sensory and perceptual detail, while imagined events are more conceptual and contain more thought- and emotion-related information.

Some current issues in this area of research revolve around the specific role of the hippocampus in imagining future events. While many amnesic patients with damage to the hippocampus are unable to construct detailed and coherent simulations of the future, some such patients are unimpaired, particularly those who sustained their hippocampal damage perinatally or in infancy. The particular task used to evaluate participants' ability to imagine the future may explain some of the inconsistencies, as might the precise nature and location of hippocampal damage. Despite these variable findings, the hippocampus is consistently active while participants imagine future events, and its role in this task may include binding, encoding, retrieval, spatial processing, or all of these processes. Further research will clarify the hippocampal contribution to episodic simulation.

Future research should also help to increase our understanding of the functions of episodic simulation. As we emphasized, this capability confers a number of advantages, including enhanced preparation for upcoming events, more farsighted decision making, the maintenance of personal goals, and improved mental health. However, episodic simulation is not without pitfalls: incomplete simulations sometimes contribute to inaccurate predictions of the future (e.g., Gilbert and Wilson, 2007) and also to mistakes in planning, such as the planning fallacy, where people underestimate how much time it will take to complete a task (e.g., Dunning, 2007). Consideration of both the benefits and limitations of future simulations led Schacter (2012) to characterize episodic simulation as an *adaptive constructive process*: it plays a functional role in cognition but can also create distortions or illusions as a consequence of doing so. The same can be also said about episodic memory. Studies that attempt to clarify the processes responsible for the benefits and limitations of both episodic simulation and episodic memory should broaden our understanding of how individuals remember the past and imagine the future.

## References

Addis, D.R., Cheng, T., Roberts, R.P., and Schacter, D.L. (2011). Hippocampal contributions to the episodic simulation of specific and general events. *Hippocampus*, 21 (10), 1045–1052. doi: 10.1002/hipo.20870.

Addis, D.R., Musicaro, R., Pan, L., and Schacter, D.L. (2010). Episodic simulation of past and future events in older adults: evidence from an experimental recombination task. *Psychology and Aging*, 25 (2), 369–376. doi: 10.1037/a0017280.

Addis, D.R., Pan, L., Vu, M.-A., *et al.* (2009). Constructive episodic simulation of the future and the past: Distinct subsystems of a core brain network mediate imagining and remembering. *Neuropsychologia*, 47 (11), 2222–2238.

Addis, D.R., Roberts, R.P., and Schacter, D.L. (2011). Age-related neural changes in autobiographical remembering and imagining. *Neuropsychologia*, 49 (13), 3656–3669. doi: 10.1016/j.neuropsychologia.2011.09.021.

Addis, D.R., and Schacter, D.L. (2008). Constructive episodic simulation: Temporal distance and detail of past and future events modulate hippocampal engagement. *Hippocampus*, 18, 227–237. doi: 10.1002/hipo.20405.

Addis, D.R., and Schacter, D.L. (2012). The hippocampus and imagining the future: Where do we stand? *Frontiers in Human Neuroscience*, 5 (173), 1–15. doi: 10.3389/fnhum.2011.00173.

Addis, D.R., and Tippett, L.J. (2004). Memory of myself: autobiographical memory and identity in Alzheimer's disease. *Memory*, 12 (1), 56–74. doi: 10.1080/09658210244000423.

Addis, D.R., Wong A.T., and Schacter, D.L. (2007). Remembering the past and imagining the future: common and distinct neural substrates during event construction and elaboration. *Neuropsychologia*, 45, 1363–1377. doi: 10.1016/j.neuropsychologia.2006.10.016.

Addis, D.R., Wong A.T., and Schacter, D.L. (2008). Age-related changes in the episodic simulation of future events. *Psychological Science*, 19 (1), 33–41.

Andelman, F., Hoofien, D., Goldberg, I., *et al.* (2010). Bilateral hippocampal lesion and a selective impairment of the ability for mental time travel. *Neurocase*, 16 (5), 426–435. doi: 10.1080/13554791003623318.

Anderson, R.J., and Dewhurst, S.A. (2009). Remembering the past and imagining the future: differences in event specificity of spontaneously generated thought. *Memory*, 17 (4), 367–373. doi: 10.1080/09658210902751669.

Andrews-Hanna, J.R. (2011). The brain's default network and its adaptive role in internal mentation. *The Neuroscientist*, 18 (3), 251–270. doi: 10.1177/1073858411403316.

Arnold, K.M., McDermott, K.B., and Szpunar, K.K. (2011). Imagining the near and far future: the role of location familiarity. *Memory and Cognition*, 39 (6), 954–967. doi: 10.3758/s13421-011-0076-1.

Atance, C.M., and Meltzoff, A.N. (2005). My future self: young children's ability to anticipate and explain future states. *Cognitive Development*, 20, 341–361. doi: doi:10.1016/j.cogdev.2005.05.001.

Atance, C.M., and O'Neill, D.K. (2001). Episodic future thinking. *Trends in Cognitive Sciences*, 5 (12), 533–538.

Atance, C.M., and O'Neill, D.K. (2005). The emergence of episodic future thinking in humans. *Learning and Motivation*, 36, 126–144. doi: 10.1016/j.lmot.2005.02.003.

Barclay, C.R. (1986). Schematization of autobiographical memory. In *Autobiographical Memory* (ed. D.C. Rubin). Cambridge: Cambridge University Press.

Bartlett, F.C. (1932). *Remembering: A Study in Experimental and Social Psychology*. Cambridge: Cambridge University Press.

Benoit, R.G., Gilbert, S.J., and Burgess, P.W. (2011). A neural mechanism mediating the impact of episodic prospection on farsighted decisions. *Journal of Neuroscience*, 31 (18), 6771–6779. doi: 10.1523/JNEUROSCI.6559-10.2011.

Berryhill, M.E., Picasso, L., Arnold, R., *et al.* (2010). Similarities and differences between parietal and frontal patients in autobiographical and constructed experience tasks. *Neuropsychologia*, 48 (5), 1385–1393. doi: 10.1016/j.neuropsychologia.2010.01.004.

Brown, A.D., Dorfman, M.L., Marmar, C.R., and Bryant, R.A. (2012). The impact of perceived self-efficacy on mental time travel and social problem solving. *Consciousness and Cognition*, 21 (1), 299–306. doi: 10.1016/j.concog.2011.09.023.

Buckner, R.L., Andrews-Hanna, J.R., and Schacter, D.L. (2008). The brain's default network: anatomy, function, and relE.nce to disease. *Annals of the New York Academy of Sciences*, 1124, 1–38. doi: 10.1196/annals.1440.011.

Busby, J., and Suddendorf, T. (2005). Recalling yesterday and predicting tomorrow. *Cognitive Development*, 20, 362–372. doi: 10.1016/j.cogdev.2005.05.002.

Conway, M.A. (2009). Episodic memories. *Neuropsychologia*, 47 (11), 2305–2313. doi: 10.1016/j.neuropsychologia.2009.02.003.

Conway, M.A., Pleydell-Pearce, C.W., Whitecross, S.E., and Sharpe, H. (2003). Neurophysiological correlates of memory for experienced and imagined events. *Neuropsychologia*, 41, 334–340. doi: 10.1016/S0028-3932(02)00165-3.

Cooper, J.M., Vargha-Khadem, F., Gadian, D.G., and Maguire, E.A. (2011). The effect of hippocampal damage in children on recalling the past and imagining new experiences. *Neuropsychologia*, 49 (7), 1843–1850. doi: 10.1016/j.neuropsychologia.2011.03.008.

D'Argembeau, A., and Demblon, J. (2012). On the representational systems underlying prospection: evidence from the event-cueing paradigm. *Cognition*, 125 (2), 160–167. doi: 10.1016/j.cognition.2012.07.008.

D'Argembeau, A., Lardi, C., and Van der Linden, M. (2012). Self-defining future projections: exploring the identity function of thinking about the future. *Memory*, 20 (2), 110–120. doi: 10.1080/09658211.2011.647697.

D'Argembeau, A., and Mathy, A. (2011). Tracking the construction of episodic future thoughts. *Journal of Experimental Psychology: General*, 140 (2), 258–271. doi: 10.1037/a0022581.

D'Argembeau, A., Stawarczyk, D., Majerus, S., *et al.* (2010). The neural basis of personal goal processing when envisioning future events. *Journal of Cognitive Neuroscience*, 22 (8), 1701–1713. doi: 10.1162/jocn.2009.21314.

D'Argembeau, A., and Van der Linden, M. (2004). Phenomenal characteristics associated with projecting oneself back into the past and forward into the future: influence of valence and temporal distance. *Consciousness and Cognition*, 13, 844–858. doi: 10.1016/j.concog.2004.07.007.

Dunning, D. (2007). Prediction: the inside view. In *Social Psychology: Handbook of Basic Principles* (ed. E.T. Higgins and A.W. Kruglanski). New York, NY: Guilford Press, pp. 69–90.

Eichenbaum, H. (2001). The hippocampus and declarative memory: cognitive mechanisms and neural codes. *Behavioural Brain Research*, 127, 199–207. doi: 10.1016/S0166-4328(01)00365-5.

Eichenbaum, H. (2007). Comparative cognition, hippocampal function, and recollection. *Comparative Cognition and Behavior Reviews*, 2, 47–66.

Eichenbaum, H., Sauvage, M., Fortin, N., *et al.* (2012). Towards a functional organization of episodic memory in the medial temporal lobe. *Neuroscience and Biobehavioral Reviews*, 36 (7), 1597–1608. doi: 10.1016/j.neubiorev.2011.07.006.

Gaesser, B., Sacchetti, D.C., Addis, D.R., and Schacter, D.L. (2011). Characterizing age-related changes in remembering the past and imagining the future. *Psychology and Aging*, 26 (1), 80–84. doi: 10.1037/a0021054.

Gamboz, N., Brandimonte, M.A., and de Vito, S. (2010). The role of past in the simulation of autobiographical future episodes. *Experimental Psychology*, 57 (6), 419–428. doi: 10.1027/1618-3169/a000052.

Gerlach, K.D., Spreng, R.N., Gilmore, A.W., and Schacter, D.L. (2011). Solving future problems: default network and executive activity associated with goal-directed mental simulations. *NeuroImage*, 55 (4), 1816–1824. doi: 10.1016/j.neuroimage.2011.01.030.

Gilbert, D.T., and Wilson, T. (2007). Prospection: experiencing the future. *Science*, 317, 1351–1354. doi: 10.1126/science.1144161.

Gilboa, A. (2004). Autobiographical and episodic memory: one and the same? Evidence from prefrontal activation in neuroimaging studies. *Neuropsychologia*, 42 (10), 1336–1349. doi: 10.1016/j.neuropsychologia.2004.02.014.

Giovanello, K.S., Schnyer, D., and Verfaellie, M. (2009). Distinct hippocampal regions make unique contributions to relational memory. *Hippocampus*, 19, 111–117. doi: 10.1002/hipo.20491.

Gollwitzer, P.M. (1999). Implementation intentions. *American Psychologist*, 54 (7), 493–503.

Hassabis, D., Kumaran, D., and Maguire, E.A. (2007). Using imagination to understand the neural basis of episodic memory. *Journal of Neuroscience*, 27 (52), 14365–14374. doi: 10.1523/jneurosci.4549-07.2007

Hassabis, D., Kumaran, D., Vann, S.D., and Maguire, E.A. (2007). Patients with hippocampal amnesia cannot imagine new experiences. *Proceedings of the National Academy of Sciences of the USA*, 104 (5), 1726–1731. doi: 10.1073/pnas.0610561104

Hassabis, D., and Maguire, E.A. (2007). Deconstructing episodic memory with construction. *Trends in Cognitive Sciences*, 11 (7), 299–306. doi: 10.1016/j.tics.2007.05.001.

Hodges, J.R., Patterson, K., Oxbury, S., and Funnell, E. (1992). Semantic dementia: Progressive fluent aphasia with temporal-lobe atrophy. *Brain*, 115, 1783–1806. doi: 10.1093/brain/115.6.1783.

Hurley, N.C., Maguire, E.A., and Vargha-Khadem, F. (2011). Patient HC with developmental amnesia can construct future scenarios. *Neuropsychologia*, 49 (13), 3620–3628. doi: 10.1016/j.neuropsychologia.2011.09.015.

Irish, M., Addis, D.R., Hodges, J.R., and Piguet, O. (2012). Considering the role of semantic memory in episodic future thinking: evidence from semantic dementia. *Brain*, 135 (7), 2178–2191. doi: 10.1093/brain/aws119.

Johnson, M.K., and Raye, C.L. (1981). Reality monitoring. *Psychological Review*, 88 (1), 67–85.

Kim, H. (2012). A dual-subsystem model of the brain's default network: self-referential processing, memory retrieval processes and autobiographical memory retrieval. *NeuroImage*, 61 (4), 966–977. doi: 10.1016/j.neuroimage.2012.03.025.

Klein, S.B., Loftus, J., and Kihlstrom, J.F. (2002). Memory and temporal experience: the effects of episodic memory loss on an amnesic patient's ability to remember the past and imagine the future. *Social Cognition*, 20 (5), 353–379. doi: 10.1521/soco.20.5.353.21125.

Klein, S.B., Robertson, T.E., and Delton, A.W. (2010). Facing the future: memory as an evolved system for planning future acts. *Memory and Cognition*, 38 (1), 13–22. doi: 10.3758/MC.38.1.13.

Konkel, A., and Cohen, N.J. (2009). Relational memory and the hippocampus: representations and methods. *Frontiers in Neuroscience*, 3 (2), 166–174. doi: 10.3389/neuro.01.023.2009.

Kwan, D., Carson, N., Addis, D.R., and Rosenbaum, R.S. (2010). Deficits in past remembering extend to future imagining in a case of developmental amnesia. *Neuropsychologia*, 48 (11), 3179–3186. doi: 10.1016/j.neuropsychologia.2010.06.011.

Kwan, D., Craver, C.F., Green, L., *et al.* (2011). Future decision-making without episodic mental time travel. *Hippocampus*, 22 (6), 1215–1219. doi: 10.1002/hipo.20981.

Lavenex, P., and Amaral, D.G. (2000). Hippocampal–neocortical interaction: a hierarchy of associativity. *Hippocampus*, 10, 420–430. doi: 10.1002/1098-1063(2000)10:4<420::AID-HIPO8>3.0.CO;2-5.

Levine, B., Svoboda, E., Hay, J., *et al.* (2002). Aging and autobiographical memory: Dissociating episodic from semantic retrieval. *Psychology and Aging*, 17 (4), 677–689. doi: 10.1037/0882-7974.17.4.677.

Maguire, E.A., Gadian, D.G., Johnsrude, I.S., *et al.* (2000). Navigation-related structural change in the hippocampi of taxi drivers. *Proceedings of the National Academy of Sciences of the USA*, 97 (8), 4398–4403. doi: 10.1073/pnas.070039597.

Maguire, E.A., Vargha-Khadem, F, and Hassabis, D. (2010). Imagining fictitious and future experiences: evidence from developmental amnesia. *Neuropsychologia*, 48 (11), 3187–3192. doi: 10.1016/j.neuropsychologia.2010.06.037.

Maguire, E.A., Vargha-Khadem, F., and Mishkin, M. (2001). The effects of bilateral hippocampal damage on fMRI regional activations and interactions during memory retrieval. *Brain*, 124 (6), 1156–1170. doi: 10.1093/brain/124.6.1156.

Martin, V.C., Schacter, D.L., Corballis, M.C., and Addis, D.R. (2011). A role for the hippocampus in encoding simulations of future events. *Proceedings of the National Academy of Sciences of the USA*, 108 (33), 13858–13863. doi: 10.1073/pnas.1105816108.

McClelland, J.L., McNaughton, B.L., and O'Reilly, R.C. (1995). Why there are complementary learning systems in the hippocampus and neocortex: insights from the successes and failures of connectionist models of learning and memory. *Psychological Review*, 102 (3), 419–457. doi: 10.1037/0033-295X.102.3.419.

McDermott, K.B., Szpunar, K.K., and Christ, S.E. (2009). Laboratory-based and autobiographical retrieval tasks differ substantially in their neural substrates. *Neuropsychologia*, 47 (11), 2290–2298. doi: 10.1016/j.neuropsychologia.2008.12.025.

Mullally, S.L., Hassabis, D., and Maguire, E.A. (2012). Scene construction in amnesia: An fMRI study. *Journal of Neuroscience*, 32 (16), 5646–5653. doi: 10.1523/jneurosci.5522-11.2012.

Nairne, J.S., VanArsdall, J.E., Pandeirada, J.N.S., and Blunt, J.R. (2012). Adaptive memory: enhanced location memory after survival processing. *Journal of Experimental Psychology: Learning, Memory, and Cognition*, 38 (2), 495–501. doi: 10.1037/0278-7393.33.2.263.

Neisser, U. (1986). Nested structure in autobiographical memory. In *Autobiographical Memory* (ed. D.C. Rubin). Cambridge: Cambridge University Press.

O'Keefe, J., and Dostrovsky, J. (1971). The hippocampus as a spatial map: preliminary evidence from unit activity in the freely-moving rat. *Brain Research*, 34, 171–175. doi: 10.1016/0006-8993(71)90358-1

O'Keefe, J. and Nadel, L. (1978). *The Hippocampus as a Cognitive Map*. Oxford: Clarendon Press.

Okuda, J., Fujii, T., Ohtake, H., *et al.* (2003). Thinking of the future and past: the roles of the frontal pole and the medial temporal lobes. *NeuroImage*, 19 (4), 1369–1380. doi: 10.1016/S1053-8119(03)00179-4.

Race, E., Keane, M.M., and Verfaellie, M. (2011). Medial temporal lobe damage causes deficits in episodic memory and episodic future thinking not attributable to deficits in narrative construction. *Journal of Neuroscience*, 31 (28), 10262–10269. doi: 10.1523/JNEUROSCI.1145-11.2011.

Raichle, M.E., MacLeod, A.M., Snyder, A.Z., *et al.* (2001). A default mode of brain function. *Proceedings of the National Academy of Sciences of the USA*, 98 (2), 676–682. doi: 10.1073/pnas.98.2.676.

Rathbone, C.J., Conway, M.A., and Moulin, C.J.A. (2011). Remembering and imagining: the role of the self. *Consciousness and Cognition*, 20 (4), 1175–1182. doi: 10.1016/j.concog.2011.02.013.

Rosenbaum, R.S., Köhler, S., Schacter, D.L., *et al.* (2005). The case of K.C.: contributions of a memory-impaired person to memory theory. *Neuropsychologia*, 43 (7), 989–1021. doi: 10.1016/j.neuropsychologia.2004.10.007.

Rosenbaum, R.S., Priselac, S., Köhler, S., *et al.* (2000). Remote spatial memory in an amnesic person with extensive bilateral hippocampal lesions. *Nature Neuroscience*, 3, 1044–1048. doi: 10.1038/79867.

Russell, J., Alexis, D., and Clayton, N. (2010). Episodic future thinking in 3- to 5-year-old children: the ability to think of what will be needed from a different point of view. *Cognition*, 114 (1), 56–71. doi: 10.1016/j.cognition.2009.08.013.

Schacter, D.L. (2012). Adaptive constructive processes and the future of memory. *American Psychologist*, 67, 603–613. doi:10.1037/a0029869.

Schacter, D.L., and Addis, D.R. (2007). The cognitive neuroscience of constructive memory: remembering the past and imagining the future. *Philosophical Transactions of the Royal Society of London, Series B: Biological Sciences*, 362, 773–786. doi: 10.1098/rstb.2007.2087.

Schacter, D.L., and Addis, D.R. (2009). On the nature of medial temporal lobe contributions to the constructive simulation of future events. *Philosophical Transactions of the Royal Society of London, Series B: Biological Sciences*, 364, 1245–1253. doi: 10.1098/rstb.2008.0308.

Schacter, D.L., Addis, D.R., and Buckner, R.L. (2007). Remembering the past to imagine the future: The prospective brain. *Nature Reviews: Neuroscience*, 8 (9), 657–661. doi: 10.1038/nrn2213.

Schacter, D.L., Addis, D.R., and Buckner, R.L. (2008). Episodic simulation of future events: concepts, data, and applications. *Annals of the New York Academy of Sciences*, 1124, 39–60. doi: 10.1196/annals.1440.001.

Schacter, D.L., Addis, D.R., Hassabis, D., *et al.* (2012). The future of memory: remembering, imagining, and the brain. *Neuron*, 76 (4), 677–694.

Schacter, D.L., Norman, K.A., and Koutstaal, W. (1998). The cognitive neuroscience of constructive memory. *Annual Review of Psychology*, 49, 289–318. doi: 10.1146/annurev.psych.49.1.289.

Schweizer, K., Beck-Seyffer, A., and Schneider, R. (1999). Cognitive bias of optimism and its influence on psychological well-being. *Psychological Reports*, 84, 627–636.

Sharot, T. (2011). The optimism bias. *Current Biology*, 21 (23), R941–R945. doi: 10.1016/j.cub.2011.10.030.

Sharot, T., Riccardi, A.M., Raio, C.M., and Phelps, E.A. (2007). Neural mechanisms mediating optimism bias. *Nature*, 450, 102–105. doi: 10.1038/nature06280.

Sheldon, S., McAndrews, M.P., and Moscovitch, M. (2011). Episodic memory processes mediated by the medial temporal lobes contribute to open-ended problem solving. *Neuropsychologia*, 49 (9), 2439–2447. doi: 10.1016/j.neuropsychologia.2011.04.021.

Spreng, R.N., and Levine, B. (2006). The temporal distribution of past and future autobiographical events across the lifespan. *Memory and Cognition*, 34 (8), 1644–1651.

Spreng, R.N., Stevens, W.D., Chamberlain, J.P., *et al.* (2010). Default network activity, coupled with the frontoparietal network, supports goal-directed cognition. *NeuroImage*, 53 (1), 303–317. doi: 10.1016/j.neuroimage.2010.06.016.

Squire, L.R., Stark, C.E.L., and Clark, R.E. (2004). The medial temporal lobe. *Annual Review of Neuroscience*, 27, 279–306. doi: 10.1146/annurev.neuro. 27.070203.144130.

Squire, L.R., van der Horst, A.S., McDuff, S.G., *et al.* (2010). Role of the hippocampus in remembering the past and imagining the future. *Proceedings of the National Academy of Sciences of the USA*, 107 (44), 19044–19048. doi: 10.1073/pnas.1014391107.

Strunk, D.R., Lopez, H., and DeRubeis, R.J. (2006). Depressive symptoms are associated with unrealistic negative predictions of future life events. *Behaviour Research and Therapy*, 44, 861–882. doi: 10.1016/j.brat.2005.07.001.

Suddendorf, T. (2010). Linking yesterday and tomorrow: preschoolers' ability to report temporally displaced events. *British Journal of Developmental Psychology*, 28 (2), 491–498. doi: 10.1348/026151009X479169.

Suddendorf, T., and Corballis, M.C. (1997). Mental time travel and the evolution of the human mind. *Genetic, Social, and General Psychology Monographs*, 123 (2), 133–167. doi: 10.1098/rstb.2008.0301.

Suddendorf, T., and Corballis, M.C. (2007). The evolution of foresight: what is mental time travel, and is it unique to humans? *Behavioral and Brain Sciences*, 30 (3), 299–313. doi: 10.1017/S0140525X07001975.

Suengas, A.G., and Johnson, M.K. (1988). Qualitative effects of rehearsal on memories for perceived and imagined complex events. *Journal of Experimental Psychology: General*, 117 (4), 377–389.

Sutin, A.R., and Robins, R.W. (2005). Continuity and correlates of emotions and motives in self-defining memories. *Journal of Personality*, 73 (3), 793–824. doi: 10.1111/ j.1467-6494.2005.00329.x.

Szpunar, K.K., Addis, D.R., and Schacter, D.L. (2012). Memory for emotional simulations: remembering a rosy future. *Psychological Science*, 23 (1), 24–29. doi: 10.1177/ 0956797611422237.

Szpunar, K.K., Chan, J.C.K., and McDermott, K.B. (2009). Contextual processing in episodic future thought. *Cerebral Cortex*, 19 (7), 1539–1548. doi: 10.1093/cercor/bhn191.

Szpunar, K.K., and McDermott, K.B. (2008). Episodic future thought and its relation to remembering: evidence from ratings of subjective experience. *Consciousness and Cognition*, 17 (1), 330–334. doi: 10.1016/j.concog.2007.04.006.

Szpunar, K.K., Watson, J.M., and McDermott, K.B. (2007). Neural substrates of envisioning the future. *Proceedings of the National Academy of Sciences of the USA*, 104 (2), 642–647. doi: 10.1073/pnas.0610082104.

Trope, Y., and Liberman, N. (2003). Temporal construal. *Psychological Review*, 110 (3), 403–421. doi: 10.1037/0033-295X.110.3.403.

Tulving, E. (1972). Episodic and semantic memory. In *Organization of Memory* (ed. E. Tulving and W. Donaldson). New York, NY: Academic Press, pp. 381–403.

Tulving, E. (1985). Memory and consciousness. *Canadian Psychology/Psychologie Canadienne*, 26 (1), 1–12. doi: 10.1037/h0080017.

Weiler, J.A., Suchan, B., and Daum, I. (2009). Foreseeing the future: Occurrence probability of imagined future events modulates hippocampal activation. *Hippocampus*, 20 (6), 685–690. doi: 10.1002/hipo.20695.

Weiler, J.A., Suchan, B., and Daum, I. (2010). When the future becomes the past: differences in brain activation patterns for episodic memory and episodic future thinking. *Behavioural Brain Research*, 212 (2), 196–203. doi: 10.1016/j.bbr.2010.04.013.

Weiler, J.A., Suchan, B., Koch, B., *et al.* (2011). Differential impairment of remembering the past and imagining novel events after thalamic lesions. *Journal of Cognitive Neuroscience*, 23 (10), 3037–3051. doi: 10.1162/jocn.2011.21633.

Wheeler, M.A., Stuss, D.T., and Tulving, E. (1997). Toward a theory of episodic memory: The frontal lobes and autonoetic consciousness. *Psychological Bulletin*, 121 (3), 331–354.

Zeman, A.Z.J., Beschin, N., Dewar, M., and Della Salla, S. (2013). Imagining the present: amnesia may impair descriptions of the present as well as of the future and the past. *Cortex*, 49 (3), 637–645. doi: 10.1016/j.cortex.2012.03.008.

# 15

# Episodic Memory Across the Lifespan

## *General Trajectories and Modifiers*

### Yana Fandakova, Ulman Lindenberger, and Yee Lee Shing

## Introduction

Episodic memory (EM) refers to memory about events that are bound to specific times and places in the past (Tulving, 2002). It allows humans to re-experience multiple aspects of events that happened from minutes to years ago. The remembering of previously experienced episodes increases during childhood (Schneider and Pressley, 1997) and declines in old and very old age (Kausler, 1994). At first sight, then, it might appear that changes in adulthood are a reversal or mirror image of changes during childhood. However, development of EM is driven by a constellation of factors, including changes in neural brain mechanisms, accumulation of experience and learning, and genetic influences (Lindenberger, Li, and Bäckman, 2006; Werkle-Bergner *et al.*, 2006). Importantly, the influences of these factors do not remain constant across the lifespan, such that the lower performance levels in children and older adults relative to younger adults may differ in etiology (Baltes, Lindenberger, and Staudinger, 2006).

In the present chapter, we provide an overview of the general trajectories of memory development across the lifespan, integrating both behavioral and neural evidence. We adopt the two-component framework (Shing *et al.*, 2010) that conceptualizes change in EM across the lifespan as the interplay of two largely independent but interacting components, one associative and the other strategic (cf. Simons and Spiers, 2003). The associative component refers to mechanisms that bind different features of an event into a coherent representation, and is mediated by areas of the medial temporal lobe (MTL) at the neural level (Zimmer, Mecklinger, and Lindenberger, 2006; see also Chapter 18). The strategic component, on the other hand, refers to control processes that aid and regulate memory functions at encoding and retrieval (Chapter 7; for more discussion of the development of strategic memory processes, see Chapter 16). Neurally, the strategic component is supported by regions of the prefrontal cortex (PFC; Miller and Cohen, 2001) and the parietal lobes (Cabeza *et al.*, 2008). A series

*The Wiley Handbook on the Cognitive Neuroscience of Memory*, First Edition.
Edited by Donna Rose Addis, Morgan Barense, and Audrey Duarte.
© 2015 John Wiley & Sons, Ltd. Published 2015 by John Wiley & Sons, Ltd.

of behavioral experiments (Brehmer *et al.*, 2007; Shing *et al.*, 2008) provided initial evidence for a dissociation in the lifespan developmental trajectories of the two components, such that the associative component is relatively functional by middle childhood (ages 10–12), but exhibits age-related decline in older adults. In contrast, the strategic component is functioning below the levels of younger adults in both children and older adults, in line with the protracted maturation and early age-related decline in PFC regions. Normative age gradients in associative and strategic components coexist with individual differences in change (de Frias *et al.*, 2007; Ghisletta *et al.*, 2012) and plasticity (Fandakova, Shing, and Lindenberger, 2012). In the second part of the present chapter we address several factors that have been shown to affect individual differences in EM mechanisms at different life periods. We attempt to interpret these findings from the perspectives of the two-component framework of EM.

## EM Across the Lifespan: General Trajectories

### Evidence for memory improvement in children

EM undergoes substantial changes from infancy to adolescence. With some tasks, performance in source memory tasks is already above chance by preschool years (Lindsay, Johnson, and Kwon, 1991), but with more difficult tasks, such as distinguishing between internally generated stimuli or making distinctions after substantial delays, developmental improvements are observed into the school years (Kovacs and Newcombe, 2006). Preschoolers have difficulties in binding together an item and its context into a coherent representation (Sluzenski, Newcombe, and Ottinger, 2004). In contrast, there seems to be little change in binding abilities after the age of six (Sluzenski, Newcombe, and Kovacs, 2006). Recollection of specific details associated with past events also improves gradually during childhood, with little or no developmental change observed in familiarity-based processing (Ghetti and Angelini, 2008). Developmental differences are also observed when memory for specific details of past events (i.e., verbatim traces) is compared to the ability to extract the general semantic meaning of past events (i.e., gist traces). While increases in verbatim traces are observed during preschool and early elementary school years, gist traces continue to develop up to adolescence (Brainerd and Reyna, 2005).

With increasing age, the use of elaborative strategies to support the formation of new memories becomes an increasingly important part of children's learning behavior, especially between late childhood and late adolescence (Schneider and Pressley, 1997). Age-related improvements in metamemory also contribute to the rise of memory accuracy during childhood (Ghetti, Castelli, and Lyons, 2010). Metamemory refers to a set of constructs, including beliefs, awareness, and knowledge about one's memory, as well as about different memory strategies and their effectiveness in a particular task setting (Nelson and Narens, 1990). While children's ability to utilize memory strategies to facilitate EM depends on a number of developmental factors such as metamemory and processing resources, temperament and motivation may also play important roles (Bjorklund *et al.*, 1997; Miller and Seier, 1994).

## Evidence for memory decline in older adults

At the other end of the lifespan, aging is associated with a pronounced decline in EM functioning (Ghisletta *et al.*, 2012; Rönnlund *et al.*, 2005; see also Chapters 17, 18, and 19). Different aspects of memory performance are disproportionally affected by aging, with memory for content showing smaller age-related decrease than memory for context (Chalfonte and Johnson, 1996; Spencer and Raz, 1995). Older adults exhibit difficulties creating and retrieving intra- and inter-item associations (Old and Naveh-Benjamin, 2008; see also Chapter 18). During retrieval, recollection of particular contextual details is more strongly affected by senescent changes than familiarity-based processing (Light *et al.*, 2000).

Age-related differences in EM are magnified under conditions that require self-initiated strategic processing (Cohn, Emrich, and Moscovitch, 2008). Older adults are less likely than younger adults to spontaneously use effective strategies to mediate memory performance (Dunlosky and Hertzog, 1998). Metamemory abilities also decline during senescence (Dodson and Krueger, 2006). A number of studies have examined cognitive decline in relation to proximity to death in older individuals (i.e., terminal decline). Increased decline in EM has been identified as early as 8.4 years prior to death (Sliwinski *et al.*, 2006), with a rate twice that observed as a function of chronological age (MacDonald, Hultsch, and Dixon, 2011). However, the paths associated with aging and terminal decline vary greatly across individuals (Ghisletta *et al.*, 2012; Lindenberger and Ghisletta, 2009) as a function of various factors, including lifestyle (e.g., Schaie, 2012), vascular risk (e.g., Raz *et al.*, 2005), and genetic influences (e.g., Deary *et al.*, 2012).

Taken together, both children and older adults perform below the level of younger adults under conditions that require the detailed recollection of specific contextual details from previous experiences. Furthermore, strategic and metacognitive abilities of both age groups seem to be less efficient compared to younger adults. However, while associative binding is relatively functional by middle childhood, older adults show difficulties in forming and retrieving associations of episodic details.

## Neural evidence from child development

**Functional differences at encoding.** Few studies have examined age differences in neural activation during EM tasks in childhood and adolescence. In general, developmental differences in memory functioning are paralleled by differences in the functional and structural integrity of the underlying brain circuitry during development. For example, Ofen and colleagues (2007) found that during the encoding of subsequently remembered scenes, PFC, but not MTL, activation increased with age in children and adults between 8 and 24 years. This finding is in contrast with a study by Ghetti and colleagues (2010), who, for both adolescents and younger adults, found higher activations in the hippocampus and the posterior parahippocampal gyrus during incidental encoding of items that were later recollected with specific detail compared to those that were later on forgotten. However, younger children (8 and 10–11 years old) did not show such discrimination, suggesting an increasing specialization of MTL regions to support recollection even in middle childhood.

**Functional differences in retrieval.** Only a few studies examined age differences in neural activation during EM retrieval. Paz-Alonso and colleagues (2008) investigated retrieval activations for true and false memories among 8-year-olds, 12-year-olds, and adults. Anterior MTL was engaged in item-specific recollection for 12-year-olds and adults, but not in the younger children. Children of both age groups engaged ventro-lateral and anterior PFC to a lesser degree than adults, suggesting continued maturation of semantic and monitoring processes during childhood. These findings were only partially supported by a recent neuroimaging study that examined retrieval of previously studied complex scenes in 8- to 21-year-olds (Ofen *et al.*, 2012). In this study, activation in ventrolateral PFC increased with age for successfully retrieved scenes, confirming the late maturation of PFC regions. However, in contrast to Paz-Alonso and colleagues (2008), no age differences in MTL activations were found. Notably, age-related increases in parietal activations across middle childhood and adolescence were consis-tently reported in both studies. More research is needed to understand the neural mechanisms by which age differences in parietal regions contribute to age-related increases in the ability to recollect past episodes that are rich in contextual details.

Taken together, the majority of studies reported developmental trends in PFC regions that support control aspects of EM. On the structural level, gray matter volume in the frontal lobes initially increases up to middle childhood and subse-quently declines during adolescence, with the most dorsal aspects of the frontal regions showing the latest maturation (Sowell *et al.*, 2003). White matter volume increases linearly in both anterior–posterior and inferior–superior directions during childhood and adolescence (Colby, Van Horn, and Sowell, 2011), probably reflecting increments in the speed and efficiency of communication among brain regions as a consequence of axon myelination.

In contrast, the findings with regard to age differences in MTL activation are mixed. One possible reason for this discrepancy might be the heterogeneity of maturational changes across subregions of the hippocampus. For instance, Gogtay and collaborators (2006) did not find changes in total hippocampal volume between 4 and 25 years, but reported that the volume of the posterior hippocampus gradually increased with age, whereas the volume of the hippocampal head decreased with age. With regard to the functional significance of these structural changes, successful retrieval of item–color associations was shown to engage distinct regions along the hippocampal axis in chil-dren (8- to 11-year-olds) and adults (DeMaster and Ghetti, 2013). While children engaged the posterior hippocampus when correctly remembering the color with which line drawings were associated when previously studied, correct source memory was associated with anterior hippocampus activation in younger adults.

## Neural evidence from aging

**Structural and functional changes in MTL.** At the other end of the lifespan, age-related changes in the functional and structural integrity of the cortical network sup-porting EM, particularly the PFC and MTL, are frequently observed in neuroimaging studies (for a review, see Chapter 17). Gray matter changes are especially pronounced in the hippocampus, and less so in the surrounding cortex (Raz *et al.*, 2005). Findings regarding MTL functional alterations during episodic encoding and retrieval in old age are contradictory, with some studies reporting age-related decreases (Daselaar *et al.*, 2006; Grady, McIntosh, and Craik, 2003), and others not (Dulas and Duarte, 2011; Persson *et al.*, 2010). One potential factor that may explain differences across studies is that differences in brain activation are often confounded by differences in memory performance, which compromise the interpretation of results at the neural level (Rugg and Morcom, 2005). In addition, age-related decreases in hippocampal activations are relatively minor before age 70 (Salami, Eriksson, and Nyberg, 2012), suggesting that differences across studies may be partly related to age range differences of the study samples.

Longitudinally, Persson and colleagues (2012) reported that for some older adults (55–79 years) examined in the context of the Betula study, memory performance decreased across a period of 10 years, whereas for others it remained stable or even increased. Importantly, a decrease in hippocampal activation and gray matter volume was observed only in the older adults who showed a pronounced decline in memory performance, but not in the older adults who remained stable in their performance. This study is important because it directly related longitudinal decline in memory performance in old age to functional and structural changes in relevant brain areas. At the same time, it underscores the need to delineate the physiological correlates that help to maintain memory performance in old age (Nyberg *et al.*, 2012).

**Structural and functional changes in PFC.** Prefrontal brain regions are among the areas that undergo the strongest atrophy in old age (Raz *et al.*, 2005). Changes in the microstructure of white matter integrity accompany these gray matter losses (Burzynska *et al.*, 2010). Older adults often show lower PFC activation during both encoding (Dennis *et al.*, 2008; Dulas and Duarte, 2011) and retrieval of past episodes (Duarte, Henson, and Graham, 2008; Fandakova, Lindenberger, and Shing, 2013). In contrast, some studies have reported additional PFC activation in older adults compared with younger adults (Cabeza *et al.*, 2002), which has been interpreted as compensatory activity for age-related decline in posterior brain regions. Alternatively, additional PFC activations might reflect decrease of neural efficiency or less differentiated processing with advancing adult age (Baltes and Lindenberger, 1997).

It is worth noting that most analyses suggesting "over-recruitment" of task-relevant brain regions with advancing adult age rely on cross-sectional evidence. Again, findings from the Betula study provide a notable exception. Nyberg and colleagues (2010) investigated longitudinal change in brain structure and function over a period of six years. While the cross-sectional analysis suggested *increased* activation of dorsal PFC in older adults, longitudinally activity in this region *decreased*, indicating that aging is associated with under- rather than over-recruitment of PFC regions. These findings are corroborated by recent evidence showing that older adults who deviate less from younger adults in the brain networks engaged during incidental picture encoding have higher recognition performance (Düzel *et al.*, 2010), suggesting that the extent of preservation in functional networks in old age is an important determinant of individual differences in memory performance. Based on this pattern of findings, Nyberg *et al.* (2012) suggested that brain maintenance (or relative lack of brain pathology) constitutes the primary determinant of successful memory aging (see also Lindenberger, Burzynska, and Nagel, 2013).

# EM Across the Lifespan: Modifiers

As reviewed above, a wide range of evidence points to substantial heterogeneity in EM performance during all age periods, and to reliable and substantial individual differences in developmental change. To understand these individual differences in level and change, researchers need to delineate the mechanisms that influence the memory development of individuals. These mechanisms are likely to unfold as epigenetic inter-actions between genetic makeup and environmental factors, and appear as lifestyle choices such as physical exercise, cognitive stimulation, nutrition, social participation, and other dimensions of daily life that influence memory performance. In the following sections, we selectively review three key factors that have been identified to influence individual differences in level and change of memory performance: one in childhood (parental style), one in adulthood (vascular risk), and one that operates at both ends of the lifespan (physical fitness). We also provide an overview of key findings from the cognitive training literature, focusing on individual differences in training, as a demonstration of memory plasticity across the lifespan (for more discussion of memory training, see Chapter 21). These factors are discussed in the context of the two-component framework. We aim to demonstrate the framework's utility for clas-sifying them according to their effect on associative and strategic aspects of EM. Doing so may foster our understanding of their common and distinctive effects, and may help generate questions and models to be tested in future research.

## Parental style

Animal models suggest that environmental enrichment in early life has long-lasting beneficial effects on brain development (Greenough, Black, and Wallace, 1987). However, the specific mechanisms by which experience shapes the brain in humans are not well understood. Enriched environment entails complexity in the sensory input and social stimulation from an individual's surroundings. In early childhood, a major share of social stimulation is related to the parents and/or primary caregivers. Of particular relevance to human memory development are retrospective data sug-gesting a link between lack of early nurturance due to maltreatment and later impaired brain development, including hippocampal volumes. Animal models of stress provide hypotheses of how the hippocampus is particularly vulnerable to the effects of adverse early environment (see review in Tottenham and Sheridan, 2009).

There are relatively few human studies that prospectively track the effect of parental care on subsequent brain and cognitive development. In a longitudinal study of depressed and healthy children, maternal support (as measured with a parent–child interaction paradigm) in early childhood was positively associated with hippocampal volume measured at school age (Luby *et al.*, 2012). The association between maternal support and hippocampal volumes was stronger in the sample of non-depressed children than in the sample of depressed children. In another longitudinal study by Rao and colleagues (2010), parental nurturance (as measured by warmth and avail-ability of parental care) and environmental stimulation (as measured by the availability of cognitively stimulating toys and activities) were measured at ages 4 and 8 years. During adolescence, the participants underwent structural brain imaging. Parental nur-turance at age 4 (but not at age 8) was associated with the volume of the left hippo-campus in adolescence, but in the unexpected direction of better nurturance associated with smaller hippocampal volume. Environment stimulation, on the other hand, showed no effect on hippocampal volume. These findings point to the possibility of sensitive periods in which parental factors show heightened influence on subsequent brain development. Furthermore, the directionality of parental influence on subsequent hippocampal volume may be nonlinear, and needs to be interpreted taking into account that the hippocampus volume undergoes an inverted U-shape trajectory across development (Gogtay *et al.*, 2006).

Taken together, adverse early experiences shape brain development, including a negative stress-related effect on the hippocampus. However, the mechanisms underlying such environment–brain relations cannot be readily generalized to the effects of less extreme environments. While the existing evidence suggests normal range variation in parental factors is associated with subsequent brain development (particularly the hippocampus, related to the associative component of EM), many questions are left open. First, the two longitudinal studies reviewed above (Luby *et al.*, 2012; Rao *et al.*, 2010) did not measure hippocampal volume in early childhood, or in the parents. Therefore, one cannot be certain that the reported results do not merely reflect common sources of variance, notably genetic differences. This is a common critical issue in studies that examine effects of parenting practices, which calls for innovative use of methodologies, including animal models (e.g., Freund *et al.*, 2013), to probe environmental influences on epigenetic effects. Second, studies that simultaneously measure parental factors, brain development, and memory development are scarce. The empirical links across neural, behavioral, and cognitive levels of analysis are yet to be demonstrated. Third, while parents and primary caregivers play an important role in the life of developing children, schooling context becomes increasingly salient in older children. Given behavioral evidence that suggests teachers' memory-relevant language is related to the development of children's memory skills (Coffman *et al.*, 2008), there is a need to better understand the influence of schooling context on neural development underlying memory functioning.

## Vascular health

Vascular changes are among the most important modifiers of normal aging. A growing body of evidence links vascular factors to age-associated changes in cognition during adulthood and old age. Indicators of vascular risk such as higher blood pressure, body mass index, cholesterol level, blood sugar level, and others have been associated with lower cognitive performance in old age, including an increased risk of being diagnosed with dementia. A number of behavioral measures are associated with lower vascular risk and maintenance of good health in old age, including exercise and refraining from smoking (for a review see Warsch and Wright, 2010).

Structural, functional, and behavioral evidence indicates that vascular health protects against accelerated forms of cognitive aging. For example, Raz *et al.* (2005) reported that hypertension is associated with shrinkage of the hippocampus in a sample of healthy older adults In this study, age-related acceleration of shrinkage in the hippocampus was limited to hypertensive participants (treated with medication). Furthermore, Shing *et al.* (2011) reported smaller CA1 subfields of hippocampus in older adults with hypertensive status, whereas normotensive older adults showed CA1 volumes within the range of younger adults. This finding demonstrates regional differences in vulnerability to vascular disease within the hippocampus (Wu *et al.*, 2008).

The extent to which vascular factors are a potential risk for cognitive decline may interact with common genetic variation. Bender and Raz (2012) found that normotensive carriers of the apolipoprotein (ApoE) ε4 allele with elevated systolic blood pressure showed lower verbal recognition than ε4 carriers with lower blood pressure.

Of note, blood pressure had a negative effect on the prefrontal volumes, but not hippocampal volumes, of ApoE ε4 carriers. Similar interactions between genetic and vascular risk in association with cognitive deficits have been reported previously. For instance, Raz *et al.* (2008) reported that elevated blood glucose predicted lower memory scores only in carriers of the 66Met allele of the BDNF gene, which is assumed to be associated with lower levels of the brain-derived neurotrophic factor in the central nervous system relative to Val homozygotes. These results suggest that the combination of a relatively mild elevation in physiological indicators of vascular risk with a genetic risk factor may lead to poorer functioning of brain and cognition.

Taken together, these studies indicate that vascular risk has a negative effect on memory functioning. Interacting with genetic burden, vascular risk seems to affect PFC and hippocampus volumes in particular, resulting in lower associative memory. Future studies should address the effect of interventions that try to reduce blood pressure, especially in individuals with genetic risk factors. In addition, future research is needed to delineate the degree to which vascular risk affects specific aspects of memory functioning. Based on the two-component framework, it would be expected that vascular risk would have a negative influence on both strategic and associative processes that strongly rely on PFC and hippocampal functioning.

## Physical fitness

Physical fitness has profound effects on brain and cognitive function, during both child development and aging. In school-aged children, physical activity is positively associated with measures of learning and general cognitive ability (Sibley and Etnier, 2003). Recent studies have attempted to link the positive effects of physical fitness on memory to underlying brain mechanisms. For instance, Chaddock and colleagues (2010) investigated the effects of physical fitness on relational memory and hippocampal volume among higher- and lower-fit 9- and 10-year-olds. Both groups did not differ in item memory, but higher-fit children performed better than lower-fit children in an associative memory task. Higher-fit children also had greater hippocampal volumes than lower-fit children, and individual differences in hippocampal volumes were positively related to relational (but not item) memory performance across all children. The effect of physical fitness on relational memory was directly tested in a subsequent study (Monti, Hillman, and Cohen, 2012), in which a group of preadolescent children underwent a nine-month after-school aerobic exercise intervention and was compared to a waiting-list control group on measures of item and relational memory for faces and scenes. The groups did not differ in memory performance for item or relational information, but the intervention group allocated a greater proportion of time on viewing the correctly recognized faces. As the proportion of viewing time in relational memory paradigms has been related to the structure and functioning of the hippocampus (Hannula and Ranganath, 2009), these group differences may reflect more efficient hippocampal involvement in relational memory following increase in aerobic fitness (Monti, Hillman, and Cohen, 2012).

The beneficial effects of physical fitness have also been documented in old age. Older adults who underwent an aerobic training intervention for six months showed reliable increases in brain gray and white matter volume (Colcombe *et al.*, 2006), and altered patterns of task-related functional activation (Colcombe *et al.*, 2004). Paralleling the results from child development, Erickson and colleagues (2009) found that the positive relationship between aerobic fitness and spatial memory performance was predicted by individual differences in hippocampal volume. The neural mechanisms driving the positive effects of aerobic fitness on brain status and cognitive performance in humans are not yet well understood. Evidence from animal studies suggests that these effects are, at least to some degree, associated with neurogenesis in the hippocampus, and the dentate gyrus in particular, due to changes in neurotransmitter and growth factor release (Kempermann, 2008; van Praag, 2009).

The extant evidence suggests that aerobic fitness has positive effects on the associative component of EM. However, studies in both children and older adults indicate that the positive effects of aerobic fitness training on brain functioning are not restricted to the hippocampus but may also affect brain networks engaged during tasks of attention and cognitive control (Chaddock *et al.*, 2012; Colcombe *et al.*, 2004). Thus, the beneficial effects of aerobic fitness may not be restricted to the associative, but also directly affect the strategic component of EM at both ends of the lifespan. Alternatively, the effects of aerobic fitness on the strategic component may not be direct, but may result from associative–strategic interactions such that a more functional associative component decreases the demand on memory control processes.

Given the importance of aerobic fitness for hippocampus and memory in old age, several studies have examined to what extent physical training may have a beneficial effect on ApoE ε4 allele carriers, who are at higher risk for developing Alzheimer's disease in old age. Initial evidence from this research indicates that physical fitness may serve as a protective factor for ApoE ε4 carriers, such that aerobic fitness is positively associated with increased functional activation (Deeny *et al.*, 2008) and better cognitive functioning in individuals with greater genetic risk for Alzheimer's disease (Etnier *et al.*, 2007). However, another study reported higher performance benefit from an aerobic training in ApoE ε4 non-carriers compared to ApoE ε4 carriers, indicating that cognitive benefits from physical exercise may be attenuated by genetic risk factors (Lautenschlager *et al.*, 2008). These results suggest that the beneficial effects of physical fitness interventions may not be linear, but may depend on the functional status of the individual at the onset of the training. Finally, a recent study with older adults revealed that executive functioning, along with use of self-regulatory strategies and self-efficacy measures, at the beginning of a physical exercise program were predictive of adherence to the intervention (McAuley *et al.*, 2011). The importance of these factors is not restricted to aerobic training programs, and should receive more attention in future developmental training studies.

## Individual differences in memory training gains

EM performance in childhood and old age can be improved through instruction and practice (e.g., Noack *et al.*, 2009; see also Chapter 21). Nevertheless, even after extensive practice, older adults do not reach the levels of performance of younger adults (Baltes and Kliegl, 1992). In contrast, when given the possibility to optimize a newly acquired strategy through extensive practice, children can advance to the level of younger adults (Brehmer *et al.*, 2007, 2008; Shing *et al.*, 2008). Importantly, there is a substantial degree of heterogeneity in training benefits in both children and older adults. Understanding the factors contributing to these age and individual differences is an important task for developmental research, as it will help identify programs and interventions that target specific mechanisms that may differ across individuals.

Instruction of an elaborative imagery strategy was shown to effectively increase memory performance in both children and older adults (Brehmer *et al.*, 2007; Shing *et al.*, 2008). In contrast, following extensive practice of the strategy, children surpassed older adults, presumably reflecting differences in associative binding mechanisms that may be relatively mature in school-aged children, but undergo age-related decline in older adults (Brehmer *et al.*, 2007; Shing *et al.*, 2008). In the samples of children and older adults originally reported by Brehmer and colleagues (2007), only children improved performance without further practice across an 11-month period of no testing, probably reflecting maturational changes in the brain networks underlying the strategic component (Brehmer *et al.*, 2008). Furthermore, individual differences in initial performance gains (i.e., immediately following mnemonic strategy instruction) correlated *negatively* with baseline performance (Lövdén *et al.*, 2012). In line with conceptual considerations (Lövdén *et al.*, 2010), this finding suggests that individuals who were already implementing efficient strategies at baseline had less to gain from strategic instruction. In contrast, the correlation between baseline performance and gains flipped its sign in both groups after extensive practice with the memory strategy, suggesting that the potential for plasticity of the associative component is higher among individuals with higher baseline performance.

In particular, the reanalysis of the Brehmer *et al.* (2007) results by Lövdén *et al.* (2012) suggests that individual differences in memory-relevant mechanisms and strategies modulate the benefits of training. For example, individuals with lower memory functioning may require a more directed strategy instruction, reflecting their greater need for environmental support (cf. Craik, 1983). In contrast, for individuals with relatively preserved strategic and associative functioning, providing the context for self-initiated strategy use followed by extensive practice may be sufficient (Fandakova, Shing, and Lindenberger, 2012; Jones *et al.*, 2006). Accordingly, in recollection strategy training with older adults, self-initiation of controlled processing predicted individual differences in training efficacy (Bissig and Lustig, 2007). These findings have received further support from neuroimaging evidence indicating that older adults who show greater performance gains after instruction in an elaborative memory strategy show patterns of neural activation during word encoding that more closely resemble the activation patterns of younger adults (Jones *et al.*, 2006; Nyberg *et al.*, 2003).

Besides specific factors associated with memory functioning, differences in other aspects of cognition may also contribute to individual differences in the ability to benefit from training interventions. For example, performance on tests of perceptual speed and working memory predicts the degree to which individuals benefit from memory training programs (Kliegl, Smith, and Baltes, 1990; Verhaeghen and Marcoen, 1996), supporting the notion that individual differences are magnified by training (Baltes, 1987; Lövdén *et al.*, 2012). These findings are in line with the observation that successful aging is associated with higher performance across different cognitive tasks as well as with higher levels of education (Ghisletta *et al.*, 2012; Habib, Nyberg, and Nilsson, 2007), presumably reflecting the ability to make flexible and efficient use of available brain resources, and to preserve structural and functional aspects of brain integrity into old age (Lindenberger, Burzynska, and Nagel, 2013; Nyberg *et al.*, 2012).

Finally, recent studies suggest that heterogeneity in training benefits are related to genetic variation. For instance, the KIBRA gene has been associated with better EM for T-allele carriers in both younger and older adults (Schaper *et al.*, 2008). In younger adults, the positive memory effect for T-allele KIBRA carriers was additionally enhanced by presence of the CLSTN2 C-allele (Preuschhof *et al.*, 2010), underscoring the need to examine interactions among multiple genes in order to understand their influence on complex cognitive functions (Lindenberger *et al.*, 2008). As both these genes exert their influence primarily on MTL regions, future research should examine the degree to which variation in these genes is associated with benefits from memory intervention in childhood and old age. In working memory, variations in the DAT1 receptor gene were not related to performance prior to an adaptive training across four weeks, but DAT1 10-repeat carriers (characterized by less active dopaminergic pathways) demonstrated smaller training-related gains compared to DAT1 9/10-repeat carriers (Brehmer *et al.*, 2009). These findings suggest that genetic effects on cognitive functioning may even be more pronounced in a training context rather than a single assessment.

Variation in dopamine modulation has also been related to individual differences in memory performance. For example, DAT1 and D2 receptor genes interactively influenced backward serial recall in younger and older adults (Li *et al.*, 2013). In line with the resource modulation hypothesis (Lindenberger *et al.*, 2008), the DAT1 and D2 genetic effects on recall were magnified in older adults, whose structural and neurochemical brain resources are compromised. Hence, genetic influence on training benefits may be crucially dependent on the available cognitive resources of the individual at the onset of the training program. Future research should determine whether differences in common genetic variation are related to distinct aspects of a training program depending on the brain networks that they are primarily targeting.

Overall, individual differences in the benefit from memory training have been more extensively investigated in aging research compared to child development. In general, training benefits seem to be positively associated with general cognitive resources. However, accumulating evidence suggests that genetic factors and factors specific to memory functioning need to be taken into consideration, as they may influence the degree to which different individuals benefit from an intervention.

# Conclusion

In this chapter we outlined the main developmental trajectory for EM across the lifespan and noted that it is largely compatible with a two-component model of memory functioning, with strategic and associative memory components following distinct trajectories across the lifespan. We then outlined some of the potential modifiers of these trajectories that may contribute to heterogeneity of memory functioning in childhood and old age. To arrive at a more complete understanding of EM development from childhood to old age, we need to (1) isolate different components of EM and track their changes across the lifespan, (2) identify factors that may underlie individual differences in performance on these EM components, and (3) understand how the interactions between general and modifying factors change across the lifespan. The presented evidence demonstrates the utility of the two-component framework not only for examining mean differences among age groups, but also for generating predictions regarding mechanisms that drive individual differences in episodic memory.

# References

Baltes, P.B. (1987). Theoretical propositions of life-span developmental psychology: on the dynamics between growth and decline. *Developmental Psychology*, 23, 611–626.

Baltes, P.B., and Kliegl, R. (1992). Further testing of limits of cognitive plasticity: negative age differences in a mnemonic skill are robust. *Developmental Psychology*, 28, 121–125. doi: 10.1037/0012-1649.28.1.121.

Baltes, P.B., and Lindenberger, U. (1997). Emergence of a powerful connection between sensory and cognitive functions across the adult life span: a new window to the study of cognitive aging? *Psychology and Aging*, 12, 12–21. doi: 10.1037/0882-7974.12.1.12.

Baltes, P.B., Lindenberger, U., and Staudinger, U.M. (2006). Lifespan theory in developmental psychology. In *Handbook of Child Psychology: Vol. 1. Theoretical Models of Human Development* (ed. William Damon and R. M. Lerner). New York, NY: John Wiley & Sons, Inc., pp. 1029–1143.

Bender, A.R., and Raz, N. (2012). Age-related differences in memory and executive functions in healthy APOE ε4 carriers: the contribution of individual differences in prefrontal volumes and systolic blood pressure. *Neuropsychologia*, 50, 704–714. doi: 10.1016/j.neuropsychologia.2011.12.025.

Bissig, D., and Lustig, C. (2007). Who benefits from memory training? *Psychological Science*, 18, 720–726. doi: 10.1111/j.1467-9280.2007.01966.x.

Bjorklund, D.F., Miller, P.H., Coyle, T.R., and Slawinski, J.L. (1997). Instructing children to use memory strategies: evidence of utilization deficiencies in memory training studies. *Developmental Review*, 17, 411–441. doi: 10.1006/drev.1997.0440.

Brainerd, C.J., and Reyna, V.F. (2005). *The Science of False Memory*. New York, NY: Oxford University Press.

Brehmer, Y., Li, S.-C., Müller, V., *et al.* (2007). Memory plasticity across the life span: uncovering children's latent potential. *Developmental Psychology*, 43, 465–478. doi: 10.1037/0012-1649.43.2.465.

Brehmer, Y., Li, S.-C., Straube, B., *et al.* (2008). Comparing memory skill maintenance across the lifespan: preservation in adults, increases in children. *Psychology and Aging*, 43, 465–478. doi: 10.1037/0012-1649.43.2.465.

Brehmer, Y., Westerberg, H., Bellander, M., *et al.* (2009). Working memory plasticity modulated by dopamine transporter genotype. *Neuroscience Letters*, 467, 117–120.

Burzynska, A.Z., Preuschhof, C., Backman, L., *et al.* (2010). Age-related differences in white matter microstructure: region-specific patterns of diffusivity. *NeuroImage*, 49 (3), 2104–2012. doi: 10.1016/j.neuroimage.2009.09.041.

Cabeza, R., Anderson, N.D., Locantore, J.K., and McIntosh, A.R. (2002). Aging gracefully: compensatory brain activity in high-performing older adults. *NeuroImage* 17, 1394–1402. doi: 10.1006/nimg.2002.1280.

Cabeza, R., Ciaramelli, E., Olson, I.R., and Moscovitch, M. (2008). The parietal cortex and episodic memory: an attentional account. *Nature Reviews Neuroscience*, 9, 613–625. doi: 10.1038/nrn2459.

Chaddock, L., Erickson, K.I., Prakash, R., *et al.* (2010). A neuroimaging investigation of the association between aerobic fitness, hippocampal volume, and memory performance in pre-adolescent children. *Brain Research*, 1358, 172–183. doi: 10.1016/j.brainres.2010.08.049.

Chaddock, L., Erickson, K., Prakash, R., *et al.* (2012). A functional MRI investigation of the association between childhood aerobic fitness and neurocognitive control. *Biological Psychology*, 89, 260–268.

Chalfonte, B.L., and Johnson, M.K. (1996). Feature memory and binding in young and older adults. *Memory and Cognition*, 24, 403–416.

Coffman, J.L., Ornstein, P.A., McCall, L.E., and Curran, P.J. (2008). Linking teachers' memory-relevant language and the development of children's memory skills. *Developmental Psychology*, 44, 1640–1654. doi: 10.1037/a0013859.

Cohn, M., Emrich, S.M., and Moscovitch, M. (2008). Age-related deficits in associative memory: the influence of impaired strategic retrieval. *Psychology and Aging*, 23, 93–103. doi: 10.1037/0882-7974.23.1.93.

Colby, J.B., Van Horn, J.D., and Sowell, E.R. (2011). Quantitative in vivo evidence for broad regional gradients in the timing of white matter maturation during adolescence. *NeuroImage*, 54, 25–31. doi: 10.1016/j.neuroimage.2010.08.014.

Colcombe, S.J., Erickson, K.I., Scalf, P.E., *et al.* (2006). Aerobic exercise training increases brain volume in aging humans. *Journals of Gerontology Series A: Biological Sciences and Medical Sciences*, 61, 1166–1170.

Colcombe, S.J., Kramer, A.F., McAuley, E., *et al.* (2004). Neurocognitive aging and cardiovascular fitness: recent findings and future directions. *Journal of Molecular Neuroscience*, 24, 9–14. doi: 10.1385/jmn:24:1:009.

Craik, F.I.M. (1983). On the transfer of information from temporary to permanent memory. *Philosophical Transactions of the Royal Society of London, Series B: Biological Sciences*, 302, 341–359.

Daselaar, S.M., Fleck, M.S., Dobbins, I.G., *et al.* (2006). Effects of healthy aging on hippocampal and rhinal memory functions: an event-related fMRI study. *Cerebral Cortex*, 16, 1771–1782. doi: 10.1093/cercor/bhj112.

Deary, I.J., Yang, J.I., Davies, G., *et al.* (2012). Genetic contributions to stability and change in intelligence from childhood to old age. *Nature*, 482, 212–215. doi: 10.1038/nature10781

Deeny, S.P., Poeppel, D., Zimmerman, J.B., *et al.* (2008). Exercise, APOE, and working memory: MEG and behavioral evidence for benefit of exercise in epsilon4 carriers. *Biological Psychology*, 78, 179–187. doi: 10.1016/j.biopsycho.2008.02.007.

de Frias, C.M., Lövdén, M., Lindenberger, U., and Nilsson, L.-G. (2007). Revisiting the dedifferentiation hypothesis with longitudinal multi-cohort data. *Intelligence*, 35, 381–392. doi: 10.1016/j.intell.2006.07.011.

DeMaster, D.M., and Ghetti, S. (2013). Developmental differences in hippocampal and cortical contributions to episodic retrieval. *Cortex*, 49(6), 1482–1493. doi: 10.1016/j.cortex.2012.08.004.

Dennis, N.A., Hayes, S.M., Prince, S.E., *et al.* (2008). Effects of aging on the neural correlates of successful item and source memory encoding. *Journal of Experimental Psychology: Learning, Memory, and Cognition*, 34, 791–808.

Dodson, C.S., and Krueger, L.E. (2006). I misremember it well: why older adults are unreliable eyewitnesses. *Psychonomic Bulletin and Review*, 13, 770–775.

Duarte, A., Henson, R.N.A., and Graham, K.S. (2008). The effects of aging on the neural correlates of subjective and objective recollection. *Cerebral Cortex*, 18, 2169–2180. doi: 10.1093/cercor/bhm243.

Dulas, M.R., and Duarte, A. (2011). The effects of aging on material-independent and material-dependent neural correlates of contextual binding. *NeuroImage*, 57, 1192–1204. doi: 10.1016/j.neuroimage.2011.05.036.

Dunlosky, J., and Hertzog, C. (1998). Aging and deficits in associative memory: what is the role of strategy production? *Psychology and Aging*, 13, 597–607. doi: 10.1037/0882-7974.13.4.597.

Düzel, E., Schutze, H., Yonelinas, A.P., and Heinze, H.J. (2010). Functional phenotyping of successful aging in long-term memory: preserved performance in the absence of neural compensation. *Hippocampus*, 21, 803–814. doi: 10.1002/hipo.20834.

Erickson, K.I., Prakash, R.S., Voss, M.W., *et al.* (2009). Aerobic fitness is associated with hippocampal volume in elderly humans. *Hippocampus*, 19, 1030–1039. doi: 10.1002/hipo.20547.

Etnier, J.L., Caselli, R.J., Reiman, E.M., *et al.* (2007). Cognitive performance in older women relative to ApoE-epsilon4 genotype and aerobic fitness. *Medicine and Science in Sports and Exercise*, 39, 199–207.

Fandakova, Y., Lindenberger, U., and Shing, Y.L. (2013). Deficits in process-specific prefrontal and hippocampal activations contribute to adult age differences in episodic memory interference. *Cerebral Cortex*, 24 (7), 1832–1844. doi: 10.1093/cercor/bht034.

Fandakova, Y., Shing, Y.L., and Lindenberger, U. (2012). Heterogeneity in memory training improvement among older adults: a latent class analysis. *Memory*, 20 (6), 554–567. doi: 10.1080/09658211.2012.687051.

Freund, J., Brandmaier, A.M., Lewejohann, L., *et al.* (2013). Emergence of individuality in genetically identical mice. *Science*, 340, 756–759. doi: 10.1126/science.1235294.

Ghetti, S., and Angelini, L. (2008). The development of recollection and familiarity in childhood and adolescence: evidence from the dual-process signal detection model. *Child Development*, 79, 339–358. doi: 10.1111/j.1467-8624.2007.01129.x.

Ghetti, S., Castelli, P., and Lyons, K.E. (2010). Knowing about not remembering: developmental dissociations in lack-of-memory monitoring. *Developmental Science*, 13, 611–621. doi: 10.1111/j.1467-7687.2009.00908.x.

Ghetti, S., DeMaster, D.M., Yonelinas, A.P., and Bunge, S.A. (2010). Developmental differences in medial temporal lobe function during memory encoding. *Journal of Neuroscience*, 30, 9548–9556. doi: 10.1523/jneurosci.3500-09.2010.

Ghisletta, P., Rabbitt, P.M.A., Lunn, M., and Lindenberger, U. (2012). Two thirds of the agebased changes in fluid and crystallized intelligence, perceptual speed, and memory in adulthood are shared. *Intelligence*, 40, 260–268.

Gogtay, N., Nugent, T.F. Herman, D.H., *et al.* (2006). Dynamic mapping of normal human hippocampal development. *Hippocampus*, 16, 664–672. doi: 10.1002/hipo.20193.

Grady, C.L., McIntosh, A.R., and Craik, F.I.M. (2003). Age-related differences in the functional connectivity of the hippocampus during memory encoding. *Hippocampus*, 13, 572–586. doi: 10.1002/hipo.10114.

Greenough, W.T., Black, J.E., and Wallace, C.S. (1987). Experience and brain development. *Child Development*, 58, 539–559. doi: 10.2307/1130197.

Habib, R., Nyberg, L., and Nilsson, L.-G. (2007). Cognitive and non-cognitive factors contributing to the longitudinal identification of successful older adults in the Betula study. *Aging Neuropsychology and Cognition*, 14, 257–273. doi: 10.1080/13825580600582412.

Hannula, D.E. and Ranganath, C. (2009). The eyes have it: hippocampal activity predicts expression of memory in eye movements. *Neuron*, 63, 592–599.

Jones, S., Nyberg, L., Sandblom, J., *et al.* (2006). Cognitive and neural plasticity in aging: general and task-specific limitations. *Neuroscience and Biobehavioral Reviews*, 30, 864–871. doi: 10.1016/j.neubiorev.2006.06.012.

Kausler, D.H. (1994). *Learning and Memory in Normal Aging*. New York, NY: Academic Press.

Kempermann, G. (2008). The neurogenic reserve hypothesis: what is adult hippocampal neurogenesis good for? *Trends in Neuroscience*, 31, 163–169.

Kliegl, R., Smith, J., and Baltes, P.B. (1990). On the locus and process of magnification of age differences during mnemonic training. *Developmental Psychology*, 26, 894–904. doi: 10.1037/0012-1649.26.6.894.

Kovacs, S.L., and Newcombe, N.S. (2006). Developments in source monitoring: the role of thinking of others. *Journal of Experimental Child Psychology*, 93, 25–44. doi: 10.1016/j.jecp.2005.06.006.

Lautenschlager, N.T., Cox, K.L., Flicker, L., *et al.* (2008). Effect of physical activity on cognitive function in older adults at risk for Alzheimer disease: a randomized trial. *JAMA*, 300, 1027–1037. doi: 10.1001/jama.300.9.1027.

Li, S.-C., Papenberg, G., Nagel, I.E., *et al.* (2013). Aging magnifies the effects of dopamine transporter and D2 receptor genes on backward serial memory. *Neurobiology of Aging*, 34, 358.e1–358.e10.

Light, L.L., Prull, M.W., La Voie, D., and Healy, M.R. (2000). Dual-process theories of memory in old age. In *Models of Cognitive Aging* (ed. T.J. Perfect and E. A. Maylor). New York, NY: Oxford University Press.

Lindenberger, U., Burzynska, A.Z., and Nagel, I.E. (2013). Heterogeneity in frontal lobe aging. In *Principles of Frontal Lobe Functions* (ed. D.T. Stuss and R.T. Knight). New York, NY: Oxford University Press, pp. 609–627.

Lindenberger, U., and Ghisletta, P. (2009). Cognitive and sensory declines in old age: gauging the evidence for a common cause. *Psychology and Aging*, 24, 1–16. doi: 10.1037/a0014986.

Lindenberger, U., Li, S.-C., and Bäckman, L. (2006). Delineating brain-behavior mappings across the lifespan: substantive and methodological advances in developmental neuroscience. *Neuroscience and Biobehavioral Reviews*, 30, 713–717. doi: 10.1016/j.neubiorev.2006.06.006.

Lindenberger, U., Nagel, I.E., Chicherio, C., *et al.* (2008). Age-related decline in brain resources modulates genetic effects on cognitive functioning. *Frontiers of Neuroscience*, 2, 234–244. doi: 10.3389/neuro.01.039.2008.

Lindsay, D.S., Johnson, M.K., and Kwon, P. (1991). Developmental changes in memory source monitoring. *Journal of Experimental Child Psychology*, 52, 297–318. doi: 10.1016/0022-0965(91)90065-Z.

Lövdén, M., Bäckman, L., Lindenberger, U., *et al.* (2010). A theoretical framework for the study of adult cognitive plasticity. *Psychological Bulletin*, 136, 659–676. doi: 10.1037/a0020080.

Lövdén, M., Brehmer, Y., Li, S.-C., and Lindenberger, U. (2012). Training-induced compensation versus magnification of individual differences in memory performance. *Frontiers in Human Neuroscience*, 6, 141. doi: 10.3389/fnhum.2012.00141.

Luby, J.L., Barch, D.M., Belden, A., *et al.* (2012). Maternal support in early childhood predicts larger hippocampal volumes at school age. *Proceedings of the National Academy of Sciences of the USA*, 109, 2854–2859. doi: 10.1073/pnas.1118003109.

MacDonald, S.W.S., Hultsch, D.F., and Dixon, R.A. (2011). Aging and the shape of cognitive change before death: terminal decline or terminal drop? *Journals of Gerontology Series B: Psychological Sciences and Social Sciences*, 66, 292–301. doi: 10.1093/geronb/gbr001.

McAuley, E., Mullen, S.P., Szabo, A.N., *et al.* (2011). Self-regulatory processes and exercise adherence in older adults: executive function and self-efficacy effects. *American Journal of Preventive Medicine*, 41, 284–290. doi: 10.1016/j.amepre.2011.04.014.

Miller, E.K., and Cohen, J.D. (2001). An Integrative theory of prefrontal cortex function. *Annual Review of Neuroscience*, 24, 167–202.

Miller, P.H., and Seier, W.L. (1994). Strategy utilization deficiencies in children: when, where, and why. *Advances in Child Development and Behaviour*, 25, 107–156.

Monti, J.M., Hillman, C.H., and Cohen, N.J. (2012). Aerobic fitness enhances relational memory in preadolescent children: the FITKids randomized control trial. *Hippocampus*, 22, 1876–1882. doi: 10.1002/hipo.22023.

Nelson, T.O., and Narens, L. (1990). Metamemory: a theoretical framework and new findings. *Psychology of Learning and Motivation*, 26, 125–173.

Noack, H., Lövdén, M., Schmiedek, F., and Lindenberger, U. (2009). Cognitive plasticity in adulthood and old age: gauging the generality of cognitive intervention effects. *Restorative Neurology and Neuroscience*, 27, 435–453. doi: 10.3233/rnn-2009-0496.

Nyberg, L., Lövden, M., Riklund, K., *et al.* (2012). Memory aging and brain maintenance. *Trends in Cognitive Sciences*, 16, 292–305. doi: 10.1016/j.tics.2012.04 005

Nyberg, L., Marklund, P., Persson, J., *et al.* (2003). Common prefrontal activations during working memory, episodic memory, and semantic memory. *Neuropsychologia*, 41, 371–377. doi: 10.1016/S0028-3932(02)00168-9.

Nyberg, L., Salami, A., Andersson, M., *et al.* (2010). Longitudinal evidence for diminished frontal cortex function in aging. *Proceedings of the National Academy of Sciences of the USA*, 107, 22682–22686. doi: 10.1073/pnas.1012651108.

Ofen, N., Chai, X.J., Schuil, K.D., *et al.* (2012). The development of brain systems associated with successful memory retrieval of scenes. *Journal of Neuroscience*, 32, 10012–10020. doi: 10.1523/jneurosci.1082-11.2012.

Ofen, N., Kao, Y.-C., Sokol-Hessner, P., *et al.* (2007). Development of the declarative memory system in the human brain. *Nature Neuroscience*, 10, 1198–1205. doi: 10.1038/nn1950

Old, S.R., and Naveh-Benjamin, M. (2008). Differential effects of age on item and associative measures of memory: a meta-analysis. *Psychology and Aging*, 23, 104–118. doi: 10.1037/0882-7974.23.1.104.

Paz-Alonso, P.M., Ghetti, S., Donohue, S.E., *et al.* (2008). Neurodevelopmental correlates of true and false recognition. *Cerebral Cortex*, 18, 2208–2216. doi: 10.1093/cercor/bhm246.

Persson, J., Kalpouzos, G., Nilsson, L.-G., *et al.* (2010). Preserved hippocampus activation in normal aging as revealed by fMRI. *Hippocampus*, 21, 753–766. doi: 10.1002/hipo.20794.

Persson, J., Pudas, S., Lind, J., *et al.* (2012). Longitudinal structure–function correlates in elderly reveal MTL dysfunction with cognitive decline. *Cerebral Cortex*, 22, 2297–2304. doi: 10.1093/cercor/bhr306.

Preuschhof, C., Heekeren, H.R., Li, S.-C., *et al.* (2010). KIBRA and CLSTN2 polymorphisms exert interactive effects on human episodic memory. *Neuropsychologia*, 48, 402–408.

Rao, H., Betancourt, L., Giannetta, J.M., *et al.* (2010). Early parental care is important for hippocampal maturation: evidence from brain morphology in humans. *NeuroImage*, 49, 1144–1150. doi: 10.1016/j.neuroimage.2009.07.003.

Raz, N., Lindenberger, U., Ghisletta, P., *et al.* (2008). Neuroanatomical correlates of fluid intelligence in healthy adults and persons with vascular risk factors. *Cerebral Cortex*, 18, 718–726. doi: 10.1093/cercor/bhm108.

Raz, N., Lindenberger, U., Rodrigue, K.M., *et al.* (2005). Regional brain changes in aging healthy adults: general trends, individual differences and modifiers. *Cerebral Cortex*, 15, 1676–1689. doi: 10.1093/cercor/bhi044.

Rönnlund, M., Nyberg, L., Bäckman, L., and Nilsson, L.-G. (2005). Stability, growth, and decline in adult life span development of declarative memory: cross-sectional and longitudinal data from a population-based study. *Psychology and Aging*, 20, 3–18. doi: 10.1037/0882-7974.20.1.3.

Rugg, M.D., and Morcom, A.M. (2005). The relationship between brain activity, cognitive performance, and aging: the case of memory. In *Cognitive Neuroscience of Aging* (ed. R. Cabeza, L. Nyberg and D.C. Park). New York, NY: Oxford University Press, pp. 132–154.

Salami, A., Eriksson, J., and Nyberg, L. (2012). Opposing effects of aging on large-scale brain systems for memory encoding and cognitive control. *Journal of Neuroscience*, 32, 10749–10757. doi: 10.1523/jneurosci.0278-12.2012.

Schaie, K.W. (2012). *Developmental influences on adult intelligence: The Seattle Longitudinal Study*, 2nd edn. New York, NY: Oxford University Press.

Schaper, K., Kölsch, H., Popp, J., *et al.* (2008). KIBRA gene variants are associated with episodic memory in healthy elderly. *Neurobiology of Aging*, 29, 1123–1125. doi: 10.1016/j.neurobiolaging.2007.02.001.

Schneider, W., and Pressley, M. (1997). *Memory Development Between Two and Twenty*. 2nd edn. Mahwah, NJ: Erlbaum.

Shing, Y.L., Rodrigue, K.M. Kennedy, K.M., *et al.* (2011). Hippocampal subfield volumes: age, vascular risk, and correlation with associative memory. *Frontiers in Aging Neuroscience*, 3, 2. doi: 10.3389/fnagi.2011.00002.

Shing, Y.L., Werkle-Bergner, M., Brehmer, Y., *et al.* (2010). Episodic memory across the lifespan: the contributions of associative and strategic components. *Neuroscience and Biobehavioral Reviews* 34, 1080–1091. doi: 10.1016/j.neubiorev.2009.11.002.

Shing, Y.L., Werkle-Bergner, M., Li, S.-C., and Lindenberger, U. (2008). Associative and strategic components of episodic memory: a life-span dissociation. *Journal of Experimental Psychology: General*, 137, 495–513. doi: 10.1037/0096-3445.137.3.495.

Sibley, B.A., and Etnier, J.L. (2003). The relationship between physical activity and cognition in children: a meta-analysis. *Pediatric Exercise Science*, 15, 243–256.

Simons, J.S., and Spiers, H.J. (2003). Prefrontal and medial temporal lobe interactions in long-term memory. *Nature Reviews Neuroscience*, 4, 637–648.

Sliwinski, M.J., Smyth, J.M., Hofer, S.M., and Stawski, R.S. (2006). Intraindividual coupling of daily stress and cognition. *Psychology and Aging*, 21, 545–557. doi: 10.1037/0882-7974.21.3.545.

Sluzenski, J., Newcombe, N.S., and Kovacs, S.L. (2006). Binding, relational memory, and recall of naturalistic events: a developmental perspective. *Journal of Experimental Psychology: Learning, Memory, and Cognition*, 32, 89–100. doi: 10.1037/0278-7393.32.1.89.

Sluzenski, J., Newcombe, N.S., and Ottinger, W. (2004). Changes in reality monitoring and episodic memory in early childhood. *Developmental Science*, 7, 225–245. doi: 10.1111/j.1467-7687.2004.00341.x.

Sowell, E.R., Peterson, B.S., Thompson, P.M., *et al.* (2003). Mapping cortical change across the human life span. *Nature Neuroscience*, 6, 309–315. doi: 10.1038/nn1008.

Spencer, W.D., and Raz, N. (1995). Differential effects of aging on memory for content and context: a meta-analysis. *Psychology and Aging*, 10, 527–539. doi: 10.1037/0882-7974.10.4.527.

Tottenham, N., and Sheridan, M.A. (2009). A review of adversity, the amygdala and the hippocampus: a consideration of developmental timing. *Frontiers in Human Neuroscience*, 3, 68. doi: 10.3389/neuro.09.068.2009.

Tulving, E. (2002). Episodic memory: from mind to brain. *Annual Review of Psychology*, 53, 1–25.

van Praag, H. (2009). Exercise and the brain: something to chew on. *Trends in Neurosciences*, 32, 283–290. doi: 10.1016/j.tins.2008.12.007.

Verhaeghen, P., and Marcoen, A. (1996). On the mechanisms of plasticity in young and older adults after instruction in the method of loci: evidence for an amplification model. *Psychology and Aging*, 11, 164–178. doi: 10.1037/0882-7974.11.1.164.

Warsch, J.R.L., and Wright, C.B. (2010). The aging mind: vascular health in normal cognitive aging. *Journal of the American Geriatrics Society*, 58, S319–S324. doi: 10.1111/j.1532-5415.2010.02983.x.

Werkle-Bergner, M., Müller, V., Li, S.-C., and Lindenberger, U. (2006). Cortical EEG correlates of successful memory encoding: implications for lifespan comparisons. *Neuroscience and Biobehavioral Reviews*, 30, 839–854. doi: 10.1016/j.neubiorev.2006.06.009.

Wu, W., Brickman, A.M., Luchsinger, J., *et al.* (2008). The brain in the age of old: the hippocampal formation is targeted differentially by diseases of late life. *Annals of Neurology*, 64, 698–706. doi: 10.1002/ana.21557.

Zimmer, H.D., Mecklinger, A., and Lindenberger, U., eds. (2006). *Handbook of Binding and Memory: Perspectives from Cognitive Neuroscience*. Oxford: Oxford University Press.

# 16

# The Development of Episodic Memory
## *Evidence from Event-Related Potentials*

Axel Mecklinger, Volker Sprondel, and
Kerstin H. Kipp

## Introduction

Remembering past experiences is an essential part of human cognition. The ability to encode new events as well as to mentally travel back in time to re-experience past events and the spatial and temporal context in which they occurred is a central aspect of daily cognitive functioning. Not all mnemonic processes show the same developmental pattern, however: while young children's performance on perceptual implicit memory tasks resembles that of young adults (see Schneider and Pressley, 1997, for a review), episodic memory shows remarkable changes during childhood and adolescence, allowing young children, who typically perform poorly on tests of episodic memory, to improve dramatically as they grow. In the current review, we will highlight distinctions between mnemonic processes in terms of their developmental patterns. Before reviewing event-related potential (ERP) studies of episodic memory development, we will briefly discuss two features that are central to the understanding of childhood episodic memory and its maturation.

The first of these concerns the differential developmental trajectories of familiarity and recollection throughout childhood and adolescence Dual-process perspectives of recognition hold that familiarity and recollection are two distinct processes that can contribute to episodic recognition judgments (Yonelinas, 2002; see also Chapter 9). Familiarity, a fast-acting process by which the strength of memory representations is assessed without retrieval of contextual details of a prior episode, appears to mature during early childhood (Ghetti and Angelini, 2008; Mecklinger, Brunnemann, and Kipp, 2011), whereas recollection, the retrieval of detailed information from a prior study episode including its spatial and temporal context, continues developing throughout adolescence (Brainerd and Reyna, 2004; Ghetti and Angelini, 2008; Sprondel, Kipp, and Mecklinger, 2011).

A second theme of central relevance in research on memory development relates to improvements in cognitive control processes that contribute to episodic memory performance (see Chapters 7 and 15). For example, children perform disproportionately

*The Wiley Handbook on the Cognitive Neuroscience of Memory*, First Edition.
Edited by Donna Rose Addis, Morgan Barense, and Audrey Duarte.
© 2015 John Wiley & Sons, Ltd. Published 2015 by John Wiley & Sons, Ltd.

worse in episodic memory tasks that require the specification of contextual information of a study episode, such as the color in which a picture was seen or the voice in which a word was spoken (Lindsay, Johnson, and Kwon, 1991). Children of early school age also encounter problems in reality monitoring tasks, in which they have to discriminate between memories of imagined and actually performed actions (Foley and Johnson, 1985). The low reliability of children in eyewitness testimony is also thought to be a reflection of their poor memory for the sources of events (Bruck and Ceci, 1999). An influential account of these difficulties is provided by the source monitoring framework, which emphasizes the role of operations involved in identifying and examining the source of remembered events, such as the time of day an event occurred or the location where an object was left (Johnson, Hashtroudi, and Lindsay, 1993; for more discussion, see Chapter 8). According to this framework, children encounter source memory difficulties because source information is not automatically reinstantiated but critically depends on cognitive control processes and purposeful retrieval strategies which are still unavailable to younger children.

## Event-Related Potential Measures of Episodic Memory

In this chapter, we review event-related potential (ERP) studies that provide important insights into the development of episodic memory in general, with a particular focus on the two themes of interest here. ERPs can reliably be recorded in a variety of explicit memory tasks, and the processes involved in encoding information into and retrieving it from episodic memory have been related to various ERP differences between experimental conditions (for reviews see Friedman and Johnson, 2000; Rugg and Curran, 2007; see also Chapter 5). An important feature of the ERP technique is its excellent temporal resolution (in the millisecond domain) by which functionally relevant brain activity can be monitored. ERPs thus allow processes of interest to be examined online, at the speed at which they unfold (Friedman, 2012), a possibility that is not available to some other neuroimaging measures such as fMRI. The ERP technique is also ideally suited for use with children, as it is easy to apply and ensures that the child finds him- or herself in a relatively comfortable laboratory environment.

ERP components are characterized by their amplitude (the magnitude by which two experimental conditions differ), their latency, and their scalp distribution (Rugg and Coles, 1995). The distortion of electrical signals by biological tissues (e.g., scalp, skull) means that the ERP technique is not well-designed for identifying functionally relevant brain regions. The use of high-density electroencephalography (EEG) recordings together with source localization techniques, however, makes the estimation of the neural generators of ERP components increasingly plausible (Luck, 2004). The ease of data collection, alongside its high temporal resolution, makes the ERP technique a valuable tool for examining developmental changes in episodic memory processes across different age groups (Friedman, 2012). Nonetheless, surprisingly few developmental ERP studies have examined commonalities and differences in encoding and retrieval-related processes across age groups to date. In this review we will focus on ERP measures of retrieval-related processes (see Friedman, 2012, for developmental aspects of encoding and memory formation).

# The Development of Episodic Recognition

To date the majority of developmental memory studies have focused on age differences in recall and recognition and have found large age-related differences in both tasks. Interpretations derived from these studies are limited, however, because comparisons between recall and recognition tasks are not process-pure, making it difficult to make specific claims about which processes are responsible for age-related changes (Ghetti and Angelini, 2008). Multiple processes are thought to contribute even to seemingly simple recognition judgments (Herron and Rugg, 2003). The dual-process view states that two distinct processes contribute to recognition memory. The first, familiarity, is a process which assesses the strength of a memory representation without the retrieval of contextual details of prior study episodes, and as such is sufficient for making adequate recognition memory judgments. A second process, however, recollection, is necessary to retrieve the context in which an event was situated. Several studies suggest that the development of recollection extends from early childhood to adolescence, whereas familiarity matures early and becomes stable during childhood (Billingsley, Smith, and McAndrews, 2002; Ghetti and Angelini, 2008; Ofen *et al.*, 2007). Data of this kind come from the remember/know (R/K) procedure (Tulving, 1985) in which participants have to evaluate their memory experience and indicate whether they recollect qualitative details from a study episode (R response) or merely have a feeling of familiarity for the test item (K response). In one study of this kind, Billingsley, Smith, and McAndrews (2002) reported that the proportion of R responses from early school age to adulthood increased while there were no differences in K responses across age groups. The procedures employed for measuring familiarity and recollection in studies with adults are not necessarily suited for use with children, however. The R/K procedure may not be appropriate in developmental or clinical studies because of its susceptibility to inter-individual variability. For example, children of early school age have been shown to be unable to distinguish between mental states such as knowing, believing, or remembering (Perner and Ruffman, 1995). Any age-related differences in familiarity and recollection as revealed by the R/K procedure may thus reflect differences in the ability to assess mental states rather than different developmental trajectories of the two processes.

An increasing number of studies indicate that familiarity and recollection can be mapped onto qualitatively different ERP old/new effects. Familiarity appears to be well reflected by more positive-going waveforms for studied than non-studied items, with a maximum difference between 300 and 500 ms at frontocentral recording sites, an effect that has been termed the mid-frontal old/new effect (for reviews see Mecklinger and Jäger, 2009; Rugg and Curran, 2007; but see Paller, Voss, and Boehm, 2007 for an alternative view of the mid-frontal old/new effect). Recollection is associated with a later-occurring effect, specifically with more positive-going ERP waveforms for old than new items between 400 and 800 ms. This effect is termed left parietal old/new effect, because it reaches its maximal amplitude at left parietal recording sites (for reviews see Friedman and Johnson, 2000; Mecklinger, 2000; Rugg and Curran, 2007). In view of the two distinct ERP effects strongly related to familiarity and recollection, and the fact that ERP measures do not presuppose the ability to distinguish between mental states, ERP measures provide a valuable tool for investigating similarities and differences between recognition memory subprocesses across age groups.

# The Development of Recollection

As will be briefly reviewed here, developmental recognition memory studies have shown that the ERP correlate of recollection, the left parietal old/new effect, can reliably be recorded at early school age. The few studies comparing ERP correlates of recollection in children and adults used item recognition tasks with pictorial materials. Using pictures of real-world objects as both study items and retrieval cues, Cycowicz, Friedmann, and Duff (2003) found highly similar parietal old/new effects in 10-year-old children, adolescents, and young adults. Similarly, Czernochowski *et al.* (2005) used line drawings of real-world objects as retrieval cues for studied words or real-world photographs. Parietal old/new effects comparable to those of adult participants were found in children as young as 6–8 years. Although these effects might suggest that recollection, as reflected by the parietal old/new effect, is relatively mature at early school age, it could be argued that, rather than reflecting recollective processing, these effects are an indication of children's greater reliance on verbatim memory traces and perceptual matching between study and test materials. To test this possibility we directly contrasted the parietal old/new effects for test blocks in which low-matching (words) or high-matching (photographs) study materials were defined as targets in the aforementioned study. No differences were found in the parietal old/new effects for high-matching and low-matching study items, suggesting that a perceptual matching account is unlikely.

Evidence of age invariance of the ERP correlate of recollection in children, adolescents, and young adults has also been reported in other episodic recognition tasks. Sprondel, Kipp, and Mecklinger (2011) employed a continuous recognition memory task in which new (un-repeated) and old (repeated) items were presented continuously and old/new judgments were required for each item. The old/new effects for children (7–8 years), adolescents (13–14 years), and adults are illustrated in Figure 16.1.

Consistent with previous studies, highly similar parietal old/new effects were found in all three age groups. The primary difference across age was a larger and delayed effect in the group of children, for whom the effect occurred 100–200 ms later. In a repeated testing paradigm designed to explore ERP indices of recognition memory across the lifespan, Friedman *et al.* (2010) tested participants on the same (pictorial) materials over four cycles. Highly similar parietal old/new effects and repetition effects were found in children (9–10 years), adolescents (13–14 years), and young adults.

Despite the broad similarities in the ERP correlates of recollection from 6–8 years to young adulthood, several ways in which this ERP effect differs with age do need to be addressed. First, in most studies the parietal old/new effect is broader, topographically less accentuated, and larger in amplitude in children than in adults. Changes in ERP components of that kind are frequently found in developmental ERP studies (see Segalowitz, Santesso, and Jetha, 2010, for a review) and may reflect functional differences across age groups. For example, children may require an increase in effortful attention towards a retrieval cue, and this may necessitate the contribution of a greater number of brain regions to the old/new effect. The larger magnitude of the parietal old/new effect in younger populations (an example is shown in Figure 16.1) and/or its more widespread topographical distribution could also reflect neurophysiological differences between developing and adult brains, however, such as

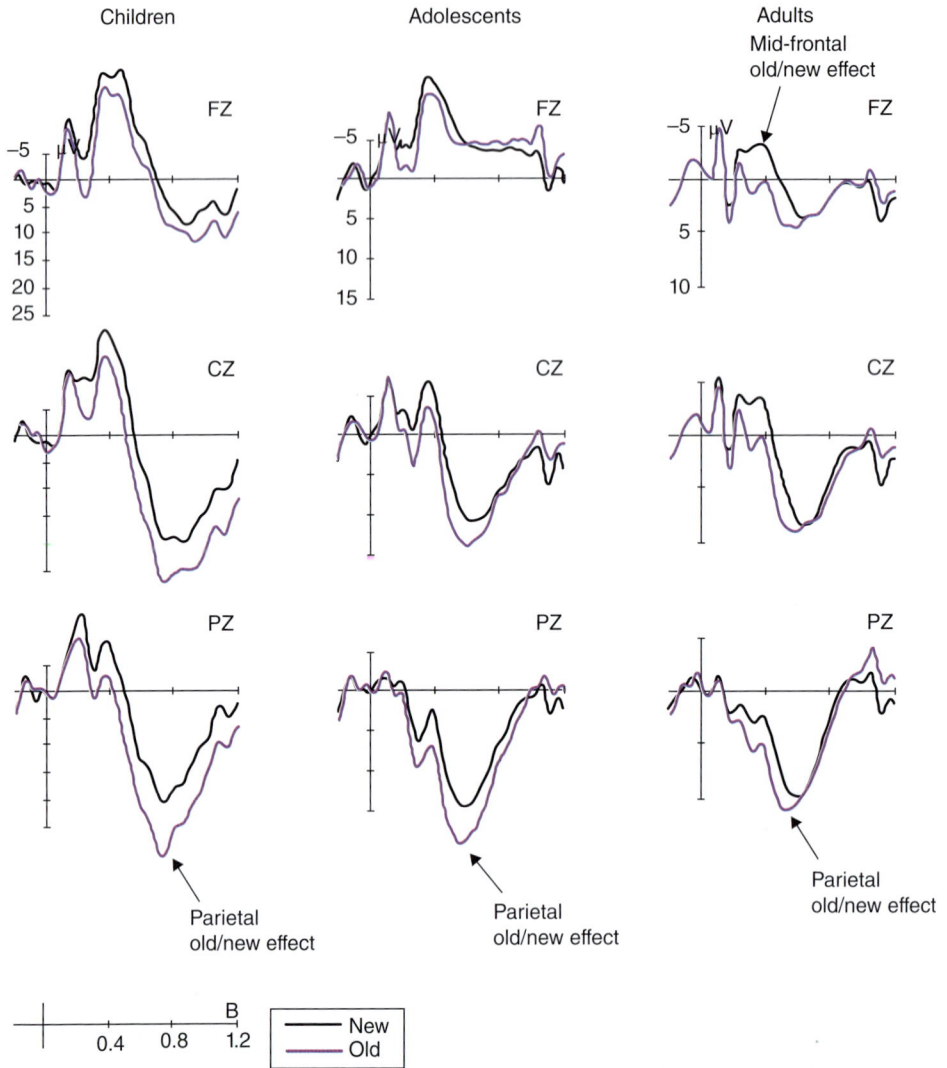

**Figure 16.1** Grand average ERP waveforms at the mid-frontal (FZ), central (CZ), and parietal (PZ) recording sites for correctly classified old (blue line) and new items (black line) in children, adolescents, and adults in the continuous recognition task employed by Sprondel, Kipp, and Mecklinger (2011). The vertical lines mark stimulus onset.

less well-refined cognitive networks, or the smaller distance between neural generators and recording sites that results from children's smaller head sizes (Picton and Taylor, 2007).

Second, irrespective of topographical differences, the parietal old/new effect, similar to other ERP effects, is often delayed in children. Delayed ERP components are accompanied by increased response latencies in most cases, and the most important determinant of the latency of information processing is thought to be the myelination of neural pathways, which starts prenatally and continues into young adulthood

(Picton and Taylor, 2007). Incomplete myelination during early childhood is likely to be a candidate factor in the delayed manifestation of the parietal old/new effect in these studies.

Interestingly, although recollection-based processes (as reflected in the parietal old/new effect) at 6–8 years of age have repeatedly been shown to be similar to those of adults, a consistent finding in developmental memory research is that recognition memory performance in item memory tasks continuously improves throughout childhood and adolescence. One interpretation of this pattern is that, rather than being a direct consequence of recollection per se, developmental improvements in recognition memory performance depend upon changes in the cognitive control of retrieval processes and strategies (Friedman, 2012; Siegler, 1998).

## The Development of Familiarity

While developmental ERP studies suggest that recollection-based processing is relatively mature at early school age, the picture is less consistent with respect to the development of familiarity. The few behavioral studies that have investigated the development of recognition memory from a dual-process perspective suggest that familiarity matures early and becomes stable during childhood (although the problems surrounding the study of mental experiences in children nonetheless apply here; Billingsley, Smith, and McAndrews, 2002; Ghetti and Angelini, 2008). Conversely, ERP studies reveal an inconsistent pattern of results. In the studies introduced above (Czernochowski *et al.*, 2005; Sprondel, Kipp, and Mecklinger, 2011) the mid-frontal old/new effect, the putative ERP correlate of familiarity, was virtually absent in the young and older child groups, but was present for adults (see also Figure 16.1). Likewise, the mid-frontal old/new effect was obtained for adolescents, young adults, and old adults in the repetition study by Friedman *et al.* (2010) but was absent for the child group. Two studies have in fact reported old/new differences between 300 and 500 ms at frontal recording sites which differ in polarity from the pattern typically observed (i.e., more positive-going ERPs for new than for old items) (Czernochowski, Mecklinger, and Johansson, 2009; Hepworth, Rovet, and Taylor, 2001). One interpretation of this finding is that children may allocate more attention to new items in some situations, and that this is reflected in an attenuated frontally distributed negativity (the so-called Nc; Czernochowski, Mecklinger, and Johansson, 2009).

In a recent study (Mecklinger, Brunnemann, and Kipp, 2011) we set out to explore whether the ERP correlate of familiarity can be reliably recorded in children of early school age using a more sensitive paradigm designed to capitalize on a widely established operational definition of familiarity. We focused on the different temporal dynamics of familiarity and recollection and tested recognition memory with a response deadline procedure in which recognition decisions have to be given very quickly. Following demonstrations that the use of familiarity is fostered and recollection is diminished under speeded response conditions (Boldini, Russo, and Avons, 2004; Light *et al.*, 2004), we predicted the ERP correlate of familiarity would be present and the correlate of recollection diminished in this condition. Children aged 8–9 years and young adults were tested in a speeded and non-speeded version of a recognition memory test with colored line drawings as stimulus materials.

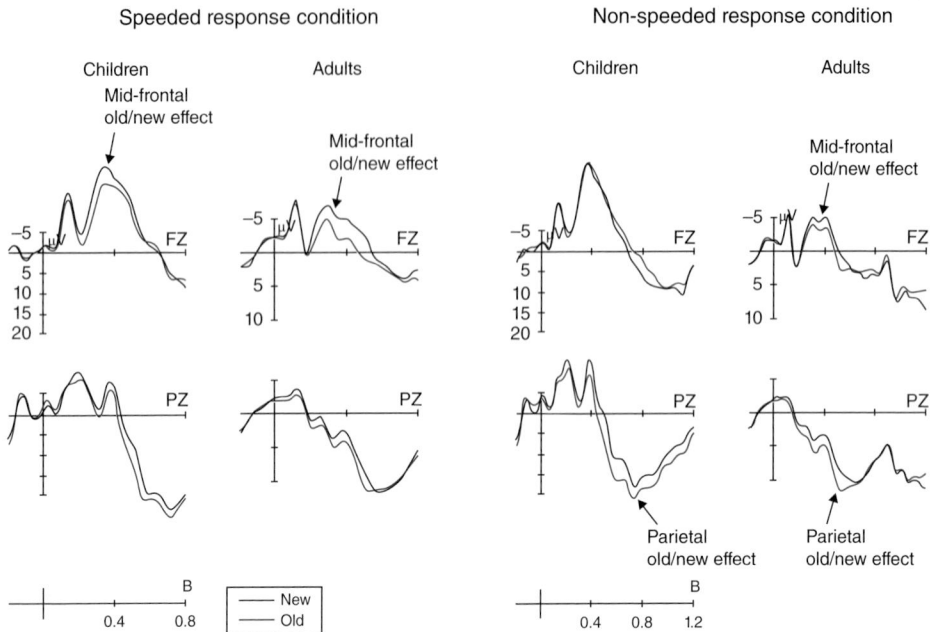

**Figure 16.2** Grand average ERP waveforms at the mid frontal (FZ) and parietal (PZ) recording sites for correctly classified old (blue line) and new items (black line) in children and adults in the speeded and non-speeded response condition in the study by Mecklinger, Brunnemann, and Kipp (2011). To take into account the delayed response latencies of children, different response deadlines were used for adults (750 ms) and children (1050 ms) in the speeded condition. The vertical lines mark stimulus onset. This is a modified version of a figure presented by Mecklinger, Brunnemann, and Kipp (2011).

As illustrated in Figure 16.2, consistent with our prediction, children and adults showed the mid-frontal old/new effect and an attenuated parietal old/new effect in the speeded condition. By showing that the ERP correlate for familiarity can be reliably recorded in children under speeded response conditions, these results show the importance of taking account of the differential temporal dynamics of familiarity and recollection when endeavoring to measure the ERP correlate of familiarity and its developmental characteristics. These findings also support models of memory development that assume familiarity matures relatively early and does not show much developmental change after 8–9 years of age (Brainerd and Reyna, 2004; Ghetti and Angelini, 2008; Shing *et al.*, 2010).

In the non-speeded condition, however, age differences were obtained: both groups showed a parietal old/new effect, whereas the mid-frontal effect was observed only for adults. The absence of an ERP correlate of familiarity in the group of children resembles earlier findings from item memory tasks and raises the question why this effect cannot reliably be found in standard episodic recognition tasks in which recognition judgments are given without time pressure. It is conceivable that in such situations children, owing to the immaturity of cognitive control processes, tend to rely more on recollection and are less flexible in using multiple memory signals for episodic recognition. In line with this notion is the finding that the absence of the ERP correlate of familiarity in children in some studies is accompanied by a more conservative decision criterion than in adults (Czernochowski *et al.*, 2004; Friedmann *et al.*, 2010). This difference might indicate that children judged items as old only when the amount of contextual information available was sufficiently high to inform that judgment. It should also be noted that most of the developmental ERP studies were not explicitly designed to explore ERP correlates of familiarity and recollection (Cycowicz, Friedmann, and Duff, 2003; Czernochowski *et al.*, 2005) and may not have been sensitive enough to dissociate both subprocesses electrophysiologically in children. Likewise, the use of relatively high-frequency words (van Strien *et al.*, 2009) might have ensured that pre-experimental familiarity was at a level that meant that familiarity increments as a function of repetition within the experiment would no longer be diagnostic for episodic recognition in children.

## The Impact of Infant Febrile Seizures on the Development of Recognition Memory

Motivated by the fact that it is possible to record the ERP correlates of familiarity and recollection in children at early school age, in a next step we explored whether these electrophysiological measures of memory can also be used to assess abnormal forms of recognition memory development (Kipp *et al.*, 2010). To this end, we investigated children who suffered from febrile seizures during infancy. Infant febrile seizures (IFS) are convulsions triggered by a fever that occurs most often in otherwise healthy children between the ages of 6 months and 5 years (Sadleir and Scheffer, 2008). IFS incidents are associated with hippocampal pathology, and a potential consequence of IFS on episodic memory development might then be disruption of memory processes that depend on the integrity of the hippocampus, such as recollection. We tested this by exploring recognition memory in a group of 17 seven- to nine-year-old children, who suffered from IFS between seven months and three years of age, and an age-matched control group. Familiarity and recollection estimates were derived from ERP measures (the mid-frontal and parietal old/new effect). An additional volumetric analysis of the hippocampus was conducted in both groups. The principal findings were as follows. No group differences were found for absolute or normalized hippo-campal volumes, but the absolute hippocampal volume (collapsed across groups) cor-related positively with recognition memory performance (hit rates), which was high and did not differ between groups. There were no behavioral differences in task performance between the patient and the control group. However, pronounced group differences were obtained in the ERP correlates of familiarity and recollection. Consistent with other ERP studies with children in this age range, we observed a large parietal old/new effect for the control group but no ERP correlate of familiarity (Figure 16.3). For the IFS group, the parietal old/new effect was absent, but a significant ERP correlate of familiarity was obtained.

To the extent that the early frontal and parietal old/new effects in children reflect familiarity and recollection in the same way as in adults, these results suggest that familiarity is preserved and recollection is impaired in school-age children who suf-fered from IFS. The highly similar recognition performance across groups despite differences in the ERP indices of familiarity and recollection may reflect the compensation of degraded recollection in IFS children by familiarity. These results

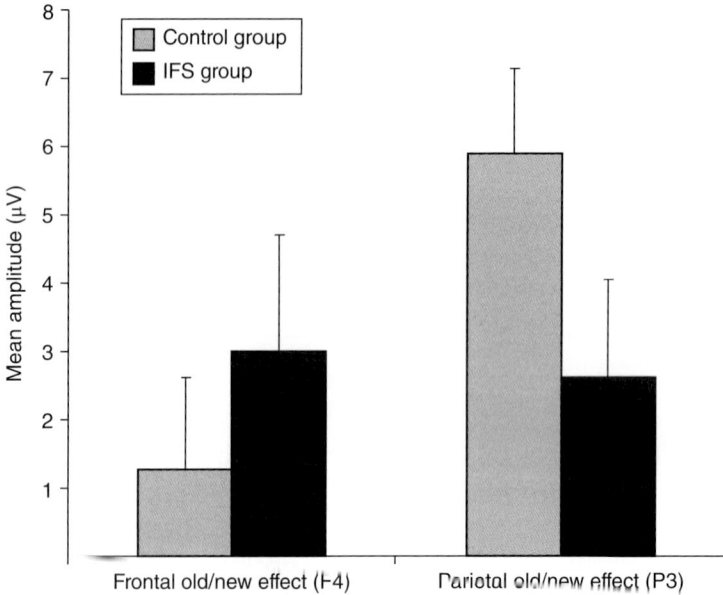

**Figure 16.3** ERP old/new amplitude differences (in microvolt) and error bars for the IFS and the control group at a frontal (F4) and a parietal (P3) recording site where the mid-frontal and late parietal effects were largest. The frontal old/new effect was significant for the IFS group but not for the control group, whereas the parietal old/new effect reached significance for the control group but not for the IFS group. This is a modified version of a figure presented by Kipp *et al.* (2010).

not only challenge the commonly held view that IFS does not have consequences for episodic memory development during childhood, they also suggest that even in the absence of structural changes in the hippocampus (as revealed by hippocampal volumetry) IFS can lead to subtle changes in the medial temporal lobe (MTL) memory network, which remain undetected by behavioral measures but can be disclosed by means of ERP measures of episodic recognition.

## Retrieval Control Processes

The engagement of memory strategies requires mentally effortful, goal-directed processes that are adapted to enhance memory performance (Bjorklund and Douglas, 2002; for more discussion of strategy use and memory training, see Chapters 15 and 21). Strategies can be used to support the encoding of information into long-term episodic memory, to improve rehearsal but also to retrieve information from memory. Retrieval strategies improve remarkably from early childhood to adolescence (Schneider and Pressley, 1997), and developmental memory studies suggest that children at early school age require more explicit retrieval cues to reinstantiate memory representations than older children. In one illustrative study, children learned pictures together with cue cards that helped to classify the pictures into categories during learning (Kobasigawa, 1974). Later they were asked to remember the pictures under three different retrieval conditions. Memory performance of the 6- to 7-year-old children was remarkably low under free recall conditions in which no explicit retrieval cues were given but improved to the level of 11- to 12-year-olds when cue cards were available and the children were informed how many pictures had been learned with each cue. Younger children thus appear to learn as much information as their older peers but require specific and explicit cues for successful remembering (Bjorklund and Douglas, 2002).

A classic approach used to investigate the control processes which support the engagement of retrieval strategies involves source memory tasks. In laboratory studies of source memory, participants have to discriminate between items studied in a particular context (e.g., words presented in a male voice or pictures studied on the left side of the screen) from items presented in another context (e.g., words spoken by a female voice or pictures on the right side of the screen) and new, unstudied items. In these tasks, being able to correctly identify the source is enhanced by the engagement of a variety of retrieval strategies. For example, cue specification processes are processes applied to retrieval cues in order to facilitate the access and recovery of task-relevant aspects of a memory trace (Mecklinger, 2010; Rugg and Wilding, 2000). Post-retrieval monitoring refers to the evaluation and verification of retrieved memory contents and is necessary for determining whether retrieved memory content meets the current task demands. It is generally assumed that lateral regions of the prefrontal cortex (PFC) are involved in this range of strategic retrieval operations (Mecklinger, 2010; Simons and Spiers, 2003) and that the generally poor ability of children to specify contextual information associated with an event (Cycowicz, Friedmann, and Duff, 2003; Czernochowski *et al.*, 2005; Drummey and Newcombe, 2002) results from the delayed maturation of the PFC (see below).

In a recent study we investigated ERP correlates of strategic retrieval in a source memory task from a developmental perspective (Sprondel, Kipp, and Mecklinger, 2011). On the basis of prior studies showing that early adolescence is a critical period for the maturation of strategic retrieval processes, this study included a group of 13- to 14-year-old adolescents as well as 7- to 8-year-old children. We used a continuous recognition memory task in which participants had to indicate by button press whether or not each item was previously presented within an experimental run. Within-run repetitions were denoted as targets. Critically, participants also completed a second run, in which repetition items from the first run were included (denoted as non-targets) alongside within-run repetitions (targets). These cross-run non-target repetitions had to be classified as new. Successful memory performance in the second run thus required discriminating between targets and non-targets on a temporal dimension. As children should have difficulties in temporal source memory, we expected target/non-target discrimination (operationalized as false alarms to non-targets) to be disproportionally lower than item memory performance (as revealed by false alarms to new items).

In line with this prediction, overall task performance in children was generally lower than in adults, and false alarms to non-targets in children were disproportionally more likely to occur than those to new items. Adolescents' item memory performance was slightly lower than for adults but no difference in source memory was found for the latter two groups. Our ERP analyses focused on the age comparison of the old/new effects for non-targets.

(a)

(b)

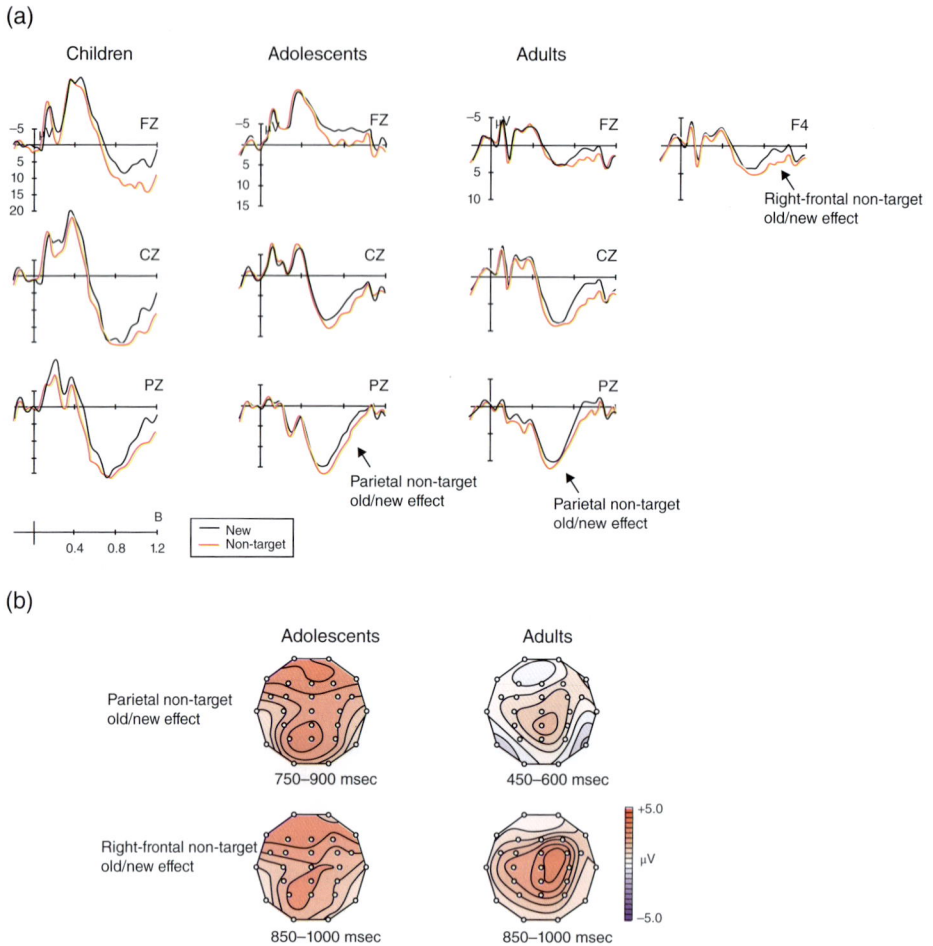

**Figure 16.4** (a) Grand average ERP waveforms at the mid-frontal (FZ), central (CZ), and parietal (PZ) recording sites for correctly classified non-targets (red line) and new items (black line) in children, adolescents, and adults in the study by Sprondel, Kipp, and Mecklinger (2011). For adults the ERP waveforms are additionally shown at a right frontal recording site (F4). (b) Scalp distributions of the parietal non-target old/new effects and the right frontal old/new effect for adolescents and adults.

As is apparent in Figure 16.4a, non-target old/new effects were absent in children but present for adults. Critically, a non-target effect was also observed for adolescents, albeit later and with a wider topographic distribution than in adults (Figure 16.4b). A further age-related finding was that an additional late old/new effect for non-targets showed a right frontal distribution for adults, was topographically more widespread in adolescents, and was virtually absent in children. According to the prevailing view, this right-frontal old/new effect reflects processes engaged to monitor and evaluate the products of retrieval (Rugg and Wilding, 2000). In line with this post-retrieval monitoring account is the fact that the effect has often been observed in paradigms that require a considerable degree of retrieval control (Hayama, Johnson, and Rugg, 2008). The observation that children failed to show this effect at all, and that adolescents did not display the typical right-frontal distribution of this late effect, therefore likely indicates that adults engaged in this kind of post-retrieval processing to a larger extent than adolescents.

Two main conclusions can be drawn from these results. First, the combination of elevated false alarm rates for non-targets and absent non-target old/new effect suggests that children of early school age were less efficient at retrieving the temporal context in which an item occurred and at using this information for adequate source memory performance. One way to solve the source memory task in this experiment is to recollect contextual information for both targets and non-targets and to reject an item as new when it does not meet the correct task demands. Children appeared to be less able to engage in this kind of recall-to-reject strategy. Second, despite comparable source memory performance for adolescents and adults, the non-target retrieval effect was delayed and topographically less focused at parietal recordings in adolescents. In addition, ERP evidence for late post-retrieval monitoring processes was found for adults but not for adolescents and children. The missing right frontal accentuation in adolescents may be a reflection of the immaturity and ongoing refinement of the neural systems supporting strategic retrieval processes during adolescence. Our results resemble those found in another ERP source memory task in which a late positivity to targets showed a clear right frontal focus in adults but was topographically more widespread in adolescence, although only marginally significant group differences in source memory performance were obtained (de Chastelaine, Friedman, and Cycowicz, 2007).

A limitation of the source memory task described above is that the examination of ERP correlates of non-target retrieval is complicated by several factors. The continuous character of the task required the simultaneous encoding of new items and retrieval of old items. Due to these interleaved encoding and retrieval demands, there were no explicit retrieval instructions. This may have induced variability across age groups with respect to the retrieval strategy adopted to perform the task. Using a similar continuous recognition memory paradigm, for example, Czernochowski, Mecklinger, and Johansson (2009) found that children allocated more attention to the encoding of novel (unrepeated) items than to the retrieval of source information associated with repeated items, and, as such, bypassed the engagement of more demanding retrieval strategies. Also, the different repetition lags for targets and non-targets may have made non-target retrieval contingent upon the general ability to retrieve an item's temporal context, thus increasing variability within and across age groups. To overcome these limitations and to explore in more detail the circumstances that determine non-target retrieval in source memory tasks and their developmental characteristics, we employed a variant of a memory exclusion task in which source-specifying features were not repeated at test and the task-relevant source feature was held constant within a test block (Sprondel, Kipp, and Mecklinger, 2012). As the previous study indicated that adolescence is a critical phase for the maturation of strategic retrieval processes, we compared the ERP correlates of target and non-target retrieval in 13- to 14-year-old adolescents and young adults.

Previous studies indicate that in tasks of this kind, the likelihood of non-target retrieval depends on the ease of target discrimination. Several studies report reliable non-target left parietal old/new effects when target discrimination was difficult but less so when target discrimination was easy (Herron and Rugg, 2003; Rosburg, Mecklinger, and Johansson, 2011). This observation implies that whenever target-specifying aspects of memory representations are difficult to reinstantiate, selective target retrieval is insufficient for adequate task performance and the recollection of both non-target and target information can boost memory performance. With these considerations in mind, we examined target and non-target retrieval in two conditions in which target/non-target discrimination was either easy or difficult. Participants learned list of words presented in one of two colors. At test they had to respond "old" for words presented in the target color and "new" to words presented in the other color and to new (unstudied) words. The color of target and non-target words was similar (red/pink) in the difficult condition and less similar in the easy source discrimination condition (green/pink). To further enhance the differential task demands, longer study and test lists were employed in the difficult condition. As expected, source memory performance was higher in the easy than in the difficult condition and was higher for adults than for adolescents. The ERP data depicting the target and non-target old/new effects for both age groups and difficulty conditions are illustrated in Figure 16.5. Adults showed reliable target old/new effects but no evidence of non-target retrieval in either condition, suggesting that

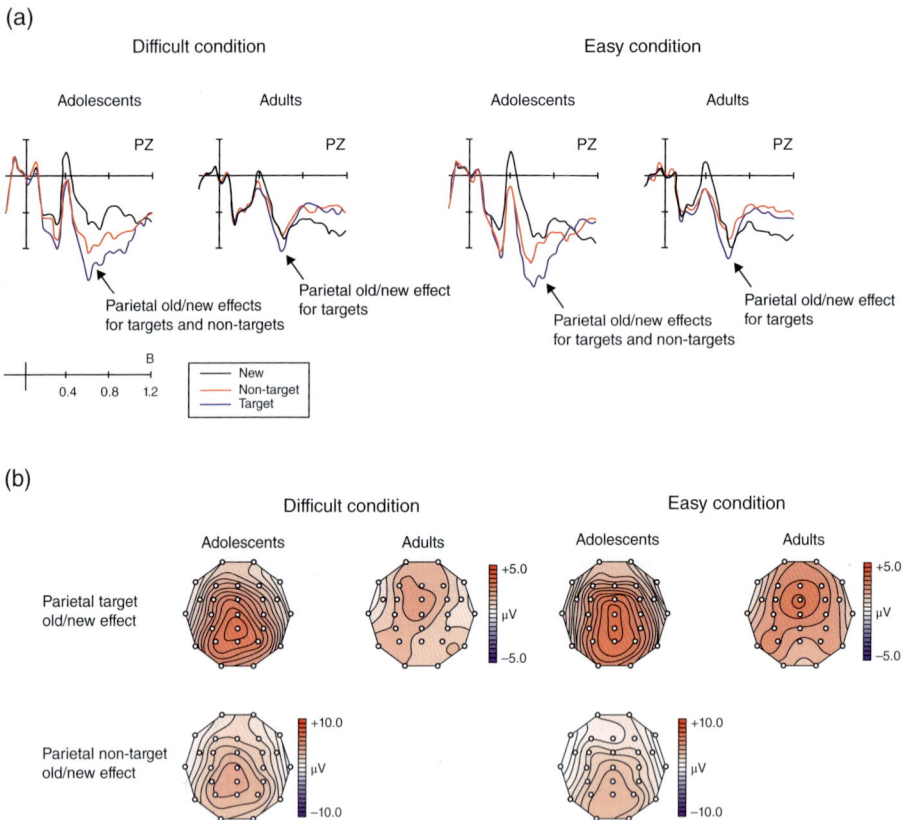

**Figure 16.5**  (a) Grand average ERP waveforms at the mid-parietal (PZ) recording sites for correctly classified targets (blue line), non-targets (red line), and new items (black line) in the easy and difficult source memory condition for adolescents and adults in the study of Sprondel, Kipp, and Mecklinger (2012). (b) Scalp distributions of the parietal target old/new effects (both age groups) and the non-target old/new effect (adolescents only). This is a modified version of a figure presented by Sprondel, Kipp, and Mecklinger (2012).

adults prioritized target over non-target retrieval irrespective of task difficulty. Conversely, adolescents showed reliable old/new effects for both targets and non-targets.

Notably, the absence of target-selective retrieval was not just a reflection of task difficulty, in the sense that the lower target discriminability boosted additional non-target retrieval for adolescents. Source memory performance for adults in the difficult condition and adolescents in the easy condition was virtually identical. Nevertheless there was a non-target retrieval effect for adolescents but not for adults in this diffi-culty-equated comparison. This striking finding indicates that rather than solely reflecting lower target discriminability, the absence of target-selective retrieval in ado-lescents is a reflection of immature strategic retrieval processes. This finding is impor-tant, because it implies that despite performance comparable to that of adults there are still immaturities in the adolescent brain which limit the flexible use of cognitive control to support episodic recognition (Luna, Padmanabhan, and O'Hearn, 2010).

Insights into the mechanisms that underlie the ERP difference between the target and non-target old/new effects come from an additional correlation analysis. We found that for adults only, the ERP target versus non-target difference amplitude correlated positively with working memory capacity as revealed by the operation span task (Turner and Engle, 1989) (Figure 16.6). In other words, the degree to which the ERP old/new effects were larger for targets than for non-targets increased as working memory capacity increased in adults but not in adolescents (see Elward and Wilding, 2010, for similar results). This finding suggests that the more resources available for cognitive control, as indexed by working memory capacity, the more likely it is that a target-selective retrieval strategy will be effectively implemented. The absence of this correlation in adolescents, whose working memory capacity scores did not differ from adults, provides further evidence for the immaturity of cognitive control during adolescence and indicates that 13- to 14-year-olds are not yet as efficient in allocating

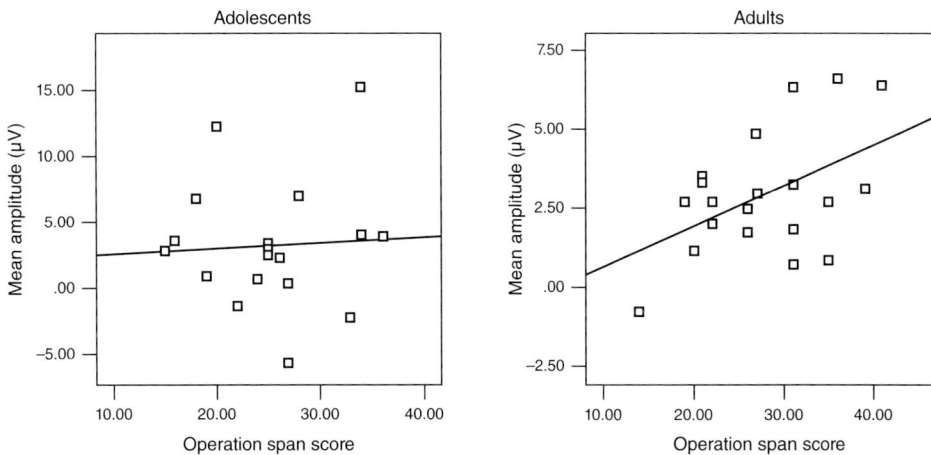

**Figure 16.6** Scatterplots showing the correlation between the ERP target/non-target difference amplitudes at a left parietal recording site (P3) and working memory capacity in the easy condition for adolescents and adults in the study of Sprondel, Kipp, and Mecklinger (2012). The correlation was significant for adults ($r=0.49$, $p<0.05$) but not for adolescents ($r=0.05$). This is a modified version of a figure presented by Sprondel, Kipp, and Mecklinger (2012).

resources for cognitive control to prioritize target over non-target recollection. An alternative yet complementary account can be derived from the recent proposal that the parietal old/new reflects the active maintenance of recollected information (Vilberg and Rugg, 2009). By this account, adult participants with high working memory capacity are more likely to allocate cognitive resources to the active maintenance of recollected task-relevant (target) information. In any event, further studies are warranted to explore the extent to which processes involved in recollecting and maintaining episodic contents depend on the availability of working memory resources and how this relationship is modulated by the maturation of cognitive control processes.

Taken together, the poorer source relative to item memory performance of children can be related to immature cognitive control operations. While children do not show evidence for the strategic use of non-target retrieval to improve source memory performance, this ability seems to develop during adolescence. In this phase of memory development, ERP correlates of strategic retrieval can be observed although they are poorly refined compared to those recorded from the adult brain (de Chastelaine, Friedman, and Cycowicz, 2007; Sprondel, Kipp, and Mecklinger, 2011). In the current task, adolescents engaged in additional, perhaps compensatory, retrieval of non-targets. The absence of a correlation between working memory capacity and the magnitude of the ERP index of selective target recollection in adolescents points to a reduced efficiency in allocating resources for cognitive control to the retrieval and maintenance of episodic memory contents. These data add to the converging evidence that adolescence is characterized by limitations in several subcomponents of cognitive control, such as response inhibition or post-error processing (Velanova, Wheeler, and Luna, 2008).

## Relationship to Other Neuroscientific Developmental Memory Studies

This brief review highlights the important insights provided by the ERP technique into the development of episodic memory, insights which cannot be inferred on the basis of behavioral data alone. The behavioral data reported by Czernochowski *et al.* (2005), for example, show that source memory performance is much poorer in children than in adults. The pattern of ERP data, in particular the correlate of target recollection alongside the absence of ERP correlates of non-target retrieval and post-retrieval monitoring in children, however, indicates that episodic recognition in children relies mainly on recollection of targets and lacks the flexibility to initiate retrieval strategies such as non-target retrieval or post-retrieval monitoring processes. Similarly, in the response deadline study by Mecklinger, Brunnemann, and Kipp (2011) we found lower memory performance for children than for adults even though the ERP correlates of familiarity and recollection were very similar in children and adults. This pattern appears to indicate that children use a less matured version of the same memory network that is used by adults in this task. ERP studies also allow inferences on the developmental trajectories of memory processes even in the absence of differences in memory performance across age groups. As reviewed above, despite the absence of performance differences between adults and adolescents, we observed changes in the topography of ERP correlates of non-target retrieval and post-retrieval monitoring which are in line with underdeveloped control processes during adolescence which differ from those of adults (Sprondel, Kipp, and Mecklinger, 2011). Similarly, in a further study in which source memory performance was equated across the two age groups, we found that adolescent but not adult ERPs were characterized by a correlate of non-target retrieval, indicating that adolescents were not yet able to strategically prioritize target over non-target retrieval (Sprondel, Kipp, and Mecklinger, 2012).

These studies have shown that all the age groups examined here engaged recollection when discriminating old and new items, and that the immaturity of episodic remembering appears to result from the slower and protracted maturation of prefrontal-based control systems that allow the flexible use of retrieval strategies. Retrieval control processes which support the engagement of retrieval strategies can operate at multiple stages, and the studies reviewed here focused on those control process that support retrieval strategies during retrieval or at post-retrieval stages. The maturation of control processes that can support successful retrieval even at pre-retrieval stages, such as retrieval orientation, is currently under investigation (Sprondel, Kipp, and Mecklinger, 2013).

The subprocesses of retrieval control that allow the flexible use of what is retrieved from memory emerge in middle childhood to adolescence and are associated with robust patterns of activation in the PFC and posterior parietal cortex (Cabeza *et al.*, 2008; Hutchinson, Uncapher and Wagner, 2010; Mecklinger, 2010; see also Chapter 7). One notable longitudinal structural neuroimaging study revealed that the volume of gray matter in the frontal and parietal lobes shows a pre-adolescence increase followed by a decline in the post-adolescence phase (Giedd *et al.*, 1999). Additional studies are necessary to clarify how these structural changes in the frontal and parietal cortex are related to the delayed maturation of cognitive control.

Evidence for the view that the delayed maturation of the PFC determines poor source memory performance in children comes from recent neuroimaging studies. While the majority of these studies have focused on memory formation (Chiu *et al.*, 2006; Menon, Boyett-Anderson, and Reiss, 2005; Ofen *et al.*, 2007) a small number have additionally or exclusively investigated retrieval-related processes (Kipp *et al.*, 2012; Ofen *et al.*, 2007, 2012; Paz-Alonso *et al.*, 2008). Using a false memory paradigm, Paz-Alonso *et al.* (2008) found less lateral PFC activation related to the retrieval of semantic features of studied words and no PFC activation related to post-retrieval monitoring in 8-year-olds as compared to older children and adults. In a seminal fMRI study by Ofen *et al.* (2007), activations in encoding-related brain structures were compared with age-related improvements in an un-scanned source memory task in children and adults ranging from 4 to 24 years. Participants viewed line drawings and made memory judgments regarding contextual features of the study episode. Source memory performance increased with age and correlated with activation in the lateral PFC (Brodmann area [BA] 9), one of the encoding-related brain structures identified before. No correlations with source memory were found in any other encoding-related brain region, and no reliable correlations between source memory and any brain activation pattern remained when the age factor was controlled for. In addition, the PFC regions critically involved in successful memory encoding and source retrieval were additionally characterized by negative correlations between gray matter and age. Together, these results speak for a strong association of childhood and adolescent memory development and both the structure and function of the PFC.

These data provide strong evidence for the view that it is the functional immaturity of lateral PFC regions that limits children's ability to discriminate between source-specifying memory representations. This notion is in line with the view of the important role the PFC plays in the maturation of episodic memory processes. In addition, several MTL regions, including the hippocampus, have been shown to be critically associated with the formation and retrieval of episodic memories. These MTL regions reach maturity during the first year of life, even though the dentate gyrus within the hippocampal formation shows prolonged development (Richmond and Nelson, 2007). Consistent with this early maturation of memory-relevant MTL regions, the imaging studies reviewed here reveal few age differences in MTL activity related to memory encoding and retrieval (Chiu *et al.*, 2006; Ofen *et al.*, 2007, 2012), although Paz-Alonso *et al.* (2008) report less recruitment of the hippocampus during item-specific recollection in 8-year-olds. This finding suggests that a network comprising MTL and PFC regions is critically involved in memory retrieval and its strategic control. MTL regions in this network show little developmental change during childhood and adolescence, and this early maturity of the MTL system may also account for the small developmental changes in familiarity and recollection and their ERP correlates. Conversely, it is the late maturation of the PFC-based brain systems that underlies the delayed developmental trajectories of strategic retrieval processes.

## Conclusions

This selective review of ERP studies on the development of episodic memory shows how the ERP technique provides important insight into the developmental trajectories of episodic retrieval and its modulation by controlled cognitive operations. The review has focused on two features which are, in our view, central for the understanding of episodic memory development: the maturation of episodic recognition memory and the development of retrieval control as revealed by source memory tasks. Investigation of the development of recognition memory reveals early maturation of recollection and familiarity and their ERP correlates at the age of 6–8 years but a limited and inflexible use of strategic retrieval at this phase of memory development. The reduced ability to specify contextual details of memory contents is likely to be a direct consequence of the immaturity of prefrontal-based systems for retrieval control. These systems show maturational changes during adolescence, a phase in which source memory performance begins approximating that of adults. These changes are assumed to be characterized by relatively poorly refined cortical networks and an inefficient allocation of resources for cognitive control to episodic remembering. From here, it is necessary to conduct more fine-grained investigations into the developmental trajectories of the cognitive control of episodic remembering during the critical adolescent phase, and to use combined ERP and brain imaging approaches to further characterize these developmental trajectories and their neural characteristics.

## Acknowledgments

We wish to thank former colleagues and co-workers for their contribution to the work reported here: Martina Becker, Nicole Brunnemann, Daniela Czernochowski and Mikael Johansson. We wish to thank Matthias Kraemer, Jerome Rimpel and Florian

Beier for assistance in data collection and analyses, Ludwig Gortner from the Department of Neonatology at Saarland University Hospital for his valuable support in the recruitment of IFS children and Emma Bridger for valuable comments on earlier versions of this manuscript. This research was supported by the German Research Foundation (KI 1399 /1–1 and 1–2).

# References

Billingsley, R.L., Smith, M.L., and McAndrews, M.P. (2002). Developmental patterns in priming and familiarity in explicit recollection. *Journal of Experimental Child Psychology*, 82 (3), 251–277.

Bjorklund, D.F., and Douglas, R.N. (2002). The development of memory strategies. In *The Development of Memory in Childhood* (ed. N. Cowan). Hove, UK: Psychology Press, pp. 201–246.

Boldini, A., Russo, R., and Avons, S. (2004). One process is not enough! A speed–accuracy tradeoff study of recognition memory. *Psychonomic Bulletin and Review*, 11 (2), 353–361.

Brainerd, C., and Reyna, V. (2004). Fuzzy-trace theory and memory development. *Developmental Review*, 24 (4), 396–439.

Bruck, M., and Ceci, S.J. (1999). The suggestibility of children's memory. *Annual Review of Psychology*, 50 (1), 419–439.

Cabeza, R., Ciaramelli, E., Olson, I.R., and Moscovitch, M. (2008). The parietal cortex and episodic memory: an attentional account. *Nature Reviews Neuroscience*, 9 (8), 613–625.

Chiu, C.-Y.P., Schmithorst, V.J., Brown, R.D., *et al.* (2006). Making memories: a cross-sectional investigation of episodic memory encoding in childhood using fMRI. *Developmental Neuropsychology*, 29 (2), 321–340.

Cycowicz, Y.M., Friedman, D., and Duff, M. (2003). Pictures and their colors: what do children remember? *Journal of Cognitive Neuroscience*, 15 (5), 759–768.

Czernochowski, D., Brinkmann, M., Mecklinger, A., and Johansson, M. (2004). When binding matters: an ERP analysis of the development of recollection and familiarity. In *Bound in Memory: Insights from Behavioral and Neuropsychological studies* (ed. A. Mecklinger, H. Zimmer, and U. Linderberger). Aachen: Shaker Verlag, pp. 93–128.

Czernochowski, D., Mecklinger, A., and Johansson, M. (2009). Age-related changes in the control of episodic retrieval: an ERP study of recognition memory in children and adults. *Developmental Science*, 12 (6), 1026–1040.

Czernochowski, D., Mecklinger, A., Johansson, M., and Brinkmann, M. (2005). Age-related differences in familiarity and recollection: ERP evidence from a recognition memory study in children and young adults *Cognitive, Affective, and Behavioral Neuroscience*, 5 (4), 417–433.

de Chastelaine, M., Friedman, D., and Cycowicz, Y.M. (2007). The development of control processes supporting source memory discrimination as revealed by event-related potentials. *Journal of Cognitive Neuroscience*, 19 (8), 1286–1301.

Drummey, A.B., and Newcombe, N.S. (2002). Developmental changes in source memory. *Developmental Science*, 5 (4), 502–513.

Elward, R., and Wilding, E. (2010). Working memory capacity is related to variations in the magnitude of an electrophysiological marker of recollection. *Brain Research*, 1342, 55–62.

Foley, M.A., and Johnson, M.K. (1985). Confusions between memories for performed and imagined actions: a developmental comparison. *Child Development*, 56 (5), 1145–1155.

Friedman, D. (2012). The development of episodic memory: an event-related brain potential (ERP) vantage point. In *Origins and Development of Recollection* (ed. S. Ghetti and P.J. Bauer). New York, NY: Oxford University Press, pp. 242–264.

Friedman, D., de Chastelaine, M., Nessler, D., and Malcolm, B. (2010). Changes in familiarity and recollection across the lifespan: an ERP perspective. *Brain Research*, 1310, 124–141.

Friedman, D., and Johnson, R. (2000). Event-related potential (ERP) studies of memory encoding and retrieval: a selective review. *Microscopy Research and Technique*, 51 (1), 6–28.

Ghetti, S., and Angelini, L. (2008). The development of recollection and familiarity in childhood and adolescence: evidence from the dual-process signal detection model. *Child Development*, 79 (2), 339–358.

Giedd, J.N., Blumenthal, J., Jeffries, N.O., *et al.* (1999). Brain development during childhood and adolescence: a longitudinal MRI study. *Nature Neuroscience*, 2 (10), 861–863.

Hayama, H.R., Johnson, J.D., and Rugg, M.D. (2008). The relationship between the right frontal old/new ERP effect and post-retrieval monitoring: specific or non-specific? *Neuropsychologia*, 46 (5), 1211–1223.

Hepworth, S.L., Rovet, J.F., and Taylor, M.J. (2001). Neurophysiological correlates of verbal and nonverbal short-term memory in children: repetition of words and faces. *Psychophysiology*, 38 (03), 594–600.

Herron, J.E., and Rugg, M.D. (2003). Strategic influences on recollection in the exclusion task: electrophysiological evidence. *Psychonomic Bulletin and Review*, 10 (3), 703–710.

Hutchinson, J.B., Uncapher, M.R., and Wagner, A.D. (2009). Posterior parietal cortex and episodic retrieval: convergent and divergent effects of attention and memory. *Learning and Memory*, 16 (6), 343–356.

Johnson, M.K., Hashtroudi, S., and Lindsay, D.S. (1993). Source monitoring. *Psychological Bulletin*, 114 (1), 3–28.

Kipp, K.H., Opitz, B., Becker, M., *et al.* (2012). Selective modifications in the neural memory network in children with febrile seizures: evidence from functional magnetic resonance imaging. *Frontiers in Human Neuroscience*, 6, 1–11.

Kipp, K.H., Mecklinger, A., Becker, M., *et al.* (2010). Infant febrile seizures: changes in declarative memory as revealed by event-related potentials. *Clinical Neurophysiology*, 121 (12), 2007–2016.

Kobasigawa, A. (1974). Utilization of retrieval cues by children in recall. *Child Development*, 45 (1), 127–134.

Light, L.L., Patterson, M.M., Chung, C., and Healy, M.R. (2004). Effects of repetition and response deadline on associative recognition in young and older adults. *Memory and Cognition*, 32 (7), 1182–1193.

Lindsay, D.S., Johnson, M.K., and Kwon, P. (1991). Developmental changes in memory source monitoring. *Journal of Experimental Child Psychology*, 52 (3), 297–318.

Luck, S.J. (2004). *An Introduction to the Event-Related Potential Technique*. Cambridge, MA: MIT Press.

Luna, B., Padmanabhan, A., and O'Hearn, K. (2010). What has fMRI told us about the development of cognitive control through adolescence? *Brain and Cognition*, 72 (1), 101–113.

Mecklinger, A. (2000). Interfacing mind and brain: a neurocognitive model of recognition memory. *Psychophysiology*, 37 (5), 565–582.

Mecklinger, A. (2010). The control of long-term memory: cognitive processes and brain systems. *Neuroscience and Biobehavioral Reviews*, 34 (7), 1055–1065.

Mecklinger, A., and Jäger, T. (2009). Episodic memory storage and retrieval: insights from electrophysiological measures. In *Neuroimaging and Psychological Theories of Human Memory* (ed. F. Rösler, C. Ranganath, B. Röder, and R.H. Kluwe). New York, NY: Oxford University Press, pp. 357–382.

Mecklinger, A., Brunnemann, N., and Kipp, K. (2011). Two processes for recognition memory in children of early school age: an event-related potential study. *Journal of Cognitive Neuroscience*, 23 (2), 435–446.

Menon, V., Boyett-Anderson, J., and Reiss, A. (2005). Maturation of medial temporal lobe response and connectivity during memory encoding. *Cognitive Brain Research*, 25 (1), 379–385.

Ofen, N., Chai, X.J., Schuil, K.D., *et al.* (2012). The development of brain systems associated with successful memory retrieval of scenes. *Journal of Neuroscience*, 32, 10012–10020.

Ofen, N., Kao, Y.-C., Sokol-Hessner, P., *et al.* (2007). Development of the declarative memory system in the human brain. *Nature Neuroscience*, 10, 1198–1205.

Paller, K.A., Voss, J.L., and Boehm, S.G. (2007). Validating neural correlates of familiarity. *Trends in Cognitive Sciences*, 11 (6), 243–250.

Paz-Alonso, P.M., Ghetti, S., Donohue, S.E., *et al.* (2008). Neurodevelopmental correlates of true and false recognition. *Cerebral Cortex*, 18, 2208–2216.

Perner, J., and Ruffman, T. (1995). Episodic memory and autonoetic conciousness: developmental evidence and a theory of childhood amnesia. *Journal of Experimental Child Psychology*, 59 (3), 516–548.

Picton, T.W., and Taylor, M.J. (2007). Electrophysiological evaluation of human brain development. *Developmental Neuropsychology*, 31 (3), 249–278.

Richmond, J., and Nelson, C.A. (2007). Accounting for change in declarative memory: a cognitive neuroscience perspective. *Developmental Review*, 27 (3), 349–373.

Rosburg, T., Mecklinger, A., and Johansson, M. (2011). Strategic retrieval in a reality monitoring task. *Neuropsychologia*, 49 (10), 2957–2969.

Rugg, M.D., and Coles, M.G.H. (1995). *Electrophysiology of Mind. Event-Related Brain Potentials and Cognition*. New York, NY: Oxford University Press.

Rugg, M.D., and Curran, T. (2007). Event-related potentials and recognition memory. *Trends in Cognitive Sciences*, 11 (6), 251–257.

Rugg, M.D., and Wilding, E.L. (2000). Retrieval processing and episodic memory. *Trends in Cognitive Sciences*, 4 (3), 108–115.

Sadleir, L.G., and Scheffer, I.E. (2008). Febrile seizures. *BMJ*, 334, 307–311.

Schneider, W., and Pressley, M. (1997). *Memory Development Between 2 and 20*. Mahwah, NJ: Erlbaum.

Segalowitz, S.J., Santesso, D.L., and Jetha, M.K. (2010). Electrophysiological changes during adolescence: a review. *Brain and Cognition*, 72 (1), 86–100.

Shing, Y.L., Werkle-Bergner, M., Brehmer, Y., *et al.* (2010). Episodic memory across the lifespan: the contributions of associative and strategic components. *Neuroscience and Biobehavioral Reviews*, 34 (7), 1080–1091.

Siegler, R.S. (1998). *Children's Thinking*. Upper Saddle River, NJ: Prentice Hall.

Simons, J.S., and Spiers, H.J. (2003). Prefrontal and medial temporal lobe interactions in long-term memory. *Nature Reviews Neuroscience*, 4 (8), 637–648.

Sprondel, V., Kipp, K.H., and Mecklinger, A. (2011). Developmental changes in item and source memory: evidence from an ERP recognition memory study with children, adolescents, and adults. *Child Development*, 82 (6), 1638–1953.

Sprondel, V., Kipp, K.H., and Mecklinger, A. (2012). Electrophysiological evidence for late maturation of strategic episodic retrieval processes. *Developmental Science*, 15 (3), 330–344.

Sprondel, V., Kipp, K.H., and Mecklinger, A. (2013). Timing matters: Age-related changes in episodic retrieval control as revealed by event-related potentials. *Brain Research*, 1537, 143–155.

Tulving, E. (1985). Memory and consciousness. *Canadian Psychology/Psychologie Canadienne*, 26 (1), 1–12.

Turner, M.L., and Engle, R.W. (1989). Is working memory capacity task dependent? *Journal of memory and language*, 28 (2), 127–154.

van Strien, J.W., Glimmerveen, J.C., Martens, V.E., and de Bruin, E.A. (2009). Age-related differences in brain activity during extended continuous word recognition in children. *NeuroImage*, 47 (2), 688–699.

Velanova, K., Wheeler, M.E., and Luna, B. (2008). Maturational changes in anterior cingulate and frontoparietal recruitment support the development of error processing and inhibitory control. *Cerebral Cortex*, 18 (11), 2505–2522.

Vilberg, K.L., and Rugg, M.D. (2009). Functional significance of retrieval-related activity in lateral parietal cortex: evidence from fMRI and ERPs. *Human Brain Mapping*, 30 (5), 1490–1501.

Yonelinas, A.P. (2002). The nature of recollection and familiarity: a review of 30 years of research. *Journal of Memory and Language*, 46 (3), 441–517.

# 17

# Episodic Memory in Healthy Older Adults

## *The Role of Prefrontal and Parietal Cortices*

### M. Natasha Rajah, David Maillet, and Cheryl L. Grady

## Introduction

Healthy aging is associated with deficits in episodic memory. These deficits may be related to changes in neural systems important for mediating episodic memory-specific processes (i.e., encoding and retrieval) and/or to deficits in neural systems implicated in other higher-order cognitive processes, which indirectly impact one's episodic memory abilities – such as attention, working memory, and cognitive control processes (Zacks *et al.*, 2000). With the advancement and increased availability of brain imaging technologies there has been a marked increase in the number of neuroimaging studies investigating the neural correlates of episodic memory decline in healthy aging. Several studies have found age-related declines in gray matter volume and functional activity of the medial temporal lobes (MTL) that have been associated with deficits in older adults' episodic memory. Chapters 5, 6, and 18 in this volume discuss the role of the MTL in episodic memory in healthy young and older adults. In the current chapter we review the functional neuroimaging studies published from 2003 to spring 2012 that have examined how age-related changes in prefrontal and parietal cortex impact episodic memory in healthy aging. The majority of studies in this field have used visual stimuli. Two functional neuroimaging studies published since 2003 examined age-related differences in episodic memory that did not employ visual stimuli, one focusing on olfactory–visual associations (Cerf-Ducastel and Murphy, 2009) and the other on auditory verbal memory (Fernandes *et al.*, 2006). These studies have not been included in the current chapter.

Also, in our review of the literature we grouped studies based on whether subsequent retrieval performance was matched between age groups, or was not matched and young adults exhibited significantly better retrieval accuracy than older adults. We did this since assessing brain activity in the context of behavior can be particularly important when there is age-related increase in brain activity in older adults. For example, when performance is matched, increased activation with age might reflect inefficient use of neural resources, but it could also indicate compensatory plasticity in older adults.

*The Wiley Handbook on the Cognitive Neuroscience of Memory*, First Edition.
Edited by Donna Rose Addis, Morgan Barense, and Audrey Duarte.
© 2015 John Wiley & Sons, Ltd. Published 2015 by John Wiley & Sons, Ltd.

In contrast, when performance is lower in older adults, over-recruitment of activity is less likely to reflect compensation but could reflect differentiation of function or the use of strategies or cognitive processes that are detrimental to performance. In the following sections we discuss the anatomy and results from functional magnetic resonance imaging (fMRI) studies of aging and episodic encoding and retrieval for the prefrontal cortex (PFC; also see Chapter 7), and then the parietal cortex. We present a summary of our observations at the end of the chapter.

## Prefrontal Cortex

### Anatomy

The PFC in humans comprises most of the frontal lobes. It is located rostral to the central sulcus, anterior to the Sylvian fissure, and excludes primary and association motor cortices. Traditionally, neuroscientists have subdivided the PFC into the following "classical" regions based on gross anatomic markers: orbitofrontal cortex (OFC), ventromedial PFC (vmPFC), ventrolateral PFC (vlPFC), medial PFC (mPFC), dorsolateral PFC (dlPFC), dorsal PFC (dPFC), and anterior PFC/frontal pole (aPFC) (Luria, 1962; Mesulam, 1986; Petrides and Pandya, 1999, 2002; Ongur, Ferry, and Price, 2003). In the current section, we focus on age-related changes in dlPFC, vlPFC, mPFC, and aPFC (see Figure 1 in Rajah and D'Esposito, 2005). We define dlPFC as being the brain area within the middle frontal gyrus (MFG) and consisting of Brodmann areas (BA) 8, 9, 46; excluding peaks in BA 10 on the MFG, which we consider to be part of aPFC. vlPFC is defined as the area within the inferior frontal gyrus (IFG), consisting of BA 47, 45, and 44. mPFC is defined as being the brain area within the medial frontal gyrus and consisting of BA 32, 24 and dorsomedial aspects of BA 10. We define aPFC as being the area within the frontal pole of the superior frontal gyrus (SFG) and consisting of BA 10.

### Age-related changes in PFC function and episodic memory encoding

Successful encoding has been related to increased activity in vlPFC in young adults, particularly in the left hemisphere (Blumenfeld and Ranganath, 2007; Fletcher, Shallice, and Dolan, 1998; Reber *et al.*, 2002; Spaniol *et al.*, 2009). Young adults also activate bilateral dlPFC during encoding, especially when the encoding tasks are more demanding and employ relational and source/context encoding paradigms (Blumenfeld *et al.*, 2011; Blumenfeld and Ranganath, 2007; Dennis *et al.*, 2008; Maillet and Rajah, 2011).

In writing this chapter we reviewed 23 fMRI studies on aging and episodic encoding. Studies examining age-related changes in episodic encoding have generally employed a subsequent memory paradigm in which encoding activity for subsequently remembered (successfully encoded) items is compared to activity for forgotten items, in young versus older adults. Seventeen of the 23 studies reviewed involved tasks in which older adults' subsequent retrieval accuracy performance was significantly worse than that of young adults (de Chastelaine *et al.*, 2011; Dennis *et al.*, 2008; Dulas and Duarte, 2011; Duverne, Motamedinia, and Rugg, 2009a; Duzel *et al.*, 2011; Fischer, Nyberg, and Backman, 2010; Grady *et al.*, 2006;

Gutchess *et al.*, 2005; Kensinger and Schacter, 2008; Kim and Giovanello, 2011; Kukolja *et al.*, 2009; Miller *et al.*, 2008; Morcom *et al.*, 2003, 2010; Murty *et al.*, 2009; Sperling *et al.*, 2003; St. Jacques, Dolcos, and Cabeza, 2009). In contrast, in only six studies was subsequent episodic retrieval accuracy matched between older and younger adults (Bangen *et al.*, 2012; Burgmans *et al.*, 2010; Dennis, Daselaar, and Cabeza, 2007; Filippini *et al.*, 2012; Kalpouzos, Persson, and Nyberg, 2012; Leshikar *et al.*, 2010). Figure 17.1 shows a bar graph in which we summarize the fMRI results reported in the 23 studies reviewed on episodic encoding. In creating this graph we tallied the number of activations reported within each PFC region of interest (ROI) (dlPFC, vlPFC, aPFC, and mPFC) from contrasts that identified group differences in regional activations. We summarize these results under conditions when performance was matched between age groups, and when performance was not matched between age groups.

*PFC encoding activation when subsequent retrieval performance is not matched*    fMRI results from studies in which retrieval performance was not matched between groups indicated that older adults exhibit increased activity in various PFC regions, compared to younger adults. Left dlPFC most markedly exhibits this pattern of age-related increased activity during encoding, when subsequent memory performance was poorer in older versus younger adults (de Chastelaine *et al.*, 2011; Duzel *et al.*, 2011; Gutchess *et al.*, 2005; Miller *et al.*, 2008; Sperling *et al.*, 2003; St. Jacques, Dolcos, and Cabeza, 2009).

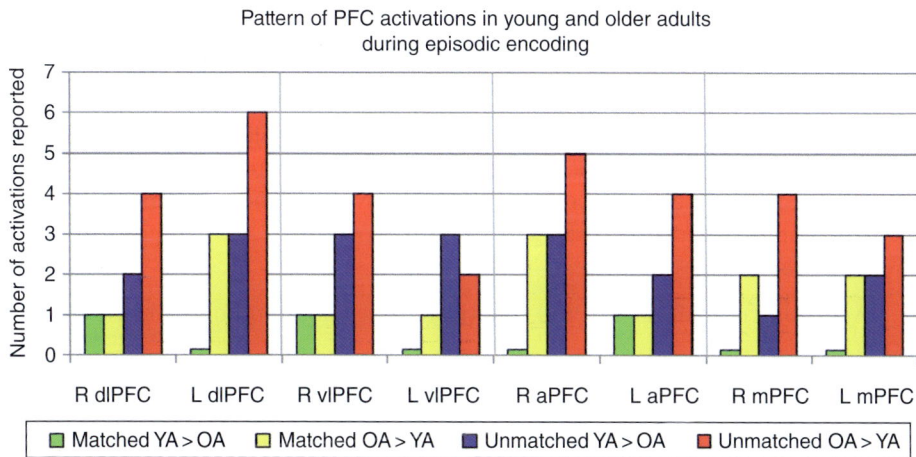

**Figure 17.1**  Pattern of prefrontal cortex (PFC) activations in young and older adults during episodic encoding. This figure summarizes the pattern of PFC activity observed in 23 fMRI studies on age-related differences in encoding (see text for details of studies reviewed). In this bar graph we report the pattern of left and right PFC activations reported in young and older adults when performance was matched ("matched") and when performance was not matched ("unmatched"). For each PFC ROI we tallied the number of activations in which young adults activated a region more than older adults, and in which older adults activated a region more than young adults. L, left; R, right. PFC abbreviations are: dl, dorsolateral; vl, ventrolateral; a, anterior; m, medial.

Also, when subsequent memory was unmatched between groups, Duverne, Motamedinia, and Rugg (2009a) and Morcom *et al.* (2003) observed that both young and older adults activated left vlPFC during successful encoding; but lower-performing older adults also activated right vlPFC to a greater degree than young and higher-performing older adults. This finding suggests that right vlPFC recruitment during encoding may reflect attempted compensation in lower-performing elders in response to deficits in left vlPFC processes (de Chastelaine *et al.*, 2011); alternatively, it may reflect dedifferentiation of function with age.

*PFC encoding activation when subsequent retrieval performance is matched*    In studies when subsequent memory was matched between age groups, the results indicate a similar pattern of age-related increases in brain activity in various PFC regions. However, only one study to our knowledge has reported greater activity in left vlPFC in older than in younger adults when performance was matched (Filippini *et al.*, 2012). Given that young adults engage this region for successful encoding, it is surprising that a greater number of studies did not report age-related increases in left vlPFC activity when performance was matched between groups. This may be due to age-invariance in left vlPFC activity once performance was matched.

Consistent with the findings for studies in which subsequent memory was unmatched (see section above), studies have also reported greater left dlPFC activity in older versus younger adults when subsequent memory was *matched* between age-groups (Burgmans *et al.*, 2010; Dennis, Daselaar, and Cabeza, 2007; Leshikar *et al.*, 2010). In two studies, greater left dlPFC activity in older adults was observed during encoding of verbal stimuli (Dennis, Daselaar, and Cabeza, 2007; Leshikar *et al.*, 2010). The study by Burgmans *et al.* (2010) reported greater bilateral dlPFC activity in older versus younger adults. This study required subjects to intentionally encode scene stimuli, which may have led participants to utilize both linguistic and spatial relational strategies at encoding.

Therefore, during episodic encoding older adults consistently over-recruit left dlPFC and right vlPFC compared to young adults when performance is unmatched between age groups, and left dlPFC when performance is matched. Again, these age-related increases in activation during encoding may reflect neural compensation or dedifferentiation of function with age.

## Age-related changes in PFC function and episodic memory retrieval

In young adults, fMRI studies have reported increases in vlPFC and dlPFC activity during retrieval (Cabeza and Nyberg, 2000; Prince, Daselaar, and Cabeza, 2005; Rajah and D'Esposito, 2005). There is evidence that, in general, the dlPFC is more active during retrieval than encoding, compared to vlPFC (Prince, Daselaar, and Cabeza, 2005; Rajah and D'Esposito, 2005; Spaniol *et al.*, 2009). However, right vlPFC activity has been consistently reported during episodic retrieval (Bunge, Burrows, and Wagner, 2004; Donohue *et al.*, 2005; Maillet and Rajah, 2011; Rajah, Ames, and D'Esposito, 2008). In young adults, dlPFC activity during retrieval has been shown to increase as a function of increasing task difficulty (Hayama and Rugg, 2009; Rajah, Ames, and D'Esposito, 2008; Rajah, Languay, and Valiquette, 2010; Spaniol *et al.*, 2009), which may reflect the role of this region in post-retrieval monitoring processes (Hayama and Rugg, 2009; Rajah, Languay, and Valiquette, 2010; Rugg, Henson, and Robb, 2003), in error processing (Garavan *et al.*, 2002), in response selection (Rajah, Ames, and D'Esposito, 2008), or in mediating relational response strategies (Blumenfeld *et al.*, 2011). Right vlPFC activity during retrieval may reflect this region's role in selection and/or inhibition of irrelevant stimuli during memory retrieval (Rajah, McIntosh, and Grady, 1999) and in novelty detection (Donohue *et al.*, 2005). However, in general, the neural/cognitive processes mediated by dlPFC and right vlPFC during retrieval remain unclear.

We reviewed 28 fMRI studies that compared the neural activity in young versus older adults during episodic memory retrieval. In 10 of these studies, memory performance was matched between young and older adults for the fMRI activation analyses discussed in this chapter (Addis, Roberts, and Schacter, 2011; Burgmans *et al.*, 2010; Cabeza *et al.*, 2004; Daselaar *et al.*, 2006; Davis *et al.*, 2008; Giovanello and Schacter, 2012; Giovanello *et al.*, 2010; Kalpouzos, Persson, and Nyberg, 2012; Spaniol and Grady, 2012; St-Laurent *et al.*, 2011). In 18 of the studies reviewed, younger adults' retrieval accuracy was significantly better than that of older adults (Daselaar *et al.*, 2003; Dew *et al.*, 2012; Brassen *et al.*, 2009; Dennis *et al.*, 2008; Duarte, Graham, and Henson, 2010; Duarte, Henson, and Graham, 2008; Dulas and Duarte, 2012; Grady, McIntosh, and Craik, 2005; Grady *et al.*, 2006; Kukolja *et al.*, 2009; McDonough, Wong, and Gallo, 2012; Morcom, Li, and Rugg, 2007; Murty *et al.*, 2009; Rajah, Ames, and D'Esposito, 2008; Rajah, Languay, and Valiquette, 2010; Tsukiura *et al.*, 2011; van der Veen *et al.*, 2006; Velanova *et al.*, 2007). Figure 17.2 shows a bar graph in which we summarize the

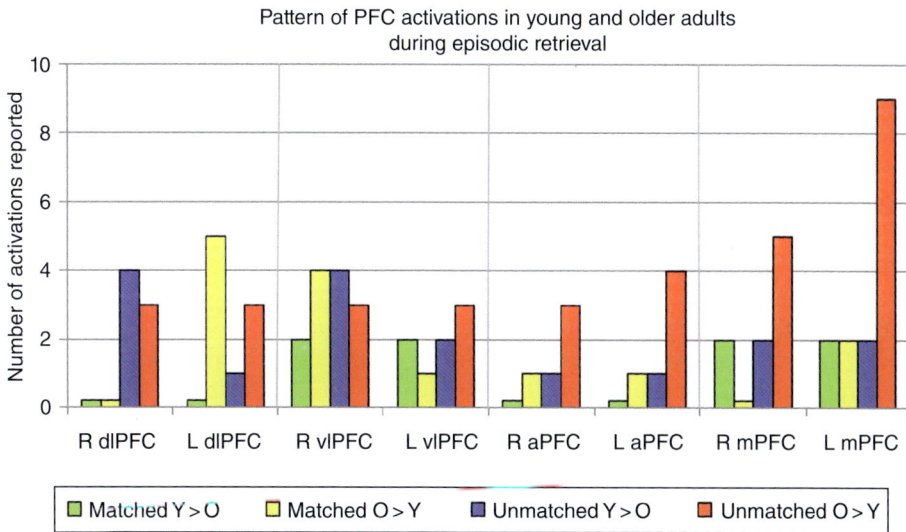

**Figure 17.2** Pattern of prefrontal cortex (PFC) activations in young and older adults during episodic retrieval. This figure summarizes the pattern of PFC activity observed in 28 fMRI studies on age-related differences in retrieval (see text for details of studies reviewed). In this bar graph, we report the pattern of left and right PFC activations reported in young and older adults when performance was matched ("matched") and when performance was not matched ("unmatched"). For each PFC ROI we tallied the number of activations in which young adults activated a region more than older adults, and in which older adults activated a region more than young adults. L, left; R, right. PFC abbreviations are: dl, dorsolateral; vl, ventrolateral; a, anterior; m, medial.

fMRI results reported in the 28 studies reviewed on episodic retrieval. In creating this graph, we tallied the number of activations reported within each PFC ROI (dlPFC, vlPFC, aPFC, and mPFC) from contrasts that identified group differences in regional activations. We summarize these results under conditions when performance was matched between age groups, and when performance was not matched between age groups.

*PFC activation during retrieval when performance is not matched*   The majority of fMRI studies of aging and episodic memory have compared brain activity during tasks in which retrieval accuracy was *not* matched between age groups, and young adults performed significantly better. In some of these studies, greater right dlPFC activity was observed in young compared to older adults during memory retrieval (Grady et al., 2006; McDonough, Wong, and Gallo, 2012; Rajah, Languay, and Valiquette, 2010; Tsukiura et al., 2011). However, other studies have reported the inverse effect (older > young adult) in this region (Duarte, Graham, and Henson, 2010; Duarte, Henson, and Graham, 2008; Rajah and McIntosh, 2008). Interestingly, the particular region of right dlPFC where there was greater activity in young compared to older adults was either BA 9 and/or BA 46. In contrast, the right dlPFC region with greater activity in older versus young adults was in more dorsal areas of dlPFC, in BA 8.

Previous studies have also reported age-related increases in left dlPFC, left vlPFC, bilateral aPFC, and bilateral mPFC at retrieval (Dew et al., 2012; Duarte, Henson, and Graham, 2008; Morcom, Li, and Rugg, 2007). Three studies have been published to date in which increased left dlPFC activity was observed in older versus young adults when performance was unmatched (Dew et al., 2012; Duarte, Henson, and Graham, 2008; Morcom, Li, and Rugg, 2007). Moreover, Dew et al. (2012) reported greater early activation of left dlPFC in young versus older adults at retrieval, but greater late activation of this same region in older versus young adults. Overall, episodic encoding and retrieval studies consistently report over-recruitment of left dlPFC in older versus younger adults, regardless of whether memory performance was matched or unmatched between age groups.

Age-related over-activations in mPFC may reflect reduced task-related deactivations in older versus younger adults (Grady et al., 2006; Rajah, Languay, and Valiquette, 2010), and therefore may be detrimental to task performance (Damoiseaux et al., 2008; Sambataro et al., 2010). Alternatively, this effect may reflect age-specific compensatory plasticity reflecting the implementation of novel process/strategies in an attempt to maintain retrieval performance when retrieval task demands are high (Rajah, Languay, and Valiquette, 2010; Stevens et al., 2008). Results from Kukolja et al. (2009) support the former interpretation. They found that young adults exhibited greater task-related decreases in mPFC compared to older adults. They concluded that deficits in task-related decreases in mPFC activity in older adults may reflect decreased attentional processing at retrieval, which may have contributed to older adults' poorer memory performance.

Age-related increases in bilateral aPFC may reflect compensation. For example, Rajah, Languay, and Valiquette (2010) reported age-specific increases in right aPFC in older versus young adults. This effect was not due to older adults showing weaker task-related decreases in aPFC activity. Moreover, in older adults, greater right aPFC activity was moderately correlated with better temporal context memory. Therefore, age-related changes in mPFC versus aPFC may differ, such that age differences in mPFC reflect deficits in task-related decreases in activation and poorer task performance, whereas age-specific increases in aPFC may reflect compensatory plasticity in the aging brain.

*PFC activation during retrieval when performance is matched*    Several fMRI studies have compared PFC activity in young versus older adults during memory retrieval, when retrieval accuracy was matched between age groups (Addis, Roberts, and Schacter, 2011; Burgmans *et al.*, 2010; Cabeza *et al.*, 2004; Daselaar *et al.*, 2006; Davis *et al.*, 2008; Giovanello *et al.*, 2010; Kalpouzos, Persson, and Nyberg, 2012; Spaniol and Grady, 2012; St-Laurent *et al.*, 2011; Giovanello and Schacter, 2012). However, only two studies to date have reported greater left vlPFC activity in young versus older adults at retrieval (Giovanello and Schacter, 2012; St-Laurent *et al.*, 2011). Another study reported the opposite age effect (Spaniol and Grady, 2012), a pattern that resembles the age-related under-recruitment of left vlPFC during episodic encoding, and suggests there may be an age-related deficit in left vlPFC during both episodic encoding and retrieval.

In contrast, several studies have reported greater right vlPFC activity in older versus younger adults, when performance was matched between age groups (Cabeza *et al.*, 2004; Giovanello *et al.*, 2010; Grady, McIntosh, and Craik, 2005; Spaniol and Grady, 2012). Verbal stimuli were used in all these studies, and in the Grady, McIntosh, and Craik (2005) study both verbal and pictorial stimuli were employed. In the Cabeza *et al.* (2004) study, greater right vlPFC activity in older versus younger adults was observed across three verbal tasks: episodic retrieval, a delayed-response working memory task, and a sustained visual attention task. During this study, young adults also activated right vlPFC across tasks, but not to the same degree as older adults. This pattern is similar to what has been found during episodic encoding; however, at encoding this pattern was observed when performance was *unmatched* between age groups.

Studies have also reported greater activity in left dlPFC in older versus younger adults during episodic retrieval when performance was matched (Burgmans *et al.*, 2010; Davis *et al.*, 2008; Kalpouzos, Persson, and Nyberg, 2012; Morcom, Li, and Rugg, 2007; Spaniol and Grady, 2012). Four studies employed verbal stimuli (Davis *et al.*, 2008; Kalpouzos, Persson, and Nyberg, 2012; Morcom, Li, and Rugg, 2007; Spaniol and Grady, 2012), and one study employed pictorial stimuli of objects and scenes (Burgmans *et al.*, 2010). Overall, greater activity in left dlPFC in older adults has been interpreted as reflecting compensation for reduced neural efficiency within this brain region and for deficits in posterior cortical regions (i.e., the hippocampus) (Morcom, Li, and Rugg, 2007).

Taken together, these findings suggest that when retrieval performance is matched between age groups, task-related increases in left dlPFC and right vlPFC activity in older versus young adults may reflect compensatory over-recruitment in response to neural inefficiency in left vlPFC with age, and in response to deficits in posterior cortical regions such as the hippocampus and occipital cortex. However, Burgmans *et al.* (2010) reported a negative correlation between left dlPFC activity and object retrieval performance in older adults. Therefore, it remains unclear if left dlPFC over-recruitment in older adults is always indicative of functional compensation. To help clarify this issue, more studies need to be conducted in which direct correlations between left dlPFC activity and memory performance are examined in young and older adults.

## Parietal Cortex

### Anatomy

The human parietal cortex is typically divided laterally into the inferior (IPL) and superior parietal lobes (SPL), and the medial portion is known as the precuneus (Talairach and Tournoux, 1988). The SPL and precuneus comprise BA 7, and anatomical studies in monkeys indicate that both are heavily connected with PFC, with the lateral parietal regions projecting to the principal and arcuate sulci and medial parietal cortex projecting to medial and superior frontal regions (Cavada and Goldman-Rakic, 1989). The IPL is more developed in humans than in other primates (Zilles and Palomero-Gallagher, 2001) and consists of BAs 40 and 39. The IPL has been further subdivided into additional regions based on cytoarchitecture (Caspers *et al.*, 2006) and gyral structure, including the supramarginal and angular gyri. For the purpose of this review we have used the parcellation published by Nelson *et al.* (2010), which was based on determining areas in the parietal lobe whose activity was related to retrieval success (hits versus correct rejections) and how these regions were functionally connected with the rest of the brain. The set of regions identified by Nelson *et al.* were SPL (anterior to the intraparietal sulcus), intraparietal sulcus (IPS), angular gyrus (AG), supramarginal gyrus (SMG), and the anterior and posterior IPL (aIPL, pIPL, superior to the SMG and AG). Of these regions, the more posterior ones (IPS, AG, aIPL, pIPL) were directly related to memory, whereas the anterior ones (SPL, SMG) were not. To assign a reported region with age differences to one of these six parietal areas, we determined the proximity of each reported set of coordinates to those reported by Nelson *et al.* for each region. That is, if a reported region had coordinates that were closest to the IPS as published in Nelson *et al.*, we labeled this region as IPS, regardless of the label ascribed to it in the source paper. We were then able to determine whether parietal age differences were specific to any particular region in the parietal lobe. In addition to these six areas, we also included the precuneus, because age differences have been reported in this area as well (the precuneus was not described by Nelson *et al.*, because their focus was on lateral parietal cortex). We labeled regions as the precuneus if the reported coordinates fell within this region in the MNI152 atlas.

### Age-related changes in parietal function and episodic memory encoding

It is not clear that the parietal lobes have a specific role in episodic encoding, except perhaps in learning new spatial routes (Shelton and Gabrieli, 2002). Indeed, a study using transcranial magnetic stimulation (TMS) to interfere with dorsal parietal activity during encoding found little disruption (Rossi *et al.*, 2006). Nevertheless, age differences in parietal activity during encoding are commonly found.

*Parietal activation during encoding when subsequent memory performance is not matched*  Eleven studies have reported age differences in parietal activity during encoding when older adults performed more poorly than young adults on subsequent memory tests. Reduced parietal subsequent memory effects in AG and SMG have been reported in older relative to younger adults for both pictures (St. Jacques, Dolcos, and Cabeza, 2009) and words (Kim and Giovanello, 2011). However, more often greater subsequent memory effects have been observed in older than in younger adults in the parietal cortex when performance was unmatched between groups. For example, larger subsequent memory effects in IPS were reported for older adults during scene encoding (Dennis *et al.*, 2008; Duzel *et al.*, 2011; Gutchess *et al.*, 2005; St. Jacques, Dolcos, and Cabeza, 2009), in the precuneus for face/name paired associate learning (Miller *et al.*, 2008), and in inferior parietal regions for words (de Chastelaine *et al.*, 2011; Morcom *et al.*, 2003). Additionally, more activity has been found in parietal cortex of older adults during encoding generally (i.e., not related to subsequent memory effects per se) during associative (Sperling *et al.*, 2003) and non-associative (Murty *et al.*, 2009) scene encoding, and during encoding of words and objects (Grady *et al.*, 2006). These age increases during encoding have been found in most regions of parietal cortex, and found bilaterally. Thus, there does not appear to be a consistent pattern of age differences during encoding, at least not based on the type of processing carried out or in the hemisphere that is engaged.

Nevertheless, there may be some specificity in terms of which region of the parietal lobe is more activated by younger versus older adults during encoding. To assess this we have plotted the number of reported age differences in each of the major subsections of the parietal lobes, based on the nomenclature used by Nelson *et al.* (2010). For encoding (Figure 17.3), it is clear that age differences have been found throughout all parietal areas of interest, although the pIPL and SPL are under-represented. This figure indicates that older adults tend to have more activity for encoding in the IPS and the precuneus, particularly when their performance is worse than that seen in younger adults (red bars). The IPS is functionally connected with dlPFC (Grady *et al.*, 2010; Nelson *et al.*, 2010) and has been implicated in top-down attentional mechanisms (Cabeza *et al.*, 2008; Corbetta, Patel, and Shulman, 2008). Over-recruitment of this region during encoding in older adults might indicate a greater additional demand relative to younger adults. Nevertheless, because all but one of these studies reported better performance in younger adults, there is no evidence that the over-recruitment of the IPS during encoding provided any benefit for later memory, but more engagement of attentional mechanisms may have aided older adults in carrying out the encoding task that was required.

The precuneus is often considered to be part of the default network, which is a set of regions that are more active during internally directed, self-referent thought and have reduced activity during externally driven tasks (Grady *et al.*, 2010; Grigg and Grady, 2010; Gusnard *et al.*, 2001). Research has shown that more activity in this region during encoding is associated with worse subsequent memory (Vannini *et al.*, 2011), and more activity here in older adults suggests less effective encoding, perhaps due to a reduced ability to suppress activity in default regions during encoding (Grady *et al.*, 2006; Miller *et al.*, 2008; Vannini *et al.*, 2012). In general, given the predominance of red bars in Figure 17.3, indicating more activity in older adults associated with worse performance, a tentative conclusion is that over-recruitment of parietal cortex during

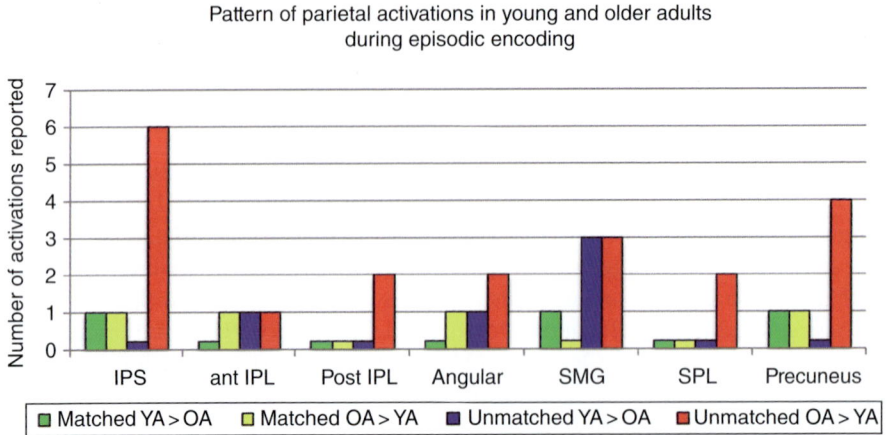

**Figure 17.3**  Pattern of parietal activations in young and older adults during episodic encoding. This figure summarizes the pattern of parietal cortex activity observed in 14 fMRI studies on age-related differences in encoding (see text for details of studies reviewed). In this bar graph we report the pattern of left and right parietal activations reported in young and older adults when performance was matched ("matched") and when performance was not matched ("unmatched"). For each parietal ROI we tallied the number of activations in which young adults activated a region more than older adults, and in which older adults activated a region more than young adults. IPS, intraparietal sulcus; IPL, inferior parietal lobule; SPL, superior parietal lobule; SMG, supramarginal gyrus.

encoding probably reflects more engagement of a number of cognitive processes, which do not necessarily support successful memory. However, these conclusions are based on only 11 studies, and further research is needed to corroborate our conclusions.

*Parietal activation during encoding when subsequent memory performance is matched*  To our knowledge 14 fMRI studies have reported age differences in parietal cortex during encoding. However, only in three of these studies was subsequent retrieval performance matched between older and younger adults (Burgmans *et al.*, 2010; Dennis, Daselaar, and Cabeza, 2007; Leshikar *et al.*, 2010). All three studies reported more activity in younger than older adults in left parietal cortex, although not in the same region. Two of these studies examined activity during encoding per se, rather than examining this activity categorized by whether the encoded item was remembered or forgotten (i.e., the subsequent memory effect). One examined brain activity during paired associate learning of object pairs, and found more activity in the left SMG in younger relative to older adults (Leshikar *et al.*, 2010), and the other found more activity in left IPS in younger adults during encoding of both neutral and emotional scenes (Burgmans *et al.*, 2010). The third found more activity during the successful encoding of words in younger adults in the left precuneus (Dennis, Daselaar, and Cabeza, 2007). In addition to these reductions, Leshikar *et al.* (2010) also found that older adults activated a number of right parietal regions more than young adults during paired associate encoding, including the AG, precuneus, and IPS. In these studies, more activity was reported in younger than in older adults in left parietal cortex.

## Age-related changes in parietal function and episodic memory retrieval

In contrast to encoding, the parietal lobes are quite active during memory retrieval (Spaniol *et al.*, 2009) and have been linked to specific memory processes. One well-known parietal effect in episodic memory retrieval is the so-called "old/new" effect in left parietal cortex that is observed using event-related potentials (ERPs; Rugg *et al.*, 1998). This old/new effect consists of greater positivity in the ERP when participants indicate that a presented stimulus has been seen at study (i.e., they judge the item to be "old": hits), relative to unseen stimuli ("new" items: correct rejections). Interestingly, studies looking at the parietal old/new effect in aging generally have found that older adults show reduced amplitude of this response (Ally *et al.*, 2008; Angel *et al.*, 2009; Duverne, Motamedinia, and Rugg, 2009b; Friedman *et al.*, 2010; Li, Morcom, and Rugg, 2004; Nessler *et al.*, 2007, 2008). Parietal cortex is also thought to play a role in familiarity, being more active for familiarity judgments than recollection (Cabeza *et al.*, 2008; Vilberg and Rugg, 2008; Wheeler and Buckner, 2004; Yonelinas *et al.*, 2005). Recently there have been suggestions that parietal activity during memory retrieval reflects specific attentional processes that are needed. Dorsal parietal cortex is thought to reflect top-down attention to retrieval search to maintain the relevant goals of the task, whereas ventral parietal cortex is thought to reflect bottom-up responses to retrieved memories (Cabeza *et al.*, 2008; Ciaramelli *et al.*, 2010; Ciaramelli, Grady, and Moscovitch, 2008). This dorsal/ventral distinction is similar to that proposed for attention in general (Corbetta, Patel, and Shulman, 2008; Fox *et al.*, 2006; Shulman *et al.*, 2009), but may not involve exactly the same regions of parietal cortex.

*Parietal activation during retrieval when subsequent memory performance is not matched*   A similar picture of both age increases and decreases was found in studies where older adults performed more poorly than younger adults (12 studies). Parietal activity during word recognition (Dennis, Kim, and Cabeza, 2008; Grady, McIntosh, and Craik, 2005; Velanova *et al.*, 2007), object recognition (Grady, McIntosh, and Craik, 2005), and paired associate retrieval (Tsukiura *et al.*, 2011) was reported to be lower in older adults in a number of areas. Some studies have found reduced parietal activity in some regions in older adults, but increased activity in other areas. For example, Kukolja *et al.* (2009) tested recall of spatial context and found that younger adults had more activity in IPS whereas older adults had more activity in SMG. Murty *et al.* (2009) examined scene recognition and found age reductions in a region of the precuneus, but age increases in more superior precuneus regions, as well as in IPS and IPL. Duarte, Graham, and Henson (2010) found reduced AG activity in older adults for object recollection, but more activity in SMG for familiarity in the older group, despite the fact that the older adults had lower measures of both recollection and familiarity. Finally, more activity in older compared to younger adults, in conjunction with age reductions in performance, has been reported for source memory (Duarte, Henson, and Graham, 2008; Morcom, Li, and Rugg, 2007) and context retrieval (Dew *et al.*, 2012).

Thus, as with encoding, there does not appear to be a consistent direction of age difference in episodic retrieval based on the type of retrieval or the kind of information that is retrieved. However, the relatively large number of published studies on memory retrieval allows an assessment of regional specificity in these age differences. Figure 17.4 plots the number of regions with more or less activity in older adults, using the same nomenclature as in Figure 17.3. For retrieval, there does not appear to be any region where younger adults have a greater tendency to show more activity. However, older adults tend to have more activity than younger adults in IPS, particularly when their performance is as good as that seen in younger adults (Figure 17.4, yellow bars), suggesting that the processes subserved by this region may be compensatory. As noted above, the IPS is thought to be involved in top-down cognitive control, which could indicate a role for attention in supporting successful memory retrieval in older adults. Additionally, its role in familiarity might indicate that more activity in IPS in older adults during retrieval could reflect the tendency for older adults to rely more heavily on familiarity rather than recollection relative to younger adults (e.g., Prull *et al.*, 2006). However, these two roles may actually reflect the same process, as Nelson *et al.* (2010) suggested that activation of the IPS during familiarity judgments may reflect control processes that are needed when individuals are uncertain about a retrieved memory, or whether a presented item has been previously encoded. The other notable aspect of Figure 17.4 is that the precuneus tends to be over-activated in older adults when their performance is worse than that of younger adults (red bar). As noted above, the precuneus is part of the default network, and older adults show smaller task-related reductions in default network activity when these tasks require responding to external stimuli (Grady *et al.*, 2010; Lustig *et al.*, 2003; Persson *et al.*, 2007; Park *et al.*, 2010). Precuneus over-recruitment in older adults during externally cued memory retrieval would be consistent with this idea of less "deactivation" in default areas with age. Additionally, Miller *et al.* (2008) found that the degree of precuneus reduction during episodic retrieval correlated with better memory in

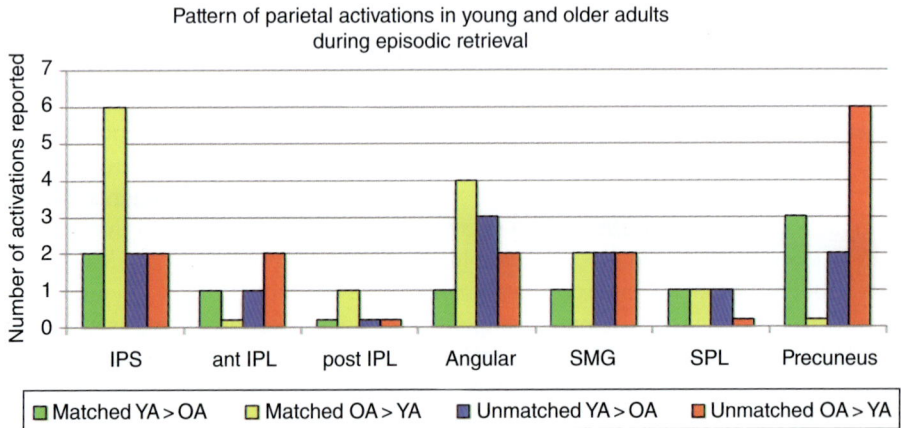

**Figure 17.4** Pattern of parietal activations in young and older adults during episodic retrieval. This figure summarizes the pattern of parietal cortex activity observed in 21 fMRI studies on age-related differences in retrieval (see text for details of studies reviewed). In this bar graph we report the pattern of left and right parietal activations reported in young and older adults when performance was matched ("matched") and when performance was not matched ("unmatched"). For each parietal ROI we tallied the number of activations in which young adults activated a region more than older adults, and in which older adults activated a region more than young adults. IPS, intraparietal sulcus; IPL, inferior parietal lobule; SPL, superior parietal lobule; SMG, supramarginal gyrus.

older adults. Thus, it seems that when older adults show over-recruitment of pre-cuneus activity, during either episodic encoding or retrieval, this provides little benefit for memory performance, making a failure to suppress default activity the most likely explanation of this increase. Aside from the precuneus, it appears that parietal over-recruitment during retrieval may have a better outcome for older adults than such activity during encoding (compare yellow and red bars in Figures 17.3 and 17.4). This finding suggests an intriguing aspect of parietal function in older age that deserves further study.

*Parietal activation during retrieval when subsequent memory performance is matched* Nine fMRI studies have reported age-related differences in parietal activation when memory performance was matched between young and older adults. In these studies both over- and under-recruitment of parietal regions in older versus younger adults has been reported. In a study that examined both autobiographical recall and "laboratory" episodic memory (St-Laurent *et al.*, 2011), more activity in younger, relative to older, adults was seen bilaterally in lateral parietal areas and medially in the precuneus. An additional study also reported less precuneus activity in older adults for autobiographical retrieval (Addis, Roberts, and Schacter, 2011). Because the precuneus, along with the rest of the default network, is activated for autobiographical memory and other self-referent tasks (Grigg and Grady, 2010; St-Laurent *et al.*, 2011; Spreng and Grady, 2010), less precuneus activity in older adults during autobiographical retrieval suggests a deficit in engaging this area during recall of personally relevant memories. On the other hand, several additional experiments looking at memory for non-personal memories, such as paired associates (Giovanello and Schacter, 2012) and word recognition (Daselaar *et al.*, 2006), also found reduced precuneus activity in older adults, as well as in lateral parietal areas, despite matched performance in the young and old groups.

However, two studies also found regions in parietal cortex where older adults had more activity, in the AG bilaterally for episodic recall (St-Laurent *et al.*, 2011) and in left SMG for autobiographical recall (Addis, Roberts, and Schacter, 2011). Other studies reporting more AG activity for older adults during memory tasks where performance was matched between groups include those examining face/name recall (Kalpouzos, Persson, and Nyberg, 2012) and word recognition (Davis *et al.*, 2008). Similarly, studies of word recognition also have reported over-recruitment in IPS and IPL by older adults when their memory performance is equivalent to that seen in younger adults (Cabeza *et al.*, 2004; Spaniol and Grady, 2012). Only one study found more SPL activity in older adults than in younger adults with matched performance (Burgmans *et al.*, 2010). Across all of these studies with matched performance, age differences were found in both right and left parietal regions, with no clear predominance of one over the other.

## General Summary of Age-related Changes in PFC and Parietal Function

Three possible patterns of results are observable when comparing task-related brain activity in young versus older adults. (1) There may be no age-related differences in activation in regional brain activations. (2) There may be less brain activity within specific brain regions in older than in younger adults (Brassen *et al.*, 2009; Dulas and Duarte, 2011; Rajah, Languay, and Valiquette, 2010). (3) There may be increased brain activity in specific brain regions in older than in younger adults (Park and Reuter-Lorenz, 2009; Dennis and Cabeza, 2008). Cognitive neuroscientists have often interpreted age-related decreases in brain activity as reflecting a deficit in brain function. In contrast, age-related increases in brain activity have often been interpreted as reflecting functional compensation in the aging brain. However, these cognitive/behavioral interpretations of between-group differences in brain activity can differ based on which neural model of age-related functional change one subscribes to: dedifferentiation (Baltes, Staudinger, and Lindenberger, 1999; Li, Lindenberger, and Sikstrom, 2001), neural inefficiency/CRUNCH model (Cappell, Gmeindl, and Reuter-Lorenz, 2010; Morcom, Li, and Rugg, 2007), or compensatory plasticity (Cabeza, 2002; Greenwood, 2007; Park and Reuter-Lorenz, 2009; Reuter-Lorenz and Cappell, 2008). For example, it is possible that age-related decreases in brain activity may be related to dedifferentiation of function, and/or to deficits in function, and/or they may reflect performance differences between age groups. In contrast, increased brain activity in older versus younger adults may be related to dedifferentiation, neural inefficiency, and/or compensatory plasticity in the aging brain. Therefore, based on functional imaging data alone, one cannot clearly interpret age-related decreases versus increases in regional brain activations.

In this chapter we have investigated the patterns of age-related changes in PFC and parietal cortex activations at episodic encoding and retrieval both when performance was matched between age groups and when it was unmatched, with younger adults performing significantly better on retrieval accuracy. Within the PFC, the majority of studies reported greater activity in older than in younger adults in most PFC regions during encoding and retrieval, regardless of whether performance was unmatched or matched between groups. The few exceptions were: (1) left vlPFC, which young adults activated more than older adults at encoding when performance was unmatched, and at retrieval when performance was matched; (2) right dlPFC and right vlPFC, which young adults activated more at retrieval when performance was unmatched; and (3) right mPFC, which young adults activated more at retrieval when performance was matched. Therefore, there appear to be performance-associated deficits in right PFC at retrieval and in left vlPFC at encoding with age. This pattern may reflect dedifferentiation and/or deficits in neural efficiency and function that limit task-related modulation of these PFC regions when task demands are high. In terms of parietal cortex there did not seem to be any specific region where younger adults consistently had more activity.

In terms of age-related over-recruitment, older adults over-activated several PFC regions, such as left dlPFC, during encoding and retrieval both when performance was matched and when it was unmatched between age groups. This age-related increase in left dlPFC activity may reflect reliance on more abstract relational strategies during encoding and retrieval to compensate for neural inefficiency within the left dlPFC itself and/or for deficits in other PFC and posterior cortical regions (i.e., parietal cortex, hippocampus, and occipital cortex). This compensatory recruitment of left dlPFC may be sufficient for maintaining older adults' performance on easier memory tasks, in which performance was matched, but not on harder tasks, in which performance was not matched. A similar argument for compensation can be made for the IPS in the parietal lobe, which was over-activated in older adults for both encoding and retrieval. However, in this region the over-recruitment during encoding was associated with poor performance, whereas during retrieval it was associated with performance equal to that seen in younger adults. Thus, like the abstract relational processes underpinned by left dlPFC, the engagement of the attentional processes in which the IPS participates might be useful for boosting performance in some circumstances, but not others. That is, one could argue that left dlPFC or IPS activity in older adults may not always be compensatory, because at times it may reflect the recruitment of cognitive processes that are deleterious to task performance. For example, if left dlPFC activation reflects the use of abstract relational strategies to support memory performance in elders, it is possible that use of such a compensatory strategy may hinder performance on tasks that require item-specific processing.

Older adults also exhibited greater recruitment in several brain regions identified as being part of the default mode network, such as mPFC and the precuneus. These "over-activations" in older adults likely reflect weaker task-related decreases in these brain regions, and may contribute to age-related deficits in memory encoding and retrieval. For example, several studies reported age-related increases in mPFC or precuneus activity at retrieval when performance was unmatched between age groups, and concluded that this may reflect reduced attentional focus in older adults during task performance.

As this review makes clear, it is still difficult to explain exactly why older adults have different patterns of brain activity compared to younger adults. However, we have uncovered some interesting aspects of age differences in our two brain areas of interest. First, older adults frequently have more activity in PFC than young adults, consistent with earlier work prior to 2003. There is now enough evidence to state with confidence that this activity is not always compensatory, if one defines this based on whether older adults can perform the memory task as well as younger adults. This observation suggests that over-recruitment of PFC is sometimes either an inefficient use of neural resources or a less selective use of such resources. Second, parietal cortex is also over-recruited by older adults, but this seems only to be beneficial for performance if it happens at retrieval. This differs from the results seen for PFC, which indicate that over-activation of PFC by older adults during both encoding and retrieval can be associated with good task performance. For both PFC and parietal cortex, it is likely that at least some of the age differences in activity during episodic memory tasks reflect the influence of older age on cognitive control processes rather than on memory processes per se.

## Conclusions

There are a number of factors that can potentially influence cognitive aging and which we have not considered here. These include, but are not limited to, health factors such as cardiovascular risk and risk for dementia, genetics, and life experience. For example, parietal over-recruitment in older adults has been linked to apoliprotein (ApoE) risk genes

(Kukolja *et al.*, 2010) and increased blood pressure (Braskie, Small, and Bookheimer, 2010), and both altered function of the default network (Hedden *et al.*, 2009; Oh *et al.*, 2011; Sheline *et al.*, 2010; Vannini *et al.*, 2011) and cognitive decline (Storandt *et al.*, 2009) have been linked to amyloid deposition in the brains of older adults.

Additionally, we have focused here on age differences as they occur in two brain areas without considering the larger picture of functional interactions among these areas. However, the field may find that using a network approach will ultimately be more useful than considering brain regions in isolation. For example, age differences in several brain networks involving parietal cortex and PFC have been reported, including the default network (Andrews-Hanna *et al.*, 2007; Grady, Grigg, and Ng, 2012; Grady *et al.*, 2010; Park *et al.*, 2010), and other networks engaged during cognitive tasks (Grady *et al.*, 2010; Rajah, Languay, and Grady, 2011; Wang *et al.*, 2010). Measures of functional connectivity are related to performance in both younger and older adults (Andrews-Hanna *et al.*, 2007; Kelly *et al.*, 2008), suggesting that the integrated activity among brain regions is important for behavior and indeed may be more important than activity in any one brain region alone. Experiments looking at functional connectivity in aging are becoming more frequent in the literature and hold great promise for our understanding of cognitive aging.

Furthermore, we have not emphasized here the studies that have assessed individual differences in brain activity in older adults and how these relate to performance, although such studies exist (e.g., Davis *et al.*, 2008; McIntosh *et al.*, 1999; Rajah, Languay, and Grady, 2011). Future fMRI studies of cognitive aging and memory should aim at directly examining correlations between regional patterns of activity and task performance in low- versus high-performing elders. Results from these studies will help us better understand whether over-recruitment of PFC or parietal cortex in general is beneficial to performance, or if over-activation in some regions reflects deleterious effects of aging on memory function.

Finally, it is notable that the majority of studies discussed in this chapter employed cross-sectional designs. Thus, the observed between-group differences in behavior or brain structure/function may not be due to the factor of age, but to developmental, historical, and other cohort factors unique to each group. One cannot determine from cross-sectional designs if age *alone* contributes to the group differences observed in cross-sectional fMRI studies of aging and episodic memory; however, comparisons of in-vivo volumetric and fMRI studies using cross-sectional versus longitudinal methods have yielded similar results (Fotenos *et al.*, 2005; Kramer *et al.*, 2007; O'Brien *et al.*, 2010; Raz *et al.*, 1997, 2005). Therefore, we argue that longitudinal designs are optimal for studying aging; but results from cross-sectional studies play an important role in providing an *initial exploration* in the most efficient, economical, and feasible manner.

# References

Addis, D.R., Roberts, R.P., and Schacter, D.L. (2011). Age-related neural changes in autobiographical remembering and imagining. *Neuropsychologia*, 49 (13), 3656–3669. doi: 10.1016/j.neuropsychologia.2011.09.021.

Ally, B.A., Simons, J.S., McKeever, J.D., *et al.* (2008). Parietal contributions to recollection: electrophysiological evidence from aging and patients with parietal lesions. *Neuropsychologia*,46 (7), 1800–1812. doi: 10.1016/j.neuropsychologia.2008.02.026.

Andrews-Hanna, J.R., Snyder, A.Z., Vincent, J.L., *et al.* (2007). Disruption of large-scale brain systems in advanced aging. *Neuron,*56 (5), 924–935.

Angel, L., Fay, S., Bouazzaoui, B., *et al.* (2009). Neural correlates of cued recall in young and older adults: an event-related potential study. *Neuroreport,* 20 (1), 75–79. doi: 10.1097/WNR.0b013e32831b6e0c.

Baltes, P.B., Staudinger, U.M., and Lindenberger, U. (1999). Lifespan psychology: theory and application to intellectual functioning. *Annual Review of Psychology,* 50, 471–507.

Bangen, K.J., Kaup, A.R., Mirzakhanian, H., *et al.* (2012). Compensatory brain activity during encoding among older adults with better recognition memory for face–name pairs: an integrative functional, structural, and perfusion imaging study. *Journal of the International Neuropsychological Society,* 18 (3), 402–413. doi: 10.1017/S1355617712000197.

Blumenfeld, R.S., Parks, C.M., Yonelinas, A.P., and Ranganath, C. (2011). Putting the pieces together: the role of dorsolateral prefrontal cortex in relational memory encoding. *Journal of Cognitive Neuroscience,* 23 (1), 257–265. doi: 10.1162/jocn.2010.21459.

Blumenfeld, R.S., and Ranganath, C. (2007). Prefrontal cortex and long-term memory encoding: an integrative review of findings from neuropsychology and neuroimaging. *Neuroscientist,* 13 (3), 280–291. doi: 10.1177/1073858407299290.

Braskie, M.N., Small, G.W., and Bookheimer, S.Y. (2010). Vascular health risks and fMRI activation during a memory task in older adults. *Neurobiology of Aging,* 31 (9), 1532–1542. doi: 10.1016/j.neurobiolaging.2008.08.016.

Brassen, S., Buchel, C., Weber-Fahr, W., *et al.* (2009). Structure–function interactions of correct retrieval in healthy elderly women. *Neurobiology of Aging,* 30 (7), 1147–1156. doi: 10.1016/j.neurobiolaging.2007.10.005.

Bunge, S.A., Burrows, B., and Wagner, A.D. (2004). Prefrontal and hippocampal contributions to visual associative recognition: interactions between cognitive control and episodic retrieval. *Brain and Cognition,* 56 (2), 141–152. doi: 10.1016/j.bandc.2003.08.001.

Burgmans, S., van Boxtel, M.P., Vuurman, E.F., *et al.* (2010). Increased neural activation during picture encoding and retrieval in 60-year-olds compared to 20-year-olds. *Neuropsychologia,* 48 (7), 2188–2197. doi: 10.1016/j.neuropsychologia.2010.04.011.

Cabeza, R. (2002). Hemispheric asymmetry reduction in older adults: the HAROLD model. *Psychology and Aging,* 17 (1), 85–100.

Cabeza, R., Ciaramelli, E., Olson, I.R., and Moscovitch, M. (2008). The parietal cortex and episodic memory: an attentional account. *Nature Reviews Neuroscience,* 9 (8), 613–625. doi: 10.1038/nrn2459.

Cabeza, R., Daselaar, S.M., Dolcos, F., *et al.* (2004). Task-independent and task-specific age effects on brain activity during working memory, visual attention and episodic retrieval. *Cerebral Cortex,* 14 (4), 364–375.

Cabeza, R., and Nyberg, L. (2000). Imaging cognition II: An empirical review of 275 PET and fMRI studies. *Journal of Cognitive Neuroscience,* 12 (1), 1–17.

Cappell, K.A., Gmeindl, L., and Reuter-Lorenz, P.A. (2010). Age differences in prefrontal recruitment during verbal working memory maintenance depend on memory load. *Cortex,* 46 (4), 462–473. doi: 10.1016/j.cortex.2009.11.009.

Caspers, S., Geyer, S., Schleicher, A., *et al.* (2006). The human inferior parietal cortex: cytoarchitectonic parcellation and interindividual variability. *NeuroImage,* 33 (2), 430–448. doi: 10.1016/j.neuroimage.2006.06.054.

Cavada, C., and Goldman-Rakic, P.S. (1989). Posterior parietal cortex in rhesus monkey: II. Evidence for segregated corticocortical networks linking sensory and limbic areas with the frontal lobe. *Journal of Comparative Neurology,* 287, 422–445.

Cerf-Ducastel, B., and Murphy, C. (2009). Age-related differences in the neural substrates of cross-modal olfactory recognition memory: an fMRI investigation. *Brain Research,* 1285, 88–98. doi: 10.1016/j.brainres.2009.05.086.

Ciaramelli, E., Grady, C., Levine, B., *et al.* (2010). Top-down and bottom-up attention to memory are dissociated in posterior parietal cortex: neuroimaging and neuropsychological evidence. *Journal of Neuroscience*, 30 (14), 4943–4956. doi: 10.1523/JNEUROSCI.1209-09.2010.

Ciaramelli, E., Grady, C.L., and Moscovitch, M. (2008). Top-down and bottom-up attention to memory: a hypothesis (AtoM) on the role of the posterior parietal cortex in memory retrieval. *Neuropsychologia*, 46 (7), 1828–1851. doi: 10.1016/j.neuropsychologia.2008.03.022.

Corbetta, M., Patel, G., and Shulman, G.L. (2008). The reorienting system of the human brain: from environment to theory of mind. *Neuron*, 58 (3), 306–324.

Damoiseaux, J.S., Beckmann, C.F., Arigita, E.J., *et al.* (2008). Reduced resting-state brain activity in the default network in normal aging. *Cerebral Cortex*, 18 (8), 1856–1864. doi: 10.1093/cercor/bhm207.

Daselaar, S.M., Fleck, M.S., Dobbins, I.G., *et al.* (2006). Effects of healthy aging on hippocampal and rhinal memory functions: an event-related fMRI study. *Cerebral Cortex*, 16 (12), 1771–1782. doi: 10.1093/cercor/bhj112.

Daselaar, S.M., Veltman, D.J., Rombouts, S.A., *et al.* (2003). Neuroanatomical correlates of episodic encoding and retrieval in young and elderly subjects. *Brain*, 126 (1), 43–56.

Davis, S.W., Dennis, N.A., Daselaar, S.M., *et al.* (2008). Que PASA? The posterior–anterior shift in aging. *Cerebral Cortex*, 18 (5), 1201–1209. doi: 10.1093/cercor/bhm155.

de Chastelaine, M., Wang, T.H., Minton, B., *et al.* (2011). The effects of age, memory performance, and callosal integrity on the neural correlates of successful associative encoding. *Cerebral Cortex*, 21 (9), 2166–2176. doi: 10.1093/cercor/bhq294.

Dennis, N.A., and Cabeza, R. (2008). Neuroimaging of healthy cognitive aging. In *The Handbook of Aging and Cognition* (ed. F. I. Craik and T.A. Salthouse). New York, NY: Psychology Press.

Dennis, N.A., Daselaar, S., and Cabeza, R. (2007). Effects of aging on transient and sustained successful memory encoding activity. *Neurobiology of Aging*, 28 (11), 1749–1758. doi: 10.1016/j.neurobiolaging.2006.07.006.

Dennis, N.A., Hayes, S.M., Prince, S.E., *et al.* (2008). Effects of aging on the neural correlates of successful item and source memory encoding. *Journal of Experimental Psychology: Learning, Memory, and Cognition*, 34 (4), 791–808. doi: 10.1037/0278-7393.34.4.791.

Dennis, N.A., Kim, H., and Cabeza, R. (2008). Age-related differences in brain activity during true and false memory retrieval. *Journal of Cognitive Neuroscience*, 20 (8), 1390–402. doi: 10.1162/jocn.2008.20096.

Dew, I.T., Buchler, N., Dobbins, I.G., and Cabeza, R. (2012). Where Is ELSA? The early to late shift in aging. *Cerebral Cortex*, 22 (11), 2542–2553. doi: 10.1093/cercor/bhr334.

Donohue, S.E., Wendelken, C., Crone, E.A., and Bunge, S.A. (2005). Retrieving rules for behavior from long-term memory. *NeuroImage*, 26 (4), 1140–1149. doi: 10.1016/j.neuroimage.2005.03.019.

Duarte, A., Graham, K.S., and Henson, R.N. (2010). Age-related changes in neural activity associated with familiarity, recollection and false recognition. *Neurobiology of Aging*, 31 (10), 1814–1830. doi: 10.1016/j.neurobiolaging.2008.09.014.

Duarte, A., Henson, R.N., and Graham, K.S. (2008). The effects of aging on the neural correlates of subjective and objective recollection. *Cerebral Cortex*, 18 (9), 2169–2180. doi: 10.1093/cercor/bhm243.

Dulas, M.R., and Duarte, A. (2011). The effects of aging on material-independent and material-dependent neural correlates of contextual binding. *NeuroImage*, 57 (3), 1192–1204. doi: 10.1016/j.neuroimage.2011.05.036.

Dulas, M.R., and Duarte, A. (2012). The effects of aging on material-independent and material-dependent neural correlates of source memory retrieval. *Cerebral Cortex*, 22 (1), 37–50. doi: 10.1093/cercor/bhr056.

Duverne, S., Motamedinia, S., and Rugg, M.D. (2009a). The relationship between aging, performance, and the neural correlates of successful memory encoding. *Cerebral Cortex* 19 (3), 733–744. doi: 10.1093/cercor/bhn122.

Duverne, S., Motamedinia, S., and Rugg, M.D. (2009b). Effects of age on the neural correlates of retrieval cue processing are modulated by task demands. *Journal of Cognitive Neuroscience* 21 (1), 1–17. doi: 10.1162/jocn.2009.21001.

Duzel, E., Schutze, H., Yonelinas, A.P., and Heinze, H.J. (2011). Functional phenotyping of successful aging in long-term memory: preserved performance in the absence of neural compensation. *Hippocampus*, 21 (8), 803–814. doi: 10.1002/hipo.20834.

Fernandes, M.A., Pacurar, A., Moscovitch, M., and Grady, C. (2006). Neural correlates of auditory recognition under full and divided attention in younger and older adults. *Neuropsychologia*, 44 (12), 2452–2464. doi: 10.1016/j.neuropsychologia.2006.04.020.

Filippini, N., Nickerson, L.D., Beckmann, C.F., *et al.* (2012). Age-related adaptations of brain function during a memory task are also present at rest. *NeuroImage*, 59 (4), 3821–3828. doi: 10.1016/j.neuroimage.2011.11.063.

Fischer, H., Nyberg, L., and Backman, L. (2010). Age-related differences in brain regions supporting successful encoding of emotional faces. *Cortex*, 46 (4), 490–497. doi: 10.1016/j.cortex.2009.05.011.

Fletcher, P.C., Shallice, T., and Dolan, R.J. (1998). The functional roles of prefrontal cortex in episodic memory. I. Encoding. *Brain*, 121 (7), 1239–1248.

Fotenos, A.F., Snyder, A.Z., Girton, L.E., *et al.* (2005). Normative estimates of cross-sectional and longitudinal brain volume decline in aging and AD. *Neurology*, 64 (6), 1032–1039.

Fox, M.D., Corbetta, M., Snyder, A.Z., *et al.* (2006). Spontaneous neuronal activity distinguishes human dorsal and ventral attention systems. *Proceedings of the National Academy of Sciences of the USA*, 103 (26), 10046–10051. doi: 10.1073/pnas.0604187103.

Friedman, D., de Chastelaine, M., Nessler, D., and Malcolm, B. (2010). Changes in familiarity and recollection across the lifespan: an ERP perspective. *Brain Research*, 1310, 124–141. doi: 10.1016/j.brainres.2009.11.016.

Garavan, H., Ross, T.J., Murphy, K., *et al.* (2002). Dissociable executive functions in the dynamic control of behavior: inhibition, error detection, and correction. *NeuroImage* 17 (4), 1820–1829.

Giovanello, K.S., Kensinger, E.A., Wong, A.T., and Schacter, D.L. (2010). Age-related neural changes during memory conjunction errors. *Journal of Cognitive Neuroscience*, 22 (7), 1348–1361. doi: 10.1162/jocn.2009.21274.

Giovanello, K.S., and Schacter, D.L. (2012). Reduced specificity of hippocampal and posterior ventrolateral prefrontal activity during relational retrieval in normal aging. *Journal of Cognitive Neuroscience*, 24 (1), 159–170. doi: 10.1162/jocn_a_00113.

Grady, C.L., Grigg, O., and Ng. C. (2012). Age differences in default and reward networks during processing of personally relevant information. *Neuropsychologia*, 50 (7), 1682–1697. doi: 10.1016/j.neuropsychologia.2012.03.024.

Grady, C.L., McIntosh, A.R., and Craik, F.I. (2005). Task-related activity in prefrontal cortex and its relation to recognition memory performance in young and old adults. *Neuropsychologia*, 43 (10), 1466–1481. doi: 10.1016/j.neuropsychologia.2004.12.016.

Grady, C.L., Protzner, A.B., Kovacevic, N., *et al.* (2010). A multivariate analysis of age-related differences in default mode and task-positive networks across multiple cognitive domains. *Cerebral Cortex*, 20 (6), 1432–1447. doi: 10.1093/cercor/bhp207.

Grady, C.L., Springer, M.V., Hongwanishkul, D., *et al.* (2006). Age-related changes in brain activity across the adult lifespan. *Journal of Cognitive Neuroscience*, 18 (2), 227–241. doi: 10.1162/089892906775783705.

Greenwood, P.M. (2007). Functional plasticity in cognitive aging: review and hypothesis. *Neuropsychology*, 21 (6), 657–673.

Grigg, O., and Grady, C.L. (2010). The default network and processing of personally relevant information: Converging evidence from task-related modulations and functional connectivity. *Neuropsychologia*, 48, 3815–3823.

Gusnard, D.A., Akbudak, E., Shulman, G.L., and Raichle, M.E. (2001). Medial prefrontal cortex and self-referential mental activity: Relation to a default mode of brain function. *Proceedings of the National Academy of Sciences of the USA*, 98, 4259–4264.

Gutchess, A.H., Welsh, R.C., Hedden, T., *et al.* (2005). Aging and the neural correlates of successful picture encoding: frontal activations compensate for decreased medial-temporal activity. *Journal of Cognitive Neuroscience*,17(1),84–96.doi:10.1162/0898929052880048.

Hayama, H.R., and Rugg, M.D. (2009). Right dorsolateral prefrontal cortex is engaged during post-retrieval processing of both episodic and semantic information. *Neuropsychologia*, 47 (12), 2409–2416. doi: 10.1016/j.neuropsychologia.2009.04.010.

Hedden, T., Van Dijk, K.R., Becker, J.A., *et al.* (2009). Disruption of functional connectivity in clinically normal older adults harboring amyloid burden. *Journal of Neuroscience*, 29 (40), 12686–12694. doi: 10.1523/JNEUROSCI.3189-09.2009.

Kalpouzos, G., Persson, J., and Nyberg, L. (2012). Local brain atrophy accounts for functional activity differences in normal aging. *Neurobiology of Aging*, 33 (3), 623.e1–623.e13. doi: 10.1016/j.neurobiolaging.2011.02.021.

Kelly, A.M., Uddin, L.Q., Biswal, B.B., *et al.* (2008). Competition between functional brain networks mediates behavioral variability. *NeuroImage*, 39 (1), 527–537. doi: 10.1016/j.neuroimage.2007.08.008.

Kensinger, E.A., and Schacter, D.L. (2008). Neural processes supporting young and older adults' emotional memories. *Journal of Cognitive Neuroscience*, 20 (7), 1161–1173. doi: 10.1162/jocn.2008.20080.

Kim, S.Y., and Giovanello, K.S. (2011). The effects of attention on age-related relational memory deficits: fMRI evidence from a novel attentional manipulation. *Journal of Cognitive Neuroscience*, 23 (11), 3637–3656. doi: 10.1162/jocn_a_00058.

Kramer, J.H., Mungas, D. Reed, B.R., *et al.* (2007). Longitudinal MRI and cognitive change in healthy elderly. *Neuropsychology*, 21 (4), 412–418. doi: 10.1037/0894-4105.21.4.412.

Kukolja, J., Thiel, C.M., Eggermann, T., *et al.* (2010). Medial temporal lobe dysfunction during encoding and retrieval of episodic memory in non-demented APOE epsilon4 carriers. *Neuroscience*, 168 (2), 487–497. doi: 10.1016/j.neuroscience.2010.03.044.

Kukolja, J., Thiel, C.M., Wilms, M., *et al.* (2009). Ageing-related changes of neural activity associated with spatial contextual memory. *Neurobiology of Aging*, 30 (4), 630–645. doi: 10.1016/j.neurobiolaging.2007.08.015.

Leshikar, E.D., Gutchess, A.H., Hebrank, A.C., *et al.* (2010). The impact of increased relational encoding demands on frontal and hippocampal function in older adults. *Cortex*, 46 (4), 507–521. doi: 10.1016/j.cortex.2009.07.011.

Li, J., Morcom, A.M., and Rugg, M.D. (2004). The effects of age on the neural correlates of successful episodic retrieval: an ERP study. *Cognitive, Affective and Behavioral Neuroscience*, 4 (3), 279–293.

Li, S.C., Lindenberger, U., and Sikstrom, S. (2001). Aging cognition: from neuromodulation to representation. *Trends in Cognitive Science*, 5 (11), 479–486.

Luria, A.R. (1962). *Higher Cortical Functions in Man*. New York, NY: Basic Books.

Lustig, C., Snyder, A.Z., Bhakta, M., *et al.* (2003). Functional deactivations: change with age and dementia of the Alzheimer type. *Proceedings of the National Academy of Sciences of the USA*, 100 (24), 14504–14509.

Maillet, D., and Rajah, M.N. (2011). Age-related changes in the three-way correlation between anterior hippocampus volume, whole-brain patterns of encoding activity and subsequent context retrieval. *Brain Research*, 1420, 68–79. doi: 10.1016/j.brainres.2011.08.071.

McDonough, I.M., Wong, J.T., and Gallo, D.A. (2012). Age-related differences in prefrontal cortex activity during retrieval monitoring: testing the compensation and dysfunction accounts. *Cerebral Cortex*, 23 (5), 1049–1060. doi: 10.1093/cercor/bhs064.

McIntosh, A.R., Sekuler, A.B., Penpeci, C., *et al.* (1999). Recruitment of unique neural systems to support visual memory in normal aging. *Current Biology*, 9, 1275–1278.

Mesulam, M.M. (1986). Frontal cortex and behavior. *Annals of Neurology*, 19, 320–325.

Miller, S.L., Celone, K., DePeau, K., *et al.* (2008). Age-related memory impairment associated with loss of parietal deactivation but preserved hippocampal activation. *Proceedings of the National Academy of Sciences of the USA*, 105 (6), 2181–2186. doi: 10.1073/pnas.0706818105.

Morcom, A.M., Bullmore, E.T., Huppert, F.A., *et al.* (2010). Memory encoding and dopamine in the aging brain: a psychopharmacological neuroimaging study. *Cerebral Cortex*, 20 (3), 743–757. doi: 10.1093/cercor/bhp139.

Morcom, A.M., Good, C.D., Frackowiak, R.S., and Rugg, M.D. (2003). Age effects on the neural correlates of successful memory encoding. *Brain*, 126 (1), 213–229.

Morcom, A.M., Li, J., and Rugg, M.D. (2007). Age effects on the neural correlates of episodic retrieval: increased cortical recruitment with matched performance. *Cerebral Cortex*, 17 (11), 2491–2506. doi: 10.1093/cercor/bhl155.

Murty, V.P., Sambataro, F., Das, S., *et al.* (2009). Age-related alterations in simple declarative memory and the effect of negative stimulus valence. *Journal of Cognitive Neuroscience*, 21 (10), 1920–1933. doi: 10.1162/jocn.2009.21130.

Nelson, S.M., Cohen, A.L., Power, J.D., *et al.* (2010). A parcellation scheme for human left lateral parietal cortex. *Neuron*, 67 (1), 156–170. doi: 10.1016/j.neuron.2010.05.025.

Nessler, D., Friedman, D., Johnson, R., Jr., and Bersick, M. (2007). Does repetition engender the same retrieval processes in young and older adults? *Neuroreport*, 18 (17), 1837–1840. doi: 10.1097/WNR.0b013e3282f16d9f.

Nessler, D., Johnson, R., Jr., Bersick, M., and Friedman, D. (2008). Age-related ERP differences at retrieval persist despite age-invariant performance and left-frontal negativity during encoding. *Neuroscience Letters*, 432 (2), 151–156. doi: 10.1016/j.neulet.2007.12.016.

O'Brien, J.L., O'Keefe, K.M., LaViolette, P.S., *et al.* (2010). Longitudinal fMRI in elderly reveals loss of hippocampal activation with clinical decline. *Neurology*, 74 (24), 1969–1976. doi: 10.1212/WNL.0b013e3181e3966e.

Oh, H., Mormino, E.C., Madison, C., *et al.* (2011). β-Amyloid affects frontal and posterior brain networks in normal aging. *NeuroImage*, 54 (3), 1887–1895. doi: 10.1016/j.neuroimage.2010.10.027.

Ongur, D., Ferry, A.T., and Price, J.L. (2003). Architectonic subdivision of the human orbital and medial prefrontal cortex. *Journal of Comparative Neurology*, 460 (3), 425–49.

Park, D.C., Polk, T.A., Hebrank, A.C., and Jenkins, L.J. (2010). Age differences in default mode activity on easy and difficult spatial judgment tasks. *Frontiers in Human Neuroscience*, 3, 75. doi: 10.3389/neuro.09.075.2009.

Park, D.C., and Reuter-Lorenz, P. (2009). The adaptive brain: aging and neurocognitive scaffolding. *Annual Review of Psychology*, 60, 173–196. doi: 10.1146/annurev.psych.59.103006.093656.

Persson, J., Lustig, C., Nelson, J.K., and Reuter-Lorenz, P.A. (2007). Age differences in deactivation: a link to cognitive control? *Journal of Cognitive Neuroscience*, 19 (6), 1021–1032.

Petrides, M., and Pandya, D.N. (1999). Dorsolateral prefrontal cortex: comparative cytoarchitectonic analysis in the human and the macaque brain and corticocortical connection patterns. *European Journal of Neuroscience*, 11 (3), 1011–1036.

Petrides, M., and Pandya, D.N. (2002). Comparative cytoarchitectonic analysis of the human and the macaque ventrolateral prefrontal cortex and corticocortical connection patterns in the monkey. *European Journal of Neuroscience*, 16 (2), 291–310.

Prince, S.E., Daselaar, S.M., and Cabeza, R. (2005). Neural correlates of relational memory: successful encoding and retrieval of semantic and perceptual associations. *Journal of Neuroscience*, 25 (5), 1203–1210. doi: 10.1523/JNEUROSCI.2540–04.2005.

Prull, M.W., Dawes, L.L., Martin, A.M. 3rd, *et al.* (2006). Recollection and familiarity in recognition memory: adult age differences and neuropsychological test correlates. *Psychology and Aging*, 21 (1), 107–118.

Rajah, M., Ames, B., and D'Esposito, M. (2008). Prefrontal contributions to domain-general executive control processes during temporal context retrieval. *Neuropsychologia*, 46 (4), 1088–1103. doi: 10.1016/j.neuropsychologia.2007.10.023.

Rajah, M., and D'Esposito, M. (2005). Region-specific changes in prefrontal function with age: a review of PET and fMRI studies on working and episodic memory. *Brain*, 128 (9), 1964–1983. doi: 10.1093/brain/awh608.

Rajah, M., Languay, R., and Grady, C. (2011). Age-related changes in right middle frontal gyrus volumes correlate with altered episodic retrieval activity. *Journal of Neuroscience*, 31, 17941–17954.

Rajah, M., Languay, R., and Valiquette, L. (2010). Age-related changes in prefrontal cortex activity are associated with behavioural deficits in both temporal and spatial context memory retrieval in older adults. *Cortex*, 46 (4), 535–549. doi: 10.1016/j.cortex.2009.07.006.

Rajah, M.N., and McIntosh, A.R. (2008). Age-related differences in brain activity during verbal recency memory. *Brain Research*, 1199, 111–125. doi: 10.1016/j.brainres.2007.12.051.

Rajah, M.N., McIntosh, A.R., and Grady, C.L. (1999). Frontotemporal interactions in face encoding and recognition. *Cognitive Brain Research*, 8 (3), 259–269.

Raz, N., Gunning, F.M., Head, D., *et al.* (1997). Selective aging of the human cerebral cortex observed in vivo: differential vulnerability of the prefrontal gray matter. *Cerebral Cortex*, 7 (3), 268–282.

Raz, N., Lindenberger, U., Rodrigue, K.M., *et al.* (2005). Regional brain changes in aging healthy adults: general trends, individual differences and modifiers. *Cerebral Cortex*, 15 (11), 1676–1689. doi: 10.1093/cercor/bhi044.

Reber, P.J., Siwiec, R.M., Gitelman, D.R., *et al.* (2002). Neural correlates of successful encoding identified using functional magnetic resonance imaging. *Journal of Neuroscience*, 22 (21), 9541–9548.

Reuter-Lorenz, P.A., and Cappell, K.A. (2008). Neurocognitive aging and the compensation hypothesis. *Current Directions in Psychological Science*, 17 (3), 177–182.

Rossi, S., Pasqualetti, P., Zito, G., *et al.* (2006). Prefrontal and parietal cortex in human episodic memory: an interference study by repetitive transcranial magnetic stimulation. *European Journal of Neuroscience*, 23 (3), 793–800. doi: 10.1111/j.1460-9568.2006.04600.x.

Rugg, M.D., Henson, R.N., and Robb, W.G. (2003). Neural correlates of retrieval processing in the prefrontal cortex during recognition and exclusion tasks. *Neuropsychologia*, 41 (1), 40–52.

Rugg, M.D., Mark, R.E., Walla, P., *et al.* (1998). Dissociation of the neural correlates of implicit and explicit memory. *Nature*, 392 (6676), 595–598.

Sambataro, F., Murty, V.P., Callicott, J.H., *et al.* (2010). Age-related alterations in default mode network: impact on working memory performance. *Neurobiology of Aging*, 31 (5), 839–852. doi: 10.1016/j.neurobiolaging.2008.05.022.

Sheline, Y.I., Raichle, M.E., Snyder, A.Z., *et al.* (2010). Amyloid plaques disrupt resting state default mode network connectivity in cognitively normal elderly. *Biological Psychiatry*, 67 (6), 584–587. doi: 10.1016/j.biopsych.2009.08.024.

Shelton, A.L., and Gabrieli, J.D. (2002). Neural correlates of encoding space from route and survey perspectives. *Journal of Neuroscience*, 22 (7), 2711–2717.

Shulman, G.L., Astafiev, S.V., Franke, D., *et al.* (2009). Interaction of stimulus-driven reorienting and expectation in ventral and dorsal frontoparietal and basal ganglia-cortical networks. *Journal of Neuroscience*, 29 (14), 4392–4407. doi: 10.1523/JNEUROSCI.5609-08.2009.

Spaniol, J., Davidson, P.S., Kim, A.S., *et al.* (2009). Event-related fMRI studies of episodic encoding and retrieval: meta-analyses using activation likelihood estimation. *Neuropsychologia*, 47 (8–9), 1765–1779. doi: 10.1016/j.neuropsychologia.2009.02.028.

Spaniol, J., and Grady, C. (2012). Aging and the neural correlates of source memory: over-recruitment and functional reorganization. *Neurobiology of Aging*, 33 (2), 425 e3–e18. doi: 10.1016/j.neurobiolaging.2010.10.005.

Sperling, R.A., Bates, J.F., Chua, E.F., *et al.* (2003). fMRI studies of associative encoding in young and elderly controls and mild Alzheimer's disease. *Journal of Neurology, Neurosurgery and Psychiatry*, 74 (1), 44–50.

Spreng, R.N., and Grady, C.L. (2010). Patterns of brain activity supporting autobiographical memory, prospection, and theory of mind, and their relationship to the default mode network. *Journal of Cognitive Neuroscience* 22 (6), 1112–1123. doi: 10.1162/jocn.2009.21282.

St. Jacques, P.L., Dolcos, F., and Cabeza, R. (2009). Effects of aging on functional connectivity of the amygdala for subsequent memory of negative pictures: a network analysis of functional magnetic resonance imaging data. *Psychological Science*, 20 (1), 74–84. doi: 10.1111/j.1467-9280.2008.02258.x.

St-Laurent, M., Abdi, H., Burianová, H., and Grady, C.L. (2011). Influence of aging on the neural correlates of autobiographical, episodic, and semantic memory retrieval. *Journal of Cognitive Neuroscience*, 23 (12), 4150–4163. doi: 10.1162/jocn_a_00079.

Stevens, W.D., Hasher, L., Chiew, K.S., and Grady, C.L. (2008). A neural mechanism underlying memory failure in older adults. *Journal of Neuroscience*, 28 (48), 12820–12824. doi: 10.1523/JNEUROSCI.2622-08.2008.

Storandt, M., Mintun, M.A., Head, D., and Morris, J.C. (2009). Cognitive decline and brain volume loss as signatures of cerebral amyloid-β peptide deposition identified with Pittsburgh compound B: cognitive decline associated with Aβ deposition. *Archives of Neurology*, 66 (12), 1476–1481. doi: 10.1001/archneurol.2009.272.

Talairach, J., and Tournoux, P. (1988). *Co-Planar Stereotaxic Atlas of the Human Brain*. Translated by Mark Rayport. New York, NY: Thieme Medical Publishers, Inc.

Tsukiura, T., Sekiguchi, A., Yomogida, Y., *et al.* (2011). Effects of aging on hippocampal and anterior temporal activations during successful retrieval of memory for face–name associations. *Journal of Cognitive Neuroscience*, 23 (1), 200–213. doi: 10.1162/jocn.2010.21476.

van der Veen, F.M., Nijhuis, F.A.P., Tisserand, D.J., *et al.* (2006). Effects of aging on recognition of intentionally and incidentally stored words: an fMRI study. *Neuropsychologia*, 44 (12), 2477–2486. doi: 10.1016/j.neuropsychologia.2006.04.023.

Vannini, P., Hedden, T., Becker, J.A., *et al.* (2011). Age and amyloid-related alterations in default network habituation to stimulus repetition. *Neurobiology of Aging*, 33(7), 1237–1252. doi: 10.1016/j.neurobiolaging.2011.01.003.

Vannini, P., Hedden, T., Huijbers, W., *et al.* (2012). The ups and downs of the posteromedial cortex: age- and amyloid-related functional alterations of the encoding/retrieval flip in cognitively normal older adults. *Cerebral Cortex*, 23 (6), 1317–1328. doi: 10.1093/cercor/bhs108.

Velanova, K., Lustig, C., Jacoby, L.L., and Buckner, R.L. (2007). Evidence for frontally mediated controlled processing differences in older adults. *Cerebral Cortex*, 17 (5), 1033–1046.

Vilberg, K.L., and Rugg, M.D. (2008). Memory retrieval and the parietal cortex: a review of evidence from a dual-process perspective. *Neuropsychologia*, 46 (7), 1787–1799. doi: 10.1016/j.neuropsychologia.2008.01.004.

Wang, L., Li, Y., Metzak, P., *et al.* (2010). Age-related changes in topological patterns of large-scale brain functional networks during memory encoding and recognition. *NeuroImage*, 50 (3), 862–872. doi: 10.1016/j.neuroimage.2010.01.044.

Wheeler, M.E., and Buckner, R.L. (2004). Functional-anatomic correlates of remembering and knowing. *NeuroImage*, 21 (4), 1337–1349.

Yonelinas, A.P., Otten, L.J., Shaw, K.N., and Rugg, M.D. (2005). Separating the brain regions involved in recollection and familiarity in recognition memory. *Journal of Neuroscience*, 25 (11), 3002–3008.

Zacks, R.T., Hasher, L., and Li, K.Z. (2000). Human memory. In *The Handbook of Aging and Cognition* (ed. F.I.M. Craik and T.A. Salthouse). Hillsdale, NJ: Erlbaum, pp. 293–358.

Zilles, K., and Palomero-Gallagher, N. (2001). Cyto-, myelo-, and receptor architectonics of the human parietal cortex. *NeuroImage*, 14 (1), S8–S20. doi: 10.1006/nimg.2001.0823.

# 18

# Relational Memory and its Relevance to Aging

## Kelly S. Giovanello and Ilana T. Z. Dew

*Memory lies in the line of elaborating each of several associates to be remembered...*

William James

## Introduction

Memory for a past event typically involves remembering the various components of the event (item memory; IM), as well the associations or links formed between the components (relational memory; RM). That is, in order to retrieve rich, detailed memories of our everyday experiences (e.g., the party you attended last week), we must recall not only the individual parts (the taste of the food, the sound of the music) but also the way in which all the components were bound together into a single event. Data from several lines of research including animal models, human neuropsychological studies, cognitive studies of normal individuals, and functional neuroimaging investigations have shaped our understanding of the cognitive processes and neural mechanisms that give rise to RM. Broadly, such studies have shown that RM depends predominantly on the prefrontal cortex (PFC) and medial temporal lobes (MTL). The PFC and MTL interact with one another, as well as with other neural regions depending on the nature of the components of the learning event (e.g., perceptual, conceptual, or affective features). Considerable emphasis has been placed on elucidating the neural processes involved in RM, as RM is more sensitive than IM to the mnemonic changes observed in several populations, including healthy aging. This chapter reviews the theoretical concepts and empirical findings concerning the neural bases of RM, and demonstrates how tasks of RM have been used to address key theoretical questions in aging research. The first section of the chapter introduces the basic paradigms or tasks used to study RM for novel associations, as well as the various forms of RM investigated in the literature. Notably, RM can be studied in the laboratory using tests of explicit (i.e., conscious, intentional) or implicit (i.e., nonconscious or incidental) retrieval. The second section of the chapter describes the contribution of PFC and MTL to explicit relational memory (ERM), while the third section discusses the contribution of these regions to implicit relational memory (IRM).

*The Wiley Handbook on the Cognitive Neuroscience of Memory*, First Edition.
Edited by Donna Rose Addis, Morgan Barense, and Audrey Duarte.
© 2015 John Wiley & Sons, Ltd. Published 2015 by John Wiley & Sons, Ltd.

Finally, a review of the findings documenting age-related neural changes during tasks of ERM and IRM is included in sections two and three, respectively.

## Testing Relational Memory

Studies of both ERM and IRM involve an initial study phase in which research participants encode novel associations in any one of a variety of ways, followed by a test phase to assess memory for the associations formed at study. At a general level, ERM and IRM are differentiated by whether or not the participants are instructed to think back to the earlier associations in order to complete the test phase successfully. Novel associations may be characterized as *inter-item* (i.e., between two independent items, such as pairs of words or names and faces), or *intra-item* (i.e., between an item and a concrete, stimulus-bound *contextual* feature). In intra-item associations, the contextual feature of interest may be a perceptual element (e.g., color or font), temporal order, or the source of information. Such intra-item associations are typically investigated under the rubric of context memory or source memory (Johnson, Hashtroudi, and Lindsay, 1993). Finally, spatial attributes (e.g., location) can be characterized as intra-item or inter-item depending upon the learning context.

ERM for inter-item associations is often tested using an associative recognition paradigm, originally used by Humphreys (1976). In the standard version of this test, subjects study unrelated pairs (e.g., "surgeon–arrow"; "lizard–cotton"; "hammer–statue"). At test, some *item–item* pairs are presented that were encoded together at study (*intact pairs*), some pairs are presented in which both units were studied but not together (*recombined pairs*), and some pairs are presented that consist of two new, unstudied units (*novel pairs*). Participants are asked to decide whether the presented pair was seen together previously. *Associative recognition* accuracy is calculated as the difference between correct recognition of intact pairs (i.e., hit rate) and incorrect recognition of recombined pairs (i.e., false-alarm rate). Importantly, both intact and recombined pairs consist of two studied items. Therefore, successful discrimination between intact and recombined pairs cannot be based on memory for individual items, but must be based on memory for the associations formed between individual items at study. In contrast, *item recognition* involves discriminating between items presented at study and those that were not. ERM for intra-item associations (i.e., an item and a feature of that item) is typically tested by having participants study single items (e.g., words) in at least two *fonts* (e.g., Arial or Forte), *locations* (e.g., upper or lower half of the computer screen), *times* (e.g., first or second word list), or *sources* (e.g., a male versus female voice), followed by an item memory and a context memory task. Whereas the item memory task requires participants to indicate which items were presented (i.e., item recognition), the context memory task necessitates selection of how (perceptual RM; source RM), where (spatial RM), or when (temporal RM) the items were presented. Accuracy on these intra-item association (or context memory) tasks is measured with the same procedures as for inter-item associations.

IRM is typically evidenced by priming, a measure of implicit memory that does not require conscious retrieval processes. For example, participants may simply be asked to complete word stems or fragments with the first word that comes to mind, and priming of new associations is seen with facilitated task performance for items presented in the same context as at study, relative to a different context. As with ERM, the associations accessed via implicit retrieval can be either inter- or intra-item. One test of inter-item IRM is speeded reading, in which participants indicate via button press when they have read two words (either alone or embedded within a sentence). In this task, associative priming (IRM) is demonstrated if subjects are faster to read previously paired (i.e., repeated) words or sentences relative to recombined words or sentences. IRM of intra-item associations is inferred if a change in a surface-level feature of an item (e.g., its font or perceptual modality) reduces the magnitude of priming. Finally, eye-tracking procedures have been employed to investigate memory for the relations among elements of prior experiences. The effects of memory on eye-movement behavior can emerge rapidly, changing the nature of visual processing, without requiring verbal reports and without conscious recollection (for a review see Hannula *et al.*, 2010). This aspect of eye-movement data is particularly useful for studying IRM with special populations (e.g., amnesic patients or older adults) because population differences are less likely to be attributed to *explicit contamination*, in which an explicit retrieval strategy may confound the interpretation of a nominally implicit test. In one paradigm that has been used in cognitive neuroscientific research (e.g., Hannula *et al.*, 2010), eye movements are monitored when participants view scenes that are either novel (i.e., not studied during a previous encoding phase), repeated (i.e., unchanged from study phase), or manipulated (i.e., a repeated scene with some features changed, such as the spatial relationship among the elements). Importantly, conditions are counterbalanced across participants such that a manipulated scene for one participant serves as a repeated scene for another participant. In this way, a comparison can be made for viewing the same scene regions across participants for whom the only difference was viewing history. Memory for elements of a stimulus is thought to occur when participants show more fixations to, and transitions into and out of, the critical region where scenes were manipulated versus repeated (Hannula *et al.*, 2010). That is, when participants spend more time viewing changed aspects of a scene it is indicative that they have memory for the prior relationship between scene elements.

## Prefrontal Cortex and Medial Temporal Lobe Contributions to Explicit Relational Memory

This section describes several of the theoretical concepts and empirical findings concerning the neural bases of ERM and IRM. However, only a subset of data is reviewed. Specifically, evidence is drawn from neuropsychological studies of focal lesion patients, as well as functional magnetic resonance imaging (fMRI) and positron emission tomography (PET) studies of healthy individuals. Findings from magneto-encephalography (MEG), electroencephalograms (EEG), single-cell recordings, and event-related potential (ERP) investigations are not reviewed (see Caplan and Glaholt, 2007; Hannula, Federmeier, and Cohen, 2006, for recent examples of electrophysiological investigations). Additionally, an emphasis is placed on the contribution of PFC and MTL to RM, with some discussion of the interaction between these structures and other neural regions. Finally, only some of the many theories that have been proposed about RM are reviewed.

## Prefrontal cortex and explicit relational memory

Broadly speaking, research in cognitive neuroscience suggests that the PFC plays a supervisory role over other brain regions, including the MTL (Miller and Cohen, 2001; Norman and Shallice, 1986), via consciously controlled bias mechanisms (Buckner, 2003; see also Chapter 7). During encoding, the PFC implements the processes that organize input to the MTL, and during retrieval, the PFC mediates search and post-retrieval monitoring processes (Cabeza, 2006; Moscovitch, 1992). In humans, focal lesions to the PFC typically produce larger RM, relative to IM, deficits (Shimamura, 2002; Stuss, Eskes, and Forster, 1994; Wheeler, Stuss, and Tulving, 1995). In monkeys, PFC lesions that lead to RM impairments tend to be in the dorsolateral PFC (dlPFC; for a review see Petrides, 1994), whereas lesions producing IM deficits are often located in the ventromedial PFC (vmPFC; Bachevalier and Mishkin, 1986).

Functional neuroimaging studies investigating the contribution of the PFC to inter-item ERM have utilized several types of stimuli, including *pairs of words* (Badgaiyan, Schacter, and Alpert, 2002; Cabeza, Locantore, and Anderson, 2003; Fletcher, Shallice, and Dolan, 2000; Mottaghy *et al.*, 1999; Park and Rugg, 2011; Prince, Daselaar, and Cabeza, 2005), *face-house pairs* (Ranganath *et al.*, 2004); *face–name pairs* (Sperling *et al.*, 2003; Tsukiura and Cabeza, 2008); *picture pairs* (Achim and Lepage, 2005; Lepage, Brodeur, and Bourgouin, 2003; Park and Rugg, 2008), and *pairs of abstract images* (Bunge, Burrows, and Wagner, 2004). The results of these studies suggest that inter-item RM is associated with activity in left PFC during encoding (Fletcher, Shallice, and Dolan, 2000; Mottaghy *et al.*, 1999; Park and Rugg, 2008, 2011; Prince, Daselaar, and Cabeza, 2005; Sperling *et al.*, 2003), even when the pair members are encoded sequentially (Hales *et al.*, 2009), and during retrieval (Badgaiyan, Schacter, and Alpert, 2002; Bunge, Burrows, and Wagner, 2004; Lepage, Brodeur, and Bourgouin, 2003; Prince, Daselaar, and Cabeza, 2005; Ranganath *et al.*, 2004), although bilateral PFC activity has been observed in at least two retrieval studies using inter-item associations (Achim and Lepage, 2005; Tsukiura and Cabeza, 2008). Left PFC activity has also been observed during functional neuroimaging studies of intra-item ERM. For example, activity in left PFC has been reported during *perceptual RM* (Nolde, Johnson, and D'Esposito, 1998; Ranganath, Johnson, and D'Esposito, 2000), as well as during *source RM* (Cansino *et al.*, 2002; Duarte, Henson, and Graham, 2011; Rugg *et al.*, 1999). However, intra-item ERM has also been associated with right PFC activity, particularly during retrieval of *spatial RM* (Hayes *et al.*, 2004; Henson, Shallice, and Dolan, 1999; Kostopoulos and Petrides, 2003) and *temporal RM* (Cabeza *et al.*, 1997b; Cabeza, Locantore, and Anderson, 2003; Ekstrom *et al.*, 2011; Hayes *et al.*, 2004). Such differences in PFC laterality may reflect the nature of the to-be-remembered information (e.g., perceptual RM versus temporal RM) or the nature of the cognitive processes engaged during the task. For example, Lekeu and colleagues (2002) showed that recognition of bound features was associated with activity in left PFC following *incidental* color encoding and with preferential right PFC activity following *intentional* color encoding. Finally, in addition to the aforementioned laterality differences in PFC, studies have also documented a differential contribution of PFC subregions to memory performance (see also Chapter 7). According to one recent account, the ventrolateral PFC (vlPFC; Brodmann areas [BA] 44, 45, 47/12) and dlPFC (BA 46, 9/46) contribute to memory, but in different ways. Whereas the vlPFC guides selection of goal-relevant, detailed item information, thereby promoting long-term IM, the dlPFC and the vlPFC are jointly recruited to guide the processing of inter-item relational information, promoting long-term RM (Blumenfeld *et al.*, 2011).

## Medial temporal lobe and explicit relational memory

The MTL has a hierarchical organization, whereby information from sensory association cortices are channeled through the parahippocampal region (perirhinal and parahippocampal cortices), to entorhinal cortex, and on to the hippocampus (Squire and Zola-Morgan, 2001; see Chapter 6 for more discussion of MTL anatomy). Although the importance of the hippocampus for memory formation and retrieval has long been established, the surrounding MTL cortex is also cited as playing a part in memory function. To date, the role of the hippocampus and surrounding cortices (perirhinal cortex, parahippocampal cortex, and entorhinal cortex) is a source of ongoing debate. According to the *hippocampal-RM* view, the hippocampus has a critical role in *relating* or binding together the various cognitive, affective, and perceptual components of a learning event into an integrated memory trace, whereas memory for item information (e.g., old/new item recognition performance) can be mediated by the parahippocampal gyrus, particularly perirhinal cortex (Aggleton and Brown, 1999; Brown and Aggleton, 2001; Eichenbaum, Otto, and Cohen, 1994). In contrast, by the *unified-MTL* view, the hippocampus is equally involved in *all* forms of episodic memory, regardless of the demands placed on relational processing (Reed and Squire, 1997; Stark, Bayley, and Squire, 2002; Stark and Squire, 2001, 2003). By this view, a critical factor for eliciting hippocampal activity is not relational processing demands, but rather the strength of a given memory (Wais, 2008, 2011; Wais, Squire, and Wixted, 2010).

Studies of amnesic patients with bilateral damage to the MTL, as well as functional neuroimaging investigations of RM in healthy populations, have provided empirical evidence supporting both theoretical views. Consistent with the hippocampal-RM view, studies of globally amnesic patients have documented a disproportionate deficit in inter-item RM relative to IM (e.g., *word pairs*: Giovanello, Verfaellie, and Keane, 2003; *word pairs and compound words*: Giovanello, Keane, and Verfaellie, 2006; *face-occupation pairs*: Turriziani *et al.*, 2004). Additionally, functional neuroimaging studies have shown greater hippocampal activity during inter-item RM than during IM (*picture pairs*: Achim and Lepage, 2005; Montaldi *et al.*, 1998; *face–name pairs*: Chua *et al.*, 2007; Henke, *et al.*, 1997; *word pairs*: Giovanello, Schnyer, and Verfaellie, 2004), with hippocampal activity shown to increase with greater relational binding demands (Addis and McAndrews, 2006; Giovanello, Schnyer, and Verfaellie, 2009; but see Tendolkar *et al.*, 2007, for an alternative finding with intra-item associations). Moreover, functional neuroimaging investigations of intra-item associations have shown greater hippocampal activity during source RM (Davachi, Mitchell, and Wagner, 2003; Davachi and Wagner, 2002) and perceptual RM (Dougal, Phelps, and Davachi, 2007; Yonelinas *et al.*, 2001) than during IM. Other evidence, however, supports the unified-MTL view. For example, Stark and Squire (2003) reported no disproportionate deficit in RM relative to IM in amnesic patients (see Kirwan, Wixted, and Squire, 2010, for a similar finding). Furthermore, several functional neuroimaging studies have reported no differential contribution of MTL structures to inter-item (Law *et al.*, 2005; Pihlajamäki *et al.*, 2003; Rombouts *et al.*, 1997; Small *et al.*, 2001) or intra-item (Stark and Squire, 2001) RM relative to IM. Rather, a differential contribution of MTL structures to RM has been attributed to differences in memory strength whereby RM reflects stronger memories and IM reflects weaker memories (e.g., Wais, 2008, 2011; Wais, Squire, and Wixted, 2010; Wais *et al.*, 2006).

Other studies have characterized the contribution of MTL cortical structures (entorhinal, perirhinal, and parahippocampal cortices) to RM compared with IM by focusing on the nature of the representations supporting feature versus context information, as well as by distinguishing between different types of binding. For example, Davachi (2006) has proposed that perirhinal cortex mediates the specific visual and conceptual features of objects, whereas parahippocampal cortex supports coding of spatial context. Information from these regions is then channeled to the hippocampus, where domain-general relational representations are formed. Consistent with this view, several studies have reported activity in perirhinal cortex for features of stimuli (Davachi, Mitchell, and Wagner, 2003; Davachi and Wagner, 2002; Staresina and Davachi, 2006, 2008, 2010; Staresina, Duncan, and Davachi, 2011) and parahippocampal activity for spatial context (e.g., scenes: Ekstrom *et al.*, 2011; Staresina, Duncan, and Davachi, 2011; or object location: Sommer *et al.*, 2005). Additionally, studies have reported activity in the hippocampus during object–background binding (e.g., Howard *et al.*, 2011). Such findings are consistent with the view that representational domain is a key factor in determining the involvement of different MTL cortical structures in IM and RM (see also Chapter 10). However, the "binding of item and context" (BIC) model, originally proposed by Eichenbaum, Yonelinas, and Ranganath (2007), and then refined by Diana, Yonelinas, and Ranganath (2007), suggests that there is no simple matching between MTL regions and RM and IM. Rather, the involvement of different MTL regions in these forms of memory depends not only on the mnemonic demands of the task, but also on the type of information to be encoded and retrieved (see also Mayes, Montaldi, and Migo, 2007). Specifically, the BIC model states that recognition of a prior event may involve two mnemonic processes (i.e., familiarity and recollection), each mediated by different neural substrates. *Familiarity* refers to the feeling that an event occurred previously, in the absence of specific associations or contextual details (IM without RM), whereas *recollection* involves retrieval of an event with its specific contextual details (IM and RM). In the BIC model, perirhinal cortex subserves familiarity-based memories, whereas the parahippocampal cortex and hippocampus both mediate recollection-based memories through their role in processing of contextual information and item–context binding, respectively. A key prediction of the BIC model is that when RM can be based on familiarity, performance should be mediated by perirhinal cortex. To date, studies have demonstrated that associative recognition (ERM) can be based on familiarity when items are unitized at encoding (Giovanello, Keane, and Verfaellie, 2006; Quamme, Yonelinas, and Norman, 2007), and that such unitization is supported by perirhinal cortex (Ford, Verfaellie, and Giovanello, 2010; Haskins *et al.*, 2008; but see Staresina and Davachi, 2010, for an alternative finding). Currently, there is no consensus as to the precise roles that MTL regions play in processing these various types of mnemonic information.

Other recent studies of ERM have highlighted the interaction between PFC and MTL regions, as well as the contribution of other neural regions, depending upon the type of information to be encoded or retrieved. Regarding functional connectivity, for example, Staresina, Gray, and Davachi (2009) demonstrated left inferior frontal gyrus–hippocampal interactions during episodic memory for congruous events that had been semantically associated and relationally integrated. Regarding other brain regions, McCormick and colleagues (2010) utilized multivariate analysis methods and showed that hippocampal–parietal networks differ during encoding and retrieval of relational information. Specifically, participants in their study encoded faces while judging the personality of the face, thereby generating relational information; at retrieval, participants viewed faces and made "old/new" followed by remember/know (R/K) judgments, a memory task in which participants are typically instructed to indicate "remember" if they remember the item along with specific contextual details of its occurrence (mapping onto RM), and "know" if they know the item was studied but cannot retrieve any contextual details (mapping onto IM). Structural equation modeling (SEM) revealed a reversal of directionality between the encoding and retrieval phases. At encoding, activation of the left hippocampus had a positive influence on left inferior parietal cortex, whereas during retrieval the reverse pattern was observed (i.e., left inferior parietal cortex positively influenced activity in left hippocampus), underscoring the complexity of the hippocampal–parietal interactions during initial binding and retrieval/reintegration of RM. Kimura *et al.* (2010) also employed network approaches, but in their study investigated the cortical networks that support relational and item-based recency judgments. Whereas relational recency judgments (i.e., retrieval of detailed temporal and relational context) was mediated by left ventral parietal and left parahippocampal regions, item recency judgments (i.e., judgments made based on the difference in familiarity of paired items) was supported by left dorsal parietal and right anterior temporal regions. Furthermore, correlations with resting blood-oxygen-level-dependent (BOLD) signals revealed significant correlations between the ventral parietal and parahippocampal regions, as well between the dorsal parietal and anterior temporal regions.

Finally, other brain regions may contribute to ERM depending on the nature of the stimuli. Park and Rugg (2011) investigated the neural correlates of encoding within- and across-domain inter-item associations. In their study, participants encoded three classes of study pairs, and judged which of the denoted objects fit into the other. Later, participants engaged in a standard associative recognition task, discriminating between intact study pairs and rearranged pairs consisting of two items encoded on two different study trials. Subsequent memory effects (independent of pair type) were observed in the left inferior frontal gyrus (see Park and Rugg, 2008, for a similar PFC finding) and hippocampus (see Holdstock *et al.*, 2010, for a similar hippocampal finding). Of interest, picture–picture pairs elicited activity in material-selective effects in fusiform cortex, whereas word–word pairs elicited activity in material-selective subsequent memory effects in left lateral temporal cortex.

## Age-related neural changes during tasks of ERM

It is generally accepted that ERM deficits are a fundamental aspect of age-related cognitive decline (Cabeza, 2006; Johnson, Hashtroudi, and Lindsay, 1993; Naveh-Benjamin, 2000). Support for this notion comes from behavioral studies demonstrating that older adults are impaired in inter-item ERM (e.g., Naveh-Benjamin, 2000; Old and Naveh-Benjamin, 2008), as well as in several aspects of intra-item or context ERM, including perceptual, spatial, and temporal RM (reviewed by Cabeza, 2006; Kausler, 1994; Old and Naveh-Benjamin, 2008; Spencer and Raz, 1995). Regarding perceptual RM, older adults are impaired in remembering the *letter case*

(Kausler and Puckett, 1980), *voice* (Kausler and Puckett, 1981), or *font* (Naveh-Benjamin, 2000) in which information was previously presented. In terms of spatial RM, older adults are impaired in remembering the location of objects (Park, Puglisi, and Lutz, 1982; Park, Puglisi, and Sovacool, 1983) or words (Denney, Dew, and Kihlstrom, 1992) on a screen, buildings and landmarks on a tourist map (Light and Zelinksi, 1983; Perlmutter al., 1981), and objects in a room (Uttl and Graf, 1993). Finally, regarding temporal RM, older adults are impaired in order recall (Kausler, Salthouse, and Saults, 1988; Naveh-Benjamin, 1990), recency (McCormack, 1982), and list-section discrimination (McCormack, 1981).

Two prominent theoretical views have been proposed to account for age-related deficits in ERM. Whereas the *binding deficit* view suggests that older adults have a fundamental deficit in linking or integrating the separate elements of a to-be-remembered episode (Bayen, Phelps, and Spaniol, 2000; Burke and Light, 1981; Chalfonte and Johnson, 1996; Lyle, Bloise, and Johnson, 2006; Mitchell *et al.*, 2000; Naveh-Benjamin, 2000; Ryan *et al.*, 2007), the *control deficit* view asserts that older adults experience more generalized age-related declines in top-down, controlled retrieval processes, including the strategic manipulation, organization, or evaluation of features or contextual attributes, as well as controlled attention, maintenance of memory goals, and conscious monitoring of retrieval accuracies (Anderson and Craik, 2000; Craik, 1986; Craik and Byrd, 1982; Dew and Giovanello, 2010; Jennings and Jacoby, 1993; Light *et al.*, 2000; Moscovitch and Winocur, 1995; Smith *et al.*, 1998).

In general, functional neuroimaging studies of memory in healthy older adults can contribute to this debate because, as described in previous sections, binding-related operations are largely seated in the MTL, and control-related operations in PFC. The use of neuroimaging to clarify age-related RM, however, is complicated by the fact that older adults frequently show general alterations in neural activity (see Cabeza, 2006; Grady, 2008; Reuter-Lorenz and Park, 2010 for a general discussion of relevant issues). Such alterations have taken the form of "under-recruitment" (i.e., failures to recruit specific brain regions to the same extent as young adults) or "non-selective recruitment" (i.e., recruitment of brain regions engaged beyond those of young adults), particularly when tasks place strong demands on relational processing.

Some evidence suggests that age-related declines in ERM may be linked to structural and functional changes in PFC. The *frontal aging hypothesis* suggests that age-related deficits are primarily due to PFC dysfunction (Dempster, 1992; Moscovitch and Winocur, 1995; West, 1996). Consistent with this view, quantitative structural MRI studies of the aging brain consistently demonstrate selective frontal atrophy (Coffey *et al.*, 1998; Convit *et al.*, 2001; Cowell *et al.*, 1994; Gur *et al.*, 2002; Raz *et al.*, 1997), with the frontal lobes showing the steepest rate of age-related atrophy (Pfefferbaum *et al.*, 1998; Raz *et al.*, 2005; Resnick *et al.*, 2003), particularly inferior frontal subregions (Resnick, *et al.*, 2003), and this atrophy corresponds to cognitive deficits (e.g., Gunning-Dixon and Raz, 2003). Additional evidence linking age-related RM deficits with PFC dysfunction comes from functional neuroimaging data showing age-related decreases in PFC during tasks of ERM. During ERM encoding, age-related decreases in PFC activity have been observed during inter-item RM (e.g., word pairs: Cabeza *et al.*, 1997a; Kim and Giovanello, 2011), perceptual RM (Iidaka *et al.*, 2001), spatial RM (Mitchell *et al.*, 2000), and source RM (Dennis *et al.*, 2008). For example, one study investigated whether a reduction in attentional resources for processing relational information (i.e., *relational attention*) underlies age-related RM deficits (Kim and Giovanello, 2011). Using fMRI, we examined whether the effect of reduced attentional resources for processing of relational information is similar to that observed in aging at both behavioral and neural levels. To do so, we utilized a divided attention task at encoding to deplete attentional resources in the young adults group. The behavioral results showed that reduced attentional resources for relational information during encoding equated young adults' RM performance to that of older adults who had encoded the information under full attention conditions. Furthermore, the fMRI results demonstrated that aging, as well as reductions in relational attention in young adults, significantly reduced activity in brain areas associated with successful RM formation, namely, the vlPFC and dlPFC, superior and inferior parietal regions, and MTL regions. That is, experimentally depleting attentional resources for relational information in young adults yielded the same patterns of behavioral performance and neural activity as that observed in the older adults. Such converging evidence from behavioral and neuroimaging studies suggests that a reduction in attentional resources for relational information is a critical factor for the RM deficit observed in aging.

During ERM retrieval, age-related changes in PFC activity have also been observed during inter-item RM (e.g., Cabeza *et al.*, 1997a, 2002; Giovanello and Schacter, 2012), and temporal RM (Cabeza *et al.*, 2000, 2002), with some studies showing age-related decreases in activity in the PFC hemisphere activated by young adults but more activity in the contralateral hemisphere. For example, Cabeza and colleagues (1997a) scanned participants while they recalled word pairs and found age-related decreases in right PFC activity. Additionally, older adults showed activation in left vlPFC that was not displayed by young adults. As a result, PFC activity during RM retrieval was unilateral for young adults and bilateral for older adults – the pattern thought to reflect "non-selective" neural activity.

Age-related declines in MTL structure and function have been also documented, and this decline is associated with impaired RM performance. Regions within the MTL (e.g., entorhinal cortex, hippocampus, and parahippocampal gyrus) undergo age-related atrophic changes, with the hippocampus in particular showing substantial atrophy (Raz *et al.*, 2005). Persson and colleagues (2006) demonstrated reduced hippocampal volume in a group of older adults whose episodic memory performance declined over time compared to that of a group whose memory performance remained stable. More recently, Yonelinas and colleagues (2007) showed that reductions in hippocampal volume resulted in decreased recollection of episodic memories. The link between age-related ERM deficits and MTL decline also is supported by age-related fMRI decreases in MTL activity during encoding (e.g., Daselaar *et al.*, 2003; Mitchell *et al.*, 2000). For example, Dennis *et al.* (2008) examined the effects of aging on the neural correlates of successful IM and source RM encoding and showed age-related reductions in both hippocampal and prefrontal regions that were more pronounced for source RM than for IM. Similar age-related reductions in hippocampal activity have been reported at retrieval (Daselaar *et al.*, 2006; Giovanello and Schacter, 2012; Tsukiura *et al.*, 2011). For example, Tsukiura *et al.* (2011) utilized face–name and face–job pairs and examined successful ERM. At encoding, participants viewed unfamiliar faces, each paired with a job title and name. At retrieval (scanned), each learned face was presented with two job titles or two names. The participants' task was to choose the correct job title or name. Retrieval success activity was identified by comparing retrieval-phase activity for hits versus misses in the name and job-title conditions. The results showed significant activity in the hippocampus for relational retrieval of both names and titles, and the activity was greater in the younger adults than older adults. Additionally, functional connectivity analyses revealed that hippocampal–anterior temporal lobe connections were stronger in younger than older adults during both retrieval tasks. More recently, Giovanello and Schacter (2012) tested the hypothesis that healthy older adults would show age-related changes in neural recruitment when the experimental task required retrieval of specific, detailed relational information (i.e., RM). At study, participants viewed two nouns and were instructed to covertly generate a sentence that related the words. At retrieval, fMRI data were acquired during RM and IM tasks. In the RM task, participants indicated whether the two words were previously seen together. In the IM task, participants indicated whether both items of a pair were previously seen. In young adults, left posterior vlPFC and bilateral hippocampal activity was modulated by the extent to which the retrieval task depended on relational processing (i.e., activity was greater during RM than during IM). In older adults, activity in these regions was equivalent for IM and RM conditions, suggesting an age-related change in the recruitment of vlPFC and hippocampal regions during RM.

## Prefrontal Cortex and Medial Temporal Lobe Contributions to Implicit Relational Memory

### Prefrontal cortex and implicit relational memory

Relative to ERM, there is considerably less evidence of a contribution of PFC to IRM, which is consistent with the role of PFC in strategic, goal-directed behaviors that are not recruited during implicit forms of memory, including IRM. Indeed, the presence of PFC activity during task performance may actually be problematic for interpreting that a given mnemonic process is implicit, rather than explicit (see Chapter 3). A recent paper by Hannula and Ranganath (2008) highlights the notion that PFC activity, even during an IRM task, is indicative of ERM. Their study assessed IRM for novel scene–face pairings using fMRI with concurrent indirect, eye-movement measures. Participants encoded several scene–face pairs and were later shown previously studied scenes and instructed to use the scene as a cue to retrieve the associated face. Next, a three-face display was superimposed on the previously studied scenes. Results showed that activity in the hippocampus during presentation of the scene cue predicted subsequent viewing of the associated face during the three-face test display, *even* when participants failed to explicitly identify the match. In contrast, activity in PFC regions was sensitive to subsequent response *accuracy* but did not predict viewing of matching faces on incorrect trials. Finally, functional connectivity between lateral PFC and hippocampus was increased during presentation of the three-face test display on correct as compared to incorrect trials. These results suggest that hippocampal activity may support the expression of IRM, but that recruitment of PFC is required to use this information to guide overt behavior (ERM).

### Medial temporal lobe and implicit relational memory

Some of the strongest evidence that MTL structures (particularly the hippocampus) support RM binding, rather than episodic memory per se, comes from studies of neuropsychological patients (Hannula and Greene, 2012; Olsen *et al.*, 2012). For example, Ryan *et al.* (2000) utilized eye-tracking procedures and operationalized relational information by manipulating the spatial location of a critical item within a picture. At encoding, control participants and amnesic patients viewed scenes. At test, a repetition priming effect was found both for normal controls and for the amnesic patients, with fewer fixations for repeated than for novel scenes. Only the normal controls showed the relational manipulation effect, however, in which the critical region in manipulated scenes received more fixations than the same regions in repeated or novel scenes. Amnesic individuals showed no difference in these fixations. Similarly, Yang *et al.* (2003) utilized a perceptual identification task to investigate novel inter-item (word–word) and intra-item (color–word) RM in patients with MTL damage. Despite normal priming of individual items (studied versus novel), relative to control participants, the amnesic patients failed to show better identification of intact versus recombined word–word or color–word pairs, indicating a role of the MTL in IRM.

Although there have been few fMRI investigations of IRM, findings as of yet have been consistent with neuropsychological studies that posit a special role of MTL structures in relational memory. In a study of non-conscious inter-item RM, Henke *et al.* (2003) asked subjects to view face–profession pairs that were flashed subliminally (i.e., below the threshold of conscious awareness) between visual masks. At test, subjects were asked to indicate whether the general semantic category of each face's profession had been an artist or an academic. Accuracy for the categories was at chance, but subjects were faster to make correct guesses relative to incorrect guesses. On control trials, for which a profession was assigned to each face but was not presented to the participants, there was no reaction time (RT) difference between correct and incorrect guesses. The RT difference for correct and incorrect face–profession pairs was taken as a measure of unaware semantic associative retrieval (IRM). Neural activity associated with this contrast revealed increases in bilateral hippocampus, as well as right perirhinal cortex. The involvement of these MTL regions coupled with the direction of activity – increases, rather than decreases in activity, which is the prototypical neural signature of item priming – was thus fundamentally different from the neural basis of item priming. Henke and colleagues extended these findings (Degonda *et al.*, 2005), and showed increased activity in anterior hippocampus and right perirhinal cortex during subliminal (non-conscious) associative encoding.

However, findings from Yang *et al.* (2008) conflict with findings from Henke and colleagues (Degonda *et al.*, 2005; Henke *et al.*, 2003). At encoding, subjects viewed two Chinese characters (familiar word stimuli for the subjects) and judged their orthographic similarity. The maximum amount of time allotted to each subject for each encoding trial was set such that it would yield only 20–40% correct on a subsequent recognition test, thus precluding the possibility of explicit contamination. The implicit test measured reaction time to reading intact (presented together), recombined (presented at study but not together), and new character pairs. IRM was defined as the overlap in neural activations for intact–recombined and intact–new contrasts. ERM was measured as neural activity for correct old responses (hits) minus correct recombined responses (correct rejections). Bilateral hippocampus and parahippocampal cortex were active during the ERM. However, the hippocampus was not involved in IRM, and the direction of activity for adjacent MTL structures was the opposite from what Henke *et al.* (2003) had found: IRM was correlated with *decreased* activity in right parahippocampal cortex (PHC), as well as anterior cingulate cortex, inferior frontal gyrus, and occipital cortex.

It is unclear what accounts for the divergent findings between Henke *et al.* (2003) and Yang *et al.* (2008). Yang *et al.* questioned whether the active involvement of the hippocampus found by Henke *et al.* may have resulted from explicit processing. Indeed, while the prototypical neural signature of priming is a reduction in activity, the RT difference for correct relative to incorrect guesses found by Henke *et al.* was associated with increased neural activity, more typical of explicit retrieval. However, the chance-level accuracy on the retrieval task used by Henke *et al.* (2003), coupled with the fact that stimuli were presented below the level of awareness at encoding, makes the possibility of explicit contamination unlikely, if not impossible. An alternative possibility is that the difference between Henke *et al.* (2003) and Yang *et al.* (2008) is a reflection of different kinds of relational information. Specifically, it is possible that the hippocampus and adjacent MTL structures are differentially engaged during implicit retrieval of conceptual (Henke *et al.*) versus perceptual (Yang *et al.*) associations. There is evidence from the explicit memory literature that a differential network of neural regions is activated during semantic versus perceptual associative retrieval. For example, Prince, Daselaar, and Cabeza (2005) found that while successful explicit retrieval of inter-item RM (word–word) and perceptual intra-item RM (word–font) both involved the hippocampus, semantic inter-item RM also involved left ventrolateral PFC, while perceptual RM involved right posterior para-hippocampal gyrus, left occipitotemporal cortex, and bilateral parietal cortex. To our knowledge, there is no direct evidence as to whether implicit retrieval of conceptual and perceptual associations may engage different neural regions, or even elicit a different direction of neural response.

Another task that has been utilized to investigate the neural correlates of IRM is sequence learning. For example, Schendan and her colleagues (2003) utilized fMRI while participants performed a serial reaction time task (SRTT) under implicit versus explicit learning conditions. In the SRTT, a color-filled square (at one of four possible locations) cued a key press at that location. On some SRTT blocks, a sequence of locations *repeated*, while on other blocks, new sequences of *random* locations were shown. For implicit learning, participants were naïve to the repeated location pattern, whereas for explicit learning participants memorized a repeating sequence. The fMRI analyses comparing repeating learning blocks with random/novel sequence blocks revealed activity in frontal, parietal, and striatal regions observed in prior SRTT studies. Of importance, however, the MTL activity observed in the study occurred under both implicit and explicit SRTT learning. Additionally, activity in the hippocampus and related cortices was observed during high-order sequence learning (operationalized in this study as learning among three or more consecutive locations) under both implicit and explicit learning conditions, regardless of conscious awareness of sequence knowledge.

Finally, a recent study by Reber and colleagues (2012) utilized a relational inference task, typically employed to assess ERM (see section on *Medial temporal lobe and explicit relational memory*, above), but in their study premise (word) pairs were presented subliminally. Specifically, in unique subliminal episodes word pairs were presented that either overlapped with another word pair (e.g., "winter–red"; "red–computer") or not. Behaviorally, the effects of unconscious (implicit) relational inference emerged in the reaction time data recorded during unconscious encoding and in the outcome of decisions made one minute later at test, when the participants were asked to judge the relatedness of two supraliminal words (i.e., words presented above the threshold of awareness). Importantly, these words were either episodically related through a common word, such as "red" (e.g., "winter–computer"), or not. At the neural level, hippocampal activity increased during unconscious encoding of overlapping versus non-overlapping word pairs, as well as during the unconscious retrieval of episodically related (versus unrelated) word pairs. Remarkably, hippocampal activity during unconscious encoding predicted the outcome of the decision made a test, suggest that unconscious inference may influence decision making in new situations. Taken together, the findings reviewed in this section suggest that, in contrast to PFC regions, the MTL is involved in RM regardless of conscious awareness of the memory representations that are formed or retrieved.

## Age-related neural changes during tasks of IRM

To date, there have been very few studies on IRM in aging using techniques from cognitive neuroscience, which is somewhat surprising, given the usefulness of IRM approaches for distinguishing between binding and control-related operations. That is, although age-related binding deficits would be evidenced by both ERM and IRM, age-related control deficits would predict declines in ERM but not IRM. Although work in this area will likely continue to grow, currently there is mixed evidence as to the mechanism underlying age-related RM deficits. Using a speeded recognition task, Trott *et al.* (1999) showed age-equivalent associative priming (behaviorally) despite large decrements on the explicit source judgment. The timing of brain activity as measured by ERPs showed no age differences on the early-onset speeded old/new judgment, but age-related differences emerged in the late-onset, long-duration, frontally oriented activity that was associated with the source judgment. These results were interpreted in line with Moscovitch's (1992) component process model, in which the earlier old/new effect could be associated with a MTL-mediated, automatic, non-strategic judgment, and the later old/new effect could be associated with a PFC-mediated, strategic, effortful search or retrieval of source information.

More recent cognitive neuroscientific studies of IRM in aging have utilized variations of the SRTT (e.g., Bennett *et al.*, 2011; Dennis and Cabeza, 2011) or the probabilistic triplets learning task (e.g., Simon *et al.*, 2012), tasks which tend to recruit the striatum. For example, Dennis and Cabeza (2011) utilized fMRI to investigate age differences in the neural correlates of explicit learning (via encoding during a semantic categorization task) and implicit learning (via a serial reaction time task). Although there were no significant age-related behavioral effects, age-related differences in neural activity were observed. Specifically, young adults recruited the MTL during explicit learning and the striatum during implicit learning, and both activations were significantly reduced in older adults. Additionally, older adults recruited the MTL during implicit learning, and this activity was significantly greater in older adults relative to young adults. Indeed, a significant task-by-age interaction was observed such that young adults preferentially recruited the MTL during explicit learning and the striatum during implicit learning, whereas older adults showed no preferential recruitment for either task. Such results demonstrate that the age-related pattern of neural dedifferentiation can occur in both ERM and IRM. In another study using the SRTT, Bennett and colleagues (2011) showed that white matter integrity correlated with IRM in aging. In their study, diffusion tensor imaging (DTI) tractography was used to reconstruct white matter connections between gray matter regions, and integrity of these tracts was related to SRTT learning in young and older adults. Both age groups showed significant sequence learning (i.e., better performance on predictable, frequently occurring sequences versus less frequent sequences), but with an age-related difference apparent in the late learning stage. Neurally, caudate–dlPFC and hippocampal–dlPFC tract integrity were related to SRTT learning. These brain–behavior relationships did not differ significantly between the age groups. Notably, age-related decreases in caudate–dlPFC tract integrity mediated age differences in late-stage sequence learning.

Finally, Simon and colleagues (2012) assessed age-related differences in IRM utilizing a probabilistic triplets learning task. In this task, participants responded only to the third (target) stimulus in sequences of three stimuli (triplets) by pressing a corresponding key. Although participants were unaware, the location of the first stimulus predicted one target location on 80% of the trials and another target location on 20% of the trials. Both young and older adults learned the associations, although age-related differences emerged with practice. Learning at the neural level was examined by identifying regions that showed greater response to triplets that occurred more frequently. Although both age groups recruited the hippocampus early in the task, with training, the younger adults recruited the caudate whereas older adults continued to recruit the hippocampus. This neural activity appears to have allowed older adults to perform at young-adult levels early in the task, but not later, when the older group failed to recruit the caudate. These findings add to prior evidence indicating that IRM is supported by distinct brain networks in young and older adults.

## Concluding Comments

In conclusion, human lesion studies and functional neuroimaging investigations have provided a wealth of knowledge regarding the cognitive processes and neural mechanisms that mediate relational memory. Such studies have shown that ERM depends predominantly on the PFC and MTL, as well as the interactions between these regions. Studies of IRM, including those utilizing subliminal presentation of stimuli, sequence learning, or eye-tracking measures, suggest that MTL regions contribute to performance, regardless of the explicit demands posed on relational memory. In contrast, the observation of PFC activity during tasks of IRM may reflect the engagement of ERM processes (e.g., conscious, intentional retrieval that guides overt behavior). Future studies are needed to address this issue. Additionally, future studies that combine methodologies (e.g., measuring EEG in the MRI scanner) or that relate different types of neuroscientific measures (e.g., fMRI-based MTL activations and EEG-based gamma oscillations) will provide important clues regarding the contribution of PFC and MTL to ERM and IRM. Finally, considerable emphasis has been placed on elucidating the neural processes involved in relational memory, as relational memory is more sensitive than item memory to the mnemonic changes observed in healthy aging. Future studies using newer statistical analyses such as functional connectivity, multi-voxel pattern analysis (MVPA; see Chapters 2 and 6) and structure–function relationships (e.g., diffusion tensor imaging) will enhance our knowledge of brain interactions and provide additional insight into the different possible mechanisms that decline in healthy aging.

# References

Achim, A.M., and Lepage, M. (2005). Neural correlates of memory for items and for associations: an event-related functional magnetic resonance imaging study. *Journal of Cognitive Neuroscience*, 17 (4), 652–667.

Addis, D.R., and McAndrews, M.P. (2006). Prefrontal and hippocampal contributions to the generation and binding of semantic associations during successful encoding. *NeuroImage*, 33 (4), 1194–1206.

Aggleton, J.P., and Brown, M.W. (1999). Episodic memory, amnesia, and the hippocampal–anterior thalamic axis. *Behavioral and Brain Sciences*, 22 (3), 425–444.

Anderson, N.D., and Craik, F.I.M. (2000). Memory in the aging brain. In *The Oxford Handbook of Memory* (ed. E. Tulving and F.I.M. Craik). New York, NY: Oxford University Press.

Bachevalier, J., and Mishkin, M. (1986). Visual recognition impairment follows ventromedial but not dorsolateral prefrontal lesions in monkeys. *Behavioural Brain Research*, 20 (3), 249–261.

Badgaiyan, R.D., Schacter, D.L., and Alpert, N.M. (2002). Retrieval of relational information: a role for the left inferior prefrontal cortex. *NeuroImage*, 17 (1), 393–400.

Bayen, U.J., Phelps, M.P., and Spaniol, J. (2000). Age-related differences in the use of contextual information in recognition memory: a global matching approach. *Journals of Gerontology, Series B: Psychological Sciences and Social Sciences*, 55 (3), 131–141.

Bennett, I.J., Madden, D.J., Vaidya, C.J., *et al.* (2011). White matter integrity correlates of implicit sequence learning in healthy aging. *Neurobiology of Aging*, 32 (12), 2317.e1–e12.

Blumenfeld, R.S., Parks, C.M., Yonelinas, A.P., and Ranganath, C. (2011). Putting the pieces together: the role of dorsolateral prefrontal cortex in relational memory encoding. *Journal of Cognitive Neuroscience*, 23 (1), 257–265.

Brown, M.W., and Aggleton, J.P. (2001). Recognition memory: what are the roles of the perirhinal cortex and hippocampus? *Nature Reviews Neuroscience*, 2 (1), 51–61.

Buckner, R.L. (2003). Functional–anatomic correlates of control processes in memory. *Journal of Neuroscience*, 23 (10), 3999–4004.

Bunge, S., Burrows, B., and Wagner, A. (2004). Prefrontal and hippocampal contributions to visual associative recognition: interactions between cognitive control and episodic retrieval. *Brain and Cognition*, 56 (2), 141–152.

Burke, D.M., and Light, L.L. (1981). Memory and aging: the role of retrieval processes. *Psychological Bulletin*, 90 (3), 513–514.

Cabeza, R. (2006). Prefrontal and medial temporal contributions to relational memory in young and older adults. In *Binding in Human Memory: a Neurocognitive Approach* (ed. D. Zimmer, A. Mecklinger, and U. Lindenberger). New York, NY: Oxford University Press, pp. 595–626.

Cabeza, R., Anderson, N.D., Houle, S., *et al.* (2000). Age-related differences in neural activity during item and temporal-order memory retrieval: A positron emission tomography study. *Journal of Cognitive Neuroscience*, 12 (1), 197–206.

Cabeza, R., Anderson, N.D., Locantore, J.K., and McIntosh, A.R. (2002). Aging gracefully: compensatory brain activity in high-performing older adults. *NeuroImage*, 17 (3), 1394–1402.

Cabeza, R., Grady, C.L., Nyberg, L., *et al.* (1997a). Age-related differences in neural activity during memory encoding and retrieval: a positron emission tomography study. *Journal of Neuroscience*, 17 (1), 391–400.

Cabeza, R., Locantore, J.K., and Anderson, N.D. (2003). Lateralization of prefrontal activity during episodic memory retrieval: evidence for the production-monitoring hypothesis. *Journal of Cognitive Neuroscience*, 15 (2), 249–259.

Cabeza, R., Mangels, J., Nyberg, L., *et al.* (1997b). Brain regions differentially involved in remembering what and when: a PET study. *Neuron*, 19 (4), 863–870.

Cansino, S., Maquet, P., Dolan, R.J., and Rugg, M.D. (2002). Brain activity underlying encoding and retrieval of source memory. *Cerebral Cortex*, 12 (10), 1048–1056.

Caplan, J.B., and Glaholt, M.G. (2007). The roles of EEG oscillations in learning relational information. *NeuroImage*, 38 (3), 604–616.

Chalfonte, B.L., and Johnson, M.K. (1996). Feature memory and binding in young and older adults. *Memory and Cognition*, 24, 403–416.

Chua, E.F., Schacter, D.L., Rand-Giovannetti, E., and Sperling, R.A. (2007). Evidence for a specific role of the anterior hippocampal region in successful associative encoding. *Hippocampus*, 17 (11), 1071–1080.

Coffey, C.E., Lucke, J.F., Saxton, J.A., *et al.* (1998). Sex differences in brain aging: a quantitative magnetic resonance imaging study. *Archives of Neurology*, 55 (2), 169–179.

Convit, A., Wolf, O.T., de Leon, M.J., *et al.* (2001). Volumetric analysis of the pre-frontal regions: findings in aging and schizophrenia. *Psychiatry Research: Neuroimaging*, 107 (2), 61–73.

Cowell, P.E., Turetsky, B.I., Gur, R.C., *et al.* (1994). Sex differences in aging of the human frontal and temporal lobes. *Journal of Neuroscience*, 14 (8), 4748–4755.

Craik, F.I.M. (1986). A functional account of age differences in memory. In *Human Memory and Cognitive Capabilities, Mechanisms, and Performances* (ed. F. Klix and H. Hagendorf). Amsterdam: North-Holland, pp. 409–422.

Craik, F.I.M., and Byrd, M. (1982). Aging and cognitive deficits: The role of attentional resources. In *Aging and Cognitive Processes* (ed. F.I.M. Craik and S. Trehub). New York, NY: Plenum Press, pp. 199–211.

Daselaar, S.M., Fleck, M.S., Dobbins, I.G., *et al.* (2006). Effects of healthy aging on hippocampal and rhinal memory functions: an event-related fMRI study. *Cerebral Cortex*, 16 (12), 1771–1782.

Daselaar, S.M., Veltman, D.J., Rombouts, S.A., *et al.* (2003). Deep processing activates the medial temporal lobe in young but not in old adults. *Neurobiology of Aging* 24 (7), 1005–1011.

Davachi, L. (2006). Item, context and relational episodic encoding in humans. *Current Opinion in Neurobiology*, 16 (6), 693–700.

Davachi, L., Mitchell, J.P., and Wagner, A.D. (2003). Multiple routes to memory: distinct medial temporal lobe processes build item and source memories. *Proceedings of the National Academy of Sciences of the USA*, 100 (4), 2157–2162.

Davachi, L., and Wagner, A.D. (2002). Hippocampal contributions to episodic encoding: insights from relational and item-based learning. *Journal of Neurophysiology*, 88 (2), 982–990.

Degonda, N., Mondadori, C.R., Bosshardt, S., *et al.* (2005). Implicit associative learning engages the hippocampus and interacts with explicit associative learning. *Neuron*, 46 (3), 505–520.

Dempster, F.N. (1992). The rise and fall of the inhibitory mechanism: toward a unified theory of cognitive development and aging. *Developmental Review*, 12 (1), 45–75.

Denney, N.W., Dew, J.R., and Kihlstrom, J.F. (1992). An adult developmental study of the encoding of spatial location. *Experimental Aging Research*, 18 (1), 25–32.

Dennis, N.A., and Cabeza, R. (2011). Age-related dedifferentiation of learning systems: an fMRI study of implicit and explicit learning. *Neurobiology of Aging*, 32 (12), 2318.e17–e30.

Dennis, N.A., Hayes, S.M., Prince, S.E., *et al.* (2008). Effects of aging on the neural correlates of successful item and source memory encoding. *Journal of Experimental Psychology: Learning, Memory, and Cognition*, 34 (4), 791–808.

Dew, I.T.Z. and Giovanello, K.S. (2010). Differential age effects for implicit and explicit associative memory. *Psychology and Aging*, 25, 911–921.

Diana, R.A., Yonelinas, A.P., and Ranganath, C. (2007). Imaging recollection and familiarity in the medial temporal lobe: a three-component model. *Trends in Cognitive Sciences*, 11 (9), 379–386.

Dougal, S., Phelps, E.A., and Davachi, L. (2007). The role of medial temporal lobe in item recognition and source recollection of emotional stimuli. *Cognitive, Affective, and Behavioral Neuroscience*, 7 (3), 233–242.

Duarte, A., Henson, R.N., and Graham, K.S. (2011). Stimulus content and the neural correlates of source memory. *Brain Research*, 1373, 110–123.

Eichenbaum, H., Otto, T., and Cohen, N.J. (1994). Two functional components of the hippocampal memory system. *Behavioral and Brain Sciences*, 17 (3), 449–471.

Eichenbaum, H., Yonelinas, A., and Ranganath, C. (2007). The medial temporal lobe and recognition memory. *Annual Review of Neuroscience*, 30, 123–152.

Ekstrom, A.D., Copara, M.S., Isham, E.A., *et al.* (2011). Dissociable networks involved in spatial and temporal order source retrieval. *NeuroImage*, 56 (3), 1803–1813.

Fletcher, P.C., Shallice, T., and Dolan, R.J. (2000). Sculpting the response space: an account of left prefrontal activation at encoding. *NeuroImage*, 12 (4), 404–417.

Ford, J.H., Verfaellie, M., and Giovanello, K.S. (2010). Neural correlates of familiarity-based associative retrieval. *Neuropsychologia*, 48 (10), 3019–3025.

Giovanello, K.S., Keane, M.M., and Verfaellie, M. (2006). The contribution of familiarity to associative memory in amnesia. *Neuropsychologia*, 44 (10), 1859–1865.

Giovanello, K.S., and Schacter, D.L. (2012). Reduced specificity of hippocampal and posterior ventrolateral prefrontal activity during relational retrieval in normal aging. *Journal of Cognitive Neuroscience*, 24 (1), 159–170.

Giovanello, K.S., Schnyer, D., and Verfaellie, M. (2009). Distinct hippocampal regions make unique contributions to relational memory. *Hippocampus*, 19 (2), 111–117.

Giovanello, K.S., Schnyer, D.M., and Verfaellie, M. (2004). A critical role for the anterior hippocampus in relational memory: evidence from an fMRI study comparing associative and item recognition. *Hippocampus*, 14 (1), 5–8.

Giovanello, K.S., Verfaellie, M., and Keane, M.M. (2003). Disproportionate deficit in associative recognition relative to item recognition in global amnesia. *Cognitive, Affective, and Behavioral Neuroscience*, 3 (3), 186–194.

Grady, C.L. (2008). Cognitive neuroscience of aging. *Annals of the New York Academy of Sciences*, 1124 (1), 127–144.

Gunning-Dixon, F.M., and Raz, N. (2003). Neuroanatomical correlates of selected executive functions in middle-aged and older adults: a prospective MRI study. *Neuropsychologia*, 41 (14), 1929–1941.

Gur, R.C., Gunning-Dixon, F., Bilker, W.B., and Gur, R.E. (2002). Sex differences in temporo-limbic and frontal brain volumes of healthy adults. *Cerebral Cortex*, 12 (9), 998–1003.

Hales, J.B., Israel, S.L., Swann, N.C., and Brewer, J.B. (2009). Dissociation of frontal and medial temporal lobe activity in maintenance and binding of sequentially presented paired associates. *Journal of Cognitive Neuroscience*, 21 (7), 1244–1254.

Hannula, D.E., Althoff, R.R., Warren, D.E., *et al.* (2010). Worth a glance: using eye movements to investigate the cognitive neuroscience of memory. *Frontiers in Human Neuroscience*, 4, 166.

Hannula, D.E., Federmeier, K.D., and Cohen, N.J. (2006). Event-related potential signatures of relational memory. *Journal of Cognitive Neuroscience* 18 (11), 1863–1876.

Hannula, D.E., and Greene, A.J. (2012). The hippocampus reevaluated in unconscious learning and memory: at a tipping point? *Frontiers in Human Neuroscience*, 6, 80.

Hannula, D.E., and Ranganath, C. (2008). Medial temporal lobe activity predicts successful relational memory binding. *Journal of Neuroscience*, 28 (1), 116–124.

Haskins, A.L., Yonelinas, A.P., Quamme, J.R., and Ranganath, C. (2008). Perirhinal cortex supports encoding and familiarity-based recognition of novel associations. *Neuron*, 59 (4), 554–560.

Hayes, S.M., Ryan, L., Schnyer, D.M., and Nadel, L. (2004). An fMRI study of episodic memory: retrieval of object, spatial, and temporal information. *Behavioral Neuroscience*, 118 (5), 885–896. doi: 10.1037/0735-7044.118.5.885.

Henke, K., Buck, A., Weber, B., and Wieser, H.G. (1997). Human hippocampus establishes associations in memory. *Hippocampus*, 7 (3), 249–256.

Henke, K., Mondadori, C.R., Treyer, V., *et al.* (2003). Nonconscious formation and reactivation of semantic associations by way of the medial temporal lobe. *Neuropsychologia*, 41 (8), 863–876.

Henson, R., Shallice, T., and Dolan, R. (1999). Right prefrontal cortex and episodic memory retrieval: a functional MRI test of the monitoring hypothesis. *Brain*, 122 (7), 1367–1381.

Holdstock, J., Crane, J., Bachorowski, J.-A., and Milner, B. (2010). Equivalent activation of the hippocampus by face–face and face–laugh paired associate learning and recognition. *Neuropsychologia*, 48 (13), 3757–3771.

Howard L.R., Kumaran, D., Ólafsdóttir, H.F., and Spiers, H.J. (2011). Equivalent activation of the hippocampus by face–face and face–laugh paired associate learning and recognition. *Journal of Neuroscience*, 31, 5253–5261

Humphreys, M.S. (1976). Relational information and the context effect in recognition memory. *Memory and Cognition*, 4 (2), 221–232.

Iidaka, T., Sadato, N., Yamada, H., *et al.* (2001). An fMRI study of the functional neuroanatomy of picture encoding in younger and older adults. *Cognitive Brain Research*, 11 (1), 1–11.

Jennings, J.M., and Jacoby, L.L. (1993). Automatic versus intentional uses of memory: aging, attention, and control. *Psychology and Aging*, 8 (2), 283–293.

Johnson, M.K., Hashtroudi, S., and Lindsay, D.S. (1993). Source monitoring. *Psychological Bulletin*, 114 (1), 3–28.

Kausler, D.H. (1994). *Learning and Memory in Normal Aging*. New York, NY: Academic Press.

Kausler, D.H., and Puckett, J.M. (1980). Adult age differences in recognition memory for a nonsemantic attribute. *Experimental Aging Research*, 6 (4), 349–355.

Kausler, D.H., and Puckett, J.M. (1981). Adult age differences in memory for sex of voice. *Journal of Gerontology*, 36 (1), 44–50.

Kausler, D.H., Salthouse, T.A., and Saults, J.S. (1988). Temporal memory over the adult lifespan. *American Journal of Psychology*, 101 (2), 207–215.

Kim, S.-Y., and Giovanello, K.S. (2011). The effects of attention on age-related memory deficits: fMRI evidence from a novel attentional manipulation. *Journal of Cognitive Neuroscience*, 23, 3637–3656.

Kimura, H.M., Hirose, S., Kunimatsu, A., *et al.* (2010). Differential temporo-parietal cortical networks that support relational and item-based recency judgments. *NeuroImage*, 49 (4), 3474–3480.

Kirwan, C.B., Wixted, J.T., and Squire, L.R. (2010). A demonstration that the hippocampus supports both recollection and familiarity. *Proceedings of the National Academy of Sciences of the USA*, 107 (1), 344–348.

Kostopoulos, P., and Petrides, M. (2003). The mid-ventrolateral prefrontal cortex: insights into its role in memory retrieval. *European Journal of Neuroscience*, 17 (7), 1489–1497.

Law, J.R., Flanery, M.A., Wirth, S., *et al.* (2005). Functional magnetic resonance imaging activity during the gradual acquisition and expression of paired-associate memory. *Journal of Neuroscience* 25 (24), 5720–5729.

Lekeu, F., Marczewski, P., Van der Linden, M., *et al.* (2002). Effects of incidental and intentional feature binding on recognition: a behavioural and PET activation study. *Neuropsychologia*, 40 (2), 131–144.

Lepage, M., Brodeur, M., and Bourgouin, P. (2003). Prefrontal cortex contribution to associative recognition memory in humans: an event-related functional magnetic resonance imaging study. *Neuroscience Letters*, 346 (1), 73–76.

Light, L.L., and Zelinski, E.M. (1983). Memory for spatial information in young and old adults. *Developmental Psychology*, 19 (6), 901–906.

Light, L. L., Prull, M.W., LaVoie, D.J., and Healy, M.R. (2000). Dual-process theories of memory in Old age. In *Models of Cognitive Aging* (ed. T.J. Perfect and E.A. Maylor). New York, NY: Oxford University Press, pp. 238–300.

Lyle, K.B., Bloise, S.M., and Johnson, M.K. (2006). Age-related binding deficits and the content of false memories. *Psychology and Aging*, 21 (1), 86–95.

Mayes, A., Montaldi, D., and Migo, E. (2007). Associative memory and the medial temporal lobes. *Trends in Cognitive Sciences*, 11 (3), 126–135.

McCormack, P. (1981). Temporal coding by young and elderly adults: a test of the Hasher–Zacks model. *Developmental Psychology*, 17 (4), 509–515.

McCormack, P. (1982). Temporal coding and study-phase retrieval in young and elderly adults. *Bulletin of the Psychonomic Society*, 22 (5), 401–402.

McCormick, C., Moscovitch, M., Protzner, A.B., and McAndrews, M.P. (2010). Hippocampal-cortical networks differ during encoding and retrieval of relational memory: Functional and effective connectivity analyses. *Neuropsychologia*, 48, 3272–3281. doi: 10.1016/j.neuropsychologia.2010.07.010

Miller, E.K., and Cohen, J.D. (2001). An integrative theory of prefrontal cortex function. *Annual Review of Neuroscience*, 24 (1), 167–202.

Mitchell, K.J., Johnson, M.K., Raye, C.L., and D'Esposito, M. (2000). fMRI evidence of age-related hippocampal dysfunction in feature binding in working memory. *Cognitive Brain Research*, 10 (1), 197–206.

Montaldi, D., Mayes, A.R., Barnes, A., *et al.* (1998). Associative encoding of pictures activates the medial temporal lobes. *Human Brain Mapping*, 6 (2), 85–104.

Moscovitch, M. (1992). Memory and working-with-memory: A component process model based on modules and central systems. *Journal of Cognitive Neuroscience*, 4 (3), 257–267.

Moscovitch, M., and Winocur, G. (1995). Frontal lobes, memory, and aging. *Annals of the New York Academy of Sciences* 769 (1), 119–150. doi: 10.1111/j.1749–6632.1995.tb38135.x.

Mottaghy, F., Shah, N., Krause, B., *et al.* (1999). Neuronal correlates of encoding and retrieval in episodic memory during a paired-word association learning task: a functional magnetic resonance imaging study. *Experimental Brain Research*, 128 (3), 332–342.

Naveh-Benjamin, M. (1990). Coding of temporal order information: An automatic process? *Journal of Experimental Psychology: Learning, Memory, and Cognition*, 16 (1), 117–126.

Naveh-Benjamin, M. (2000). Adult age differences in memory performance: tests of an associative deficit hypothesis. *Journal of Experimental Psychology: Learning, Memory, and Cognition*, 26 (5), 1170–1187.

Nolde, S.F., Johnson, M.K., and D'Esposito, M. (1998). Left prefrontal activation during episodic remembering: an event-related fMRI study. *Neuroreport*, 9 (15), 3509–3514.

Norman, D.A. and Shallice, T. (1986). Attention to action: willed and automatic control of behavior. In *Consciousness and Self-Regulation: Advances in Research and Theory* (ed. R.J. Davidson, G.E. Schwartz, and D. Shapiro). New York, NY: Plenum Press, pp. 1–18.

Old, S.R., and Naveh-Benjamin, M. (2008). Differential effects of age on item and associative measures of memory: a meta-analysis. *Psychology and Aging*, 23 (1), 104–118.

Olsen, R.K., Moses, S.N., Riggs, L., and Ryan, J.D. (2012). The hippocampus supports multiple cognitive processes through relational binding and comparison. *Frontiers in Human Neuroscience* 6, 146.

Park, D.C., Puglisi, J.T., and Lutz, R. (1982). Spatial memory in older adults: Effects of intentionality. *Journal of Gerontology*, 37 (3), 330–335.

Park, D.C., Puglisi, J.T., and Sovacool, M. (1983). Memory for pictures, words, and spatial location in older adults: evidence for pictorial superiority. *Journal of Gerontology*, 38 (5), 582–588.

Park, H., and Rugg, M.D. (2008). Neural correlates of successful encoding of semantically and phonologically mediated inter-item associations. *NeuroImage*, 43 (1), 165–172.

Park, H., and Rugg, M.D. (2011). Neural correlates of encoding within- and across-domain inter-item associations. *Journal of Cognitive Neuroscience* 23 (9), 2533–2543.

Perlmutter, M., Metzger, R., Nezworski, T., and Miller, K. (1981). Spatial and temporal memory in 20 and 60 year olds. *Journal of Gerontology*, 36 (1), 59–65.

Persson, J., Nyberg, L., Lind, J., *et al.* (2006). Structure–function correlates of cognitive decline in aging. *Cerebral Cortex*, 16 (7), 907–915.

Petrides, M. (1994). Frontal lobes and working memory: evidence from investigations of the effects of cortical excisions in nonhuman primates. In *Handbook of Neuropsychology* (ed. F. Boller and J. Grafman). Amsterdam: Elsevier, pp. 59–82.

Pfefferbaum, A., Sullivan, E.V., Rosenbloom, M.J., *et al.* (1998). A controlled study of cortical gray matter and ventricular changes in alcoholic men over a 5-year interval. *Archives of General Psychiatry*, 55 (10), 905–912.

Pihlajamäki, M., Tanila, H., Hänninen, T., *et al.* (2003). Encoding of novel picture pairs activates the perirhinal cortex: an fMRI study. *Hippocampus*, 13 (1), 67–80.

Prince, S.E., Daselaar, S.M., and Cabeza, R. (2005). Neural correlates of relational memory: successful encoding and retrieval of semantic and perceptual associations. *Journal of Neuroscience*, 25 (5), 1203–1210.

Quamme, J.R., Yonelinas, A.P., and Norman, K.A. (2007). Effect of unitization on associative recognition in amnesia. *Hippocampus*, 17 (3), 192–200.

Ranganath, C., Cohen, M.X., Dam, C., and D'Esposito, M. (2004). Inferior temporal, prefrontal, and hippocampal contributions to visual working memory maintenance and associative memory retrieval. *Journal of Neuroscience*, 24 (16), 3917–3925.

Ranganath, C., Johnson, M.K., and D'Esposito, M. (2000). Left anterior prefrontal activation increases with demands to recall specific perceptual information. *Journal of Neuroscience*, 20 (22), 19–57.

Raz, N., Gunning, F.M., Head, D., *et al.* (1997). Selective aging of the human cerebral cortex observed in vivo: differential vulnerability of the prefrontal gray matter. *Cerebral Cortex*, 7 (3), 268–282.

Raz, N., Lindenberger, U. Rodrigue, K.M., *et al.* (2005). Regional brain changes in aging healthy adults: general trends, individual differences and modifiers. *Cerebral Cortex*, 15 (11), 1676–1689.

Reber, T.P., Luechinger, R., Boesiger, P., and Henke, K. (2012). Unconscious relational inference recruits the hippocampus. *Journal of Neuroscience*, 32 (18), 6138–6148.

Reed, J.M., and Squire, L.R. (1997). Impaired recognition memory in patients with lesions limited to the hippocampal formation. *Behavioral Neuroscience*, 111 (4), 667–675.

Resnick, S.M., Pham, D.L. Kraut, M.A., *et al.* (2003). Longitudinal magnetic resonance imaging studies of older adults: a shrinking brain. *Journal of Neuroscience*, 23 (8), 3295–3301.

Reuter-Lorenz, P.A., and Park, D.C. (2010). Human neuroscience and the aging mind: a new look at old problems. *Journals of Gerontology Series B: Psychological Sciences and Social Sciences*, 65 (4), 405–415.

Rombouts, S.A., Machielsen, W., Witter, M.P., *et al.* (1997). Visual association encoding activates the medial temporal lobe: a functional magnetic resonance imaging study. *Hippocampus*, 7 (6), 594–601.

Rugg, M.D., Fletcher, P.C., Chua, P.M., and Dolan, R.J. (1999). The role of the prefrontal cortex in recognition memory and memory for source: an fMRI study. *NeuroImage*, 10 (5), 520–529.

Ryan, J.D., Althoff, R.R., Whitlow, S., and Cohen, N.J. (2000). Amnesia is a deficit in relational memory. *Psychological Science*, 11 (6), 454–461.

Ryan, J.D., Leung, G., Turk-Browne, N.B., and Hasher, L. (2007). Assessment of age-related changes in inhibition and binding using eye movement monitoring. *Psychology and Aging*, 22 (2), 239–250.

Schendan, H.E., M.M. Searl, R.J. Melrose, and C.E. Stern. (2003). An fMRI study of the role of the medial temporal lobe in implicit and explicit sequence learning. *Neuron* 37 (6), 1013–1025.

Shimamura, A.P. (2002). Memory retrieval and executive control processes. In *Principles of Frontal Lobe Function* (ed. D. T. Stuss and R. T. Knight). New York, NY: Oxford University Press, pp. 210–220.

Simon, J.R., Vaidya, C.J., Howard, J.H., Jr, and Howard, D.V. (2012). The effects of aging on the neural basis of implicit associative learning in a probabilistic triplets learning task. *Journal of Cognitive Neuroscience*, 24 (2), 451–463.

Small, S.A., Nava, A.S., Perera, G.M., *et al.* (2001). Circuit mechanisms underlying memory encoding and retrieval in the long axis of the hippocampal formation. *Nature Neuroscience*, 4 (4), 442–449.

Smith, A.D., Park, D.C., Earles, J.L., *et al.* (1998). Age differences in context integration in memory. *Psychology and Aging*, 13 (1), 21–28.

Sommer, T., Rose, M., Gläscher, J., *et al.* (2005). Dissociable contributions within the medial temporal lobe to encoding of object–location associations. *Learning and Memory*, 12 (3), 343–351.

Spencer, W.D., and Raz, N. (1995). Differential effects of aging on memory for content and context: a meta-analysis. *Psychology and Aging*, 10 (4), 527–539.

Sperling, R., Chua, E., Cocchiarella, A., *et al.* (2003). Putting names to faces: successful encoding of associative memories activates the anterior hippocampal formation. *NeuroImage*, 20 (2), 1400–1410.

Squire, L.R., and Zola-Morgan, S. (1991). The medial temporal lobe memory system. *Science*, 253 (5026), 1380–1386.

Staresina, B.P., and Davachi, L. (2006). Differential encoding mechanisms for subsequent associative recognition and free recall. *Journal of Neuroscience*, 26 (36), 9162–9172.

Staresina, B.P., and Davachi, L. (2008). Selective and shared contributions of the hippocampus and perirhinal cortex to episodic item and associative encoding. *Journal of Cognitive Neuroscience*, 20 (8), 1478–1489.

Staresina, B.P., and Davachi, L. (2010). Object unitization and associative memory formation are supported by distinct brain regions. *Journal of Neuroscience*, 30 (29), 9890–9897.

Staresina, B.P., Duncan, K.D., and Davachi, L. (2011). Perirhinal and parahippocampal cortices differentially contribute to later recollection of object- and scene-related event details. *Journal of Neuroscience*, 31 (24), 8739–8747.

Staresina, B.P., Gray, J.C., and Davachi, L. (2009). Event congruency enhances episodic memory encoding through semantic elaboration and relational binding. *Cerebral Cortex*, 19 (5), 1198–1207.

Stark, C.E., Bayley, P.J., and Squire, L.R. (2002). Recognition memory for single items and for associations is similarly impaired following damage to the hippocampal region. *Learning and Memory*, 9 (5), 238–242.

Stark, C.E., and Squire, L.R. (2001). Simple and associative recognition memory in the hippocampal region. *Learning and Memory* 8 (4), 190–197.

Stark, C.E., and Squire, L.R. (2003). Hippocampal damage equally impairs memory for single items and memory for conjunctions. *Hippocampus*, 13 (2), 281–292.

Stuss, D.T., Eskes, G.A., and Forster, J.K. (1994). Experimental neuropsychological studies of frontal lobe functions. In *Handbook of Neuropsychology* (ed. F. Boller and J. Grafman). Amsterdam: Elsevier, pp. 149–185.

Tendolkar, I., Arnold, J., Petersson, K.M., *et al.* (2007). Probing the neural correlates of associative memory formation: a parametrically analyzed event-related functional MRI study. *Brain Research*, 1142, 159–168.

Trott, C.T., Friedman, D., Ritter, W., *et al.* (1999). Episodic priming and memory for temporal source: Event-related potentials reveal age-related differences in prefrontal functioning. *Psychology and Aging*, 14 (3), 390–413.

Tsukiura, T. and Cabeza, R. (2008). Orbitofrontal and hippocampal contributions to memory for face–name associations: the rewarding power of a smile. *Neuropsychologia*, 46, 2310–2319.

Tsukiura, T., Sekiguchi, A., Yomogida, Y., *et al.* (2011). Effects of Aging on Hippocampal and Anterior Temporal Activations during Successful Retrieval of Memory for Face–Name Associations. *Journal of Cognitive Neuroscience*, 23 (1), 200–213.

Turriziani, P., Fadda, L., Caltagirone, C., and Carlesimo, G.A. (2004). Recognition memory for single items and for associations in amnesic patients. *Neuropsychologia*, 42 (4), 426–433.

Uttl, B., and Graf, P. (1993). Episodic spatial memory in adulthood. *Psychology and Aging*, 8 (2), 257–273.

Wais, P.E. (2008). fMRI signals associated with memory strength in the medial temporal lobes: a meta-analysis. *Neuropsychologia*, 46 (14), 3185–3196.

Wais, P.E. (2011). Hippocampal signals for strong memory when associative memory is available and when it is not. *Hippocampus*, 21 (1), 9–21.

Wais, P.E., Squire, L.R., and Wixted, J.T. (2010). In search of recollection and familiarity signals in the hippocampus. *Journal of Cognitive Neuroscience*, 22 (1), 109–123.

Wais, P.E., Wixted, J.T., Hopkins, R.O., and Squire, L.R. (2006). The hippocampus supports both the recollection and the familiarity components of recognition memory. *Neuron*, 49 (3), 459–466.

West, R.L. (1996). An application of prefrontal cortex function theory to cognitive aging. *Psychological Bulletin*, 120 (2), 272–292.

Wheeler, M.A., Stuss, D.T., and Tulving, E. (1995). Frontal lobe damage produces episodic memory impairment. *Journal of the International Neuropsychological Society*, 1 (6), 525–536.

Yang, J., Meckinger, A., Xu, M., *et al.* (2008). Decreased parahippocampal activity in associative priming: Evidence from an event-related fMRI study. *Learning and Memory*, 15 (9), 703–710.

Yang, J., Weng, X., Guan, L., *et al.* (2003). Involvement of the medial temporal lobe in priming for new associations. *Neuropsychologia*, 41 (7), 818–829.

Yonelinas, A., Hopfinger, J., Buonocore, M., *et al.* (2001). Hippocampal, parahippocampal and occipital–temporal contributions to associative and item recognition memory: an fMRI study. *Neuroreport*, 12 (2), 359–363.

Yonelinas, A.P., Widaman, K., Mungas, D., *et al.* (2007). Memory in the aging brain: doubly dissociating the contribution of the hippocampus and entorhinal cortex. *Hippocampus*, 17 (11), 1134–1140.

# 19

# Memory for Emotional and Social Information in Adulthood and Old Age

## Elizabeth A. Kensinger and Angela Gutchess

## Introduction

Many events have emotional meaning or social importance. While there is a long tradition of investigating the effects of aging on memory, and much of the research discussed in this chapter builds on that strong base (see also Chapters 15, 17, and 18), the patterns of age-related changes in emotional and social memory do not exactly parallel those in other domains of memory. On the one hand, the changes may be related to motivational changes: we want to process information differently as we age and our top-down goal states shift the way we view the world and retain past experiences; for example, socioemotional selectivity theory suggests that people prioritize meaningful relationships as the time remaining in their lives is limited (Carstensen, Isaacowitz, and Charles, 1999). On the other hand, the changes in memory for socioemotional information may be related to age-related changes in brain structure and function; these brain changes may force us to process the socioemotional world in a different way as we age. Memory for emotional and social information is supported by regions that extend beyond those that comprise the traditional memory system (Macrae *et al.*, 2004; Todorov and Olson, 2008), with the amygdala and medial prefrontal cortex (mPFC) being key additions to the typical memory network. It is thus possible that the systems subserving memory for socioemotional information may respond differently to age-related changes compared to memory systems that have been better characterized in the literature thus far.

To date, the literature on memory for emotional information has been kept largely distinct from the literature on memory for social experiences, and for this reason we will mostly discuss age-related changes in these domains separately. However, there will often be overlap in the events that are emotional and social, and so we briefly discuss when it would be most productive to research these dimensions separately and when it would be more advantageous to investigate them as an integrated domain.

*The Wiley Handbook on the Cognitive Neuroscience of Memory*, First Edition.
Edited by Donna Rose Addis, Morgan Barense, and Audrey Duarte.
© 2015 John Wiley & Sons, Ltd. Published 2015 by John Wiley & Sons, Ltd.

## Emotion, Episodic Memory, and Aging

Memory benefits from emotion in many ways: emotional events are more likely than neutral events to be recalled or recognized (Buchanan, 2007; Hamann, 2001), and to be remembered vividly (Kensinger, 2009). These enhancements appear to occur throughout the adult lifespan (see Kensinger, Allard, and Krendl, 2014, for recent review), although there are some important differences in the ways that young and older adults process and remember emotional information. In the following sections, we note the points of convergence and divergence in emotion processing across the adult lifespan, and their implications for emotional memory.

## The Neuroanatomy of Emotional Memory

Although once viewed narrowly as a "threat detector" (Öhman and Mineka, 2001), it is now thought that the amygdala serves a more general role in information processing, providing salience detection (Sander, Grafman, and Zalla, 2003) or the resolution of ambiguity or uncertainty (e.g., Herry *et al.*, 2007). The amygdala and hippocampus are strongly interconnected, enabling interactions between emotion processing and memory (reviewed by LaBar and Cabeza, 2006). These links – anatomical and functional – have been identified in animal models, and there is evidence for similar links in humans (Phelps, 2004). The amygdala and hippocampus work in concert with many other brain regions, including the prefrontal cortex (PFC) and sensory regions (see Murty *et al.*, 2010, for meta-analysis), to influence episodic memory, and throughout this chapter, we use the shorthand of "emotional memory network" to refer to their interactions.

Given the historical focus on the role of the amygdala in emotional memory (McGaugh, 2004), initial examinations of age-related changes in this domain focused on the amygdala, with mixed results. Some studies noted disproportionate atrophy in the amygdala with age (e.g., Malykhin *et al.*, 2008) while others found levels on par with whole-brain atrophy (e.g., Chow and Cummings, 2000). In terms of amygdala function, there has been more consistent evidence for age-related differences in the valence of information to which the amygdala is most responsive, with the amygdalar response to positive information (Mather *et al.*, 2004) and to novelty (Wright *et al.*, 2006) being relatively preserved with age but its response to negative information declining (reviewed by Kensinger and Leclerc, 2009).

Changes in amygdala *connectivity* may also underlie many age-related changes in emotional memory. For example, St. Jacques, Dolcos, and Cabeza (2009) noted weakened connections between the amygdala and hippocampus as older (versus younger) adults encoded negative information, while Addis *et al.* (2010) reported that, during the encoding of positive information, hippocampal activity was more strongly correlated with activity in the amygdala and ventromedial PFC (vmPFC) in older adults than in young adults. These connectivity changes often occur even when there are not age differences in the activity level within the amygdala (e.g., Waring, Addis, and Kensinger, 2013). Thus, older adults may sometimes remember positive information better than negative information not because of how the amygdala activates to that information but because of how the amygdala connects to other regions during the encoding of the information.

Age differences in PFC recruitment are also pronounced, both in terms of the connectivity during emotion processing (Addis *et al.*, 2010; Waring, Addis, and Kensinger, 2013) and also in terms of activity levels seen during emotion processing (reviewed by Kensinger and Leclerc, 2009; St. Jacques, Bessette-Symons, and Cabeza, 2009). There have been two types of age differences in PFC recruitment noted. The first is age differences in the valence of information to which the PFC is most responsive: whereas young adults show greater activity in PFC to negative than to positive information, older adults often show the opposite pattern (Leclerc and Kensinger, 2008b, 2010; Ritchey *et al.*, 2011). The second is that older adults often over-recruit the PFC regardless of the type of emotional information being processed (e.g., Gutchess, Kensinger, and Schacter, 2007; St. Jacques *et al.*, 2008; Tessitore *et al.*, 2005; Williams *et al.*, 2006). This enhanced engagement of PFC is often coupled with reduced engagement of sensory and attentional regions (discussed in Nashiro, Sakaki, and Mather, 2012) and sometimes with reduced engagement of the amygdala as well (reviewed by St. Jacques *et al.*, 2009). There continue to be debates about whether older adults' over-recruitment of PFC is a function of a domain-general shift toward reliance on PFC with aging (reviewed by Davis *et al.*, 2008) or whether the shift reflects a more domain-specific shift in the way that emotional information is processed or regulated by older adults (see Nashiro, Sakaki, and Mather, 2012 for discussion).

Although we have been able to note some generalizations about age-related changes in the emotional memory network, one difficulty with trying to characterize age-related changes in such a sweeping way is that these regions interact with one another at many different points in the formation of emotional memories. Thus, the next section describes the cognitive processes that are thought to yield effects of emotion on memory and discusses the effects of age on these processes, at both a behavioral and neural level.

## Age-Related Changes in Emotional Memory: Information Processing, Retention, and Retrieval

In order to have conscious access to a memory of an emotional event, that event must be encoded into memory, stored in memory over time, and accessed from a retrieval cue (Buchanan, 2007; Hamann, 2001; McGaugh, 2004). To date, most of the research on age-related changes in the cognitive neuroscience of emotional memory has focused on the initial encoding-stage processes, and so we will focus much of our discussion on that phase. Where relevant we will bring in relevant studies that have examined age-related changes in the retention and retrieval of emotional information as well.

### Encoding of emotional information

At the most basic level, the events we remember will be the events we experience. In this regard, it is interesting to note that aging often affects the types of events that are selected for experience. Older adults are more likely than young adults to avoid situations likely to evoke negative emotions (Urry and Gross, 2010), such as negative interpersonal interactions (Charles and Carstensen, 2009). Although this difference in situation selection may have a large effect on the frequency with which young and older adults experience different emotions, we will set aside this difference for the time being, focusing instead on what young and older adults encode when they experience the same event.

## Detection of emotional information

Young and older adults detect threatening and angry faces more rapidly than neutral faces (e.g., Hahn *et al.*, 2006), and they notice high-arousal objects within a visual array faster than low-arousal objects (Leclerc and Kensinger, 2008a). This rapid detection is proposed to be supported by connections between the amygdala and the visual processing stream; although these connections were first conceived of as a "fear module" that led to the rapid detection of threatening stimuli (Öhman and Mineka, 2001), it is now believed to be a more general enhancement of detection triggered by an arousal response, and not a response limited to fear.

Only one study has compared the neural processes supporting young and older adults' detection of high-arousal targets. This study revealed that young and older adults showed overlapping activity within the fusiform gyrus and the thalamus when detecting high-arousal, emotional targets (e.g., guns, snakes, money; Leclerc and Kensinger, 2010). This enhanced activity relative to low-arousal or neutral stimuli is consistent with the proposal that arousal can modulate visual processing within the fusiform gyrus (e.g., Talmi *et al.*, 2008) as well as a host of attentional and sensory processes mediated by the medial thalamus (e.g., Fredrikson, Wik, and Andersson, 1995), suggesting some preservation in the way that emotion modulates attention and sensory processing throughout the adult lifespan.

However, there were age differences based on the valence of the targets being detected. During the visual search task, activity within the amygdala and the mPFC was greater when young adults detected negative targets and when older adults detected positive targets (Leclerc and Kensinger, 2010). These results suggest that age-related valence reversals in neural engagement can be present even on tasks that rely on relatively automatic processes and that yield no behavioral effects of aging. An important caveat, however, is that because of the sluggish time-course of fMRI, these results could be influenced by age-related changes in elaborative processes that individuals engage after they detect the emotional information. At this point what can be ruled out is that the reversal is tied to changes in the elaborative processes that are implemented in the service of *task-related* goals, but it cannot be ruled out that the reversal is tied to changes in elaborative processes that stem from internal goal states. As we discuss in the next sections, age differences become more pronounced when considering how information is processed after its initial detection, and there is some evidence to suggest that these age-related valence reversals in PFC recruitment are most likely to occur when elaborative processing of information is encouraged.

## Sustained attention on emotional information

Age differences in emotion processing become more pronounced when examining how attention is sustained on positive or negative information. The late positive potential (LPP) is an event-related potential (ERP) component thought to reflect selective attention and to relate to the motivational relevance of stimuli (Lang, Bradley, and Cuthbert, 1997). Using the "extreme age group design" (i.e., where membership in an age group at either end of adulthood is treated as a categorical variable), Wood and Kisley (2006) demonstrated that whereas young adults showed a stronger LPP to negative images than positive ones (see also Ito *et al.*, 1998), older adults showed no such negativity bias. Langeslag and van Strien (2009) similarly found an interactive effect of age and valence on the LPP response, with young adults showing a stronger LPP response to negative images than to positive ones and older adults showing the opposite pattern of response. Using a continuous age design, Kisley, Wood, and Burrows (2007) provided evidence that age effects are particularly pronounced for negative stimuli, with age reducing the LPP response to negative stimuli while having a lesser effect on the LPP response to positive stimuli.

Consistent with these LPP findings, a number of studies have suggested that older adults have an easier time disengaging their attention from negative stimuli and are less distracted by negative stimuli than are young adults (Ashley and Swick, 2009; Hahn *et al.*, 2006; Wurm *et al.*, 2004). There are at least three explanations for older adults' enhanced ability to disengage from negative stimuli. The first is that – perhaps because older adults show a blunted amygdala response to negative stimuli (e.g., Cacioppo *et al.*, 2011) – there is less capture of attention by these stimuli in older adults than in younger adults, making it easier for older adults to divert their attention away from these stimuli. A problem for this explanation is that older adults seem to detect negative information just as readily as young adults (Hahn *et al.*, 2006; Leclerc and Kensinger, 2008a), and they often show short-term interference from negative information (e.g., slowing on an emotional Stroop task; Ashley and Swick, 2009; Wurm *et al.*, 2004; but see LaMonica *et al.*, 2010 for evidence of reduced interference with age). Moreover, young and older adults show comparable amygdala activity in response to rapidly-presented novel, fearful faces (Wright *et al.*, 2006) whereas older adults show a blunted amygdala response when the faces are presented more slowly (e.g., Tessitore *et al.*, 2005); this is the opposite pattern, as would be expected if the key age-related change were in the initial processing or detection of the negative information (see Kensinger and Leclerc, 2009, for further discussion).

The second explanation is that – perhaps because they show a shift toward PFC-based processing of emotional information – older adults are better poised to exert control over their processing of negative information, disengaging attention from those stimuli when the task demands it. This explanation is supported by studies that have found older adults to be less susceptible to distraction from *any* type of emotional stimulus, positive or negative (e.g., LaMonica *et al.*, 2010; Samanez-Larkin *et al.*, 2009). This pattern would be consistent with their general shift toward PFC processing of emotional information, which may provide them with better control over its processing.

A challenge to the generality of this second explanation, however, is that sometimes older adults *fail* to disengage from positive stimuli (e.g., Ebner and Johnson, 2010), and it is hard to imagine how increased engagement of PFC would create a *difficulty* disengaging from emotional material. In one task, young and older adults were asked to perform a Posner cuing task (Posner, 1980), with the cues superimposed on faces with varying expressions (Brassen, Gamer, and Buchel, 2010). Older adults were more distracted by the presence of the happy faces, and they showed greater anterior cingulate activity to those faces, than young adults. Critically, these age differences arose only on the subset of trials when the cue provided no helpful information about the target. Brassen and colleagues argued that on those trials, more processing resources would have been granted to the face than on trials where the superimposed cue provided important information about the target location. On this basis, the authors suggested that older adults may have difficulty disengaging from positive information specifically once it has become the focus of cognitive processing.

The third explanation is that – perhaps because of an internal goal state related to emotional wellbeing (Mather and Carstensen, 2005) – older adults regulate their affective response to an event by diverting their resources away from the processing of negative information and toward the processing of positive information. Indeed, there is evidence that older adults in a negative mood are more likely than those in a neutral mood to avoid negative stimuli and to focus on positive stimuli, perhaps because the negative-mood participants are more motivated to use gaze as an emotion regulation strategy (Isaacowitz *et al.*, 2008). In fact, some have proposed that older adults may be more likely than young adults to use eye gaze as an emotion regulation strategy (Urry and Gross, 2010); older adults may find this type of regulatory strategy easier to implement than other strategies such as detached reappraisal (Shiota and Levenson, 2009), perhaps because it does not require extensive cognitive control (Allard and Isaacowitz, 2008).

There may be instances where each of these three explanations is correct. Older adults may sometimes show faster disengagement from negative stimuli than young adults, sometimes show slower disengagement from positive stimuli, and sometimes be more likely to use gaze as a regulatory strategy. Although each of these outcomes ultimately leads to older adults' greater focus on positive relative to negative information, the mechanism underlying each pattern may differ.

## Details retained about events

Although older adults are less likely than young adults to "recollect" events (see Chapter 18), they show a boost in their ability to recollect emotional events compared to neutral ones. While some of these effects may reflect a bias to report vivid memories for emotional information (Sharot, Delgado, and Phelps, 2004), emotion seems to enhance not only the subjective vividness of older adults' memories but also their ability to bind disparate elements of an experience together. Older adults are more likely to remember the locations of arousing images than the locations of neutral images (Nashiro and Mather, 2011), and their source memory deficits are ameliorated if older adults must remember an affective detail, such as whether a person is "good" or "bad" (Rahhal, May, and Hasher, 2002) or whether food is "safe" or "unsafe" to eat (May *et al.*, 2005).

It may be that binding of at least some event details can occur automatically when information has arousing content, creating a binding process that is less taxing for older adults. This proposal would be consistent with priority binding theory (MacKay *et al.*, 2004) and in keeping with the arousal-biased competition model, which says in part that arousal focuses encoding resources on the most relevant features in the environment, facilitating their binding into a mnemonic representation (Mather and Sutherland, 2011).

An alternative explanation for older adults' good binding of affective details relates to the types of details they attend to. Whereas young adults tend to focus on the external, event-related details, older adults may encode the internal, affective details of an event (e.g., Carstensen and Turk-Charles, 1994; Yoder and Elias, 1987). This finding is consistent with older adults' shift from recruitment of posterior occipito-temporal regions and toward recruitment of anterior PFC ("posterior-to-anterior shift in aging" or PASA; Davis *et al.*, 2008), and with their reduced early "old/new" ERP components emanating from occipital cortices (Schefter *et al.*, 2012). This shift away from posterior recruitment and toward frontal recruitment is revealed in many cognitive domains, including long-term memory retrieval and emotion processing (Grady, McIntosh, and Craik, 2003; St. Jacques *et al.*, 2008), and may explain why older adults remember less about how an event unfolded and more about what they were thinking or feeling during the event.

Older adults' reflection on feelings may be particularly pronounced when information is of positive valence (Tomaszczyk and Fernandes, 2012). Even in young adults, positive information is more likely than negative information to be remembered at a "gist" level or with reference to the global event properties (e.g., Storbeck and Clore, 2005), and so older adults' pattern of memory performance may reflect an exaggeration of this general pattern. At a neural level, this pattern may relate to older adults' engagement of the mPFC, a region connected to self-referential processing and to the processing of internal thoughts and feelings (see below). Although older adults sometimes over-engage the mPFC for the processing of negative information (Williams *et al.*, 2006), older adults may be even more likely to engage it for positive information (e.g., Leclerc and Kensinger, 2008b, 2010), particularly during tasks that encourage deep, elaborative encoding of positive items (Ritchey *et al.*, 2011). The processes reflected by this engagement have not been delimited, although likely candidates include self-referential processing (see Kensinger and Leclerc, 2009, for review), emotion regulation (see Kaszniak and Menchola, 2012; Nashiro, Sakaki, and Mather, 2012, for recent reviews), and semantic elaboration (see Ritchey *et al.*, 2011, for discussion).

Changes in older adults' connectivity between the amygdala and other regions may also influence the types of details they retain about emotional experiences. For instance, older adults show stronger connections between the mPFC, amygdala, and hippocampus during the encoding of positive information than do young adults (Addis *et al.*, 2010), and this may enhance older adults' memories for internal and affective details of these pleasurable experiences.

## Retrieval of emotional information: discrimination versus bias

Relatively little research has examined the effects of aging on the neural processes recruited during retrieval. Behavioral research has revealed that older adults are even more likely than young adults to remember past events in a positive fashion (Kennedy, Mather, and Carstensen, 2003) and to be susceptible to choice-supportive memory biases (Mather and Johnson, 2000). More generally, older adults may be biased to endorse positive information as studied (Fernandes *et al.*, 2008; Kapucu *et al.*, 2008; Werheid *et al.*, 2010) and to perceive positive information as familiar (Spaniol, Voss, and Grady, 2008; Werheid *et al.*, 2010). In some situations, older adults may even have greater familiarity signals for all emotional stimuli, unpleasant or pleasant. Langeslag and van Strien (2008) revealed that emotion enhanced young adults' parietal and late frontal old/new effects but older adults' early old/new effect, which the authors interpreted as a demonstration of a stronger influence of emotion on familiarity in older adults. Murty *et al.* (2010) found further evidence for age differences in the neural processes implemented during emotional memory retrieval, demonstrating an age-related shift toward prefrontal processing of negative information during both encoding and retrieval phases of memory. These studies provide intriguing evidence that age and emotion may interact to influence the neural processes that guide recognition, although more research is needed to specify the nature of those interactions.

### Summary of emotional memory in aging

As has been outlined above, motional memory changes in aging may be best understood as a reflection of broader age-related changes in emotion processing. Age affects how attention is sustained on emotional information, and how internal details of experiences are elaborated. Many of these changes appear consistent with a shift from posterior to PFC functioning. Although this shift is also noted in other domains of cognition, it remains an open question whether it is the same mechanisms that lead to these shifts in the emotional domain and in other cognitive domains.

## "Social" as Distinct from "Emotional"

The separability of "social" and "emotional" is debated. Some work finds overlap, with regions such as the amygdala responding to emotional and more mundane social information (e.g., Somerville *et al.*, 2006). Other work (e.g., Harvey, Fossati, and Lepage, 2007) finds some support for their separation. An investigation of the neural substrates implicated in encoding socially relevant information (Macrae *et al.*, 2004) highlighted the distributed nature of memory systems, with largely distinct regions contributing to memory for verbal, nonverbal, and emotional modalities, as well as self-referential information. Much of the work, however, relies on indirect comparisons, or fails to account for each. Indeed, it is difficult to fully separate out these domains, as many social interactions will be inherently emotional.

Emotional information may affect cognition more automatically, due to its biological relevance, whereas social information may operate through elaborated, resource-intensive processes (Sakaki, Niki, and Mather, 2012). This framework accounts for largely separable neural effects; despite amygdala involvement in both domains, the region connects with lower-level visual cortices for biologically relevant emotional pictures but with higher-level mPFC for social ones. These findings also provide a basis to predict different effects of aging across domains.

## Neural Regions Implicated in Social Memory for Young Adults

While the hippocampus is widely implicated in explicit memory, memory for social information may rely on distinct mechanisms. Neuroimaging research in young adults finds that the amygdala, temporal pole, and mPFC contribute to the encoding of social information (Gilron and Gutchess, 2012; Harvey, Fossati, and Lepage, 2007; Johnson, Kim, and Risse, 1985; Macrae *et al.*, 2004; Mitchell, Macrae, and Banaji, 2004; Todorov and Olson, 2008). Patient data indicate a dissociation between social and nonsocial memory systems, with amnesics forming accurate impressions of individuals. Korsakoff's patients preferred an individual characterized as a "good guy" over the "bad guy," despite having negligible recall of information (Johnson, Kim, and Risse, 1985). A patient with a hippocampal lesion formed positive and negative impressions of individuals much like normal adults. However, learning of impressions was impaired in patients who had left amygdala or temporal pole lesions (Todorov and Olson, 2008). These results suggest that learning affective impressions may not require the hippocampus, indicating that memory for social information may rely on a neural system that is separable from that used in memory for nonsocial information.

Neuroimaging data also suggest that a separable system contributes to memory for social information. mPFC is involved in memory for socially relevant information, with vmPFC implicated in self-referencing (Fossati *et al.*, 2004; Kelley *et al.*, 2002; Macrae *et al.*, 2004) and a dorsal mPFC (dmPFC) underlying the encoding of face–behavior associations (Gilron and Gutchess, 2012; Mitchell, Macrae and Banaji, 2004). Furthermore, dorsal and orbital mPFC regions are implicated in the encoding of social versus nonsocial pictures, while the amygdala underlies the encoding of emotional versus neutral pictures (Harvey, Fossati, and Lepage, 2007). Learning information consistent with the subsequent evaluation of an individual engages posterior cingulate cortex (PCC) and the amygdala (Schiller *et al.*, 2009), but not dmPFC, despite the role of the region in encoding and updating impressions (Ma *et al.*, 2011).

Supplementing the few studies of social memory, there is a large body of research identifying a "social network" involved in mentalizing, inferring intentions, self-reflection (Mitchell, 2008; Van Overwalle, 2009), and social event knowledge (Krueger, Barbey, and Grafman, 2009). Reviews highlight the engagement of cortical midline structures (mPFC and precuneus/PCC), and temporoparietal junction. Other neural regions such as PFC (Wood *et al.*, 2003) and anterior temporal lobes (e.g., Olson, Plotzker, and Ezzyat, 2007) may have distinct subregions for social information.

Largely overlapping neural regions underlie mentalizing and autobiographical memory (Buckner and Carroll, 2007; Rabin *et al.*, 2010; Spreng and Grady, 2010; Spreng and Mar, 2012; Spreng, Mar, and Kim, 2009). Conceptually, theory of mind and autobiographical memory should share some processes in common, in that a sense of oneself across time relies on the abilities to represent one's knowledge state as changing (Spreng, Mar, and Kim, 2009) and to plan for the future (Spreng and Mar, 2012) (see also Chapter 14).

# Review of Social Domains

In this section, we review research on the topics of thinking about the self, thinking about others, and the intersection between self and other. Because little aging research investigates the neural regions implicated in social memory, we draw from the young adult and behavioral literatures to speculate on promising directions for aging research.

## Thinking about the self

Relating information to oneself is an effective strategy for encoding information (Rogers, Kuiper, and Kirker, 1977), and benefits memory similarly for younger and older adults for trait words (Glisky and Marquine, 2009; Gutchess *et al.*, 2007; Mueller, Wonderlich, and Dugan, 1986) as well as visual objects, source or perceptual details, and self-performed actions (Hamami, Serbun, and Gutchess, 2011; Rosa and Gutchess, 2011). Although the self-reference effect emerges regardless of attention or emotion (Yang *et al.*, 2012), older adults over 75 or with reduced cognitive resources may benefit less (Glisky and Marquine, 2009; Gutchess *et al.*, 2007).

vmPFC and PCC are engaged during judgments about the self, relative to others (Kelley *et al.*, 2002). mPFC responds during the successful encoding of self-referential information (Macrae *et al.*, 2004), including source details (Leshikar and Duarte, 2012) in young adults. During recognition of previously studied words, there are distinct peaks in mPFC for positive and negative words studied in regard to the self versus social desirability (Fossati *et al.*, 2004). Like the young, older adults engage ventral mPFC and mid-cingulate when making judgments about self versus other (Gutchess, Kensinger, and Schacter, 2007). The effects of aging are mixed, depending on the method. With ERP, younger and older adults exhibit similar engagement of neural regions during self-referencing (Dulas, Newsome, and Duarte, 2011), but with fMRI, differences emerge in regions including dmPFC (Gutchess, Kensinger, and Schacter, 2010).

Different hubs of the self-referencing network may subserve qualitatively different types of self-reflective thought and agendas. mPFC, as well as anterior cingulate cortex, reflects a promotion (internal) focus, emphasizing hopes and aspirations, whereas PCC/precuneus governs a prevention (external) focus concerning duties and obligations (Johnson *et al.*, 2006). Age-related changes in motivation affect neural activation patterns such that young, but not old, engage mPFC during promotion more than prevention. This is consistent with self-reports indicating less internal focus for older than for younger adults (Mitchell *et al.*, 2009).

These differences in regulatory focus could influence encoding. For example, information consistent with one's regulatory focus might invoke more elaborative encoding processes, perhaps triggering retrieval of focus-consistent autobiographical memories as an effect of self-relevance (Touryan *et al.*, 2007). PCC, implicated in self-referencing, was more engaged by a prevention-focused group during judgments of negative versus neutral words, but by a promotion-focused group during judgments of positive versus neutral words (Touryan *et al.*, 2007). Furthermore, a region of right parahippocampal gyrus was more engaged during the successful encoding of negative words by the prevention group, but by positive words by the promotion group. While this study suggests ways in which regulatory focus could impact memory for young adults, it also has implications for aging in that chronic differences in regulation (as in Mitchell *et al.*, 2009) could underlie age differences in emotional memory and neural engagement.

## Thinking about others

One important socially relevant ability is mentalizing from another's perspective, or theory of mind. Mentalizing may be impaired with age (e.g., Maylor *et al.*, 2002), although findings of age-related declines, behaviorally or neurally, are not universal (e.g., Castelli *et al.*, 2010). Older adults exhibit reductions in dmPFC activity across several mentalizing tasks (i.e., animate movement, moral judgments, and false beliefs) (Moran, Jolly, and Mitchell, 2012). The authors interpret this as evidence of impaired mentalizing ability with age, which should also impact memory for socially relevant information. Impairments in engaging dmPFC could be context-specific, perhaps reflecting age-related differences in the prioritization of different types of information. For example, during impression formation, young adults increase dmPFC activity for negative, relative to positive, impressions whereas older adults exhibit the reverse pattern (positive over negative) (Cassidy *et al.*, 2013). This pattern is consistent with socioemotional selectivity theory (Carstensen, Isaacowitz, and Charles, 1999) and fMRI data revealing age differences in vmPFC activity as an effect of valence (Leclerc and Kensinger, 2008b).

Research in young adults has begun to investigate the neural regions involved in forming and remembering impressions of others. Research with young adults (e.g., Winston *et al.*, 2002) and lesion patients (Adolphs, Tranel, and Damasio, 1998) implicates the amygdala in judgments of trustworthiness. Behavioral research suggests young and old similarly rate faces on traits (e.g., trustworthiness), although older adults generally rate more positively (Zebrowitz *et al.*, 2013). However, it is not known how aging affects the neural regions engaged by appearance-based information.

Learning about others based on more than facial appearance engages additional social cognition regions. When tested on faces with neutral expressions, previous encounters with the faces impact neural engagement. The amygdala is engaged for faces that had been threatening, as opposed to the ventral striatum for non-threatening ones (Satterthwaite *et al.*, 2009). Learning about a person also implicates regions associated with theory of mind (i.e., anterior paracingulate cortex and superior temporal gyrus) as well as orbitofrontal cortex, hippocampus, and middle temporal gyrus (Todorov *et al.*, 2007). Explicitly recalling information about an individual, compared to when it was forgotten, exacerbated neural activity; this was especially true for left superior temporal gyrus for negative, as opposed to positive, information (Todorov *et al.*, 2007). Explicit recall did not impact all of the implicated neural regions; some regions responded to particular traits (e.g., anterior insula activity for disgusting behaviors) regardless of memory.

Interactions with individuals, as through neuroeconomic games, can further influence the regions implicated in learning about others. Encounters with game partners who previously had acted as "cooperators" versus "defectors" or neutral players in a Prisoner's Dilemma game evoked more activity in the regions associated with emotion (amygdala, orbitofrontal cortex, and insula), reward (striatum), face perception (fusiform gyrus), and mentalizing (superior temporal sulcus), particularly when opponents acted intentionally (Singer *et al.*, 2004). Learning to trust engages the caudate (King-Casas *et al.*, 2005). Previous encounters with an individual as an ally or opponent also engage reward regions, such as caudate and anterior cingulate cortex, along with regions involved in face perception (e.g., fusiform, PCC, amygdala) (Vrticka *et al.*, 2009). Outside of an economic game context, previously learned valenced information about behaviors (e.g., "deadbeat dad") engages the right amygdala more than neutral information (Somerville *et al.*, 2006). Right amygdala dissociates from right hippocampus, which responds to all faces encountered previously with additional information, and also responds more when information is explicitly remembered.

Effects in regions responding to socioemotionality and reward emerge even when individuals cannot explicitly retrieve behaviors of others (e.g., Satterthwaite *et al.*, 2009; Somerville *et al.*, 2006; Vrticka *et al.*, 2009). These studies generally compare activations across different types of prior experience with individuals. Results indicate that remembering information about socially relevant behaviors of others engages systems associated with reward and social cognition rather than hippocampally based explicit memory systems. However, it is necessary to assess whether this pattern of neural activity also occurs when information is explicitly retrieved. If retrieval of socially relevant information is supported by implicit memory processes, these processes may be relatively spared with healthy aging (e.g., Light and Singh, 1987).

The few aging studies of memory for others suggest that older adults may exhibit intact explicit memory under some conditions. Encoding in a self-relevant or socio-emotionally meaningful context eliminates age differences in memory for impressions of others (Cassidy and Gutchess, 2012). While the effects of aging have not been assessed for neural regions supporting impression memory, some evidence indicates that young and older adults engage similar neural regions during impression formation. When making social as opposed to nonsocial evaluations, regions associated with mentalizing and impression formation (dorsal and ventral mPFC, precuneus, and temporoparietal junction) are engaged by young and older adults (Cassidy, Shih, and Gutchess, 2012). The largely similar pattern of neural activity across the age groups sets the stage for the meaningful evaluation of neural regions implicated during memory for impressions. Morality is an interesting domain in that older adults exhibit better memory for morality information (Narvaez *et al.*, 2011). Older adults might be expected to effectively engage neural regions implicated in memory, or recruit reward regions that modulate memory, for morality-relevant information.

Although there may be some conditions under which person memory can be age-equivalent, much of the literature suggests age-related declines. Compared to younger adults, older adults have more difficulty remembering inconsistent information about others (Hess and Tate, 1991), but use trait diagnostic information more (Hess and Auman, 2001) and update impressions when given new information (Hess, Osowski, and Leclerc, 2005). The relevant cognitive processes, generating explanations and relying on specific information, require cognitive resources, which are limited with age (Hess, 2006; Hess *et al.*, 2009). Task demands and cognitive ability may contribute to older adults' memory for impressions; for example, age differences in integrating inconsistent information into memory were eliminated for older adults with high working memory capacity under a meaningful job evaluation condition (Hess, Follett, and McGee, 1998).

## Intersection of self and other

A small body of work investigates the neural substrates involved in social interaction. For example, the hippocampus is engaged to the same extent when making judgments about self and similar, but not dissimilar, others; this pattern was particularly evident when participants retrieved a related autobiographical memory (Perry, Hendler, and Shamay-Tsoory, 2011). Autobiographical memories may contribute to the ways in which we mentalize about others, depending on the similarity of the other person to oneself. Given potential changes to mentalizing ability with age (e.g., Moran, Jolly, and Mitchell, 2012), thinking about dissimilar others may be more demanding than thinking about similar others.

mPFC activity may be modulated by the similarity of others to oneself, with more activity for similar others (Mitchell, Macrae, and Banaji, 2006). This pattern extends to own-age versus different-age individuals, consistent with the idea that own-age peers are thought to be more similar to the self (Ebner *et al.*, 2011). Memory is typically better for same-age faces, which may reflect greater exposure to members of one's own age group (Rhodes and Anastasi, 2012), as these individuals have greater personal and social relevance (He, Ebner, and Johnson, 2011).

In terms of interactions with the self, smiling faces (Tsukiura and Cabeza, 2008) and direct, as opposed to averted, gaze (Conty and Grèzes, 2012) enhance young adults' memory for information about others. The hippocampus contributes to both effects (Conty and Grèzes, 2012), and acts in conjunction with orbitofrontal cortex in response to smiling, possibly reflecting reward system engagement (Tsukiura and Cabeza, 2008). Prioritization of socially meaningful information (Hess, 2006; Hess *et al.*, 2009) may preserve, or enhance, these effects with age.

Neural regions responding to interactions with others have also been investigated using pictures of social scenes. Young and older adults activate mPFC and temporal pole, regions related to self-referencing and theory of mind, in response to scenes depicting affiliation or isolation (Beadle, Yoon, and Gutchess, 2012). Yet social content affects engagement with age, with older adults engaging temporal pole more than young for isolation pictures, which may indicate more mentalizing due to concerns about loneliness. Young and older adults differ in precuneus recruitment, with older adults activating it more for affiliation and young for isolation. This may reflect differences with age in what type of social information evokes self-referencing.

The social context of learning has begun to be explored. Retrieval of information encoded in a social context (e.g., generating a narrative with another person versus alone) engages right mPFC more than information learned in a nonsocial context, perhaps reflecting the contribution of familiar scripts and people to memory (Mano *et al.*, 2011). Work on social interactions extends to false memory. The same neural regions support the formation of both true and false nonsocial memories (e.g., Schacter and Slotnick, 2004; for a review, see Chapter 8). In the social domain, a number of regions, including mPFC and bilateral frontal cortex, are engaged at encoding and predict whether spoken sentences accompanied with gestures will be remembered as communicated directly to the participant versus presented to an unseen third party (Straube *et al.*, 2011). These regions emerge regardless of whether memory for the communication context is accurate.

Personality traits likely affect memory and the engagement of neural resources, although this has not been investigated with aging. Traits related to interpersonal relationships may be most subject to change, in that older adults prioritize close relationships more than information acquisition (Carstensen, Isaacowitz, and Charles, 1999). Because higher levels of interdependence are more strongly linked to the number of close social partners one has as one ages (Yeung, Fung, and Lang, 2008), this trait could particularly impact older adults' motivation to remember social information. In young adults, interdependent self-construal is associated with greater engagement of mPFC and PCC for self than for close others (Ray *et al.*, 2010). While this result seems counterintuitive, the authors suggest that trait judgments evoke effortful retrieval of socially relevant memories in interdependent individuals, whereas independent individuals rely on retrieval of general semantic memories about the self.

## Summary of social memory and aging

Exploration has barely begun into the effects of aging on the neural regions implicated in social memory. While research on traditionally "cognitive" tasks reveals rich patterns of preservation and change with age (see Chapter 17), it is unclear whether these findings will characterize the social domain. If memory for social information recruits a distinct network (e.g., Mitchell, Macrae, and Banaji, 2004; Todorov and Olson, 2008), the effects of aging on the social domain may diverge from the cognitive domain. Thus far, substantial overlap occurs across young and older adults in the regions implicated in social memory tasks (e.g., Cassidy, Shih, and Gutchess, 2012; Gutchess, Kensinger, and Schacter, 2007). However, age-related differences occur in regions associated with theory of mind (Moran, Jolly, and Mitchell, 2012) and motivational relevance (e.g., Beadle, Yoon, and Gutchess, 2012; Mitchell *et al.*, 2009) suggesting that research has only scratched the surface in investigating potential changes to neural recruitment in the social domain with age.

# Emotional and Social Processing in Aging: Conclusions and Future Directions

The effects of age on emotional and social processing have typically been considered separately. While emotion and social processes have some common effects, such as their ability to engage the amygdala or enhance the amount or vividness of information encoded and retrieved from memory, aging differently affects neural engagement during their processing. While older adults show enhanced PFC engagement or connectivity during emotion processing (Ritchey *et al.*, 2011; St. Jacques *et al.*, 2008), younger and older adults similarly activate mPFC in social contexts (Cassidy *et al.*, 2013; Gutchess *et al.*, 2007). Aside from differences in recruiting neural regions, the two domains differ in the extent to which age-related changes occur in early versus late stages of processing. Young and old generally do not differ in their initial detection of emotional information, and the age differences emerge in their later response to the emotional information. Social information, on the other hand, seems to require higher-order processing even at its first encounter, such that the initial orientation to information can differ greatly across young and older adults. When encountering information about other people, for example, young adults could evoke mentalizing processes from the start, whereas older adults may only do so when the task necessitates it or the information is highly self-relevant. Thus, social and emotional memory may differ in the extent to which they are affected by deliberative versus automatic processing, which in turn affects which stage(s) of information processing will be affected by age-related changes.

Although emotional and social domains are largely separable, the effects of age in these domains share one important commonality, which is in the coherence of cortical midline regions. Whereas older adults often fail to show connectivity among midline regions that comprise the "default network," in the context of social or emotional processing, older adults seem capable of engaging these regions and, in some instances, even relying disproportionately on them. This commonality may reflect the fact that there are important ways in which social and emotional processing overlap. For instance, Parkinson (1996) argued that emotions may be best conceived as social phenomena for three reasons: interactions – real or anticipated – with other people are one of the most common causes of emotion (e.g., Shaver, Wu, and Schwartz, 1992), they have consequences for other people (e.g., influence their emotional state either directly or through social referencing), and they serve social purposes. There also are particular classes of emotions referred to as "social emotions": this class of emotions guides social behavior and can also fuel moral decision making. To date, there is little understanding of how aging may affect these emotional reactions or the neural circuitry underlying them.

In conclusion, while research on aging has begun to reveal how memory is impacted by emotional and social information, much work remains to be done in order to fully understand the ways in which these processes may support accurate memory and the robust engagement of neural systems with age. The extant research suggests important distinctions in the stages of processing in which age differences occur and the recruitment of networks that contribute to social versus emotional processing, yet there remain open avenues for future research that more specifically examine how age affects processing at the intersection of the social and emotional domains.

# Acknowledgments

This chapter was supported by funding from NIMH grant R01 MH080833 and the McKnight Foundation (to E.A.K.) and NIA grant R21 AG032382 (to A.H.G.).

# References

Addis, D.R., Leclerc, C.M., Muscatell, K.A., and Kensinger, E.A. (2010). There are age-related changes in neural connectivity during the encoding of positive, but not negative, information. *Cortex*, 46 (4), 425–433.

Adolphs, R., Tranel, D., and Damasio, A. (1998). The human amygdala in social judgment. *Nature*, 393, 470–474.

Allard, E.S., and Isaacowitz, D.M. (2008). Are preferences in emotional processing affected by distraction? Examining the age-related positivity effect in visual fixation within a dual-task paradigm. *Aging, Neuropsychology, and Cognition*, 15 (6), 725–743.

Ashley, V., and Swick, D. (2009). Consequences of emotional stimuli: age differences on pure and mixed blocks of the emotional Stroop. *Behavioral and Brain Functions*, 5, 14.

Beadle, J., Yoon, C., and Gutchess, A. (2012). Age-related neural differences in affiliation and isolation. *Cognitive, Affective, and Behavioral Neuroscience*, 12, 269–279.

Brassen, S., Gamer, M., and Büchel, C. (2011). Anterior cingulate activation is related to a positivity bias and emotional stability in successful aging. *Biological Psychiatry*, 70 (2), 131–137.

Buchanan, T.W. (2007). Retrieval of emotional memories. *Psychological Bulletin*, 133 (5), 761.

Buckner, R.L., and Carroll, D.C. (2007). Self-projection and the brain. *Trends in Cognitive Sciences*, 11 (2), 49–57.

Cacioppo, J. T., Berntson, G.G., Bechara, A., *et al.* (2011). Could an aging brain contribute to subjective well-being? The value added by a social neuroscience perspective. In *Social Neuroscience: Toward Understanding the Underpinnings of the Social Mind* (ed. A. Todorov, S.T. Fiske, and D. Prentice). New York, NY: Oxford University Press, pp. 249–262.

Carstensen, L., Isaacowitz, D., and Charles, S. (1999). Taking time seriously: a theory of socioemotional selectivity. *American Psychologist*, 54 (3), 165–181.

Carstensen, L.L., and Turk-Charles, S. (1994). The salience of emotion across the adult life span. *Psychology and Aging*, 9 (2), 259.

Cassidy, B.S., and Gutchess, A. (2012). Social relevance enhances memory for impressions in older adults. *Memory*, 20 (4), 332–345.

Cassidy, B.S., Leshikar, E.D., Shih, J.Y., *et al.* (2013). Valence-based age differences in medial prefrontal activity during impression formation. *Social Neuroscience*, 8 (5), 462–473.

Cassidy, B.S., Shih, J., and Gutchess, A. (2012). Age-related changes to the neural correlates of social evaluation. *Social Neuroscience*, 7 (6), 552–564.

Castelli, I., Baglio, F. Blasi, V., *et al.* (2010). Effects of aging on mindreading ability through the eyes: an fMRI study. *Neuropsychologia*, 48 (9), 2586–2594.

Charles, S.T. and L.L. Carstensen (2009). Socioemotional selectivity theory. In *Encyclopedia of Human Relationships* (ed. H. Reis and S. Sprecher). Thousand Oaks, CA: Sage Publications, pp. 1578–1581.

Chow, T.W., and Cummings, J.L. (2000). The amygdala and Alzheimer's disease. In *The Amygdala: A Functional Analysis* (ed. J.P. Aggleton). Oxford: Oxford University Press, pp. 656–680.

Conty, L., and Grèzes, J. (2012). Look at me, I'll remember you: The perception of self-relevant social cues enhances memory and right hippocampal activity. *Human Brain Mapping*, 33 (10), 2428–2440.

Davis, S.W., Dennis, N.A., Daselaar, S.M., *et al.* (2008). Que PASA? The posterior–anterior shift in aging. *Cerebral Cortex*, 18 (5), 1201–1209.

Dulas, M.R., Newsome, R.N., and Duarte, A. (2011). The effects of aging on ERP correlates of source memory retrieval for self-referential information. *Brain Research*, 1377, 84–100. doi: 10.1016/j.brainres.2010.12.087.

Ebner, N.C., Gluth, S., Johnson, M.R., *et al.* (2011). Medial prefrontal cortex activity when thinking about others depends on their age. *Neurocase*, 17 (3), 260–269. doi: 10.1080/13554794.2010.536953.

Ebner, N.C., and Johnson, M.K. (2010). Age-group differences in interference from young and older emotional faces. *Cognition and Emotion*, 24 (7), 1095–1116.

Fernandes, M., Ross, M., Wiegand, M., and Schryer, E. (2008). Are the memories of older adults positively biased? *Psychology and Aging*, 23 (2), 297.

Fossati, P., Hevenor, S.J., Lepage, M., *et al.* (2004). Distributed self in episodic memory: neural correlates of successful retrieval of self-encoded positive and negative personality traits. *NeuroImage*, 22 (4), 1596–1604. doi: 10.1016/j.neuroimage.2004.03.034.

Fredrikson, M., Wik, G., and Andersson, J. (1995). Affective and attentive neural networks in humans: a PET study of Pavlovian conditioning. *Neuroreport*, 7 (1), 97–101.

Gilron, R., and Gutchess, A. (2012). Remembering first impressions: effects of intentionality and diagnosticity of subsequent memory. *Cognitive, Affective, and Behavioral Neuroscience*, 12 (1), 85–98.

Glisky, E., and Marquine, M. (2009). Semantic and self-referential processing of positive and negative adjectives in older adults. *Memory*, 17 (2), 144–157.

Grady, C.L., McIntosh, A.R., and Craik, F.I. (2003). Age-related differences in the functional connectivity of the hippocampus during memory encoding. *Hippocampus*, 13 (5), 572–586.

Gutchess, A., Kensinger, E., and Schacter, D. (2007). Aging, self-referencing, and medial prefrontal cortex. *Social Neuroscience*, 2 (2), 117–133.

Gutchess, A., Kensinger, E., and Schacter, D.L. (2010). Functional neuroimaging of self-referential encoding with age. *Neuropsychologia*, 48, 211–219.

Gutchess, A., Kensinger, E., Yoon, C., and Schacter, D.L. (2007). Aging and the self-reference effect in memory. *Memory*, 15 (8), 822–837.

Hahn, S., Carlson, C., Singer, S., and Gronlund, S.D. (2006). Aging and visual search: automatic and controlled attentional bias to threat faces. *Acta Psychologica*, 123 (3), 312–336.

Hamami, A., Serbun, S., and Gutchess, A. (2011). Self-referencing processing and memory specificity with age. *Psychology and Aging*, 26, 636–646.

Hamann, S. (2001). Cognitive and neural mechanisms of emotional memory. *Trends in Cognitive Sciences*, 5 (9), 394–400.

Harvey, P.O., Fossati, P., and Lepage, M. (2007). Modulation of memory formation by stimulus content: specific role of the medial prefrontal cortex in the successful encoding of social pictures. *Journal of Cognitive Neuroscience*, 19 (2), 351–362.

He, Y., Ebner, N.C., and Johnson, M.K. (2011). What predicts the own-age bias in face recognition memory? *Social Cognition*, 29 (1), 97–109.

Herry, C., Bach, D.R., Esposito, F., *et al.* (2007). Processing of temporal unpredictability in human and animal amygdala. *Journal of Neuroscience*, 27, 5958–5966.

Hess, T. (2006). Adaptive aspects of social cognitive functioning in adulthood: age-related goal and knowledge influences. *Social Cognition*, 24 (3), 279–309.

Hess, T., and Auman, C. (2001). Aging and social expertise: the impact of trait-diagnostic information on impressions of others. *Psychology and Aging*, 16 (3), 497–510.

Hess, T., Follett, K., and McGee, K. (1998). Aging and impression formation: the impact of processing skills and goals. *Journals of Gerontology Series B: Psychological Sciences and Social Sciences*, 53 (3), 175–187.

Hess, T., Germain, C., Swaim, E., and Osowski, N. (2009). Aging and selective engagement: the moderating impact of motivation on older adults' resource utilization. *Journals of Gerontology Series B: Psychological Sciences and Social Sciences*, 64 (4), 447–456. doi: 10.1093/geronb/gbp020.

Hess, T., Osowski, N., and Leclerc, C. (2005). Age and experience influences on the complexity of social inferences. *Psychology and Aging*, 20 (3), 447–459.

Hess, T., and Tate, C. (1991). Adult age-differences in explanations and memory for behavioral information. *Psychology and Aging*, 6 (1), 86–92.

Isaacowitz, D.M., Toner, K., Goren, D., and Wilson, H.R. (2008). Looking while unhappy mood-congruent gaze in young adults, positive gaze in older adults. *Psychological Science*, 19 (9), 848–853.

Ito, T.A., Larsen, J.T., Smith, N.K., and Cacioppo, J.T. (1998). Negative information weighs more heavily on the brain: the negativity bias in evaluative categorizations. *Journal of Personality and Social Psychology*, 75 (4), 887.

Johnson, M., Kim, J., and Risse, G. (1985). Do alcoholic Korsakoff's syndrome patients acquire affective reactions? *Journal of Experimental Psychology: Learning, Memory, and Cognition* 11 (1), 22–36.

Johnson, M.K., Raye, C.L., Mitchell, K.J., *et al.* (2006). Dissociating medial frontal and posterior cingulate activity during self-reflection. *Social Cognitive and Affective Neuroscience*, 1 (1), 56–64. doi: 10.1093/scan/nsl004.

Kapucu, A., Rotello, C.M., Ready, R.E., and Seidl, K.N. (2008). Response bias in remembering emotional stimuli: a new perspective on age differences. *Journal of Experimental Psychology: Learning, Memory, and Cognition*, 34 (3), 703.

Kaszniak, A.W., and Menchola, M. (2012). Behavioral neuroscience of emotion in aging. *Current Topics in Behavioral Neurosciences*, 10, 51–66.

Kelley, W.M., Macrae, C.N., Wyland, C.L., *et al.* (2002). Finding the self? An event-related fMRI study. *Journal of Cognitive Neuroscience*, 14 (5), 785–794.

Kennedy, Q., Mather, M., and Carstensen, L.L. (2004). The role of motivation in the age-related positivity effect in autobiographical memory. *Psychological Science* 15 (3), 208–214.

Kensinger, E.A. (2009). How emotion affects older adults' memories for event details. *Memory*, 17 (2), 208–219.

Kensinger, E.A., Allard, E.R., and Krendl, A.C. (2014). The effects of age on memory for socio-emotional material: an affective neuroscience perspective. In *The Oxford Handbook of Emotion, Social Cognition, and Problem Solving in Adulthood* (ed. P. Verhaeghen and C.K. Hertzog). New York, NY: Oxford University Press.

Kensinger, E.A., and Leclerc, C.M. (2009). Age-related changes in the neural mechanisms supporting emotion processing and emotional memory. *European Journal of Cognitive Psychology*, 21 (2–3), 192–215.

King-Casas, B., Tomlin, D., Anen, C., *et al.* (2005). Getting to know you: Reputation and trust in a two-person economic exchange. *Science*, 308 (5718), 78–83. doi: 10.1126/science.1108062.

Kisley, M.A., Wood, S., and Burrows, C.L. (2007). Looking at the sunny side of life: age-related change in an event-related potential measure of the negativity bias. *Psychological Science*, 18 (9), 838–843.

Krueger, F., Barbey, A.K., and Grafman, J. (2009). The medial prefrontal cortex mediates social event knowledge. *Trends in Cognitive Sciences*, 13 (3), 103–109. doi: 10.1016/j.tics.2008.12.005.

LaBar, K.S., and Cabeza, R. (2006). Cognitive neuroscience of emotional memory. *Nature Reviews Neuroscience*, 7 (1), 54–64.

LaMonica, H.M., Keefe, R.S., Harvey, P.D., *et al.* (2010). Differential effects of emotional information on interference task performance across the life span. *Frontiers in Aging Neuroscience*, 2, 141. doi: 10.3389/fnagi.2010.00141.

Lang, P.J., Bradley, M.M., and Cuthbert, M.M. (1997). Motivated attention: affect, activation and action. In *Attention and Orienting: Sensory and Motivational Processes* (ed. P.J. Lang, R.F. Simons, and M.T. Balaban). Hillsdale, NJ: Lawrence Erlbaum Associates, Inc, pp. 97–135.

Langeslag, S.J., and van Strien, J.W. (2008). Age differences in the emotional modulation of ERP old/new effects. *International Journal of Psychophysiology*, 70 (2), 105–114.

Langeslag, S.J., and van Strien, J.W. (2009). Aging and emotional memory: the co-occurrence of neurophysiological and behavioral positivity effects. *Emotion*, 9 (3), 369.

Leclerc, C.M., and Kensinger, E.A. (2008a). Age-related differences in medial prefrontal activation in response to emotional images. *Cognitive, Affective, and Behavioral Neuroscience*, 8 (2), 153–164.

Leclerc, C.M., and Kensinger, E.A. (2008b). Effects of age on detection of emotional information. *Psychology and Aging*, 23 (1), 209.

Leclerc, C.M., and Kensinger, E.A. (2010). Age-related valence-based reversal in recruitment of medial prefrontal cortex on a visual search task. *Social Neuroscience*, 5 (5–6), 560–576.

Leshikar, E.D., and Duarte, A. (2012). Medial prefrontal cortex supports source memory accuracy for self-referenced items. *Social Neuroscience*, 7 (2), 126–145. doi: 10.1080/17470919.2011.585242.

Light, L., and Singh, A. (1987). Implicit and explicit memory in young and older adults. *Journal of Experimental Psychology: Learning, Memory, and Cognition*, 13 (4), 531–541.

Ma, N., Vandekerckhove, M., Van Overwalle, F., *et al.* (2011). Spontaneous and intentional trait inferences recruit a common mentalizing network to a different degree: Spontaneous inferences activate only its core areas. *Social Neuroscience*, 6 (2), 123–138. doi: 10.1080/17470919.2010.485884.

Mackay, D.G., Shafto, M., Taylor, J.K., *et al.* (2004). Relations between emotion, memory, and attention: Evidence from taboo Stroop, lexical decision, and immediate memory tasks. *Memory and Cognition*, 32 (3), 474–488.

Macrae, C.N., Moran, J.M., Heatherton, T.F., *et al.* (2004). Medial prefrontal activity predicts memory for self. *Cerebral Cortex*, 14 (6), 647–654. doi: 10.1093/cercor/bhh025.

Malykhin, N.V., Bouchard, T.P., Camicioli, R., and Coupland, N.J. (2008). Aging hippo-campus and amygdala. *Neuroreport*, 19 (5), 543–547.

Mano, Y., Sugiura, M., Tsukiura, T., *et al.* (2011). The representation of social interaction in episodic memory: A functional MRI study. *NeuroImage*, 57 (3), 1234–1242. doi: 10.1016/j.neuroimage.2011.05.016.

Mather, M., Canli, T., English, T., *et al.* (2004). Amygdala responses to emotionally valenced stimuli in older and younger adults. *Psychological Science*, 15 (4), 259–263.

Mather, M., and Carstensen, L.L. (2005). Aging and motivated cognition: the positivity effect in attention and memory. *Trends in Cognitive Sciences*, 9 (10), 496–502.

Mather, M., and Johnson, M.K. (2000). Choice-supportive source monitoring: do our decisions seem better to us as we age? *Psychology and Aging*, 15 (4), 596.

Mather, M., and Sutherland, M.R. (2011). Arousal-biased competition in perception and memory. *Perspectives on Psychological Science*, 6 (2), 114–133.

May, C.P., Rahhal, T., Berry, E.M., and Leighton, E.A. (2005). Aging, source memory, and emotion. *Psychology and Aging*, 20 (4), 571.

Maylor, E.A., Moulson, J.M., Muncer, A.M., and Taylor, L.A. (2002). Does performance on theory of mind tasks decline in old age? *British Journal of Psychology*, 93, 465–485. doi: 10.1348/000712602761381358.

McGaugh, J.L. (2004). The amygdala modulates the consolidation of memories of emotionally arousing experiences. *Annual Review of Neuroscience*, 27, 1–28.

Mitchell, J.P. (2008). Contributions of functional neuroimaging to the study of social cognition. *Current Directions in Psychological Science*, 17 (2), 142–146. doi: 10.1111/j.1467-8721.2008.00564.x.

Mitchell, J.P., Macrae, C.N., and Banaji, M.R. (2004). Encoding-specific effects of social cognition on the neural correlates of subsequent memory. *Journal of Neuroscience*, 24 (21), 4912–4917.

Mitchell, J.P., Macrae, C.N., and Banaji, M.R. (2006). Dissociable medial prefrontal contributions to judgments of similar and dissimilar others. *Neuron*, 50 (4), 655–663. doi: 10.1016/j.neuron.2006.03.040.

Mitchell, K.J., Raye, C.L., Ebner, N.C., *et al.* (2009). Age-group differences in medial cortex activity associated with thinking about self-relevant agendas. *Psychology and Aging*, 24 (2), 438–449. doi: 10.1037/a0015181.

Moran, J., Jolly, E., and Mitchell, J.P. (2012). Social-cognitive deficits in normal aging. *Journal of Neuroscience*, 32 (16), 5553–5561.

Mueller, J.H., Wonderlich, S., and Dugan, K. (1986). Self-referent processing of age-specific material. *Psychology and Aging*, 1 (4), 293–299.

Murty, V.P., Ritchey, M., Adcock, R.A., and LaBar, K.S. (2010). fMRI studies of successful emotional memory encoding: a quantitative meta-analysis. *Neuropsychologia*, 48 (12), 3459–3469.

Narvaez, D., Radvansky, G.A., Lynchard, N.A., and Copeland, D.E. (2011). Are older adults more attuned to morally charged information? *Experimental Aging Research*, 37 (4), 398–434. doi: 10.1080/0361073x.2011.590756.

Nashiro, K., and Mather, M. (2011). The effect of emotional arousal on memory binding in normal aging and Alzheimer's disease. *American Journal of Psychology*, 124 (3), 301.

Nashiro, K., Sakaki, M., and Mather, M. (2012). Age differences in brain activity during emotion processing: reflections of age-related decline or increased emotion regulation. *Gerontology*, 58 (2), 156–163.

Öhman, A., and Mineka, S. (2001). Fears, phobias, and preparedness: toward an evolved module of fear and fear learning. *Psychological Review*, 108 (3), 483.

Olson, I., Plotzker, A., and Ezzyat, Y. (2007). The enigmatic temporal pole: a review of findings on social and emotional processing. *Brain*, 130, 1718–1731.

Parkinson, B. (1996). Emotions are social. *British Journal of Psychology*, 87 (4), 663–683.

Perry, D., Hendler, T., and Shamay-Tsoory, S.G. (2011). Projecting memories: The role of the hippocampus in emotional mentalizing. *NeuroImage*, 54 (2), 1669–1676. doi: 10.1016/j.neuroimage.2010.08.057.

Phelps, E.A. (2004). Human emotion and memory: interactions of the amygdala and hippocampal complex. *Current Opinion in Neurobiology*, 14 (2), 198–202.

Posner, M.I. (1980). Orienting of attention. *Quarterly Journal of Experimental Psychology*, 32, 3–25.

Rabin, J.S., Gilboa, A., Stuss, D.T., *et al.* (2010). Common and unique neural correlates of autobiographical memory and theory of mind. *Journal of Cognitive Neuroscience*, 22 (6), 1095–1111. doi: 10.1162/jocn.2009.21344.

Rahhal, T.A., May, C.P., and Hasher, L. (2002). Truth and character: sources that older adults can remember. *Psychological Science*, 13 (2), 101–105.

Ray, R.D., Shelton, A.L., Hollon, N.G., *et al.* (2010). Interdependent self-construal and neural representations of self and mother. *Social Cognitive and Affective Neuroscience*, 5 (2–3), 318–323. doi: 10.1093/scan/nsp039.

Rhodes, M.G., and Anastasi, J.S. (2012). The own-age bias in face recognition: a meta-analytic and theoretical review. *Psychological Bulletin*, 138 (1), 146–174. doi: 10.1037/a0025750.

Ritchey, M., Bessette-Symons, B., Hayes, S.M., and Cabeza, R. (2011). Emotion processing in the aging brain is modulated by semantic elaboration. *Neuropsychologia*, 49 (4), 640–650.

Rogers, T., Kuiper, N., and Kirker, W. (1977). Self-reference and the encoding of personal information. *Journal of Personality and Social Psychology*, 35 (9), 677–688.

Rosa, N., and Gutchess, A. (2011). Source memory for action in young and older adults: Self vs. close or unknown others. *Psychology and Aging*, 26, 625–630.

Sakaki, M., Niki, K., and Mather, M. (2012). Beyond arousal and valence: The importance of the biological versus social relevance of emotional stimuli. *Cognitive Affective and Behavioral Neuroscience*, 12 (1), 115–139. doi: 10.3758/s13415-011-0062-x.

Samanez-Larkin, G.R., Robertson, E.R., Mikels, J.A., *et al.* (2009). Selective attention to emotion in the aging brain. *Psychology and Aging*, 24 (3), 519.

Sander, D., Grafman, J., and Zalla, T. (2003). The human amygdala: an evolved system for relevance detection. *Reviews in the Neurosciences*, 14 (4), 303–316.

Satterthwaite, T.D., Wolf, D.H., Gur, R.C., *et al.* (2009). Frontolimbic responses to emotional face memory: The neural correlates of first impressions. *Human Brain Mapping*, 30 (11), 3748–3758.

Schacter, D.L., and Slotnick, S.D. (2004). The cognitive neuroscience of memory distortion. *Neuron*, 44 (1), 149–160.

Schefter, M., Knorr, S., Kathmann, N., and Werheid, K. (2012). Age differences on ERP old/ new effects for emotional and neutral faces. *International Journal of Psychophysiology*, 85 (2), 257–269.

Schiller, D., Freeman, J., Mitchell, J., *et al.* (2009). A neural mechanism of first impressions. *Nature Neuroscience*, 12, 508–514.

Sharot, T., Delgado, M.R., and Phelps, E.A. (2004). How emotion enhances the feeling of remembering. *Nature Neuroscience*, 7 (12), 1376–1380.

Shaver, P.R., Wu, S., and Schwartz, J.C. (1992). Cross-cultural similarities and differences in emotion and its representation: a prototype approach. In *Review of Personality and Social Psychology* (ed. M.S. Clark). Thousand Oaks, CA: Sage, vol. 13, pp. 175–212.

Shiota, M.N., and Levenson, R.W. (2009). Effects of aging on experimentally instructed detached reappraisal, positive reappraisal, and emotional behavior suppression. *Psychology and Aging*, 24 (4), 890.

Singer, T., Kiebel, S.J., Winston, J.S., *et al.* (2004). Brain responses to the acquired moral status of faces. *Neuron*, 41 (4), 653–662.

Somerville, L.H., Wig, G.S., Whalen, P.J., and Kelley, W.M. (2006). Dissociable medial temporal lobe contributions to social memory. *Journal of Cognitive Neuroscience*, 18 (8), 1253–1265.

Spaniol, J., Voss, A., and Grady, C.L. (2008). Aging and emotional memory: cognitive mechanisms underlying the positivity effect. *Psychology and Aging*, 23 (4), 859.

Spreng, R.N., and Grady, C.L. (2010). Patterns of brain activity supporting autobiographical memory, prospection, and theory of mind, and their relationship to the default mode network. *Journal of Cognitive Neuroscience*, 22 (6), 1112–1123. doi: 10.1162/jocn. 2009.21282.

Spreng, R.N., and Mar, R.A. (2012). I remember you: a role for memory in social cognition and the functional neuroanatomy of their interaction. *Brain Research*, 1428, 43–50. doi: 10.1016/j.brainres.2010.12.024.

Spreng, R.N., Mar, R.A., and Kim, A.S.N. (2009). The common neural basis of autobiographical memory, prospection, navigation, theory of mind, and the default mode: a quantitative meta-analysis. *Journal of Cognitive Neuroscience*, 21 (3), 489–510. doi: 10.1162/jocn.2008.21029.

St. Jacques, P.L., Bessette-Symons, B., and Cabeza, R. (2009). Functional neuroimaging studies of aging and emotion: fronto-amygdalar differences during emotional perception and episodic memory. *Journal of the International Neuropsychological Society*, 15 (06), 819–825.

St. Jacques, P.L., Dolcos, F., and Cabeza, R. (2009). Effects of aging on functional connectivity of the amygdala for subsequent memory of negative pictures a network analysis of functional magnetic resonance imaging data. *Psychological Science*, 20 (1), 74–84.

St. Jacques, P.L., Rubin, D.C., LaBar, K.S., and Cabeza, R. (2008). The short and long of it: neural correlates of temporal-order memory for autobiographical events. *Journal of Cognitive Neuroscience* 20 (7), 1327–1341.

Storbeck, J., and Clore, G.L. (2005). With sadness comes accuracy; with happiness, false memory mood and the false memory effect. *Psychological Science*, 16 (10), 785–791.

Straube, B., Green, A., Chatterjee, A., and Kircher, T. (2011). Encoding social interactions: the neural correlates of true and false memories. *Journal of Cognitive Neuroscience*, 23 (2), 306–324. doi: 10.1162/jocn.2010.21505.

Talmi, D., Anderson, A.K., Riggs, L., *et al.* (2008). Immediate memory consequences of the effect of emotion on attention to pictures. *Learning and Memory*, 15 (3), 172–182.

Tessitore, A., Hariri, A.R., Fera, F., *et al.* (2005). Functional changes in the activity of brain regions underlying emotion processing in the elderly. *Psychiatry Research: Neuroimaging*, 139 (1), 9–18.

Todorov, A., Gobbini, M., Evans, K., and Haxby, J. (2007). Spontaneous retrieval of affective person knowledge in face perception. *Neuropsychologia*, 45 (1), 163–173. doi: 10.1016/j.neuropsychologia.2006.04.018.

Todorov, A., and Olson, I. (2008). Robust learning of affective trait associations with faces when the hippocampus is damaged, but not when the amygdala and temporal pole are damaged. *Social Cognitive and Affective Neuroscience*, 3, 195–203.

Tomaszczyk, J.C., and Fernandes, M.A. (2012). A positivity effect in autobiographical memory, but not phonemic fluency, in older adults. *Aging, Neuropsychology, and Cognition*, 19 (6), 699–722.

Touryan, S.R., Johnson, M.K., Mitchell, K.J., *et al.* (2007). The influence of self-regulatory focus on encoding of, and memory for, emotional words. *Social Neuroscience*, 2 (1), 14–27. doi: 10.1080/17470910601046829.

Tsukiura, T., and Cabeza, R. (2008). Orbitofrontal and hippocampal contributions to memory for face–name associations: The rewarding power of a smile. *Neuropsychologia*, 46 (9), 2310–2319. doi: 10.1016/j.neuropsychologia.2008.03.013.

Urry, H.L., and Gross, J.J. (2010). Emotion regulation in older age. *Current Directions in Psychological Science*, 19 (6), 352–357.

Van Overwalle, F. (2009). Social cognition and the brain: a meta-analysis. *Human Brain Mapping*, 30 (3), 829–858. doi: 10.1002/hbm.20547.

Vrticka, P., Andersson, F., Sander, D., and Vuilleumier, P. (2009). Memory for friends or foes: the social context of past encounters with faces modulates their subsequent neural traces in the brain. *Social Neuroscience*, 4 (5), 384–401. doi: 10.1080/17470910902941793.

Waring, J.D., Addis, D.R., and Kensinger, E.A. (2013). Effects of aging on neural connectivity underlying selective memory for emotional scenes. *Neurobiology of Aging*, 34 (2), 451–467.

Werheid, K., Gruno, M., Kathmann, N., *et al.* (2010). Biased recognition of positive faces in aging and amnestic mild cognitive impairment. *Psychology and Aging*, 25 (1), 1.

Williams, L.M., Brown, K.J., Palmer, D., *et al.* (2006). The mellow years? Neural basis of improving emotional stability over age. *Journal of Neuroscience*, 26 (24), 6422–6430.

Winston, J., Strange, B., O'Doherty, J., and Dolan, R. (2002). Automatic and intentional brain responses during evaluation of trustworthiness of faces. *Nature Neuroscience*, 5, 277–283.

Wood, J.N., Romero, S.G., Makale, M., and Grafman, J. (2003). Category-specific representations of social and nonsocial knowledge in the human prefrontal cortex. *Journal of Cognitive Neuroscience*, 15 (2), 236–248. doi: 10.1162/089892903321208178.

Wood, S., and Kisley, M.A. (2006). The negativity bias is eliminated in older adults: age-related reduction in event-related brain potentials associated with evaluative categorization. *Psychology and Aging*, 21 (4), 815.

Wright, C.I., Wedig, M.M., Williams, D., *et al.* (2006). Novel fearful faces activate the amygdala in healthy young and elderly adults. *Neurobiology of Aging*, 27 (2), 361–374.

Wurm, L.H., Labouvie-Vief, G., Aycock, J., *et al.* (2004). Performance in auditory and visual emotional stroop tasks: a comparison of older and younger adults. *Psychology and Aging*, 19 (3), 523.

Yang, L., Truong, L., Fuss, S., and Bislimovic, S. (2012). The effects of aging and divided attention on the self-reference effect in emotional memory: spontaneous or effortful mnemonic benefits? *Memory*, 20 (6), 596–607.

Yeung, D.Y., Fung, H.H., and Lang, F.R. (2008). Self-construal moderates age differences in social network characteristics. *Psychology and Aging*, 23 (1), 222–226. doi: 10.1037/0882-7974.23.1.222.

Yoder, C.Y., and Elias, J.W. (1987). Age, affect, and memory for pictorial story sequences. *British Journal of Psychology*, 78 (4), 545–549.

Zebrowitz, L.A., Franklin, R.G. Jr, Hillman, S., and Boc, H. (2013). Older and younger adults' first impressions from faces: similar in agreement but different in positivity. *Psychology and Aging*, 28 (1), 202.

# 20

# Episodic Memory in Neurodegenerative Disorders
## Past, Present, and Future
### Muireann Irish and Michael Hornberger

## Introduction

Neurodegenerative disorders offer a compelling view of the cognitive architecture of the brain when specific neural systems break down in a coordinated fashion. The study of neurodegenerative cohorts can therefore provide important insights into the underlying mechanisms supporting episodic memory. In this chapter, we examine the systematic and progressive degeneration of episodic memory processes in the most common subtypes of dementia, namely Alzheimer's disease (AD) and frontotemporal dementia (FTD). We discuss behavioral and neuroimaging studies of anterograde and retrograde episodic memory deficits in these dementia subtypes, as well as recent advances in which the ability to imagine the future is posited to represent a key expression of the episodic memory system.

### Alzheimer's disease

The dementia syndrome of AD has long been heralded as a lesion model for episodic memory, particularly given the characteristic pattern of medial temporal lobe (MTL) neural degeneration evident from a very early stage in the pathological process (Braak and Braak, 1991; Butters *et al.*, 1987). Clinically, the most common presentation of AD is an amnesic profile in which anterograde memory difficulties concerning the encoding and retrieval of recent events are prominent. A decline in episodic memory function emerges as a consequence of neurofibrillary tangles, beginning in the allocortex of the MTL (entorhinal cortex and hippocampus), progressing across the hippocampus, and spreading to the neocortex (Ewers *et al.*, 2011; Sperling *et al.*, 2011) (Figure 20.1). Diffusion tensor imaging (DTI) of white matter tracts has pointed to decreased fractional anisotropy in the left anterior temporal lobe (Damoiseaux *et al.*, 2009) and in the left anterior and posterior cingulum tracts, bilateral descending cingulum tracts, and left uncinate tracts (Zhang *et al.*, 2009) in

*The Wiley Handbook on the Cognitive Neuroscience of Memory*, First Edition.
Edited by Donna Rose Addis, Morgan Barense, and Audrey Duarte.
© 2015 John Wiley & Sons, Ltd. Published 2015 by John Wiley & Sons, Ltd.

Pre-clinical stages

Phase 1                    Phase 2                    Phase 3

Clinical stages

Phase 4                         Phase 5

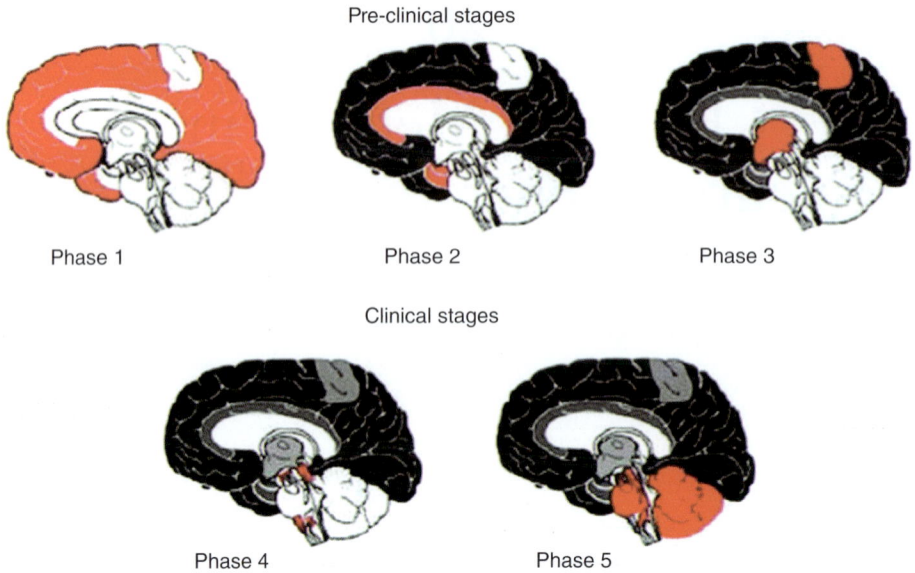

**Figure 20.1**    The progression of amyloid deposits as assessed at different stages of Alzheimer's disease (AD) in postmortem brain tissue using immunohistochemical techniques against amyloid beta (Ab). Phases (1–5) of postmortem histological appearance of Ab in clinical AD. In phase 1, Ab is largely restricted to neocortical brain areas. In phases 2 and 3, when clinical signs of cognitive decline have yet to appear, Ab deposits are localized throughout the neocortex and allocortex, including brain areas such as the medial temporal lobe, and also begin to occur in the motor cortex and subcortical brain structures. In the clinical stages of AD (phases 4 and 5), Ab deposits are observed globally in the brain, including the brainstem and the cerebellum in the final stage of the disease (phase 5). Key: white, no Ab deposits; red, novel Ab deposition; gray, Ab deposits that were missing in phase 1; black, Ab deposits that were present already in phase 1. Reproduced with the permission of Elsevier Ltd., from Ewers, M., Sperling, R.A., Klunk, W.E., *et al.* (2011). Neuroimaging markers for the prediction and early diagnosis of Alzheimer's disease dementia. *Trends in Neurosciences*, 34 (8), 430–442. Copyright (2011).

AD compared with healthy older adults. Further, resting-state functional connectivity studies corroborate the disruption of connectivity between the MTL, lateral temporoparietal, posterior cingulate, and medial frontal cortices in AD (Seeley *et al.*, 2009; Zhou *et al.*, 2010).

## Semantic dementia

The hallmark clinical feature of semantic dementia (SD) concerns the progressive and amodal loss of semantic memory, that is, general conceptual knowledge of the world (Hodges and Patterson, 2007). SD is a language variant within the FTD spectrum in which a progressive decline in semantic processing is theoretically attributable to the degeneration of a central amodal semantic hub (Patterson, Nestor, and Rogers, 2007; Rogers *et al.*, 2004). Despite striking semantic impairments, in the early stages of the disease, SD patients nevertheless display a wide range of relatively

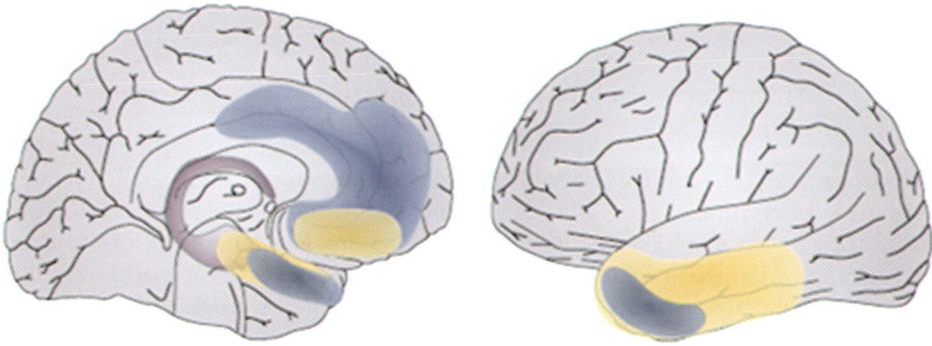

**Figure 20.2** Characteristic profiles of atrophy in the behavioral variant of frontotemporal dementia (bvFTD) and semantic dementia (SD). In bvFTD, atrophy typically begins in the medial and orbital prefrontal cortices, extending to the temporal pole and hippocampal formation with disease progression (blue). In SD, atrophy is typically lateralized, with the left hemisphere generally more affected than the right, and chiefly affects the anterior temporal lobes and temporal pole, including the hippocampal formation and amygdala, gradually spreading to ventral prefrontal cortical regions as the disease progresses (yellow). Reproduced with the permission of Macmillan Publishers Ltd., from Irish, M., Piguet, O., and Hodges, J.R. (2012). Self-projection and the default network in frontotemporal dementia. *Nature Reviews Neurology*, 8 (3), 152–161. Copyright (2012).

preserved cognitive abilities, including relatively intact episodic retrieval, particularly on nonverbal tasks (Bozeat *et al.*, 2000). On a neural level, SD is characterized by the progressive degeneration of the anterior temporal lobes (Hodges and Patterson, 2007), most severe on the ventral surface and including the perirhinal cortex and anterior fusiform gyrus (Mion *et al.*, 2010; Whitwell *et al.*, 2005), and typically lateralized to the left more than the right hemisphere (Figure 20.2). The severity of atrophy in the anterior temporal lobes in SD is directly correlated with the extent to which semantic memory is compromised (Davies *et al.*, 2004; Mion *et al.*, 2010). Importantly, volumetric MRI studies have confirmed that the degree of hippocampal atrophy in SD is equivalent to, or greater than, that seen in disease-matched cases of AD, albeit in the context of much more severe temporal lobe atrophy (Chan *et al.*, 2001; Galton *et al.*, 2001).

## Behavioral-variant frontotemporal dementia

Behavioral-variant FTD (bvFTD) is characterized by the progressive deterioration of social functioning and personality, reflecting the disintegration of the underlying neural circuits known to support social cognition, emotion processing, motivation, and decision making (Piguet *et al.*, 2011). Clinically, bvFTD patients often present with a dysexecutive syndrome, displaying disinhibited impulsive behaviors and an apparent lack of regard for others (Rascovsky *et al.*, 2011). The burden of neural atrophy in bvFTD emerges first in the anterior cingulate and frontoinsular cortices, the medial prefrontal cortices (PFC), frontal pole, striatum, and thalamus (Seeley *et al.*, 2008). With disease progression, atrophy encroaches into the temporal cortices, typically on the right hand side (Rabinovici *et al.*, 2007) (Figure 20.2).

# Anterograde Memory

## Medial temporal lobe contributions to episodic memory in neurodegeneration

Overwhelmingly, AD patients have been studied to investigate anterograde memory processes. Interestingly, the earliest experimental memory studies in AD focused mainly on implicit memory function (e.g., Graf, Squire, and Mandler, 1984), before the demonstration that explicit memory processes (i.e., episodic memory) were disproportionately affected in AD (Knight, 1998). This finding triggered subsequent AD studies, in particular, once it became apparent that the early hippocampal damage in AD made these patients a good lesion model to investigate the dual-process theory of recognition memory (Jacoby, 1991; Yonelinas, 1997). Indeed, several studies have found that recollection is disproportionately affected compared to familiarity in AD (Ally, Gold, and Budson, 2009; Tse *et al.*, 2010; Westerberg *et al.*, 2006). Similar to findings in hippocampal lesion patients (Yonelinas *et al.*, 2010), AD patients showed severe deficits in recollecting encoded information. Nevertheless, familiarity-related processes are also disrupted in AD (though see Westerberg *et al.*, 2006). These additional familiarity deficits might be explained by the AD disease etiology, in which hippocampal, as well as entorhinal, cortices are affected from early on (Braak and Braak, 1991). Dual-process theories state that recollection is only subserved by the hippocampus, while familiarity should be processed via extra-hippocampal regions, including perirhinal and entorhinal areas (Yonelinas *et al.*, 2010). A recent study confirmed this notion by showing a strong relationship between recollection performance and hippocampal volumes, whereas familiarity performance was strongly related to entorhinal intactness (Wolk *et al.*, 2011) (Figure 20.3). Thus, evidence from AD patients reveals a dissociation of episodic memory processes across MTL regions, supporting dual-process theories.

Recollection is commonly assumed to involve the mnemonic association of contextual information (e.g., time, space) with the actual memory trace (see also Chapter 18). Given the commonly observed hippocampal degradation in AD, one can predict that AD patients should show more general associative memory problems. Indeed, neuropsychological associative memory tasks, such as the Paired Associates Learning task, have revealed severe impairments in AD (e.g., Lee *et al.*, 2003). A further study of associative memory in AD required patients to encode word pairs that were presented at test either in their original, or re-arranged, configurations. AD patients showed a disproportionate impairment for the association of the word pairs in comparison to age-matched controls (Gallo *et al.*, 2004). These findings are further corroborated by fMRI associative memory studies in AD (Sperling *et al.*, 2003), which show that AD patients display reduced hippocampal activation compared to age-matched controls for the encoding of associative information (though see Pihlajamaki *et al.*, 2008). Taken together, the recollective deficits observed in AD appear to stem from a general associative memory deficit, which fails to "link" different mnemonic material to create a full recollective experience.

One issue that arises from the associative memory findings concerns the origin of these deficits, more specifically, whether associative memory deficits emanate from an inability to retrieve the to-be-remembered items together, or due to an impaired capacity to perceptually link the presented information into a memory trace via the perirhinal cortex (see also Chapter 10). The neurodegenerative condition of SD

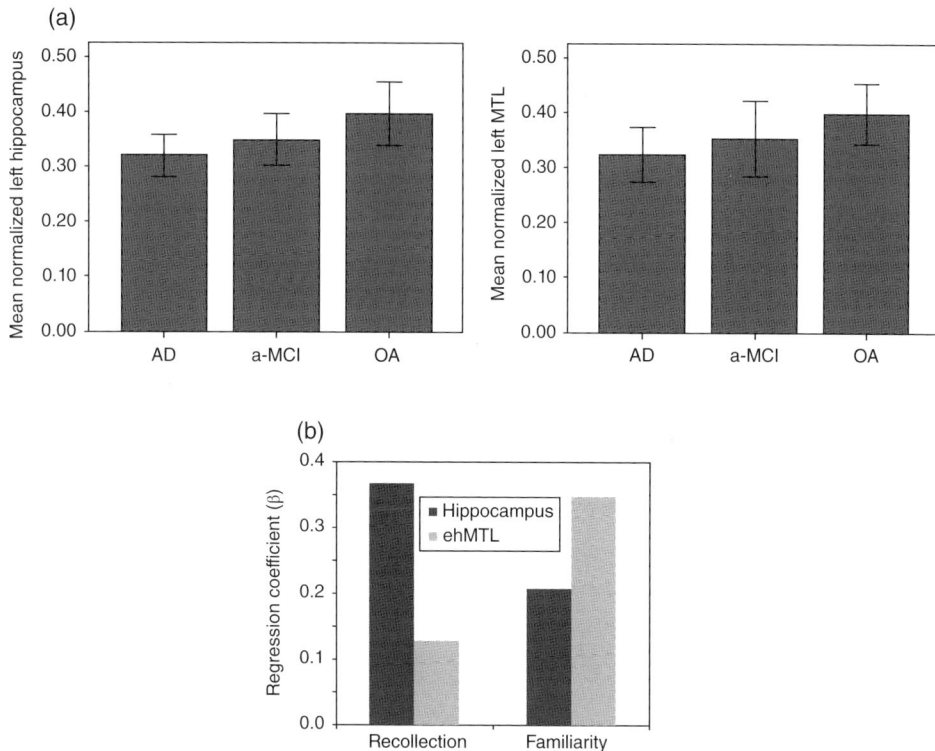

**Figure 20.3** Relationship between left hippocampus and entorhinal cortex (ehMTL) volumes in Alzheimer's disease (AD) and recollection and familiarity performance, respectively. a-MCI, amnestic mild cognitive impairment; OA, older adults. Reproduced with permission from Wolk, D.A., Dunfee, K.L., Dickerson, B.C., *et al.* (2011). A medial temporal lobe division of labor: insights from memory in aging and early Alzheimer disease. *Hippocampus*, 21 (5), 461–466. Copyright (2011) John Wiley & Sons, Ltd.

represents an ideal patient group to investigate the perirhinal contribution to episodic memory, given the atrophy seen in this region (Davies *et al.*, 2004). Overall, SD patients show relatively intact episodic memory performance (Graham *et al.*, 2000; Simons *et al.*, 2001) and often perform better than AD patients (Scahill, Hodges, and Graham, 2005) with the exception of verbally loaded tasks. While semantic memory is severely impaired in SD, intact episodic memory performance in this syndrome may rely almost exclusively on perceptual information. Indeed, this hypothesis was originally advanced by Warrington (1975) in one of the earliest descriptions of the SD syndrome. It follows that episodic memory should be affected in SD patients when the retrieval demand for perceptual information is increased. This hypothesis was explored by Graham and colleagues (2000), who investigated recognition memory in SD patients using color pictures. Crucially, while some target items were perceptually identical at study and test (e.g., the same telephone), others were perceptually different (e.g., telephones of different colors or shapes). Despite their profound semantic memory problems, SD patients showed relatively preserved episodic memory for perceptually identical pictures. By contrast, recognition performance was much poorer for the items that were perceptually different at study and test, some patients performing at chance level. These findings demonstrate that SD patients rely heavily on perceptual inputs for anterograde memory, and therefore show high rates of false recognition when perceptually similar objects are used for episodic memory testing (Simons *et al.*, 2005). These findings can also account for the impaired recognition memory for words found in SD, given the few distinctive perceptual features written words have in comparison to pictures.

### Frontal lobe contributions to episodic memory in neurodegeneration

Although the MTL plays a major role in episodic memory functioning, it is also strongly supported by various PFC regions, and this is evident across many episodic memory paradigms (Simons and Spiers, 2003). The specific functions of distinct PFC regions in supporting episodic memory, however, remain unknown. One putative PFC episodic memory function is memory monitoring (Burgess and Shallice, 1996; Wagner *et al.*, 2001), which checks that mnemonic details are veridical and is, therefore, particularly in demand when the attribution of mnemonic details is difficult to verify (e.g., confabulation) (Burgess and Shallice, 1996). Increasing evidence demonstrates that such monitoring functions fail to some degree in AD. In particular, the failure to retrieve specific mnemonic details in AD manifests in over-familiarization and, consequently, false alarms in memory performance (e.g., Budson *et al.*, 2001). For example, patients display increased false-alarm rates by accepting more distractors as previously learned (Tse *et al.*, 2010), suggesting that AD patients show specific problems with rejecting or suppressing irrelevant information (reviewed by Souchay, 2007).

This finding converges with reports from false-recognition studies in AD (Budson *et al.*, 2001, 2003; Gallo *et al.*, 2004; Plancher *et al.*, 2009; see Chapter 8 for a review of false memory in aging). For example, Budson and colleagues (2001) found that compared with healthy younger and older adults, AD patients showed higher levels of uncorrected false recognition of semantic associates across five trials. These results suggested that over the study-test trials, the patients with AD built up gist memories that led to more false alarms, while healthy younger and older adults could reduce their false memories with increased item-specific memory. This failure to reject false memories in AD patients may stem from deficits in PFC-dependent monitoring systems. Indeed, recent studies show that memory monitoring deficits can even outweigh memory accuracy deficits in AD (Dodson *et al.*, 2011), and thus AD patients often have more liberal memory biases than age-matched controls (Deason *et al.*, 2012). AD patients appear largely to rely on familiarity-based memory, due to their severe impairments in recollective memory processes. This over-familiarization of memory information is corroborated on a neural level by a recent fMRI study (Pihlajamaki *et al.*, 2011), which revealed that healthy older participants show a suppression of MTL activation after multiple stimulus repetition at encoding. By contrast, AD patients show no such MTL suppression, leading to poorer subsequent associative memories for the learned information. An obvious candidate for such modulation of MTL activity at encoding and retrieval is the PFC. The question remains, however, as to the specific contributions of the MTL and PFC in episodic memory processing in AD.

Episodic memory deficits in bvFTD provide an ideal contrast against the AD findings, given the substantial PFC degeneration in bvFTD. On a neuropsychological level, many studies have shown that bvFTD patients perform better than AD patients on standard verbal and visuospatial memory tasks (reviewed by Hornberger and Piguet, 2012), and that bvFTD patients tend not to show the accelerated forgetting which is typical of AD (Hutchinson and Mathias, 2007). Importantly, however, recent more thorough investigations demonstrate that the majority of bvFTD patients show impaired episodic memory (Hornberger *et al.*, 2010). These episodic memory deficits are mostly attributed to their substantial PFC pathology and are related to defective memory monitoring processes rather than true amnesia (e.g., Collette, Van der Linden, and Salmon, 2010). This finding is corroborated by structural MRI studies showing that disturbance in the strategic aspects of episodic memory recall and retrieval processes is associated with PFC atrophy in bvFTD, in particular, orbitofrontal cortex atrophy (Kramer *et al.*, 2005; Pennington, Hodges, and Hornberger, 2011). The failure of these prefrontally mediated retrieval control mechanisms can also account for the increased false-recognition rates (de Boysson *et al.*, 2011) and confabulations (Nedjam, Devouche, and Dalla Barba, 2004) found in bvFTD.

The strongest evidence to date for predominantly frontally mediated episodic memory deficits in bvFTD comes from source memory studies that require participants to encode and retrieve information about the context in which items were studied. Previous studies have reported severe impairments in source recollection in bvFTD (Söderlund *et al.*, 2008), with temporal source attributions being particularly affected (Simons *et al.*, 2002). A more recent study (Irish *et al.*, 2012b) replicated the temporal source finding in bvFTD by Simons and colleagues and revealed that a subgroup of patients presented with additional deficits in retrieval of spatial source contextual details. Neuroimaging and patient studies have implicated the PFC in supporting retrieval of temporal source information (Duarte *et al.*, 2010; Ekstrom *et al.*, 2011). In contrast, the MTL, particularly the parahippocampal cortex, has been implicated in the successful retrieval of spatial source details (Ekstrom *et al.*, 2011; Spiers and Maguire, 2007). Thus, the source memory data in bvFTD indicate that, overwhelmingly, these patients exhibit significant prefrontal damage, which can adversely influence their episodic memory performance. Additionally, however, a subgroup of bvFTD patients shows evidence of substantial MTL involvement and concomitant severe episodic memory processing deficits. To our knowledge, no study to date has directly contrasted bvFTD and AD patients on specific tasks which differentially stress prefrontal versus MTL aspects of episodic memory functioning. The creation of such tasks, in conjunction with neuroimaging techniques, will permit the investigation of PFC and MTL contributions to episodic memory in more detail, and represent a promising avenue in anterograde memory research.

## Retrograde Memory in Neurodegenerative Disorders

Autobiographical memory (AM) refers to the complex ability to mentally project backwards in subjective time to recollect personal episodes from the past (Greenberg and Rubin, 2003). Such events are typically accompanied by visual imagery, emotional connotations, and a sense of reliving of the original event (Conway, 2001; Tulving, 2002; Wheeler, Stuss, and Tulving, 1997) and rely on a widespread neural network including the hippocampus, parahippocampal gyrus, lateral temporal cortices, posterior parietal cortex, retrosplenial cortex, posterior cingulate cortex, precuneus, thalamus, and the medial PFC (Cabeza and St. Jacques, 2007; Maguire, 2001;

Svoboda, McKinnon, and Levine, 2006; see also Chapter 13). Accordingly, the study of AM in neurodegenerative disorders with varying patterns of damage to this distributed network represents an important line of enquiry for understanding the neural and cognitive mechanisms supporting this branch of episodic memory.

## Autobiographical memory in Alzheimer's disease

The loss of recent personal memories is a hallmark feature of AD, and has been reliably demonstrated across a range of AM paradigms. An ongoing debate within the literature pertains to the temporal profile of the episodic AM deficit in AD, and whether recent events are disproportionately disrupted in comparison with more remote memories. The presence or absence of temporal gradients during AM retrieval is informative for understanding mechanisms of consolidation and whether the MTL, more specifically the hippocampus, plays a time-limited or a permanent role in the storage and recollection of remote memories (Nadel *et al.*, 2000; Squire and Alvarez, 1995). Temporal gradients have been reported widely in the literature (Eustache *et al.*, 2004; Graham and Hodges, 1997; Greene, Hodges, and Baddeley, 1995; Irish *et al.*, 2011b; Kopelman, Wilson, and Baddeley, 1989; Leyhe *et al.*, 2009), but other studies using more detailed probing methods have failed to reliably demonstrate a temporal gradient in AD (Irish *et al.*, 2011a; Piolino *et al.*, 2003). Such conflicting findings may reflect methodological differences in probing and scoring across assessments (Barnabe *et al.*, 2012).

While a large body of evidence confirms the association between MTL volumes and anterograde memory performance in AD (de Toledo-Morrell *et al.*, 2000; Gallagher and Koh, 2011), comparatively few studies have directly investigated the neural substrates of retrograde memory performance in AD. Using a partial least squares approach with structural MRI scans of AD patients, Gilboa and colleagues found significant associations between episodic AM retrieval and the integrity of temporal lobe structures. Specifically, retrieval of events, irrespective of time period, was associated with the combined volume of anterior temporal lobe and MTL structures, more pronounced on the right (Gilboa *et al.*, 2005). More recently, an fMRI study of AM retrieval in AD has revealed enhanced activation of the ventromedial PFC (vmPFC), left inferior frontal gyrus, right precuneus, and left lingual gyrus during AM retrieval when compared with semantic retrieval (Meulenbroek *et al.*, 2010). Interestingly, this study demonstrated that in concert with decreases in hippocampal volume, activity in the vmPFC and left inferior frontal gyrus increased, indicating a possible compensatory mechanism and increased demands on semantic processing (Meulenbroek *et al.*, 2010).

AM impairment in AD reflects extensive pathology involving multiple neural regions necessary for the recollection of the past, the most important of which are the MTL, retrosplenial cortex, and posterior cingulate cortex (Pengas *et al.*, 2010). The posterior cingulate cortex, for example, appears to be particularly important in the retrieval of past AMs (Maddock, Garrett, and Buonocore, 2001) and represents a site of early amyloid deposition in AD using PiB uptake as an in-vivo biomarker (Rowe *et al.*, 2007). Further, FDG-PET imaging studies have detected metabolic changes in the posterior cingulate from early in the course of AD (Nestor, Fryer, and Hodges, 2006; Salmon *et al.*, 2009). Therefore, while AD has typically been studied in relation to hippocampal degeneration, consideration of structures beyond the MTL is important to fully comprehend the nature of AM deficits in this syndrome.

## Remote memory deficits in semantic dementia

Studies of AM in SD have yielded inconsistent results, with the majority of studies documenting a reverse temporal gradient, or more accurately a step function, whereby recent memories are relatively preserved in comparison with remote memories (Graham and Hodges, 1997; Hou, Miller, and Kramer, 2005; Irish *et al.*, 2011a; Matuszewski *et al.*, 2009; Nestor *et al.*, 2002; Piolino *et al.*, 2003). The relative sparing of recent episodic memory in SD has been interpreted as reflecting preserved anterograde processes and encoding and retrieval mechanisms (Adlam, Patterson, and Hodges, 2009; Matuszewski *et al.*, 2009). It has further been suggested that older memories become semanticized, whereby the repeated recollection of past events allows for abstraction of the gist of the episode without the accompanying contextual details (Rosenbaum, Winocur, and Moscovitch, 2001; Winocur and Moscovitch, 2011). By this reasoning, remote memory deficits in SD can be interpreted as reflecting a loss of semantic information that is integral to the memory trace (Westmacott *et al.*, 2001). Remote-period deficits are unlikely to stem primarily from executive dysfunction, given that the provision of structured probing does not appear to eradicate remote memory deficits in SD (Irish *et al.*, 2011a; Nestor *et al.*, 2002). The mechanisms supporting the relative preservation of recent AM in SD remain contentious, although it has been suggested that recent memories encompass more perceptual elements rather than over-general or semanticized information (Hodges and Graham, 2001; Nestor *et al.*, 2002). As such. SD patients rely on perceptual features for recent retrieval.

The reverse temporal gradient has been questioned in SD, with a number of studies failing to demonstrate this profile of ABM recall (Maguire *et al.*, 2010; McKinnon *et al.*, 2006; Moss *et al.*, 2003; Westmacott *et al.*, 2001). While such inconsistencies in the literature may reflect variation in disease severity across cohorts (Matuszewski *et al.*, 2009), the methods used to probe AM are also of relevance. When nonverbal stimuli, such as family photographs, are used to elicit AMs in SD, this approach tends to produce a flat profile with remote and recent memory recalled equally well (Greenberg *et al.*, 2011; Maguire *et al.*, 2010; Moss *et al.*, 2003; Westmacott *et al.*, 2001). This finding is concordant with the proposition that SD patients may harness perceptual elements of such visual cues to bypass their language and verbal impairments, and access sensory-perceptual details at a higher level in the AM system (Conway, 2001; Nestor *et al.*, 2002). A recent longitudinal fMRI study of AM in a single case of SD suggests that extra-hippocampal regions, such as the vmPFC, may compensate to some degree for hippocampal damage in SD, and as such, may assume some of those duties previously undertaken by the hippocampus, such as the integration of information (Maguire *et al.*, 2010) (Figure 20.4).

## Disruption of autobiographical memory in bvFTD

Studies of AM in bvFTD have revealed relatively consistent results, most studies reporting deficits irrespective of methodology or the age of the memories (Hou, Miller, and Kramer, 2005; Irish *et al.*, 2011a; Nestor *et al.*, 2002; Piolino *et al.*, 2003, 2007; Thomas-Anterion, Jacquin, and Laurent, 2000). The absence of a temporal gradient in bvFTD has been ascribed to impairments in strategic retrieval processes related to executive dysfunction (Matuszewski *et al.*, 2006; Piolino *et al.*, 2003,

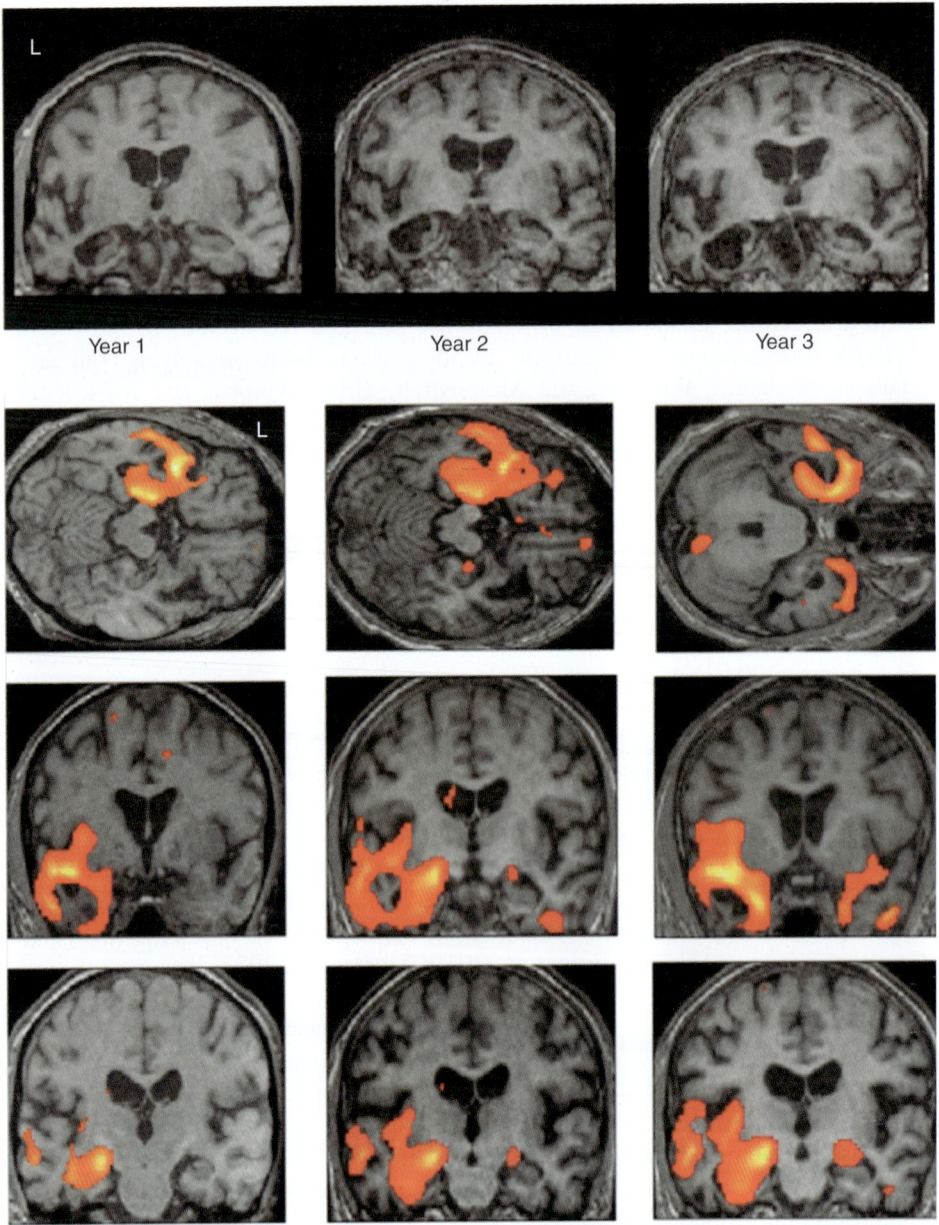

**Figure 20.4** Results from Maguire *et al.*'s (2010) longitudinal fMRI study of autobiographical memory (AM) retrieval in a case of semantic dementia (SD). At year 1, recollection of personal memories correlated with activation in the anterior temporal lobe, including residual tissue in the hippocampus. AM retrieval at years 2 and 3 was associated with upregulation of other regions in the AM network including the ventromedial and ventrolateral prefrontal cortex, right lateral temporal cortex, and precuneus. Reproduced with the permission of Elsevier Ltd., from Maguire, E.A., Kumaran, D., Hassabis, D., and Kopelman, M.D. (2010). Autobiographical memory in semantic dementia: a longitudinal fMRI study. *Neuropsychologia*, 48 (1), 123–136. Copyright (2010).

2007), which impact on the capacity to retrieve personally relevant episodes across all life epochs equally.

The importance of frontally mediated retrieval processes in AM has been reinforced by studies incorporating neuroimaging data in bvFTD. A positron emission tomography (PET) study demonstrated that the global AM impairments in bvFTD correlated with dysfunction in the left orbitofrontal cortex, left dorsolateral PFC, and lateral temporal cortex regardless of time period (Piolino *et al.*, 2007). Selective functions crucial for the recollection of AMs were ascribed to subregions of the PFC, beyond those implicated in executive functioning. Specifically, Piolino and colleagues proposed that the degeneration of the orbitofrontal cortex disrupts the selection, comparison, and decision on information stored in long-term memory, while dorsolateral PFC dysfunction underpins a failure to monitor output from long-term memory and its subsequent manipulation in working memory. Given the widespread cerebral dysfunction in bvFTD, it is unlikely that frontal lobe atrophy alone can account for the gross impairments in ABM retrieval demonstrated by bvFTD patients, particularly as the provision of structured probing does not seem to ameliorate their AM deficits (Irish *et al.*, 2011a).

McKinnon and colleagues investigated the neural substrates of AM dysfunction in a combined sample of bvFTD, FTD/SD mixed, and progressive non-fluent aphasic cases using a partial least squares approach. Their results underscored the importance of a left-lateralized posterior network, which was centered on the temporal lobes including the hippocampus and surrounding structures, but also included the posterior cingulate cortex, and left inferior parietal and occipital regions (McKinnon *et al.*, 2008). While the amalgamation of different FTD variants in this study precludes interpretations specific to the bvFTD group, the finding that MTL dysfunction correlates with AM deficits in FTD syndromes points to an additional disruption to the memory trace, in concert with frontally mediated generative and strategic retrieval deficits (Irish *et al.*, 2011a). The involvement of anterior temporal regions in the genesis of AM deficits in bvFTD concords with observations of the encroachment of the pathological process into temporal regions with disease progression (Rabinovici *et al.*, 2007; Williams, Nestor, and Hodges, 2005), potentially disrupting semantic elements necessary for AM retrieval. An interesting, but as yet unanswered, question concerns the multifactorial nature of AM disruption in bvFTD (Irish *et al.*, 2011a), specifically how potential impairments in the evaluation of internally generated information (Christoff and Gabrieli, 2000) and self-referential processing (Northoff and Bermpohl, 2004) in bvFTD patients contribute to their global AM deficits (Irish, Piguet, and Hodges, 2012).

## Memory for the Future: Episodic Future Thinking

As previously described (Chapter 14), the conception of episodic memory has undergone a radical revision in recent years, which has led to the reframing of the episodic memory system from a predominantly past-oriented system to one that appears equally suited to future-oriented thinking (Schacter, Addis, and Buckner, 2007). Despite this relatively recent paradigm shift, studies of future simulation in AD and SD have revealed important new insights into the component processes underlying the capacity for prospection.

## Parallel deficits in past and future thinking in AD

Damage to the episodic memory system produces parallel impairments in past auto-biographical retrieval and simulation of personal future events in mild AD (Addis *et al.*, 2009; Irish *et al.*, 2012a) and in mild cognitive impairment (Gamboz *et al.*, 2010). The neural underpinnings of these parallel episodic past and future thinking deficits in AD were recently elucidated using voxel-based morphometry. Atrophy in a widespread neural network including the frontal pole, posterior cingulate cortex, supramarginal gyrus, and lateral temporal cortices correlated with deficits in recent autobiographical memory retrieval in AD. Importantly, the integrity of the posterior cingulate cortex, posterior parahippocampal gyrus, and frontal pole emerged as regions crucial for future-oriented thought in AD (Irish *et al.*, 2012a), reflecting commonalities in the neural regions important for past retrieval and future simulation. The demonstration that atrophy in specific MTL and frontopolar regions manifests in a compromised capacity for future simulation dovetails with functional neuroimaging studies in which MTL regions and the frontal pole have been consistently shown to activate during future sim-ulation in healthy individuals (Addis, Wong, and Schacter, 2007; Okuda *et al.*, 2003).

## Asymmetric impairments of future thinking in SD

The first empirical demonstration of impairments in future thinking in SD arose from a study investigating the capacity to form self-representations across past, present, and future contexts (Duval *et al.*, 2012). Although recall of past self-representations was largely intact, SD patients displayed striking impairments when envisaging their pos-sible future selves, manifesting in a marked inability to construct a self-image in the future or to provide relevant details to support their future self-representations (Duval *et al.*, 2012). More recently, the asymmetric impairment of future thinking with respect to past retrieval was confirmed in SD using an episodic future simulation task in which patients were asked to imagine personally relevant future events (Irish *et al.*, 2012a). Voxel-based morphometry analyses of structural brain scans revealed that episodic future thinking deficits in SD robustly correlated with those brain regions known to underpin semantic representations (Visser *et al.*, 2010), namely the left anterior inferior temporal gyrus and bilateral temporal poles (Irish *et al.*, 2012a). Crucially, these results suggest that the retrieval of episodic information alone may not be sufficient to imagine the future, and point towards the pivotal role of semantic processing in mediating much of our internally driven cognition (Binder *et al.*, 2009; Irish and Piguet, 2013).

# Conclusions and Future Directions

We conclude this chapter at an exciting juncture in episodic memory research. The evidence to date highlights the importance of studying neurodegenerative conditions for understanding structure–function relationships within episodic memory. Patients with AD have provided significant insights into the recollection and familiarity com-ponents of episodic memory, fueling debate regarding the process by which remote memories are encoded and stored. In contrast, the syndrome of SD has proved illu-minating for understanding the role of perceptual processes in episodic retrieval and the fundamental contribution of semantic memory to past and future episodic thinking. Finally, the predominantly PFC dysfunction in bvFTD has furthered our knowledge of how strategic and executive functions influence episodic memory processing.

With advances in neuroimaging techniques, the future of episodic memory research in neurodegenerative conditions is bright. In particular, the coupling of resting-state fMRI techniques, and task-based fMRI incorporating sophisticated effective connectivity analyses, represents an important avenue for studying the breakdown of specific memory processes within distributed neural networks across dementia syndromes. We propose that this synthesis of functional and structural connectivity approaches will further elucidate those specific networks which are vulnerable in different neurodegenerative conditions, and ultimately will shed light on how we remember the past and imagine the future.

# References

Addis, D.R., Sacchetti, D.C., Ally, B.A., *et al.* (2009). Episodic simulation of future events is impaired in mild Alzheimer's disease. *Neuropsychologia*, 47 (12), 2660–2671.

Addis, D.R., Wong A.T., and Schacter, D.L. (2007). Remembering the past and imagining the future: common and distinct neural substrates during event construction and elaboration. *Neuropsychologia*, 45, 1363–1377.

Adlam, A.L.R., Patterson, K., and Hodges, J.R. (2009). I remember it as if it were yesterday: Memory for recent events in patients with semantic dementia. *Neuropsychologia*, 47 (5), 1344–1351.

Ally, B.A., Gold, C.A., and Budson, A.E. (2009). An evaluation of recollection and familiarity in Alzheimer's disease and mild cognitive impairment using receiver operating characteristics. *Brain and Cognition*, 69 (3), 504–513.

Barnabe, A., Whitehead, V., Pilon, R., *et al.* (2012). Autobiographical memory in mild cognitive impairment and Alzheimer's disease: a comparison between the Levine and Kopelman interview methodologies. *Hippocampus*, 22 (9), 1809–1825.

Binder, J.R., Desai, R.H., Graves, W.W., and Conant, L.L. (2009). Where is the semantic system? A critical review and meta-analysis of 120 functional neuroimaging studies. *Cerebral Cortex*, 19 (12), 2767–2796.

Bozeat, S., Gregory, C.A., Ralph, M.A., and Hodges, J.R. (2000). Which neuropsychiatric and behavioural features distinguish frontal and temporal variants of frontotemporal dementia from Alzheimer's disease? *Journal of Neurology, Neurosurgery and Psychiatry*, 69 (2), 178–186.

Braak, H., and Braak, E. (1991). Neuropathological stageing of Alzheimer-related changes. *Acta Neuropathologica*, 82, 239–249.

Budson, A.E., Desikan, R., Daffner, K.R., and Schacter, D.L. (2001). Perceptual false recognition in Alzheimer's disease: impairment of gist-based memory. *Neuropsychology*, 15, 230–243.

Budson, A.E., Sullivan, A.L., Daffner, K.R., and Schacter, D.L. (2003). Semantic versus phonological false recognition in aging and Alzheimer's disease. *Brain and Cognition*, 51 (3), 251–261.

Burgess, P.W., and Shallice, T. (1996). Confabulation and the control of recollection. *Memory*, 4 (4), 359–411.

Butters, N., Granholm, E., Salmon, D.P., *et al.* (1987). Episodic and semantic memory: a comparison of amnesic and demented patients. *Journal of Clinical and Experimental Neuropsychology*, 9 (5), 479–497.

Cabeza, R., and St. Jacques, P. (2007). Functional neuroimaging of autobiographical memory. *Trends in Cognitive Sciences*, 11 (5), 219–227.

Chan, D., Fox, N.C., Scahill, R.I., *et al.* (2001). Patterns of temporal lobe atrophy in semantic dementia and Alzheimer's disease. *Annals of Neurology*, 49 (4), 433–442.

Christoff, K., and Gabrieli, J.D.E. (2000). The frontopolar cortex and human cognition: Evidence for a rostrocaudal hierarchical organization within the human prefrontal cortex. *Psychobiology*, 28 (2), 168–186.

Collette, F., Van der Linden, M., and Salmon, E. (2010). Dissociation between controlled and automatic processes in the behavioral variant of fronto-temporal dementia. *Journal of Alzheimer's Disease*, 22 (3), 897–907.

Conway, M.A. (2001). Sensory-perceptual episodic memory and its context: Autobiographical memory. *Philosophical Transactions of the Royal Society of London, Series B: Biological Sciences* 356 (1413), 1356–1384.

Damoiseaux, J.S., Smith, S.M., Witter, M.P., *et al.* (2009). White matter tract integrity in aging and Alzheimer's disease. *Human Brain Mapping*, 30 (4), 1051–1059.

Davies, R.R., Graham, K.S., Xuereb, J.H., *et al.* (2004). The human perirhinal cortex and semantic memory. *European Journal of Neuroscience*, 20 (9), 2441–2446.

de Boysson, C., Belleville, S., Phillips, N.A., *et al.* (2011). False recognition in Lewy-body disease and frontotemporal dementia. *Brain and Cognition*, 75 (2), 111–118.

de Toledo-Morrell, L., Dickerson, B., Sullivan, M.P., *et al.* (2000). Hemispheric differences in hippocampal volume predict verbal and spatial memory performance in patients with Alzheimer's disease. *Hippocampus*, 10 (2), 136–142.

Deason, R.G., Hussey, E.P., Ally, B.A., and Budson, A.E. (2012). Changes in response bias with different study–test delays: evidence from young adults, older adults, and patients with Alzheimer's disease. *Neuropsychology*, 26 (1), 119–126.

Dodson, C.S., Spaniol, M., O'Connor, M.K., *et al.* (2011). Alzheimer's disease and memory-monitoring impairment: Alzheimer's patients show a monitoring deficit that is greater than their accuracy deficit. *Neuropsychologia*, 49 (9), 2609–2618.

Duarte, A., Henson, R.N., Knight, R.T., *et al.* (2010). Orbito-frontal cortex is necessary for temporal context memory. *Journal of Cognitive Neuroscience*, 22 (8), 1819–1831.

Duval, C., Desgranges, B., de la Sayette, V., *et al.* (2012). What happens to personal identity when semantic knowledge degrades? A study of the self and autobiographical memory in semantic dementia. *Neuropsychologia*, 50, 254–265.

Ekstrom, A.D., Copara, M.S., Isham, E.A., *et al.* (2011). Dissociable networks involved in spatial and temporal order source retrieval. *NeuroImage*, 56 (3), 1803–1813.

Eustache, F., Piolino, P., Giffard, B., *et al.* (2004). "In the course of time": a PET study of the cerebral substrates of autobiographical amnesia in Alzheimer's disease. *Brain*, 127 (7), 1549–1560.

Ewers, M., Sperling, R.A., Klunk, W.E., *et al.* (2011). Neuroimaging markers for the prediction and early diagnosis of Alzheimer's disease dementia. *Trends in Neurosciences*, 34 (8), 430–442.

Gallagher, M., and Koh, M.T. (2011). Episodic memory on the path to Alzheimer's disease. *Current Opinion in Neurobiology*, 21 (6), 929–934.

Gallo, D.A., Sullivan, A.L., Daffner, K.R., *et al.* (2004). Associative recognition in Alzheimer's disease: evidence for impaired recall-to-reject. *Neuropsychology*, 18 (3), 556–563.

Galton, C.J., Patterson, K., Graham, K., *et al.* (2001). Differing patterns of temporal atrophy in Alzheimer's disease and semantic dementia. *Neurology*, 57 (2), 216–225.

Gamboz, N., De Vito, S., Brandimonte, M.A., *et al.* (2010). Episodic future thinking in amnesic mild cognitive impairment. *Neuropsychologia*, 48 (7), 2091–2097.

Gilboa, A., Ramirez, J., Kohler, S., *et al.* (2005). Retrieval of autobiographical memory in Alzheimer's disease: relation to volumes of medial temporal lobe and other structures. *Hippocampus*, 15 (4), 535–550.

Graf, P., Squire, L.R., and Mandler, G. (1984). The information that amnesic patients do not forget. *Journal of Experimental Psychology, Learning, Memory and Cognition*, 10 (1), 164–178.

Graham, K.S., and Hodges, J.R. (1997). Differentiating the roles of the hippocampal complex and the neocortex in long-term memory storage: evidence from the study of semantic dementia and Alzheimer's disease. *Neuropsychology*, 11 (1), 77–89.

Graham, K.S., Simons, J.S., Pratt, K.H., *et al.* (2000). Insights from semantic dementia on the relationship between episodic and semantic memory. *Neuropsychologia*, 38 (3), 313–324.

Greenberg, D.L., and Rubin, D.C. (2003). The neuropsychology of autobiographical memory. *Cortex*, 39 (4), 687–728.

Greenberg, D.L., Ogar, J.M., Viskontas, I.V., *et al.* (2011). Multimodal cuing of autobiographical memory in semantic dementia. *Neuropsychology*, 25 (1), 98–104.

Greene, J.D.W., Hodges, J.R., and Baddeley, A.D. (1995). Autobiographical memory and executive function in early dementia of Alzheimer type. *Neuropsychologia*, 33 (12), 1647–1670.

Hodges, J.R., and Graham, K.S. (2001). Episodic memory: insights from semantic dementia. *Philosophical Transactions of the Royal Society of London, Series B: Biological Sciences*, 356 (1413), 1423–1434.

Hodges, J.R., and Patterson, K. (2007). Semantic dementia: a unique clinicopathological syndrome. *Lancet Neurology*, 6 (11), 1004–1014.

Hornberger, M., and Piguet, O. (2012). Episodic memory in frontotemporal dementia: a critical review. *Brain*, 135 (3), 678–692.

Hornberger, M., Piguet, O., Graham, A.J., *et al.* (2010). How preserved is episodic memory in behavioral variant frontotemporal dementia? *Neurology*, 74 (6), 472–479.

Hou, C.E., Miller, B.L., and Kramer, J.H. (2005). Patterns of autobiographical memory loss in dementia. *International Journal of Geriatric Psychiatry*, 20 (9), 809–815.

Hutchinson, A.D., and Mathias, J.L. (2007). Neuropsychological deficits in frontotemporal dementia and Alzheimer's disease: a meta-analytic review. *Journal of Neurology, Neurosurgery and Psychiatry*, 78 (9), 917–928.

Irish, M., Addis, D.R., Hodges, J.R., and Piguet, O. (2012a). Considering the role of semantic memory in episodic future thinking: evidence from semantic dementia. *Brain*, 135 (7), 2178–2191.

Irish, M., Graham, A., Graham, K.S., *et al.* (2012b). Differential Impairment of Source Memory in Progressive Versus Non-progressive Behavioral Variant Frontotemporal Dementia. *Archives of Clinical Neuropsychology*, 27 (3), 338–347.

Irish, M., Hornberger, M., Lah, S., *et al.* (2011a). Profiles of recent autobiographical memory retrieval in semantic dementia, behavioural-variant frontotemporal dementia, and Alzheimer's disease. *Neuropsychologia*, 49 (9), 2694–2702.

Irish, M., Lawlor, B.A., O'Mara, S.M., and Coen, R.F. (2011b). Impaired capacity for autonoetic reliving during autobiographical event recall in mild Alzheimer's disease. *Cortex*, 47 (2), 236–249.

Irish, M., and Piguet, O. (2013). The pivotal role of semantic memory in remembering the past and imagining the future. *Frontiers in Behavioral Neuroscience*, 7, 27.

Irish, M., Piguet, O., and Hodges, J.R. (2012). Self-projection and the default network in frontotemporal dementia. *Nature Reviews Neurology*, 8 (3), 152–161.

Jacoby, L.L. (1991). A Process Dissociation Framework: Separating Automatic from Intentional Uses of Memory. *Journal of Memory and Language*, 30 (5), 513–541.

Knight, R.G. (1998). Controlled and automatic memory process in Alzheimer's disease. *Cortex*, 34 (3), 427–435.

Kopelman, M.D., Wilson, B.A., and Baddeley, A.D. (1989). The autobiographical memory interview: a new assessment of autobiographical and personal semantic memory in amnesic patients. *Journal of Clinical and Experimental Neuropsychology*, 11 (5), 724–744.

Kramer, J.H., Rosen, H.J., Du, A.T., *et al.* (2005). Dissociations in hippocampal and frontal contributions to episodic memory performance. *Neuropsychology*, 19 (6), 799–805.

Lee, A.C., Rahman, S., Hodges, J.R., *et al.* (2003). Associative and recognition memory for novel objects in dementia: implications for diagnosis. *European Journal of Neuroscience*, 18 (6), 1660–1670.

Leyhe, T., Muller, S., Milian, M., *et al.* (2009). Impairment of episodic and semantic autobiographical memory in patients with mild cognitive impairment and early Alzheimer's disease. *Neuropsychologia*, 47 (12), 2464–2469.

Maddock, R.J., Garrett, A.S., and Buonocore, M.H. (2001). Remembering familiar people: the posterior cingulate cortex and autobiographical memory retrieval. *Neuroscience*, 104 (3), 667–676.

Maguire, E.A. (2001). Neuroimaging studies of autobiographical event memory. *Philosophical Transactions of the Royal Society of London, Series B: Biological Sciences*, 356 (1413), 1441–1451.

Maguire, E.A., Kumaran, D., Hassabis, D., and Kopelman, M.D. (2010). Autobiographical memory in semantic dementia: a longitudinal fMRI study. *Neuropsychologia*, 48 (1), 123–136.

Matuszewski, V., Piolino, P., Belliard, S., *et al.* (2009). Patterns of autobiographical memory impairment according to disease severity in semantic dementia. *Cortex*, 45 (4), 456–472.

Matuszewski, V., Piolino, P., de la Sayette, V., *et al.* (2006). Retrieval mechanisms for autobiographical memories: insights from the frontal variant of frontotemporal dementia. *Neuropsychologia*, 44 (12), 2386–2397.

McKinnon, M.C., Black, S.E., Miller, B., *et al.* (2006). Autobiographical memory in semantic dementia: Implications for theories of limbic-neocortical interaction in remote memory. *Neuropsychologia*, 44 (12), 2421–2429.

McKinnon, M.C., Nica, E.I., Sengdy, P., *et al.* (2008). Autobiographical memory and patterns of brain atrophy in fronto-temporal lobar degeneration. *Journal of Cognitive Neuroscience*, 20 (10), 1839–1853.

Meulenbroek, O., Rijpkema, M., Kessels, R.P., *et al.* (2010). Autobiographical memory retrieval in patients with Alzheimer's disease. *NeuroImage*, 53 (1), 331–340.

Mion, M., Patterson, K., Acosta-Cabronero, J., *et al.* (2010). What the left and right anterior fusiform gyri tell us about semantic memory. *Brain*, 133 (11), 3256–3268.

Moss, H.E., Kopelman, M.D., Cappelletti, M., *et al.* (2003). Lost for words or loss of memories? Autobiographical memory in semantic dementia. *Cognitive Neuropsychology*, 20 (8), 703–732.

Nadel, L., Samsonovich, A., Ryan, L., and Moscovitch, M. (2000). Multiple trace theory of human memory: computational, neuroimaging, and neuropsychological results. *Hippocampus*, 10 (4), 352–368.

Nedjam, Z., Devouche, E., and Dalla Barba, G. (2004). Confabulation, but not executive dysfunction discriminate AD from frontotemporal dementia. *European Journal of Neurology*, 11 (11), 728–733.

Nestor, P.J., Fryer, T.D., and Hodges, J.R. (2006). Declarative memory impairments in Alzheimer's disease and semantic dementia. *NeuroImage*, 30 (3), 1010–1020.

Nestor, P.J., Graham, K.S., Bozeat, S., *et al.* (2002). Memory consolidation and the hippocampus: further evidence from studies of autobiographical memory in semantic dementia and frontal variant frontotemporal dementia. *Neuropsychologia*, 40 (6), 633–654.

Northoff, G., and Bermpohl, F. (2004). Cortical midline structures and the self. *Trends in Cognitive Sciences*, 8 (3), 102–107.

Okuda, J., Fujii, T., Ohtake, H., *et al.* (2003). Thinking of the future and past: the roles of the frontal pole and the medial temporal lobes. *NeuroImage*, 19 (4), 1369–1380.

Patterson, K., Nestor, P.J., and Rogers, T.T. (2007). Where do you know what you know? The representation of semantic knowledge in the human brain. *Nature Reviews Neuroscience*, 8 (12), 976–987.

Pengas, G., Hodges, J.R., Watson, P., and Nestor, P.J. (2010). Focal posterior cingulate atrophy in incipient Alzheimer's disease. *Neurobiology of Aging*, 31 (1), 25–33.

Pennington, C., Hodges, J.R., and Hornberger, M. (2011). Neural correlates of episodic memory in behavioral variant frontotemporal dementia. *Journal of Alzheimers Disease*, 24 (2), 261–268.

Piguet, O., Hornberger, M., Mioshi, E., and Hodges, J.R. (2011). Behavioural-variant fronto-temporal dementia: diagnosis, clinical staging, and management. *Lancet Neurology*, 10 (2), 162–172.

Pihlajamaki, M., DePeau, K.M., Blacker, D., and Sperling, R.A. (2008). Impaired medial temporal repetition suppression is related to failure of parietal deactivation in Alzheimer disease. *American Journal of Geriatric Psychiatry*, 16 (4), 283–292.

Pihlajamaki, M., O'Keefe, K., O'Brien, J., *et al.* (2011). Failure of repetition suppression and memory encoding in aging and Alzheimer's disease. *Brain Imaging and Behaviour*, 5 (1), 36–44.

Piolino, P., Chételat, G., Matuszewski, V., *et al.* (2007). In search of autobiographical memories: a PET study in the frontal variant of frontotemporal dementia. *Neuropsychologia*, 45 (12), 2730–2743.

Piolino, P., Desgranges, B., Belliard, S., *et al.* (2003). Autobiographical memory and autonoetic consciousness: triple dissociation in neurodegenerative diseases. *Brain*, 126 (10), 2203–2219.

Plancher, G., Guyard, A., Nicolas, S., and Piolino, P. (2009). Mechanisms underlying the production of false memories for famous people's names in aging and Alzheimer's disease. *Neuropsychologia*, 47 (12), 2527–2536.

Rabinovici, G. D., Seeley, W.W., Kim, E.J., *et al.* (2007). Distinct MRI atrophy patterns in autopsy-proven Alzheimer's disease and frontotemporal lobar degeneration. *American Journal of Alzheimer's Disease and Other Dementias*, 22 (6), 474–488.

Rascovsky, K., Hodges, J.R., Knopman, D., *et al.* (2011). Sensitivity of revised diagnostic criteria for the behavioural variant of frontotemporal dementia. *Brain*, 134 (9), 2456–2477.

Rogers, T.T., Lambon Ralph, M.A., Garrard, P., *et al.* (2004). Structure and deterioration of semantic memory: a neuropsychological and computational investigation. *Psychological Review*, 111 (1), 205–235.

Rosenbaum, R.S., Winocur, G., and Moscovitch, M. (2001). New views on old memories: re-evaluating the role of the hippocampal complex. *Behavioural Brain Research*, 127 (1–2), 183–197.

Rowe, C.C., Ng, S., Ackermann, U., *et al.* (2007). Imaging beta-amyloid burden in aging and dementia. *Neurology*, 68 (20), 1718–1725.

Salmon, E., Kerrouche, N., Perani, D., *et al.* (2009). On the multivariate nature of brain metabolic impairment in Alzheimer's disease. *Neurobiology of Aging*, 30 (2), 186–197.

Scahill, V.L., Hodges, J.R., and Graham, K.S. (2005). Can episodic memory tasks differentiate semantic dementia from Alzheimer's disease? *Neurocase*, 11 (6), 441–451.

Schacter, D.L., Addis, D.R., and Buckner, R.L. (2007). Remembering the past to imagine the future: the prospective brain. *Nature Reviews Neuroscience*, 8 (9), 657–661.

Seeley, W.W., Crawford, R., Rascovsky, K., *et al.* (2008). Frontal paralimbic network atrophy in very mild behavioral variant frontotemporal dementia. *Archives of Neurology*, 65 (2), 249–255.

Seeley, W.W., Crawford, R.K., Zhou, J., *et al.* (2009). Neurodegenerative diseases target large-scale human brain networks. *Neuron*, 62 (1), 42–52.

Simons, J.S., Graham, K.S., Owen, A.M., *et al.* (2001). Perceptual and semantic components of memory for objects and faces: a PET study. *Journal of Cognitive Neuroscience*, 13 (4), 430–443.

Simons, J.S., and Spiers, H.J. (2003). Prefrontal and medial temporal lobe interactions in long-term memory. *Nature Reviews Neuroscience*, 4 (8), 637–648.

Simons, J.S., Verfaellie, M., Galton, C.J., *et al.* (2002). Recollection-based memory in frontotemporal dementia: implications for theories of long-term memory. *Brain*, 125 (11), 2523–2536.

Simons, J.S., Verfaellie, M., Hodges, J.R., *et al.* (2005). Failing to get the gist: reduced false recognition of semantic associates in semantic dementia. *Neuropsychology*, 19 (3), 353–361.

Söderlund, H., Black, S.E., Miller, B.L., *et al.* (2008). Episodic memory and regional atrophy in frontotemporal lobar degeneration. *Neuropsychologia*, 46 (1), 127–136.

Souchay, C. (2007). Metamemory in Alzheimer's disease. *Cortex*, 43 (7), 987–1003.

Sperling, R.A., Aisen, P.S., Beckett, L.A., *et al.* (2011). Toward defining the preclinical stages of Alzheimer's disease: recommendations from the National Institute on Aging–Alzheimer's Association workgroups on diagnostic guidelines for Alzheimer's disease. *Alzheimer's and Dementia*, 7 (3), 280–292.

Sperling, R.A., Bates, J.F., Chua, E.F., *et al.* (2003). fMRI studies of associative encoding in young and elderly controls and mild Alzheimer's disease. *Journal of Neurology, Neurosurgery and Psychiatry*, 74 (1), 44–50.

Spiers, H.J., and Maguire, E.A. (2007). The neuroscience of remote spatial memory: a tale of two cities. *Neuroscience*, 149 (1), 7–27.

Squire, L.R., and Alvarez, P. (1995). Retrograde amnesia and memory consolidation: a neurobiological perspective. *Current Opinion in Neurobiology*, 5 (2), 169–177.

Svoboda, E., McKinnon, M.C., and Levine, B. (2006). The functional neuroanatomy of autobiographical memory: a meta-analysis. *Neuropsychologia*, 44 (12), 2189–2208.

Thomas-Anterion, C., Jacquin, K., and Laurent, B. (2000). Differential mechanisms of impairment of remote memory in Alzheimer's and frontotemporal dementia. *Dementia and Geriatric Cognitive Disorders*, 11 (2), 100–106.

Tse, C.S., Balota, D.A., Moynan, S.C., *et al.* (2010). The utility of placing recollection in opposition to familiarity in early discrimination of healthy aging and very mild dementia of the Alzheimer's type. *Neuropsychology*, 24 (1), 49–67.

Tulving, E.T. (2002). Episodic memory: from mind to brain. *Annual Review of Psychology*, 53, 1–25.

Visser, M., Embleton, K.V., Jefferies, E., *et al.* (2010). The inferior, anterior temporal lobes and semantic memory clarified: novel evidence from distortion-corrected fMRI. *Neuropsychologia*, 48 (6), 1689–1696.

Wagner, A.D., Maril, A., Bjork, R.A., and Schacter, D.L. (2001). Prefrontal contributions to executive control: fMRI evidence for functional distinctions within lateral Prefrontal cortex. *NeuroImage*, 14 (6), 1337–1347.

Warrington, E.K. (1975). The selective impairment of semantic memory. *Quarterly Journal of Experimental Psychology*, 27 (4), 635–657.

Westerberg, C.E., Paller, K.A., Weintraub, S., *et al.* (2006). When memory does not fail: familiarity-based recognition in mild cognitive impairment and Alzheimer's disease. *Neuropsychology*, 20 (2), 193–205.

Westmacott, R., Leach, L., Freedman, M., and Moscovitch, M. (2001). Different patterns of autobiographical memory loss in semantic dementia and medial temporal lobe amnesia: a challenge to consolidation theory. *Neurocase*, 7 (1), 37–55.

Wheeler, M.A., Stuss, D.T., and Tulving, E.T. (1997). Toward a theory of episodic memory: the frontal lobes and autonoetic consciousness. *Psychological Bulletin*, 121, 331–354.

Whitwell, J.L., Josephs, K.A., Rossor, M.N., *et al.* (2005). Magnetic resonance imaging signatures of tissue pathology in frontotemporal dementia. *Archives of Neurology*, 62 (9), 1402–1408.

Williams, G.B., Nestor, P.J., and Hodges, J.R. (2005). Neural correlates of semantic and behavioural deficits in frontotemporal dementia. *NeuroImage*, 24 (4), 1042–1051.

Winocur, G., and Moscovitch, M. (2001). Memory transformation and systems consolidation. *Journal of the International Neuropsychological Society*, 17 (5), 766–780.

Wolk, D.A., Dunfee, K.L., Dickerson, B.C., *et al.* (2011). A medial temporal lobe division of labor: insights from memory in aging and early Alzheimer disease. *Hippocampus*, 21 (5), 461–466.

Yonelinas, A.P. (1997). Recognition memory ROCs for item and associative information: the contribution of recollection and familiarity. *Memory and Cognition*, 25 (6), 747–763.

Yonelinas, A.P., Aly, M., Wang, W.C., and Koen, J.D. (2010). Recollection and familiarity: examining controversial assumptions and new directions. *Hippocampus*, 20 (11), 1178–1194.

Zhang, Y., Schuff, N., Du, A.T., *et al.* (2009). White matter damage in frontotemporal dementia and Alzheimer's disease measured by diffusion MRI. *Brain*, 132 (9), 2579–2592.

Zhou, J., Greicius, M.D., Gennatas, E.D., *et al.* (2010). Divergent network connectivity changes in behavioural variant frontotemporal dementia and Alzheimer's disease. *Brain*, 133 (5), 1352–1367.

# 21

# Memory Rehabilitation in Neurological Patients

## Laurie A. Miller and Kylie A. Radford

## Introduction

Memory problems are common in patients with neurological disorders. This is because, first, there are many types of memory (e.g., anterograde memory, retrograde memory, prospective memory). Second, there are usually several steps/cognitive processes in each type of memory, with different parts of the brain involved in the various processes. At its core, memory depends on encoding, storing, and retrieving new information, and it is clear from both lesion studies (Graff-Radford *et al.*, 1985; Scoville and Milner, 1957; Winocur, Moscovitch, and Bontempi, 2010; Zola-Morgan and Squire, 1993) and more recent imaging work (Jenkins and Ranganath, 2010; Park *et al.*, 2012; Park and Rugg, 2011; Westerberg *et al.*, 2012) that the hippocampus and its connections with other medial temporal lobe (MTL) structures, as well as retrosplenial cortex and anteromedial thalamus, are crucial to these processes (see Chapter 5). Successful remembering in everyday life also requires the capacity to pay attention to the environment (both to ensure encoding and to elicit recall), to comprehend new information, and to self-monitor responses (to avoid repetition, judge appropriateness, etc.). These processes depend on a widespread network of cortical and subcortical structures (see Chapter 5). Hence, memory can be affected by many types of acquired brain injury (ABI).

Interventions to improve memory have been evaluated mainly using pre- and post-treatment scores from behavioral tests or from questionnaires concerning everyday memory abilities, but also (more recently) using pre- and post-treatment results from functional brain imaging. When memory outcome is used to evaluate success, measures can range from the very specific to the more generalized: (1) memory for trained items; (2) memory for untrained items of the same type used during training; (3) performance on laboratory-based memory tasks with material or response demands that differ in nature from those employed in the intervention; (4) everyday memory ability. Outcome in terms of changes in brain functioning has come from neuroimaging techniques including functional magnetic resonance imaging (fMRI), positron emission tomography (PET), and magnetic resonance spectroscopy. When an intervention increases the functioning of the hippocampal network, this is likely to be particularly noteworthy with regard to improving memory.

*The Wiley Handbook on the Cognitive Neuroscience of Memory*, First Edition.
Edited by Donna Rose Addis, Morgan Barense, and Audrey Duarte.
© 2015 John Wiley & Sons, Ltd. Published 2015 by John Wiley & Sons, Ltd.

In this chapter, we will examine the outcomes of different types of memory rehabilitation, primarily in relation to treating adults with mild to moderate memory deficits as a result of neurological disorders. A comprehensive systematic review of this literature would exceed the limits of the present chapter, and so we set out to provide an overview of key issues and findings. The focus will be on remediation of declarative memory (i.e., memory for events, information, etc. that one can consciously recall/describe) and prospective memory (i.e., remembering to carry out tasks at the right time). When considering the evidence that a particular intervention is better than none, we will avoid considering results from studies that failed to include either a control group or multiple baseline measures (i.e., those where post-training gains could simply be the result of test–retest practice effects). Because there have been so few neuroimaging studies investigating the effects of interventions in neurological patients, we will consider functional imaging results from memory interventions in both patients and healthy subjects.

To date, most interventions used with neurological patients have involved teaching strategies to improve memory. This includes internal/mental strategies, external memory aids, and more holistic/diversified training that incorporates a range of strategies as well as psychoeducation. In this chapter, we will first review the results of strategy training in terms of memory outcome and, where possible, in terms of neuroimaging findings. Next, baseline factors that influence the results from these types of interventions will be examined. Lastly, we will consider the more limited outcome results from some newer interventions (i.e., physical exercise, computerized training).

# Strategy Training

Results from traditional studies in experimental psychology have informed the design of interventions centred on teaching memory strategies. Whereas simple repetitive practice is not very effective in ensuring longer-term retention (Craik and Watkins, 1973), distributed practice (i.e., several short periods of practice spread over time) (Payne and Wenger, 1992) and staggered rehearsal/spaced retrieval (Landauer and Bjork, 1978) are known to improve retention in healthy subjects. Mnemonic strategies that require the generation of associations have been found to facilitate retention of face–name stimuli and other types of paired stimuli (Bellezza, 1981; Brooks *et al.*, 1999; for more on associative memory, see Chapter 18). Furthermore, depth of encoding influences retention, such that material that is processed to a deeper level (e.g., semantically as opposed to lexographically) will be remembered better (Craik and Lockhart, 1972). Hence, semantic elaboration (e.g., forming a story out of individual elements or considering the meaning of a word/name and its associations) should aid memory. Similarly, it has been shown that dual encoding (e.g., combining verbal with nonverbal encoding modalities) improves subsequent recall (Paivio and Begg, 1974). For example, one might form visual images to help with the retention of verbal material (Wilson, 1987). Another mental strategy that improves memory in healthy subjects is the method of loci, first described by Cicero in ~40 BCE. For this technique, one takes a mental walk along a highly familiar route and landmarks serve as the cues for the recall of sequential information, with associations between items and places recalled having been formed at encoding.

The first type of interventions we will present here are those that have involved encouraging participants to use the above-mentioned internal/mental strategies, also known as mnemonics. Outcome evidence in the form of memory performance and brain activity (as seen on functional imaging) will be considered. Subsequently, we will add results from interventions that include training in the use of external memory aids.

### Using internal/mental strategies to enhance encoding: memory outcome

In patients with severe memory impairments, it has been found that teaching specific ways of making associations to learn environmentally relevant stimuli (e.g., faces and names of hospital staff they regularly encounter) improves retention (Glisky and Glisky, 2002; Wilson, 1987). Memory-impaired patients can also use *supplied* associations (as illustrated in Figure 21.1) to enhance memory for *previously unfamiliar* faces and names (Hampstead *et al.*, 2008) or between objects and their locations (Hampstead *et al.*, 2012a). We are not aware of any published studies evaluating whether neurological patients can use the method of loci strategy to learn specified information.

Although it is good to know that some mnemonic strategies can aid patients' recall of trained items, it is important to determine whether being taught these strategies leads to more generalized memory improvement. Reassuringly, many studies have also found positive effects for untrained items, such as word lists (Wilson, 1987), paired-word associates (Jones, 1974), stories (Kaschel *et al.*, 2002), prospective memory tasks (Goldstein, McCue, and Turner, 1988; Kaschel *et al.*, 2002), and associations between faces and verbal information (Milders, Deelman and Berg, 1998) when neurological patients have been trained to use a single new mental encoding

Name to learn: **Thomas**
Notable facial feature: **Goatee and moustache**
Association: **shaped like a T– which is the first letter of his name**

Name to learn: **Marina**
Notable facial feature: **Long, wavy hair**
Association: **like water – and marina is a place in the water**

**Figure 21.1** Example of possible associations between facial features and names. These stimuli can either be generated for the subject, to enhance learning of specific people's names, or used to illustrate the nature of the strategy with the intention that subjects generate future associations on their own.

strategy. Furthermore, there is evidence of generalization of benefits following interventions that have taught a variety of internal memory strategies. In several such studies, patients (including those with mild cognitive impairment [MCI], stroke, and traumatic brain injury [TBI]) who received several weeks of training with multiple internal/mental strategies showed improvements on laboratory-based measures of anterograde memory relative to wait-list control patients (Belleville *et al.*, 2006; Berg, Koning-Haanstra, and Deelman, 1991; Doornhein and De Haan, 1998; Hildebrandt, Bussmann-Mork, and Schwendemann, 2006; O'Neil-Pirozzi *et al.*, 2010; Ryan and Ruff, 1988).

Unfortunately, there is less evidence that patients with ABI can make use of these mental encoding strategies in everyday life. When Richardson (1980, 1995) reviewed results on the effectiveness of mental imagery, he noted that although training in the use of this strategy may result in improved performance on memory tasks (e.g., word-list recall), brain-damaged patients tended to need explicit prompting to use imagery mnemonics and often failed to generalize their use to new learning situations. Only a few studies have examined changes in "everyday memory" as a result of multiple-mental-strategies training. The Rivermead Behavioral Memory Test (RBMT) (Wilson, Cockburn, and Baddeley, 1985), which was designed to be a more ecologically valid measure of everyday memory (e.g., includes measures of face–name association memory and prospective memory), was employed in some of these studies. O'Neil-Pirozzi *et al.* (2010) found that TBI patients improved compared to wait-listed control patients on the RBMT following six weeks of group-based, internal/mental strategy training sessions. Also, Berg, Koning-Haanstra, and Deelman (1991) reported improvements on objective measures of everyday memory (e.g., face–name learning, shopping-list recall) after a similar intervention in TBI outpatients. In other studies, however, ABI patients have failed to show significant improvements on the RMBT or everyday memory questionnaires after internal strategy training (Doornhein and De Haan, 1998; Kaschel *et al.*, 2002). And, in the study by Belleville *et al.* (2006), MCI patients reported everyday memory improvements in only 1 out of 10 domains (i.e., memory for personal events).

## Using internal/mental strategies to enhance encoding: neuroimaging outcomes

To understand how training in the use of mental strategies changes brain function, neuroimaging techniques have been applied in a few investigations of patients and healthy subjects. Hampstead and colleagues (2012a, 2012b) used training on mnemonic linkages between object and location pictorial pairs to look at changes in brain functioning. Twenty-eight patients with MCI were randomized to one of two groups. In the first group, subjects received training in specific (verbal) associative links for 45 of the pairs. In the second group, subjects were simply shown the 45 objects in their locations repeatedly (to control for exposure). Both before and after training, subjects were shown 90 object–location pairs for six seconds each for "encoding" and later, during a "retrieval" scan, asked to choose from three locations the one associated with each object. For 18 patients (nine trained and nine repeat-exposure only), the pre- and post-training encoding sessions were performed during fMRI scanning. Imaging analyses restricted to the hippocampus revealed that the group who received training in object–location associations showed increased activity in the left hippocampus during both encoding and retrieval relative to baseline levels (Hampstead *et al.*, 2012b). This neural effect was evident for both trained and untrained stimuli, but memory gains were seen only on the trained items. The authors concluded that the intervention facilitated hippocampal functioning in a partially restorative manner, and speculated that the short exposure time for the untrained items was insufficient for strategy application to be accomplished.

There have been a few investigations using functional neuroimaging to look for changes in healthy subjects trained to use method of loci (but none involving neuro-logical patients). Valenzuela *et al.* (2003) taught healthy older adults to memorize word lists using this technique. Participants practiced the strategy (utilizing a mental representation of their home city) for five weeks, with ever-lengthening word lists. Magnetic resonance spectroscopy revealed significant biochemical changes post training: choline and creatine signals in the medial temporal lobes were higher. The authors postulated that these changes related to increases in cellular energy and cell-membrane turnover. Additional evidence of changes in the hippocampal region after training in method of loci came from a study where healthy subjects underwent PET scanning at various stages in the training of word-list encoding (Nyberg *et al.*, 2003). In the baseline condition, subjects were scanned while trying to memorize an 18-word list, presented on a computer screen. Recall was assessed directly after scanning. Next, these same subjects were shown 18 words denoting locations in a home (e.g., bed, cupboard, sofa), which they were asked to memorize in order. They were repeatedly shown and tested on this list, and a series of PET images was obtained. Finally, the subjects were scanned during encoding of a new 18-item word list, which they were to learn using location associations. Again, recall was requested immediately after-wards. Activity in the left hippocampal region increased over the course of acquisition of the 18 location items, and improved word-list retention was associated with increased activity in the left occipitoparietal region and the left retrosplenial cortex (a major projection area of the hippocampus). Changes in the left inferomedial temporal and retrosplenial regions were also found using fMRI in conjunction with a similar paradigm (Kondo *et al.*, 2005). It is important to keep in mind that in terms of memory outcome, these studies demonstrated only that subjects could learn to use the method of loci to memorize trained word lists. None of these studies looked at success for untrained items and, as yet, the usefulness of method of loci for everyday memory has not been verified.

Belleville and colleagues (2011) looked for changes in neural activity in patients with MCI who underwent a six-week group-based training course focusing on mental strategies. One week before and one week after training, patients were scanned while trying to encode a word list (a different list pre- and post-training). Increased activation after the intervention was evident within a large network including frontal, temporal, and parietal areas, and word-list memory improved. There was a correlation between activity in the right inferior parietal lobule (a brain area newly activated post-training in these patients) and word-list recall performance. The authors concluded that memory training resulted in significant neural changes that are measurable using neuroimaging.

In summary, it is intriguing that changes in the hippocampus and related structures have been evident with functional neuroimaging when the intervening training involved strategies emphasizing memory for places (i.e., either object–location pair associations [Hampstead *et al.*, 2012b] or method of loci [Kondo *et al.*, 2005; Nyberg *et al.*, 2003; Valenzuela *et al.*, 2003]). This observation might be consistent with evidence that the hippocampus plays a role in acquiring spatial maps (Astur *et al.*, 2002; Burgess, Maguire, and O'Keefe, 2002; Ekstrom *et al.*, 2003) and object–location associations (Postma, Kessels, and van Asselen, 2008). In contrast, the findings to date suggest that training with nonspatial association strategies results in increased activation across broad cortical association areas (Belleville *et al.*, 2011), possibly reflecting the fact that these brain regions were involved in conjuring the associations.

## Memory interventions that involve training in the use of external memory aids

If we take a moment to consider the usefulness of mental encoding strategies as discussed in the previous section, it becomes obvious that the application of a mental strategy for storing a new memory takes more time than might normally be available. For example, in everyday life, one might be introduced to two or three people at a time, with conversation following directly afterwards – not an easy situation for pausing to consider associative links. Furthermore, not all pairs are easy to link with an association. Perhaps it is not too surprising, then, that interventions teaching new mental strategies are more likely to enhance performance on laboratory-based tasks involving word-list memory, item-association learning, or prospective memory, rather than memory in everyday life. In contrast, the use of external memory aids is becoming more acceptable and pervasive in the general population, and there are numerous studies which show that neurological patients are able to learn to use such aids to improve their everyday functioning (Kapur, 1995; Sohlberg *et al.*, 2007; Stapleton, Adams, and Atterton, 2007; Wade and Troy, 2001; Wilson *et al.*, 2001). In particular, recent work highlights how patients can be taught to use Smartphone technologies via errorless fading-of-cues protocols to support their memory in a variety of ways (Svoboda and Richards, 2009; Svoboda *et al.*, 2012).

For many patients, however, reliance on a device seems an incomplete solution, and they seek exercises or strategies that can improve their brain's functioning. Hence, several studies have evaluated more holistic instructional approaches involving training in both internal/mental strategies and external memory aids. Many of these also include educational components on how factors such as sleep, alcohol, exercise, and mood impact on memory (see Chapter 11 for more discussion of sleep and memory). We refer to this approach as "diversified" strategy training. Diversified strategy training usually takes place over several sessions and may be administered to individuals or small groups of subjects. Each session will usually include background information on memory function and everyday influences on memory, therapy to reduce stress and improve self-efficacy, as well as practice with different types of strategies, and homework to encourage generalization. See Table 21.1 for an example (Radford *et al.*, 2010).

As was found for those studies that emphasized internal/mental strategies alone, following diversified memory strategy training, patients with ABI tend to show significant gains on laboratory-based, anterograde memory measures such as word-list learning or figure recall (Engelberts *et al.*, 2002; Helmstaedter *et al.*, 2008; Radford *et al.*, 2011, 2012b; Thickpenny-Davis and Barker-Collo, 2007; Wilson and Moffat, 1984, 1992). Furthermore, when everyday memory has been assessed, most studies have found that patients who undergo diversified training improve more than

**Table 21.1**　Overview of a memory training program. Based on Radford *et al.*, 2010. Reproduced with permission

| Session | Component | Content summary |
|---|---|---|
| 1 | Psychoeducation | Stages and types of memory |
| | Lifestyle issue | Optimizing the home/office environment |
| | Internal strategies | Repetition; clustering |
| | External strategies | Note-taking; diaries; calendars |
| | Homework | Learn new name; bring back letter; change home environment; review notes (assigned each week) |
| 2 | Psychoeducation | Prospective memory |
| | Lifestyle issue | Physical exercise |
| | Internal strategies | Attending to details; staggered rehearsal |
| | External strategies | Physical reminders; lists; organization systems |
| | Homework | Make phone call and leave particular message; modify home filing system; add physical exercise; bring in photographs |
| 3 | Psychoeducation | How neurological conditions affect memory |
| | Lifestyle issue | Diet and herbal therapies |
| | Internal strategies | Remembering the context, self-prompting |
| | External strategies | Use of photographs; clocks; alarms, post-it notes |
| | Homework | Look at family photographs; eat fish; bring in mobile phone |
| 4 | Psychoeducation | How stress and mood affect memory |
| | Lifestyle issue | Managing stress |
| | Internal strategies | Method of loci, elaboration; word association |
| | External strategies | Electronic devices including phones |
| | Homework | Learn new words; try herbal tea; alleviate some stress |
| 5 | Psychoeducation | The importance of sleep |
| | Lifestyle issue | How to improve sleep |
| | Internal strategies | Recalling names – rehearsal, alphabet scanning, categorical prompting; learning names– repetition, elaboration, association |
| | External strategies | Make phone call and leave particular message; keep sleep diary; complete celebrity naming sheet |
| 6 | Revision | Memory function and lifestyle |
| | Revision | Internal and external memory strategies |
| | Debrief | Sources of additional help and support |

wait-listed controls (e.g., Engelberts *et al.*, 2002; Kinsella *et al.*, 2009; Ownsworth and McFarland, 1999; Radford *et al.*, 2011, 2012b; Rapp, Brenes, and Marsh, 2002; Thickpenny-Davis and Barker-Collo, 2007).

There is some evidence that it takes time for participants to discover ways to use newly learned strategies to improve their everyday functioning. Following six weeks of diversified training, we found that relatives of patients indicated some further improvement in the patients' everyday memory when they were re-evaluated at three-month follow-up (Radford *et al.*, 2011), compared to the initial post-training evaluation. Similarly, Berg, Koning-Haanstra, and Deelman (1991) noted additional improvements on objective memory tasks when subjects were retested three months after diversified training.

To our knowledge, no functional neuroimaging studies have been carried out after diversified training or training in the use of external aids alone. As the aids represent compensatory strategies rather than restorative ones, one might not expect to see changes on imaging as a result of such training.

## Baseline factors that influence the behavioral outcomes of strategy training

Several investigators have looked for variables that predict which patients will benefit from strategy-based memory rehabilitation (for discussion of genetic factors and other individual differences that influence memory training, see Chapter 15). When baseline memory function has been considered as a predictor of outcome, patients with moderate memory impairments seem to be more likely to improve than those with either mild or very severe impairments (Berg, Koning-Haanstra, and Deelman, 1991; Jennett and Lincoln, 1991; Malec, Goldstein, and McCue, 1991; O'Neil-Pirozzi *et al.*, 2010; Radford *et al.*, 2011; Ryan and Ruff, 1988). In fact, completely different approaches (using procedural or errorless learning), which are beyond the scope of this chapter, are recommended for densely amnesic patients (e.g., Wilson *et al.*, 1994).

Younger age has also been predictive of greater gains in several studies of strategy-based interventions (Belleville *et al.*, 2006; Radford *et al.*, 2011; Verhaeghen, Marcoen, and Goossens, 1992; Yesavage *et al.*, 1990). Some indication of differences in the ways in which younger and older brains respond to method of loci training was obtained on PET imaging by Nyberg *et al.* (2003). They found that both younger (mean age 26 years) and older (mean age 69 years) healthy volunteers were able to learn the strategy and locations, but different brain regions were activated in the two groups when they acquired a word list using the strategy. After training, the younger adults showed increased activity in occipitoparietal and frontal brain regions. In contrast, the older participants did not show increased frontal activity, and only those elderly who performed better post training (8/16 subjects) showed increased left occipitoparietal activity. Determining which interventions are most beneficial to different age groups would obviously add to their efficacy.

General intellectual function (IQ) or education level also seems to influence outcome – possibly in different ways, depending on the type of outcome being considered. Those with fewer years of education report more gains in everyday memory post training (Engelberts *et al.*, 2002; Radford *et al.*, 2011). It may be that participants with lower educational levels have not discovered appropriate strategies to help them cope with everyday tasks and therefore show benefits once they are taught. In contrast, a higher IQ/level of education has been found to be related to better outcome on laboratory-based anterograde verbal memory measures (Belleville *et al.*, 2006; Radford *et al.*, 2011). Given that improvements on these sorts of tasks probably depend on increases in internal/mnemonic strategies, perhaps those who are more intelligent and/or more educated are better able to learn these sorts of strategies. Exploring these possible relationships in future studies would help to tailor interventions to maximize effectiveness.

Mood and self-awareness of memory ability can also be important predictors of outcome. For a mixed group of neurological patients who underwent six weeks of diversified strategy training, we found that lower levels of depression at baseline predicted greater gains on everyday prospective memory (Radford *et al.*, 2012a). In addition, better self-awareness of memory function was associated with greater pre- to post-training gains for objective measures of verbal memory and prospective memory.

Etiology might also be important. Fish *et al.* (2008) found that patients with TBI, but not those with stroke, showed a sustained benefit from using a pager as an external memory aid. When we examined outcome in patients with stroke versus epilepsy undergoing a diversified training program, we found that although both showed training-related gains in anterograde memory that were sustained at three-month follow-up, only the epilepsy patients showed improvements on other variables, including self-report of everyday memory and number of strategies used (Radford *et al.*, 2012a). Both of these studies suggest lesser benefits for patients with stroke, but Stringer (2011) found no difference in post-strategy training gains when patients with stroke were compared to those with TBI. Very few other studies involving groups with differing etiologies have been carried out.

With regard to etiology, the effectiveness of memory training in patients with MCI is particularly controversial. A recent review paper (Stott and Spector, 2011) concluded that although there was some indication that people with MCI could learn specific information with training, there was little evidence to suggest that they demonstrated generalization of strategy application when attempting to learn new stimuli. However, Li and colleagues (2011), using meta-analysis, and Teixeira *et al.* (2012), using systematic review, find more evidence of positive outcomes for patients with MCI. Obviously, given the burgeoning population with neurodegenerative diseases, more research is necessary with MCI patients, many of whom are likely to be in the earliest stages of these disorders.

Extent of lesion is another baseline variable that has been explored with relation to memory outcome. Strangman *et al.* (2010) used volumetric MRI from TBI patients to predict outcome. They found that baseline volumes of several brain regions (hippocampus, lateral prefrontal cortex, thalamus, and several subregions of the cingulate cortex) were correlated with post-training scores after 12 weeks of training. However, they found that these structural imaging indications of brain damage were not as good as the baseline memory performance at predicting post-training scores. For MCI patients who were taught object–location associations by Hampstead and colleagues (2012a) in the fMRI study mentioned earlier, a negative correlation was found between volume of the inferior lateral ventricle (where greater volume indicated hippocampal atrophy) and training gains, implying that those with greater atrophy in the medial temporal region were less likely to benefit from training. Whether the baseline atrophy contributed to predictions of outcome independently of baseline memory levels was not tested. Thus, although structural imaging might contribute as a predictor, whether it contributes in addition to other baseline measures remains to be clarified.

## Summary of results for strategy training

With regard to memory outcome, interventions that train and encourage practice of internal/mental strategies usually result in improvements on laboratory-based memory tests. There is less evidence that this sort of intervention results in changes in everyday memory. On the other hand, a number of studies have indicated that patients can be trained to use external, compensatory memory aids, and that these facilitate everyday memory performance. Interventions that combine training in both internal strategies and the use of external devices have been particularly successful at demonstrating positive outcomes at various levels. Baseline predictors of successful training-related gains include moderate levels of memory impairment, younger age, low levels of depression and better self-awareness. Intellectual level, etiology, and extent of structural damage probably also influence outcome, but this might be affected by the nature of the intervention and the type of outcome being considered.

There is some evidence from neuroimaging that training in the use of elaborative encoding strategies changes neural activation in response to to-be-learned stimuli. Strategies that involve location information (e.g., method of loci) seem particularly likely to change hippocampal functioning (Kondo *et al.*, 2005; Nyberg *et al.*, 2003; Valenzuela *et al.*, 2003). However, given the effort involved in some of the encoding strategies, it is unlikely that they would be very helpful in everyday life. For example, the method of loci strategy could certainly facilitate oral presentations where one has to deliver messages in a particular order, but it is unlikely to replace written notes or lists to meet everyday needs. Similarly, using associations to remember where one has placed important objects is less reliable than learning to store such items routinely in the same spot. Nonetheless, it seems possible that practicing a strategy that has been shown to upregulate hippocampal function might be beneficial to memory in a more general way. Whether this sort of approach would work in patients with hippocampal damage is yet another question. The extent, location, and nature of the damage to the hippocampus might influence outcome.

## Other Interventions to Improve Everyday Memory

Now we turn our focus away from results of strategy-based interventions to some newer techniques for improving cognition that have mainly been used in healthy populations. We raise these approaches as potentially useful for memory-impaired patients as well.

### Physical exercise

There is good evidence from the animal literature that physical exercise increases brain-derived neurotrophic factor (BDNF) in the hippocampus (important for long-term potentiation) and improves learning and retention in maze tasks (Albeck *et al.*, 2006; Cotman and Berchtold, 2002; Neeper *et al.*, 1995; Van Praag *et al.*, 2005). Consistent with the findings in animals, increased cerebral blood volume in the dentate gyrus of the hippocampus was found in a small group of middle-aged healthy adults following three months of fitness training, and the change was associated with improvements in verbal learning and memory (Pereira *et al.*, 2007). More recently, Erickson and colleagues (2011) have shown that for older adults, one year of aerobic exercise training (i.e., walking) was associated with increased hippocampal volume, higher serum levels of BDNF, and improvements in spatial memory. In other studies, increases in gray matter volume have been noted in elderly individuals following a period of regular aerobic exercise sessions (Colcombe *et al.*, 2006; Ruscheweyh *et al.*, 2011). A survey of the literature on exercise interventions in healthy subjects concluded that there were post-intervention gains in cognition, though these were not necessarily specific to memory (Colcombe and Kramer, 2003). However, as others have noted, the general effects of exercise on aspects of cognition and mood might serve to improve everyday memory performance (Deslandes *et al.*, 2009; Kramer, Erickson, and Colcombe, 2006).

Only a few studies have looked for effects of exercise on memory in neurological patients. In patients with MCI, van Uffelen and colleagues (2008) found that improvements in memory on a word-list learning task were associated with increased attendance at a walking intervention. In another randomized intervention for patients with MCI, however, aerobic exercise had no effect on memory when compared to a stretching control condition (Baker *et al.*, 2010). Hence, more evidence is needed to support the postulation that physical exercise benefits memory function in neurological patients (for reviews, see Cumming *et al.*, 2012; McDonnell *et al.*, 2011).

## Computer-based "cognitive exercise"

We hear much about staving off memory decline by keeping our brains active, and many studies have used computer games as interventions (see Lustig *et al.*, 2009, for a summary). Typically this training involves repetitive practice aimed at remediation/restoration of function. However, there is not much proof that this sort of practice improves everyday memory. Certainly in healthy adults, studies have indicated post-intervention improvements in computer task performance after these interventions, but little evidence of generalization or of specific improvements in memory (Owen *et al.*, 2010; Papp, Walsh, and Snyder, 2009; Unverzagt *et al.*, 2012).

Alternatively, computer-administered, titrated tasks designed to target attention and memory skills have also been assigned for practice. These tasks have been used in a few studies of patients with MCI, but they too seem to have met with only limited success with regard to changes in memory abilities. Barnes *et al.* (2009) found improvement in general cognitive function, but only a nonsignificant trend toward better memory performance on a laboratory-based measure after 50 hours of computerized training focused on processing speed. Rozzini *et al.* (2007) delivered a more varied computerized intervention (60 hours spaced over seven months), focusing on several domains including memory, and found increases in verbal but not nonverbal memory. In contrast, Talassi and colleagues (2007) found only nonverbal memory improvements using a similar, but briefer, computerized intervention. Both these latter studies incorporated additional treatment elements (i.e., cholinesterase inhibitors or other behavioral treatments), which were also part of the control condition.

Computer-based training has also been tried with other types of neurological patients. Using computer-based presentation and practice of strategies (e.g., ways of making associations between faces and names, ways of remembering to do something) to train patients with TBI, Tam and Man (2004) found no post-training benefits on the RBMT. In a study of patients with relapsing–remitting multiple sclerosis, Hildebrandt *et al.* (2007) found that six weeks of almost daily home-based practice with computerized memory tasks (very similar to the outcome measures) resulted in improvements on a test of working memory (Paced Auditory Serial Addition Test), but not on the California Verbal Learning Test (a measure of verbal anterograde memory). And, following stroke, although computerized cognitive training was found to improve working memory and attention in one study (Westerberg *et al.*, 2007) and general cognitive function in another (Prokopenko *et al.*, 2013), there is currently no evidence that this type of intervention improves other aspects of memory function (e.g., anterograde or prospective memory).

On the other hand, using approaches that combined education on the effects of life-style factors on memory with computerized games and exercises, at least two studies have indicated post-intervention memory improvement compared to wait-list control subjects. First, using the Neuropsychological Educational Approach to Remediation (NEAR) model (Medalia and Freilich, 2008; Medalia and Revheim, 1999), Naismith and colleagues (2011) examined memory outcome in older participants with a lifetime history of major depression, three-quarters of whom met criteria for MCI. Improvements were found for the trained group (but not the wait-list control group) on standardized memory tasks involving both verbal and visual material. Furthermore, the training out-comes were fairly specific to memory, as no changes in response inhibition, problem solving, or mood were evident. Second, in patients with gliomas, Gehring *et al.* (2009) used a six-week (individualized) intervention that combined computer-based attention training with instruction on compensatory memory strategies (and homework). Although they found no group difference in memory improvement when the trained and untrained subject groups ($n = 70$ each) were compared shortly after the training, at six-month follow-up testing the trained group showed improved performance on a list-learning test. Unfortunately, it is not possible to know the extent to which the computer-based training versus the educational components regarding lifestyle factors contributed to these improvements.

Brooks and Rose (2003) were among the first to describe the potential for using computer-based virtual environments in memory rehabilitation, both as training tools and as instruments for measuring memory in everyday scenarios. The possibility that exposure to a navigational task might change hippocampal functioning and memory was recently explored in a single-case fMRI study using a virtual-reality environment in a videogame driving simulator (Caglio *et al.*, 2012). Memory for spatial and nonspatial material and neural activity during encoding of word pairs were examined. The patient was a 24-year-old man whose recovery had plateaued one year following a moderately severe TBI. The driving game involved exploring a town from a ground-level perspective, with the goal of cutting down poles and trees found along the way. The subject played the game for three 90-minute sessions per week for five weeks. Increases in hippocampal and parahippocampal activation were evident during the word-pair list learning task when pre- and post-training images were compared. The patient showed improvements on some standard neuropsychological measures involving spatial memory (i.e., memory for a newly learned route, recall of a spatial block-tapping sequence) compared to multiple baseline measures. Even more importantly, he also showed evidence of generalization of memory skills, in that he was also better on word-list learning. Some of these gains were still evident at one-year follow-up.

From a different (but potentially related) line of research, Maguire *et al.* (2000) found that training to be a London taxi driver (i.e., learning the layout of the city) was associated with increased volume in the posterior hippocampus. This volumetric increase is presumably related to practice on navigational tasks. However, her team has also recently shown that after training, although the drivers were very skilled at London navigation, their performance on object–location memory tasks was impaired relative to control subjects (Woollett and Maguire, 2012). Hence, training on navigational tasks might possibly result in improvements in some aspects of memory, though potentially at a cost to others. We would suggest that the potential for engagement in navigational tasks (possibly via virtual reality or computer-based simulated environments) to improve memory in patients is highly speculative at this stage, but possibly worth further investigation.

## Summary of non-strategy-based interventions

Most computer-based cognitive training seems to result in fairly limited changes in specifically trained skills. There is little evidence that such training facilitates everyday memory. On the other hand, games that involve navigation or moving through virtual reality environments may stimulate the hippocampus and possibly result in memory gains. This theory remains to be tested. There is also evidence that physical exercise improves brain functioning, including changes in the hippocampal region, but again, little is known about whether these techniques are helpful in memory-impaired patients.

# Conclusions and Future Directions

A number of rehabilitation techniques have the potential to improve memory in adults with neurological conditions. However, as has been pointed out in this chapter, the choice of outcome measure is important: gains on laboratory-based tests and activation changes on neuroimaging measures are most likely to be seen after training on internal/mental strategies, whereas everyday memory gains seem to have been documented more often following training on the use of external aids. Although changes in the hippocampus and related structures have been found in a few neuroimaging studies after training on tasks involving navigation or spatial memory, whether such interventions will improve memory functioning in neurological patients needs to be investigated.

The extent to which strategy-based interventions are successful depends on several factors, including the participant's baseline memory, age, mood, self-awareness, level of education, and etiology. Clinically, consideration of these predictor variables could be used to fine-tune rehabilitation approaches and goals for different individuals.

There are multiple possible reasons that diversified interventions result in memory improvement. The psychoeducation components of these programs tend to include advice on lifestyle factors, such as how to improve sleep, reduce stress, and increase physical exercise, any of which might have an important independent effect. In addition, some internal/mental strategies probably help more than others; training that includes practice with spatial/navigational memory might be particularly effective. Because of the multiple possible influences from this sort of diversified training, it is difficult to know the relative importance of each. Large-scale trials that randomize subjects to different combinations of treatments are needed.

At the beginning of the chapter, we pointed out that because everyday memory has so many forms and depends on so many neural processes, nearly anything that disrupts brain function can cause impairment. On the other hand, it is also apparent that a variety of techniques that enhance neural functioning might also improve memory in some way. For now, diversified/holistic memory strategy training has the greatest support for improving everyday memory function, with most "real-world" benefits demonstrated via compensation using external memory aids. However, given that functional neuroimaging now provides the potential to observe neural plasticity, more effective interventions targeted at restoring or re-routing functional connections in the brain might be identified in future.

# References

Albeck, D.S., Sano, K., Prewitt, G.E. and Dalton, L. (2006). Mild forced treadmill exercise enhances spatial learning in the aged rat. *Behavioural Brain Research*, 168, 345–348.

Astur, R.S., Taylor, L.B., Mamelak, A.N., *et al.* (2002). Humans with hippocampus damage display severe spatial memory impairments in a virtual Morris water task. *Behavioural Brain Research*, 132 (1), 77–84.

Baker, L.D., Frank, L.L., Foster-Schubert, K., *et al.* (2010). Effects of Aerobic Exercise on Mild Cognitive Impairment A Controlled Trial. *Archives of Neurology*, 67 (1), 71–79.

Barnes, D.E., Yaffe, K., Belfor, N., *et al.* (2009). Computer-based cognitive training for mild cognitive impairment: results from a pilot randomized, controlled trial. *Alzheimer Disease and Associated Disorders*, 23 (3), 205–210.

Belleville, S., Clement, F., Mellah, S., *et al.* (2011). Training-related brain plasticity in subjects at risk of developing Alzheimer's disease. *Brain*, 134, 1623–1634.

Belleville, S., Gilbert, B., Fontaine, F., *et al.* (2006). Improvement of episodic memory in persons with Mild Cognitive Impairment and healthy older adults: evidence from a cognitive intervention program. *Dementia and Geriatric Cognitive Disorders*, 22 (5–6), 486–499.

Bellezza, F.S. (1981). Mnemonic devices: classification, characteristics, and criteria. *Review of Educational Research*, 51, 247–275.

Berg, I.J., Koning-Haanstra, M., and Deelman, B.G. (1991). Long-term effects of memory rehabilitation: a controlled study. *Neuropsychological Rehabilitation*, 1 (2), 97–111.

Brooks, B.M., and Rose, F.D. (2003). The use of virtual reality in memory rehabilitation: current findings and future directions. *Neurorehabilitation*, 18 (2), 147–57.

Brooks, J.O., Friedman, L., Pearman, A.M., *et al.* (1999). Mnemonic training in older adults: effects of age, length of training, and type of cognitive pretraining. *International Psychogeriatrics*, 11 (1), 75–84.

Burgess, N., Maguire, E.A., and O'Keefe, J. (2002). The human hippocampus and spatial and episodic memory. *Neuron*, 35 (4), 625–641.

Caglio, M., Latini-Corazzini, L., D'Agata, F., *et al.* (2012). Virtual navigation for memory rehabilitation in a traumatic brain injured patient. *Neurocase*, 18 (2), 123–131. doi: 10.1080/13554794.2011.568499.

Colcombe, S., and Kramer, A.F. (2003). Fitness effects on the cognitive function of older adults: a meta-analytic study. *Psychological Science*, 14 (2), 125–130.

Colcombe, S.J., Erickson, K.I., Scalf, P.E., *et al.* (2006). Aerobic exercise training increases brain volume in aging humans. *Journals of Gerontology Series A: Biological Sciences and Medical Sciences*, 61 (11), 1166–1170.

Cotman, C.W., and Berchtold, N.C. (2002). Exercise: a behavioral intervention to enhance brain health and plasticity. *Trends in Neuroscience*, 25, 295–301.

Craik, F.I.M., and Lockhart, R.S. (1972). Levels of processing: a framework for memory research. *Journal of Verbal Learning and Verbal Behavior*, 11, 671–684.

Craik, F.I.M., and Watkins, M.J. (1973). The role of rehearsal in short-term memory. *Journal of Verbal Learning and Verbal Behavior*, 12, 599–607.

Cumming, T.B., Tyedin, K., Churilov, L., *et al.* (2012). The effect of physical activity on cognitive funciton after stroke: a systematic review. *International Psychogeriatrics*, 24 (4), 557–567.

Deslandes, A., Moraes, H., Ferreira, C., *et al.* (2009). Exercise and mental health: many reasons to move. *Neuropsychobiology*, 59 (4), 191–8.

Doornhein, K., and De Haan, E.H.F. (1998). Cognitive training for memory deficits in stroke patients. *Neuropsychological Rehabilitation*, 8 (4), 393–400.

Ekstrom, A.D., Kahana, M.J., Caplan, J.B., *et al.* (2003). Cellular networks underlying human spatial navigation. *Nature*, 425 (6954), 184–187.

Engelberts, N.H., Klein, M., Ader, H.J., *et al.* (2002). The effectiveness of cognitive rehabilitation for attention deficits in focal seizures: a randomized controlled study. *Epilepsia*, 43 (6), 587–595. doi: epi29401 [pii].

Erickson, K.I., Voss, M.W., Prakash, R.S., *et al.* (2011). Exercise training increases size of hippocampus and improves memory. *Proceedings of the National Academy of Sciences of the USA*, 108 (7), 3017–3022.

Fish, J., Manly, T., Emslie, H., *et al.* (2008). Compensatory strategies for acquired disorders of memory and planning: differential effects of a paging system for patients with brain injury of traumatic versus cerebrovascular aetiology. *Journal of Neurology, Neurosurgery, and Psychiatry*, 79, 930–935.

Gehring, K., Sitskoorn, M.M., Gundy, C.M., *et al.* (2009). Cognitive rehabilitation in patients with gliomas: a randomized, controlled trial. *Journal of Clinical Oncology*, 27 (22), 3712–3722.

Glisky, E.L., and Glisky, M.L. (2002). Learning and memory impairments. In *Neuropsychological Interventions: Clinical Research and Practice* (ed. P.J. Eslinger). New York, NY: Guilford Press, pp. 137–162.

Goldstein, G., McCue, M., and Turner, S.M. (1988). An efficacy study of memory training for patients with closed head injury. *Clinical Neuropsychologist*, 2, 251–259.

Graff-Radford, N., Damasio, H., Yamada, T., *et al.* (1985). Nonhaemorrhagic thalamic infarction: clinical neuropsychological and electrophysiological findings in four anatomical groups defined by computerized tomography. *Brain*, 108, 485–516.

Hampstead, B.M., Sathian, K., Moore, A.B., *et al.* (2008). Explicit memory training leads to improved memory for face–name pairs in patients with mild cognitive impairment: results of a pilot investigation. *Journal of the International Neuropsychological Society*, 14, 883–889.

Hampstead, B.M., Sathian, K., Phillips, P.A., *et al.* (2012a). Mnemonic strategy training improves memory for object location associations in both healthy elderly and patients with amnestic mild cognitive impairment: a randomized, single-blind study. *Neuropsychology*, 26 (3), 385–399. doi: 10.1037/a0027545.

Hampstead, B.M., Stringer, A.Y., Stilla, R.F., *et al.* (2012b). Mnemonic strategy training partially restores hippocampal activity in patients with mild cognitive impairment. *Hippocampus*, 22 (8), 1652–1658. doi: 10.1002/hipo.22006.

Helmstaedter, C., Loer, B., Wohlfahrt, R., *et al.* (2008). The effects of cognitive rehabilitation on memory outcome after temporal lobe epilepsy surgery. *Epilepsy and Behavior*, 12 (3), 402–409. doi: 10.1016/j.yebeh.2007.11.010.

Hildebrandt, H., Bussmann-Mork, B., and Schwendemann, G. (2006). Group therapy for memory impaired patients: a partial remediation is possible. *Journal of Neurology*, 253 (4), 512–519.

Hildebrandt, H., Lanz, M., Hahn, H.K., *et al.* (2007). Cognitive training in MS: eand relation to brain atrophy. *Restorative Neurology and Neuroscience*, 25 (1), 33–43.

Jenkins, L.J., and Ranganath, C. (2010). Prefrontal and medial temporal lobe actvity at encoding predicts temporal context memory. *Journal of Neuroscience*, 30 (46), 15558–15565.

Jennett, S.M., and Lincoln, N.B. (1991). An evaluation of the effectiveness of group therapy for memory problems. *International Disability Studies*, 13, 83–86.

Jones, M.K. (1974). Imagery as a mnemonic aid after left temporal lobectomy: contrast between material-specific and generalized memory disorders. *Neuropsychologia* 12, 21–30.

Kapur, N. (1995). Memory aids in the rehabilitation of memory disordered patients. In *Handbook of Memory Disorders* (ed. A.D. Baddeley, B.A. Wilson, and F.N. Watts). Chichester, UK: John Wiley & Sons, Ltd pp. 533–556.

Kaschel, R., Della Sala, S., Cantagallo, A., *et al.* (2002). Imagery mnemonics for the rehabilitation of memory: a randomised group controlled trial. *Neuropsychological Rehabilitation*, 12, 127–153.

Kinsella, G.J., Mullaly, E., Rand, E. *et al.* (2009). Early intervention for mild cognitive impairment: a randomised controlled trial. *Journal of Neurology, Neurosurgery and Psychiatry*, 80 (7), 730–736. doi: jnnp.2008.148346 [pii] 10.1136/jnnp.2008.148346.

Kondo, Y., Suzuki, M., Mugikura, S., *et al.* (2005). Changes in brain activation associated with use of a memory strategy: a functional MRI study. *NeuroImage*, 24 (4), 1154–1163. doi: 10.1016/j.neuroimage.2004.10.033.

Kramer, A.F., Erickson, K.I., and Colcombe, S.J. (2006). Exercise, cognition, and the aging brain. *Journal of Applied Physiology*, 101, 1237–1242.

Landauer, T.K., and Bjork, R.A. (1978). Optimum rehearsal patterns and name learning. In *Practical Aspects of Memory* (ed. P.E. Morris, M.M. Gruneberg, and R.N. Sykes). London: Academic Press, pp. 625–632.

Li, H., Li, J., Li, N., *et al.* (2011). Cognitive intervention for persons with mild cognitive impairment: a meta-analysis. *Ageing Research Reviews*, 10 (2), 285–296. doi: 10.1016/j.arr.2010.11.003.

Lustig, C., Shah, P., Seidler, R., and Reuter-Lorenz, P.A. (2009). Aging, training, and the brain: A review and future directions. *Neuropsychological Review*, 19, 504–522.

Maguire, E.A., Gadian, D.G., Johnsrude, I.S., *et al.* (2000). Navigation-related structural change in the hippocampi of taxi drivers. *Proceedings of the National Academy of Sciences of the USA*, 97 (8), 4398–4403. doi: 10.1073/pnas.070039597.

Malec, E.A., Goldstein, G., and McCue, M. (1991). Predictors of memory training success in patients with closed-head injury. *Neuropsychology*, 5, 29–34.

McDonnell, M.N., Bryan, J., Smith, A.E., and Esterman, A.J. (2011). Assessing cognitive impairment following stroke. *Journal of Clinical and Experimental Neuropsychology*, 33 (9), 945–953.

Medalia, A., and Freilich, B. (2008). The neuropsychological educational approach to cognitive remediation (NEAR) model: practice principles and outcome studies. *American Journal of Psychiatric Rehabilitation*, 11, 123–143.

Medalia, A., and Revheim, N. (1999). Computer assisted learning in psychiatric rehabilitation. *American Journal of Psychiatric Rehabilitation*, 3, 77–98.

Milders, M., Deelman, B., and Berg, I. (1998). Rehabilitation of memory for people's names. *Memory*, 6, 21–36.

Naismith, S.L., Diamond, K., Carter, P.E., *et al.* (2011). Enhancing memory in late-life depression: the effects of a combined psychoeducation and cognitive training program. *American Journal of Geriatric Psychiatry*, 19 (3), 240–248. doi: 10.1097/JGP.0b013e3181dba587.

Neeper, S., Gomez-Pinilla, F., Choi, J., and Cotman, J.C. (1995). Exercise and brain neurotrophins. *Nature*, 373, 109.

Nyberg, L., Sandblom, J., Jones, S., *et al.* (2003). Neural correlates of training-related memory improvements in adulthood and aging. *Proceedings of the National Academy of Sciences of the USA*, 100 (23), 13728–13733.

O'Neil-Pirozzi, T.M., Strangman, G.E., Goldstein, R., *et al.* (2010). A controlled treatment study of internal memory strategies (I-MEMS) following traumatic brain injury. *Journal of Head Trauma Rehabilitation*, 25 (1), 43–51.

Owen, A.M., Hampshire, A., Grahn, J.A., *et al.* (2010). Putting brain training to the test. *Nature*, 465 (7299), 775–778. doi: 10.1038/nature09042.

Ownsworth, T.L., and McFarland, K. (1999). Memory rehabilitation in long-term acquired brain injury: two approaches in diary training. *Brain Injury*, 13 (8), 605–626.

Paivio, A., and Begg, I. (1974). Pictures and words in visual search. *Memory and Cognition*, 2 (3), 515–521. doi: 10.3758/BF03196914.

Papp, K.V., Walsh, S.J., and Snyder, P.J. (2009). Immediate and delayed effects of cognitive interventions in healthy elderly: a review of current literature and future directions. *Alzheimers and Dementia*, 5 (1), 50–60. doi: 10.1016/j.jalz.2008.10.008

Park, H., and Rugg, M.D. (2011). Neural correlates of encoding within- and across-domain inter-item associations. *Journal of Cognitive Neuroscience*, 23 (9), 2533–2543.

Park, H., Shannon, V., Biggan, J., and Spann, C. (2012). Neural activity supporting the formation of associative memory versus source memory. *Brain Research*, 1471, 81–92.

Payne, D.G., and Wenger, M.J. (1992). Improving memory through practice. In *Memory improvement: Implications for memory theory* (ed. H. Weingartner, D.J. Herrmann, A. Searleman, and C.L. McEvoy). New York, NY: Springer-Verlag, pp. 187–209.

Pereira, A.C., Huddleston, D.E., Brickman, A.M., *et al.* (2007). An in vivo correlate of exercise-induced neurogenesis in the adult dentate gyrus. *Proceedings of the National Academy of Sciences of the USA*, 104 (13), 5638–5643. doi: 10.1073/pnas.0611721104.

Postma, A., Kessels, R.P.C., and van Asselen, M. (2008). How the brain remembers and forgets where things are: the neurocognition of object-location memory. *Neuroscience and Biobehavioral Reviews*, 32, 1339–1345.

Prokopenko, S.V., Mozheyko, E.Y., Petrova, M.M., *et al.* (2013). Correction of post-stroke cognitive impairments using computer programs. *Journal of the Neurological Sciences*, 325 (1–2), 148–153. doi: 10.1016/j.jns.2012.12.024.

Radford, K., Lah, S., Thayer, Z., and Miller, L.A. (2011). Effective group-based memory training for patients with epilepsy. *Epilepsy and Behavior*, 22 (2), 272–278. doi: 10.1016/j.yebeh.2011.06.021.

Radford, K., Lah, S., Thayer, Z., and Miller, L.A. (2012a). Comparing the effectiveness of group-based memory training and predictors of outcome for patients with stroke versus epilepsy. *Neurorehabilitation and Neural Repair*, 26 (6), 756.

Radford, K., Lah, S., Thayer, Z., *et al.* (2012b). Improving memory in outpatients with neurological disorders using a group-based training program. *Journal of the International Neuropsychological Society*, 18 (4), 738–748. doi: 10.1017/S1355617712000379.

Radford, K., Say, M.J., Thayer, Z., and Miller, L.A. (2010). *Making the Most of Your Memory: An Everyday Memory Skills Program*. Sydney: ASSBI Resources.

Rapp, S., Brenes, G., and Marsh, A.P. (2002). Memory enhancement training for older adults with mild cognitive impairment: a preliminary study. *Aging and Mental Health*, 6 (1), 5–11. doi: 10.1080/13607860120101077.

Richardson, J.T. (1980). *Mental Imagery and Human Memory*. London: Macmillan.

Richardson, J.T. (1995). The efficacy of imagery mnemonics in memory remediation. *Neuropsychologia*, 33, 1345–1357.

Rozzini, L., Costardi, D., Chilovi, B.V., *et al.* (2007). Efficacy of cognitive rehabilitation in patients with mild cognitive impairment treated with cholinesterase inhibitors. *International Journal of Geriatric Psychiatry*, 22, 356–360.

Ruscheweyh, R., Willemer, C., Kruger, K., *et al.* (2011). Physical activity and memory functions: An interventional study. *Neurobiology of Aging*, 32, 1304–1319.

Ryan, T.V., and Ruff, R.M. (1988). The efficacy of structured memory retraining in a group comparison of head trauma patients. *Archives of Clinical Neuropsychology*, 3, 165–179.

Scoville, W.B., and Milner, B. (1957). Loss of recent memory after bilateral hippocampal lesions. *Journal of Neurology, Neurosurgery, and Psychiatry*, 20 (1), 11–21. doi: 10.1136/jnnp.20.1.11.

Sohlberg, M.M., Kennedy, M., Avery, J., *et al.* (2007). Evidence-based practice for the use of external aids as a memory compensation technique. *Journal of Medical Speech-Language Pathology*, 15, xv–li.

Stapleton, S., Adams, M., and Atterton, L. (2007). A mobile phone as a memory aid for individuals with traumatic brain injury: a preliminary investigation. *Brain Injury*, 21, 401–411.

Stott, J., and Spector, A. (2011). A review of the effectiveness of memory interventions in mild cognitive impairment (MCI). *International Psychogeriatrics*, 23 (4), 526–538. doi: 10.1017/S1041610210001973.

Strangman, G.E., O'Neil-Pirozzi, T.M., Supelana, C., *et al.* (2010). Regional brain morphometry predicts memory rehabilitation outcome after traumatic brain injury. *Frontiers in Human Neuroscience*, 4, 1–11.

Stringer, A.Y. (2011). Ecologically-oriented neurorehabilitation of memory: robustness of outcome across diagnosis and severity. *Brain Injury*, 25 (2), 169–178.

Svoboda, E., and Richards, B. (2009). Compensating for anterograde amnesia: a new training method that capitalizes on emerging smartphone technologies. *Journal of the International Neuropsychological Society*, 15, 629–638.

Svoboda, E., Richards, B., Leach, L., and Mertens, V. (2012). PDA and smartphone use by individuals with moderate-to-severe memory impairment: application of a theory-driven training programme. *Neuropsychological Rehabilitation*, 22 (3), 408–427.

Talassi, E., Guerreschi, M., Feriani, M., *et al.* (2007). Effectiveness of a cognitive rehabilitation program in mild dementia (MD) and mild cognitive impairment (MCI): a case control study. *Archives of Gerontology and Geriatrics*, 44, 391–399. doi: 10.1016/j.archger.2007.01.055.

Tam, S.-F., and Man, W.-K. (2004). Evaluating computer-assisted memory retraining programmes for people with post-head injury amnesia. *Brain Injury*, 18 (5), 461–470. doi: doi:10.1080/02699050310001646099.

Teixeira, C.V.L., Gobbi, L.T.B., Corazza, D.I. *et al.* (2012). Non-pharmacological interventions on cognitive functions in older people with mild cognitive impairment (MCI). *Archives of Gerontology and Geriatrics*, 54 (1), 175–180. doi: http://dx.doi.org/10.1016/j.archger.2011.02.014.

Thickpenny-Davis, K.L., and Barker-Collo, S.L. (2007). Evaluation of a structured group format memory rehabilitation program for adults following brain injury. *Journal of Head Trauma Rehabilitation*, 22 (5), 303–313.

Unverzagt, F.W., Guey, L.T., Jones, R.N., *et al.* (2012). ACTIVE cognitive training and rates of incident dementia. *Journal of the International Neuropsychological Society*, 18 (4), 669–677. doi: doi:10.1017/S1355617711001470.

Valenzuela, M.J., Jones, M., Wen, W., *et al.* (2003). Memory training alters hippocampal neurochemistry in healthy elderly. *NeuroReport*, 14 (10), 1333–1337.

Van Praag, H., Shubert, T., Zhao, C., and Gage, F.H. (2005). Exercise enhances learning and hippocampal neurogenesis in aged mice. *Journal of Neuroscience*, 25, 8680–8685.

van Uffelen, J.G.Z., Chinapaw, M.J.M., van Mechelen, W., and Hopman-Rock, M. (2008). Walking or vitamin B for cognition in older adults with mild cognitive impairment? *British Journal of Sports Medicine*, 42, 344–351.

Verhaeghen, P., Marcoen, A., and Goossens, L. (1992). Improving memory performance in the aged through mnemonic training: a meta-analytic study. *Psychology and Aging*, 7 (2), 242–251.

Wade, T.K., and Troy, J.C. (2001). Mobile phones as a new memory aid: a preliminary investigation using case studies. *Brain Injury*, 15, 305–320.

Westerberg, C.E., Voss, J.L., Reber, P.J., and Paller, K.A. (2012). Medial temporal contributions to successful face–name learning. *Human Brain Mapping*, 33 (7), 1717–1726.

Westerberg, H., Jacobaeus, H., Hirvikoski, T., *et al.* (2007). Computerized working memory training after stroke: a pilot study. *Brain Injury*, 21 (1), 21–29. doi: 10.1080/02699050601148726.

Wilson, B. (1987). *Rehabilitation of Memory*. New York, NY: Guilford Press.

Wilson, B.A., Baddeley, A., Evans, J., and Shiel, A. (1994). Errorless learning in the rehabilitation of memory impaired people. *Neuropsychological Rehabilitation* 4 (3), 307–326.

Wilson, B.A., Cockburn, J., and Baddeley, A. (1985). *The Rivermead Behavioural Memory Test*. Bury St. Edmunds, UK: Thames Valley Test.

Wilson, B.A., Emslie, H., Quirk, K., and Evans, J.J. (2001). Reducing everyday memory and planning problems by means of a paging system: a randomised control crossover study. *Journal of Neurology, Neurosurgery and Psychiatry*, 70, 477–482.

Wilson, B.A., and Moffat, N. (1984). *Clinical Management of Memory Problems*. London: Croom Helm.

Wilson, B.A., and Moffat, N. (1992). The development of group memory therapy. In *Clinical Management of Memory Problems* (ed. B.A. Wilson and N. Moffat). London: Chapman and Hall, pp. 243–273.

Winocur, G., Moscovitch, M., and Bontempi, B. (2010). Memory formation and long-term retention in humans and animals: convergence towards a transformation account of hippocampal–neocortical interactions. *Neuropsychologia*, 48 (8), 2339–2356.

Woollett, K., and Maguire, E.A. (2012). Exploring anterograde associative memory in London taxi drivers. *NeuroReport*, 23 (15), 885–888. doi: 10.1097/WNR.0b013e328359317e.

Yesavage, J.A., Sheikh, J.I., Friedman, L.F., and Tanke, E. (1990). Learning mnemonics: roles of aging and subtle cognitive impairment. *Psychology and Aging*, 5 (1), 133–137.

Zola-Morgan, S., and Squire, L.R. (1993). Neuroanatomy of memory. *Annual Review of Neurosciences*, 16, 547–563.

# Index

*The Wiley Handbook on the Cognitive Neuroscience of Memory*, First Edition.
Edited by Donna Rose Addis, Morgan Barense, and Audrey Duarte.
© 2015 John Wiley & Sons, Ltd. Published 2015 by John Wiley & Sons, Ltd.